Mathematics
for GCSE

Hundreds of practice questions and
worked examples covering every GCSE Maths topic.

Foundation Level

Contents

Number and Algebra

Geometry and Measures

Section 14 — Angles and 2D Shapes

Section 15 — Units, Measuring and Estimating

Section 16 — Speed, Distance and Time

Section 17 — Pythagoras, Bearings and Scale Drawings

Section 18 — Constructions

Section 19 — Area and Perimeter

Statistics and Probability

Throughout the book, the more challenging questions are marked like this: **❶**

Editors
Sarah Blackwood, Chris Burton, Helena Hayes, Paul Jordin, Kirstie McHale, Matteo Orsini Jones,
Ali Palin, Andy Park, Charlotte Whiteley, Jonathan Wray

Contributors:
Alida Allen, Jane Appleton, Cath Brown, Katharine Brown, Pamela Chatley, Eva Cowlishaw,
Alastair Duncombe, Stephen Green, Philip Hale, Phil Harvey, Judy Hornigold, Louise Irons,
Claire Jackson, Mark Moody, Charlotte O'Brien, Philip Potten, Rosemary Rogers, Manpreet Sambhi,
Neil Saunders, Jonathan Stevens, Jan Walker, Kieran Wardell, Jeanette Whiteman

Proofreaders:
Peter Caunter, Sharon Keeley-Holden, Glenn Rogers

Published by CGP

ISBN: 978 1 84762 686 8

Groovy Website: www.cgpbooks.co.uk
Jolly bits of clipart from CorelDRAW®
Printed by Elanders Ltd, Newcastle upon Tyne.

Based on the classic CGP style created by Richard Parsons.

Section 1 — Non-Calculator Arithmetic

1.1 Negative Numbers

Adding and Subtracting Negative Numbers

Negative numbers are numbers which are **less than zero**.
You can count places on a **number line** to help with calculations involving negative numbers.

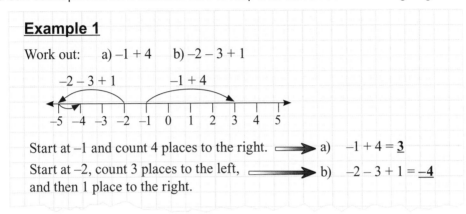

Example 1

Work out: a) $-1 + 4$ b) $-2 - 3 + 1$

Start at -1 and count 4 places to the right. ⟹ a) $-1 + 4 = \underline{\mathbf{3}}$

Start at -2, count 3 places to the left, ⟹ b) $-2 - 3 + 1 = \underline{\mathbf{-4}}$
and then 1 place to the right.

Exercise 1

Answer **Questions 1-6** without using your calculator.

1   Work out the following.
   a) $-4 + 3$ **b)** $-1 + 5$ **c)** $-2 + 1$ **d)** $2 - 6$
   e) $-5 + 9$ **f)** $-5 - 3$ **g)** $-9 - 2$ **h)** $4 - 8$
   i) $-12 + 15$ **j)** $6 - 17$ **k)** $-13 + 18$ **l)** $11 - 19$

2   Work out the following.
   a) $-3 + 2 - 1$ **b)** $-2 + 8 - 5$ **c)** $8 - 5 - 3$ **d)** $6 - 2 + 1$
   e) $-1 - 7 - 4$ **f)** $-5 + 8 - 12$ **g)** $-9 + 13 + 11$ **h)** $7 - 18 + 11$

The thermometer on the right shows temperature. Use it to answer **Questions 3-6**.

3   **a)** Find the temperature that is 3 °C lower than -1 °C.
    b) Find the temperature that is 8 °C higher than -5 °C.

4   Find the difference between the following temperatures.
   a) -6 °C and 3 °C   **b)** -2 °C and -5 °C

5   At midday the temperature was 6 °C. By midnight, the temperature had decreased
   by 7 °C. What was the temperature at midnight?

6   At 5 am, the temperature was -6 °C. At 11 pm, the temperature was -1 °C.
   What was the difference in temperature between these two times?

°C
7
6
5
4
3
2
1
0
-1
-2
-3
-4
-5
-6

Rules for Adding and Subtracting Negative Numbers

Adding a negative number is the same as subtracting a positive number. **'+' next to '−' means subtract**

Subtracting a negative number is the same as adding a positive number. **'−' next to '−' means add**

Example 2

Work out: a) $1 - (-4)$ b) $-5 + (-2)$.

1. − next to − means add.

2. + next to − means subtract.

a) $1 - (-4) = 1 + 4$
$= \underline{5}$

b) $-5 + (-2) = -5 - 2$
$= \underline{-7}$

Exercise 2

Answer **Questions 1-4** without using your calculator.

1   Work out the following.

a) $4 - (-2)$ b) $-3 - (-5)$ c) $-7 + (-2)$ d) $-6 - (-2)$

e) $-5 + (-5)$ f) $-5 - (-5)$ g) $9 + (-2)$ h) $3 - (-7)$

i) $-13 - (-3)$ j) $8 + (-2)$ k) $-6 + (-3)$ l) $1 - (-12)$

2   Work out the following.

a) $-1 + (-4) - 1$ b) $3 + (-2) + (-5)$ c) $6 - (-2) + (-3)$ d) $7 + (-6) - (-8)$

e) $-2 - (-9) - (-1)$ f) $-8 + (-8) - (-12)$ g) $9 - (-13) + (-2)$ h) $-3 + (-11) + (-6)$

3   Find the difference between the following numbers by subtracting one from the other.

a) 6 and −5   b) −10 and −6   c) −8 and 4   d) −5 and −12

4   Copy the following calculations and fill in the blanks.

a) $-3 + \square = -5$ b) $5 - \square = 10$ c) $\square + (-7) = 4$ d) $\square - (-2) = -6$

Multiplying and Dividing Negative Numbers

When you multiply or divide two numbers which have the **same** sign, the answer is **positive**.
When you multiply or divide two numbers which have **opposite** signs, the answer is **negative**.

Example 3

Work out:

a) $24 \div (-6)$ The signs are opposite (one positive, one negative), so the answer is negative. $24 \div -6 = \underline{-4}$

b) $-5 \times (-8)$ The signs are the same (both negative), so the answer is positive. $-5 \times -8 = \underline{40}$

Exercise 3

Answer **Questions 1-3** without using your calculator.

1 Work out the following.

a) $3 \times (-4)$ b) $(-15) \div (-3)$ c) $12 \div (-4)$ d) $2 \times (-8)$

e) $5 \div (-5)$ f) $(-15) \div 3$ g) $(-9) \times 6$ h) $(-11) \times (-8)$

i) $(-72) \div (-6)$ j) $56 \div (-8)$ k) $(-7) \times (-3)$ l) $(-81) \div (-9)$

m) $(-24) \div 4$ n) $(-18) \div (-2)$ o) $6 \times (-3)$ p) $(-96) \div (-12)$

q) $(-12) \times (-3)$ r) $7 \times (-6)$ s) $45 \div (-9)$ t) $(-12) \times 2$

2 Copy the following calculations and fill in the blanks.

a) $-3 \times \square = -6$ b) $-14 \div \square = -2$ c) $\square \times 4 = -16$ d) $\square \div (-2) = -5$

e) $-8 \times \square = -24$ f) $-18 \div \square = 3$ g) $\square \times (-3) = 36$ h) $\square \div 11 = -7$

3 Work out the following.

a) $(-3) \times 4 \div 2$ b) $2 \times 4 \div (-2)$ c) $(-3) \times 7 \div (-21)$ d) $(-5) \times (-6) \div 3$

e) $(-6) \times 5 \div (-2)$ f) $(-3) \times (-5) \times (-6)$ g) $(-63) \times (-2) \div (-9)$ h) $(-12) \times 3 \times (-2)$

i) $(-60) \times (-10) \div 12$ j) $[35 \div (-7)] \times (-8)$ k) $[55 \div (-11)] \times (-9)$ l) $[(-24) \div 8)] \div 3$

1.2   Whole Number Arithmetic

Addition and Subtraction

When adding or subtracting large numbers, write one number above the other, then add or subtract one column at a time.

Example 1

Work out: a) $145 + 28$ b) $364 - 128$

1. Write one number above the other, making sure the columns line up.

2. Add or subtract one column at a time — you may have to 'carry' numbers when adding, or 'borrow' numbers when subtracting.

a)
$$\begin{array}{r} 145 \\ + 28 \\ \hline 3 \end{array} \quad \begin{array}{r} 145 \\ + 28 \\ \hline 73 \end{array} \quad \begin{array}{r} 145 \\ + 28 \\ \hline 173 \end{array}$$
So $145 + 28 = \underline{\mathbf{173}}$.

b)
$$\begin{array}{r} 3\,\overset{5}{\cancel{6}}\,\overset{1}{4} \\ - 128 \\ \hline 6 \end{array} \quad \begin{array}{r} 3\,\overset{5}{\cancel{6}}\,\overset{1}{4} \\ - 128 \\ \hline 36 \end{array} \quad \begin{array}{r} 3\,\overset{5}{\cancel{6}}\,\overset{1}{4} \\ - 128 \\ \hline 236 \end{array}$$
So $364 - 128 = \underline{\mathbf{236}}$.

Exercise 1

Answer these questions without using your calculator.

1 Copy and work out the following.

a)
$$\begin{array}{r} 23 \\ + 56 \\ \hline \end{array}$$

b)
$$\begin{array}{r} 47 \\ + 36 \\ \hline \end{array}$$

c)
$$\begin{array}{r} 122 \\ + 97 \\ \hline \end{array}$$

d)
$$\begin{array}{r} 243 \\ + 178 \\ \hline \end{array}$$

2 Copy and work out the following.

a)
$$\begin{array}{r} 9\,8 \\ -\ 3\,5 \\ \hline \end{array}$$

b)
$$\begin{array}{r} 7\,3 \\ -\ 2\,7 \\ \hline \end{array}$$

c)
$$\begin{array}{r} 1\,8\,1 \\ -\ \ 3\,5 \\ \hline \end{array}$$

d)
$$\begin{array}{r} 2\,3\,3 \\ -\,1\,8\,7 \\ \hline \end{array}$$

3 Work out the following.

a) $25 + 68$ b) $256 + 312$ c) $342 + 679$ d) $614 + 288$

e) $138 - 26$ f) $262 - 54$ g) $841 - 346$ h) $307 - 128$

i) $2513 + 241$ j) $1358 + 1296$ k) $2942 - 324$ l) $4003 - 1235$

4 Work out the following.

a) $41 + 112 + 213$ b) $123 + 478 + 215$ c) $341 + 162 - 145$ d) $764 + 138 - 345$

e) $221 + 126 - 98$ f) $(498 - 137) + 556$ g) $(1841 - 346) + 141$ h) $(987 - 451) + 221$

5 Lisa has 38 marbles, John has 52 marbles and Bina has 65 marbles.
How many marbles do they have altogether?

6 An art club has £2146 in the bank. It spends £224 on art supplies.
How much money does it have left?

7 The village of Great Missingham has a population of 1845. The neighbouring village of Fentley has a population of 1257. How many more people live in Great Missingham than Fentley?

Multiplication

There are different methods for multiplying large numbers.
Example 2 uses traditional **long multiplication**, while Example 3 uses a **grid method**.

Example 2

Work out 254×26.

1. Write one number above the other, making sure the columns line up.

2. Multiply each digit of 254 by 6, working from right to left. If the answer is 10 or more, carry the ten's digit. This is 254×6.

3. Now put a 0 in the right-hand column, and multiply each digit of 254 by 2, carrying digits where necessary. This is 254×20.

4. Add the two rows to find the final answer.

$$\begin{array}{r} 2\,5\,4 \\ \times\ 2\,6 \\ \hline \end{array} \qquad \begin{array}{r} 2\,5\,4 \\ \times\ 2\,6 \\ \hline \end{array} \qquad \begin{array}{r} 2\,5\,4 \\ \times\ 2\,6 \\ \hline \end{array}$$

$$\begin{array}{r} {}_2 4 \end{array} \qquad \begin{array}{r} {}_3 {}_2 4 \end{array} \qquad \begin{array}{r} 1\,{}_3{}_2 4 \end{array}$$

$$\begin{array}{r} 2\,5\,4 \\ \times\ 2\,6 \\ \hline 1\,5_3\,2_2\,4 \\ 0 \end{array} \quad \begin{array}{r} 2\,5\,4 \\ \times\ 2\,6 \\ \hline 1\,5_3\,2_2\,4 \\ 8\,0 \end{array} \quad \begin{array}{r} 2\,5\,4 \\ \times\ 2\,6 \\ \hline 1\,5_3\,2_2\,4 \\ {}_1 0\,8\,0 \end{array} \quad \begin{array}{r} 2\,5\,4 \\ \times\ 2\,6 \\ \hline 1\,5_3\,2_2\,4 \\ 5_1\,0\,8\,0 \end{array}$$

$$\begin{array}{r} 1\,5\,4 \\ \times\ 2\,6 \\ \hline 1\,5_3\,2_2\,4 \\ 5_1\,0\,8\,0 \\ \hline 6\,6_1\,0\,4 \end{array} \qquad \text{So } 254 \times 26 = \underline{\textbf{6604}}.$$

Example 3

Work out 254 × 26.

1. Split each number up into units, tens, hundreds etc.

2. Put these around the outside of a grid.

3. Multiply the numbers at the edge of each box. To multiply by 200, multiply by 2, then by 100. To multiply by 50, multiply by 5, then by 10.

4. Add the numbers from the boxes to find the final answer.

	200	50	4
20	20 × 200 = 4000	20 × 50 = 1000	20 × 4 = 80
6	6 × 200 = 1200	6 × 50 = 300	6 × 4 = 24

```
    4 0 0 0
    1 0 0 0
        8 0
    1 2 0 0
      3 0 0
  +     2 4
   ─────────
    6 6ₗ0 4
```

So 254 × 26 = **6604**.

Exercise 2

Answer **Questions 1-8** without using your calculator.

1 Work out the following.

a) 52 × 10 b) 11 × 17 c) 13 × 12 d) 16 × 24
e) 37 × 19 f) 43 × 15 g) 32 × 53 h) 87 × 24
i) 64 × 67 j) 71 × 49 k) 88 × 76 l) 93 × 98
m) 66 × 72 n) 79 × 86 o) 86 × 98 p) 83 × 81

2 Work out the following.

a) 100 × 26 b) 114 × 30 c) 125 × 71 d) 216 × 54
e) 245 × 31 f) 311 × 59 g) 409 × 63 h) 415 × 41
i) 367 × 62 j) 498 × 69 k) 511 × 55 l) 568 × 74

3 In November, Jilly tells her friend that there are 46 days until Christmas. How many hours is this?

4 Dom's monthly electricity bill is £33. How much does he spend on electricity each year?

5 Sheila earns £243 per week. How much does she earn in 52 weeks?

6 The weight of a storage container is 14 tonnes. A cargo ship can carry 230 of these containers. How many tonnes can the cargo ship carry?

7 A box of matches contains 85 matches. There are 160 boxes in a carton. How many matches are there in a carton?

8 Work out the following.

a) 1347 × 20 b) 2271 × 25 c) 3669 × 21 d) 5624 × 42
e) 3000 × 21 f) 1211 × 34 g) 2623 × 42 h) 4526 × 19

Division

There are different ways to divide numbers without using a calculator.
Example 4 shows '**short division**'. Example 5 shows '**long division**'.

Example 4

Work out $3144 \div 8$.

Using short division:

1. 8 doesn't go into 3, so look at the first <u>two</u> digits.

$$8 \overline{)3\,1^74\,4} \quad \begin{smallmatrix}0\ 3\end{smallmatrix}$$

2. 8 goes into 31 three times, with remainder 7.

$$8 \overline{)3\,1^74^24} \quad \begin{smallmatrix}0\ 3\ 9\end{smallmatrix}$$

3. 8 goes into 74 nine times, with remainder 2.

4. 8 goes into 24 three times exactly.

$$8 \overline{)3\,1^74^24} \quad \begin{smallmatrix}0\ 3\ 9\ 3\end{smallmatrix}$$

So $3144 \div 8 = \underline{\textbf{393}}$.

Example 5

Work out $7657 \div 34$.

Using long division:

1. 34 goes into 76 twice.
    $34 \times 2 = 68$, so subtract 68 from 76 to find the remainder.

$$
\begin{array}{r}
2 \\
34)\overline{7\,6\,5\,7} \\
-\,6\,8 \\
\hline
8
\end{array}
$$

2. Bring the 5 down from above.

$$
\begin{array}{r}
2 \\
34)\overline{7\,6\,5\,7} \\
-\,6\,8\downarrow \\
\hline
8\,5
\end{array}
$$

3. 34 goes into 85 twice.
    $34 \times 2 = 68$, so subtract 68 from 85 to find the remainder.

$$
\begin{array}{r}
2\,2 \\
34)\overline{7\,6\,5\,7} \\
-\,6\,8 \\
\hline
8\,5 \\
-\,6\,8 \\
\hline
1\,7
\end{array}
$$

4. Bring the 7 down from above.

$$
\begin{array}{r}
2\,2 \\
34)\overline{7\,6\,5\,7} \\
-\,6\,8 \\
\hline
8\,5 \\
-\,6\,8\downarrow \\
\hline
1\,7\,7
\end{array}
$$

5. 34 goes into 177 five times. $34 \times 5 = 170$, so subtract 170 from 177 to find the remainder.

$$
\begin{array}{r}
2\,2\,5 \\
34)\overline{7\,6\,5\,7} \\
-\,6\,8 \\
\hline
8\,5 \\
-\,6\,8 \\
\hline
1\,7\,7 \\
-\,1\,7\,0 \\
\hline
7
\end{array}
$$

So $7657 \div 34 = \underline{\textbf{225 remainder 7}}$

$= \underline{\textbf{225}\frac{\textbf{7}}{\textbf{34}}}$

Exercise 3

Answer **Questions 1-10** without using your calculator.

1 Use short division to work out the following.

   a) $7 \overline{)357}$ **b)** $7 \overline{)238}$ **c)** $9 \overline{)603}$ **d)** $8 \overline{)3616}$

   e) $4 \overline{)1312}$ **f)** $6 \overline{)1350}$ **g)** $4 \overline{)2240}$ **h)** $6 \overline{)3732}$

2 Use short division to work out the following. In each case, give the remainder as a fraction.

  a) $361 \div 5$ **b)** $5213 \div 3$ **c)** $4198 \div 5$ **d)** $4609 \div 9$

  e) $300 \div 7$ **f)** $671 \div 9$ **g)** $2545 \div 6$ **h)** $2674 \div 8$

3 Use long division to work out the following.

  a) $23\overline{)644}$ **b)** $19\overline{)608}$ **c)** $18\overline{)738}$ **d)** $17\overline{)816}$

  e) $20\overline{)4120}$ **f)** $33\overline{)6633}$ **g)** $24\overline{)9624}$ **h)** $31\overline{)7936}$

  i) $22\overline{)6842}$ **j)** $34\overline{)9146}$ **k)** $28\overline{)8680}$ **l)** $26\overline{)9152}$

4 Use long division to work out the following. Give any remainders as fractions.

  a) $945 \div 45$ **b)** $846 \div 32$ **c)** $711 \div 21$ **d)** $648 \div 18$

  e) $608 \div 16$ **f)** $1159 \div 19$ **g)** $1218 \div 21$ **h)** $1552 \div 33$

  i) $7131 \div 18$ **j)** $6718 \div 25$ **k)** $8323 \div 31$ **l)** $8539 \div 44$

5 A postage stamp costs 41p. How many stamps could you buy for £5.00, and how much change would you receive?

6 672 people are to be divided into 24 equal groups. How many people will be in each group?

7 Eggs are packed into boxes that hold 6 eggs each. How many boxes are needed for 1350 eggs?

8 22 identical washing machines cost £7634 in total. How much does each washing machine cost?

9 **a)** Mike earns £22 464 per year. How much does he earn per week? (Assume 1 year = 52 weeks.)

  b) Andrea earns £24 636 per year. How much does she earn per month?

10 The local team played 14 games on their home ground. The same number of people went to each game and 17 584 people in total attended the games. How many people went to each game?

1.3 Decimals

Decimals are a way of showing parts of a whole number.

$$\underset{\text{Hundreds}}{6} \; \underset{\text{Tens}}{2} \; \underset{\text{Units}}{7} . \underset{\text{Tenths}}{3} \; \underset{\text{Hundredths}}{8} \; \underset{\text{Thousandths}}{1}$$

Decimal Point

Example 1

What is the value of each of the digits in 0.692?

The 6 is in the tenths column.   Six tenths $= \frac{6}{10}$

The 9 is in the hundredths column.   Nine hundredths $= \frac{9}{100}$

The 2 is in the thousandths column.   Two thousandths $= \frac{2}{1000}$

Exercise 1

1 Write down the value of the 7 in 4.271.

2 Write down the value of the 3 in 6.382.

3 Write down the value of the 8 in 0.718.

4 Write down the value of the 1 in 9.0361.

5 Write down the value of the 2 in 2.37.

6 Write down the value of the 6 in 0.956.

7 Write down the following as decimal numbers.

    a) one tenth   **b)** two hundredths   **c)** five thousandths   **d)** seven tenths

    e) $\dfrac{7}{100}$ **f)** $\dfrac{1}{1000}$ **g)** $\dfrac{9}{100}$ **h)** $\dfrac{8}{10}$

Ordering Decimals

Use the **place value** of digits to put decimals in order of size — digits further to the left are 'worth more'.

Example 2

Put the decimals 8.09, 8.2, 8.092 and 8.9 in order of size, from smallest to largest.

1. Arrange the numbers in columns and fill in any gaps with 0's.

                                                                  8.090

2. Compare the numbers one column at a time, from left to right.

                                                                  8.200

                                                                  8.092

3. Write the numbers in the correct order.

                                                                  8.900

The correct order is
8.09, 8.092, 8.2, 8.9

Example 3

Put the decimals –1.02, –1.2, –0.12 and –2.1 in order, from lowest to highest.

1. Arrange the numbers in columns and fill in any gaps with 0's.

                                                                 –1.02

2. Compare the numbers one column at a time, from left to right.

                                                                  –1.20

                                                                  –0.12

3. With negative numbers, the larger the digit the lower the number is. For example, –2 is lower than –1.

                                                                  –2.10

4. Write the numbers in the correct order.

The correct order is
–2.1, –1.2, –1.02, –0.12

Exercise 2

1 Write down the larger number in each of the following pairs.

    a) 0.3, 0.31   **b)** 0.21, 0.12   **c)** 0.09, 0.009   **d)** 0.427, 0.472

    e) 8.3, 8.03   **f)** 0.006, 0.05   **g)** 0.1, 0.01   **h)** 0.11, 0.09

    i) 3.7, 3.07   **j)** 7.19, 7.091   **k)** 12.1, 12.099   **l)** 18.07, 17.08

2 Put each of the following lists of decimals in order of size, from smallest to largest.

    a) 0.02, 0.2, 0.15   **b)** 0.61, 0.51, 0.16   **c)** 0.59, 0.591, 0.559

    d) 0.03, 0.035, 0.04   **e)** 0.07, 0.007, 0.017, 0.7   **f)** 1.4, 1.14, 0.41, 1.41

    g) 2.3, 2.03, 0.09, 0.75   **h)** 0.78, 0.782, 0.708, 0.078   **i)** 0.09, 0.101, 0.1, 0.11

    j) 1.6, 1.66, 0.61, 1.09   **k)** 0.3, 0.31, 3.01, 3.1   **l)** 4.05, 5.04, 5.4, 4.5

3 Put each of the following lists of decimals in order of size, from lowest to highest.

a) 1.05, 1.5, −1.5, 1.55   **b)** 0.6, 6.1, −0.6, −6   **c)** −0.01, 0.1, −0.09, −0.1

d) −0.5, −0.45, −0.55, −5   **e)** −7, −7.1, −7.07, 0.007   **f)** 0.9, −0.05, −0.09, −0.095

1.4   Adding and Subtracting Decimals

Adding and subtracting decimals is similar to using whole numbers
— just make sure you line up the decimal points.

Example 1

Work out 4.53 + 1.6

1. Write one number above the other,
    lining up the decimal points.

2. Fill in any gaps with 0's.

3. Add the digits one column at a time.

$$
\begin{array}{r} 4.53 \\ +\,1.60 \\ \hline .\;3 \end{array}
\qquad
\begin{array}{r} 4.53 \\ +\,1.60 \\ \hline {}_1.13 \end{array}
\qquad
\begin{array}{r} 4.53 \\ +\,1.60 \\ \hline 6{}_1.13 \end{array}
$$

So 4.53 + 1.6 = **6.13**

Example 2

Work out 8.5 − 3.07

1. Write one number above the other,
    lining up the decimal points.

2. Fill in any gaps with 0's.

3. Subtract the digits one column at a time.

$$
\begin{array}{r} 8.\overset{4}{\cancel{5}}{}^{1}0 \\ -\,3.07 \\ \hline .\;3 \end{array}
\qquad
\begin{array}{r} 8.\overset{4}{\cancel{5}}{}^{1}0 \\ -\,3.07 \\ \hline .43 \end{array}
\qquad
\begin{array}{r} 8.\overset{4}{\cancel{5}}{}^{1}0 \\ -\,3.07 \\ \hline 5.43 \end{array}
$$

So 8.5 − 3.07 = **5.43**

Exercise 1

Answer these questions without using your calculator.

1 Copy and work out the following.

a)
$$\begin{array}{r} 5.1 \\ +\,1.8 \\ \hline \end{array}$$

b)
$$\begin{array}{r} 6.3 \\ +\,5.4 \\ \hline \end{array}$$

c)
$$\begin{array}{r} 11.7 \\ +\,\;\;8.2 \\ \hline \end{array}$$

d)
$$\begin{array}{r} 2.5 \\ +\,4.1 \\ \hline \end{array}$$

e)
$$\begin{array}{r} 0.4 \\ +\,0.7 \\ \hline \end{array}$$

f)
$$\begin{array}{r} 8.9 \\ +\,3.2 \\ \hline \end{array}$$

g)
$$\begin{array}{r} 5.7 \\ +\,12.6 \\ \hline \end{array}$$

h)
$$\begin{array}{r} 4.8 \\ +\,5.3 \\ \hline \end{array}$$

2 Copy and work out the following.

a)
$$\begin{array}{r} 5.6 \\ -\,0.3 \\ \hline \end{array}$$

b)
$$\begin{array}{r} 9.9 \\ -\,4.2 \\ \hline \end{array}$$

c)
$$\begin{array}{r} 16.8 \\ -\,7.5 \\ \hline \end{array}$$

d)
$$\begin{array}{r} 6.7 \\ -\,5.1 \\ \hline \end{array}$$

e)
$$\begin{array}{r} 6.45 \\ -\,3.23 \\ \hline \end{array}$$

f)
$$\begin{array}{r} 7.98 \\ -\,6.12 \\ \hline \end{array}$$

g)
$$\begin{array}{r} 5.3 \\ -\,2.8 \\ \hline \end{array}$$

h)
$$\begin{array}{r} 8.5 \\ -\,1.9 \\ \hline \end{array}$$

3 Work out the following.

a) 10.83 + 7.4   b) 0.029 + 1.8   c) 91.7 + 0.492   d) 6.474 + 0.92

e) 2.191 + 4.1   f) 14.799 + 0.08   g) 1.581 + 15.8   h) 11.1 + 12.902

i) 7.89 + 4.789   j) 0.888 + 1.02   k) 0.02 + 0.991   l) 3.41 + 22.169

4 Work out the following.

a) 24.63 − 7.5   b) 6.78 − 5.6   c) 9.915 − 3.7   d) 73.46 − 8.5

e) 67.5 − 4.31   f) 16.3 − 5.16   g) 9.241 − 2.8   h) 0.946 − 0.07

i) 3.52 − 0.126   j) 9.1 − 7.02   k) 11.2 − 1.89   l) 1.1 − 0.839

5 Work out the following.

a) 3.81 + 9.54   b) 2.75 + 9.45   c) 8.67 + 0.95   d) 2.81 − 0.16

e) 4.32 − 2.17   f) 8.72 − 5.94   g) 6.31 − 5.83   h) 1.6 + 4.35

i) 9.6 + 3.12   j) 0.78 + 1.3   k) 6.78 − 5.6   l) 4.21 − 1.9

m) 3.8 − 0.59   n) 15.1 − 0.08   o) 6.25 + 5.6   p) 1.97 + 21.7

Example 3

Work out 4 − 0.91

1. Write any whole numbers as decimals by adding 0's, then line up the decimal points.

2. Subtract the digits one column at a time. As you can't borrow from 0, borrow from the 4 instead.

$$\begin{array}{r} 4.00 \\ -\ 0.91 \\ \hline . \end{array}$$

$$\begin{array}{r} {}^{3}4.{}^{9}0{}^{1}0 \\ -\ 0.91 \\ \hline .\ 9 \end{array}$$

$$\begin{array}{r} {}^{3}4.{}^{9}0{}^{1}0 \\ -\ 0.91 \\ \hline 3.09 \end{array}$$

So 4 − 0.91 = **3.09**

---

6 Work out the following.

a) 6 − 5.1   b) 23 − 18.51   c) 12 − 5.028   d) 13 − 6.453

7 Work out the following.

a) 2 + 1.8   b) 3.7 + 6   c) 12.7 + 7.34   d) 9.49 + 13

e) 38 + 6.92   f) 5 − 0.8   g) 9 − 4.2   h) 24 − 5.7

8 Work out the following.

a) 6.474 + 0.92 + 1.1   b) 2.39 + 8.8 + 0.26   c) 12.24 + 3.7 + 1.2   d) 13.56 + 1.5 + 7.06

e) 2 + 4.123 + 1.86   f) 16.8 + 4.17 + 2   g) 2.64 + 13 + 1.012   h) 1 + 0.07 + 0.012

9 Copy the following calculations and fill in the blanks.

a)
$$\begin{array}{r} \square . 6\ \square \\ +\ 0 . \square\ 0 \\ \hline 8 . 2\ 1 \end{array}$$

b)
$$\begin{array}{r} 5 . \square\ 8 \\ +\ \square . 4\ \square \\ \hline 6 . 4\ 0 \end{array}$$

c)
$$\begin{array}{r} 6 . 7\ 5 \\ +\ \square . 4\ \square \\ \hline 9 . \square\ 3 \end{array}$$

d)
$$\begin{array}{r} 5 . \square\ 3 \\ -\ 2 . 1\ \square \\ \hline \square . 3\ 1 \end{array}$$

Exercise 2

Answer **Questions 1-6** without using your calculator.

1   Malcolm travels 2.3 km to the shops, then a further 4.6 km to his aunt's house.
    How far does he travel in total?

2   Sunita buys a hat for £18.50 and a bag for £31. How much does she spend altogether?

3   A plank of wood is 4 m long. A 2.75 m long piece is cut from the plank.
    What length of wood is left?

4   Joan goes out for a meal. The bill for the meal comes to £66.50. She uses a voucher which
    entitles her to £15 off her meal. How much does she have left to pay?

5   Ashkan spends £71.42 at the supermarket. His receipt says that he has saved £11.79 on special
    offers. How much would he have spent if there had been no special offers?

6   On his first run, Ted sprints 100 m in 15.32 seconds. On his second run, he is 0.47 seconds
    quicker. How long did he take on his second run?

1.5   Multiplying and Dividing Decimals

Multiplying and Dividing by 10, 100, 1000

When multiplying by 10, 100 or 1000, each digit in the number moves to the **left**.

   × 10   each digit moves **one place** to the left
   × 100   each digit moves **two places** to the left
   × 1000   each digit moves **three places** to the left

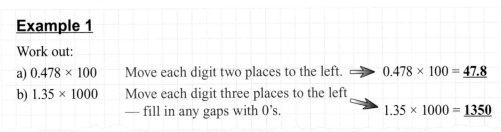

Example 1

Work out:

a) 0.478 × 100   Move each digit two places to the left. ⟹ 0.478 × 100 = **47.8**

b) 1.35 × 1000   Move each digit three places to the left
                   — fill in any gaps with 0's.   ⟹ 1.35 × 1000 = **1350**

When dividing by 10, 100 or 1000, each digit in the number moves to the **right**.

   ÷ 10   each digit moves **one place** to the right
   ÷ 100   each digit moves **two places** to the right
   ÷ 1000   each digit moves **three places** to the right

Example 2

Work out:

a) 923.1 ÷ 100   Move each digit two places to the right. ⟹ 923.1 ÷ 100 = **9.231**

b) 51.4 ÷ 1000   Move each digit three places to the right — fill
                   in any gaps after the decimal point with 0's. ⟹ 51.4 ÷ 1000 = **0.0514**

Exercise 1

Answer **Questions 1-2** without using your calculator.

1 Work out the following.

    a) 0.92×10 **b)** 1.41×100 **c)** 72.5×10 **d)** 0.023×100

    e) 0.019×1000 **f)** 14.6×100 **g)** 6.07×1000 **h)** 9.9×100

    i) 13.04×10 **j)** 7.8×1000 **k)** 0.006×100 **l)** 0.23×1000

2 Work out the following.

    a) $25.9 \div 10$ **b)** $861.5 \div 100$ **c)** $381.7 \div 10$ **d)** $549.1 \div 1000$

    e) $901.5 \div 100$ **f)** $6.3 \div 10$ **g)** $5.1 \div 1000$ **h)** $0.94 \div 100$

    i) $0.08 \div 10$ **j)** $23.2 \div 1000$ **k)** $601.2 \div 100$ **l)** $17 \div 1000$

Multiplying Decimals

When multiplying two decimals, ignore the decimal point and multiply them as whole numbers. Then add in the decimal point in the right place at the end.

Example 3

Work out 0.32×0.6

1. Ignore the decimal points and treat it as a whole number multiplication.

2. There are three digits in total after the decimal points in the question (two in 0.32 and one in 0.6).

3. The answer should also have three digits after the decimal point.

$$\begin{array}{r} 3\,2 \\ \times \quad 6 \\ \hline {}_1 2 \end{array} \qquad \begin{array}{r} 3\,2 \\ \times \quad 6 \\ \hline 1\,9_1 2 \end{array}$$

So $0.32 \times 0.6 = \underline{\textbf{0.192}}$

Exercise 2

Answer **Questions 1-8** without using your calculator.

1 You are given that $132 \times 238 = 31\,416$. Use this information to work out the following.

    a) 13.2×238 **b)** 1.32×23.8 **c)** 1.32×0.238 **d)** 0.132×0.238

2 You are given that $401 \times 119 = 47\,719$. Use this information to work out the following.

    a) 40.1×11.9 **b)** 4.01×1.19 **c)** 0.401×1.19 **d)** 0.401×0.119

3   **a)** Work out 21×6.

    b) Use your answer to work out the following.

        (i) 2.1×6 **(ii)** 2.1×0.6 **(iii)** 0.21×0.06

4   **a)** Work out 11×23.

    b) Use your answer to work out the following.

        (i) 1.1×2.3 **(ii)** 1.1×0.23 **(iii)** 0.11×0.23

5 Work out the following.
   a) 6.7×8 **b)** 3.2×6 **c)** 8.8×3 **d)** 5.6×8
   e) 0.65×9 **f)** 9.7×2 **g)** 2.7×4 **h)** 9.3×5

6 Work out the following.
   a) 0.6×0.3 **b)** 0.9×0.8 **c)** 0.01×0.6 **d)** 0.05×0.04
   e) 0.08×0.5 **f)** 0.2×0.03 **g)** 0.04×0.02 **h)** 0.007×0.006

7 Work out the following.
   a) 2.1×0.6 **b)** 3.5×0.4 **c)** 8.1×0.5 **d)** 2.2×0.3
   e) 3.6×0.3 **f)** 0.51×0.3 **g)** 1.6×0.04 **h)** 8.2×0.008
   i) 0.61×0.6 **j)** 0.33×0.02 **k)** 5.2×0.09 **l)** 4.7×0.002

8 Work out the following.
   a) 6.3×2.1 **b)** 1.4×2.3 **c)** 1.5×2.7 **d)** 2.4×1.8
   e) 3.9×8.3 **f)** 8.6×6.9 **g)** 0.16×3.3 **h)** 5.1×0.23
   i) 0.52×0.12 **j)** 0.64×0.42 **k)** 0.029×0.61 **l)** 0.017×0.034

Example 4

Work out 1.36×200

1. $1.36 \times 200 = 1.36 \times 2 \times 100$, so break the multiplication down into two stages.
2. First calculate 1.36×2 by ignoring the decimal point and adding it in at the end.
3. Then multiply by 100 by moving each digit two places to the left.

$$\begin{array}{r} 1\,3\,6 \\ \times\quad 2 \\ \hline {}_1 2 \end{array} \qquad \begin{array}{r} 1\,3\,6 \\ \times\quad 2 \\ \hline 7_1 2 \end{array} \qquad \begin{array}{r} 1\,3\,6 \\ \times\quad 2 \\ \hline 2\,7_1 2 \end{array}$$

$136 \times 2 = 272$, so $1.36 \times 2 = 2.72$
So $1.36 \times 200 = 2.72 \times 100$
$$= \underline{\mathbf{272}}$$

Exercise 3

Answer **Questions 1-2** without using your calculator.

1 **a)** Work out 6.412×4.
   b) Use your answer to work out the following.
      (i) 6.412×40 **(ii)** 6.412×400 **(iii)** 6.412×4000

2 Work out the following.
   a) 3.1×40 **b)** 0.7×600 **c)** 12.1×30 **d)** 11.06×80
   e) 0.061×2000 **f)** 1.007×400 **g)** 101.8×60 **h)** 0.903×5000
   i) 4.112×90 **j)** 0.003×8000 **k)** 12.225×70 **l)** 30.303×20

Dividing Decimals

When dividing decimals, you need to make sure you put the decimal point in the correct place.

When the number you're **dividing by** is a decimal, convert the calculation into a division by a whole number by multiplying both numbers by a power of 10.

Example 5

Work out 5.16 ÷ 8

1. Position the decimal point in the answer directly above the one inside the division.

$$\begin{array}{r} 0. \\ 8\overline{)5.\,^5 1\,6} \end{array}$$

2. Divide as you would with whole numbers.

$$\begin{array}{r} 0.\,6 \\ 8\overline{)5.\,^5 1\,^3 6} \end{array} \qquad \begin{array}{r} 0.\,6\,4 \\ 8\overline{)5.\,^5 1\,^3 6\,^4 0} \end{array} \qquad \begin{array}{r} 0.\,6\,4\,5 \\ 8\overline{)5.\,^5 1\,^3 6\,^4 0} \end{array}$$

3. You may need to add zeros to the decimal inside the division sign.

So 5.16 ÷ 8 = **0.645**

Example 6

Work out 8.16 ÷ 0.2

1. Multiply both numbers by 10, so you are dividing by a whole number.

$$\times 10 \left(\begin{array}{c} 8.16 \div 0.2 \\ = 81.6 \div 2 \end{array} \right) \times 10$$

2. Divide as usual.

$$\begin{array}{r} 4. \\ 2\overline{)8\,1.\,6} \end{array} \qquad \begin{array}{r} 4\,0. \\ 2\overline{)8\,1.\,^1 6} \end{array} \qquad \begin{array}{r} 4\,0.\,8 \\ 2\overline{)8\,1.\,^1 6} \end{array}$$

So 8.16 ÷ 0.2 = **40.8**

Exercise 4

Answer **Questions 1-12** without using your calculator.

1 Copy and work out the following.

    a) $2\overline{)5.4}$ **b)** $3\overline{)9.6}$ **c)** $6\overline{)9.24}$ **d)** $5\overline{)2.65}$

    e) $7\overline{)7.21}$ **f)** $9\overline{)4.05}$ **g)** $7\overline{)98.7}$ **h)** $4\overline{)0.924}$

2 Work out the following.

    a) 8.52 ÷ 4   **b)** 0.0612 ÷ 6   **c)** 112.8 ÷ 4   **d)** 1.02 ÷ 3

    e) 2.14 ÷ 4   **f)** 8.62 ÷ 5   **g)** 17.1 ÷ 6   **h)** 0.081 ÷ 9

    i) 0.84 ÷ 5   **j)** 49.35 ÷ 7   **k)** 1.25 ÷ 4   **l)** 89.1 ÷ 2

    m) 5.62 ÷ 8   **n)** 0.052 ÷ 5   **o)** 12.06 ÷ 8   **p)** 3.061 ÷ 5

3 Consider the calculation 6.4 ÷ 0.4.

    a) Multiply both numbers by 10 to form an equivalent calculation which involves dividing by a whole number.

    b) Use your answer to work out 6.4 ÷ 0.4.

4 Consider the calculation 0.384 ÷ 0.12.

    a) Multiply both numbers by 100 to form an equivalent calculation which involves dividing by a whole number.

    b) Use your answer to work out 0.384 ÷ 0.12.

5 Consider the calculation 3.8 ÷ 0.008.

    a) Write down an equivalent calculation which involves dividing by a whole number.

    b) Use your answer to work out 3.8 ÷ 0.008.

6 Work out the following.

    a) 6.4 ÷ 0.2   **b)** 1.56 ÷ 0.2   **c)** 0.624 ÷ 0.3   **d)** 8.8 ÷ 0.2

    e) 3.54 ÷ 0.4   **f)** 3.774 ÷ 0.4   **g)** 5.75 ÷ 0.5   **h)** 0.275 ÷ 0.5

7 Work out the following.

    a) 22.56 ÷ 0.03   **b)** 16.42 ÷ 0.02   **c)** 0.028 ÷ 0.07   **d)** 0.257 ÷ 0.05

    e) 1.08 ÷ 0.08   **f)** 7.665 ÷ 0.03   **g)** 0.252 ÷ 0.05   **h)** 0.039 ÷ 0.06

8 Work out the following.

    a) 0.81 ÷ 0.009   **b)** 4.68 ÷ 0.006   **c)** 7.5 ÷ 0.005   **d)** 50.4 ÷ 0.007

9 Work out the following.

    a) 0.9 ÷ 0.03   **b)** 0.71 ÷ 0.002   **c)** 63 ÷ 0.09   **d)** 108 ÷ 0.4

    e) 1.76 ÷ 0.008   **f)** 4.151 ÷ 0.7   **g)** 15.33 ÷ 0.07   **h)** 8.006 ÷ 0.2

    i) 20.16 ÷ 0.007   **j)** 0.008 ÷ 0.4   **k)** 0.01 ÷ 0.8   **l)** 1.44 ÷ 1.2

10 Consider the calculation 7.3 ÷ 50.

    a) By dividing both numbers by 10, write down an equivalent calculation which involves dividing by 5.

    b) Use your answer to work out 7.3 ÷ 50.

11 Consider the calculation 2.41 ÷ 400.

    a) Write down an equivalent calculation which involves dividing by a one-digit number.

    b) Use your answer to work out 2.41 ÷ 400.

12 Work out the following.

    a) 6.08 ÷ 40   **b)** 5.74 ÷ 700   **c)** 3.552 ÷ 80   **d)** 13.722 ÷ 3000

    e) 25.47 ÷ 900   **f)** 33.708 ÷ 6000   **g)** 14.016 ÷ 120   **h)** 28.6 ÷ 13 000

1.6   Order of Operations

Operations in mathematics are things like addition, subtraction, multiplication and division. The order in which each of these is carried out within a calculation is very important.

BODMAS tells you the correct order to carry out these operations.

        Brackets, **O**ther, **D**ivision, **M**ultiplication, **A**ddition, **S**ubtraction

Example 1

Work out:

a) 20 − 3 × 4   Multiply first, then subtract. ⟹ 20 − 3 × 4 = 20 − 12 = **8**

b) 30 ÷ (15 − 12)   Work out what's in the   ⟹ 30 ÷ (15 − 12) = 30 ÷ 3 = **10**
                      brackets first, then divide.

Exercise 1

Answer **Questions 1-5** without using your calculator.

1 Work out the following.

a) $5 + 1 \times 3$ b) $11 - 2 \times 5$ c) $5 + 6 \times 2$ d) $18 - 10 \div 5$

e) $24 \div 4 + 2$ f) $35 \div 5 + 2$ g) $4 + 9 \times 2$ h) $36 - 12 \div 4$

2 Work out the following.

a) $2 \times (4 + 10)$ b) $(7 - 2) \times 3$ c) $4 + (48 \div 8)$ d) $5 + (3 \times 7)$

e) $56 \div (2 \times 4)$ f) $(3 + 2) \times (9 - 4)$ g) $(9 + 15) \div 4$ h) $20 \div (5 - 3)$

i) $6 \times (4 + 3)$ j) $11 - (2 + 3)$ k) $(8 - 7) \times (6 + 5)$ l) $(8 \times 4) - 11$

3 Work out the following.

a) $2 \times (8 + 4) - 7$ b) $5 \times 6 - 8 \div 2$ c) $18 \div (9 - 12 \div 4)$ d) $100 \div (8 + 3 \times 4)$

e) $7 + (10 - 9 \div 3)$ f) $20 - (5 \times 3 + 2)$ g) $48 \div 3 - 7 \times 2$ h) $36 - (7 + 4 \times 4)$

4 Copy each of the following and insert brackets to make the calculation correct.

a) $9 \times 7 - 5 = 18$ b) $18 - 6 \div 3 = 4$ c) $21 \div 4 + 3 = 3$

d) $5 + 2 \times 6 - 2 = 28$ e) $13 - 5 \times 13 - 1 = 96$ f) $6 + 8 - 7 \times 5 = 35$

5 Copy each of the following and: **(i)** fill in the blanks with either $+$, $-$, $\times$ or $\div$,

(ii) add any brackets necessary to complete the calculation.

a) $6 + 7 \,\square\, 2 = 20$ b) $16 \,\square\, 6 \div 3 = 14$ c) $11 \,\square\, 3 + 5 = 38$ d) $5 + 16 \,\square\, 2 = 13$

e) $3 \,\square\, 6 \,\square\, 9 = 9$ f) $18 \,\square\, 4 \,\square\, 6 = 8$ g) $8 \,\square\, 2 \,\square\, 6 = 10$ h) $35 \,\square\, 7 \,\square\, 2 = 56$

i) $3 \,\square\, 7 \,\square\, 4 = 40$ j) $13 \,\square\, 4 \,\square\, 1 = 10$ k) $14 \,\square\, 6 \,\square\, 8 = 1$ l) $45 \,\square\, 6 \,\square\, 3 = 5$

Example 2

Work out $\dfrac{2 \times 4 + 12}{9 - 5}$.

1. You need to divide the top line by the bottom line.
2. Work out what's on the top and the bottom separately
   — imagine brackets around the two parts.

$$\frac{2 \times 4 + 12}{9 - 5} = (2 \times 4 + 12) \div (9 - 5)$$
$$= (8 + 12) \div (9 - 5)$$
$$= 20 \div 4 = \underline{\mathbf{5}}$$

Exercise 2

Answer **Question 1** without using your calculator.

1 Work out the following.

a) $\dfrac{4 + 5}{3}$ b) $\dfrac{7 \times 4}{2 + 5}$ c) $\dfrac{4 - 1 + 5}{2 \times 2}$ d) $\dfrac{12 - 5 \times 2}{4 - 2}$

e) $\dfrac{16}{4 \times (5 - 3)}$ f) $\dfrac{8 + 2}{15 \div 3}$ g) $\dfrac{4 \times (7 + 5)}{6 + 3 \times 2}$ h) $\dfrac{6 + (11 - 8)}{7 - 5}$

i) $\dfrac{12 \div (9 - 5)}{25 \div 5}$ j) $\dfrac{8 \times 2 \div 4}{5 - 6 + 7}$ k) $\dfrac{3 \times 3}{21 \div (12 - 5)}$ l) $\dfrac{36 \div (11 - 2)}{8 - 8 \div 2}$

1.7 Non-Calculator Arithmetic Problems

Exercise 1

Answer **Questions 1-20** without using your calculator.

1 Work out the following.
   a) $-5 + 8$ **b)** $3 \times (-7)$ **c)** $-9 + (-4)$ **d)** $-48 \div 3$
   e) $6 - (-2)$ **f)** $-8 \times (-5)$ **g)** $54 \div (-9)$ **h)** $-11 - 3$

2 In New York, the evening temperature was -4 °C. During the night, the temperature dropped by 7 °C. What was the lowest temperature that night?

3 The melting point of nitrogen is -210 °C. The melting point of magnesium is 650 °C. What is the difference in melting points of the two elements?

4 Six supermarket shelves each contain 75 tins of soup. How many tins are there in total?

5 Tickets for the school play cost £6 each. £570 worth of tickets were sold altogether. How many tickets were sold?

6 Laura receives £14 pocket money each week. How much money does she get in 52 weeks?

7 462 pupils are going on a school trip. A coach can seat 54 children. How many coaches will be needed for the trip?

Carry out the calculations in **Questions 8-10**.

8   **a)** $-8.7 + 3.94$ **b)** $7.6 + (-3.82)$ **c)** $16 - (-8.74)$ **d)** $-6 + 0.9 - (-12.53)$
9   **a)** 3.4×0.01 **b)** $3.48 \div 0.1$ **c)** -9.5×1.14 **d)** $86.2 \div (-0.04)$
10 **a)** $-0.051 \div 0.5$ **b)** -0.09×8.2 **c)** $-0.048 \div (-0.12)$ **d)** $-0.072 \times (-0.5)$

11 Asha bought 2 CDs. One cost £11.95 and the other cost £6.59. She paid with a £20 note. How much change did she receive?

12 1 litre is equal to 1.76 pints. How many pints are there in 5 litres?

13 A car uses 9 litres of petrol to travel 80 km. Petrol costs £1.35 per litre. How much does it cost to travel 400 km?

14 A school jumble sale raises £412.86. The money is to be split equally between three charities. How much will each charity receive?

15 A box of chocolates costs £4.65. A bunch of flowers costs £12.95. Mr O'Brien buys his wife six boxes of chocolates and 3 bunches of flowers. How much does he spend altogether?

16 It costs £35.55 to buy nine identical books. How much would it cost to buy seven of these books?

17 You are given that $221 \times 168 = 37\ 128$. Work out the following.
   a) 2.21×1.68 **b)** 0.221×1.68 **c)** 221×0.168 **d)** 22.1×16.8

18 A shop sells apples for £1.18 per kg. How much would it cost to buy 2.5 kg of apples?

19 A 2.72 m ribbon is cut into pieces of length 0.08 m. How many pieces will there be?

20 Work out the following.
   a) $3 - 8 \times 2$ **b)** $2 - 18 \div 3$ **c)** $6 + 4 \times (-2)$ **d)** $0.5 \times 3 - 1.2$
   e) $3.4 \div 1.7 - 2$ **f)** $0.48 \div (5 + 1)$ **g)** $(5 - 13) \times 1.2$ **h)** $12.8 \div [3 - (-1)]$

Section 2 — Approximations

2.1   Rounding — Whole Numbers

Numbers are sometimes **approximated** (or **rounded**) to make them easier to work with.

For example, a number like 5468.9 could be rounded:
- to the nearest **whole number** (= 5469)
- to the nearest **ten** (= 5470)
- to the nearest **hundred** (= 5500)
- to the nearest **thousand** (= 5000)

Example 1

a)   Round 18.6 to the nearest whole number.
     Look at the digit in the <u>tenths</u> column.
     It's <u>greater than 5</u>, so round <u>up</u>.

b)   Round 34.2 to the nearest ten.
     Look at the digit in the <u>units</u> column.
     It's <u>less than 5</u>, so round <u>down</u>.

c)   Round 150 to the nearest hundred.
     Look at the digit in the <u>tens</u> column.
     It's <u>equal to 5</u>, so round <u>up</u>.

a) 18.⑥ — rounds up to **19**

b) 3④.2 — rounds down to **30**

c) 1⑤0 — rounds up to **200**

Exercise 1

1   Write down all the numbers from the box that round to 14 to the nearest whole number.

14.1	13.3	14.02	15.499	14.5	15.01
13.7	14.09	14.9	13.4999	14.4999	13.901

2   Round the following to the nearest whole number.
   a) 9.7   **b)** 8.4   **c)** 12.2   **d)** 7.5   **e)** 39.8
   f) 7.8   **g)** 45.5   **h)** 1.1   **i)** 117.4   **j)** 662.5

3   Round the following to the nearest whole number.
   a) 11.79   **b)** 7.41   **c)** 25.12   **d)** 45.58   **e)** 11.04

4   Round the following to the nearest ten.
   a) 27   **b)** 32   **c)** 78   **d)** 68   **e)** 48.5
   f) 55   **g)** 54   **h)** 485   **i)** 658   **j)** 187 523

5   Round the following to the nearest hundred.
   a) 158   **b)** 596   **c)** 650   **d)** 449   **e)** 486
   f) 5685   **g)** 6321   **h)** 4714   **i)** 2369   **j)** 12 345

6   Round the following to the nearest thousand.
   a) 2536   **b)** 8516   **c)** 7218   **d)** 9500   **e)** 8596
   f) 1658   **g)** 4328   **h)** 12   **i)** 3258   **j)** 56 985

7 Round the numbers on these calculator displays to the nearest: **(i)** whole number **(ii)** ten

a) `18.2`   b) `16.479`   c) `20150001`   d) `14999999`

Exercise 2

1 378 people visited a museum. Round this number to the nearest 10.

2 Flora picked 417 blackberries. How many is this to the nearest 10?

3 Raj says Italy has an area of 301 225 km². Round this figure to the nearest thousand.

4 Seven thousand four hundred and fifty-two people attended a football match.

    a) Write this number in digits.

    b) Round this number to the nearest:

      (i) ten   **(ii)** hundred   **(iii)** thousand

5 At its closest, Jupiter is about 390 682 810 miles from Earth. Write this distance to the nearest million miles.

6 The number of sweets in a jar is 670, to the nearest 10.

    a) What is the maximum possible number of sweets in the jar?

    b) What is the minimum possible number of sweets in the jar?

7 Bryony keeps 1600 chickens, rounded to the nearest hundred. What is the maximum number of chickens Bryony could have?

2.2 Rounding — Decimal Places

You can also round to different numbers of decimal places (d.p.).

For example, a number like 8.9471 could be rounded:
- to **one** decimal place (= 8.9)
- to **two** decimal places (= 8.95)
- to **three** decimal places (= 8.947)

Example 1

    a)   Round 4.7625 to one decimal place.
          Look at the digit in the <u>second</u> decimal place.   a) 4.7⑥25 — rounds <u>up</u> to **4.8**
          It's greater than 5, so round up.

    b)   Round 4.7625 to two decimal places.
          Look at the digit in the <u>third</u> decimal place.   b) 4.76②5 — rounds <u>down</u> to **4.76**
          It's less than 5, so round down.

    c)   Round 4.7625 to three decimal places.
          Look at the digit in the <u>fourth</u> decimal place.   c) 4.762⑤ — rounds <u>up</u> to **4.763**
          It's equal to 5, so round up.

Exercise 1

1 Write down all the numbers from the box that round to 0.4 to one decimal place.

0.41	0.45	0.347	0.47204	0.335	0.405
0.35	0.4295	0.5216	0.4124	0.4671	0.307

2 Round the following numbers to one decimal place.

a) 0.23   **b)** 0.678   **c)** 2.6893   **d)** 7.147

e) 13.5561   **f)** 1.3493   **g)** 72.355   **h)** 8.3812

i) 0.0324   **j)** 5.6023   **k)** 1.85223   **l)** 4.69999

Exercise 2

1 Write down all the numbers from the box that round to 0.35 to two decimal places.

0.362	0.357	0.345	0.359	0.3493	0.3509
0.355	0.3405	0.339	0.3498	0.3545	0.3573

2 Round the following numbers to two decimal places.

a) 4.567   **b)** 0.0424   **c)** 6.2571   **d)** 0.35273

e) 3.103695   **f)** 23.74902   **g)** 0.34457   **h)** 0.666666

i) 0.07953   **j)** 10.30436   **k)** 1.165725   **l)** 0.087462

3 Round the following numbers to three decimal places.

a) 0.96734   **b)** 0.25471   **c)** 2.43658   **d)** 6.532561

e) 0.03056   **f)** 3.638205   **g)** 5.68414   **h)** 3.26861

i) 0.008723   **j)** 13.68543   **k)** 5.855486   **l)** 4.57034

4 Round these numbers to the number of decimal places (d.p.) specified.

a) 0.13475 — to 2 d.p.   **b)** 0.68361 — to 1 d.p.

c) 5.73174 — to 3 d.p.   **d)** 0.000635 — to 3 d.p.

e) 21.3532 — to 2 d.p.   **f)** 0.25623 — to 1 d.p.

g) 0.39641 — to 2 d.p.   **h)** 3.3041 — to 2 d.p.

i) 0.00563 — to 2 d.p.   **j)** 3.25953 — to 3 d.p.

k) 11.399627 — to 3 d.p.   **l)** 29.5425 — to 2 d.p.

m) 5.9998 — to 2 d.p.   **n)** 0.0045789 — to 4 d.p.

5 The mass of the field vole on the right is 0.0384 kg.
Round this mass to two decimal places.

6 The length of a snake is 1.245 metres. Round this length to one decimal place.

7 The average distance that a group of students live from a school is 2.4575 km.
Round this figure to three decimal places.

8 A number, when rounded to two decimal places, equals 0.40.
Write down the smallest possible value of the number.

Not shown
actual size.

2.3 Rounding — Significant Figures

You can also round to different numbers of **significant figures** (s.f.).

For example, 217 304 could be rounded:
- to **one** significant figure (= 200 000)
- to **two** significant figures (= 220 000)
- to **three** significant figures (= 217 000)

Example 1

a) Round 52 691 to one significant figure.
Look at the <u>second</u> digit.
It's less than 5, so round down.

b) Round 6.578 to two significant figures.
Look at the <u>third</u> digit.
It's more than 5, so round up.

c) Round 958 542 to three significant figures.
Look at the <u>fourth</u> digit.
It's equal to 5, so round up.

a) 5②691 — rounds <u>down</u> to **50 000**

b) 6.5⑦8 — rounds <u>up</u> to **6.6**

c) 958 ⑤42 — rounds <u>up</u> to **959 000**

Exercise 1

1 Round the following numbers to one significant figure.
- **a)** 476
- **b)** 31
- **c)** 7036
- **d)** 867
- **e)** 3729
- **f)** 79 975
- **g)** 146 825
- **h)** 993

2 Round the following numbers to two significant figures.
- **a)** 741
- **b)** 6551
- **c)** 7067
- **d)** 2649
- **e)** 11.806
- **f)** 674.81
- **g)** 136 164
- **h)** 974.008

3 Round the following numbers to three significant figures.
- **a)** 4762
- **b)** 46.874
- **c)** 5067
- **d)** 594.5
- **e)** 35 722
- **f)** 693 704
- **g)** 80.569
- **h)** 925 478

4 Round the following numbers to the number of significant figures (s.f.) indicated.
- **a)** 45.89 — to 1 s.f.
- **b)** 5689.6 — to 3 s.f.
- **c)** 6.792 — to 1 s.f.
- **d)** 360.8 — to 2 s.f.
- **e)** 6527 — to 2 s.f.
- **f)** 756 557 — to 3 s.f.
- **g)** 146.745 — to 1 s.f.
- **h)** 376.25 — to 2 s.f.
- **i)** 79 477 — to 2 s.f.
- **j)** 624 595 — to 1 s.f.
- **k)** 579 — to 1 s.f.
- **l)** 4 567 296 — to 3 s.f.

5 The speed of sound is approximately 1236 km/h. Round this speed to two significant figures.

6 The diameter of Saturn is 120 536 km.
Round this diameter to three significant figures.

7 The average length of a dragon's tail is 258 cm.
Round this length to two significant figures.

8 The table on the right shows the areas of five European countries.
Round each area to two significant figures.

Country	Area (km²)
Austria	83 871
Greece	131 960
Italy	301 263
Luxembourg	2586
Sweden	449 960

Rounding Decimals to Significant Figures

Zeros at the start of a decimal do **not** count as significant figures.
The first significant figure is the first **non-zero** digit.

For example, 0.00152839 could be rounded: • to **one** significant figure (= 0.002)
• to **two** significant figures (= 0.0015)
• to **three** significant figures (= 0.00153)

Example 2

a) Round 0.06826 to one significant figure.
Look at the <u>second</u> significant figure.
It's more than 5, so round up.

a) 0.06⑧26 — rounds <u>up</u> to **0.07**

b) Round 0.006325 to two significant figures.
Look at the <u>third</u> significant figure.
It's less than 5, so round down.

b) 0.0063②5 — rounds <u>down</u> to **0.0063**

c) Round 0.00097151 to three significant figures.
Look at the <u>fourth</u> significant figure.
It's equal to 5, so round up.

c) 0.000971⑤1 — rounds <u>up</u> to **0.000972**

Exercise 2

1 Round the following numbers to one significant figure.

a) 0.0672   b) 0.349   c) 0.000555   d) 0.0197
e) 0.47892   f) 0.000798   g) 0.11583   h) 0.00825

2 Round each of the following numbers to two significant figures.

a) 0.003753   b) 0.02644   c) 0.0001792   d) 0.08735
e) 3570.4   f) 0.5635   g) 0.0007049   h) 167 489

3 Round each of the following numbers to three significant figures.

a) 0.5787   b) 0.08521   c) 0.10653   d) 0.00041769
e) 146.83   f) 34.726   g) 0.0084521   h) 0.437501

4 Round the following numbers to the number of significant figures (s.f.) indicated.

a) 0.004567 — to 1 s.f.   b) 0.1932 — to 2 s.f.   c) 0.0043862 — to 3 s.f.
d) 0.006204 — to 1 s.f.   e) 0.009557 — to 2 s.f.   f) 0.00060384 — to 3 s.f.
g) 1567.9 — to 2 s.f.   h) 2364.8 — to 1 s.f.   i) 0.57863 — to 3 s.f.
j) 0.02727 — to 1 s.f.   k) 0.0348657 — to 4 s.f.   l) 0.04962 — to 2 s.f.
m) 0.35952 — to 3 s.f.   n) 0.09625 — to 1 s.f.   o) 0.069496 — to 2 s.f.

5 The table shows the masses (in kilograms) of some mammals. ⟹
Round each mass to two significant figures.

6 The density of the hydrogen gas in a balloon is 0.0899 kg/m³.
Round this density to one significant figure.

Mammal	Mass (kg)
Common vole	0.0279
Gerbil	0.1472
Meerkat	0.7751
Red squirrel	0.1998
Shrew	0.00612

2.4 Estimating Answers

An **approximate** answer to a calculation can be obtained by rounding all the numbers in the calculation to **one significant figure**. Even though the answer isn't exact, it can still be useful.

Example 1

By rounding each number to one significant figure, estimate the following:

a) $43 + 28.7$

Replace: 43 with 40
28.7 with 30

$43 + 28.7 \approx 40 + 30$
$= \underline{\textbf{70}}$

b) $\dfrac{78.43 \times 6.24}{19.76}$

Replace: 78.43 with 80
6.24 with 6
19.76 with 20

$\dfrac{78.43 \times 6.24}{19.76} \approx \dfrac{80 \times 6}{20}$

$= \dfrac{480}{20} = \underline{\textbf{24}}$

Exercise 1

1 By rounding each number to one significant figure, estimate the following.

   a) $437 + 175$ **b)** $310 + 876$ **c)** $784 - 279$

   d) $0.516 - 0.322$ **e)** $184 + 722$ **f)** $838 - 121$

2 By rounding each number to one significant figure, estimate the following.

   a) 23×36 **b)** 59×5.7 **c)** 40.4×4.9

   d) 18×81 **e)** 276×19 **f)** 587×9.23

   g) 413×78 **h)** 51.87×88.43 **i)** 67.4×312

3 Sam has done the calculation 56.2×34.7 on his calculator.
His calculator display is shown on the right.
Beth says Sam must have pressed the wrong button at some point.

   a) By rounding each number in the calculation to one significant figure, estimate 56.2×34.7.

   b) Do you think Sam pressed the wrong button at some point? Explain your answer.

4 Use rounding to choose the correct answer (A, B or C) for each of the following calculations.

   a) 1.76×6.3 A: 1.328   B: 5.788   C: 11.088

   b) 68.5×24.6 A: 145.9   B: 1685.1   C: 3492.1

   c) 582×2.1 A: 119.52   B: 1222.2   C: 4545.2

   d) $337.84 \div 41.2$ A: 8.2   B: 15.6   C: 23.2

   e) $\dfrac{57.5 \times 3.78}{16.1}$ A: 1.65   B: 6.3   C: 13.5

5 By rounding each number to one significant figure, estimate the following.

a) $\dfrac{18}{4.8}$

b) $\dfrac{8.9}{3.1}$

c) $\dfrac{32}{5.1}$

d) $\dfrac{38}{9.7}$

e) $\dfrac{57}{18}$

f) $\dfrac{37.3}{5.2}$

g) $\dfrac{39.4}{3.86}$

h) $\dfrac{9.98}{2.14}$

i) $\dfrac{605}{28.4}$

j) $\dfrac{765.4}{18.2}$

k) $\dfrac{420.7}{5.14}$

l) $\dfrac{586.2}{186}$

6 The decimal points have been missed out from each of the answers to these calculations. Use rounding to find an approximate answer in each case, and then decide where the decimal point should be.

a) $18.5 \times 3.2 = 592$

b) $\dfrac{325.26}{5.2} = 6255$

c) $82.2 \times 1.8 = 14796$

d) $41 \times 4.85 = 19885$

e) $7.2 \times 69 = 4968$

f) $\dfrac{160.05}{3.75} = 4268$

g) $\dfrac{85.399}{11.5} = 7426$

h) $4.2 \times 5.1 = 2142$

i) $\dfrac{19.74}{2.4} = 8225$

j) $\dfrac{19.8 \times 27.4}{3.3} = 1644$

k) $\dfrac{52.668 \times 36.6}{4.697} = 4104$

l) $\dfrac{12.6 \times 127.5}{20.4} = 7875$

7 Pens cost 32 pence each. Estimate the cost of 18 pens. Give your answer in pounds.

8 It costs £4.70 to buy the toys needed for one 'Child's Party Bag'.
If 21 children attend a party, estimate how much it would cost to buy all the toys for the party bags.

9 Karen works 42 hours one week, and earns £6.85 per hour.
Estimate the amount of money she earns for the week.

10 A total of 6922 people enter a city-centre marathon.

a) They each pay a fee of £10.50 to enter.
Estimate the total amount of money paid to enter the marathon.

b) The average amount of sponsorship money collected by each runner is £217.
Estimate the total amount of sponsorship money collected by the runners.

11 A group of 28 children are going on a trip to watch a pantomime.
The total cost of the trip to the pantomime is £584.
Estimate the cost per child for the trip.

12 A smoothie factory operates for 62 hours per week.
It makes 324 litres of smoothie per hour.
Each litre of smoothie contains 18 strawberries.
Estimate the number of strawberries used each week.

Section 3 — Powers and Roots

3.1 Squares and Cubes

Squares and **cubes** show that a number is multiplied by itself.

For example, $4 \times 4 = 4^2$ is the **square** of 4. The square of a number is always **positive**.

And $4 \times 4 \times 4 = 4^3$ is the **cube** of 4.
The cube of a **positive** number is **positive**, but the cube of a **negative** number is **negative**.

Example 1

Find: a) 4^2 $4^2 = 4 \times 4 = \underline{\mathbf{16}}$

        b) $(-4)^2$ $(-4)^2 = -4 \times -4 = \underline{\mathbf{16}}$

        c) 4^3 $4^3 = 4 \times 4 \times 4 = \underline{\mathbf{64}}$

        d) $(-4)^3$ $(-4)^3 = -4 \times -4 \times -4 = \underline{\mathbf{-64}}$

Exercise 1

1   Copy and complete the table below without using a calculator.

x	1	2	3	4	5	6	7	8	9	10
x^2				16						

2   Evaluate the following. Use a calculator where necessary.

   a) 11^2 **b)** 12^2 **c)** 15^2 **d)** 20^2 **e)** 30^2

3   Evaluate the following. Use a calculator where necessary.

   a) $(-4)^2$ **b)** 0.1^2 **c)** $(-10)^2$ **d)** 0.3^2 **e)** 0.8^2

   f) 0.6^2 **g)** $(-3)^2$ **h)** $(-0.2)^2$ **i)** $(-0.4)^2$ **j)** $(-15)^2$

4   Copy and complete the table below. Use a calculator where necessary.

x	1	2	3	4	5
x^3				64	

5   Evaluate the following. Use a calculator where necessary.

   a) 6^3 **b)** 10^3 **c)** 11^3 **d)** 20^3 **e)** 30^3

6   Evaluate the following. Use a calculator where necessary.

   a) $(-3)^3$ **b)** $(-5)^3$ **c)** $(-10)^3$ **d)** 0.4^3 **e)** 0.5^3

   f) $(-0.5)^3$ **g)** $(-6)^3$ **h)** $(-0.3)^3$ **i)** $(-0.8)^3$ **j)** $(-12)^3$

7   Evaluate the following. Use a calculator where necessary.

   a) $(-2)^2$ **b)** $(-2)^3$ **c)** $(-0.1)^2$ **d)** $((-2)^2)^3$ **e)** $((-2)^3)^2$

Square Roots

Finding the **square root** of a number is the opposite of squaring it.
Every **positive** number has **two** square roots — one **positive** ($\sqrt{x}$) and one **negative** ($-\sqrt{x}$).

For example, the positive square root of 2 is $\sqrt{2}$.
And the negative square root of 2 is $-\sqrt{2}$.

Negative numbers **don't have** square roots.

$$\sqrt{x} \times \sqrt{x} = (\sqrt{x})^2 = x$$
$$(-\sqrt{x}) \times (-\sqrt{x}) = (-\sqrt{x})^2 = x$$

Example 2

Find both square roots of 16.

1. $4^2 = 16$, so the positive square root is 4. $\sqrt{16} = \underline{4}$
2. There's also the negative square root.
   Remember, $(-4) \times (-4) = 16$ too. $-\sqrt{16} = \underline{-4}$

Exercise 2

1 Copy and complete the table below without using a calculator.

x	1	4	9	16	25	36	100
$\sqrt{x}$		2					
$-\sqrt{x}$		-2					

2 Without using a calculator, find:

a) $\sqrt{49}$ b) $-\sqrt{49}$ c) $\sqrt{81}$ d) $-\sqrt{81}$
e) $\sqrt{121}$ f) $\sqrt{169}$ g) $-\sqrt{144}$ h) $\sqrt{400}$

3 Find both square roots of the following numbers. Use a calculator where necessary.

a) 64   b) 121   c) 169   d) 10 000   e) 196

Cube Roots

Every number has exactly one **cube root**. The symbol $\sqrt[3]{}$ is used for cube roots.

$$\sqrt[3]{x} \times \sqrt[3]{x} \times \sqrt[3]{x} = (\sqrt[3]{x})^3 = x$$

Example 3

Find the cube root of: a) 64   b) −64

a) $4^3 = 64$, so the cube root of 64 is 4.   a) $\sqrt[3]{64} = \underline{4}$

b) $(-4)^3 = -64$, so the cube root of −64 is −4.   b) $\sqrt[3]{-64} = \underline{-4}$

Exercise 3

1 Copy and complete this table.
Use a calculator
where necessary.

x	1	8	27	1000	−1	−8	−27	−1000
$\sqrt[3]{x}$				10				

2 Find the following cube roots. Use a calculator where necessary.

a) $\sqrt[3]{64}$ b) $\sqrt[3]{125}$ c) $\sqrt[3]{1331}$ d) $\sqrt[3]{-64}$

e) $\sqrt[3]{-125}$ f) $\sqrt[3]{512}$ g) $\sqrt[3]{216}$ h) $\sqrt[3]{-729}$

Exercise 4 — Mixed Exercise

In this exercise use a calculator where you need to.

1 Evaluate the following.

a) 16^2 b) 12^3 c) $\sqrt[3]{729}$ d) $\sqrt{10000}$

e) $\sqrt[3]{-343}$ f) 13^2 g) 15^3 h) $\sqrt[3]{-1000000}$

2 Work out the following.

a) 2.7^3 b) 1.9^2 c) $\sqrt{10}$ d) $\sqrt[3]{80}$

e) 0.1^2 f) 0.1^3 g) $\sqrt{0.000001}$ h) $\sqrt[3]{-0.000001}$

3 Work out which number in each pair is greater.

a) 5^2 or $\sqrt{5}$ b) 0.5^2 or $\sqrt{0.5}$ c) $\sqrt{27}$ or $\sqrt[3]{125}$

d) 5^2 or 5^3 e) 0.5^2 or 0.5^3 f) $\sqrt{200}$ or $\sqrt[3]{2000}$

g) 100^2 or 10^3 h) $\sqrt{1000}$ or 3^3 i) 4^3 or $\sqrt[3]{250000}$

3.2 Indices

Squares and cubes are two examples of **powers**.

Powers show something that is being multiplied by itself. Powers are usually written using '**index notation**' — involving a **base** and an **index**.

base $\Rightarrow 2^3 \Leftarrow$ index

For example, $2 \times 2 \times 2 \times 2 = 2^4$ — this is four 2's multiplied together, and is read as "**2 to the power 4**". And $5 \times 5 \times 5 \times 5 \times 5 \times 5 = 5^6$ — this is six 5's multiplied together, and is read as "**5 to the power 6**".

Example 1

a) Rewrite $3 \times 3 \times 3 \times 3 \times 3$ using index notation.

$3 \times 3 \times 3 \times 3 \times 3 = \underline{\mathbf{3^5}}$

b) Rewrite 100 000 using powers of 10.

$100\,000 = 10 \times 10 \times 10 \times 10 \times 10 = \underline{\mathbf{10^5}}$

c) Evaluate 5^4.

$5^4 = 5 \times 5 \times 5 \times 5 = \underline{\mathbf{625}}$

Exercise 1

1 Write the following using index notation.

a) 3×3 b) $2 \times 2 \times 2$ c) $7 \times 7 \times 7 \times 7 \times 7$

d) $9 \times 9 \times 9 \times 9 \times 9 \times 9$ e) $12 \times 12 \times 12 \times 12$ f) $17 \times 17 \times 17$

2 Use a calculator to evaluate these powers.

a) 2^4 b) 2^5 c) 3^4 d) 4^6

e) 6^4 f) 17^3 g) 5^5 h) 3^5

3 **a)** Use a calculator to evaluate these powers of 10.

    (i) 10^2 **(ii)** 10^3 **(iii)** 10^4 **(iv)** 10^5

    (v) 10^6 **(vi)** 10^7 **(vii)** 10^8 **(viii)** 10^9

b) Copy and complete the following sentences. (Here, n is a positive whole number.)

    (i) "10^{15} can be written as a '1' followed by _____ zeros."

    (ii) "10^n can be written as a '1' followed by _____ zeros."

4 Rewrite the following as powers of 10.

  a) 100   **b)** 1000   **c)** 10 000   **d)** 100 000

  e) 1 million   **f)** 10 million   **g)** 1 000 000 000   **h)** 1 000 000 000 000

5 Evaluate the following using a calculator.

(Remember to work out powers **before** carrying out any addition or subtraction.)

  a) $3^2 + 2^3$ **b)** $2^3 + 3^3$ **c)** $3^4 - 4^2$ **d)** $5^2 + 6^2$ **e)** $10^3 - 6^2$

  f) $2^6 + 10^3$ **g)** $3^5 - 5^3$ **h)** $10^4 - 7^3$ **i)** $3^4 - 9^2$ **j)** $2^7 + 10^5$

6 Evaluate the following using a calculator.

  a) $3^2 - 2^3$ **b)** $5^2 - 6^2$ **c)** $2^6 - 10^2$ **d)** 3×2^8 **e)** 8×5^4

  f) $8 + 2^5$ **g)** $150 - 3^4$ **h)** $2^7 + 10^6$ **i)** $3^4 \times 2^5$ **j)** $7^5 + 8^4$

  k) $8^7 \div 4^6$ **l)** $10^4 \times 10^3$ **m)** $2^4 \times 2^2$ **n)** $9^3 + 4^2$ **o)** $3^4 \div 5^4$

(7) Evaluate the following using a calculator.

  a) $(5 - 2)^3$ **b)** $(5 - 6)^2$ **c)** $(2^2)^2$ **d)** $(3^2)^2$ **e)** $(8 - 5)^4$

  f) $(7 + 3)^5$ **g)** $6^4 - 7^2$ **h)** $2 + 10^5$ **i)** $3^5 \times 2^3$ **j)** $(150 - 50)^6$

Example 2

a)   Rewrite $a \times a \times a \times a \times a \times a$ using index notation.
There are 6 a's multiplied together.

                                    $a \times a \times a \times a \times a \times a = \underline{\boldsymbol{a^6}}$

b)   Rewrite $b \times b \times b \times b \times c \times c$ using index notation.
There are 4 b's multiplied together, and 2 c's.

                                      $b \times b \times b \times b \times c \times c = b^4 \times c^2$

                                                 $= \underline{\boldsymbol{b^4 c^2}}$

Exercise 2

1 Rewrite the following using index notation.

  a) $h \times h \times h \times h$ **b)** $t \times t \times t \times t \times t$ **c)** $s \times s \times s \times s \times s \times s \times s$

  d) $k \times k \times k \times k \times k \times k$ **e)** $y \times y \times y \times y$ **f)** $m \times m \times m \times m \times m$

2 Rewrite the following using index notation.

  a) $a \times a \times b \times b \times b$ **b)** $k \times k \times k \times k \times f \times f \times f$ **c)** $m \times m \times m \times m \times n \times n$

  d) $s \times s \times s \times s \times t$ **e)** $w \times w \times w \times v \times v \times v$ **f)** $p \times p \times q \times q \times q \times q \times q$

(3) Evaluate these powers using a calculator, given that $x = 2$ and $y = 5$.

  a) $x^2 y^2$ **b)** $x^3 y^2$ **c)** $x^2 y^3$

  d) $x^5 y^2$ **e)** $x^4 y^3$ **f)** $x^4 y^4$

3.3 Laws of Indices

Use the **laws of indices** ('indices' = plural of 'index') to multiply and divide powers with the **same base**.

1) To **multiply** two powers with the same base, **add** the indices: $a^m \times a^n = a^{m+n}$

2) To **divide** two powers with the same base, **subtract** the indices: $a^m \div a^n = a^{m-n}$

3) To **raise** one power to another power, **multiply** the indices: $(a^m)^n = a^{m \times n}$

There are two other important index facts you need to know.

1) Anything to the **power 1** is itself: $a^1 = a$

2) Anything to the **power 0** is 1: $a^0 = 1$

Example 1

Simplify the following, leaving the answers in index form.

a) $3^8 \times 3^5$
This is multiplication, so add the indices.
$$3^8 \times 3^5 = 3^{8+5} = \underline{\mathbf{3^{13}}}$$

b) $\dfrac{10^8}{10^5}$
This is division ($\frac{10^8}{10^5} = 10^8 \div 10^5$), so subtract the indices.
$$10^8 \div 10^5 = 10^{8-5} = \underline{\mathbf{10^3}}$$

c) $(2^7)^2$
For one power raised to another power, multiply the indices.
$$(2^7)^2 = 2^{7 \times 2} = \underline{\mathbf{2^{14}}}$$

d) $a^7 \times a^3$
The laws of indices work in exactly the same way with variables.
$$a^7 \times a^3 = a^{7+3} = \underline{\mathbf{a^{10}}}$$

Exercise 1

1 Simplify these without using a calculator. Leave your answers in index form.
  a) $3^2 \times 3^6$
  b) $10^7 \times 10^3$
  c) $4^7 \times 4^4$
  d) 7×7^6
  e) $2^3 \times 2^{10}$

2 Simplify these without using a calculator. Leave your answers in index form.
  a) $6^7 \div 6^4$
  b) $8^6 \div 8^3$
  c) $5^7 \div 5^2$
  d) $6^8 \div 6^6$
  e) $2^{18} \div 2^{11}$

3 Simplify these without using a calculator. Leave your answers in index form.
  a) $(4^3)^3$
  b) $(11^2)^5$
  c) $(100^3)^{23}$
  d) $(14^7)^4$
  e) $(9^{11})^8$

4 Simplify these without using a calculator. Leave your answers in index form.
  a) $4^5 \times 4^{11}$
  b) $12^7 \div 12^3$
  c) $8^2 \times 8^9$
  d) $(6^8)^4$
  e) $(3^{12})^4$
  f) $7^{11} \div 7^6$
  g) $4^{15} \div 4^7$
  h) $(11^2)^9$
  i) $8^8 \div 8^4$
  j) $15^{12} \times 15^{14}$
  k) $129^5 \times 129^2$
  l) $72^{13} \div 72^7$
  m) $(145^2)^9$
  n) $188^8 \times 188^4$
  o) $\dfrac{20^{222}}{20^{210}}$

5 For each of the following, find the number that should replace the square.
  a) $3^3 \times 3^6 = 3^{\blacksquare}$
  b) $8^{\blacksquare} \times 8^{10} = 8^{12}$
  c) $(6^{10})^4 = 6^{\blacksquare}$
  d) $(15^6)^{\blacksquare} = 15^{24}$
  e) $(9^{\blacksquare})^{10} = 9^{30}$
  f) $5^{\blacksquare} \div 5^6 = 5^7$
  g) $6^5 \times 6^{\blacksquare} = 6^{12}$
  h) $10^{\blacksquare} \div 10^2 = 10^4$
  i) $12^{14} \div 12^{\blacksquare} = 12^7$
  j) $13^6 \div 13^{\blacksquare} = 13$
  k) $(2^{\blacksquare})^5 = 2^{40}$
  l) $2^{24} \div 12^{\blacksquare} = 2^{17}$

6 Simplify the following.

a) $a^6 \times a^4$ b) $e^{12} \div e^3$ c) $(c^5)^4$ d) $b^8 \div b^5$ e) $(m^6)^8$

f) $y^8 \div y^2$ g) $h^{17} \times h^2$ h) $g^7 \times g^5$ i) $(k^3)^6$ j) $\dfrac{b^8}{b^5}$

7 For each of the following, find the number that should replace the square.

a) $s^9 \times s^{\blacksquare} = s^{14}$ b) $t^5 \div t^{\blacksquare} = t^3$ c) $r^7 \times r^{\blacksquare} = r^{13}$ d) $(p^7)^{\blacksquare} = p^{49}$

e) $k^{\blacksquare} \div k^5 = k^3$ f) $a^{\blacksquare} \times a^7 = a^{15}$ g) $m^5 \times m^{\blacksquare} = m^8$ h) $(q^5)^{\blacksquare} = q^{25}$

Example 2

Simplify each expression without using a calculator. Leave your answers in index form.

a) $2^6 \times 2^8 \div 2^2$

The index of the result will be $6 + 8 - 2$. $\qquad\qquad 2^6 \times 2^8 \div 2^2 = 2^{6+8-2} = \underline{\mathbf{2^{12}}}$

b) $\dfrac{2^3 \times 2^5}{2^8 \div 2^6}$

1. Work out the top and bottom lines of the fraction separately. $\qquad \dfrac{2^3 \times 2^5}{2^8 \div 2^6} = \dfrac{2^{3+5}}{2^{8-6}} = \dfrac{2^8}{2^2}$

2. Then you can do the final division. $\qquad\qquad\qquad\qquad\qquad\qquad = 2^{8-2}$

$\qquad\qquad\qquad\qquad\qquad\qquad\qquad\qquad\qquad\qquad\qquad\qquad\qquad\qquad = \underline{\mathbf{2^6}}$

Exercise 2

In **Questions 1-3**, simplify each expression without using a calculator.
Leave your answers in index form.

1 a) $3^2 \times 3^5 \times 3^7$ b) $5^4 \times 5 \times 5^8$ c) $(8^6)^2 \times 8^5$ d) $(9^4 \times 9^3)^5$

e) $7^3 \times 7^5 \div 7^6$ f) $8^3 \times 8^7 \div 8^9$ g) $(12^8 \div 12^4)^3$ h) $(4^3)^6 \div 4^4$

2 a) $\dfrac{3^4 \times 3^5}{3^6}$ b) $\dfrac{8^5 \times 8^4}{8^2 \times 8^3}$ c) $\dfrac{2^5 \times 2^5}{2^3}$ d) $\dfrac{4^4 \times 4^6}{4^8 \times 4}$

e) $\dfrac{7 \times 7^8}{7^2 \times 7^3}$ f) $\dfrac{5^5 \times 5^5}{5^8 \div 5^3}$ g) $\dfrac{10^8 \div 10^3}{10^4 \div 10^4}$ h) $\dfrac{8^{25} \div 8^2}{8^6 \times 8^{10}}$

3 a) $\left(\dfrac{6^3 \times 6^9}{6^7}\right)^3$ b) $\dfrac{2^3 \times 2^4}{(2^2)^2}$ c) $\dfrac{(8^5)^7 \div 8^{12}}{8^6 \times 8^{10}}$ d) $\dfrac{(5^{10} \div 5^8)^4}{5^4 \div 5^2}$

4 Which of the expressions in the box below are equal to 1?

$$\dfrac{4^4 \div 4^3}{4} \qquad \dfrac{7^{16}}{7^8 \times 7^2} \qquad \dfrac{3^8 - 3^7}{3} \qquad \dfrac{5^5 \times 5^9}{(5^2)^7} \qquad \dfrac{(9^2)^2 - 9^0}{9^3}$$

Simplify each of the expressions in **Questions 5-6**.

5 a) $a^6 \times a^5 \div a^4$ b) $z^8 \div z^2 \times z$ c) $(m^4)^3 \times m^3$ d) $(p^5 \div p^3)^6$

6 a) $\dfrac{r \times r^4}{r^2}$ b) $\dfrac{s^{18} \div s^4}{s^3 \times s^6}$ c) $\dfrac{y^8 \div y^3}{y^4 \div y^4}$ d) $\dfrac{(t^6 \div t^3)^4}{t^9 \div t^4}$

Section 4 — Factors and Multiples

4.1 Multiples

A **multiple** of a number is one that is in its times table.
So the multiples of 2 are: 2, 4, 6, 8, 10, 12, 14... and the multiples of 5 are: 5, 10, 15, 20, 25, 30, 35...

10 is in both lists, so 10 is a **common multiple** of 2 and 5. Both 2 and 5 divide into 10 exactly.

Example 1

a) List the multiples of 5 between 23 and 43.
    Starting at 20, the times table of 5 is: 20, 25, 30, 35, 40, 45...
    — so the multiples between 23 and 43 are: **25, 30, 35, 40**

b) Which of the numbers in the box on the right are: | 24   7   28   35   39 |
    (i) multiples of 3?
    3 divides into 24 and 39 exactly — so 24 and 39 are multiples of 3.
    But 3 doesn't divide exactly into 7, 28 or 35 — these aren't multiples of 3. (i) **24 and 39**

    (ii) multiples of 5?
    The only number in the box that 5 divides into exactly is 35.   (ii) **35**

    (iii) common multiples of 4 and 7?
    The multiples of 4 are 24 and 28, while the multiples of 7   (iii) **28**
    are 7, 28 and 35. So the only common multiple is 28.

Exercise 1

1 List the first five multiples of: **a)** 4   **b)** 10   **c)** 3   **d)** 6   **e)** 7

2 Write down the numbers from the box that are:

   a) multiples of 3
   b) multiples of 4
   c) multiples of 5

   | 2   5   8   9   11   12 |
   | 14   15   16   18   20   21 |

3 **a)** List the multiples of 8 between 10 and 20.
   b) List the multiples of 9 between 20 and 50.
   c) List the multiples of 6 between 25 and 35.

4 Write down the numbers from the box that are:
   a) multiples of 10
   b) multiples of 15
   c) common multiples of 10 and 15

   | 5   10   15   20   25   30   35 |
   | 40   45   50   55   60   65   70 |
   | 75   80   85   90   95   100 105 |

5 **a)** List the multiples of 3 between 19 and 35.
   b) List the multiples of 4 between 19 and 35.
   c) List the common multiples of 3 and 4 between 19 and 35.

6 List all the common multiples of 5 and 6 between 1 and 40.

7 List all the common multiples of 8 and 10 between 1 and 100.

Least Common Multiple (LCM)

The **least common multiple** (**LCM**) of a set of numbers is the smallest of their common multiples. It's the lowest number that they all divide into exactly.

Example 2

Find the least common multiple (LCM) of 4, 6 and 8.

1. Find the multiples of 4, 6 and 8.

   Multiples of 4 are: 4, 8, 12, 16, 20, 24, 28...
   Multiples of 6 are: 6, 12, 18, 24, 30, 36...
   Multiples of 8 are: 8, 16, 24, 32, 40, 48...

2. The LCM is the smallest number that appears in all three lists.

   So the LCM of 4, 6 and 8 is **24**.

Exercise 2

1 Find the LCM of each of the following pairs of numbers.

   a) 3 and 4   **b)** 3 and 5   **c)** 6 and 8   **d)** 2 and 10

   e) 6 and 7   **f)** 4 and 9   **g)** 10 and 15   **h)** 15 and 20

2 Find the LCM of each of the sets of numbers below.

   a) 3, 6, 8   **b)** 2, 5, 6   **c)** 3, 5, 6

   d) 4, 9, 12   **e)** 5, 7, 10   **f)** 5, 6, 9

Example 3

Jane and Alec are running around a small circular track.
It takes Jane 10 seconds to run one lap and Alec 12 seconds.

If they both start from the same point on the track at exactly the same time, how long will it be before they next cross the start line together?

Jane crosses the start line after the following numbers of seconds: 10, 20, 30, 40, 50, 60, 70...
Alec crosses the start line after the following numbers of seconds: 12, 24, 36, 48, 60, 72...

So they will next cross the start line together after **60 seconds**.

Exercise 3

1 Laurence and Naima are cycling around a circular course. They leave the start-line at the same time and need to do 10 laps. It takes Laurence 8 minutes to do one lap and Naima 12 minutes.

   a) After how many minutes does Laurence pass the start-line? Write down all possible answers.

   b) After how many minutes does Naima pass the start-line? Write down all possible answers.

   c) When will they first pass the start-line together?

2 Mike visits Oscar every 4 days, while Narinda visits Oscar every 5 days. If they both visited today, how many days will it be before they visit on the same day again?

3 Jill divides a pile of sweets into 5 equal piles. Kay then divides the same sweets into 7 equal piles. What is the smallest number of sweets there could be?

4.2 Factors

A number's **factors** divide into it exactly.

For example, the factors of 12 are 1, 2, 3, 4, 6 and 12 — all these numbers divide into 12 exactly.

5 is a factor of both 15 and 20, so 5 is a **common factor** of 15 and 20.

Example 1

Write down all the factors of: a) 18   b) 16

1. Check if 1, 2, 3, 4... divide into the number. Write down each number that divides in exactly, and also its 'factor partner' in a multiplication.

2. Stop checking when you reach a number already in an earlier multiplication, or when a factor is repeated in a multiplication.

3. List all the numbers in your multiplications.

a) $18 = 1 \times 18$ $18 = 2 \times 9$ $18 = 3 \times 6$
4 and 5 don't divide exactly into 18.
So the factors of 18 are **1, 2, 3, 6, 9, 18**.

b) $16 = 1 \times 16$ $16 = 2 \times 8$ $16 = 4 \times 4$
3 doesn't divide exactly into 16.
So the factors of 16 are **1, 2, 4, 8, 16**.

Exercise 1

1 List the numbers from the box on the right that are factors of:

a) 8
b) 15
c) 21
d) 40
e) 28
f) 25

$$\boxed{1 \quad 3 \quad 4 \quad 7 \quad 8 \quad 20}$$

2 List the numbers from the box on the right that are factors of:

a) 6
b) 24
c) 30
d) 36
e) 20
f) 45

$$\boxed{2 \quad 3 \quad 5 \quad 6 \quad 12 \quad 15}$$

3 List all the factors of the following numbers.

a) 10
b) 4
c) 13
d) 20
e) 25
f) 24
g) 35
h) 32
i) 40
j) 50
k) 9
l) 15
m) 36
n) 49
o) 48

4 a) Which number is a factor of all other numbers?

b) Which two numbers are factors of all even numbers?

c) Which two numbers must be factors of all numbers whose last digit is 5?

d) Which four numbers must be factors of all numbers whose last digit is 0?

Example 2

Find the common factors of 6 and 20.

1. Find the factors of 6 and 20.

2. The common factors are the numbers that appear in both lists.

$6 = 1 \times 6$ $6 = 2 \times 3$
So the factors of 6 are: 1, 2, 3, 6

$20 = 1 \times 20$ $20 = 2 \times 10$ $20 = 4 \times 5$
So the factors of 20 are: 1, 2, 4, 5, 10, 20

So the common factors of 6 and 20 are **1 and 2**.

5 **a)** List all the factors of 15.

 b) List all the factors of 21.

 c) List the common factors of 15 and 21.

6 List the common factors of the following pairs of numbers.

 a) 15, 20   **b)** 12, 15   **c)** 30, 45   **d)** 50, 90   **e)** 25, 50

7 List the common factors of the following sets of numbers.

 a) 15, 20, 25   **b)** 12, 18, 20   **c)** 30, 45, 50   **d)** 15, 16, 17

Highest Common Factor (HCF)

The **highest common factor** (HCF) of a set of numbers is the largest of their common factors. It's the biggest number that divides into all of them exactly.

Example 3

Find the highest common factor of: a) 12 and 15   b) 4 and 8

1. Find the factors of both numbers. The common factors are the numbers in both lists.

a)   The factors of 12 are: ① 2, ③ 4, 6, 12
     The factors of 15 are: ① ③ 5, 15
     So the highest common factor of 12 and 15 is **3**.

2. The HCF is the biggest number that appears in both lists.

b)   The factors of 4 are: ① ② ④
     The factors of 8 are: ① ② ④ 8
     So the highest common factor of 4 and 8 is **4**.

Exercise 2

1 **a)** Find the common factors of 12 and 20.

 b) Hence find the highest common factor (HCF) of 12 and 20.

2 **a)** List the common factors of 20 and 30.

 b) Use your list to find the HCF of 20 and 30.

3 Find the HCF of the following pairs of numbers.

 a) 8 and 12   **b)** 24 and 32   **c)** 18 and 24   **d)** 36 and 60

 e) 14 and 15   **f)** 12 and 36   **g)** 35 and 42   **h)** 56 and 63

4 Write down the following:

 a) the HCF of 5 and 6

 b) the HCF of 11 and 12

 c) the HCF of 21 and 22

5 Find the HCF of the following sets of numbers.

 a) 6, 8, 16   **b)** 12, 15, 18   **c)** 24, 30, 36

 d) 18, 36, 72   **e)** 36, 48, 60   **f)** 25, 50, 75

Exercise 3 – Mixed Exercise

1 **a)** Find the highest common factor of the following pairs of numbers.

    (i) 5 and 9   **(ii)** 9 and 12   **(iii)** 10 and 15   **(iv)** 12 and 20

  b) Find the least common multiple of the following pairs of numbers.

    (i) 5 and 9   **(ii)** 9 and 12   **(iii)** 10 and 15   **(iv)** 12 and 20

2 Anna has 36 identical sweets, and wants to arrange them all into equal piles.

  a) First she makes piles of 2 sweets. How many piles could she make?

  b) Could she make piles of 5 sweets using all the sweets? Explain your answer.

  c) In total, how many different ways are there for Anna to divide the 36 sweets into equal piles? List all the different possibilities.

3 A baker has 12 identical cakes. In how many different ways can he divide them up into equal packets (without cutting them up)? List the possibilities.

4 In how many different ways can 100 identical chairs be arranged in rows of equal length? List all the ways the chairs can be arranged.

5 A zoo has between 95 and 155 animals. The number of animals divides exactly by 20 and exactly by 30.

  a) Write down all the multiples of 20 between 95 and 155.

  b) Write down all the multiples of 30 between 95 and 155.

  c) How many animals are there?

6 A garden centre has between 95 and 205 potted plants. They can be arranged exactly in rows of 25 and exactly in rows of 30. How many plants are there?

7 There are between 240 and 300 decorated plates hanging on a wall, and the number of plates divides exactly by both 40 and 70. How many plates are there?

4.3 Prime Numbers

A **prime number** is a number that has no factors except itself and 1.
In other words, the only numbers that divide exactly into a prime number are itself and 1.

But remember... 1 is **not** a prime number.

Example 1

Which of the numbers in the box on the right are prime? | 16   17   18   19   20 |

1. Look for factors of each of the numbers.

2. If you can find factors other than 1 and the number itself, then the number isn't prime.

3. If there are no factors other than 1 and the number itself, then the number is prime.

$16 = 2 \times 8$, and so 16 isn't prime
$18 = 3 \times 6$, and so 18 isn't prime
$20 = 4 \times 5$, and so 20 isn't prime

17 has no factors other than 1 and 17.
19 has no factors other than 1 and 19.

So the prime numbers are **17 and 19**

Exercise 1

1 Look at the following list of numbers: 11, 13, 15, 17, 19

  a) Which number in the list is <u>not</u> prime?

  b) Find two factors greater than 1 that can be multiplied together to give this number.

2 **a)** Which three numbers in the box on the right are <u>not</u> prime?   31 33 35 37 39

  b) Find two factors greater than 1 that multiply together to give each of your answers to **a)**.

3 Write down the prime numbers in this list: 5, 15, 22, 34, 47, 51, 59

4 **a)** Write down all the prime numbers less than 10.

  b) Find all the prime numbers between 20 and 30.

5 **a)** For each of the following, find a factor greater than 1 but less than the number itself:

  (i) 4   **(ii)** 14   **(iii)** 34   **(iv)** 74

  b) Explain why any number with last digit 4 <u>cannot</u> be prime.

6 Without doing any calculations, explain how you can tell that none of the numbers in this list are prime.   20 30 40 50 70 90 110 130

Writing a Number as a Product of Primes

Whole numbers which are **not** prime can be broken down into **prime factors**. The **product** of these prime factors is the original number. (Remember, 'product' means the result of multiplying things.)

Example 2

Write 12 as the product of prime factors.

Make a factor tree.

1. First find <u>any</u> two factors whose product is 12 (here, 12 = 2 × 6). Circle any of these factors that are prime.

2. Repeat step 1 for any factors you didn't circle (here, 6 = 2 × 3).

3. Stop when all the factor tree's branches end in a circle. The product of all the circled primes is the number you started with.

$12 = 2 \times 2 \times 3$, or $12 = 2^2 \times 3$

Exercise 2

In the following questions, write any repeated prime factors as powers.

1 **a)** Copy and complete the following factor trees.

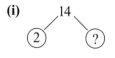

b) Use your factor trees to write the following as products of prime factors.

  (i) 14   **(ii)** 33   **(iii)** 10   **(iv)** 25

2 Write the following numbers as the product of two prime factors.

  a) 15   **b)** 21   **c)** 22   **d)** 35   **e)** 39

3 **a)** Copy and complete the following factor trees.

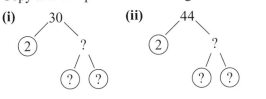

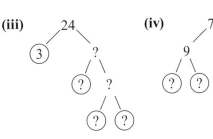

b) Use your factor trees to write the following as the product of prime factors.

   (i) 30   **(ii)** 44   **(iii)** 24   **(iv)** 72

4 **a)** Copy and complete the three factor trees below.

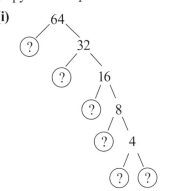 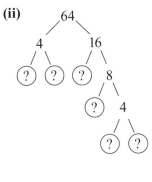 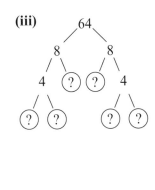

b) Use each of your factor trees to write 64 as the product of prime factors.
What do you notice?

5 Use factor trees to write the following numbers as the product of prime factors.

   a) 42   **b)** 66   **c)** 70   **d)** 190   **e)** 210

6 Use factor trees to write the following numbers as the product of prime factors.

   a) 18   **b)** 50   **c)** 36   **d)** 150   **e)** 32

7 Write the following as the product of prime factors.

   a) 8   **b)** 6   **c)** 28   **d)** 27   **e)** 16

   f) 60   **g)** 40   **h)** 98   **i)** 24   **j)** 128

   k) 168   **l)** 225   **m)** 325   **n)** 1000   **o)** 46

8 Square numbers have all their prime factors raised to even powers.
For example, $36 = 2^2 \times 3^2$ and $64 = 2^6$.

   a) Write 75 as a product of prime factors.

   b) What is the smallest number you could multiply 75 by to form a square number?
Explain your answer.

Section 5 — Fractions

5.1 Equivalent Fractions

The fraction $\frac{a}{b}$ means 'a out of b' or 'a divided by b'. The top number in a fraction (a) is called the **numerator**. The bottom number (b) is called the **denominator**.

Equivalent fractions are fractions that are equal in value.

To find an equivalent fraction, multiply or divide the numerator and denominator by the **same thing**.

Example 1

Find the value that needs to replace the square: $\frac{1}{5} = \frac{\blacksquare}{20}$

1. Find what you need to multiply by to get from one denominator to the other.

$$\frac{1}{5} = \frac{\blacksquare}{20} \quad \times 4$$

2. Multiply the numerator by the same number.

$$\frac{1}{5} \overset{\times 4}{=} \frac{4}{20}$$

Example 2

Find the value of b if $\frac{12}{30} = \frac{4}{b}$

1. Find what you need to divide by to get from one numerator to the other.

$$\frac{12}{30} \overset{\div 3}{=} \frac{4}{b}$$

2. Divide the denominator by the same number.

$$\frac{12}{30} = \frac{4}{10} \quad \div 3 \qquad \text{So } \boldsymbol{b = 10}$$

Exercise 1

1 **a)** How many sections of each square do you need to shade to show a fraction equivalent to $\frac{1}{2}$?

  b) Use your answers to replace the stars and make fractions equivalent to $\frac{1}{2}$.

$$\frac{1}{2} \quad = \quad \frac{\bigstar}{4} \quad = \quad \frac{\bigstar}{6} \quad = \quad \frac{\bigstar}{8}$$

2 Replace the stars and make fractions equivalent to $\frac{1}{3}$. Use the circles to help.

$$\frac{1}{3} \quad = \quad \frac{\bigstar}{6} \quad = \quad \frac{\bigstar}{9} \quad = \quad \frac{\bigstar}{12}$$

3 Find the values of the letters in the following fractions.

a) $\frac{1}{5} = \frac{a}{10}$

b) $\frac{1}{4} = \frac{b}{12}$

c) $\frac{3}{4} = \frac{c}{16}$

d) $\frac{1}{20} = \frac{d}{60}$

e) $\frac{1}{5} = \frac{5}{e}$

f) $\frac{1}{6} = \frac{3}{f}$

g) $\frac{7}{12} = \frac{35}{g}$

h) $\frac{9}{10} = \frac{81}{h}$

4 Find the values of the letters in the following fractions.

a) $\frac{1}{a} = \frac{5}{15}$

b) $\frac{3}{b} = \frac{12}{20}$

c) $\frac{c}{3} = \frac{10}{15}$

d) $\frac{d}{14} = \frac{9}{42}$

e) $\frac{e}{9} = \frac{15}{27}$

f) $\frac{f}{51} = \frac{9}{17}$

g) $\frac{11}{g} = \frac{55}{80}$

h) $\frac{1}{h} = \frac{11}{121}$

Simplifying Fractions

Simplifying a fraction by **cancelling down** means writing an equivalent fraction using the smallest possible numbers. This is also known as 'expressing a fraction in its **lowest terms**'.

Example 3

Express $\frac{24}{30}$ as a fraction in its lowest terms.

1. Divide the numerator and denominator by any common factor. Here, 3 is a common factor of 24 and 30.
2. Repeat this until the numerator and denominator have no more common factors. Here, 2 is a common factor of 8 and 10.
3. 4 and 5 have no common factors, so this is in its lowest terms.
4. Dividing 24 and 30 by their highest common factor (= 6) will get the answer in a single step.

Exercise 2

Answer **Questions 1-4** without using a calculator.

1 a) Find a common factor of 2 and 10 that's greater than 1.

b) Use your answer to simplify $\frac{2}{10}$.

c) Is your answer to **b)** in its lowest terms? Explain your answer.

2 a) Which of the following is a common factor of 45 and 75? [9   25   2   5]

b) (i) Simplify $\frac{45}{75}$ by dividing the numerator and denominator by your answer to **a)**.

   (ii) Is this fraction in its lowest terms?
   If not, find another common factor of the numerator and denominator and simplify the fraction again. Repeat this process until the fraction is in its lowest terms.

3 Write the following fractions in their lowest terms.

a) $\frac{3}{9}$

b) $\frac{5}{20}$

c) $\frac{8}{16}$

d) $\frac{4}{32}$

e) $\frac{9}{45}$

f) $\frac{15}{36}$

g) $\frac{15}{20}$

h) $\frac{12}{15}$

i) $\frac{21}{35}$

j) $\frac{24}{64}$

k) $\frac{30}{40}$

l) $\frac{25}{100}$

4   Simplify these fractions. Then state which fraction is not equivalent to the other two.

a) $\frac{6}{18}$, $\frac{5}{20}$, $\frac{9}{27}$ b) $\frac{6}{8}$, $\frac{9}{15}$, $\frac{15}{25}$ c) $\frac{4}{18}$, $\frac{6}{33}$, $\frac{10}{45}$ d) $\frac{18}{24}$, $\frac{60}{80}$, $\frac{24}{40}$

5   Simplify each of these fractions. Use a calculator where necessary.

a) $\frac{91}{130}$ b) $\frac{175}{230}$ c) $\frac{204}{348}$ d) $\frac{1029}{3486}$

5.2   Mixed Numbers

A **mixed number** is a whole number combined with a fraction. ⇒

A fraction where the numerator is bigger than the denominator is a **top-heavy** or **improper** fraction. → $\frac{5}{2}$

> ### Example 1
>
> Write the mixed number $4\frac{3}{5}$ as an improper fraction.
>
> 1. Find the fraction which is equivalent to 4 and which has 5 as the denominator. Remember, $4 = \frac{4}{1}$.
>
> $\overset{\times 5}{\frac{4}{1}} = \frac{20}{5}$
> $\underset{\times 5}{}$
>
> 2. Combine the two fractions into one improper fraction.
>
>   So $4\frac{3}{5} = \frac{20}{5} + \frac{3}{5} = \frac{23}{5}$

Exercise 1

Answer **Questions 1-6** without using the fractions button on your calculator.

1   Use the diagrams to form improper fractions equivalent to the whole numbers.

a) $2 = \frac{\bigstar}{3}$

b) $3 = \frac{\bigstar}{4}$

Clue: *How many thirds are there in 2?*   Clue: *How many quarters are there in 3?*

2   Find the values of the letters to write the following whole numbers as improper fractions.

a) $2 = \frac{a}{6}$ b) $5 = \frac{b}{5}$ c) $6 = \frac{30}{c}$ d) $13 = \frac{65}{d}$

3   a) Find the value of a if $4 = \frac{a}{3}$.

b) Use your answer to write the mixed number $4\frac{1}{3}$ as an improper fraction.

4   a) Find the value of b if $3 = \frac{b}{5}$.

b) Use your answer to write the mixed number $3\frac{2}{5}$ as an improper fraction.

5   Find the values of the letters to write the following mixed numbers as improper fractions.

a) $1\frac{1}{3} = \frac{a}{3}$ b) $1\frac{2}{7} = \frac{b}{7}$ c) $2\frac{1}{2} = \frac{c}{2}$ d) $3\frac{4}{7} = \frac{d}{7}$

6 Write the following mixed numbers as improper fractions.

a) $1\frac{4}{5}$ b) $1\frac{5}{12}$ c) $2\frac{9}{10}$ d) $5\frac{3}{10}$

e) $4\frac{3}{4}$ f) $9\frac{5}{6}$ g) $12\frac{2}{5}$ h) $15\frac{5}{7}$

i) $6\frac{5}{6}$ j) $3\frac{1}{9}$ k) $10\frac{3}{10}$ l) $7\frac{2}{3}$

Example 2

Write the improper fraction $\frac{13}{5}$ as a mixed number in its simplest terms.

1. Split the numerator into:
   (i) a multiple of the denominator,
   plus   (ii) a 'remainder' (since $13 \div 5 = 2$, with <u>remainder 3</u>).

$$\frac{13}{5} = \frac{10 + 3}{5}$$
$$= \frac{10}{5} + \frac{3}{5}$$

2. Separate the fraction to write it as a mixed number.
   The first part will always simplify to a whole number.

$$= 2 + \frac{3}{5} = 2\frac{3}{5}$$

Exercise 2

Answer **Questions 1-7** without using your calculator.

1 Write the whole number that is equivalent to these improper fractions.

a) $\frac{14}{2}$ b) $\frac{22}{11}$ c) $\frac{45}{5}$ d) $\frac{72}{12}$

2 a) Write down the value of a if $\frac{11}{7} = \frac{7 + a}{7}$.

   b) Use your answer to write $\frac{11}{7}$ as a mixed number in its simplest terms.

3 a) Write down the value of c if $\frac{17}{3} = \frac{c + 2}{3}$.

   b) Use your answer to write $\frac{17}{3}$ as a mixed number in its simplest terms.

4 Write the following improper fractions as mixed numbers.

a) $\frac{5}{3}$ b) $\frac{9}{5}$ c) $\frac{17}{10}$ d) $\frac{12}{7}$ e) $\frac{13}{11}$

f) $\frac{9}{4}$ g) $\frac{13}{6}$ h) $\frac{16}{5}$ i) $\frac{20}{9}$ j) $\frac{11}{3}$

5 a) Simplify the improper fraction $\frac{26}{4}$ so that it is in its lowest terms.

   b) Use your answer to write $\frac{26}{4}$ as a mixed number.

6 Write the following improper fractions as mixed numbers in their lowest terms.

a) $\frac{18}{12}$ b) $\frac{10}{4}$ c) $\frac{50}{15}$ d) $\frac{18}{4}$ e) $\frac{24}{18}$

f) $\frac{35}{25}$ g) $\frac{18}{8}$ h) $\frac{51}{12}$ i) $\frac{34}{6}$ j) $\frac{98}{8}$

7 Find the number in each list that is not equivalent to the other two.

a) $\frac{5}{2}$, $\frac{6}{4}$, $1\frac{1}{2}$ b) $2\frac{1}{3}$, $3\frac{1}{2}$, $\frac{7}{3}$ c) $\frac{19}{4}$, $4\frac{3}{4}$, $\frac{15}{4}$ d) $2\frac{2}{3}$, $\frac{11}{3}$, $\frac{16}{6}$

5.3 Ordering Fractions

Finding a Common Denominator

Putting two (or more) fractions over a **common denominator** means rewriting them so they have the same denominator (the number on the bottom of the fraction).

The common denominator will be a **multiple** of both fractions' denominators.

Example 1

Rewrite the following pairs of fractions so they have a common denominator.

a) $\frac{1}{2}$ and $\frac{1}{8}$

You can use 8 as the common denominator, since 8 is a multiple of 2 and 8. So find a fraction equivalent to $\frac{1}{2}$ with 8 as the denominator.

So these fractions are equivalent to $\frac{4}{8}$ and $\frac{1}{8}$.

b) $\frac{5}{6}$ and $\frac{3}{8}$

24 is a multiple of both 6 and 8, so use this as the common denominator. Rewrite the two fractions so that they have 24 as the denominator.

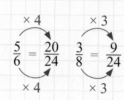

These fractions are equivalent to $\frac{20}{24}$ and $\frac{9}{24}$.

Exercise 1

Answer **Questions 1-4** without using a calculator.

1 Rewrite the following pairs of fractions so they have a common denominator.

a) $\frac{1}{3}, \frac{1}{6}$
b) $\frac{1}{5}, \frac{3}{10}$
c) $\frac{1}{4}, \frac{5}{16}$
d) $\frac{2}{5}, \frac{7}{20}$

e) $\frac{3}{8}, \frac{1}{4}$
f) $\frac{1}{12}, \frac{2}{3}$
g) $\frac{5}{18}, \frac{2}{9}$
h) $\frac{2}{7}, \frac{5}{28}$

2 Rewrite the following pairs of fractions so they have a common denominator.

a) $\frac{1}{2}, \frac{1}{5}$
b) $\frac{1}{3}, \frac{1}{4}$
c) $\frac{1}{7}, \frac{1}{10}$
d) $\frac{1}{3}, \frac{1}{7}$

e) $\frac{1}{8}, \frac{2}{5}$
f) $\frac{1}{4}, \frac{1}{12}$
g) $\frac{1}{6}, \frac{1}{4}$
h) $\frac{1}{8}, \frac{1}{6}$

3 Rewrite the following pairs of fractions so they have a common denominator.

a) $\frac{2}{9}, \frac{1}{3}$
b) $\frac{2}{3}, \frac{3}{4}$
c) $\frac{5}{6}, \frac{1}{7}$
d) $\frac{2}{9}, \frac{1}{2}$

e) $\frac{3}{8}, \frac{4}{5}$
f) $\frac{5}{6}, \frac{7}{12}$
g) $\frac{7}{8}, \frac{3}{10}$
h) $\frac{2}{5}, \frac{4}{9}$

4 Rewrite the following groups of fractions so they have a common denominator.

a) $\frac{3}{4}, \frac{5}{8}, \frac{7}{12}$
b) $\frac{1}{5}, \frac{7}{10}, \frac{9}{20}$
c) $\frac{1}{7}, \frac{4}{21}, \frac{5}{14}$
d) $\frac{1}{2}, \frac{3}{8}, \frac{2}{3}$

e) $\frac{2}{5}, \frac{5}{12}, \frac{11}{30}$
f) $\frac{1}{8}, \frac{7}{20}, \frac{3}{5}$
g) $\frac{2}{3}, \frac{5}{7}, \frac{5}{6}$
h) $\frac{5}{18}, \frac{7}{24}, \frac{11}{30}$

If fractions have a common denominator, then you can use their **numerators** to put them in order.

Example 2

Put the fractions $\frac{1}{2}$, $\frac{3}{8}$, and $\frac{3}{4}$ in order, from smallest to largest.

1. Put the fractions over a common denominator first.
   Use 8 as the common denominator, since 8 is a multiple of
   2, 4 and 8. So rewrite $\frac{1}{2}$ and $\frac{3}{4}$ as fractions with a denominator of 8.

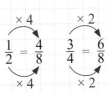

So the fractions are equivalent to $\frac{4}{8}$, $\frac{3}{8}$ and $\frac{6}{8}$.

2. Use the numerators to put the fractions in order.   In order, these are: $\frac{3}{8}$, $\frac{4}{8}$, $\frac{6}{8}$.

3. Write the ordered fractions in their original form.   So in order, the original

fractions are $\frac{3}{8}$, $\frac{1}{2}$, $\frac{3}{4}$.

Exercise 2

Answer **Questions 1-9** without using a calculator.

1 **a)** Rewrite the fractions $\frac{5}{6}$ and $\frac{2}{3}$ so they have a common denominator.

b) Which of the fractions $\frac{5}{6}$ and $\frac{2}{3}$ is larger?

2 **a)** Rewrite the fractions $\frac{2}{5}$ and $\frac{3}{8}$ so they have a common denominator.

b) Which of the fractions $\frac{2}{5}$ and $\frac{3}{8}$ is larger?

3 Write down the larger fraction in each pair below.

a) $\frac{1}{4}$, $\frac{5}{8}$ **b)** $\frac{3}{5}$, $\frac{7}{10}$ **c)** $\frac{4}{7}$, $\frac{9}{14}$ **d)** $\frac{11}{18}$, $\frac{2}{3}$

e) $\frac{5}{6}$, $\frac{3}{4}$ **f)** $\frac{2}{3}$, $\frac{3}{5}$ **g)** $\frac{2}{3}$, $\frac{3}{4}$ **h)** $\frac{7}{10}$, $\frac{3}{4}$

4 **a)** Rewrite the fractions $\frac{1}{3}$, $\frac{4}{15}$ and $\frac{2}{9}$ so they have a common denominator.

b) Use your answer to write the fractions $\frac{1}{3}$, $\frac{4}{15}$ and $\frac{2}{9}$ in order, from smallest to largest.

In **Questions 5-7**, put each of the sets of fractions in order, from smallest to largest.

5 **a)** $\frac{1}{2}$, $\frac{5}{8}$, $\frac{7}{16}$ **b)** $\frac{2}{5}$, $\frac{3}{10}$, $\frac{7}{20}$ **c)** $\frac{3}{4}$, $\frac{7}{12}$, $\frac{5}{8}$ **d)** $\frac{5}{6}$, $\frac{11}{12}$, $\frac{19}{24}$

6 **a)** $\frac{4}{9}$, $\frac{5}{12}$, $\frac{2}{3}$ **b)** $\frac{9}{10}$, $\frac{11}{12}$, $\frac{4}{5}$ **c)** $\frac{1}{4}$, $\frac{3}{11}$, $\frac{5}{22}$ **d)** $\frac{7}{9}$, $\frac{4}{5}$, $\frac{13}{15}$

7 **a)** $\frac{7}{8}$, $\frac{5}{6}$, $\frac{13}{16}$ **b)** $\frac{4}{15}$, $\frac{7}{27}$, $\frac{13}{45}$ **c)** $\frac{5}{16}$, $\frac{7}{20}$, $\frac{9}{25}$ **d)** $\frac{11}{36}$, $\frac{4}{15}$, $\frac{9}{24}$

8 Annette scores $\frac{5}{6}$ on a test. Ben scores $\frac{7}{8}$. Who does better?

9 Charlene runs $\frac{3}{4}$ of a mile, while Dave runs $\frac{7}{10}$ of a mile. Who runs further?

5.4 Adding and Subtracting Fractions

Add or subtract fractions with a **common denominator** by adding or subtracting the **numerators**.
If fractions have **different denominators**, then rewrite them with a common denominator first.

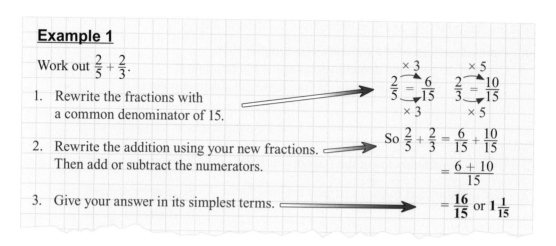

Example 1

Work out $\frac{2}{5} + \frac{2}{3}$.

1. Rewrite the fractions with a common denominator of 15.

2. Rewrite the addition using your new fractions. Then add or subtract the numerators.

3. Give your answer in its simplest terms.

$$\overset{\times 3}{\underset{\times 3}{\frac{2}{5} = \frac{6}{15}}} \qquad \overset{\times 5}{\underset{\times 5}{\frac{2}{3} = \frac{10}{15}}}$$

So $\frac{2}{5} + \frac{2}{3} = \frac{6}{15} + \frac{10}{15}$

$= \frac{6 + 10}{15}$

$= \frac{16}{15}$ or $1\frac{1}{15}$

Exercise 1

Answer **Questions 1-7** without using your calculator.

1 Work out the following. Give your answers in their simplest form.

a) $\frac{1}{3} + \frac{1}{3}$ b) $\frac{4}{5} - \frac{2}{5}$ c) $\frac{5}{11} - \frac{3}{11}$ d) $\frac{1}{10} + \frac{3}{10}$

e) $\frac{1}{12} + \frac{5}{12}$ f) $\frac{8}{9} - \frac{2}{9}$ g) $\frac{3}{20} + \frac{7}{20}$ h) $\frac{11}{16} - \frac{5}{16}$

2 Work out the following. Give your answers as mixed numbers in their simplest form.

a) $\frac{5}{8} + \frac{7}{8}$ b) $\frac{3}{4} + \frac{3}{4}$ c) $\frac{7}{10} + \frac{9}{10}$ d) $\frac{11}{20} + \frac{13}{20}$

e) $\frac{5}{11} + \frac{8}{11} + \frac{7}{11}$ f) $\frac{5}{7} + \frac{4}{7} + \frac{6}{7}$ g) $\frac{8}{15} + \frac{13}{15} - \frac{2}{15}$ h) $\frac{17}{20} + \frac{19}{20} - \frac{7}{20}$

3 a) Rewrite the fractions $\frac{1}{2}$ and $\frac{1}{4}$ with a common denominator.

    b) Work out $\frac{1}{2} + \frac{1}{4}$.

4 Work out the following. Give your answers in their simplest form.

a) $\frac{3}{5} + \frac{1}{10}$ b) $\frac{1}{4} + \frac{3}{8}$ c) $\frac{1}{6} + \frac{1}{2}$ d) $\frac{3}{14} + \frac{2}{7}$

e) $\frac{4}{9} - \frac{1}{3}$ f) $\frac{3}{4} - \frac{3}{8}$ g) $\frac{7}{10} - \frac{2}{5}$ h) $\frac{5}{18} - \frac{2}{9}$

5 a) Rewrite the fractions $\frac{9}{10}$ and $\frac{5}{6}$ with a common denominator.

    b) Work out $\frac{9}{10} - \frac{5}{6}$. Give your answer in its simplest form.

6 Work out the following. Give your answers in their simplest form.

a) $\frac{1}{5} + \frac{1}{3}$

b) $\frac{9}{10} - \frac{5}{6}$

c) $\frac{1}{2} + \frac{3}{5}$

d) $\frac{2}{3} - \frac{1}{4}$

e) $\frac{2}{3} + \frac{4}{5}$

f) $\frac{5}{6} + \frac{9}{10}$

g) $\frac{3}{7} + \frac{3}{4}$

h) $\frac{6}{11} + \frac{7}{9}$

i) $\frac{23}{24} - \frac{7}{10}$

j) $\frac{8}{9} + \frac{12}{21}$

k) $\frac{3}{5} + \frac{6}{7}$

l) $\frac{15}{16} + \frac{3}{5}$

7 Work out the following. Give your answers in their simplest form.

a) $\frac{1}{9} + \frac{5}{9} + \frac{11}{18}$

b) $\frac{3}{4} + \frac{1}{8} - \frac{7}{16}$

c) $\frac{6}{7} + \frac{1}{14} - \frac{1}{2}$

d) $\frac{1}{4} + \frac{2}{3} + \frac{5}{6}$

Example 2

A maths exam has 24 questions. $\frac{1}{2}$ of the questions are on number topics, $\frac{1}{3}$ of the questions are on algebra, and the rest are on geometry.

What fraction of the questions are geometry questions?

1. The fractions of number questions, algebra questions and geometry questions must add up to 1.

$$\text{Fraction of geometry questions} = 1 - \frac{1}{2} - \frac{1}{3}$$

2. Put the fractions over a common denominator. (Remember, anything divided by itself is 1, so you can write $1 = \frac{6}{6}$.)

$$1 = \frac{6}{6} \qquad \frac{1}{2} = \frac{3}{6} \qquad \frac{1}{3} = \frac{2}{6}$$
($\times 3$)   ($\times 2$)

3. Subtract to find the fraction of geometry questions.

$$\text{Fraction of geometry questions} = \frac{6}{6} - \frac{3}{6} - \frac{2}{6} = \frac{6 - 3 - 2}{6}$$
$$= \frac{1}{6}$$

Exercise 2

1 $\frac{4}{9}$ of the pupils in one class are boys. What fraction of the class are girls?

2 Jake, Frank and Olga are sharing a cake. Jake eats $\frac{2}{7}$ of the cake, Frank eats $\frac{3}{7}$ and Olga eats the rest. What fraction of the cake does Olga eat?

3 $\frac{1}{5}$ of the flowers in a garden are roses. $\frac{3}{10}$ of the flowers are tulips. What fraction of the flowers are neither roses nor tulips?

4 A bag contains a mixture of sweets. $\frac{2}{5}$ of the sweets are chocolates, $\frac{1}{4}$ are toffees and the rest are mints. What fraction of the sweets are mints?

5 In a school survey, $\frac{1}{2}$ of the pupils said they walk to school. $\frac{1}{5}$ said they catch the bus. The rest arrive by car. What fraction come to school by car?

Adding and Subtracting Mixed Numbers

To add or subtract mixed numbers, first change them into **improper fractions** with a **common denominator**.

Example 3

Work out $1\frac{1}{3} + 2\frac{5}{6}$.

1. Write the mixed numbers as improper fractions.

   $1 = \frac{3}{3}$, so $1\frac{1}{3} = \frac{3}{3} + \frac{1}{3} = \frac{4}{3}$

   $2 = \frac{12}{6}$, so $2\frac{5}{6} = \frac{12}{6} + \frac{5}{6} = \frac{17}{6}$

2. Rewrite the improper fractions with a common denominator of 6.

   $$\frac{4}{3} \overset{\times 2}{\underset{\times 2}{=}} \frac{8}{6}$$

3. Add the numerators.

   So $1\frac{1}{3} + 2\frac{5}{6} = \frac{8}{6} + \frac{17}{6} = \frac{25}{6}$

4. Give your answer as a mixed number in its simplest form.

   $$= \frac{24}{6} + \frac{1}{6} = 4\frac{1}{6}$$

Exercise 3

Answer **Questions 1-8** without using your calculator.

1 **a)** Write the mixed number $1\frac{4}{5}$ as an improper fraction.

   b) Use your answer to work out $1\frac{4}{5} + \frac{3}{5}$.

2 Work out the following. Give your answers in their simplest form.

   a) $1\frac{2}{3} + \frac{1}{3}$ **b)** $2\frac{3}{8} + \frac{7}{8}$ **c)** $3\frac{1}{5} + \frac{2}{5}$

   d) $1\frac{5}{6} + 1\frac{1}{6}$ **e)** $1\frac{3}{7} - \frac{4}{7}$ **f)** $2\frac{5}{9} - \frac{8}{9}$

3 **a)** Write the following as improper fractions: **(i)** $2\frac{1}{5}$ **(ii)** $1\frac{3}{5}$

   b) Use your answers to work out $2\frac{1}{5} - 1\frac{3}{5}$.

4 Work out the following. Give your answers in their simplest form.

   a) $2\frac{1}{5} + 1\frac{3}{5}$ **b)** $4\frac{5}{12} - 2\frac{11}{12}$ **c)** $5\frac{7}{11} + \frac{5}{11}$

   d) $3\frac{2}{5} - \frac{4}{5}$ **e)** $4\frac{1}{3} + \frac{2}{3}$ **f)** $6\frac{3}{8} - \frac{7}{8}$

5 **a)** Write the following as improper fractions: **(i)** $2\frac{3}{4}$ **(ii)** $1\frac{1}{2}$

   b) Rewrite your answers to part **a)** with a common denominator.

   c) Work out $2\frac{3}{4} + 1\frac{1}{2}$.

6 Work out the following. Give your answers in their simplest form.

a) $3\frac{3}{10} + \frac{2}{5}$ b) $2\frac{5}{9} + \frac{1}{3}$ c) $3\frac{1}{2} + 1\frac{3}{4}$ d) $2\frac{5}{8} + 3\frac{3}{4}$

e) $2\frac{3}{8} - \frac{3}{4}$ f) $4\frac{5}{12} - 2\frac{5}{6}$ g) $4\frac{3}{14} - 1\frac{6}{7}$ h) $7\frac{5}{9} - 1\frac{11}{18}$

7 a) Write the following as improper fractions: **(i)** $1\frac{1}{6}$ **(ii)** $3\frac{1}{8}$

b) Rewrite your answers to part **a)** with a common denominator.

c) Work out $1\frac{1}{6} + 3\frac{1}{8}$.

8 Work out the following. Give your answers in their simplest form.

a) $1\frac{3}{5} + \frac{3}{4}$ b) $2\frac{5}{8} + \frac{2}{3}$ c) $3\frac{1}{5} + 2\frac{3}{7}$ d) $1\frac{1}{6} + 4\frac{7}{15}$

e) $3\frac{3}{4} - \frac{5}{7}$ f) $5\frac{2}{5} - 3\frac{7}{9}$ g) $2\frac{1}{4} - 1\frac{6}{7}$ h) $2\frac{5}{11} + 3\frac{2}{3}$

i) $5\frac{7}{12} + 3\frac{2}{5}$ j) $4\frac{3}{8} - 1\frac{2}{9}$ k) $1\frac{4}{7} + 3\frac{5}{9}$ l) $5\frac{3}{20} - 1\frac{7}{12}$

5.5 Multiplying and Dividing Fractions

Multiplying by Unit Fractions

A **unit fraction** has 1 as its numerator — for example, these are all unit fractions: $\frac{1}{2}, \frac{1}{3}, \frac{1}{5}, \frac{1}{10}$

Multiplying by a **unit fraction** is the same as **dividing** by a **whole number**.

For example, multiplying by $\frac{1}{2}$ is the same as dividing by 2.

Example 1

Work out:

a) $12 \times \frac{1}{3}$ Multiplying by $\frac{1}{3}$ is the same as dividing by 3. $12 \times \frac{1}{3} = \frac{12}{3}$

Remember, $\frac{12}{3}$ means the same as $12 \div 3$. $= \underline{\mathbf{4}}$

b) $10 \times \frac{1}{4}$ Multiplying by $\frac{1}{4}$ is the same as dividing by 4. $10 \times \frac{1}{4} = \frac{10}{4}$

Remember, $\frac{10}{4}$ means the same as $10 \div 4$. $= \underline{\mathbf{2\frac{1}{2}}}$

Exercise 1

Answer **Questions 1-2** without using your calculator.

1 Work out the following.

a) $8 \times \frac{1}{4}$ b) $10 \times \frac{1}{5}$ c) $15 \times \frac{1}{5}$ d) $45 \times \frac{1}{3}$

e) $27 \times \frac{1}{9}$ f) $40 \times \frac{1}{8}$ g) $16 \times \frac{1}{4}$ h) $35 \times \frac{1}{5}$

i) $39 \times \frac{1}{3}$ j) $42 \times \frac{1}{7}$ k) $48 \times \frac{1}{6}$ l) $80 \times \frac{1}{10}$

2 Work out the following. Write your answers as mixed numbers.

a) $18 \times \frac{1}{4}$ b) $15 \times \frac{1}{6}$ c) $17 \times \frac{1}{2}$ d) $25 \times \frac{1}{10}$

e) $16 \times \frac{1}{5}$ f) $21 \times \frac{1}{4}$ g) $39 \times \frac{1}{4}$ h) $29 \times \frac{1}{5}$

i) $10 \times \frac{1}{3}$ j) $20 \times \frac{1}{9}$ k) $25 \times \frac{1}{6}$ l) $40 \times \frac{1}{3}$

Multiplying Whole Numbers by Fractions

To multiply a whole number by any fraction: • **multiply** by the **numerator**
                                          • **divide** by the **denominator**

You can do these two steps in any order.

Example 2

Work out:

a) $15 \times \frac{2}{5}$ You need to multiply 15 by 2, and then divide by 5. $15 \times \frac{2}{5} = \frac{15 \times 2}{5} = \frac{30}{5}$
             (Or you can divide by 5, and then multiply by 2
             — you'll get the same answer.) $= \mathbf{6}$

b) $5 \times \frac{3}{4}$ You need to multiply 5 by 3, and then divide by 4. $5 \times \frac{3}{4} = \frac{5 \times 3}{4} = \frac{15}{4}$
           (Or you can divide by 4, and then multiply by 3.)
                                                    $= \mathbf{3\frac{3}{4}}$

Exercise 2

Answer **Questions 1-3** without using your calculator.

1 Work out the following. Write your answers as simply as possible.

a) $12 \times \frac{2}{3}$ b) $28 \times \frac{3}{4}$ c) $15 \times \frac{4}{5}$ d) $48 \times \frac{3}{8}$

e) $60 \times \frac{5}{12}$ f) $32 \times \frac{7}{16}$ g) $35 \times \frac{3}{7}$ h) $40 \times \frac{9}{10}$

i) $18 \times \frac{2}{9}$ j) $24 \times \frac{5}{6}$ k) $100 \times \frac{7}{25}$ l) $96 \times \frac{7}{12}$

2 Work out the following. Write your answers as mixed numbers.

a) $15 \times \frac{3}{4}$ b) $22 \times \frac{2}{5}$ c) $42 \times \frac{3}{10}$ d) $38 \times \frac{3}{5}$

e) $48 \times \frac{2}{7}$ f) $27 \times \frac{5}{6}$ g) $32 \times \frac{2}{3}$ h) $34 \times \frac{4}{5}$

i) $80 \times \frac{2}{9}$ j) $45 \times \frac{5}{12}$ k) $72 \times \frac{3}{11}$ l) $62 \times \frac{5}{8}$

Example 3

Find $\frac{3}{5}$ of 20.

You can replace 'of' with a multiplication sign. $\frac{3}{5}$ of $20 = \frac{3}{5} \times 20 = \frac{3 \times 20}{5} = \frac{60}{5} = \mathbf{12}$

3   Find the following.

a) $\frac{3}{4}$ of 36   b) $\frac{2}{3}$ of 33   c) $\frac{3}{8}$ of 64   d) $\frac{5}{12}$ of 72

e) $\frac{5}{6}$ of 18   f) $\frac{3}{5}$ of 15   g) $\frac{5}{6}$ of 33   h) $\frac{7}{12}$ of 45

Multiplying Fractions and Mixed Numbers

To multiply two or more fractions, multiply the numerators and denominators **separately**.
To multiply **mixed numbers**, change them to improper fractions first.

Example 4

Work out:

a) $\frac{2}{3} \times \frac{4}{5}$ The numerator of the result will be 2 × 4. $\frac{2}{3} \times \frac{4}{5} = \frac{2 \times 4}{3 \times 5} = \frac{8}{15}$
    The denominator of the result will be 3 × 5.

b) $\frac{3}{4} \times \frac{2}{9}$ The numerator of the result will be 3 × 2. $\frac{3}{4} \times \frac{2}{9} = \frac{3 \times 2}{4 \times 9} = \frac{6}{36} = \frac{1}{6}$
    The denominator of the result will be 4 × 9.
    Simplify your answer as much as possible.

Exercise 3

Answer **Questions 1-6** without using your calculator.

1   Work out the following.

a) $\frac{1}{6} \times \frac{1}{3}$ b) $\frac{2}{5} \times \frac{1}{3}$ c) $\frac{3}{4} \times \frac{1}{7}$ d) $\frac{1}{5} \times \frac{3}{5}$

e) $\frac{5}{6} \times \frac{1}{4}$ f) $\frac{4}{5} \times \frac{2}{7}$ g) $\frac{2}{7} \times \frac{5}{7}$ h) $\frac{3}{8} \times \frac{7}{10}$

2   Work out the following. Give your answers in their lowest terms.

a) $\frac{1}{4} \times \frac{2}{3}$ b) $\frac{3}{5} \times \frac{1}{6}$ c) $\frac{5}{6} \times \frac{2}{15}$ d) $\frac{5}{12} \times \frac{3}{4}$

e) $\frac{4}{7} \times \frac{3}{8}$ f) $\frac{2}{5} \times \frac{15}{16}$ g) $\frac{6}{7} \times \frac{7}{8}$ h) $\frac{7}{10} \times \frac{5}{14}$

Example 5

Work out $4\frac{1}{2} \times 3\frac{3}{5}$.

1. Write the mixed numbers $4\frac{1}{2} = \frac{8}{2} + \frac{1}{2} = \frac{9}{2}$
   as improper fractions.
                                  $3\frac{3}{5} = \frac{15}{5} + \frac{3}{5} = \frac{18}{5}$

2. Multiply the two fractions.   So $4\frac{1}{2} \times 3\frac{3}{5} = \frac{9}{2} \times \frac{18}{5} = \frac{9 \times 18}{2 \times 5} = \frac{162}{10}$

3. Simplify your answer and $\frac{162}{10} = \frac{81}{5} = \frac{80}{5} + \frac{1}{5} = \mathbf{16\frac{1}{5}}$
   write it as a mixed number.

3 **a)** Write the mixed number $1\frac{3}{7}$ as an improper fraction.

   b) Use your answer to work out $1\frac{3}{7} \times \frac{2}{3}$.

4 Work out the following.

   a) $1\frac{1}{2} \times \frac{1}{3}$ **b)** $2\frac{1}{5} \times \frac{3}{4}$ **c)** $1\frac{5}{6} \times \frac{2}{3}$ **d)** $3\frac{3}{4} \times \frac{2}{5}$

   e) $2\frac{1}{7} \times \frac{2}{9}$ **f)** $1\frac{11}{12} \times \frac{1}{4}$ **g)** $4\frac{3}{5} \times \frac{4}{5}$ **h)** $2\frac{4}{9} \times \frac{3}{8}$

5 **a)** Write the mixed number $3\frac{2}{5}$ as an improper fraction.

   b) Write the mixed number $1\frac{1}{2}$ as an improper fraction.

   c) Use your answer to work out $3\frac{2}{5} \times 1\frac{1}{2}$.

6 Work out the following.

   a) $1\frac{1}{5} \times 1\frac{1}{4}$ **b)** $2\frac{2}{5} \times 1\frac{2}{3}$ **c)** $1\frac{1}{9} \times 2\frac{2}{3}$ **d)** $1\frac{3}{5} \times 1\frac{3}{4}$

   e) $2\frac{3}{7} \times 3\frac{1}{6}$ **f)** $3\frac{4}{9} \times 1\frac{7}{8}$ **g)** $2\frac{6}{7} \times 2\frac{1}{9}$ **h)** $4\frac{3}{10} \times 3\frac{5}{6}$

Dividing by Fractions

Swapping the numerator and the denominator of a fraction gives you the **reciprocal** of that fraction.
Dividing by a fraction is the same as **multiplying by its reciprocal**.

Example 6

Find the reciprocal of:

a) $\frac{3}{5}$ Swap the numerator and denominator.   The reciprocal of $\frac{3}{5}$ is $\frac{5}{3}$.

b) 6   Remember, $6 = \frac{6}{1}$.   The reciprocal of 6 is $\frac{1}{6}$.

Exercise 4

1 Find the reciprocal of each of the following.

   a) $\frac{1}{3}$ **b)** $\frac{1}{7}$ **c)** $\frac{4}{5}$ **d)** $\frac{5}{8}$

   e) $\frac{12}{27}$ **f)** $\frac{9}{10}$ **g)** $\frac{6}{19}$ **h)** $\frac{84}{107}$

2 Find the reciprocal of each of the following.

   a) 5   **b)** 12   **c)** 9   **d)** 27

3 **a)** Write the mixed number $1\frac{1}{4}$ as an improper fraction.

   b) Use your answer to find the reciprocal of $1\frac{1}{4}$.

4 By first writing them as improper fractions, find the reciprocal of each of the following.

a) $1\frac{3}{5}$ b) $2\frac{1}{7}$ c) $1\frac{4}{9}$ d) $2\frac{3}{4}$

e) $1\frac{11}{12}$ f) $3\frac{1}{4}$ g) $5\frac{2}{3}$ h) $4\frac{2}{7}$

Example 7

Work out:

a) $\frac{1}{2} \div \frac{2}{3}$ Multiply $\frac{1}{2}$ by the reciprocal of $\frac{2}{3}$. $\frac{1}{2} \div \frac{2}{3} = \frac{1}{2} \times \frac{3}{2} = \frac{1 \times 3}{2 \times 2} = \frac{3}{4}$

b) $\frac{4}{7} \div 2$ Multiply $\frac{4}{7}$ by the reciprocal of 2. $\frac{4}{7} \div 2 = \frac{4}{7} \times \frac{1}{2} = \frac{4 \times 1}{7 \times 2} = \frac{4}{14} = \frac{2}{7}$
Simplify your answer if possible.

Exercise 5

Answer **Questions 1-7** without using your calculator.

1 Work out the following.

a) $\frac{1}{5} \div \frac{2}{3}$ b) $\frac{1}{6} \div \frac{2}{5}$ c) $\frac{1}{4} \div \frac{3}{7}$ d) $\frac{2}{3} \div \frac{5}{7}$

e) $\frac{5}{12} \div \frac{4}{5}$ f) $\frac{2}{7} \div \frac{5}{6}$ g) $\frac{3}{8} \div \frac{2}{5}$ h) $\frac{7}{10} \div \frac{5}{7}$

2 Work out the following. Give your answers in their simplest form.

a) $\frac{1}{6} \div \frac{3}{8}$ b) $\frac{1}{4} \div \frac{1}{2}$ c) $\frac{2}{5} \div \frac{7}{10}$ d) $\frac{4}{7} \div \frac{8}{21}$

e) $\frac{3}{8} \div \frac{9}{11}$ f) $\frac{3}{5} \div \frac{9}{20}$ g) $\frac{3}{4} \div \frac{9}{16}$ h) $\frac{5}{7} \div \frac{11}{14}$

3 Work out the following.

a) $1 \div \frac{1}{2}$ b) $2 \div \frac{2}{3}$ c) $3 \div \frac{3}{5}$ d) $4 \div \frac{7}{8}$

e) $\frac{2}{3} \div 4$ f) $\frac{2}{5} \div 3$ g) $\frac{1}{4} \div 4$ h) $\frac{3}{7} \div 6$

4 a) Write the mixed number $1\frac{3}{4}$ as an improper fraction.

b) Find the reciprocal of $1\frac{3}{4}$.

c) Use your answer to work out $\frac{2}{5} \div 1\frac{3}{4}$.

5 By first writing any mixed numbers as improper fractions, work out the following.

a) $1\frac{1}{2} \div 4$ b) $3\frac{1}{3} \div 6$ c) $2\frac{3}{7} \div 3$ d) $4\frac{4}{9} \div 6$

e) $5 \div 1\frac{3}{5}$ f) $2 \div 1\frac{7}{8}$ g) $6 \div 2\frac{1}{3}$ h) $4 \div 4\frac{1}{5}$

6 a) Write the mixed numbers $2\frac{1}{3}$ and $1\frac{4}{5}$ as improper fractions.

b) Find the reciprocal of $1\frac{4}{5}$.

c) Hence work out $2\frac{1}{3} \div 1\frac{4}{5}$. Give your answer as a mixed number in its simplest form.

7 By first writing any mixed numbers as improper fractions, work out the following.

a) $1\frac{1}{3} \div \frac{2}{5}$ b) $2\frac{1}{2} \div \frac{1}{3}$ c) $1\frac{1}{6} \div \frac{1}{4}$ d) $3\frac{1}{5} \div \frac{2}{3}$

e) $\frac{2}{3} \div 3\frac{2}{5}$ f) $\frac{3}{4} \div 2\frac{1}{3}$ g) $\frac{4}{7} \div 3\frac{1}{2}$ h) $\frac{4}{9} \div 1\frac{3}{5}$

i) $1\frac{1}{4} \div 1\frac{1}{5}$ j) $2\frac{2}{3} \div 1\frac{1}{4}$ k) $4\frac{5}{6} \div 2\frac{1}{3}$ l) $3\frac{2}{3} \div 2\frac{1}{10}$

m) $4\frac{3}{4} \div 1\frac{1}{6}$ n) $6\frac{2}{5} \div 2\frac{3}{10}$ o) $5\frac{1}{7} \div 1\frac{4}{5}$ p) $3\frac{3}{10} \div 2\frac{1}{7}$

5.6 Fractions and Decimals

All fractions can be written as either a **terminating** or **recurring** decimal. In a terminating decimal the digits stop. A recurring decimal has a repeating pattern in its digits which goes on forever.

A recurring decimal is shown using a dot above the first and last repeated digits.

For example, $0.111... = 0.\dot{1}$, $0.151515... = 0.\dot{1}\dot{5}$, $0.12341234... = 0.\dot{1}23\dot{4}$.

Converting Fractions to Decimals Using a Calculator

Use a calculator to convert a fraction to a decimal by **dividing** the numerator by the denominator.

Example 1

Use a calculator to convert the following fractions to decimals:

a) $\frac{5}{16}$ Divide the numerator by the denominator. $\frac{5}{16} = 5 \div 16 = \mathbf{0.3125}$

b) $1\frac{2}{5}$ Either: Think of this as $1 + (2 \div 5) = 1 + 0.4$. $1\frac{2}{5} = 1 + (2 \div 5) = 1 + 0.4 = \underline{\mathbf{1.4}}$
Or: Convert this to the improper fraction $\frac{7}{5}$, and use your calculator to find $7 \div 5 = 1.4$.

Exercise 1

1 Use a calculator to help decide whether these decimals are terminating or recurring.

a) $\frac{3}{8}$ b) $\frac{2}{5}$ c) $\frac{5}{6}$ d) $\frac{5}{8}$

e) $\frac{2}{11}$ f) $\frac{11}{20}$ g) $\frac{5}{9}$ h) $\frac{13}{16}$

i) $\frac{15}{32}$ j) $\frac{6}{11}$ k) $\frac{23}{40}$ l) $\frac{1}{15}$

2 Use a calculator to convert the following fractions to decimals.

a) $\frac{3}{4}$ b) $\frac{4}{5}$ c) $\frac{5}{8}$ d) $\frac{7}{20}$

e) $\frac{7}{16}$ f) $\frac{5}{32}$ g) $\frac{7}{40}$ h) $\frac{23}{50}$

i) $\frac{176}{200}$ j) $\frac{53}{64}$ k) $\frac{329}{500}$ l) $\frac{97}{128}$

3 Use a calculator to convert the following mixed numbers to decimals.

a) $1\frac{3}{5}$ b) $2\frac{1}{8}$ c) $6\frac{7}{20}$ d) $2\frac{37}{100}$

e) $4\frac{719}{1000}$ f) $5\frac{19}{25}$ g) $7\frac{11}{32}$ h) $8\frac{7}{16}$

Example 2

Use a calculator to convert the following fractions to decimals:

a) $\frac{1}{6}$ This is a 'recurring decimal' — one that repeats forever. The calculator tells you the answer is 0.1666... Show the repeating digit with a dot. $\frac{1}{6} = 1 \div 6 = 0.1666... = \mathbf{0.1\dot{6}}$

b) $\frac{41}{333}$ The calculator tells you the answer is 0.123123123... Show the repeating pattern by putting dots over the first and last digits of the repeated group. $\frac{41}{333} = 41 \div 333$
$= 0.123123123... = \mathbf{0.\dot{1}2\dot{3}}$

4 Use a calculator to convert the following fractions to decimals.

a) $\frac{1}{3}$ b) $\frac{2}{11}$ c) $\frac{5}{6}$ d) $\frac{4}{9}$

5 By first writing these fractions as decimals, put each of the following lists in order, from smallest to largest.

a) $\frac{3}{10}, \frac{1}{4}, \frac{7}{16}$ b) $\frac{7}{8}, \frac{17}{20}, \frac{5}{6}$ c) $\frac{4}{10}, \frac{3}{8}, \frac{9}{25}$

6 Use a calculator to convert the following fractions to decimals.

a) $\frac{67}{111}$ b) $\frac{1111}{9000}$ c) $\frac{4}{15}$ d) $\frac{1234}{9999}$

Converting Fractions to Decimals Without Using a Calculator

There are a couple of ways to convert fractions to decimals if you don't have a calculator.

1) You can use the following to convert fractions with denominators of **10**, **100** or **1000**.

$$\frac{1}{10} = 0.1, \qquad \frac{1}{100} = 0.01, \qquad \frac{1}{1000} = 0.001$$

For fractions with **other denominators**, you can first convert them to an equivalent fraction whose denominator is 10, 100 or 1000.

2) Or you can divide the numerator by the denominator using **pen and paper** (instead of a calculator).

Example 3

Write the following fractions as decimals.

a) $\frac{7}{10}$ Write the fraction as a multiple of $\frac{1}{10}, \frac{1}{100}$ or $\frac{1}{1000}$. Then rewrite as a decimal. $\frac{7}{10} = 7 \times \frac{1}{10} = 7 \times 0.1 = \mathbf{0.7}$

b) $\frac{9}{100}$ $\frac{9}{100} = 9 \times \frac{1}{100} = 9 \times 0.01 = \mathbf{0.09}$

Exercise 2

Answer **Questions 1-10** without using your calculator.

Write the fractions in **Questions 1-4** as decimals.

1 a) $\frac{9}{10}$ b) $\frac{2}{10}$ c) $\frac{3}{10}$ d) $\frac{8}{10}$

2 a) $\frac{91}{100}$ b) $\frac{42}{100}$ c) $\frac{99}{100}$ d) $\frac{8}{100}$

3 a) $\frac{7}{1000}$ b) $\frac{201}{1000}$ c) $\frac{41}{1000}$ d) $\frac{27}{1000}$

4 a) $\frac{52}{100}$ b) $\frac{6}{10}$ c) $\frac{635}{1000}$ d) $\frac{34}{100}$

   e) $\frac{86}{1000}$ f) $\frac{46}{100}$ g) $\frac{9}{10}$ h) $\frac{492}{1000}$

Example 4

Write these fractions as decimals.

a) $\frac{4}{5}$
  1. Multiply top and bottom to find an equivalent fraction with a denominator of 10.

$$\frac{4}{5} \overset{\times 2}{\underset{\times 2}{=}} \frac{8}{10}$$

  2. Then rewrite as a decimal.

$$\frac{8}{10} = 8 \times \frac{1}{10} = 8 \times 0.1 = \underline{\mathbf{0.8}}$$

b) $\frac{123}{300}$
  1. Divide top and bottom to find an equivalent fraction with a denominator of 10.

$$\frac{123}{300} \overset{\div 3}{\underset{\div 3}{=}} \frac{41}{100}$$

  2. Then rewrite as a decimal.

$$\frac{41}{100} = 41 \times \frac{1}{100} = 41 \times 0.01 = \underline{\mathbf{0.41}}$$

5 a) Find the value of a if $\frac{13}{20} = \frac{a}{100}$.
   b) Use your answer to write the fraction $\frac{13}{20}$ as a decimal.

6 a) Find a fraction which is equivalent to $\frac{8}{25}$ and which has a denominator of 100.
   b) Use your answer to write $\frac{8}{25}$ as a decimal.

Write the fractions in **Questions 7-10** as decimals.

7 a) $\frac{1}{5}$ b) $\frac{9}{30}$ c) $\frac{45}{50}$ d) $\frac{3}{5}$

8 a) $\frac{17}{50}$ b) $\frac{22}{25}$ c) $\frac{43}{50}$ d) $\frac{96}{300}$

9 a) $\frac{1}{500}$ b) $\frac{33}{250}$ c) $\frac{103}{200}$ d) $\frac{306}{3000}$

10 a) $\frac{2}{5}$ b) $\frac{12}{25}$ c) $\frac{333}{500}$ d) $\frac{24}{50}$

   e) $\frac{180}{2000}$ f) $\frac{43}{50}$ g) $\frac{7}{20}$ h) $\frac{123}{200}$

Example 5

Write $\frac{1}{8}$ as a decimal.

You need to work out $1 \div 8$.

1. 8 doesn't go into 1.

$$8\overline{)1.{}^10}$$
$$0.$$

2. 8 goes into 10 once, with remainder 2.

$$8\overline{)1.{}^10{}^20}$$
$$0.\,1$$

3. 8 goes into 20 twice, with remainder 4.

$$8\overline{)1.{}^10{}^20{}^40}$$
$$0.\,1\,2$$

4. 8 goes into 40 exactly 5 times.
    Remember, the decimal point in the answer goes
    directly above the decimal point in 1.000.

$$8\overline{)1.{}^10{}^20{}^40}$$
$$0.\,1\,2\,5$$

So $\frac{1}{8} = \mathbf{\underline{0.125}}$

Exercise 3

Answer **Questions 1-3** without using your calculator.

1   Write $\frac{5}{16}$ as a decimal by finding $5 \div 16$.

2   Write $\frac{3}{8}$ as a decimal by finding $3 \div 8$.

3   Write the following fractions as decimals by dividing the numerator by the denominator.

a) $\frac{1}{4}$ b) $\frac{3}{4}$ c) $\frac{1}{20}$ d) $\frac{1}{40}$

e) $\frac{1}{16}$ f) $\frac{7}{8}$ g) $\frac{7}{40}$ h) $\frac{13}{80}$

Converting Terminating Decimals to Fractions

You can quickly convert a **terminating decimal** to a fraction with a denominator of 10, 100, 1000 or another power of 10.

Example 6

Write the following decimals as fractions.

a) 0.24   The final digit is in the 'hundredths' column — so write as a fraction with denominator 100. Then simplify your answer.

$$0.24 = \frac{24}{100} = \frac{6}{25}$$

b) 0.025   The final digit is in the 'thousandths' column — so write this as a fraction with denominator 1000.

$$0.025 = \frac{25}{1000} = \frac{1}{40}$$

Exercise 4

Convert the decimals in **Questions 1-4** to fractions without using your calculator.
Give your answers in their simplest form.

1   a) 0.7   b) 0.9   c) 0.1   d) 0.4

2   a) 0.93   b) 0.07   c) 0.23   d) 0.47

3 **a)** 0.004 **b)** 0.801 **c)** 0.983 **d)** 0.098

4 **a)** 0.6 **b)** 0.12 **c)** 0.236 **d)** 0.35

  e) 0.05 **f)** 0.084 **g)** 0.24 **h)** 0.175

  i) 0.014 **j)** 0.08 **k)** 0.125 **l)** 0.375

Converting Fractions to Recurring Decimals

Example 7

Write $\frac{3}{11}$ as a decimal without using a calculator.

1. Work out $3 \div 11$ using a written method.

$$\text{①}\quad 11\overline{)3.^30}^{\;\;0.}$$

2. The digits in your answer have started to repeat — first 2, then 7, then 2, then 7, and so on. The remainders are repeating as well — 3, 8, 3, 8.

$$\text{②}\quad 11\overline{)3.^30^80}^{\;\;0.\,2}\qquad\text{③}\quad 11\overline{)3.^30^80^30}^{\;\;0.\,2\,7}$$

3. You've found the repeating pattern of the recurring decimal — so mark the first and last digits of the repeating group.

$$\text{④}\quad 11\overline{)3.^30^80^30^80}^{\;\;0.\,2\,7\,2}\qquad\text{⑤}\quad 11\overline{)3.^30^80^30^80^30}^{\;\;0.\,2\,7\,2\,7}$$

So $\frac{3}{11} = \mathbf{0.\dot{2}\dot{7}}$

Exercise 5

Answer **Questions 1-4** without using your calculator.

1 Write $\frac{6}{11}$ as a recurring decimal by finding $6 \div 11$.

Write the fractions in **Questions 2-3** as recurring decimals.

2 **a)** $\frac{1}{3}$ **b)** $\frac{1}{9}$ **c)** $\frac{1}{12}$ **d)** $\frac{4}{9}$

  e) $\frac{1}{6}$ **f)** $\frac{1}{11}$ **g)** $\frac{2}{3}$ **h)** $\frac{4}{11}$

  i) $\frac{7}{15}$ **j)** $\frac{5}{6}$ **k)** $\frac{4}{15}$ **l)** $\frac{7}{9}$

3 **a)** $\frac{11}{30}$ **b)** $\frac{28}{45}$ **c)** $\frac{47}{90}$ **d)** $\frac{27}{110}$

4 **a)** Write the following fractions as recurring decimals.

  (i) $\frac{1}{7}$ **(ii)** $\frac{2}{7}$ **(iii)** $\frac{3}{7}$ **(iv)** $\frac{4}{7}$ **(v)** $\frac{5}{7}$

  b) What do you notice about the repeating pattern?

  c) Use your answers to parts **a)** and **b)** to write down the decimal which is equivalent to $\frac{6}{7}$.

5.7 Fractions Problems

Exercise 1

Unless told otherwise, answer the questions in this Exercise without using your calculator.

1 Which of the fractions on the right are equivalent to $\frac{2}{3}$?
$\boxed{\dfrac{18}{27} \quad \dfrac{21}{31} \quad \dfrac{40}{60} \quad \dfrac{4}{9} \quad \dfrac{12}{18}}$

2 Which of the fractions on the right are equivalent to $1\frac{1}{4}$?
$\boxed{\dfrac{11}{4} \quad \dfrac{10}{8} \quad \dfrac{18}{16} \quad \dfrac{17}{12} \quad \dfrac{25}{20}}$

3 Use a calculator to write the following fractions as decimals.

  a) $\frac{7}{20}$ **b)** $\frac{21}{250}$ **c)** $\frac{3}{40}$ **d)** $\frac{7}{8}$

4 Use equivalent fractions to write $\frac{3}{4}$, $\frac{2}{3}$, $\frac{5}{6}$ and $\frac{11}{16}$ in order, from smallest to largest.

5 **a)** Convert the fractions $\frac{39}{100}$, $\frac{7}{20}$, $\frac{8}{25}$ and $\frac{3}{10}$ into decimals.

  b) Put the fractions in order, from smallest to largest.

6 Copy the scale on the right, making sure it's divided into 24 parts. Then mark the positions of the following fractions on the scale.

  a) $\frac{1}{3}$ **b)** $\frac{5}{8}$ **c)** $\frac{5}{12}$ **d)** $\frac{5}{6}$

Evaluate the expressions in **Questions 7-10**.

7 **a)** $\frac{5}{7} + \frac{2}{3}$ **b)** $\frac{3}{8} - \frac{2}{9}$ **c)** $\frac{6}{10} + \frac{3}{6}$ **d)** $\frac{2}{5} - \frac{1}{8}$

8 **a)** $\frac{7}{12} \times \frac{6}{11}$ **b)** $\frac{3}{5} \div \frac{7}{15}$ **c)** $\frac{4}{7} \times \frac{6}{8}$ **d)** $\frac{5}{9} \div \frac{15}{24}$

9 **a)** $2\frac{1}{8} + 3\frac{2}{5}$ **b)** $2\frac{3}{10} - 1\frac{7}{8}$ **c)** $3\frac{2}{5} + 4\frac{1}{4}$ **d)** $4\frac{5}{8} - 2\frac{1}{2}$

10 **a)** $1\frac{1}{6} \times 2\frac{1}{3}$ **b)** $3\frac{3}{4} \div 1\frac{1}{2}$ **c)** $3\frac{1}{2} \times 6\frac{7}{8}$ **d)** $5\frac{1}{2} \div 1\frac{1}{4}$

11 A plank of wood is 20 inches long. Three pieces of length $7\frac{3}{4}$ inches, $5\frac{5}{16}$ inches and $2\frac{1}{8}$ inches are cut from the plank. What length of wood is left over?

12 Work out the following (remembering the rules of BODMAS).

  a) $\frac{1}{4} \times \frac{2}{3} + \frac{5}{12}$ **b)** $\frac{7}{30} + \frac{2}{3} \times \frac{4}{5}$ **c)** $\frac{2}{3} \div \frac{5}{6} - \frac{1}{5}$ **d)** $\frac{15}{16} - \frac{3}{8} \div \frac{1}{3}$

  e) $1\frac{1}{2} + \frac{2}{5} \times \frac{3}{4}$ **f)** $1\frac{1}{2} \times \frac{2}{5} + \frac{3}{4}$ **g)** $1\frac{1}{6} - 3\frac{3}{4} \div \frac{3}{8}$ **h)** $3\frac{3}{4} \div 1\frac{1}{6} - \frac{3}{8}$

13 **a)** Find the reciprocal of each of these fractions. Give your answers in their simplest form.

  (i) $\frac{2}{5}$ **(ii)** $\frac{1}{3}$ **(iii)** $\frac{4}{5}$

  b) Multiply each fraction by its reciprocal. What do you notice?

14 This question involves the fractions $\frac{2}{7}$, $\frac{4}{5}$, $\frac{1}{3}$ and $\frac{1}{6}$.

   a) Put these fractions in order, starting with the smallest.

   b) Find the reciprocal of each of the fractions.

   c) Put the reciprocals in order, starting with the largest. What do you notice?

15 Using a calculator, find which of these fractions are equivalent to recurring decimals, and which are equivalent to terminating decimals.

   a) $\frac{7}{8}$ **b)** $\frac{1}{3}$ **c)** $\frac{3}{11}$ **d)** $\frac{4}{21}$ **e)** $\frac{7}{32}$

16 Which of the fractions $\frac{4}{5}$, $\frac{5}{6}$, $\frac{9}{16}$, $\frac{17}{40}$ and $\frac{2}{9}$ are equivalent to recurring decimals?

17 The length of a rectangle is $3\frac{3}{5}$ cm and the width is $1\frac{5}{8}$ cm.

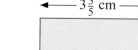

   a) Find the rectangle's perimeter.

   b) Find the rectangle's area.

18 Amy, Ben and Carl are sharing a bar of chocolate. They each eat $\frac{1}{5}$ of the bar.

   a) What fraction of the bar of chocolate is left?

   Dave joins the group and the four of them share the rest of the bar equally.

   b) What fraction of the whole bar does Dave eat?

19 Pat's cat eats $\frac{2}{3}$ of a tin of cat food every morning and every evening.

   How many tins of cat food will Pat need to buy to feed the cat for a week?

20 It takes Ella $1\frac{1}{4}$ minutes to answer each question on her maths homework.

   How many questions can she answer in 20 minutes?

21 A bag contains a mixture of different coloured counters. $\frac{1}{3}$ of the counters are red, $\frac{2}{5}$ are blue, and the rest are yellow.

   a) What fraction of the counters are yellow?

   b) If there are 60 counters altogether, work out how many of each colour are in the bag.

22 Which of the fractions on the right is closest to $\frac{3}{4}$? $\boxed{\dfrac{11}{15} \quad \dfrac{7}{10} \quad \dfrac{4}{5} \quad \dfrac{5}{6}}$

23 What numbers need to go in the boxes to make the following true?

   a) $\frac{1}{3}$ of $60 = \frac{1}{2}$ of $\Box$ **b)** $\frac{2}{5}$ of $100 = \Box$ of 50 **c)** $\frac{3}{4}$ of $\Box = \frac{2}{3}$ of 90

24 In ancient Egypt, fractions were written using sums of unit fractions.

   For example, instead of writing $\frac{3}{5}$, ancient Egyptians would write $\frac{1}{2} + \frac{1}{10}$.

   Find the fractions that ancient Egyptians would have written in the following ways:

   a) $\frac{1}{2} + \frac{1}{5}$ **b)** $\frac{1}{3} + \frac{1}{12}$ **c)** $\frac{1}{2} + \frac{1}{3} + \frac{1}{7}$

Section 6 — Ratio and Proportion

6.1 Ratios and Simplifying

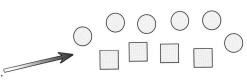

Ratios are used to compare quantities.
For example, here the ratio of circles to squares is 6:4.

You can simplify ratios by dividing the numbers by common factors, just like you do with fractions.

Example 1

There are 15 fiction books and 10 non-fiction books on a shelf.

a) Write down the ratio of fiction books to non-fiction books.
It's fiction to non-fiction, so the '15' comes first. ⟹ The ratio is **15:10**

b) Write this ratio in its simplest form.
1. Look for a number that divides into both 15 and 10.   5 divides into both 15 and 10.
2. Divide both sides of the ratio by this number, and rewrite the ratio. $15 \div 5 = 3$ and $10 \div 5 = 2$
3. When no other numbers divide into both sides of the ratio, the ratio is in its simplest form.   So the ratio can be written **3:2**, and this is the ratio's simplest form.

Exercise 1

1 Write down the ratio of stars to triangles.

2 Write down the ratio of triangles to stars.

3 Write down the ratio of people to pigeons.

4 There are 17 boys and 14 girls in a class. Write down the ratio of boys to girls.

5 On a farm there are 15 pigs and 23 cows. Write down the ratio of cows to pigs.

For questions **6** and **7**, write down the given ratio. Then simplify your answer.

6 Shaded squares to white squares.

7 Shaded circles to white circles.

8 Write down each of the following ratios in its simplest form.
  a) 2:8 **b)** 5:15 **c)** 40:10 **d)** 4:6 **e)** 24:6
  f) 20:8 **g)** 7:28 **h)** 15:9 **i)** 16:12 **j)** 25:3
  k) 40:60 **l)** 21:35 **m)** 55:5 **n)** 16:40 **o)** 18:27
  p) 48:36 **q)** 18:72 **r)** 80:32 **s)** 150:350 **t)** 121:33

9 Write down each of the following ratios in its simplest form.
  a) 6:2:4 **b)** 15:12:3 **c)** 14:10:2 **d)** 24:12:20 **e)** 6:3:15
  f) 30:10:25 **g)** 16:24:80 **h)** 21:49:42 **i)** 12:32:16 **j)** 27:30:54

10 A floor is made up of 24 black tiles and 8 white tiles. Find the ratio of black tiles to white tiles in its simplest form.

11 At a party there are 36 girls and 27 boys. What is the ratio of girls to boys? Give your answer in its simplest form.

12 A school has 595 pupils and 170 computers. Write down the ratio of computers to pupils in its simplest form.

13 There are 18 boys in a class of 33 pupils. Find the ratio of boys to girls, giving your answer in its simplest form.

14 Isabel and Sophia share a bag of 42 sweets. Isabel has 16 sweets and Sophia has the rest. Find the ratio of Sophia's sweets to Isabel's sweets, giving your answer in its simplest form.

Example 2

Write the ratio 1 m : 40 cm in its simplest form.

1. Rewrite the ratio so that the units are the same on both sides. Then remove the units altogether.

2. Simplify as normal.

1 m : 40 cm is the same as 100 cm : 40 cm. This is the same as 100 : 40.

$$\div 20 \begin{array}{c} 100 : 40 \\ 5 : 2 \end{array} \div 20$$

So the simplest form is **5 : 2**

Exercise 2

1 Write these ratios in their simplest form.
 a) 10p : £1
 b) 20 mm : 4 cm
 c) 10 g : 1 kg
 d) 2 weeks : 7 days
 e) 40p : £1
 f) 30 cm : 2 m
 g) 18 mins : 1 hour
 h) 6 days : 3 weeks

2 Give the following ratios in their simplest form.
 a) 1 m : 150 mm
 b) 12 weeks : 1 year
 c) 8 cm : 1.1 m
 d) 9 g : 0.3 kg
 e) 2.5 hours : 20 mins
 f) £1.25 : 75p
 g) 65 m : 1.3 km
 h) 1.2 kg : 480 g

3 A jug of orange squash is made using 50 ml of orange concentrate and 1 litre of water. Find the ratio of concentrate to water in its simplest form.

4 A model of a house has a height of 15 cm. The actual house is 6 m tall. Write the ratio of the model's height to the actual height in its simplest form.

5 Emma's mass is 54 kg. Her award-winning pumpkin has a mass of 6000 g. Find the ratio of the pumpkin's mass to Emma's mass. Give your answer in its simplest form.

6 Alexsy runs in two cross-country races. He runs the first in 45 minutes and the second in 3½ hours. Find the ratio of his first race time to his second race time in its simplest form.

7 A small bag of crisps costs 44p and a king-size bag costs £1.21. Find the ratio of the cost of the small bag to the cost of the king-size bag in its simplest form.

8 The icing for some cupcakes is made by mixing 1.6 kg of icing sugar with 640 g of butter. Find the ratio of butter to icing sugar. Give your answer in its simplest form.

Writing Ratios in the Form 1 : n

Another way to simplify ratios is to write them in the form 1 : n, where n is a number.
In making the left-hand side equal to 1, you might end up with a fraction or a decimal on the right.

Example 3

Write the ratio 16 : 24 in the form 1 : n.

1. To get '1' on the left-hand side, divide both sides by 16.

2. Now the ratio is in the form 1 : n, where n = 1.5.

$$\div 16 \underset{\mathbf{1 : 1.5}}{\overparen{16 : 24}} \div 16$$

Example 4

Nigel makes his favourite smoothie by mixing half a litre of blueberry juice with 100 millilitres of plain yoghurt. How much yoghurt does he use for every millilitre of juice?

1. Write down the ratio of juice to yoghurt.   0.5 l : 100 ml

2. Rewrite the ratio so that it's all in millilitres.   0.5 l : 100 ml is the same
   Then get rid of the units altogether.   as 500 ml : 100 ml, or just 500 : 100

3. Simplify the ratio.
   And remember to give the units in your answer.

$$\div 500 \underset{\mathbf{1 : 0.2}}{\overparen{500 : 100}} \div 500$$

So he uses 0.2 ml for every 1 ml of juice.

Exercise 3

1 Write down the following ratios in the form 1 : n.

   a) 2 : 6   **b)** 7 : 35   **c)** 6 : 24   **d)** 30 : 120

   e) 2 : 7   **f)** 4 : 26   **g)** 8 : 26   **h)** 2 : 1

   i) 10 : 3   **j)** 6 : 21   **k)** 8 : 5   **l)** 5 : 9

2 Write down each of these ratios in the form 1 : n.

   a) 10 mm : 5 cm   **b)** 12p : £6   **c)** 30 mins : 2 hours   **d)** 500 g : 20 kg

   e) 90 m : 7.2 km   **f)** 14 cm : 5.6 m   **g)** 50p : £6.25   **h)** 4.5 m : 900 mm

3 In a pond there are 7 frogs and 56 fish. Find the ratio of frogs to fish in the form 1 : n.

4 On a garage forecourt there are 15 red cars and 45 silver cars. Find the ratio of red cars to silver cars in the form 1 : n.

5 A recipe uses 125 ml of chocolate syrup and 2½ litres of milk. Write the ratio of chocolate syrup to milk in the form 1 : n.

6 Two towns 4.8 km apart are shown on a map 12 cm apart. Find the ratio of the map distance to the true distance in the form 1 : n.

7 A shade of purple paint is made using 4 parts of red paint to 5 parts of blue paint. How much blue paint is needed for every 1 part of red paint?

8 When Ellie went on holiday to Denmark she changed £50 into 425 Danish krone. Write down a ratio showing the exchange rate in the form £1 : n krone.

9 An animal sanctuary has 120 animals, 40 of which are donkeys. Write the ratio of donkeys to other animals in the form 1 : n.

6.2 Using Ratios

If you know the **ratio** of one quantity to another and you know **how big** one of them is, you can use the ratio to find the size of the other.

Example 1

The ratio of men to women in an office is $3:4$.
If there are 9 men in the office, how many women are there?

1. Write down what you know and what you need to find out.

2. Work out what you have to multiply the left-hand side by to get from 3 to 9.

3. Multiply the right-hand side by the same number.

$$3:4$$
$$= 9:?$$

$$\times 3 \binom{3:4}{9:12} \times 3$$

So there are **12 women**.

Example 2

A cereal contains raisins, nuts and oats in the ratio $2:3:5$. If a box of the cereal contains 200 g of raisins and 300 g of nuts, find how many grams of oats it contains.

1. Write the ratio of one of the quantities you know to the one you want to find. $\Longrightarrow$ The ratio of nuts to oats is $3:5$

2. Find the number both sides of the ratio have to be multiplied by.
And remember to give the mass in grams.

$$3:5$$
$$= 300:? \Longrightarrow \times 100 \binom{3:5}{300:500} \times 100$$

So it contains **500 g oats**

Exercise 1

1 For a class of pupils, the ratio of blue eyes to brown eyes is $2:3$. If 8 pupils have blue eyes, how many pupils have brown eyes?

2 Ben feeds his horses carrots. For every 12 carrots they eat, Ben eats 1. If the horses eat 24 carrots, how many does Ben eat?

3 The ages of a father and son are in the ratio $8:3$. If the father is 48, how old is the son?

4 The ratio of red to yellow sweets in a bag is $3:4$. If the bag contains 12 yellow sweets, how many red sweets are there?

5 In a wood there are oak trees and beech trees in the ratio $2:9$. If there are 42 oak trees, how many beech trees are there?

6 In a supermarket the ratio of apples to bananas is $5:3$. If there are 450 bananas, how many apples are there?

For questions **7–18**, remember to give the correct units in your answer.

7 A recipe uses sugar and butter in the ratio $2:1$. How much butter would be needed with 100 g of sugar?

8 A photo of width 10 cm is enlarged so that the ratio of the two pictures' widths is $2:7$.

How wide is the enlarged picture?

9 Meera and Sabrina share a holiday job. They split the money they make in the ratio $7:6$. If Sabrina gets £48, how much does Meera get?

10 Tim has a cardboard cut-out of his favourite footballer. The height of the cut-out and the footballer's actual height are in the ratio $5:6$. If the cut-out is 165 cm high, find the footballer's actual height in metres.

Section 6 — Ratio and Proportion

11 A fruit punch is made by mixing pineapple juice, orange juice, and lemonade in the ratio $1:3:6$. If 500 ml of pineapple juice is used, how much orange juice is needed?

12 Jem is unusually fussy about pizza toppings. She always orders olives, slices of courgette and slices of goat's cheese in the ratio $8:3:4$. How many slices of courgette and goat's cheese would she order with 24 olives?

13 Mai, Lizzy and Dave have heights in the ratio $31:33:37$. Mai is 155 cm tall. How tall are Lizzy and Dave?

14 Max, Molly and Maisie are at a bus stop. The number of minutes they have waited can be represented by the ratio $3:7:2$. Molly has been waiting for 1 hour and 10 minutes. Calculate how long Max and Maisie have been waiting for.

15 The ratio of children to adults in a swimming pool must be $5:1$ or less. If there are 32 children, how many adults must there be?

16 A TV-show producer is selecting a studio audience. He wants the ratio of under 30s to those aged 30 or over to be at least $8:1$. If 100 under 30s are selected, find the maximum number of people aged 30 or over.

17 Harry is cooking for friends. His recipe says to use 1 aubergine for every 3 people. How many aubergines should he buy if there are 10 people eating?

18 Olga allows herself no more than 5 minutes of reality TV for every minute of news programmes she watches. If she watches 45 minutes of reality TV, what's the least amount of news she should watch?

Using Ratios to Find Fractions

You can use a ratio to express a quantity as a fraction of a total amount.
Or you can start with a fraction and use it to write a ratio between two quantities.

Example 3

A box of doughnuts contains jam doughnuts and chocolate doughnuts in the ratio $3:5$.
What fraction of the doughnuts are chocolate flavoured?

1. Add the numbers to find the total number of parts. $3 + 5 = 8$ parts altogether.

2. Divide the number of parts that are chocolate by the total number of parts. 5 of the parts are chocolate. Fraction that are chocolate is $\frac{5}{8}$.

Exercise 2

1 A tiled floor has blue and white tiles in the ratio $1:3$. What fraction of the tiles are blue?

2 A necklace has yellow beads and red beads in the ratio $3:2$. What fraction of the beads are yellow?

3 The ratio of girls to boys in a class is $4:3$. What fraction of the class are girls?

4 A recipe uses white flour and brown flour in the ratio $2:1$. What fraction of the flour is brown?

5 A zoo has Gentoo penguins and King penguins in the ratio $9:4$. What fraction of the penguins are King penguins?

6 The ratio of women to men in a tennis club is $13:7$. What fraction of the players are men?

7 In a football tournament the numbers of home wins, away wins and draws were in the ratio $7:2:5$. What fraction of the games were home wins?

8 In Amy's sock drawer there are spotty, stripy and plain socks in the ratio $5:1:4$. What fraction of Amy's socks are stripy?

9 At a music festival there are men, women and children in the ratio $13:17:5$. What fraction of the people are children?

10 James has peaches, pears and pomegranates in the ratio of $5:3:2$.
  a) What fraction of the fruit are peaches?
  b) What fraction of the fruit are pears?

11 At a birthday party there are purple, red and blue balloons in the ratio $3:8:11$.
  a) What fraction of the balloons are blue?
  b) What fraction of the balloons are purple?
  c) What fraction of the balloons aren't red?

Example 4

All of Hannah's DVDs are either horror films or comedies.
If $\frac{2}{7}$ of her DVDs are horror films, find the ratio of comedies to horror films.

1. Use the fraction to find the number of parts corresponding to each type of film.

$\frac{2}{7}$ = 2 parts out of 7 are horror

So $7 - 2 = 5$ parts are comedies

2. Write this in ratio form, making sure you put the numbers the right way round.

Ratio of comedies to horror is **5:2**

Exercise 3

1 Aiden has a bag of red and green jelly babies. $\frac{1}{3}$ of the jelly babies are red. Write down the ratio of red to green jelly babies.

2 $\frac{1}{8}$ of the items made in a factory have defects. What is the ratio of items with defects to items without defects?

3 Jack has watched $\frac{3}{10}$ of the episodes in a DVD box set. Write down the ratio of episodes he's watched to episodes he hasn't watched.

4 $\frac{5}{12}$ of the children at a school eat school dinners and the rest bring a packed lunch. What is the ratio of children who bring a packed lunch to those who eat school dinners?

5 $\frac{3}{19}$ of the members of a chess club are left handed. Write down the ratio of right-handed club members to left-handed club members.

6 $\frac{1}{8}$ of the balls in a bag are red, $\frac{5}{8}$ are blue and the rest are green. What is the ratio of red to blue to green balls in the bag?

7 A cycling challenge has three routes — A, B and C. $\frac{3}{5}$ of the competitors choose route A, $\frac{1}{5}$ choose route B and the rest choose route C. What is the ratio of competitors choosing route A to those choosing route C?

8 A rugby team won half of their matches by more than 10 points, won a quarter of their matches by less than 10 points, and lost the rest. Write the ratio of games they won to games they lost.

9 During one day at a pizza restaurant, $\frac{3}{8}$ of the pizzas ordered were pepperoni, $\frac{1}{2}$ were cheese and tomato and the rest were spicy chicken. Write down the ratio of pepperoni to cheese and tomato to spicy chicken.

6.3 Dividing in a Given Ratio

Ratios can be used to divide an amount into two or more shares.
The numbers in the ratio show how many parts of the whole each share gets.

Example 1

Divide £54 in the ratio $4:5$.

1. Add the numbers to find the total number of parts.

   $4 + 5 = 9$ parts altogether

2. Work out the amount for one part.

   9 parts = £54
   So 1 part = £54 ÷ 9 = £6

3. Then multiply the amount for one part by the number of parts for each share.
   (Check the shares add up to the original amount: £20 + £34 = £54)

   £6 × 4 = £24
   £6 × 5 = £30
   So the shares are **£24** and **£30**.

Example 2

A drink is made using apple juice, blackcurrant juice and lemonade in the ratio $3:2:5$.
How much lemonade is needed to make 5 litres of the drink?

1. Add the numbers to find the total number of parts.

   $3 + 2 + 5 = 10$ parts altogether

2. Work out the amount for one part.

   10 parts = 5 litres
   So 1 part = 0.5 litres

3. Then multiply the amount for one part by the 'lemonade number' in the ratio.

   0.5 litres × 5
   = **2.5 litres of lemonade**

Exercise 1

1 Divide £48 in the following ratios.

   a) $2:1$ **b)** $1:3$ **c)** $5:1$ **d)** $7:5$

2 Share 90 kg in these ratios.

   a) $4:1$ **b)** $7:2$ **c)** $8:7$ **d)** $12:18$

3 Share 56 m in these ratios.

   a) $1:7$ **b)** $4:4$ **c)** $10:4$ **d)** $22:6$

4 Divide 1000 ml in these ratios.

   a) $1:9$ **b)** $25:25$ **c)** $3:17$ **d)** $57:43$

5 Divide 72 cm in the following ratios.

   a) $2:3:1$ **b)** $2:2:5$ **c)** $5:3:4$ **d)** $7:6:5$

6 Share £150 in these ratios.

   a) $1:4:5$ **b)** $15:5:30$ **c)** $6:7:2$ **d)** $13:11:6$

7 Find the smallest share when each amount below is divided in the given ratio.

a) £22 in the ratio $5:6$

b) 450 g in the ratio $22:28$

c) 45 kg in the ratio $2:3:4$

d) 1800 ml in the ratio $5:6:7$

8 Find the largest share when each amount below is divided in the given ratio.

a) £30 in the ratio $1:3$

b) 36 g in the ratio $3:2$

c) 150 kg in the ratio $10:7:3$

d) 24 000 ml in the ratio $5:7:20$

Exercise 2

1 Kat and Lindsay share 30 cupcakes in the ratio $3:2$. How many do they each get?

2 Share 32 sandwiches in the ratio $3:5$.

3 There are 112 people in an office. The ratio of men to women is $9:5$. How many men and how many women are there?

4 Lauren is 16 and Cara is 14. Their grandad gives them £1200 to share in the ratio of their ages. How much money do they each get?

5 Orange paint is made by mixing yellow and red paint in the ratio $4:3$. How much of each colour is needed to make 42 litres of orange paint?

6 There are 28 passengers on a bus. The ratio of passengers talking on their phones to those not talking on their phones is $5:2$. How many passengers are on their phones?

7 In a school of 600 pupils, the ratio of right-handed pupils to left-handed pupils is $7:1$. How many right-handed pupils are there?

8 Elsa and Daniel put money into their business in the ratio $2:3$. If they share the profits in the same ratio, how much of a £5700 profit would Daniel get?

Exercise 3

1 Nicky, Jacinta and Charlie share a bag of 36 sweets in the ratio $2:4:3$. How many sweets does each of them get?

2 Three friends win £6000 between them. They decide to share the money in the ratio $3:5:4$. Calculate the amounts they receive.

3 Gemma, Alisha and Omar have a combined height of 490 cm. If their heights are in the ratio $31:32:35$, how tall are they?

4 A fruit salad is made from raspberries, strawberries and redcurrants in the ratio $2:3:1$. How much of each fruit is needed to make 450 g of fruit salad?

5 A quiz team share their prize money in the ratio $2:4:6$. What is the least amount any team member wins if the prize is £150?

6 A box of 48 chocolates contains dark, milk and white chocolates in the ratio $2:7:3$. Jeff doesn't like dark chocolates. How many of the chocolates can he happily eat?

7 Claire owns 20 handbags, which are black brown and purple in the ratio $5:3:2$. She is choosing a bag and doesn't want it to be brown. How many bags does she have to choose from?

8 The four angles in a quadrilateral are in the ratio $2:4:1:3$. Calculate the sizes of all four angles.

9 The length and width of a rectangle are in the ratio $5:1$. If the perimeter of the rectangle is 72 cm, calculate the length and the width of the rectangle.

6.4 Proportion

If the **ratio** between two things is always the same, then they're in **direct proportion**.
For example, if 1 item costs £2, then 2 items will cost £4, 3 items will cost £6, etc. The ratio is
always 1 item : £2. You can use this relationship between quantities to convert from one to another.

Example 1

If 8 chocolate bars cost £6, calculate the cost of 10 chocolate bars.

1. Calculate the cost of one bar by dividing the total cost by the number of bars.

    8 bars cost £6
    so 1 bar costs £6 ÷ 8 = £0.75

2. Then multiply this by the new number of bars.

    10 bars cost £0.75 × 10 = **£7.50**

Example 2

If £100 is worth $160, convert £40 into dollars ($).

1. Calculate how much £1 is worth.

    £100 is worth $160
    so £1 is worth $160 ÷ 100 = $1.60

2. Then multiply this by the new amount.

    £40 is worth 40 × $1.60 = **$64**

Exercise 1

1   If 1 pair of jeans costs £35, find the cost of the following:

   a) 2 pairs of jeans   **b)** 5 pairs of jeans   **c)** 20 pairs of jeans

2   If £1 is worth €1.14, convert the following amounts into euros (€).

   a) £10   **b)** £20   **c)** £100   **d)** £850

3   The cost of 8 identical books is £36. What is the cost of 12 of these books?

4   The cost of 5 concert tickets is £210. How much would 9 of these tickets cost?

5   6 jackets cost £480. Find the cost of 11 of these jackets.

6   If it takes 1.8 kg of flour to make 3 loaves of bread, how much flour is needed to make 5 loaves?

7   To make 4 jugs of squash you need 5 litres of water. How much water is needed to make 3 jugs of squash?

8   30 m of material costs £21.60. How much would 18 m of this material cost?

9   Convert £7 into Japanese yen given that £20 is worth 2620 Japanese yen.

10   If 10 litres of paint costs £45, find the cost of:
   a) 3 litres,   **b)** 14 litres,   **c)** 60 litres.

11   Ryan earns £192 for cleaning 12 cars. How much more will he earn if he cleans another 5 cars?

12   Grace buys 11 pens for £12.32 and 6 note pads for £5.88. How much would she pay altogether for 8 pens and 5 note pads?

Example 3

Oliver has 30 euros (€) left over from a holiday in France. Assuming the exchange rate is £1 = €1.14, how many pounds can he exchange his euros for?

1. Work out how many pounds €1 is worth by dividing both sides of the equation "£1 = €1.14" by 1.14.

   €1.14 = £1
   so €1 = £1 ÷ 1.14 = £0.877...

2. Then multiply this by the number of euros Oliver has. €30 = 30 × £0.877 = **£26.32**

   (to the nearest penny)

Exercise 2

1   If 1 book costs £7.50, work out how many books you can buy for:
    a) £22.50   **b)** £60   **c)** £187.50

2   If £1 is worth €1.14, convert the following amounts in euros (€) into pounds.
    a) €10   **b)** €100   **c)** €250

3   1 kg is equal to 2.2 pounds (lbs). Calculate the weight of 8.25 lbs of sugar in kg?

4   At the end of her holiday Poppy had 45 euros left. She changed the money back into pounds using the exchange rate £1 = €1.14. How many pounds did she get back?

5   If 7 of the same DVDs cost £84, how many DVDs can be bought for £48?

6   If 24 houses can be built by 6 builders, how many builders would it take to build 52 houses in the same amount of time?

7   A recipe for four people uses 75 g of cheese. Helen has 375 g of cheese. How many people does she have enough cheese to make the recipe for?

8   Using an exchange rate of £100 = 1055 Chinese yuan, convert 65 Chinese yuan into pounds.

9   Two-and-a-half kilos of apples cost £6.85. Leroy bought some of these apples and paid a total of £13.70. How many kilos of apples did he buy?

Exercise 3

1   A bus travels 50 km in 40 minutes. Assuming the bus continues to travel at the same average speed, calculate the following:
    a) the time it would take to travel 65 km
    b) the distance the bus would travel in 16 minutes

2   A car uses 35 litres of petrol to travel 250 km.
    a) How far, to the nearest km, can the car travel on 50 litres of petrol?
    b) How many litres of petrol would the car use to travel 400 km?

3   Philip changed £50 into Swiss francs before going on holiday to Switzerland. The exchange rate was £1 = 1.47 Swiss francs.

    a) How many Swiss francs did he get?

    At the end of his holiday, Philip changed his remaining 30 Swiss francs back into pounds.
    b) Given that the exchange rate was now £1 = 1.50 Swiss francs, how much money did he get back in pounds?

6.5 Ratio and Proportion Problems

Exercise 1

1 A builder mixes 10 bags of cement with 25 bags of sand. Write down the ratio of cement to sand:

  a) in its simplest form

  b) in the form $1:n$

  c) in the form $n:1$

2 During one day, a shop has 63 customers. 18 of them are men.

  a) Write down the ratio of male to female customers. Give your answer in its simplest form.

  b) What fraction of the customers are men?

3 A field of sheep contains white sheep and black sheep in the ratio $8:1$.

  a) What fraction of the sheep are white?

  b) If there are 7 black sheep in the field, how many white sheep are there?

4 Evie is making wedding invitation cards in three different colours — blue, green and purple. She uses the different colours in the ratio $2:7:3$. Evie has made 12 green cards so far and has 72 more green cards to make. Work out how many purple cards she will need to make.

5 Here is a recipe for cupcakes:

> **Cupcakes** (makes 25)
> Butter, 200 g
> Caster sugar, 250 g
> Plain flour, 280 g
> Eggs, 4

  a) How much butter would you need to make 10 cupcakes?

  b) How much flour would you need to make 35 cupcakes?

  c) If you only had 1 egg, how many cupcakes could you make?

6 It costs me £20 to put 12.5 litres of petrol in my car. How much will it cost me for a full tank of petrol if the tank holds 60 litres?

7 Natasha and Arun share a holiday job. They share the hours in the ratio $4:5$. If Natasha works for 12 hours, and they're each paid £6 an hour, how much does Arun earn?

8 Emma changed £500 into rand before going on holiday to South Africa. The rate of exchange at the time was £1 = 10.4 rand.

  a) How many rand did she get for her £500?

On holiday Emma spent 4000 rand. When she got home, she changed the rand she had left (from her original amount) back into pounds. The exchange rate had changed to £1 = 9.8 rand.

  b) How much money did she get back in pounds?

9 A map has a scale of $1:200\,000$. The real distance between two towns is 60 km. How many centimetres apart are the towns on the map?

10 Jordan has 30 books. 18 of them are fiction books and 12 of them are non-fiction books. Jade's collection of non-fiction books is shown below.

If Jade has the same ratio of fiction to non-fiction books as Jordan, how many books does she have altogether?

11 Jonathan makes orange squash by mixing orange concentrate and water in the ratio $1:10$. Caroline mixes the concentrate and water in the ratio $2:15$. Whose squash is stronger?

Section 7 — Percentages

7.1 Percentages

Writing One Number as a Percentage of Another

'Per cent' means 'out of 100'. Writing an amount as a **percentage** means writing it as a number out of 100.

Example 1

Out of 100 cars in a car park, 38 are red. What percentage of the cars are red?

1. Write the amount as a fraction. ⟶ $\frac{38}{100}$
2. The amount is already written 'out of 100'.
3. Write the amount as a percentage. So **38%** of the cars are red.

Example 2

Express 15 as a percentage of 50.

1. Write the amount as a fraction.
2. Write an equivalent fraction which is 'out of 100' by multiplying the top and bottom by the same number.
3. Write the amount as a percentage.

$$\frac{15}{50} = \frac{30}{100}$$
$\times 2$

So 15 is **30%** of 50.

Exercise 1

Answer **Questions 1-11** without using your calculator.

1 Each grid below is made up of 100 small squares.
Find the percentage of each grid that is shaded.

a) 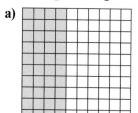 b) 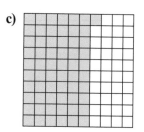 c) 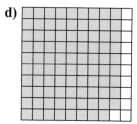 d)

2 Write each of the following amounts as a percentage.

a) 13 out of 100 b) 27 out of 100 c) 76 out of 100 d) 99 out of 100

3 A football team scored 100 goals in one season. 13 of these goals were penalties.
What percentage of the goals scored were penalties?

4 a) Find the fraction equivalent to $\frac{23}{50}$ which has 100 as the denominator.
  b) Use your answer to express '23 out of 50' as a percentage.

5 A chess club has 25 members. 12 of these members are female.

   a) Write the number of female members as a fraction of the total number of members.

   b) Find the fraction equivalent to your answer to part **a)** which has 100 as the denominator.

   c) Hence express the number of female members of the club as a percentage.

6 There are 300 coloured counters in a bag. 45 of these counters are green.

   a) Write the number of green counters as a fraction of the total number of counters.

   b) Find the fraction equivalent to your answer to part **a)** which has 100 as the denominator.

   c) Hence express the amount of green counters as a percentage.

7 Write each of the following amounts as a percentage.

   a) 11 out of 25   **b)** 33 out of 50   **c)** 3 out of 20   **d)** 8 out of 10

   e) 12 out of 200   **f)** 99 out of 300   **g)** 100 out of 400   **h)** 890 out of 1000

Example 3

Express 45 as a percentage of 180.

1. Write the amount as a fraction.
2. It may take more than one step to write the fraction out of 100.
3. Write the amount as a percentage.

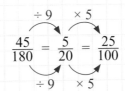

So 45 is **25%** of 180.

8 Write each of the following amounts as a percentage.

   a) 8 out of 32   **b)** 36 out of 60   **c)** 24 out of 40   **d)** 30 out of 150

   e) 27 out of 45   **f)** 56 out of 80   **g)** 63 out of 75   **h)** 120 out of 160

   i) 48 out of 120   **j)** 34 out of 170   **k)** 14 out of 35   **l)** 54 out of 180

9 Out of 24 pupils in a class, 18 walk to school.

   a) What percentage of the class walk to school?

   b) What percentage of the class do not walk to school?

10 There are 55 chocolates in a tin. 33 of the chocolates are milk chocolate.
   The rest are dark chocolate. What percentage are dark chocolate?

11 39 out of 65 people in a book club have blonde hair. What percentage do not have blonde hair?

Example 4

Express 333 as a percentage of 360.

1. Write the amount as a fraction.
2. It's not easy to rewrite this as a fraction out of 100. So instead, divide the top number by the bottom number, using a calculator if necessary.
3. Multiply by 100% to write as a percentage.

$\frac{333}{360}$

$333 \div 360 = 0.925$

$0.925 \times 100\% = 92.5$

So 333 is **92.5%** of 360.

Exercise 2

You may use a calculator to answer these questions.

1   Write each of the following amounts as a percentage.

   a) 15 out of 24   **b)** 221 out of 260   **c)** 61 out of 500   **d)** 328 out of 800

   e) 258 out of 375   **f)** 77 out of 275   **g)** 323 out of 850   **h)** 101 out of 250

2   A school has 875 pupils. 525 are boys. What is this as a percentage?

3   Express £252 as a percentage of £560.

4   171 out of 180 raffle tickets were sold for a summer fete.
   What percentage of the tickets were sold?

5   Write each of the following amounts as a percentage.

   a) 116.6 out of 212   **b)** 41.6 out of 128   **c)** 53.5 out of 428   **d)** 16.8 out of 210

   e) 47.25 out of 126   **f)** 315.15 out of 382   **g)** 85.86 out of 265   **h)** 17.92 out of 512

6   **a)** Express 31.36 as a percentage of 32.

   b) Express £117.30 as a percentage of £782.

7   The jackpot for a lottery was £10 250. John won £1896.25.
   What percentage of the total jackpot did he win?

8   Curtis receives £5.60 pocket money per week from his parents, and £2.40 pocket money per week from his grandparents. What percentage of his total pocket money comes from his grandparents?

Finding a Percentage without a Calculator

You can find some percentages without a calculator using the following rules.

- **50%** = $\frac{1}{2}$, so find 50% of something by **dividing by 2** (which is the same as multiplying by $\frac{1}{2}$).
- **25%** = $\frac{1}{4}$, so find 25% of something by **dividing by 4** (which is the same as multiplying by $\frac{1}{4}$).
- **10%** = $\frac{1}{10}$, so find 10% of something by **dividing by 10** (which is the same as multiplying by $\frac{1}{10}$).

Example 5

Find 75% of 44.

1. First find 25% by dividing by 4.   25% of 44 = 44 ÷ 4 = 11
2. 75% = 3 × 25%, so multiply by 3.   So 75% of 44 = 3 × 11 = **33**

Example 6

Find 35% of 70.

1. First find 10% of 70 by dividing by 10.   10% of 70 = 70 ÷ 10 = 7
2. 30% = 3 × 10%, so multiply 7 by 3 to find 30%.   30% of 70 = 3 × 7 = 21
3. 5% = 10% ÷ 2, so divide 7 by 2 to find 5%.   5% of 70 = 7 ÷ 2 = 3.5
4. 35% = 30% + 5%, so add the two amounts to find 35%.   So 35% of 70 = 21 + 3.5 = **24.5**

Exercise 3

Answer **Questions 1-7** without using your calculator.

1 Find each of the following.
   a) 50% of 24
   b) 50% of 82
   c) 50% of 15
   d) 25% of 36
   e) 25% of 80
   f) 25% of 120
   g) 10% of 90
   h) 10% of 270

2 a) Find 25% of 48.
   b) Use your answer to find 75% of 48.

3 a) Find 10% of 120.
   b) Use your answer to find the following.
      (i) 5% of 120
      (ii) 20% of 120
      (iii) 25% of 120
      (iv) 40% of 120

4 Find each of the following.
   a) 75% of 12
   b) 75% of 20
   c) 5% of 140
   d) 5% of 260
   e) 30% of 90
   f) 40% of 150
   g) 70% of 110
   h) 80% of 70
   i) 15% of 220
   j) 35% of 340
   k) 45% of 500
   l) 65% of 120

5 What is 85% of £70?

6 A wooden plank is 9 m long. 55% of the plank is cut off.
   What length of wood has been cut off?

7 Shima has £1400 in her savings account. She gives 95% of her savings to charity.
   How much does she give to charity?

Finding a Percentage with a Calculator

To find a percentage of an amount, **divide** the amount by 100 to find 1%,
then **multiply** by the percentage you need to find.

Example 7

Find 67% of 138.

Divide by 100, then multiply by 67. $138 \div 100 \times 67 = \underline{\textbf{92.46}}$

Exercise 4

You may use a calculator to answer these questions.

1 Find each of the following.
   a) 17% of 200
   b) 9% of 11
   c) 3% of 210
   d) 41% of 180
   e) 68% of 320
   f) 21% of 370
   g) 79% of 615
   h) 73% of 801
   i) 59% of 713
   j) 82% of 823
   k) 91% of 769
   l) 96% of 911

2 What is 12% of 68 kg?

3 Jeff is on a journey of 385 km. So far, he has completed 31% of his journey.
   How far has he travelled?

4   125 people work in an office. 12% of the office workers are men. How many workers is this?

5   The cost of an adult's ticket for a theme park is £42. A child's ticket is 68% of the price of an adult's ticket. How much does a child's ticket cost?

6   Which is larger, 22% of £57 or 46% of £28? By how much?

7   A jug can hold 2.4 litres of water. It is 34% full. How much more water will fit in the jug?

7.2   Percentage Increase and Decrease

To **increase** an amount by a percentage — (i) **calculate** the percentage,
(ii) **add** it to the original amount.
To **decrease** an amount by a percentage, **subtract** the percentage from the original amount.

Example 1

Increase 450 by 15% without using your calculator.

1.   Find 10% and 5% of 450.   10% of 450 = 450 ÷ 10 = 45
                                  5% of 450 = 45 ÷ 2 = 22.5

2.   Add these to find 15% of 450.   So 15% of 450 = 45 + 22.5 = 67.5
3.   Add this to the original amount.   450 + 67.5 = **517.5**

Exercise 1

Answer **Questions 1-6** without using your calculator.

1   **a)** Find 50% of 360.   **3**   **a)** Find 10% of 160.
       b) Increase 360 by 50%.   **b)** Decrease 160 by 10%.

2   **a)** Find 30% of 120.   **4**   **a)** Find 20% of 84.
       b) Increase 120 by 30%.   **b)** Decrease 84 by 20%.

5   Increase each of the following amounts by the percentage given.
       a) 90 by 10%   **b)** 30 by 50%   **c)** 60 by 25%   **d)** 80 by 75%
       e) 270 by 20%   **f)** 110 by 60%   **g)** 150 by 40%   **h)** 25 by 30%
       i) 11 by 80%   **j)** 480 by 15%   **k)** 140 by 45%   **l)** 100 by 85%

6   Decrease each of the following amounts by the percentage given.
       a) 60 by 50%   **b)** 55 by 10%   **c)** 24 by 25%   **d)** 48 by 75%
       e) 25 by 30%   **f)** 75 by 20%   **g)** 120 by 60%   **h)** 125 by 40%
       i) 11 by 70%   **j)** 150 by 55%   **k)** 140 by 35%   **l)** 520 by 15%

You may use a calculator to answer **Questions 7 and 8**.

7   Increase each of the following amounts by the percentage given.
       a) 490 by 11%   **b)** 101 by 16%   **c)** 55 by 37%   **d)** 89 by 61%
       e) 139 by 28%   **f)** 426 by 34%   **g)** 854 by 89%   **h)** 761 by 77%

8   Decrease each of the following amounts by the percentage given.

   a) 77 by 8%   **b)** 36 by 21%   **c)** 82 by 13%   **d)** 101 by 43%

   e) 189 by 38%   **f)** 313 by 62%   **g)** 645 by 69%   **h)** 843 by 91%

Example 2

Fabian deposits £150 into an account which pays 5% interest per year.
How much will be in the account after one year?

1. Find 5% of £150.   10% of 150 = 15

                             So 5% of 150 = 15 ÷ 2 = 7.5

2. Add this to £150.   £150 + £7.50 = **£157.50**

Exercise 2

Answer **Questions 1-6** without using your calculator.

1   Leroy deposits £230 into an account which pays 5% interest per year.
     How much will be in the account after one year?

2   Damelza's salary of £24 500 is increased by 15%. What is her new salary?

3   A farmer has 380 acres of land. He sells 35% of his land. How much does he have left?

4   A kettle originally costing £42 is reduced by 75% in a sale.
     What is the sale price of the kettle?

5   20% VAT is added to the basic price of a TV to give the selling price.
     The basic price of the TV is £485. What is the selling price?

6   A population decreases by 15% from 2400. What is the new population?

You may use a calculator to answer **Questions 7-13**.

7   Kimberley deposits £895 into an account which pays 3% interest per year.
     How much will be in the account after one year?

8   A computer costing £365 is reduced by 7% in a sale. What is the sale price of the computer?

9   A household spends £643 on electricity per year. The electricity company increases its prices
     by 11%. How much would the same amount of electricity now cost the family?

10 A couple go out for a meal in a restaurant. The bill is £63, but the restaurant adds a
     13% service charge. How much are the couple being asked to pay in total?

11 David's height increased by 20% between the ages of 6 and 10.
     He was 50 inches tall when he was 6. How tall was he when he was 10?

12 A dining room suite costs £975. One week, it is reduced by 11% in a sale.
     The following week, it is reduced by a further 8% of the new price.

   a) How much does it cost after the first reduction?

   b) How much does it cost after the second reduction?

13 Alison earns £31 000 per year. One year, she gets a pay rise of 3%.
     The following year, she gets a pay cut of 2%. How much does she now earn?

Example 3

Shop A sells a type of oven for £300 and then increases its prices by 5%.
Shop B sells the same type of oven for £290 and increases its prices by 10%.
Which shop now sells the oven more cheaply?

	Shop A:	Shop B:
1. Calculate the new price in Shop A.	10% of 300 = 30	10% of 290 = 29
2. Calculate the new price in Shop B.	So 5% of 300 = 15	£290 + £29 = £319
	£300 + £15 = £315	
3. Compare the new prices to see which is cheaper.	So **Shop A** is cheaper.	

Exercise 3

Answer **Questions 1-4** without using your calculator.

1   Roberto's weekly wage of £400 is **decreased** by 5%.
Mary's weekly wage of £350 is **increased** by 10%.

   a) How much does Roberto now earn?

   b) How much does Mary now earn?

   c) Who now earns more? By how much?

2   A car priced at £11 000 decreases in value at a rate of 10% per year.
A van priced at £12 400 decreases in value at a rate of 15% per year.

   a) Find the cost of the car after one year.

   b) Find the cost of the van after one year.

   c) Which costs more after one year? By how much?

3   At the start of a journey, Natalie's car had 8 gallons of fuel, and Jason's car had 12 gallons of fuel.
During the journey, Natalie used 25% of her fuel, and Jason used 40% of his fuel.
Who had more fuel left at the end of the journey? By how much?

4   Gerry puts £5500 into an account which pays 10% interest per year.
Raj puts £6000 into an account which pays 5% interest per year.
Who has more money in their account after one year? By how much?

You may use a calculator to answer **Questions 5-7**.

5   House A is valued at £245 000. Over the next year, it increases in value by 2%.
House B is valued at £225 000. Over the next year, it increases in value by 9%.
Which house is worth more at the end of the year? By how much?

6   Last year, Elsie's gas bill was £480 and her electricity bill was £612.
This year, her gas bill has increased by 2% and her electricity bill has decreased by 4%.
Which is now the more expensive bill? By how much?

7   The population of Barton is 152 243, and increases by 11% each year.
The population of Meristock is 210 059, and decreases by 8% each year.
Which town has the larger population after one year? By how much?
Give your answer to the nearest whole number.

Finding a Percentage Increase or Decrease

To find a percentage increase:
    (i) calculate the **difference** between the new amount and the original amount,
    (ii) find this as a percentage of the **original** amount.

Example 4

In a sale, the cost of a CD is reduced from £15 to £9. Find the percentage decrease.

1. Find the difference between the new cost and the original cost.

    $15 - 9 = 6$

2. Write the difference as a fraction of the original cost...

    $\dfrac{6}{15} = \dfrac{2}{5} = \dfrac{40}{100} = 40\%$

    $\div 3 \quad \times 20$

3. ...then write the fraction out of 100 to find the percentage decrease.

    So it is a **40%** decrease.

Exercise 4

Answer **Questions 1-7** without using your calculator.

1 Find the percentage increase when:
    a) a price of £10 is increased to £12.
    b) a price of £20 is increased to £22.
    c) a price of £140 is increased to £161.

2 Find the percentage decrease when:
    a) a price of £10 is decreased to £8.
    b) a price of £25 is decreased to £22.
    c) a price of £150 is decreased to £138.

3 The number of people working for a company increases from 45 to 72.
    a) Find the difference in the number of people working for the company.
    b) Write your answer to part **a)** as a fraction of the original amount.
    c) Find the percentage increase in the number of people working for the company.

4 Percy is on a healthy eating plan. His weight drops from 80 kg to 68 kg.
    a) Find the amount of weight Percy has lost.
    b) Find the percentage decrease in Percy's weight.

5 In an experiment, the mass of a chemical drops from 75 g to 69 g. Find the percentage decrease.

6 The price of a local newspaper increases from 80p to £1. Find the percentage increase.

7 In a sale, the price of a toaster is reduced from £50 to £30. Find the percentage reduction.

Example 5

A house price increases from £145 000 to £187 050. Find the percentage increase.

1. Calculate the difference.

    $187\,050 - 145\,000 = 42\,050$

2. Write as a fraction of the original amount, then divide the top number by the bottom number.

    $\dfrac{42\,050}{145\,000} = 42\,050 \div 145\,000$
    $= 0.29$

3. Multiply by 100% to write as a percentage.

    $0.29 \times 100\% = 29\%$
    So it is a **29%** increase.

You may use a calculator to answer **Questions 8-12**.

8 The price of a holiday increases from £320 to £364.80. Find the percentage increase.

9 The price of a pair of trainers is reduced from £80 to £70.40. What is the percentage reduction?

10 The height of a sunflower increases from 1.3 m to 2.08 m over the course of summer. What is the percentage increase in its height?

11 During a season, the average attendance for a local sports team's matches was 11 350. The following season, the average attendance was 11 123. Find the percentage decrease.

12 A car is bought for £12 950. Three years later, it is sold for £8806. After another three years, it is sold again for £4403.

  a) Find the percentage decrease in the car's price over the first three years.

  b) Find the percentage decrease in the car's price over the next three years.

  c) Find the percentage decrease in the car's price over the whole six years.

7.3 Percentages, Fractions and Decimals

You can switch between percentages, fractions and decimals in the following ways.

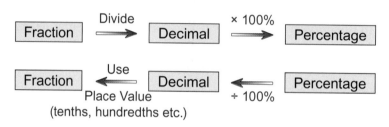

Example 1

Write 24% as: a) a decimal   b) a fraction in its simplest terms.

1. Divide by 100% to write as a decimal.

  a) $24\% \div 100\% = \underline{\textbf{0.24}}$

2. The final digit of 0.24 (the '4') is in the hundredths column, so write 0.24 as 24 hundredths, and then simplify.

  b) $0.24 = \dfrac{24}{100} = \dfrac{6}{25}$ ($\div 4$)

Example 2

Write $\dfrac{3}{8}$ as: a) a decimal   b) a percentage.

1. Calculate $3 \div 8$ to write as a decimal.

  a) $8\overline{)3.^{3}0^{6}0^{4}0}$ gives 0.375 So $\dfrac{3}{8} = \underline{\textbf{0.375}}$

2. Multiply the decimal by 100% to write as a percentage.

  b) $0.375 \times 100\% = \underline{\textbf{37.5\%}}$

Exercise 1

1 Each grid below is made up of 100 small squares. Find the proportion of each grid that is shaded as **(i)** a percentage, **(ii)** a decimal, and **(iii)** a fraction in its simplest terms.

a) 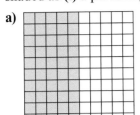   **b)** 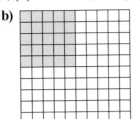   **c)** 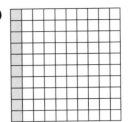   **d)**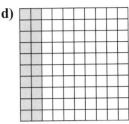

2 **a)** Find the fraction equivalent to $\frac{3}{20}$ which has 100 as the denominator.
    b) Write $\frac{3}{20}$ as **(i)** a percentage, and **(ii)** a decimal.

3 **a)** By calculating $5 \div 11$, write $\frac{5}{11}$ as a recurring decimal.
    b) Hence write $\frac{5}{11}$ as a percentage.

4 Write each of the following percentages as **(i)** a decimal, and **(ii)** a fraction in its simplest terms.

a) 75%	**b)** 30%	**c)** 40%	**d)** 65%
e) 85%	**f)** 95%	**g)** 24%	**h)** 32%
i) 48%	**j)** 12%	**k)** 2%	**l)** 6%
m) 5%	**n)** 13%	**o)** 96%	**p)** 74%

5 Write each of the following fractions as **(i)** a decimal, and **(ii)** a percentage.

a) $\frac{79}{100}$	**b)** $\frac{43}{100}$	**c)** $\frac{3}{10}$	**d)** $\frac{7}{10}$
e) $\frac{1}{2}$	**f)** $\frac{1}{5}$	**g)** $\frac{2}{5}$	**h)** $\frac{4}{5}$
i) $\frac{3}{4}$	**j)** $\frac{7}{8}$	**k)** $\frac{1}{3}$	**l)** $\frac{1}{9}$
m) $\frac{2}{15}$	**n)** $\frac{7}{11}$	**o)** $\frac{1}{6}$	**p)** $\frac{4}{25}$

6 Write each of the following decimals as **(i)** a percentage, and **(ii)** a fraction in its simplest terms.

a) 0.35	**b)** 0.86	**c)** 0.7	**d)** 0.52
e) 0.6	**f)** 0.48	**g)** 0.05	**h)** 0.72
i) 0.36	**j)** 0.4	**k)** 0.01	**l)** 0.68
m) 0.14	**n)** 0.13	**o)** 0.125	**p)** 0.325

7 Raj answers 86% of the questions in a test correctly. Write this as a decimal.

8 8% of the members of a drama group have green eyes. Write this as a decimal.

9 $\frac{3}{5}$ of the pupils in a class are right-handed. What percentage of the class are right-handed?

10 Raphael eats 36% of a cake. Write this percentage as a fraction in its lowest terms.

11 The probability of it raining tomorrow is $\frac{17}{25}$. Write this probability as a percentage.

Example 3

Put $\frac{1}{3}$, 33% and 0.3 in order, from smallest to largest.

Write the amounts in the same form.
(Here, I've chosen to write them all as decimals.)

1. Calculate $1 \div 3$ to write $\frac{1}{3}$ as a decimal.

$$\begin{array}{r} 0.\ 3\ 3 \\ 3\overline{)1.^10^10^10} \end{array}$$ So $\frac{1}{3} = 0.33... = 0.\dot{3}$

2. Calculate $33\% \div 100\%$ to write 33% as a decimal.

$33\% \div 100\% = 0.33$

3. Put the decimals in order, from smallest to largest.

$0.3, 0.33, 0.\dot{3}$

4. Rewrite in their original forms.

0.3, 33%, $\frac{1}{3}$

Exercise 2

Answer **Questions 1-8** without using your calculator.

1 **a)** Write 24% as a decimal.

   b) Write $\frac{1}{5}$ as a decimal.

   c) Hence put 24%, $\frac{1}{5}$ and 0.25 in order, from smallest to largest.

2 For each of the following pairs, write down which is larger.

   a) 0.35, 32%　　　　**b)** 0.58, 68%　　　　**c)** 0.4, 4%　　　　**d)** 0.09, 90%

   e) 0.2, $\frac{21}{100}$　　　**f)** 0.6, $\frac{7}{10}$　　　**g)** 0.7, $\frac{3}{4}$　　　**h)** 0.55, $\frac{3}{5}$

3 For each of the following lists, write down which amount is not equal to the others.

   a) 0.25, 40%, $\frac{1}{4}$　　**b)** 0.5, 20%, $\frac{1}{2}$　　**c)** 0.125, 1.25%, $\frac{1}{8}$　　**d)** 0.44, 44%, $\frac{4}{9}$

   e) 0.8, 8%, $\frac{4}{5}$　　**f)** 0.615, 40%, $\frac{6}{15}$　　**g)** 0.22, 22%, $\frac{22}{50}$　　**h)** 0.25, 25%, $\frac{4}{24}$

4 Put the numbers in each of the following lists in order, from smallest to largest.

   a) 0.42, 25%, $\frac{2}{5}$　　**b)** 0.505, 45%, $\frac{1}{2}$　　**c)** 0.15, 0.2%, $\frac{1}{5}$　　**d)** 0.37, 38%, $\frac{3}{8}$

   e) 0.2, 22%, $\frac{2}{9}$　　**f)** 0.07, 0.7%, $\frac{7}{10}$　　**g)** 0.111, 11%, $\frac{1}{9}$　　**h)** 0.13, 12.5%, $\frac{3}{20}$

   i) 0.25, 23%, $\frac{9}{40}$　　**j)** 0.02, 0.5%, $\frac{1}{20}$　　**k)** 0.4, 2.5%, $\frac{1}{25}$　　**l)** 0.006, 0.06%, $\frac{3}{50}$

5 Two shops are having a sale. Shop A is offering $\frac{1}{8}$ off all items, while Shop B is offering 15% off all items. Which shop is reducing its prices by the greater percentage?

6 Margaret is buying a car. She needs to pay $\frac{2}{5}$ of the total cost as a deposit. Her parents give her 35% of the cost of the car to help her buy it. Is this enough to pay the deposit?

7 In a game, the winner is the person who transfers more of their 60 counters from one box to another. Oliver transfers 65% of his counters. Jen transfers $\frac{11}{20}$ of her counters. Who has won?

8 In a season, Team X won 14 out of the 20 matches they played. Team Y won 60% of their matches. Which team had the higher proportion of wins?

Example 4

$\frac{1}{4}$ of pupils in a school bring a packed lunch, 65% have school dinners, and the rest go home for lunch. What percentage of pupils go home for lunch?

1. Write $\frac{1}{4}$ as a percentage by writing it as a fraction out of 100. (Or you could divide the top number by the bottom number and multiply by 100%.)

2. Find the percentage that don't go home for lunch by adding the percentages for 'packed lunches' and 'school dinners'.

3. Subtract this from 100% to find the percentage who <u>do</u> go home for lunch.

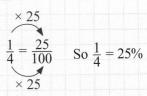

$$\frac{1}{4} = \frac{25}{100} \quad \text{So } \frac{1}{4} = 25\%$$

$$25\% + 65\% = 90\%$$
$$100\% - 90\% = \underline{\mathbf{10\%}}$$

Exercise 3

Answer **Questions 1-9** without using your calculator.

1 In a school survey of food preferences, 50% of pupils said they prefer pizza, $\frac{1}{5}$ said they prefer shepherd's pie and the rest said they prefer roast chicken.

   a) Write the percentage of pupils that prefer shepherd's pie.

   b) Use your answer to find the percentage that prefer roast chicken.

2 In a car park, $\frac{2}{5}$ of the cars are red, 0.12 are white, 15% are blue, and the rest are black.

   a) Write the proportion of red cars as a percentage.

   b) Write the proportion of white cars as a percentage.

   c) Use your answers to find the percentage of cars in the car park that are black.

3 A bag contains coloured counters. 0.37 of the counters are green, 12% are pink and the rest are yellow. What percentage of the counters are yellow?

4 Ainslie is keeping a record of the birds in his garden. Of the birds he has seen this month, $\frac{3}{8}$ were sparrows, 41.5% were blackbirds, and the rest were robins. What percentage were robins?

5 $\frac{3}{4}$ of the people at a concert arrived by train, 0.05 walked, and the rest came by car. What percentage came by car?

6 $\frac{3}{5}$ of the chocolates in a tin are milk chocolate, 20% are white chocolate, and the rest are dark chocolate. What percentage are dark chocolate?

7 Beverley eats 0.3 of a pie, Victoria eats $\frac{1}{10}$, Patrick eats 20%, and Gus eats the rest. What percentage of the pie does Gus eat?

8 $\frac{1}{2}$ of Jay's music collection is rap, 30% is jazz, 12% is blues, and the rest is classical. Find the percentage of Jay's music collection that is classical.

9 $\frac{1}{4}$ of Hattie's jackets are leather, $\frac{1}{5}$ are denim, 30% are suede, and the rest are corduroy. Find the percentage of Hattie's jackets that are corduroy.

7.4 Percentages Problems

Exercise 1

Answer **Questions 1-6** without using your calculator.

1 Sandra gets paid £1385 per month. In December she gets a Christmas bonus of £138.50. What percentage of her monthly wage is this bonus?

2 A coat normally costs £160. In a sale, the coat's price was reduced by 35%.
 a) What is 35% of £160?
 b) What is the new price of the coat?

3 A pot of yoghurt normally contains 450 g. A special offer pot contains 35% extra free. How many grams of yoghurt does the special offer pot contain?

4 A newborn baby weighs 3.2 kg. His weight increases by 5% over the next fortnight. What does he weigh at the end of the fortnight?

5 House A is valued at £420 000 and House B is valued at £340 000. After 5 years the value of House A has **decreased** by 15% and the value of House B has **increased** by 5%. What is the difference in value of the two houses after 5 years?

6 Each grid below is made up of 25 small squares. Find the proportion of each grid that is shaded as **(i)** a fraction in its simplest terms, **(ii)** a percentage, and **(iii)** a decimal.

 a)   **b)**   **c)** 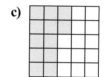   **d)**

You may use a calculator to answer **Questions 7-13**.

7 The insurance for a car normally costs £356. With a no-claims discount, the cost is reduced by 27%. What is the reduced cost of the insurance?

8 Tony deposits £3250 into a savings account that earns 8.5% interest per year. How much will he have at the end of the year?

9 The population of an island is 12 500. Each year, the population increases by 8%.
 a) What is the population of the island after 1 year?
 b) What is the population of the island after 2 years?

10 Write $\frac{2}{33}$, 0.061 and 6% in order, from smallest to largest.

11 Kelly and Nasir both had maths tests last week. Kelly scored $\frac{47}{68}$ and Nasir scored $\frac{35}{52}$. Who got the higher percentage score?

12 Two shops had a sale on a suit that had previously cost £92. Shop A had 70% off the original price, while Shop B had $\frac{7}{8}$ off. Which shop had the lower price, and by how much?

13 Last summer, 385 000 people visited a holiday resort. $\frac{1}{8}$ were German, 0.11 were French and the rest were British.
 a) What percentage were British?
 b) How many British people visited the resort?

Section 8 — Algebraic Expressions

8.1 Collecting Like Terms

An **algebraic expression** involves letters that represent numbers.

For example, these are all algebraic expressions: a $\quad$ $6b$ $\quad$ xyz $\quad$ $a + b$ $\quad$ $x^2 + y^2 + z^2$

(Remember — a is the same as **1a**, and **6b** is the same as **6 × b**.)

Expressions do **not** contain an equals sign (=).

Expressions can sometimes be simplified by **collecting like terms**.
'**Like terms**' contain exactly the same combination of letters.

Example 1

Simplify these expressions by collecting like terms: $\quad$ a) $5p - 2p + 4p$ $\quad$ b) $4a + 3b - a - 7b$

a) This expression contains three 'like terms'
— each only contains the letter p.
They combine to give a total of $7p$.

a) $\quad 5p - 2p + 4p = \underline{\mathbf{7p}}$

b) First write the like terms next to each other.

'4a' and '–a' are like terms — they just contain a.
Together these give $4a - a = 3a$.

And '3b' and '–7b' are like terms — they just contain b.
Together these give $3b - 7b = -4b$.

Remember, the + or – sign in front of a term actually
belongs to that term.

b) $\quad 4a + 3b - a - 7b$

$\quad = 4a - a + 3b - 7b$

$\quad = \underline{\mathbf{3a - 4b}}$

Exercise 1

1 Simplify these expressions by collecting like terms.

    a) $b + b + b + b$ $\qquad$ **b)** $a + a + a$ $\qquad$ **c)** $2x + 3x + x$

    d) $p + 7p + 2p + 4p$ $\qquad$ **e)** $4s + s + 2s + 7s$ $\qquad$ **f)** $11n + 8n + n$

2 Simplify these expressions by collecting like terms.

    a) $3y + 5y - 2y$ $\qquad$ **b)** $8z + 7z - 3z$ $\qquad$ **c)** $7p - 2p + 3p - 4p$

    d) $10m - 7m + 2m$ $\qquad$ **e)** $8y - y - 3y$ $\qquad$ **f)** $3x + 5x - 8x$

    g) $q - 3q - 2q$ $\qquad$ **h)** $5m - 2m + 8m - 6m$ $\qquad$ **i)** $2y - y - 3y - 5y + 6y$

3 Simplify these expressions by collecting like terms.

    a) $c + c + c + d + d$ $\qquad$ **b)** $a + b + a - a + b$ $\qquad$ **c)** $x + y + x + y + x - y$

    d) $3m + m + 2n$ $\qquad$ **e)** $5x + 2y + 3x$ $\qquad$ **f)** $3a + 5b + 8a + 2b$

    g) $6p + q + p + 3q$ $\qquad$ **h)** $5a - 2a + 5b + 2b$ $\qquad$ **i)** $4b + 8c - b - 5c$

Example 2

Simplify the expression $x + 4y + 4 - 2x - y - 3$ by collecting like terms.

1. Terms involving no letters at all are like terms.
2. Collect them together in the same way as terms containing letters.

$$x + 4y + 4 - 2x - y - 3$$
$$= x - 2x + 4y - y + 4 - 3$$
$$= \underline{-x + 3y + 1}$$

4 Simplify these expressions by collecting like terms.

a) $2c + 4 + c + 7$ b) $3x + 6 - 6x - 4$ c) $5y + 12 - 9y - 7$

d) $-m + 5 - 8m + 16$ e) $-4x - 2 + 7x + 12$ f) $13a + 8 + 8a + 2$

5 Simplify these expressions by collecting like terms.

a) $x + 7 + 4x + y + 5$ b) $a + 2b + b - 8 - 5a$ c) $5x + 2y + 6 + 4y + 2x - 9$

d) $13m + 7 + 2n - 8m - 3$ e) $5x + 2y + 3x - 2y - 3$ f) $13a - 5b + 8a + 12b + 7$

6 Simplify these expressions.

a) $16p + 4q + 4 - 2p + 3q - 8$ b) $5a - 7b + 5b - 2 + 2a + 11$

c) $14b + 8c - b + 3 - 5c - 5b + 4$ d) $-3x + 9y + 2z - 2x - 5 + 4y - 8x$

e) $-5m + 3 - 6n - 4 + 3n - 6m - 2n$ f) $8p + 6q + 14 - 6r - 4p - 14r - 2q - 23$

Example 3

Simplify the expression $x + x^2 + yx + 7 + 4x + 2xy - 3$ by collecting like terms.

There are four sets of like terms:
(i) terms involving just x
(ii) terms involving x^2
(iii) terms involving xy (or yx, which means the same)
(iv) terms involving just numbers

Collect the different sets together separately.

$$x + x^2 + xy + 7 + 4x + 2xy - 3$$
$$= (x + 4x) + x^2 + (xy + 2xy) + (7 - 3)$$
$$= \underline{5x + x^2 + 3xy + 4}$$

7 Simplify the following expressions by collecting like terms.

a) $x^2 + 3x + 2 + 2x + 3$ b) $x^2 + 4x + 1 + 3x - 3$ c) $x^2 + 4x + x^2 + 2x + 4$

d) $x^2 + 2x^2 + 4x - 3x$ e) $p^2 - 5p + 2p^2 + 3p$ f) $3p^2 + 6q + p^2 - 4q + 3p^2$

g) $8 + 6p^2 - 5 + pq + p^2$ h) $4p + 5q - pq + p^2 - 7q$ i) $6b^2 + 7b + 9 - 4b^2 + 5b - 2$

8 Simplify the following expressions by collecting like terms.

a) $ab + cd - xy + 3ab - 2cd + 3yx + 2x^2$ b) $pq + 3pq + p^2 - 2qp + q^2$

c) $3ab - 2b + ab + b^2 + 5b$ d) $4abc - 3bc + 2ab + b^2 + 5b + 2abc$

8.2 Expanding Brackets

You can **expand** (or remove) brackets by multiplying everything **inside** the brackets by the letter or number **in front**.

$$a(b + c) = ab + ac$$
$$a(b - c) = ab - ac$$

Remember, **powers** work with **letters** in exactly the same way as they work with numbers.

$$a^2 = a \times a$$
$$a^3 = a \times a \times a$$

$$a^m \times a^n = a^{m+n}$$

Example 1

Expand the brackets in these expressions: a) $3(a + 2)$ b) $8(n - 3)$

a) Multiply both a and 2 by 3.

b) Multiply both n and 3 by 8.

a) $3(a + 2) = (3 \times a) + (3 \times 2) = \underline{\mathbf{3a + 6}}$

b) $8(n - 3) = (8 \times n) - (8 \times 3) = \underline{\mathbf{8n - 24}}$

Exercise 1

1 Expand the brackets in these expressions.

a) $2(a + 5)$ b) $4(b + 3)$ c) $5(d + 7)$ d) $3(p + 4)$

e) $4(x + 8)$ f) $6(5 - r)$ g) $2(7 + y)$ h) $8(h - 2)$

i) $9(q - 3)$ j) $2(t + 6)$ k) $4(b - 4)$ l) $3(k + 6)$

m) $3(5 + p)$ n) $7(6 + g)$ o) $5(3 - y)$ p) $8(a - b)$

Example 2

Expand the brackets in these expressions: a) $m(n + 7)$ b) $a(a - 4)$

a) Multiply both n and 7 by m.

b) Multiply both a and 4 by a.

a) $m(n + 7) = (m \times n) + (m \times 7) = \underline{\mathbf{mn + 7m}}$

b) $a(a - 4) = (a \times a) - (a \times 4) = \underline{\mathbf{a^2 - 4a}}$

2 Expand the brackets in these expressions.

a) $x(y + 5)$ b) $p(q + 2)$ c) $a(b + 4)$ d) $m(p + 8)$

e) $q(p - 4)$ f) $s(5 - t)$ g) $y(5 + x)$ h) $n(n - 7)$

i) $x(x - 2)$ j) $p(8 - q)$ k) $x(8 - x)$ l) $a(b - 12)$

Example 3

Simplify these expressions: a) $b \times b \times b \times b$ b) $4a \times 5b$ c) $3a \times 6a$

1. If the same letter is multiplied by itself, write it as a power.

2. Multiply numbers and letters separately.

a) $b \times b \times b \times b = \underline{\mathbf{b^4}}$

b) $4a \times 5b = 4 \times 5 \times a \times b = \underline{\mathbf{20ab}}$

c) $3a \times 6a = 3 \times 6 \times a \times a = \underline{\mathbf{18a^2}}$

Exercise 2

1 Simplify the following expressions.

a) $a \times a \times a$
b) $2a \times 3a$
c) $8p \times 2q$
d) $3a \times 7a$
e) $5x \times 3y$
f) $m \times m \times m \times m$
g) $12a \times 4b$
h) $6p \times 8p$

2 Simplify the following expressions.

a) $a \times ab$
b) $4a^2 \times 5a$
c) $2p \times 7q^2$
d) $4ab \times 2ab$

Example 4

Expand the brackets in the following expressions.

a) $4(5a + 3)$
b) $3(4 - 7n)$

a) Multiply both $5a$ and 3 by 4.

b) Multiply both 4 and $7n$ by 3.

a) $4(5a + 3) = (4 \times 5a) + (4 \times 3)$
$\quad = \underline{\mathbf{20a + 12}}$

b) $3(4 - 7n) = (3 \times 4) - (3 \times 7n)$
$\quad = \underline{\mathbf{12 - 21n}}$

Exercise 3

1 Expand the brackets in the following expressions.

a) $3(2p + 4)$
b) $5(4t - 8)$
c) $7(3h + 9)$
d) $2(5d + 4)$
e) $8(7k - 5)$
f) $4(7 + 4p)$
g) $4(5 + 7b)$
h) $3(4 - 2z)$
i) $2(8 - 6m)$
j) $9(2 + 8v)$
k) $6(n - 6m)$
l) $9(u + 8v)$

2 Expand the brackets in the following expressions.

a) $3(2n - 6m)$
b) $5(4u + 8v)$
c) $7(5n - 6m)$
d) $3(u + 8v)$
e) $4(4x - 7y)$
f) $3(2p - 11q)$
g) $8(2s - 12t)$
h) $6(4x + 5y)$

Example 5

Expand the brackets in the following expressions: a) $-(q + 4)$ b) $-3(4 - 2a)$

a) You can think of $-(q + 4)$ as $-1 \times (q + 4)$.
See how a minus sign outside the brackets
reverses the sign of everything inside the brackets.

a) $-(q + 4) = (-1 \times q) + (-1 \times 4)$
$\quad = (-q) + (-4)$
$\quad = \underline{\mathbf{-q - 4}}$

b) Again, the sign of everything
inside the brackets changes.
Remember: $-(-6a) = 6a$.

b) $-3(4 - 2a) = (-3 \times 4) - (-3 \times 2a)$
$\quad = (-12) - (-6a)$
$\quad = \underline{\mathbf{-12 + 6a}}$

---

3 Expand the brackets in the following expressions.

a) $-(q + 2)$
b) $-(x + 7)$
c) $-(h + 3)$
d) $-(g + 3)$
e) $-4(n + 2)$
f) $-2(7 + r)$
g) $-8(3 + 5a)$
h) $-5(4 + z)$
i) $-6(a + 4)$
j) $-7(b + 2)$
k) $-2(11 + c)$
l) $-5(12 + d)$

4 Expand the brackets in the following expressions.

a) $-(p-3)$ b) $-(q-5)$ c) $-(r-6)$ d) $-(s-2)$

e) $-4(u-7)$ f) $-2(12-v)$ g) $-8(7-w)$ h) $-5(5-x)$

5 Expand the brackets in the following expressions.

a) $-(m+3)$ b) $-(n-11)$ c) $-(p+4)$ d) $-(q-7)$

e) $-4(r-9)$ f) $-2(13+s)$ g) $-8(2-t)$ h) $-5(6+u)$

i) $-v(v+4)$ j) $-v(v-5)$ k) $-x(12-x)$ l) $-y(4+y)$

6 Expand the brackets in the following expressions.

a) $-6(5g-3)$ b) $-7(4v+8)$ c) $-2(5+4m)$ d) $-5(10-8v)$

e) $-5(2+3n)$ f) $-4z(8-2z)$ g) $-2(6b-3)$ h) $-4y(2y+6)$

Example 6

Simplify the following expressions.

a) $2(a+5)+3(a+2)$ b) $3(x+2)-5(2x+1)$

a) Multiply out both sets of brackets.

Then collect like terms.

a) $2(a+5)+3(a+2)=(2a+10)+(3a+6)$
$$=2a+10+3a+6$$
$$=\underline{\mathbf{5a+16}}$$

b) Multiply out the individual brackets.

The minus sign before the second set of brackets reverses the sign of each term inside those brackets.

b) $3(x+2)-5(2x+1)=(3x+6)-(10x+5)$
$$=3x+6-10x-5$$
$$=\underline{\mathbf{-7x+1}}$$

Exercise 4

1 Simplify the following expressions.

a) $2(z+3)+4(z+2)$ b) $3(c+1)+5(c+7)$ c) $4(u+6)+8(u+5)$

d) $2(c+2)+3(c+5)$ e) $3(v+5)+6(v+7)$ f) $3(w+4)+5(w+2)$

g) $5(b-6)+7(b+4)$ h) $7(t-3)+2(t+12)$ i) $8(m-2)+9(m+5)$

2 Simplify the following expressions.

a) $5(p-3)-(p+6)$ b) $2(c-6)-(c+5)$ c) $5(q-3)-(q+1)$

d) $2(j-5)-(j-3)$ e) $5(y-4)-(y-2)$ f) $5(3c-6)-(c-3)$

3 Simplify the following expressions.

a) $5(2q+5)-2(q-2)$ b) $2(3c-8)-8(c+4)$ c) $4(5q-1)-2(q+2)$

d) $3(a-6)-4(a-1)$ e) $5(4z-3)-3(z-5)$ f) $5(q-2)-3(q-4)$

4 Simplify the following expressions.

a) $2(z+2)+3(z+6)$ b) $8(c+4)-(c+2)$ c) $4(u+4)+3(u+5)$

d) $4p(3p+5)-3(p+1)$ e) $6(4m+5)+7m(2m+3)$ f) $4(3k+1)-k(7k+9)$

g) $9b(2b+5)+4b(6b+6)$ h) $4(t+1)-7t(8t-11)$ i) $7h(3h+2)-10h(4h-1)$

8.3 Factorising

Factorising is the opposite of expanding brackets.
You look for a **common factor** of all the terms in an expression, and 'take it outside' the brackets.
If there is more than one common factor, the **highest common factor** goes outside the brackets.

For a lot of these questions, you'll need to remember how to **divide** two powers: $a^m \div a^n = \dfrac{a^m}{a^n} = a^{m-n}$

Example 1

Factorise these expressions: a) $6p + 8$ b) $12x - 18y$

a) 2 is a common factor of $6p$ and 8.
    So 2 goes outside the brackets.

    Divide each term by the common factor, and write
    the results inside the brackets: $6p \div 2 = 3p$ and $8 \div 2 = 4$

a) $6p + 8 = 2(\quad + \quad)$
    $= 2(3p + \quad)$
    $= \mathbf{2(3p + 4)}$

b) 6 is the highest common factor of $12x$ and $18y$.
    So 6 goes outside the brackets.

    Divide each term by the common factor, and write the
    results inside the brackets: $12x \div 6 = 2x$ and $18y \div 6 = 3y$

b) $12x - 18y = 6(\quad - \quad)$
    $= 6(2x - \quad)$
    $= \mathbf{6(2x - 3y)}$

Exercise 1

1 Factorise the following expressions.

a) $2a + 10$ b) $3b + 12$ c) $5c + 15$ d) $4 + 12x$

e) $15 + 3y$ f) $28 + 7v$ g) $10d + 35$ h) $8x + 12$

i) $8c - 20$ j) $21p - 84$ k) $14 - 7x$ l) $24x + 12$

2 Factorise the following expressions.

a) $5a + 15b$ b) $9c + 12d$ c) $3x + 12y$ d) $21u + 7v$

e) $8c + 12f$ f) $25d + 35e$ g) $12x + 16y$ h) $3x + 9y$

3 Factorise the following expressions.

a) $4a^2 + 12b$ b) $3c + 15d^2$ c) $5c^2 + 25f$ d) $6x + 12y^2$

Example 2

Factorise $3x^2 + 2x$.

1. x is a common factor of $3x^2$ and $2x$.
    So x goes outside the brackets.

2. Divide each term by the common factor, and write the
    results inside the brackets: $3x^2 \div x = 3x$ and $2x \div x = 2$

$3x^2 + 2x = x(\quad + \quad)$
$= x(3x + \quad)$
$= \mathbf{x(3x + 2)}$

4 Simplify the following.

a) $x^2 \div x$ b) $2y^2 \div y$ c) $8p^2 \div p$ d) $35n^2 \div 7n$

e) $10d^2 \div 2d$ f) $24m^2 \div 3m$ g) $12a^2 \div 2a$ h) $22b^2 \div 11b$

5 Factorise the following expressions.

a) $3a^2 + 7a$ **b)** $4b^2 + 19b$ **c)** $2x^2 + 9x$ **d)** $7y + 15y^2$

e) $10d^2 + 27d$ **f)** $4y^2 + 13y$ **g)** $11y + 3y^2$ **h)** $22w + 5w^2$

i) $4x^2 - 9x$ **j)** $21q^2 - 16q$ **k)** $15y - 7y^2$ **l)** $27z^2 + 11z$

Example 3

Factorise these expressions: a) $6p + 9p^2$ b) $15x^2 - 10xy$

a) 3 <u>and</u> p are common factors of $6p$ and $9p^2$.
So $3p$ goes outside the brackets.

Divide each term by the common factor, and write the
results inside the brackets: $6p \div 3p = 2$ and $9p^2 \div 3p = 3p$

a) $6p + 9p^2 = 3p(\ + \ )$

$= 3p(2 + \ )$

$= \underline{\mathbf{3p(2 + 3p)}}$

b) 5 <u>and</u> x are common factors of $15x^2$ and $10xy$.
So $5x$ goes outside the brackets.

Divide each term by the common factor, and write the results
inside the brackets: $15x^2 \div 5x = 3x$ and $10xy \div 5x = 2y$

b) $15x^2 - 10xy = 5x(\ - \ )$

$= 5x(3x - \ )$

$= \underline{\mathbf{5x(3x - 2y)}}$

Exercise 2

1 Factorise these expressions.

a) $5a^2 + 10a$ **b)** $4b + 8b^2$ **c)** $3c^2 - 9c$ **d)** $9d - 18d^2$

e) $6f^2 + 2f$ **f)** $7p^2 + 21p$ **g)** $2y + 18y^2$ **h)** $3h - 15h^2$

2 Factorise these expressions.

a) $10c^2 - 5cd$ **b)** $20x^2 - 10xy$ **c)** $9x^2 + 6xy$ **d)** $12x^2 + 8xy$

e) $2ab - 6b^2$ **f)** $6a^2 + 3a$ **g)** $4xy - 8x^2$ **h)** $2ab + 12b^2$

3 Factorise these expressions.

a) $10p^2 + 15pq$ **b)** $12xy + 8y^2$ **c)** $15ab - 20a^2$ **d)** $12q^2 - 18pq$

e) $6a^2 + 9ab$ **f)** $12pq - 8p^2$ **g)** $8a^2 + 6ab$ **h)** $24x^2y - 16x$

i) $30ab^2 + 25ab$ **j)** $14x^2 - 28xy^2$ **k)** $12xy^2 + 8x^2y$ **l)** $8ab^2 + 10a^2b$

Exercise 3 — Mixed Exercise

1 Factorise these expressions.

a) $2x + 4y$ **b)** $2x + x^2$ **c)** $2x + 4x^2$ **d)** $8x + 24$

e) $6a + 9b$ **f)** $7x - x^2$ **g)** $7y - 4xy$ **h)** $pq + p^2q$

i) $7m^2n + 4m^2p$ **j)** $4y - 6y^2$ **k)** $20y + 12xy$ **l)** $9pr + 6pq$

2 Factorise these expressions.

a) $28a - 35b$ **b)** $15ab - 10a^2$ **c)** $60x + 144y$ **d)** $28rst + 40r^2s$

e) $4abc^2 - 6a^2bc$ **f)** $5pq + 10qr$ **g)** $20m^2n - 24m$ **h)** $23pq - 92p$

3 Factorise these expressions.

a) $10pq^2 - 15p^2q$ **b)** $8cd^2 - 6c^2d$ **c)** $14m^2n - 35mn^2$ **d)** $16pq^2 - 6q^2p$

Section 9 — Equations and Inequalities

9.1 Solving Equations

Solving an equation means finding the value of an unknown letter that makes both sides **equal**.

For example, the solution to $2x + 3 = 11$ is $x = 4$ — because if $x = 4$, **both** sides equal 11.

Example 1

Solve the equation $x + 8 = 15$.

1. You need to get x on its own on one side of the equation, so you need to subtract 8 from the left-hand side.
2. But you must always do the same to both sides of an equation. So subtract 8 from the right-hand side too.
3. Check your answer by putting it in the original equation. $x + 8 = 7 + 8 = 15$, which is the same as the right-hand side.

$$x + 8 = 15$$
$$x + 8 - 8 = 15 - 8$$
$$x = 15 - 8$$
$$\underline{x = 7}$$

Exercise 1

1 Get x alone on one side of the equation to solve these equations.

a) $x + 9 = 12$
b) $x + 5 = 16$
c) $x - 2 = 14$
d) $x - 7 = 19$
e) $x - 3 = 12$
f) $x + 8 = 14$
g) $x - 5 = -3$
h) $x - 12 = -1$
i) $6 = x + 10$
j) $18 = x - 8$
k) $-2 = 7 + x$
l) $40 = x - 12$
m) $24 = x - 11$
n) $32 = x - 17$
o) $x - 22 = 27$
p) $x + 31 = 30$

Example 2

Solve the equation $15 - x = 7$.

1. Add x to both sides of the equation — this means you don't have a minus sign in front of x.
2. Now you can solve the equation as before.
3. Don't forget to check your answer.

$$15 - x = 7$$
$$15 = x + 7$$
$$\underline{x = 8}$$

2 Solve these equations. Start by adding x to both sides.

a) $12 - x = 9$
b) $4 - x = 2$
c) $15 - x = 14$
d) $14 - x = 19$
e) $2 - x = 7$
f) $4 - x = 12$
g) $8 - x = 14$
h) $5 - x = 7$

3 Solve the following equations.

a) $x + 7 = 12$
b) $x + 8 = 26$
c) $5 - x = 21$
d) $28 = 20 - x$
e) $16 = x + 10$
f) $18 - x = 9$
g) $28 = 7 + x$
h) $12 - x = 23$
i) $x - 9 = 12$
j) $x - 8 = 14$
k) $35 = 31 - x$
l) $32 - x = 17$

4 Solve the following equations.

a) $x + 2.5 = 2$
b) $x - 7.3 = 1.6$
c) $5.6 + x = 2.1$
d) $5.2 = 2.8 - x$
e) $1.6 = x + 2.3$
f) $6.2 - x = 9.8$
g) $3.47 = 7.18 + x$
h) $6.03 - x = 0.58$

Example 3

Solve the equation $5x = 15$.

1. Get x on its own by dividing both sides of the equation by 5.

2. Remember: $5x \div 5 = x$

$5x = 15$

$5x \div 5 = 15 \div 5$

$\underline{x = 3}$

Exercise 2

1 Get x alone on one side of the equation to solve these equations.

    a) $7x = 35$ **b)** $8x = 24$ **c)** $9x = 54$ **d)** $10x = 110$

    e) $11x = 143$ **f)** $12x = 18$ **g)** $16x = 56$ **h)** $14x = 91$

    i) $4x = 6$ **j)** $9x = 1.8$ **k)** $2x = 1.5$ **l)** $5x = 22.5$

2 Solve the following equations.

    a) $3.5x = 49$ **b)** $4.5x = 81$ **c)** $7.5x = 75$ **d)** $10.5x = 126$

    e) $12.5x = 250$ **f)** $22.5x = 180$ **g)** $37.5x = 600$ **h)** $62.5x = 1125$

3 Solve the following equations.

    a) $6x = -18$ **b)** $5x = -20$ **c)** $7x = -14$ **d)** $15x = -150$

    e) $2.5x = -25$ **f)** $1.5x = -1.8$ **g)** $3.5x = -7$ **h)** $6.5x = -1.3$

Example 4

Solve the equation $-6x = 9$.

1. This time, divide both sides by -6.

2. Remember: $-6x \div (-6) = x$

$-6x = 9$

$-6x \div (-6) = 9 \div (-6)$

$\underline{x = -1.5}$

4 Solve these equations by dividing both sides by a negative number.

    a) $-5x = 50$ **b)** $-8x = 24$ **c)** $-3x = 27$ **d)** $-7x = 35$

    e) $-4x = -16$ **f)** $-7x = -56$ **g)** $-9x = 108$ **h)** $-13x = 195$

5 Solve the following equations.

    a) $-3x = -12$ **b)** $40x = -32$ **c)** $-4.5x = -2.7$ **d)** $50x = -3.4$

    e) $60x = -36$ **f)** $-6.4x = -0.48$ **g)** $75x = -45$ **h)** $-80x = -56$

Example 5

Solve the equation $\dfrac{x}{5} = 3$.

1. Multiply both sides by 5.

2. Remember: $\dfrac{x}{5} \times 5 = x$

$\dfrac{x}{5} = 3$

$\dfrac{x}{5} \times 5 = 3 \times 5$

$\underline{x = 15}$

Exercise 3

1 Solve the following equations.

    a) $\dfrac{x}{3} = 2$ **b)** $\dfrac{x}{10} = 4$ **c)** $\dfrac{x}{4} = 11$ **d)** $\dfrac{x}{6} = -3$

    e) $\dfrac{x}{5} = 1.5$ **f)** $\dfrac{x}{3} = 0.4$ **g)** $\dfrac{x}{11} = -0.5$ **h)** $\dfrac{x}{2} = -3.2$

2 Solve these equations by multiplying both sides by a negative number.

    a) $-\dfrac{x}{4} = 3$ **b)** $-\dfrac{x}{5} = 6$ **c)** $-\dfrac{x}{10} = 1.1$ **d)** $-\dfrac{x}{3} = 0.5$

    e) $-\dfrac{x}{2.1} = 2.5$ **f)** $-\dfrac{x}{3.3} = 1.4$ **g)** $-\dfrac{x}{0.2} = 3.2$ **h)** $-\dfrac{x}{2.5} = 6.3$

Example 6

Solve the equation $\dfrac{3x}{4} = 6$.

                                                       $\dfrac{3x}{4} = 6$

1. Multiply both sides by 4. $3x = 6 \times 4 = 24$

2. Then divide both sides by 3. $x = 24 \div 3 = 8$

                                                     $\underline{x = 8}$

3 Solve the following equations.

    a) $\dfrac{4x}{3} = 12$ **b)** $\dfrac{2x}{5} = 6$ **c)** $\dfrac{6x}{7} = 12$ **d)** $\dfrac{5x}{6} = 3$

    e) $\dfrac{7x}{5} = 1.4$ **f)** $\dfrac{2x}{1.5} = -0.2$ **g)** $\dfrac{3x}{0.1} = -0.6$ **h)** $\dfrac{11x}{2.2} = 6.3$

Two-Step Equations

"Two-step equations" need to be solved in two stages — and you need to do them in the **right order**.

Example 7

Solve the equation $2x + 3 = 11$.

1. $2x + 3$ means "take your value of x and then: (i) multiply it by 2,
                                                       (ii) add 3".

    To get x on its own, "undo" these steps, but in the opposite order. $2x + 3 = 11$

2. First, subtract 3. $2x = 11 - 3 = 8$

3. Then divide by 2. $x = 8 \div 2 = 4$

4. Check your answer: $(2 \times 4) + 3 = 8 + 3 = 11$ $\underline{x = 4}$

Exercise 4

1 Solve the following two-step equations.

    a) $8x + 10 = 66$ **b)** $10x + 15 = 115$ **c)** $12x + 9 = 105$ **d)** $15x + 12 = 72$

    e) $20x + 86 = 6$ **f)** $25x + 140 = 15$ **g)** $27x + 99 = 18$ **h)** $35x + 80 = 10$

2 Solve the following equations.

    a) $16x - 6 = 10$ **b)** $15x - 8 = 22$ **c)** $14x - 17 = 25$ **d)** $28x - 14 = 42$

    e) $1.5x - 3 = -24$ **f)** $1.8x - 8 = -62$ **g)** $2.6x - 7 = -59$ **h)** $4.8x - 9 = -57$

3 Solve the following equations.

    a) $6x - 12 = 48$ **b)** $8x + 15 = 71$ **c)** $10x - 7 = 73$ **d)** $12x + 8 = 44$

    e) $18x - 6 = -60$ **f)** $20x - 12 = -132$ **g)** $4x + 12 = -8$ **h)** $2x + 9 = -2$

4 The expression $\frac{x}{2} - 1$ means: (i) divide x by 2,   (ii) subtract 1.

    "Undo" these two steps in the opposite order to solve the equation: $\frac{x}{2} - 1 = 3$

5 Solve the following equations

    a) $\frac{x}{2} + 1 = 7$ **b)** $\frac{x}{3} - 2 = 2$ **c)** $\frac{x}{6} + 4 = 16$ **d)** $\frac{x}{10} - 3 = -1$

    e) $\frac{x}{4} - 5 = -9$ **f)** $\frac{x}{2} - 1 = 3.5$ **g)** $\frac{x}{5} + 3 = -5$ **h)** $\frac{x}{7} - 8 = -11$

6 **a)** Write down the equation you get if you add $5x$ to both sides of the equation $20 - 5x = 10$.

    b) Solve your equation to find x.

7 Solve the following equations.

    a) $12 - 4x = 8$ **b)** $47 - 9x = 11$ **c)** $8 - 7x = 22$ **d)** $17 - 10x = 107$

Example 8

Solve the equation $8(x + 2) = 36$.

There are two ways to do this — you'll get the same result both ways.

Either:

1. $8(x + 2)$ means: "add 2 to x, then multiply by 8". $8(x + 2) = 36$
2. So to find x, first divide by 8. $x + 2 = 36 \div 8 = 4.5$
3. And then subtract 2. $x = 4.5 - 2 = 2.5$

                                           $\underline{x = 2.5}$

Or:

1. Multiply out the brackets. $8x + 16 = 36$
2. Subtract 16. $8x = 36 - 16 = 20$
3. And then divide by 8. $x = 20 \div 8 = 2.5$

                                           $\underline{x = 2.5}$

Exercise 5

1 Solve the following equations.

   a) $7(x + 4) = 63$ **b)** $8(x + 4) = 88$ **c)** $11(x + 3) = 132$ **d)** $14(x + 5) = 98$

   e) $16(x - 3) = -80$ **f)** $13(x - 4) = -91$ **g)** $14(x - 2) = -98$ **h)** $18(x - 3) = -180$

   i) $2.5(x + 4) = 30$ **j)** $1.5(x + 2) = 12$ **k)** $3.5(x + 6) = 63$ **l)** $4.5(x + 3) = 72$

   m) $7.5(x - 4) = 60$ **n)** $4.2(x - 5) = 63$ **o)** $12.5(x - 4) = 75$ **p)** $6.5(x - 6) = 78$

   q) $98 = 7(2 - x)$ **r)** $165 = 15(4 - x)$ **s)** $315 = 21(6 - x)$ **t)** $171 = 4.5(8 - x)$

9.2   Solving Harder Equations

Sometimes equations have an 'unknown' on both sides.

Example 1

Solve the equation $5x + 6 = 2x + 18$.

1. First subtract $2x$ from both sides.
   This leaves x on only one side of the equation.

2. Now you can solve the equation as before.
   Subtract 6 from both sides...
   ...and then divide by 3.

3. Remember to check your answer:
   $(5 \times 4) + 6 = 26$ and $(2 \times 4) + 18 = 26$.

$5x + 6 = 2x + 18$

$3x + 6 = 18$

$3x = 12$

$x = 12 \div 3$

$\underline{x = 4}$

Exercise 1

1 Solve these equations. Start by subtracting a multiple of x from both sides.

   a) $6x - 4 = 2x + 16$ **b)** $17x - 2 = 7x + 8$ **c)** $9x - 26 = 5x - 14$

   d) $10x - 5 = 3x + 9$ **e)** $14x - 7 = 6x + 41$ **f)** $15x - 12 = 6x + 15$

   g) $8x - 4 = 2x + 44$ **h)** $15x - 8 = 4x + 47$ **i)** $21x - 5 = 5x + 11$

2 Solve the following equations. Start by adding a multiple of x to both sides.

   a) $13x - 35 = 45 - 3x$ **b)** $20x - 18 = 54 - 16x$ **c)** $17x - 9 = 57 - 5x$

   d) $14x - 9 = 31 - 6x$ **e)** $6x - 12 = 51 - 3x$ **f)** $5x - 13 = 87 - 5x$

   g) $82 - 8x = 10 - 6x$ **h)** $7x - 8 = 70 - 6x$ **i)** $4x - 15 = 147 - 14x$

3 Solve the following equations.

   a) $4x - 3 = 0.5 - 3x$ **b)** $10x - 18 = 10.2 + 4x$ **c)** $4x + 9 = 6 - x$

   d) $6x - 2 = -18 - 2x$ **e)** $11x - 1 = 5.3 + 2x$ **f)** $2x - 2 = -11.6 - 2x$

   g) $56 - 7x = -48 + 6x$ **h)** $4x - 8.6 = 48.1 - 5x$ **i)** $-x + 1 = 28 + 2x$

Example 2

Solve the equation $4(x + 2) = 2(x + 6)$.

1. Multiply out the brackets.

2. Now you can solve the equation as before.

3. Remember to check your answer:
   $4 \times (2 + 2) = 16$ and $2 \times (2 + 6) = 16$.

$$4(x + 2) = 2(x + 6)$$
$$4x + 8 = 2x + 12$$
$$2x + 8 = 12$$
$$2x = 4$$
$$\underline{x = 2}$$

Exercise 2

1 Solve the following equations by first multiplying out the brackets.

a) $3(x + 2) = x + 14$

b) $9(x - 1) = x + 15$

c) $6(x + 2) = 3x + 48$

d) $5(x + 3) = 2x + 57$

e) $7(x - 2) = 2x + 36$

f) $10(x + 2) = 5x + 90$

g) $8(x - 8) = 2(x - 2)$

h) $6(x - 3) = 3(x + 8)$

i) $20(x - 2) = 5(x + 1)$

2 Solve the following equations.

a) $5(x - 5) = 2(x - 14)$

b) $4(x - 3) = 2(x - 8)$

c) $6(x - 2) = 3(x + 6)$

d) $6(x - 1.5) = 2(x - 3.5)$

e) $7(x - 2.5) = 14(x - 3)$

f) $9(x - 3.3) = -6(x + 1.7)$

g) $-4(x - 3) = 8(0.7 - x)$

h) $6(x - 1) = 4(6.2 - 2x)$

i) $8(x + 3) = 9(12.3 - x)$

3 Solve the following equations.

a) $4(2x + 1) = 2x + 34$

b) $11(3x - 5) = 5x - 195$

c) $5(4x - 1) = 2x + 7$

d) $5(6x - 2) = 2(2x - 31)$

e) $7(3x + 2) = 5(9x - 0.08)$

f) $7(2x + \frac{1}{7}) = 14(3x - 0.5)$

g) $10(x - 2) = -2(\frac{4}{3} + 7x)$

h) $4(3x - 3) = -2(\frac{76}{9} + 5x)$

Example 3

Solve the equation $\frac{x}{3} = 7 - 2x$.

1. Multiply both sides by 3.

2. Then solve in the normal way.

3. Remember to check your answer.

$$\frac{x}{3} = 7 - 2x$$
$$x = 3(7 - 2x)$$
$$x = 21 - 6x$$
$$7x = 21$$
$$\underline{x = 3}$$

Exercise 3

1 Solve the following equations. Start by multiplying both sides by a number.

a) $\frac{x}{4} = 1 - x$

b) $\frac{x}{3} = 8 - x$

c) $\frac{x}{5} = 11 - 2x$

d) $\frac{x}{2} = 5 - x$

e) $\frac{x}{6} = 1 - 2x$

f) $\frac{x}{3} = x + 4$

g) $\frac{x}{4} = 10 - x$

h) $\frac{x}{5} = x + 4$

i) $\frac{x}{5} = -22 - 2x$

2 Solve the following equations.

a) $\frac{x}{3} = 2(x - 5)$

b) $\frac{x}{2} = 4(x - 7)$

c) $\frac{x}{5} = 2(x + 9)$

d) $\frac{x}{2} = 2(x + 5)$

e) $\frac{x}{4} = -2(x + 18)$

f) $\frac{x}{4} = 3(x - 55)$

Example 4

Solve the equation $\frac{x - 2}{2} = \frac{6 - x}{6}$.

1. Cross-multiply — multiply the top of each fraction by the bottom of the other.
    (This is the same as first multiplying both sides by 2 and then multiplying both sides by 6.)

    $$\frac{x - 2}{2} = \frac{6 - x}{6}$$

    $$6(x - 2) = 2(6 - x)$$
    $$6x - 12 = 12 - 2x$$

2. Then solve in the normal way.

    $$8x = 24$$

3. Remember to check your answer.

    $$\underline{x = 3}$$

Exercise 4

1 Solve the following equations.

a) $\frac{x + 4}{2} = \frac{x + 10}{3}$

b) $\frac{x + 2}{2} = \frac{x + 4}{6}$

c) $\frac{x + 3}{4} = \frac{x + 9}{7}$

d) $\frac{x - 2}{3} = \frac{x + 4}{5}$

e) $\frac{x - 3}{4} = \frac{x + 2}{8}$

f) $\frac{x - 6}{5} = \frac{x + 3}{8}$

2 Solve the following equations.

a) $\frac{x - 17}{4} = \frac{8 - x}{5}$

b) $\frac{x - 2}{4} = \frac{15 - 2x}{3}$

c) $\frac{x - 4}{6} = \frac{12 - 3x}{2}$

d) $\frac{x - 6}{2} = \frac{8 - 2x}{4}$

e) $\frac{x - 9}{2} = \frac{2 - 3x}{4}$

f) $\frac{x - 12}{6} = \frac{4 - 2x}{3}$

Exercise 5 — Mixed Exercise

Solve the following.

1 **a)** $24x - 3 = -21$

b) $32x - 8 = -16$

c) $35x - 14 = -42$

d) $45x - 7 = -52$

e) $7 - 6x = 43$

f) $14 - 8x = 46$

g) $8 - 3x = 47$

h) $10 - 2.5x = 27.5$

i) $5.5x + 0.8 = 7.2$

2 **a)** $12(x - 3) = 4x + 92$

b) $15(x - 4) = 6x + 21$

c) $9(x - 4) = 4(x + 6)$

d) $7(x - 2) = 3(2 - x)$

e) $9(x - 1) = 3(-8 - x)$

f) $12(x - 2) = 4(3 - x)$

3 **a)** $\frac{x}{2} = 5$

b) $\frac{x}{3} = 18$

c) $\frac{x}{12} = 3.7$

d) $\frac{x}{7} = 1.8$

4 **a)** $\frac{3x}{7} = x + 4$

b) $\frac{2x}{3} = 4 - 5x$

c) $\frac{x}{4} = 2(4.5 - x)$

d) $\frac{5x}{2} = 2(6.75 - x)$

5 **a)** $\frac{x + 5}{3} = \frac{x + 9}{2}$

b) $\frac{x + 7}{3} = \frac{x + 13}{6}$

c) $\frac{7x + 3}{2} = \frac{x + 19}{4}$

9.3 Writing Your Own Equations

Sometimes you'll need to write your own equation based on a description of a situation.
Always read the question very carefully. And always **simplify** your equations as much as possible.

Example 1

I think of a number, double it, and add 3. The result equals 17.
What is the number I thought of?

1. You don't know what the number is yet.   Call the number x.

2. Doubling x gives $2x$.   Then: $2x + 3 = 17$
   Then adding 3 gives $2x + 3$.
   The result is 17.
                                              So: $2x = 14$
3. Solve the equation in the normal way. $x = 14 \div 2$
   Then check your answer. $\underline{x = 7}$

Exercise 1

1 Which number did I think of in each situation below?
"*I think of a number, and then...*"

   a) ...I add 5 to it. The result equals 12.   **b)** ...I add 8 to it. The result equals 23.
   c) ...I subtract 12 from it. The result equals 7.   **d)** ...I subtract 14 from it. The result equals 15.
   e) ...I multiply it by 2. The result equals 22.   **f)** ...I multiply it by 6. The result equals 54.
   g) ...I divide it by 3. The result equals 12.   **h)** ...I divide it by 7. The result equals 16.

2 Which number did I think of in each situation below?
"*I think of a number, and then...*"

   a) ...I double it, and then add 3. The result equals 19.
   b) ...I multiply it by 3, and then add 7. The result equals 43.
   c) ...I multiply it by 2, and then subtract 5. The result equals 15.
   d) ...I multiply it by 4, and then subtract 10. The result equals 44.

Example 2

Use the triangle to write an equation involving x.
Solve your equation to find x.

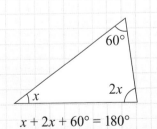

1. The angles in a triangle always add up to 180°. $x + 2x + 60° = 180°$

2. Simplify your equation. $3x + 60° = 180°$

3. Solve the equation in the normal way. $3x = 180° - 60° = 120°$
   Then check your answer. $x = 120° \div 3$

                                                      $\underline{x = 40°}$

Exercise 2

1 For each triangle below:

    (i) Write an equation involving x. (All the angles are measured in degrees.)

    (ii) Solve your equation to find x.

a)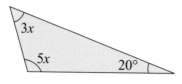

b)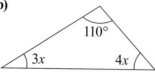

c)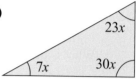

d)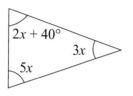

e)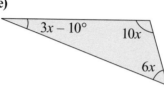

f)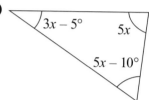

Example 3

The perimeter of this rectangle is 78 cm.

Write an equation involving x to show this.
Then solve your equation to find x.

$(x + 12)$ cm

$(x + 3)$ cm

1. Find the perimeter by adding together the lengths of all the sides. This must equal 78.

    Perimeter $= (x + 12) + (x + 3) + (x + 12) + (x + 3)$
                $= 4x + 30$

    So $4x + 30 = 78$.

2. Solve the equation in the normal way. Then check your answer.

    $4x = 78 - 30 = 48$

    $x = 48 \div 4$

    $\underline{x = 12}$

---

2 For each shape below:

    (i) Write an equation involving x.

    (ii) Solve your equation to find x.

a)
    $4x$ cm

    Perimeter $= 146$ cm $(x + 8)$ cm

b)
    $(x + 10)$ cm

    Perimeter $= 196$ cm $(x + 3)$ cm

3 The length of each side of this regular hexagon is $(x + 4)$ cm, and the total perimeter is 180 cm.

    a) Write an equation involving x.

    b) Solve your equation to find the value of x.

4 A regular octagon has a perimeter of 320 cm. Each side measures $(2x + 4)$ cm. Find the value of x.

9.4 Solving Inequalities

Write **inequalities** using these symbols:
> greater than   ≥ greater than or equal to
< less than   ≤ less than or equal to

Solving inequalities is very similar to solving equations. Your answer will also be an inequality.

Example 1

Show the following inequalities on a number line: a) $x > 1$ b) $x \leq 1$

The empty circle shows 1 is **not** included —
$x = 1$ does **not** make the inequality true.

a)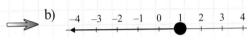

The solid circle shows 1 **is** included —
$x = 1$ **does** make the inequality true.

b)

Exercise 1

1 Insert $>$ or $<$ in each of the boxes to complete the following inequalities.

a) 6 ☐ 1   **b)** 2 ☐ 8   **c)** −1 ☐ −3   **d)** −7 ☐ 1

2 Describe in words what is meant by the following inequalities.

a) $x \geq 1$ **b)** $x < 7$ **c)** $x > -4$ **d)** $x \leq 9$
e) $x < 8$ **f)** $x \leq -5$ **g)** $x \geq 3$ **h)** $x > -4$

3 Write each of the following as an inequality.

a) x is greater than 4   **b)** x is less than or equal to 12
c) x is greater than or equal to 8   **d)** x is less than 3

4 Show the following inequalities on a number line.

a) $x \geq 12$ **b)** $x < 22$ **c)** $x > -6$ **d)** $x \leq -3$
e) $x < 18$ **f)** $x > -25$ **g)** $x \leq 34$ **h)** $x < 45$
i) $x \geq 57$ **j)** $x < 65$ **k)** $x \geq -7$ **l)** $x \leq -4$

Example 2

Solve the inequalities: a) $x + 4 < 8$ b) $x - 7 \geq 2$
Show your solutions on a number line.

1. You need to get x on its own on one side. But you must always do the same to both sides of an inequality.

a) $x + 4 < 8$
$x + 4 - 4 < 8 - 4$
$\underline{x < 4}$

2. If the question uses < or >, so will your answer. If the question uses ≤ or ≥, so will your answer.

b) $x - 7 \geq 2$
$x - 7 + 7 \geq 2 + 7$
$\underline{x \geq 9}$

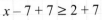

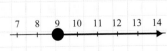

Exercise 2

1 Solve the following inequalities. Show each of your solutions on a number line.

a) $x + 9 > 14$ b) $x + 3 \leq 12$ c) $x - 2 \geq 14$ d) $x - 7 < 19$

e) $x - 13 \geq 17$ f) $x + 5 > 2$ g) $x - 5 < -3$ h) $x + 1 \leq -1$

2 Solve the following inequalities.

a) $x - 9 > 8$ b) $x + 7 < 17$ c) $x + 4 \geq 5$ d) $x - 2 \leq 11$

e) $x + 16 \geq 20$ f) $x - 4 > 9$ g) $x + 12 < -18$ h) $x - 8 \leq -3$

Example 3

Solve the inequality $2 > x - 5$. Show your solution on a number line.

1. This time x is on the right-hand side of the inequality. But as before, just do the same to both sides (so here, add 5).

    $2 > x - 5$

    $2 + 5 > x - 5 + 5$

2. So $7 > x$ (that is, '7 is greater than x').

    $7 > x$

3. To move x to the left-hand side, you have to swap the direction that the inequality points (showing that 'x is less than 7').

    <u>$x < 7$</u>

---

3 This question is about the inequality $6 > x$.

a) Describe in words what is meant by this inequality.

b) Rewrite the inequality by completing the following: $x \boxed{} 6$

c) Show the solution to this inequality on a number line.

4 Rewrite each of these inequalities with x on the left-hand side.

a) $12 \geq x$ b) $4 < x$ c) $15 \leq x$ d) $14 > x$

5 Solve the following inequalities. Show each of your solutions on a number line.

a) $18 < x + 2$ b) $12 \leq x - 4$ c) $1 > x - 17$ d) $31 \geq x + 30$

Example 4

Solve the following inequalities: a) $4x < 12$ b) $\frac{x}{3} \geq 5$

1. Do the same to both sides of an inequality.   a) $4x < 12$ b) $\frac{x}{3} \geq 5$

2. Multiplying or dividing by a positive number doesn't change the direction of the inequality sign. $4x \div 4 < 12 \div 4$ $\frac{x}{3} \times 3 \geq 5 \times 3$

    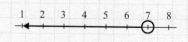

    <u>$x < 3$</u>   <u>$x \geq 15$</u>

---

6 Solve the following inequalities by dividing both sides by a positive number.

a) $3x \geq 9$ b) $5x < 25$ c) $2x > 8$ d) $7x \leq 21$

e) $4x < -16$ f) $9x > -72$ g) $11x \leq 33$ h) $2x < 45$

i) $6x \geq 57$ j) $2x < 15$ k) $4x \geq -32$ l) $2x \leq -1.5$

7 Solve the following inequalities by multiplying both sides by a positive number.

a) $\frac{x}{2} \geq 3$ b) $\frac{x}{5} < 2$ c) $\frac{x}{3} < 8$ d) $\frac{x}{7} \leq 5$

e) $\frac{x}{8} < -1$ f) $\frac{x}{6} \leq 0.5$ g) $\frac{x}{1.1} \geq 10$ h) $\frac{x}{0.2} < -3.2$

i) $\frac{x}{5.5} < 1.2$ j) $\frac{x}{4} \geq -0.3$ k) $\frac{x}{0.1} \leq 1.8$ l) $\frac{x}{0.3} < -2.3$

Example 5

Solve the following inequalities: a) $2x + 4 > 10$ b) $\frac{x+4}{2} \leq 3$

1. Solve these in the same way that you'd solve two-step equations.

2. In a), first subtract 4, then divide by 2.
   In b), first multiply by 2, then subtract 4.

a) $2x + 4 > 10$

$2x > 6$

$\underline{x > 3}$

b) $\frac{x+4}{2} \leq 3$

$x + 4 \leq 6$

$\underline{x \leq 2}$

Solve each of the inequalities in **Questions 8-10**.

8   a) $4x + 11 < 23$ b) $5x + 3 \leq 43$ c) $3x - 7 \geq -1$ d) $7x - 12 > 65$

e) $2x + 16 \geq -8$ f) $9x - 14 > -5$ g) $8x - 4.2 < 12.6$ h) $4x + 2.6 \leq 28.6$

9   a) $\frac{x+2}{3} < 1$ b) $\frac{x+4}{5} \geq 2$ c) $\frac{x-8}{2} > 7$ d) $\frac{x-8}{4} \leq 0.5$

10   a) $\frac{x}{4} - 2.5 \geq 1$ b) $\frac{x}{2} + 5.5 > 7$ c) $\frac{x}{8} - 3.1 < -1$ d) $\frac{x}{3.2} + 1.3 \leq 5$

Compound Inequalities

A compound inequality is like "two inequalities in one".
For example, $3 < x \leq 9$ means that **both** the following are true: $3 < x$ **and** $x \leq 9$.

So $3 < x \leq 9$ means: x is between 3 and 9 (including 9, but not including 3).

Example 6

Show the inequality $2 \leq x < 4$ on a number line.

1. Write down the two separate inequalities.

2. Find the number x is greater than...
   ...and the number x is less than.

3. Draw the number line. Here, x is between 2 and 4 (including 2, but not including 4).

$2 \leq x < 4$ means $2 \leq x$ and $x < 4$.

$2 \leq x$ is the same as $x \geq 2$
So $x \geq 2$ and $x < 4$.

Example 7

Solve the inequality $-1 < 2x + 2 < 4$. Show your solution on a number line.

1. Write down the two separate inequalities.

$-1 < 2x + 2$ and $2x + 2 < 4$
Or: $2x + 2 > -1$ and $2x + 2 < 4$

2. Solve the inequalities separately.

① $2x + 2 > -1$
$2x > -3$
$x > -1.5$

② $2x + 2 < 4$
$2x < 2$
$x < 1$

3. Draw the number line.

So $\underline{x > -1.5 \text{ and } x < 1}$.
Or you can write: $\underline{-1.5 < x < 1}$.

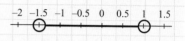

Exercise 3

1 Show the following inequalities on a number line.

a) $1 < x \le 6$
b) $12 \le x \le 15$
c) $-1 \le x < 8$
d) $25 \le x \le 30$
e) $4 \le x < 9$
f) $35 < x < 40$
g) $0 < x < 7$
h) $36 < x \le 42$
i) $-2.4 \le x < 1.6$

2 Solve the following inequalities. Show each of your solutions on a number line.

a) $7 < x + 3 \le 15$
b) $2 \le x - 4 \le 12$
c) $-1 \le x + 5 \le 4$
d) $21 \le x - 16 \le 44$
e) $5.1 \le x + 2.5 < 9.7$
f) $-5.6 < x - 6.8 < 12.9$

3 Solve the following inequalities.

a) $16 < 4x < 28$
b) $32 < 2x \le 42$
c) $-24 < 8x \le 40$
d) $27 < 4.5x \le 72$
e) $-22.5 \le 7.5x < 30$
f) $62.72 < 11.2x \le 94.08$

4 Solve the following inequalities.

a) $17 < 6x + 5 < 29$
b) $8 < 3x - 4 \le 26$
c) $-42 < 7x + 7 \le 91$
d) $9 < 1.5x + 3 \le 9.9$
e) $-18.8 \le 10x + 14.2 < -6.8$
f) $61.7 < 12x - 6.3 \le 101.7$

Exercise 4 — Mixed Exercise

Solve the following inequalities.

1 a) $x + 7 > 22$
b) $x - 6 \le 14$
c) $x + 11 \ge 17$
d) $x - 7 < 21$
e) $x + 5.6 \le 14.6$
f) $x - 6.23 \ge 9.75$
g) $x + 7.01 < 33.25$
h) $x + 11.08 > 21.82$

2 a) $4x \ge 84$
b) $3x < 28.5$
c) $9x \ge -56$
d) $6x \le -5.4$
e) $\frac{x}{2} \le 6$
f) $\frac{x}{3} > 25$
g) $\frac{x}{5} \ge -4$
h) $\frac{x}{4} < -16$

3 a) $5x + 12 < 37$
b) $11x + 7 \le -15$
c) $21x - 33 \ge -12$
d) $4x - 5 > 2$
e) $4x + 11 < 11$
f) $12x - 3 \le -8$
g) $17x + 8 \ge -9$
h) $4.6x - 5.6 > 2.3$

4 a) $\frac{x + 5}{5} < 5$
b) $\frac{x - 5.6}{3} \ge 6$
c) $\frac{x}{3} - 4 \le 6.2$
d) $\frac{x}{4} + 3.7 > 8.4$

5 a) $-2 < 2x + 3 < 5$
b) $-30 < 7x + 12 \le 61$
c) $-9 < 13x - 9 \le 17$
d) $-12 < 5x + 3 \le 58$

9.5 Trial and Improvement

Some equations are best solved by **trial and improvement**.

This involves trying out a value for x and seeing if it satisfies the equation.
If it doesn't, then you try other values for x.

By choosing the values to try carefully, you can quickly get close to the correct solution.

Example 1

The area (in cm²) of the rectangle on the right is $x(x + 1) = x^2 + x$.
The rectangle's area is 30 cm².

Use trial and improvement to find x.

$(x + 1)$ cm

Area = 30 cm² x cm

1. Try out some possible values for x.
   Here, $x = 3$ is too small.
   But $x = 6$ is too big.
   So x must be between 3 and 6.

2. Now try other values between 3 and 6.
   Try $x = 5$. This works — this is the solution.

3. So here, you could find the exact solution
   using trial and improvement.

Need to solve: $x^2 + x = 30$

Try $x = 3$:
$3^2 + 3 = 9 + 3 = 12$ — too small
Try $x = 6$:
$6^2 + 6 = 36 + 6 = 42$ — too big
Try $x = 5$:
$5^2 + 5 = 25 + 5 = 30$ — the solution

So **$x = 5$**.

Exercise 1

1 Solve the following equations by trial and improvement.

   a) $x^2 + 2x = 35$ **b)** $x^2 + 3x = 28$ **c)** $x^2 + 4x = 96$ **d)** $x^2 + 5x = 176$

   e) $x^2 + 6x = 91$ **f)** $x^2 + 7x = 170$ **g)** $x^2 + 8x = -7$ **h)** $x^2 + 9x = -8$

2 For this rectangle, x satisfies the equation $x^2 + 8x = 105$.

   a) Use trial and improvement to find the value of x.

   b) Find the lengths of the sides of the rectangle.

$(x + 8)$ cm

Area = $(x^2 + 8x)$ cm²
= 105 cm²

x cm

3 Solve the following equations by trial and improvement.

   a) $x^3 + x = 30$ **b)** $x^3 + 5x = 18$ **c)** $x^3 + 3x = 76$ **d)** $x^3 + 2x = 357$

4 A ball is thrown upwards from the ground.
   After x seconds, its height (h) in metres is given by the formula $h = 50x - 5x^2$.
   It starts to fall back to the ground after 5 seconds.

   a) After how many seconds does the ball first reach a height of 105 metres?

   b) How many seconds after it's thrown does the ball reach a height of
   105 metres for the second time?

Example 2

The area (in cm²) of the rectangle on the right is $x(x + 1) = x^2 + x$.
The rectangle's area is 18 cm².

The value of x lies between 3 and 4.
Give the solution correct to one decimal place.

$(x + 1)$ cm

Area = 18 cm² x cm

1. Try out some possible values for x.
   Here, $x = 3.5$ is too small.
   And $x = 3.7$ is also too small.
   But $x = 3.8$ is too big.
   So x must be between 3.7 and 3.8.

2. Now try $x = 3.75$ — this is too small.

3. This means x lies between 3.7 and 3.8,
   but is closer to 3.8 — so 3.8 is the answer
   correct to 1 decimal place.

Need to solve: $x^2 + x = 18$

Try $x = 3.5$:
$3.5^2 + 3.5 = 15.75$ — too small.

Try $x = 3.7$:
$3.7^2 + 3.7 = 17.39$ — too small.

Try $x = 3.8$:
$3.8^2 + 3.8 = 18.24$ — too big.

Try $x = 3.75$:
$3.75^2 + 3.75 = 17.8125$ — too small.

So $\underline{x = \mathbf{3.8}}$ *(to 1 d.p.)*

Exercise 2

1 A solution to the equation $x^2 + x = 10$ lies between 2 and 3.

  a) Evaluate $x^2 + x$ for $x = 2.5$.

  b) Is the solution to $x^2 + x = 10$ greater than or less than 2.5?

  c) State whether the solution to $x^2 + x = 10$ is greater than or less than the following.

  (i) 2.6   **(ii)** 2.7   **(iii)** 2.8

  d) By evaluating $x^2 + x$ for one more value of x, find the solution to the equation $x^2 + x = 10$ correct to 1 decimal place.

2 Use trial and improvement to solve the following. Give your answers to 1 decimal place.

  a) Find the solution to $x^2 + 2x = 30$ that lies between 4 and 5.

  b) Find the solution to $x^2 + 3x = 16$ that lies between 2 and 3.

  c) Find the solution to $x^2 + 4x = 100$ that lies between 8 and 9.

  d) Find the solution to $x^2 - 6x = 130$ that lies between 14 and 15.

3 The following equations all have a solution between $x = 0$ and $x = 10$.
   Find this solution correct to 1 decimal place.

  a) $x^2 + x = 23$ **b)** $x^2 + 2x = 17$ **c)** $x^2 + 5x = 62$ **d)** $x^2 + 8x = 95$

4 The rectangle on the right has an area of 100 cm².

  a) Write down an equation involving x
     for the area of the rectangle in cm².

  b) Use trial and improvement to find x, correct to 1 decimal place.

  c) Find the lengths of the sides of the rectangle.

$(x + 7)$ cm

x cm

5 These equations have a solution between 0 and 5. Find these solutions correct to 1 decimal place.

  a) $x^3 + 3x = 20$ **b)** $x^3 - 4x = 52$ **c)** $x^3 + 6x = 17$ **d)** $x - x^3 = -0.17$

6 A cannonball is fired upwards from the ground. After x seconds, its height (h) in metres is given by the formula $h = 100x - 5x^2$. It starts to fall back to the ground after 10 seconds.

a) After how many seconds does the ball first reach a height of 200 metres?
Give your answer correct to 1 decimal place.

b) After how many seconds does the ball first reach a height of 400 metres?
Give your answer correct to 1 decimal place.

c) As it falls back down to the ground, it reaches a height of 200 metres for a second time.
Find the number of seconds after being fired that it reaches this height.
Give your answer correct to 1 decimal place.

Example 3

A solution to the equation $x^2 + 6x = 50$ lies between 4.6 and 4.7.
Give this solution correct to two decimal places (d.p.).

1. Since the solution lies between 4.6 and 4.7, try $x = 4.65$.

   Try $x = 4.65$:
   $4.65^2 + 6 \times 4.65 = 49.5225$ — too small.

   Try $x = 4.68$:
   $4.68^2 + 6 \times 4.68 = 49.9824$ — too small.

2. Eventually, you find that x lies between 4.68 and 4.69.

   Try $x = 4.69$:
   $4.69^2 + 6 \times 4.69 = 50.1361$ — too big.

   Try $x = 4.685$:
   $4.685^2 + 6 \times 4.685 = 50.059...$ — too big.

3. So try $x = 4.685$. Since this is too big, the solution must be closer to 4.68.

   So $\underline{x = 4.68}$ *(to 2 d.p.)*

Exercise 3

1 A solution to the equation $x^2 + x = 14$ lies between 3.2 and 3.3.

a) Evaluate $x^2 + x$ for $x = 3.25$.

b) Is the solution to $x^2 + x = 14$ greater than or less than 3.25?

c) State whether the solution to $x^2 + x = 14$ is greater than or less than the following.

   (i) 3.27   **(ii)** 3.28

d) By evaluating $x^2 + x$ for one more value of x, determine whether the solution to the equation $x^2 + x = 14$ is closer to 3.27 or 3.28.

e) Hence give the solution of the equation $x^2 + x = 14$ correct to 2 decimal places.

2 Use trial and improvement to solve the following. Give your answers to 2 decimal places.

a) Find the solution to $x^2 + 2x = 30$ that lies between 4.5 and 4.6.

b) Find the solution to $x^2 + 3x = 16$ that lies between 2.7 and 2.8.

c) Find the solution to $x^3 + 4x = 45$ that lies between 3.1 and 3.2.

d) Find the solution to $x^3 - 6x = 152$ that lies between 5.7 and 5.8.

9.6 Equations and Inequalities Problems

Exercise 1

1 Solve the following equations.

a) $\dfrac{x+8}{3} = 4$ b) $\dfrac{x-5}{6} = 5$ c) $\dfrac{x-2.5}{7} = 3$ d) $\dfrac{x+6}{5} = 4.2$

e) $9 + 5x = 54$ f) $12 - 6x = 84$ g) $30 + 7x = 9$ h) $13 - 3.5x = 34$

i) $\dfrac{x+3}{5} = -12$ j) $\dfrac{x-3}{7} = -5$ k) $24 - 8x = -16$ l) $17 - 12x = 149$

2 Solve the following equations.

a) $72 = 4.5(8 + 2x)$ b) $7(x-3) = 3(x-6)$ c) $6(x-2) = 4(x-3)$

d) $12(x+3) = 6(x+15)$ e) $108 = 6(2-x)$ f) $9x - 144 = 42 + 15x$

g) $5x - 9 = 54 - 8x$ h) $12(x-3) = 4(6+2x)$ i) $12(4x-3) = 4(2x+1)$

3 Solve the following equations.

a) $\dfrac{x-2}{5} = \dfrac{9-x}{3}$ b) $\dfrac{x-5}{6} = \dfrac{12-3x}{4}$ c) $\dfrac{x-7}{8} = \dfrac{15-4x}{6}$

d) $\dfrac{x}{7} = 10 - 3x$ e) $\dfrac{3x}{8} = 16 + 3x$ f) $\dfrac{2x}{5} = 18 - 2x$

4 An electrician charges £x for each hour worked plus a £35 call-out charge. He does a job lasting 4 hours for which his total bill is £170. How much does the electrician charge per hour?

5 Jane bought 7 cereal bars costing x pence each. She also bought 4 cans of drink for 45p each. The total cost was £4.25. How much does each cereal bar cost?

6 a) Use the triangle to write an equation involving x.

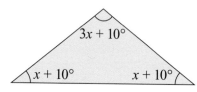

b) Use your equation to find the sizes of the triangle's angles.

7 Find the sizes of this triangle's angles.

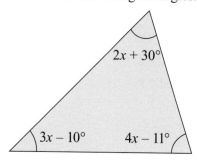

8 The perimeter of this rectangle is 158 cm. What is the value of x?

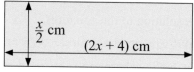

9 The perimeter of this rectangle is 191 m. Find the value of x.

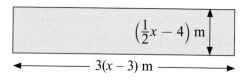

10 The area of this rectangle is 12 cm². Find x.

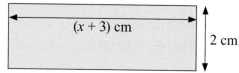

Exercise 2

1 Solve the following inequalities. Show each of your solutions on a number line.

 a) $x - 8 > 17$ **b)** $x - 11 \le -3$ **c)** $x + 24 \ge 6$ **d)** $x + 7 > -3$

 e) $x + 2.7 \ge 6.2$ **f)** $x + 6.9 < -3.1$ **g)** $x - 6.2 \le 81.6$ **h)** $x - 3.25 < -7.48$

 i) $\frac{x}{7} \ge 4$ **j)** $7x < 84$ **k)** $\frac{x}{9} < 7$ **l)** $6.5x \le 45.5$

 m) $5x \ge 35$ **n)** $\frac{x}{40} < 20$ **o)** $2.5x > 20$ **p)** $\frac{x}{2.5} \le 6$

2 Solve the following inequalities.

 a) $3x + 6 \le 39$ **b)** $8x - 7 \ge 33$ **c)** $9x - 6 < 111$ **d)** $18x + 24 > 132$

 e) $0.4x + 2.3 > 12.3$ **f)** $7 \le 33 - x$ **g)** $3x - 5 < -11$ **h)** $0.24x + 3.7 \ge 1.5$

3 Solve the following inequalities. Show each of your solutions on a number line.

 a) $70 < 13x + 5 \le 96$ **b)** $49 < 15x + 4 < 79$ **c)** $-5 \le 12x + 7 < 43$

 d) $-37 \le 7x + 12 \le -2$ **e)** $15 < 12x + 3 < 27$ **f)** $-17 < 6x + 7 \le 49$

4 Use trial and improvement to solve the following. Give your answers to 1 decimal place.

 a) Find the solution to $x^2 - 7x = 26$ that lies between 9 and 10.

 b) Find the solution to $x^2 - 8x = 30$ that lies between -3 and -2.

 c) Find the solution to $x^3 + 5x = 175$ that lies between 5 and 6.

 d) Find the solution to $x^3 - 3x = 1$ that lies between -2 and -1.

5 The area of this rectangular garden is 54 m². What is the value of x to 1 decimal place?

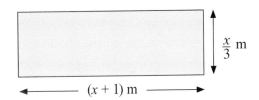

6 The solution to the equation $3^x = 50$ lies between 3 and 4.
Find x, correct to 1 decimal place.

7 **a)** The area of Sam's rectangular swimming pool (shown below) is 50 m². What is the value of x to 1 decimal place?

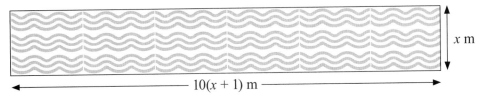

 b) Sam decides he needs a new swimming pool (shown on the right).

  Its area is given by the formula $A = 0.79(y^2 + 10y)$, but this pool has the same area as his rectangular pool.

  Find y, correct to 1 decimal place.

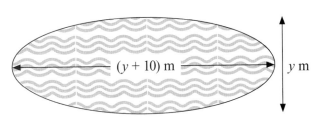

Section 10 — Formulas

10.1 Writing Formulas

A **formula** is like a set of instructions for working something out.
For example, $s = 4t + 3$ is a formula for s — it tells you how to find s, assuming you know the value of t.

The part after the equals sign is an **algebraic expression** — here, the algebraic expression involves t.

Example 1

Write an expression for the number of marbles I have in each case below.

a) I have a bag containing m marbles. I then lose 8 marbles.

    1. "I have a bag containing m marbles." m

    2. "I then lose 8 marbles" — so you need to subtract 8. $\underline{m - 8}$

b) My brother has 12 marbles, which is m marbles more than I own.

    1. "My brother has 12 marbles..."   12

    2. "...which is m marbles more than I own."
       This means I have m marbles less than my brother. $\underline{12 - m}$

Exercise 1

1   Write an algebraic expression for each of the quantities asked for below.

    a) I have c carrots. Su has 6 carrots more than me. How many carrots does Su have?

    b) Harry has s sugar cubes. Zurab takes 3 of them. How many sugar cubes does Harry now have?

    c) Daisy has p plants. Iris has 8 fewer plants. How many plants does Iris have?

    d) Elmer has r rabbits. Sam gives him 20 more rabbits. How many rabbits does Elmer have now?

2   Write an algebraic expression for each of the quantities asked for below.

    a) Genevieve has d daffodils, which is 8 more than Mariella has.
       How many daffodils does Mariella have?

    b) Jessica has 6 shirts, which is s more than Becky. How many shirts does Becky have?

    c) George spends m minutes on his maths homework, which is half as long as Chris.
       How many minutes does Chris spend on his homework?

    d) Emily has c chairs, which is 3 times more than Sara. How many chairs does Sara have?

Example 2

I have m marbles. I lose half of those marbles, but then someone gives me
6 of their marbles. Write an expression for how many marbles I have now.

    1. "I have m marbles." m

    2. "I lose half of those marbles" — so divide m by 2. $\dfrac{m}{2}$

    3. "...someone gives me 6 of their marbles" — so add 6. $\dfrac{m}{2} + 6$

---

3 Claudia owns f films. Barry owns twice as many films as Claudia.

    a) How many films does Barry own?

    b) How many films do Claudia and Barry own in total?

    c) How many films would they own in total if they each gave away 3 of their films?

4 I have b flower bulbs. To find the number of flowers that should grow from them, multiply the number of bulbs by 3 and then add 5. How many flowers can I expect?

5 Alf has £18. He then works in a shop for h hours. For each hour he works, he is paid £8. How much money (in pounds) does Alf have now?

6 To hire a go-kart, you have to pay: (i) 25p for each lap of the track you do (the variable charge)
                                  plus (ii) a fixed fee of £7

    I do n laps of the track.

    a) Write an expression for the cost (in pounds) of the variable charge.

    b) Write an expression for the total cost (in pounds) I will have to pay.

Example 3

Write a formula to show how much it costs to hire a boat for h hours if the total cost in pounds (C) is made up of: i)   a charge of £5 for each hour
                          plus   ii)   a fixed cost of £25

1. You need an expression showing the total cost.   Cost (in pounds) for 1 hour = 5
2. Multiply the number of hours (h) by 5.   → Cost (in pounds) for h hours $= h \times 5 = 5h$
   Then you need to add the fixed cost of £25. → Fixed cost (in pounds) = 25
3. A formula for C must start with "$C = ...$".   So $C = 5h + 25$

Exercise 2

1 It costs £3 per hour to park a car. Write a formula for the cost in pounds (C) to park for h hours.

2 It takes 2 minutes to drive 1 km. Write a formula for the time taken in minutes (T) to drive k km.

3 Tom gets paid w pounds for each hour he works in his local shop.
Write a formula for the total amount he gets paid in pounds (P) if he works for 8 hours.

4 Katie always eats 2 more apples for her pudding than Laura does.
Write a formula for the number of apples (n) that Katie eats if Laura eats a apples.

5 Sue runs r km, but Ellie runs 5 km less. Write a formula for the distance in km (d) that Ellie runs.

6 Write a formula for the cost in pounds (C) of hiring a minibus
for n hours if it costs £5.50 for each hour plus a fixed charge of £F.

7 Write a formula for the cost in pounds (C) of having t trees
cut down if it costs p pounds per tree plus a fixed amount of £25.

8 To hire a boat costs a £10 fixed fee plus 22 pence per mile for each mile covered.
Write a formula for finding the cost in pounds (C) of hiring a boat and covering m miles.

9 To hire a bouncy castle costs a £125 fixed fee plus 80 pence per minute it is used.
Write a formula for the cost in pounds (C) of hiring a bouncy castle for h hours.

10.2 Substituting into a Formula

Substituting numbers into a formula means replacing any letters with numbers.

Example 1

The area (A) of a rectangle is given by the formula $A = bh$.
Find the value of A when $b = 5$ and $h = 6$.

1. Write down the formula.
2. Replace each letter with its value, and carry out the calculation.

$$A = bh = b \times h$$
$$= 5 \times 6$$
$$= \underline{\mathbf{30}}$$

Exercise 1

1 Find the value of y in each of the following given that $x = 7$.

    a) $y = x + 4$ **b)** $y = x - 3$ **c)** $y = 12 - x$ **d)** $y = 6x$

2 Find the value of y in each of the following given that $m = -3$.

    a) $y = m - 8$ **b)** $y = m + 2$ **c)** $y = -4 + m$ **d)** $y = \dfrac{12}{m}$

3 If $x = 4$ and $y = 3$, then find the value of z in each of the following.

    a) $z = x + 2$ **b)** $z = y - 1$ **c)** $z = x + y$ **d)** $z = y - x$

    e) $z = 2x$ **f)** $z = 3y$ **g)** $z = 3y - 2$ **h)** $z = 6x - y$

4 The area (A, in cm²) of this rectangle is given by the formula $A = 6w$.
Find A for the values of w below.

    a) $w = 7$ **b)** $w = 8$ **c)** $w = 14$

    d) $w = 23$ **e)** $w = 37$ **f)** $w = 41$

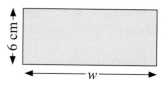

5 The temperature in degrees Fahrenheit (f) is given by the formula $f = 1.8c + 32$, where c is the temperature in degrees Celsius (°C).

Convert the following temperatures to degrees Fahrenheit.

    a) 15 °C   **b)** 6 °C   **c)** 24 °C   **d)** 100 °C

6 The formula for working out the speed (s, in metres per second) of a moving object is $s = \dfrac{d}{t}$, where d is the distance travelled (in metres) and t is the time taken (in seconds).
Find the speed (in metres per second) of each of the following.
(Give your answers to 3 significant figures.)

    a) a runner who travels 800 metres in 110 seconds

    b) a cheetah that travels 400 metres in 14 seconds

    c) a car that travels 1000 metres in 60 seconds

    d) a plane that travels 640 000 metres in 3600 seconds

    e) a satellite that travels 40 000 000 metres in 5000 seconds

Example 2

The sum of the first n square numbers is $1^2 + 2^2 + 3^2 + 4^2 + ... + n^2$.

This sum (S) is given by the formula $S = \frac{n}{6}(2n^2 + 3n + 1)$.

Use the formula to find S when $n = 10$.

1. Write down the formula.

$$S = \frac{n}{6}(2n^2 + 3n + 1)$$

2. Replace n with 10.

$$= \frac{10}{6}(2 \times 10^2 + 3 \times 10 + 1)$$

3. Remember BODMAS:
   Evaluate the brackets first.
   Inside the brackets: (i) Find 10^2 first.

$$= \frac{10}{6}(2 \times 100 + 3 \times 10 + 1)$$

   (ii) Then do the multiplications.
   (iii) Then do the additions.

$$= \frac{10}{6}(200 + 30 + 1) = \frac{10}{6} \times 231$$

   Now evaluate the rest.

$$S = \frac{10}{6} \times 231 = \underline{\mathbf{385}}$$

7 If $m = 4$ and $n = 3$, then find the value of p in each of the following.

    a) $p = mn$ **b)** $p = m^2$ **c)** $p = m - n^2$ **d)** $p = \frac{3m}{n}$

    e) $p = m(m - n)$ **f)** $p = n^2 + n$ **g)** $p = \frac{n}{m}$ **h)** $p = mn^2$

8 Use the formula $S = \frac{1}{2}n(n + 1)$ to find S when:

    a) $n = 10$ **b)** $n = 100$ **c)** $n = 1000$ **d)** $n = 5000$

Example 3

Use the formula $f = 1.8c + 32$ to find the temperature in degrees Fahrenheit (f) equivalent to the following temperatures in degrees Celsius (c).

a) $c = -17$ b) $c = 37.4$

1. Write down the formula.

    a) $f = 1.8c + 32$ b) $f = 1.8c + 32$

2. Replace each letter with its value, and do the calculation.

    $= 1.8 \times (-17) + 32$ $= 1.8 \times 37.4 + 32$

    $= -30.6 + 32 = \underline{\mathbf{1.4}}$ $= 67.32 + 32 = \underline{\mathbf{99.32}}$

9 If $a = -4$ and $b = -3$, then find the value of c in each of the following.

    a) $c = a - 4$ **b)** $c = b + a$ **c)** $c = 4b$ **d)** $c = 6b - a$

    e) $c = b^3$ **f)** $c = -\frac{4b}{3a}$ **g)** $c = 5a - b^2$ **h)** $c = 6a^2 - 2ab + 2b^2$

10 If $p = -4.8$ and $q = 3.2$, then find the value of r in each of the following.

    a) $r = p + 6.7$ **b)** $r = q - p$ **c)** $r = -4q$ **d)** $r = 8.4q - p$

    e) $r = -q^3$ **f)** $r = \frac{2.1q}{3.5p}$ **g)** $r = -3.2p + q^2$ **h)** $r = 4.1p^2 - 2.8pq$

11 Find the value of x in each of the following given that $r = \frac{3}{4}$ and $s = -\frac{1}{3}$.

  a) $x = 4r$ **b)** $x = -2s$ **c)** $x = \frac{s}{r}$ **d)** $x = rs$

  e) $x = r + s$ **f)** $x = r - s$ **g)** $x = 4r + s$ **h)** $x = 3s + 2r$

12 Use the formula $c = \frac{5}{9}(f - 32)$ to convert the following temperatures in degrees Fahrenheit (f) to degrees Celsius (c).

  a) 212 °F   **b)** 64.4 °F   **c)** −40 °F   **d)** 98.6 °F

13 The area (A, in cm²) of this circle is given by the formula $A = \pi r^2$.
Find A for the values of r below. Give your answers to 1 decimal place.

  a) $r = 5$ cm   **b)** $r = 3.5$ cm

  c) $r = 11.1$ cm   **d)** $r = 6.4$ cm

14 The number of seconds (T) taken for a pendulum to swing forwards and then backwards once is given by the formula $T = 2\pi\sqrt{\dfrac{l}{10}}$, where l is the length of the pendulum in metres.

Taking π to be 3.142, calculate (to 1 decimal place) how long it will take a pendulum to swing backwards and forwards once if:

  a) $l = 1$ metre   **b)** $l = 0.5$ metres   **c)** $l = 0.25$ metres   **d)** $l = 16$ metres

15 Use the formula $A = \frac{1}{2}bh$ to find the area (A, in m²) of a triangle with base b and height h, if:

  a) $b = 4$ m, $h = 6$ m   **b)** $b = 2$ m, $h = 3$ m   **c)** $b = 4$ m, $h = 6$ m   **d)** $b = 0.4$ m, $h = 1.8$ m

16 Find the volumes (V, in cm³) of the cylinders below, using the formula on the left.
Give your answers to 3 significant figures.

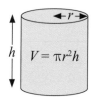
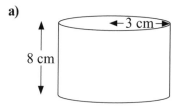
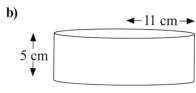

17 Find the volumes (V, in cm³) of the cones below, using the formula on the left.
Give your answers to 3 significant figures.

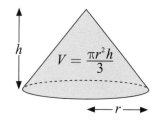
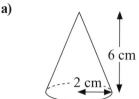
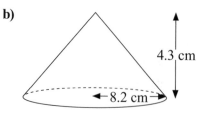

Example 4

Use the formula $v = u + at$ to find v if $u = 2.6$, $a = -18.3$ and $t = 4.9$.

1. You have three values to substitute this time — u, a and t.
2. Replace each letter with its value...
3. ...and carry out the calculation.

$$v = u + at$$
$$= 2.6 + (-18.3 \times 4.9)$$
$$= 2.6 + (-89.67)$$
$$= \underline{\mathbf{-87.07}}$$

18 Use the formula $v = u + at$ to find v if:

   a) $u = 3$, $a = 7$ and $t = 5$
   b) $u = 12$, $a = 17$ and $t = 15$
   c) $u = 2.3$, $a = 4.1$ and $t = 3.4$
   d) $u = 5.25$, $a = 9.81$ and $t = 4.39$
   e) $u = 3$, $a = -10$ and $t = 5.6$
   f) $u = -34$, $a = -1.37$ and $t = 63.25$

19 Use the formula $s = ut + \frac{1}{2}at^2$ to find s if:

   a) $u = 7$, $a = 2$ and $t = 4$
   b) $u = 24$, $a = 11$ and $t = 13$
   c) $u = 3.6$, $a = 5.3$ and $t = 14.2$
   d) $u = 9.8$, $a = 48.2$ and $t = 15.4$
   e) $u = -11$, $a = -9.81$ and $t = 12.2$
   f) $u = 66.6$, $a = -1.64$ and $t = 14.2$

10.3 Rearranging Formulas

Making a letter the **subject** of a formula means rearranging the formula so that that letter is on its own.

It's a bit like solving an equation — you always have to do the same thing on **both sides**.

Example 1

Make b the subject of the formula $A = bh$.

1. Write down the original formula.
2. Divide both sides by h.
   Then b is on its own, since $bh \div h = b$.
3. In your final answer, always write the letter that's on its own on the left-hand side of the formula.
   All the other letters should be on the right-hand side.

$$A = bh$$
$$\frac{A}{h} = b$$
$$\mathbf{b = \frac{A}{h}}$$

Exercise 1

1 Make x the subject of the following formulas. All your answers should begin "$x =$".

   a) $y = x + 2$
   b) $b = x - 5$
   c) $z = 7 + x$
   d) $m = x + 2.3$
   e) $p = x - 8.4$
   f) $z = 12 + x$

2 Make x the subject of the following formulas.

a) $z = x + r$ **b)** $3y = x + 4r$ **c)** $16r = 23t + x$

3 Make x the subject of the following formulas.

a) $z = 4x$ **b)** $p = 17x$ **c)** $r = 4.2x$

d) $s = 3.7x$ **e)** $s = 6x$ **f)** $s = 3.5x$

4 Make x the subject of the following formulas.

a) $y = \dfrac{x}{8}$ **b)** $z = \dfrac{x}{17}$ **c)** $t = \dfrac{x}{8.6}$

d) $m = \dfrac{x}{4}$ **e)** $n = \dfrac{x}{6.1}$ **f)** $p = \dfrac{x}{17.4}$

5 Make x the subject of the following formulas.

a) $abc = 2x$ **b)** $t = xy$ **c)** $uv + y = 4.2x$

d) $v = 7.3wx$ **e)** $vwy = 6x$ **f)** $2z + 4 = 2.2xy$

Example 2

Make x the subject of the formula $y = -2x$.

1. Write down the original formula. $y = -2x$
2. Divide both sides by –2.
   Then x is on its own, since $\dfrac{-2x}{-2} = x$. $\dfrac{y}{-2} = x$
3. Write your final answer with x on the left-hand side. $x = -\dfrac{y}{2}$
   Remember, $\dfrac{y}{-2} = -\dfrac{y}{2}$.

Example 3

Make x the subject of the formula $c = \dfrac{5}{6}x$.

1. Write down the original formula. $c = \dfrac{5}{6}x$
2. Multiply both sides by 6.
   Remember, $\dfrac{5}{6} \times 6 = 5$. $6c = 5x$
3. Divide both sides by 5. Remember, $\dfrac{6c}{5} = \dfrac{6}{5}c$. $\dfrac{6}{5}c = x$
4. Write your final answer with x on the left-hand side. $x = \dfrac{6}{5}c$
   You could also write this as $x = \dfrac{6c}{5}$.

6 Make x the subject of the following formulas.

a) $p = -3x$ b) $q = -\dfrac{x}{5}$ c) $n = -6x$

d) $m = -\dfrac{x}{9}$ e) $r = -2.1x$ f) $s = -\dfrac{x}{2.5}$

7 Make y the subject of the following formulas.

a) $a = \dfrac{4}{5}y$ b) $b = \dfrac{3}{4}y$ c) $c = \dfrac{2}{3}y$

d) $d = \dfrac{7}{11}y$ e) $e = \dfrac{10}{3}y$ f) $f = \dfrac{20}{7}y$

8 Make s the subject of the following formulas.

a) $y = s - 4$ b) $t = \dfrac{s}{11}$ c) $d = \dfrac{3}{4}s$

d) $m = \dfrac{4}{5}s$ e) $r = -16s$ f) $p = -14.2s$

g) $a = \dfrac{5}{4}s$ h) $b = -\dfrac{6}{7}s$ i) $c = -11.6s$

9 The volume (V) of a cylinder is given by the formula $V = \pi r^2 h$, where r is the radius of the cylinder and h is its height.

a) Make h the subject of the formula.

b) Find the height of each of these cylinders.

(i)   ←3 cm→   (ii)

h $V = 18\pi$ cm³

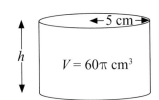

←5 cm→

h $V = 60\pi$ cm³

Two-Step Rearrangements

Example 4

Make x the subject of the formula $y = 4 + bx$.

1. $4 + bx$ means "take your value of x and then: (i) multiply by b $y = 4 + bx$
                                                         (ii) add 4"

     To get x on its own, undo these steps, but in the opposite order.

2. First, subtract 4 from both sides. $y - 4 = bx$

3. Then divide both sides by b. $\dfrac{y-4}{b} = x$

4. Write x on the left-hand side of the formula. $x = \dfrac{y-4}{b}$

Exercise 2

1 Make x the subject of the following formulas.

a) $y = 5x + 3$ **b)** $z = 8x - 2$ **c)** $p = 15x + 18$

d) $m = 6x + 3$ **e)** $n = 5x + 4$ **f)** $r = 2x - 8$

2 Make y the subject of the following formulas.

a) $z = \dfrac{y + 4}{3}$ **b)** $x = \dfrac{7 + y}{4}$ **c)** $s = \dfrac{y - 2}{9}$

d) $t = \dfrac{y - 5.3}{9.7}$ **e)** $v = \dfrac{y + 11}{-3}$ **f)** $w = \dfrac{-65 + y}{5}$

3 Make x the subject of the following formulas.

a) $u = 4(x - 2)$ **b)** $v = 8(x + 4)$ **c)** $w = 3(x - 4)$

d) $p = -6(x - 8)$ **e)** $q = -5(x + 1)$ **f)** $r = -0.2(x + 5)$

4 Make y the subject of the following formulas.

a) $p + 3 = 4y - 2$ **b)** $q + 7 = 9y + 11$ **c)** $r - 5 = 21y - 9$

d) $s - 8 = 8y + 7$ **e)** $t + 6 = 3y - 2$ **f)** $u - 11 = 13y - 14$

5   **a)** Rearrange the formula $v = u + at$ to make a the subject.

     b) Find a if $u = 3$, $v = 38$ and $t = 5$.

     c) Find a if $u = 2.3$, $v = 16.24$ and $t = 3.4$.

     d) Find a if $u = 5.25$, $v = 48.32$ and $t = 4.39$.

6 The temperature in degrees Fahrenheit (f) is given by the formula $f = \frac{9}{5}c + 32$, where c is the temperature in degrees Celsius.

     a) Rearrange the formula to make c the subject.

     b) Find c if:

         (i) $f = 50$ **(ii)** $f = 80$ **(iii)** $f = -30$ **(iv)** $f = 32$

7 The surface area (A) of the shape on the right is given approximately by the formula $A = 21.5d^2$.

     a) Rearrange the formula to make d the subject.

     b) Find d if:

         (i) $A = 344$ cm²

         (ii) $A = 134.375$ cm²

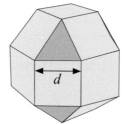

8 The perimeter (P) of the shape on the right is given by the formula $P = 2(2x + y)$.

     a) Rearrange the formula to make x the subject.

     b) Find x if:

         (i) $P = 14$ and $y = 3$

         (ii) $P = 32$ and $y = 4$

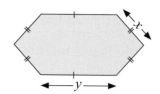

Example 1

An isosceles triangle with one angle of size x has two angles of size y.

a) Write a formula for y in terms of x.
  1. The angles in a triangle add up to 180°, so first subtract x from 180.
  2. Then divide by 2 to find the size of y.

$$y = \frac{180 - x}{2}$$

b) Find y when $x = 30°$.
  Substitute $x = 30$ into the formula.

$$y = \frac{180 - x}{2} = \frac{180 - 30}{2} = \frac{150}{2} = \underline{75°}$$

c) Rearrange the formula to make x the subject.

$$y = \frac{180 - x}{2}$$

  1. Multiply both sides by 2.
  2. Add x to both sides.
  3. Subtract $2y$ from both sides.

$2y = 180 - x$

$2y + x = 180$

$\underline{x = 180 - 2y}$

Exercise 1

1 Chloe gets 45 fewer free minutes on her mobile phone each month than Wassim.
  a) If Wassim gets w free minutes, write a formula for the number of free minutes (c) Chloe gets.
  b) Find c when $w = 125$.

2 The number of matchsticks (m) needed to make h hexagons as shown is given by the formula $m = 5h + 1$.
  a) Rearrange this formula to make h the subject.
  b) Use your formula to find h when $m = 36$.

3 The formula for calculating the cost (C, in £) of gas is $C = 0.06n + 7.5$, where n is the units used.
  a) Find the cost if 275 units of gas were used.
  b) Rearrange this formula to make n the subject.
  c) Use your formula to find how many units of gas were used if the gas bill is £40.50.

4 To book a swimming pool for a party, there is a fixed charge of £30 plus a fee of £1.25 for each person who attends.
  a) Write a formula to calculate the hire cost (C, in £) for n people.
  b) Calculate the hire cost when $n = 32$.
  c) Rearrange your formula to make n the subject.
  d) If the total cost of hiring the pool was £80, how many people attended the party?

5 A joint of beef needs to be cooked for 35 minutes for each kilogram it weighs, plus an extra 25 minutes.
  a) Write a formula for the cooking time needed (T, in minutes) for a joint weighing w kilograms.
  b) Use your formula to find the cooking time needed for a joint weighing 5.2 kg.
  c) Rearrange your formula to make w the subject.
  d) Use your formula to find the weight of a joint that must be cooked for 3 hours and 48 minutes.

Section 11 — Sequences

11.1 Sequences — Term-to-Term Rules

A **sequence** is a list of numbers or shapes which follows a particular **rule**. Each number or shape in the sequence is called a **term**.

Example 1

The first term of a sequence is 3. The rule for finding the next term in the sequence is 'add 4 to the previous term'. Write down the first 5 terms of the sequence.

1. The first term is 3, so write this down.
2. Add 4 each time to find the terms.

3, 7, 11, 15, 19
+4 +4 +4 +4

Example 2

Consider the sequence 2, 6, 18, 54...

a) Explain the rule for finding the next term in the sequence.

b) Write down the next three terms in the sequence.

1. This time the rule for finding the next term involves multiplication.

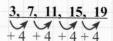

2. Multiply each term by 3 to get the next term.

a) Multiply the previous term by 3.

b) 54, **162, 486, 1458**.
×3 ×3 ×3

Exercise 1

1 The first term of a sequence is 5. The rule for finding the next term in the sequence is 'add 4 to the previous term'. Write down the first 5 terms of the sequence.

2 The first term of a sequence is 2. The rule for finding the next term in the sequence is 'multiply the previous term by 2'. Write down the first 5 terms of the sequence.

3 Write down the first 5 terms of the sequence with:
   a) first term = 100; further terms generated by the rule 'subtract 6 from the previous term'.
   b) first term = 40; further terms generated by the rule 'divide the previous term by 2'.
   c) first term = 11; further terms generated by the rule 'multiply the previous term by –2'.

4 The first four terms of a sequence are 3, 6, 9, 12.
   a) Write down what you add to each term in the sequence to find the next term.
   b) Write down the next three terms in the sequence.

5 The first four terms of a sequence are 3, 6, 12, 24.
   a) Write down what you multiply each term in the sequence by to find the next term.
   b) Write down the next three terms in the sequence.

For **Questions 6-7**: **(i)** explain the rule for finding the next term in the sequence.
(ii) find the next three terms in the sequence.

6 **a)** 3, 5, 7, 9...   **b)** 1, 2, 4, 8...   **c)** 4, 12, 36, 108...   **d)** 4, 7, 10, 13...
   e) 5, 3, 1, –1...   **f)** 1, 1.5, 2, 2.5...   **g)** 0.01, 0.1, 1, 10...   **h)** 192, 96, 48, 24...

7 **a)** 0, –4, –8, –12...   **b)** –1, –3, –9, –27...   **c)** 16, 8, 4, 2...   **d)** 1, –2, 4, –8...

8 The first four terms of a sequence are 4, 10, 16, 22.
   a) Explain the rule for finding the next term in this sequence.
   b) Use your rule to find: **(i)** the 5th term   **(ii)** the 6th term   **(iii)** the 8th term

9 The first four terms of a sequence are 1, 3, 9, 27.
   a) Explain the rule for finding the next term in this sequence.
   b) Use your rule to find: **(i)** the 5th term   **(ii)** the 7th term   **(iii)** the 9th term

10 Copy the following sequences and fill in the blanks.
   a) 7, 13, 19 , 25, ☐, 37   **b)** 9, 5, ☐, –3, –7, –11   **c)** ☐, –3, –9, –27, ☐, –243
   d) –72, ☐, –18, –9, ☐, –2.25   **e)** ☐, 0.8, 3.2, 12.8, ☐, 204.8   **f)** –63, –55, ☐, ☐, ☐, –23

Example 3

Find the next three terms in the sequence 4, 5, 7, 10...

1. Try finding the difference between neighbouring terms.

2. Here, the difference is **increasing by 1** each time.

3. Use this to find the next three terms in the sequence.
   Start with 10. Then add 4. Then add 5. Then add 6.

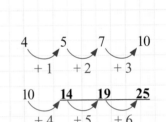

Exercise 2

1 Consider the sequence 7, 8, 10, 13, 17...
   a) Find the difference between each term and the next for the first 5 terms.
   b) Find the next three terms in the sequence.

2 For each sequence below, find: **(i)** the difference between neighbouring terms for the first 5 terms,
                                       (ii) the next three terms in the sequence.
   a) 4, 5, 7, 10, 14...   **b)** 5, 7, 11, 17, 25...   **c)** 20, 18, 15, 11, 6...

3 Consider the sequence 1, 2, 0, 3, –1...
   a) Find the difference between each term and the next for the first 5 terms.
   b) Find the next three terms in the sequence.

4 The sequence 1, 1, 2, 3, 5... is known as the Fibonacci sequence. Each term in the sequence is found by adding together the previous two terms. Find the next three terms in the sequence.

5 The first 5 terms of a sequence are 1, 1, 2, 6, 24.
   a) For the first 5 terms, find the number you multiply by each time to get the next term.
   b) Find the next two terms in the sequence.

Example 4

The matchstick shapes below form the first three patterns in a sequence.

a) Draw the fourth and fifth patterns in the sequence.

b) How many matchsticks are needed to make the sixth pattern in the sequence?

1. You have to add an extra square to the previous pattern.

a)

2. Adding an extra square means you have to add 3 matchsticks to the previous pattern.

3. There are 16 + 3 = 19 matchsticks in the sixth pattern.

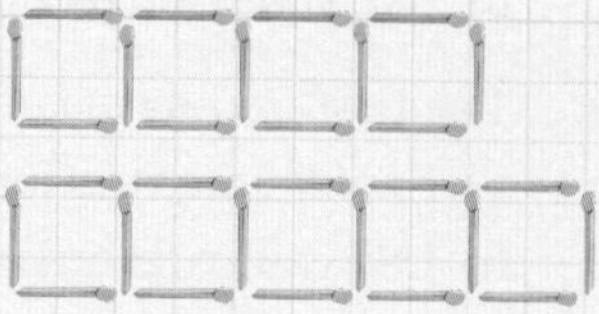

b) **19 matchsticks**.

Exercise 3

1 The first three patterns of several sequences are shown below.

For each of the sequences: **(i)** explain the rule for making the next pattern,

(ii) draw the fourth and fifth patterns in the sequence,

(iii) find the number of matches needed to make the sixth pattern.

a)

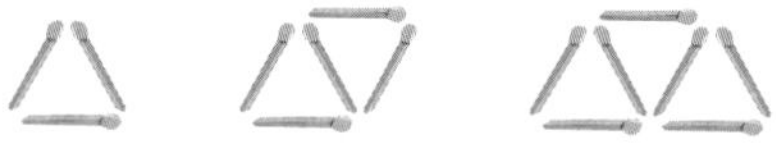

b)

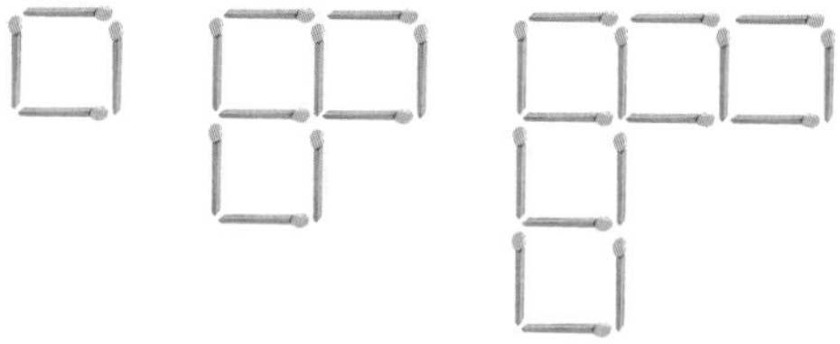

c)

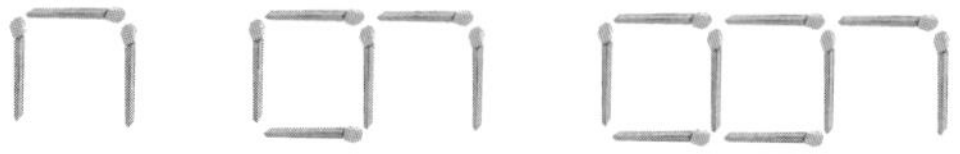

2 Below is a sequence of triangles made up of different numbers of circles.

The numbers of circles in each triangle form a sequence called the 'triangle numbers'.

For example, the first three triangle numbers are 1, 3 and 6.

a) Draw the next three triangles in the sequence, and write down the corresponding triangle numbers.

b) Explain the rule for generating the next triangle number in the sequence.

c) Find the 7th triangle number.

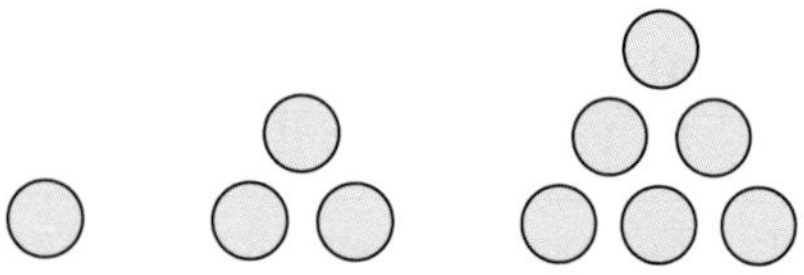

3 For each of the sequences below:

(i) Draw the next three patterns in the sequence.

(ii) Explain the rule for generating the number of circles in the next pattern.

(iii) Work out how many circles there are in the 7th pattern.

(iv) Work out how many circles there are in the 10th pattern.

a)

b)

c)

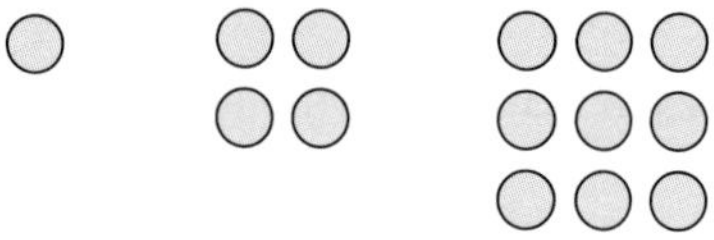

You can also work out a term by using its **position** (n) in the sequence.
For example, the 1st term has $n = 1$, the 2nd term has $n = 2$, the 10th term has $n = 10$, and so on.

Example 1

The nth term of a sequence is $2n - 1$. Find the first four terms of the sequence.

1. To find the 1st, 2nd, 3rd and 4th terms of the sequence, substitute the values $n = 1$, $n = 2$, $n = 3$ and $n = 4$ into the formula.

$(2 \times 1) - 1 = 1$
$(2 \times 2) - 1 = 3$
$(2 \times 3) - 1 = 5$
$(2 \times 4) - 1 = 7$

2. Write the terms in order to form the sequence. So the first four terms are **1, 3, 5, 7**.

Exercise 1

1 The nth term of a sequence is $2n + 3$.
Find the value of the nth term when:
   a) $n = 1$ **b)** $n = 2$ **c)** $n = 3$ **d)** $n = 4$.

2 The nth term of a sequence is $20 - 2n$.
Find the value of:
   a) the 1st term   **b)** the 2nd term   **c)** the 3rd term   **d)** the 4th term

3 The nth term of a sequence is $7n - 11$. Write down the first four terms of the sequence.

4 Find the first four terms of a sequence if the nth term is given by:
   a) $n + 5$ **b)** $3n + 2$ **c)** $4n - 2$ **d)** $5n - 1$
   e) $10 - n$ **f)** $3 - 4n$ **g)** $10n - 8$ **h)** $-7 - 3n$

5 Find the first four terms of a sequence if the nth term is given by:
   a) $n^2 + 1$ **b)** $2n^2 + 1$ **c)** $3n^2 - 1$ **d)** $n(n - 1)$

6 The nth term of a sequence is $2n + 20$. Find the value of:
   a) the 5th term   **b)** the 10th term   **c)** the 20th term   **d)** the 100th term

7 The nth term of a sequence is $100 - 3n$. Find the value of:
   a) the 3rd term   **b)** the 10th term   **c)** the 30th term   **d)** the 40th term

8 Each of the following gives the nth term for a different sequence.
For each sequence, find: **(i)** the 5th term   **(ii)** the 10th term   **(iii)** the 100th term
   a) $n + 11$ **b)** $2n + 3$ **c)** $6n - 1$ **d)** $4n + 12$
   e) $100 - n$ **f)** $30 - 3n$ **g)** $100n - 8$ **h)** $-20 + 2n$

9 Each of the following gives the nth term for a different sequence.
For each sequence, find: **(i)** the 2nd term   **(ii)** the 5th term   **(iii)** the 20th term
   a) $2n^2$ **b)** $2n^2 + 3$ **c)** $4n^2 - 5$ **d)** $n(n + 1)$

Example 2

The nth term of a sequence is $4n + 5$. Which term has the value 41?

1. Make the nth term equal to 41.

2. Solve the equation to find n.

$4n + 5 = 41$

$4n = 36$

$n = 9$

So the **9th term** is 41.

Exercise 2

1   **a)** Find the value of n when $2n + 6 = 20$.

    b) The nth term of a sequence is $2n + 6$. Write down which term has the value 20.

2   **a)** Find the value of n when $6n - 3 = 15$.

    b) The nth term of a sequence is $6n - 3$. Write down which term has the value 15.

3   **a)** The nth term of a sequence is $7n + 4$. Which term of the sequence has the value 53?

    b) The nth term of a sequence is $5n - 8$. Which term of the sequence has the value 37?

    c) The nth term of a sequence is $4n + 3$. Which term of the sequence has the value 27?

    d) The nth term of a sequence is $2n - 5$. Which term of the sequence has the value 11?

4   The nth term of a sequence is $17 - 2n$.

    a) Which term of the sequence has the value 3?

    b) Which term of the sequence has the value 9?

5   The nth term of a sequence is $50 - 6n$. Find which terms have the following values.

    a) 2   **b)** 8   **c)** 14   **d)** 26

6   The nth term of a sequence is $n^2 - 1$.

    a) Which term of the sequence has the value 8?

    b) Which term of the sequence has the value 99?

7   The nth term of a sequence is $n^2 + 1$. Find which terms have the following values.

    a) 5   **b)** 26   **c)** 50   **d)** 82

8   The formulas for the number of matches in the nth pattern of the following 'matchstick sequences' are shown below. For each of the sequences:

    (i) find the number of matches needed to make the 6th pattern,

    (ii) find the number of matches needed to make the 100th pattern.

a)

Number of matches in nth pattern = $2n + 1$

b)

Number of matches in nth pattern = $4n - 1$

9   The formula for the number of circles in the nth triangle in this sequence is $\dfrac{n(n + 1)}{2}$.

    a) Find the number of circles needed to make the 6th triangle.

    b) Find the number of circles needed to make the 10th triangle.

11.3 Finding a Position-to-Term Rule

You need to be able to write a formula for the nth term of a sequence.

Example 1

Find the nth term of the sequence 5, 7, 9, 11...

1. Find the difference between each term and the next.

    $$5 \quad 7 \quad 9 \quad 11$$
    $$+2 \quad +2 \quad +2$$

2. Here, the terms increase by 2 each time, so the formula for the nth term must include '$2n$'.
    The complete formula for the nth term will be '$2n + a$', where a is a number you need to find using the first term of the sequence.

    nth term is $2n + a$
    $(2 \times 1) + a = 5$
    $a = 5 - 2 = 3$

3. Substitute $n = 1$ into $2n + a$, and put it equal to 5. Then solve your equation to find a.

    So the nth term is **$2n + 3$**.

4. Check your formula by using it to find another term.   (Check: 2nd term is $2 \times 2 + 3 = 7$ ✔)

Example 2

Find the nth term of the sequence 45, 42, 39, 36...

1. Find the difference between each term and the next.

    $$45 \quad 42 \quad 39 \quad 36$$
    $$-3 \quad -3 \quad -3$$

2. Here, the terms decrease by 3 each time, so the nth term is $-3n + a$.

    nth term is $-3n + a$

3. Use the first term of the sequence to find a.
    Substitute $n = 1$ into $-3n + a$ and put it equal to 45.
    Solve the equation to find a.

    $(-3 \times 1) + a = 45$
    $a = 45 + 3 = 48$

4. Write down and check your formula.

    So the nth term is **$-3n + 48$**, or **$48 - 3n$**.

    (Check: 2nd term is $-3 \times 2 + 48 = 42$ ✔)

Exercise 1

1   The first 4 terms of a sequence are: 9, 13, 17, 21
    a) Find the difference between each term and the next.
    b) Copy and complete this formula for the nth term of the sequence: $\boxed{} n + a$
    c) Use the first term of the sequence to find the value of a.
    d) Write down and check your formula for the nth term of the sequence.

2   Find the formula for the nth term of each of the following sequences.
    a) 7, 13, 19, 25...   b) 3, 10, 17, 24...   c) 4, 8, 12, 16...   d) 6, 16, 26, 36...
    e) 5, 10, 15, 20...   f) 7, 27, 47, 67...   g) 41, 81, 121, 161...   h) 3, 11, 19, 27...

3   Find the formula for the nth term of each of the following sequences.
    a) –1, 1, 3, 5...   b) –2, 1, 4, 7...   c) –9, –5, –1, 3...   d) –45, –26, –7, 12...

4 Find the formula for the nth term of each of the following sequences.
   a) 10, 8, 6, 4...   **b)** 5, 4, 3, 2...   **c)** 15, 10, 5, 0...   **d)** 40, 37, 34, 31...
   e) 70, 60, 50, 40...   **f)** 78, 69, 60, 51... **g)** 60, 55, 50, 45...   **h)** 100, 92, 84, 76...

5 Find the formula for the nth term of each of the following sequences.
   a) 4, −1, −6, −11...   **b)** 6, 3, 0, −3...   **c)** −10, −25, −40, −55...   **d)** −39, −51, −63, −75...

6 Find the number of matchsticks in the nth pattern of the following sequences.

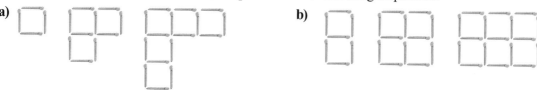

   a)   **b)**

7 **a)** Find the nth term of sequence A, which starts 4, 7, 10, 13...
   b) Find the nth term of sequence B, which starts 5, 8, 11, 14...
   c) **(i)** How does each term in sequence B compare with the corresponding term in sequence A?
      (ii) What do you notice about the formulas giving the nth term for these two sequences?

8 **a)** Find the nth term of the sequence 6, 11, 16, 21...
   b) Use your answer to part **a)** to write down the nth term of the sequence 7, 12, 17, 22...

9 **a)** Find the nth term of the sequence 13, 9, 5, 1...
   b) Use your answer to part **a)** to write down the nth term of the sequence 11, 7, 3, −1...

Example 3

A sequence has nth term $3n + 2$. Is 37 a term in the sequence?

1. Make an equation by setting the formula for the nth term equal to 37. $3n + 2 = 37$
    Then solve your equation to find n. $3n = 35$
                                                                                $n = 11.666...$

2. Since n is not a whole number, 37 is not a term in the sequence.   So 37 **is not** a term
                                                                                in the sequence.

Exercise 2

1 A sequence has nth term $2n + 1$. Show that 54 is **not** a term in this sequence.

2 Show that 80 is a term in the sequence with nth term equal to $3n - 1$.

3 A sequence has nth term $21 - 2n$.
   Show that −1 is a term in this sequence, and write down the corresponding value of n to show its position.

4 **a)** Find the nth term of the sequence whose first four terms are 4, 9, 14, 19...
   b) Is 34 a term in this sequence? If so, write down its position.

5 **a)** Find the nth term of the sequence whose first four terms are 12, 18, 24, 30...
   b) Is 34 a term in this sequence?

6 A sequence has nth term equal to $17 + 3n$.
   Determine whether each of the following is a term in this sequence.
   a) 52   **b)** 98   **c)** 105   **d)** 248   **e)** 996

7 A sequence starts −5, −1, 3, 7...
   Determine whether each of the following is a term in this sequence. For those that are, state the corresponding value of n.
   a) 43   **b)** 71   **c)** 138   **d)** 384   **e)** 879

Section 12 — Graphs and Equations

12.1 Coordinates

Coordinates describe the **position** of a point. They are written in pairs inside brackets, with the x-coordinate (left or right) first and the y-coordinate (up or down) second.

Example 1

Write down the coordinates of the vertices of the triangle *ABC* shown below.

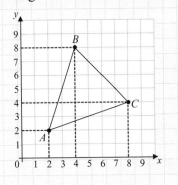

1. Follow the grid line down from each point and read off the x-coordinate.

2. Follow the grid line across from each point and read off the y-coordinate.

3. Write the coordinates in brackets with the x-coordinate first.

The coordinates are **A(2, 2)**, **B(4, 8)**, **C(8, 4)**.

Example 2

Draw the shape *WXYZ* with vertices *W*(–4, 5), *X*(3, 2), *Y*(4, –3) and *Z*(–5, –2).

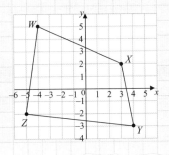

1. Here, some of the coordinates are negative, so your axes need to go below zero.

2. Read across the horizontal axis for the x-coordinates.

3. Read up and down the vertical axis for the y-coordinates.

4. Plot the points and connect them to draw the shape.

Exercise 1

1 Use the grid on the right to answer this question.

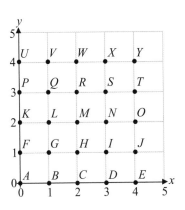

a) Write down the coordinates of the following points.

   (i) *A*   **(ii)** *M*   **(iii)** *Q*   **(iv)** *U*   **(v)** *Y*

b) Write down the sentence given by the letters with the following coordinates.

   (3, 4) - (2, 0) (4, 2) (4, 2) (2, 3) (3, 0) (3, 1) (3, 2) (0, 0) (4, 3) (4, 0)
   (2, 0) (4, 2) (2, 2) (4, 0) (3, 3)
   (0, 1) (3, 1) (2, 3) (3, 3) (4, 3)

2 On separate copies of the grid on the right, draw the shapes whose vertices are given by the following sets of coordinates.

a) $A(2, 1)$, $B(2, 4)$, $C(5, 4)$, $D(5, 1)$

b) $E(1, 1)$, $F(6, 3)$, $G(3, 5)$

c) $H(1, 3)$, $I(3, 5)$, $J(6, 3)$, $K(3, 1)$

d) $L(2, 6)$, $M(5, 5)$, $N(5, 3)$, $O(2, 1)$

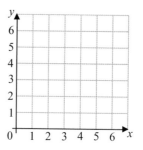

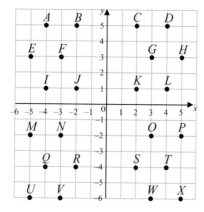

3 Use the grid on the left for this question.

a) The following sets of coordinates spell out the names of shapes. Write down the name of each shape.

(i) $(2, -4)$ $(-4, -4)$ $(-5, -6)$ $(-4, 5)$ $(-2, -4)$ $(-5, 3)$

(ii) $(2, 5)$ $(-4, 1)$ $(-2, -4)$ $(2, 5)$ $(4, 1)$ $(-5, 3)$

(iii) $(2, 5)$ $(-5, -6)$ $(-2, 5)$ $(3, -2)$ $(-4, 1)$ $(4, 5)$

b) Write down the sets of coordinates which spell out the names of the following shapes.

(i) kite   (ii) sphere   (iii) triangle

4 Draw a coordinate grid ranging from –5 to 5 on the x-axis and y-axis. Plot the following points on your grid. Join the points you have plotted.

$A(0, 5)$ $B(1, 1)$ $C(5, 1)$ $D(2, -1)$ $E(3, -4)$

$F(0, -2)$ $G(-3, -4)$ $H(-2, -1)$ $I(-5, 1)$ $J(-1, 1)$

Midpoint of a Line Segment

The midpoint of a line segment is **halfway** between the end points. The midpoint's x- and y-coordinates equal the **average** of the end points' **x-coordinates** and the **average** of the end points' **y-coordinates**.

Example 3

Find the midpoint of the line segment AB.

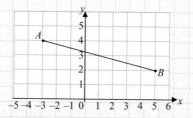

1. Write down the coordinates of the end points A and B. $A(-3, 4)$ and $B(5, 2)$

2. Find the average of the x-coordinates by adding them together and dividing by 2.

   $\left(\dfrac{-3 + 5}{2}, \dfrac{4 + 2}{2}\right) = (1, 3)$

3. Find the average of the y-coordinates in the same way.

   The midpoint has coordinates **(1, 3)**.

Exercise 2

1 A line segment XY is shown on the grid on the right.

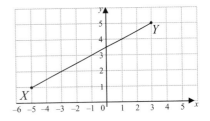

   a) Write down the coordinates of the points X and Y.

   b) Use the coordinates of X and Y to calculate the coordinates of M, the midpoint of XY.

   c) Plot the point M on a copy of the diagram. Use a ruler to check that the distances XM and MY are equal.

2 The points P and Q have coordinates $P(1, 0)$ and $Q(3, 5)$.

   a) Find the coordinates of M, the midpoint of PQ.

   b) Check your answer: **(i)** Plot P and Q on a square grid.
Join the points to form the line segment PQ.

                   (ii) Plot the point M. Check that M is the midpoint of PQ.

3 Find the coordinates of the midpoint of the line segment AB, where A and B have coordinates:

   a) $A(1, 1)$, $B(3, 5)$ **b)** $A(0, 1)$, $B(6, 3)$ **c)** $A(0, 0)$, $B(4, 4)$ **d)** $A(2, 7)$, $B(6, 7)$

4 Find the coordinates of the midpoint of the line segment AB, where A and B have coordinates:

   a) $A(-1, 2)$, $B(1, 2)$ **b)** $A(-2, 3)$, $B(-4, 5)$

   c) $A(-1, -6)$, $B(5, 8)$ **d)** $A(3, -2)$, $B(-1, 4)$

   e) $A(-1, -9)$, $B(-3, -4)$ **f)** $A(2, 5)$, $B(-7, -8)$

   g) $A(0, -4)$, $B(-5, 1)$ **h)** $A(-2, 0)$, $B(1, -8)$

5 Use the diagram on the right to find the midpoints of the following line segments.

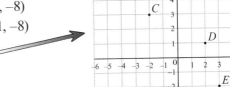

   a) AF **b)** AC **c)** DF

   d) BE **e)** BF **f)** CE

12.2   Horizontal and Vertical Graphs

All **horizontal** lines on a graph have the equation $y = a$ (where a is a number), since every point on the same horizontal line has the same y-coordinate (a).

All **vertical** lines on a graph have the equation $x = b$ (where b is a number), since every point on the same vertical line has the same x-coordinate (b).

Example 1

Write down the equations of the lines marked A and B.

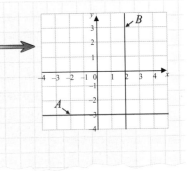

1. Every point on the line marked A has y-coordinate -3. $\implies$ A is the line $\underline{y = -3}$

2. Every point on the line marked B has x-coordinate 2. $\implies$ B is the line $\underline{x = 2}$

Example 2

Plot the graphs of the equations: a) $x = -1$ b) $y = 3$

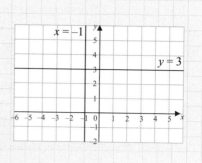

1. The line with equation $x = -1$ is a
    vertical line through -1 on the x-axis.

2. The line with equation $y = 3$ is a
    horizontal line through 3 on the y-axis.

Exercise 1

1 Write down the equations of each of the
lines labelled A to E on this diagram.

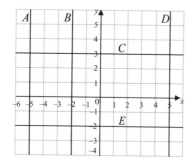

2 Draw a set of coordinate axes and plot the
graphs with the following equations.

a) $y = 3$ b) $y = -6$ c) $y = -1$

d) $x = 2$ e) $x = 4$ f) $x = -4$

3 a) What is the y-coordinate of every point
on the x-axis?

b) Write down the equation of the x-axis.

4 Write down the equation of the y-axis.

5 Draw a set of coordinate axes.

a) Plot the line which is parallel to the
x-axis, and which passes through the
point $(2, -2)$.

b) What is the equation of this line?

6 Draw a set of coordinate axes.

a) Plot the line which is parallel to the
y-axis, and which passes through the
point $(1, -3)$.

b) What is the equation of this line?

7 Write down the equation of the line which
is parallel to the x-axis, and which passes
through the point $(4, 8)$.

8 Write down the equation of the line which
is parallel to the y-axis, and which passes
through the point $(-2, -6)$.

9 Write down the equation of the line which is
parallel to the line $x = 4$, and which passes
through the point $(1, 2)$.

10 Write down the equation of the line which is
parallel to the line $y = -5$, and which passes
through the point $(0, 6)$.

11 Draw a set of coordinate axes.

a) Plot the points $P(3, -1)$ and $Q(-1, -1)$.

b) What is the equation of the line that
contains points P and Q?

12 Find the equation of the line containing
points $M(2, 0)$ and $N(2, -3)$.

13 Draw a set of coordinate axes.

a) Plot the lines with the equations
$x = -2$ and $y = 4$.

b) Write down the coordinates of the point
where the two lines intersect (cross).

14 Write down the coordinates of the points
where the following pairs of lines intersect.

a) $x = 2$ and $y = 4$

b) $x = -3$ and $y = 7$

c) $x = 8$ and $y = -11$

d) $x = -5$ and $y = -13$

12.3 Other Straight-Line Graphs

The equation of a straight line which **isn't** horizontal or vertical contains **both** x **and** y.

Example 1

a) Complete the table to show the value of $y = 2x + 1$ for values of x from 0 to 5.

b) Draw the graph of $y = 2x + 1$ for values of x from 0 to 5.

x	0	1	2	3	4	5
y						
Coordinates						

a)

x	0	1	2	3	4	5
y	$2 \times 0 + 1$ $= 1$	$2 \times 1 + 1$ $= 3$	$2 \times 2 + 1$ $= 5$	$2 \times 3 + 1$ $= 7$	$2 \times 4 + 1$ $= 9$	$2 \times 5 + 1$ $= 11$
Coordinates	$(0, 1)$	$(1, 3)$	$(2, 5)$	$(3, 7)$	$(4, 9)$	$(5, 11)$

b)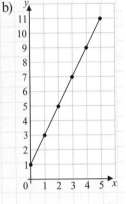

1. Use the equation $y = 2x + 1$ to find the y-value corresponding to each value of x.

2. Use the numbers from the first and second rows to fill in the third row.

3. Plot the coordinates from your table on a grid, and join them up to draw the graph.

Exercise 1

1 a) Copy and complete the table below to show the value of $y = x + 2$ for values of x from 0 to 5.

x	0	1	2	3	4	5
y	2	3				
Coordinates	$(0, 2)$					

b) Copy the grid on the right and plot the coordinates from your table.

c) Join up the points to draw the graph of $y = x + 2$ for values of x from 0 to 5.

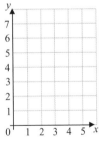

2 a) Copy and complete the table below to show the value of $y = x - 4$ for values of x from 0 to 5.

x	0	1	2	3	4	5
y	-4					
Coordinates						

b) Copy the grid on the right and plot the coordinates from your table.

c) Join up the points to draw the graph of $y = x - 4$ for values of x from 0 to 5.

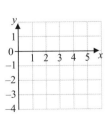

3 **a)** Copy and complete this table to show the value of $y = 2x$ for values of x from –2 to 2.

x	–2	–1	0	1	2
y					
Coordinates					

b) Draw a set of axes with x-values from –5 to 5 and y-values from –10 to 10.
Plot the coordinates from your table.

c) Join up the points to draw the graph with equation $y = 2x$ for values of x from –2 to 2.

d) Use a ruler to extend your line to show the graph of $y = 2x$ for values of x from –5 to 5.

e) Use your graph to fill in the missing coordinates of these points on the line:

    (i) $(4, \boxed{})$ **(ii)** $(-3, \boxed{})$ **(iii)** $(\boxed{}, -10)$

4 **a)** Copy and complete the table on the right to show the value of $y = 8 - x$ for values of x from 0 to 4.

x	0	1	2	3	4
y					
Coordinates					

b) Draw a set of axes with x-values from –5 to 5 and y-values from 0 to 13.
Plot the coordinates from your table.

c) Join up the points to draw the graph of $y = 8 - x$ for values of x from 0 to 4.
Use a ruler to extend your line to show the graph of $y = 8 - x$ for values of x from –5 to 5.

5 For each of the following equations:

    (i) complete a table like the one on the right to show the value of y for values of x from –1 to 2,

    (ii) draw a graph of the equation for values of x from –5 to 5.

x	–1	0	1	2
y				
Coordinates				

a) $y = x + 3$ **b)** $y = x + 5$ **c)** $y = x - 1$ **d)** $y = x - 3$

e) $y = 3x$ **f)** $y = 4x$ **g)** $y = \frac{x}{2}$ **h)** $y = 3x - 1$

i) $y = 2x + 5$ **j)** $y = 4x - 3$ **k)** $y = 3 - x$ **l)** $y = 4 - x$

m) $y = 6 - 2x$ **n)** $y = 8 - 3x$ **o)** $y = 1 - 2x$ **p)** $y = 5 - \frac{x}{2}$

6 Draw a graph of the following equations for the given range of x-values.

    a) $y = x$ for x from –4 to 4

    b) $y = x - 2$ for x from 0 to 6

    c) $y = x + 7$ for x from –7 to 0

    d) $y = 3x - 5$ for x from 0 to 4

    e) $y = 7 - 5x$ for x from 0 to 2

    f) $y = -2x + 8$ for x from 0 to 5

12.4 Gradients

The **gradient** of a straight line is a measure of **how steep** it is.

To find the gradient of a line divide the 'vertical distance' between two points on the line by the 'horizontal distance' between those points.

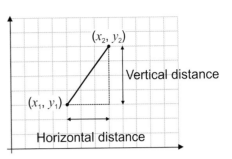

$$\text{Gradient} = \frac{\textbf{Vertical distance}}{\textbf{Horizontal distance}} = \frac{y_2 - y_1}{x_2 - x_1}$$

A line sloping upwards from left to right has a **positive gradient**.
A line sloping downwards from left to right has a **negative gradient**.

Example 1

Find the gradient of the line segment AB.
Each square on the grid measures 1 unit.

1. The vertical distance between A and B is 3 squares.
   The horizontal distance between A and B is 4 squares.

   $$\frac{\text{Vertical distance}}{\text{Horizontal distance}} = \frac{3}{4}$$

2. The line slopes downwards from left to right, so the gradient is negative.

   $$\text{Gradient of } AB = -\frac{3}{4}$$

Exercise 1

1 The grid spacing in this question is 1 unit.
   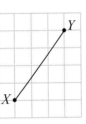
   a) Write down the vertical distance between the points X and Y.
   b) Write down the horizontal distance between X and Y.
   c) State whether the gradient is positive or negative.
   d) Calculate the gradient of the line segment XY.

2 Find the gradient of each of the following line segments. The grid spacing is 1 unit.

a)

b)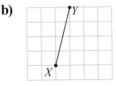

c)

d)

e)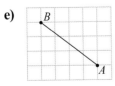

f)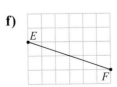

g)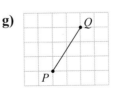

h)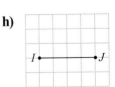

Example 2

Find the gradient of the line containing points $P(-3, 1)$ and $Q(4, 5)$.

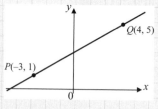

1. Call the coordinates of P (x_1, y_1), and the coordinates of Q (x_2, y_2).

2. Use the formula for the gradient.

3. The line slopes upwards from left to right. So you should get a positive answer.

$$\text{Gradient} = \frac{y_2 - y_1}{x_2 - x_1}$$

$$= \frac{5 - 1}{4 - (-3)}$$

$$= \frac{4}{7}$$

3 Points $P(x_1, y_1)$ and $Q(x_2, y_2)$ are plotted on this graph.
  a) Without doing any calculations, state whether the gradient of the line containing P and Q is positive or negative.
  b) Calculate the vertical distance $y_2 - y_1$ between P and Q.
  c) Calculate the horizontal distance $x_2 - x_1$ between P and Q.
  d) Find the gradient of the line containing P and Q.

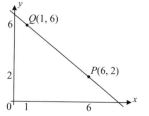

4 Use the points shown to find the gradient of each of the following lines.

a)
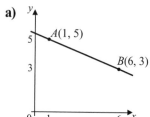

b)
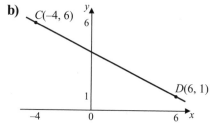

c)
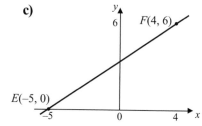

5 For each line shown below:
  (i) Use the axes to find the coordinates of each of the marked points.
  (ii) Find the gradient of each of the lines.

a)
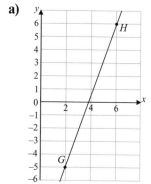

b)
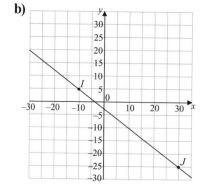

c)
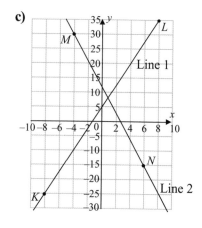

6 a) Plot the points $U(-1, 2)$ and $V(2, 5)$ on a square grid.
b) Find the gradient of the line containing points U and V.

7 Use the gradient formula to find the gradient of the line containing the points $Y(2, 0)$ and $Z(-4, -3)$.

8 Find the gradients of the lines containing the following points.
a) $A(0, 4)$, $B(2, 10)$
b) $C(1, 3)$, $D(5, 11)$
c) $E(-1, 3)$, $F(5, 7)$
d) $G(-3, -2)$, $H(1, -5)$
e) $I(5, -2)$, $J(-1, 1)$
f) $K(-4, -3)$, $L(-8, -6)$

$y = mx + c$

The equation of a straight line is often written in the form $y = mx + c$, where m and c are numbers — for example, $y = 3x + 5$ ($m = 3$ and $c = 5$), or $y = -7x + 1$ ($m = -7$ and $c = 1$).

When written in this form: • m is the **gradient** of the line,
• c tells you the **y-intercept** — the point where the line crosses the y-axis.

Example 3

Find the gradient and coordinates of the y-intercept of the line $y = 3x + 1$.

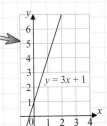

1. Comparing $y = 3x + 1$ to $y = mx + c$
    gives $m = 3$ and $c = 1$.   gradient is **3**

2. Since $c = 1$, the line crosses the y-axis
    when $y = 1$. So the y-intercept has y-intercept is at **(0, 1)**
    coordinates (0, 1).

Exercise 2

For each of the lines in **Questions 1 and 2**, write down:
    (i) the gradient   **(ii)** the coordinates of the y-intercept

1 a) $y = 3x + 2$
b) $y = 2x - 4$
c) $y = 5x - 11$
d) $y = -3x + 7$
e) $y = 4x$
f) $y = \frac{1}{2}x - 1$

2 a) $y = -x - \frac{1}{2}$
b) $y = 3 - x$
c) $y = 3$

3 Parallel lines have the same gradient.
Match the letters to show which of the following lines are parallel.

A: $y = 3x + 1$ B: $y = -x$ C: $y = -2x - 9$

D: $y = -x - 9$ E: $y = 3x - 2$ F: $y = -2x + 2$

4 Match the graphs to the correct equation from the box.

$$y = x + 2 \qquad y = \tfrac{7}{3}x - 1 \qquad y = -x + 6 \qquad y = 3x \qquad y = -\tfrac{1}{3}x + 4 \qquad y = \tfrac{1}{3}x + 2$$

A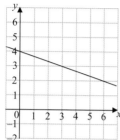

B

C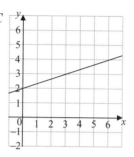

D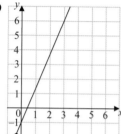

E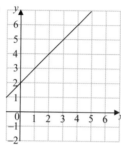

F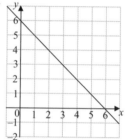

12.5 Quadratic Graphs

Drawing Quadratic Graphs

Quadratic functions always involve an x^2 **term** (but no higher powers of x, such as x^3, x^4...).

The graph of a quadratic function is always a curve called a **parabola**.
A parabola can be **u-shaped** or **n-shaped**.

Example 1

a) Complete the table to find the value of $y = x^2 - 3$ for values of x from –3 to 3.

x	–3	–2	–1	0	1	2	3
x^2							
$x^2 - 3$							

b) Draw the graph of $y = x^2 - 3$ for values of x from –3 to 3.

1. Fill in the table one row at a time.

2. Now plot each x-value from the first row against the corresponding y-value ($= x^2 - 3$) from the third row, and join the points with a smooth curve.

x	–3	–2	–1	0	1	2	3
x^2	9	4	1	0	1	4	9
$x^2 - 3$	6	1	–2	–3	–2	1	6

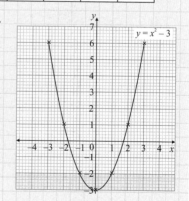

Exercise 1

1 **a)** Copy and complete the table below to find the value of $y = x^2 + 2$ for values of x from -3 to 3.

x	-3	-2	-1	0	1	2	3
x^2	9		1			4	
$x^2 + 2$	11		3			6	

b) Copy the grid on the right and plot the points from your table.

c) Join up the points to draw the graph of $y = x^2 + 2$ for values of x from -3 to 3.

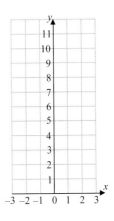

2 **a)** Copy and complete the table to show the value of $y = x^2 - 1$ for values of x from -3 to 3.

b) Draw a set of axes with x-values from -3 to 3 and y-values from -1 to 8.
Draw the graph of $y = x^2 - 1$ on your axes.

x	-3	-2	-1	0	1	2	3
x^2		4					9
$x^2 - 1$		3					8

3 For each of the following equations: **(i)** Complete a table like the one below to show the value of y for values of x from -3 to 3.

(ii) Draw a graph of the equation on suitable axes.

x	-3	-2	-1	0	1	2	3
x^2							
y							

a) $y = x^2$ **b)** $y = x^2 + 3$

c) $y = x^2 - 2$ **d)** $y = x^2 + 4$

e) $y = 5 - x^2$ **f)** $y = 10 - x^2$

Example 2

a) Complete the table to find the value of $y = x^2 - x$ for values of x from -3 to 3.

x	-3	-2	-1	0	1	2	3
x^2		4			1		
$-x$		2			-1		
$x^2 - x$		6			0		

b) Draw the graph of $y = x^2 - x$ for values of x from -3 to 3.

1. Fill in the table one row at a time. Find the entry for the '$x^2 - x$' row by adding the entries in the 'x^2' and '$-x$' rows.

2. Now plot each x-value from the first row against the corresponding y-value ($= x^2 - x$) from the fourth row. Join the points with a smooth curve.

x	-3	-2	-1	0	1	2	3
x^2	9	4	1	0	1	4	9
$-x$	3	2	1	0	-1	-2	-3
$x^2 - x$	12	6	2	0	0	2	6

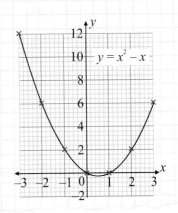

Exercise 2

1 a) Copy and complete the table below to find the value of $y = x^2 + x$ for values of x from -3 to 3.

x	-3	-2	-1	0	1	2	3
x^2	9					4	
x	-3					2	
$x^2 + x$	6					6	

b) Copy the grid on the right and plot the points from your table.

c) Join up the points to draw the graph of $y = x^2 + x$ for values of x from -3 to 3.

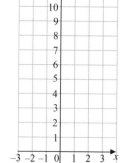

2 a) Copy and complete the table to show the value of $y = x^2 - 2x$ for values of x from -3 to 3.

b) Draw a set of axes with x-values from -3 to 3 and y-values from -1 to 15.
Draw the graph of $y = x^2 - 2x$ on your axes.

x	-3	-2	-1	0	1	2	3
x^2		4					9
$-2x$		4					-6
$x^2 - 2x$		8					3

3 For each of the following quadratic equations:

    (i) Complete a table to show the value of y for values of x from -3 to 3.

    (ii) Draw a graph of the equation on suitable axes.

a) $y = x^2 + 3x$ **b)** $y = x^2 + 2x$ **c)** $y = x^2 - 4x$

d) $y = x^2 + 5x$ **e)** $y = x^2 - 3x$ **f)** $y = x^2 + 4x$

Example 3

Draw the graph of $y = x^2 + 3x - 2$ for values of x from -3 to 3.

1. Make a table — include separate rows for x^2, $3x$ and -2.
   The last row should add the three entries above.

x	-3	-2	-1	0	1	2	3
x^2	9	4	1	0	1	4	9
$3x$	-9	-6	-3	0	3	6	9
-2	-2	-2	-2	-2	-2	-2	-2
$x^2 + 3x - 2$	-2	-4	-4	-2	2	8	16

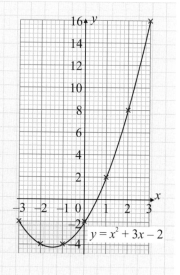

2. Now plot each x-value from the first row against the corresponding y-value ($= x^2 + 3x - 2$) from the final row.
   Join the points with a smooth curve.

4 For each of the following quadratic equations:

    (i) Complete a table to show the value of y for values of x from -3 to 3.

    (ii) Draw a graph of the equation on suitable axes.

a) $y = x^2 + 2x + 5$ **b)** $y = x^2 + x - 3$ **c)** $y = x^2 - 3x - 2$

d) $y = x^2 - 2x - 3$ **e)** $y = x^2 - 3x - 1$ **f)** $y = -x^2 - x - 1$

Using Quadratic Graphs to Solve Quadratic Equations

Example 4

This graph shows the curve $y = x^2 - 2x + 2$.
Use the graph to find the solution of $x^2 - 2x + 2 = 3$.

1. $x^2 - 2x + 2 = 3$ when the graph $y = x^2 - 2x + 2$ crosses the line $y = 3$.

2. So draw the line $y = 3$...

3. ...and write down the x-values of the points where the line and the curve intersect.

$$x = -0.4 \text{ and } x = 2.4$$

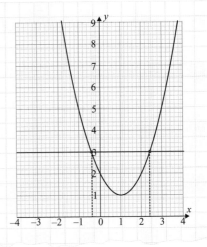

Exercise 3

1 The graph on the right shows the curve $y = x^2 + 1$.
Use the graph to solve these equations.

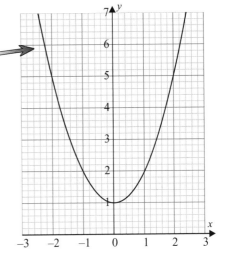

a) $x^2 + 1 = 2$ b) $x^2 + 1 = 3$
c) $x^2 + 1 = 4$ d) $x^2 + 1 = 5$
e) $x^2 + 1 = 6$ f) $x^2 + 1 = 7$

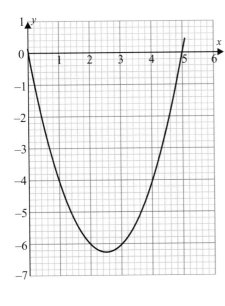

2 The graph on the left shows the curve $y = x^2 - 5x$.

Use the graph to solve these equations.

a) $x^2 - 5x = -1$ b) $x^2 - 5x = -4$
c) $x^2 - 5x = -2$ d) $x^2 - 5x = -5$
e) $x^2 - 5x = -3$ f) $x^2 - 5x = -6$

The graph on the right shows the curve $y = 9 - x^2$.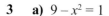
Use this graph to solve the equations in **Questions 3-4**.

3   **a)** $9 - x^2 = 1$ **b)** $9 - x^2 = 2$

     c) $9 - x^2 = 4$ **d)** $9 - x^2 = 5$

     e) $9 - x^2 = 6$ **f)** $9 - x^2 = 8$

4   **a)** $9 - x^2 = 5.6$ **b)** $9 - x^2 = 7.8$

     c) $9 - x^2 = 1.2$ **d)** $9 - x^2 = 4.4$

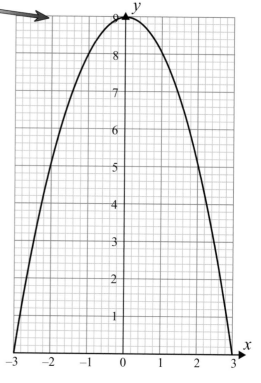

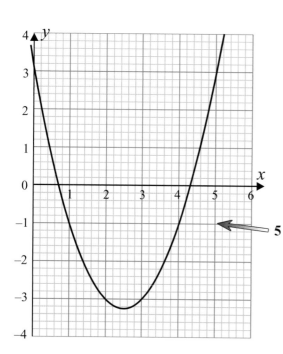

5   The graph on the left shows
the curve $y = x^2 - 5x + 3$.

Use the graph to solve these equations.

   a) $x^2 - 5x + 3 = 3$ **b)** $x^2 - 5x + 3 = 0$

   c) $x^2 - 5x + 3 = 2$ **d)** $x^2 - 5x + 3 = -1$

   e) $x^2 - 5x + 3 = 1.8$ **f)** $x^2 - 5x + 3 = -2.4$

6   **a)** Copy and complete the table to show
the value of $y = x^2 - 4x$ for values of x
from -1 to 5.

     b) Draw a set of axes with x-values
from -1 to 5 and y-values from -4 to 5.
Plot the graph of $y = x^2 - 4x$ on your axes.

x	-1	0	1	2	3	4	5
x^2					9		
$-4x$					-12		
$x^2 - 4x$					-3		

     c) Use your graph to solve these equations.

       (i) $x^2 - 4x = 3$ **(ii)** $x^2 - 4x = 1$ **(iii)** $x^2 - 4x = 2$

       (iv) $x^2 - 4x = 4$ **(v)** $x^2 - 4x = 2.4$ **(vi)** $x^2 - 4x = -3.6$

7   **a)** Find the value of $y = x^2 - 3x + 2$ for values of x from -1 to 4.

     b) Use your results to draw the graph of $y = x^2 - 3x + 2$ for x between -1 and 4.

     c) Use your graph to solve these equations.

       (i) $x^2 - 3x + 2 = 4$ **(ii)** $x^2 - 3x + 2 = 1$

       (iii) $x^2 - 3x + 2 = 5$ **(iv)** $x^2 - 3x + 2 = 2.5$

8 By drawing a suitable graph, solve these equations.

   a) $x^2 + x + 1 = 4$　　**b)** $x^2 + x + 1 = 3$　　**c)** $x^2 + x + 1 = 1.5$　　**d)** $x^2 + x + 1 = 2.4$

9 By drawing a suitable graph, solve these equations.

   a) $x^2 - x - 2 = 2$　　**b)** $x^2 - x - 2 = 5$　　**c)** $x^2 - x - 2 = 4.2$　　**d)** $x^2 - x - 2 = 3.6$

12.6 Graphs and Equations Problems

Exercise 1

1　**a)** Plot the points $A(0, 4)$, $B(2, 6)$, $C(4, 4)$ and $D(2, 0)$ on a set of axes.

   b) Join the points. What kind of shape have you made?

2　The points A and B have coordinates $A(2, 5)$ and $B(-4, 1)$.
   Find the coordinates of the midpoint of the line segment AB.

3　For each of the following equations, write down:

   (i)　the gradient of the line
   (ii)　the coordinates of the line's y-intercept

   a) $y = 2x + 3$　　　　**b)** $y = 3x + 8$　　　　**c)** $y = 4x - 5$

   d) $y = 3 - x$　　　　**e)** $y = 3x + \dfrac{1}{2}$　　　**f)** $y = -\dfrac{2}{3}x - 1$

4　Find the equation of the line which is parallel to the y-axis which passes through the point $(11, -4)$.

5　A horizontal line is drawn on a coordinate grid. The line passes through the point $(3, 7)$.
   What is the equation of the line?

6　Find the gradient of each of the line segments shown in the diagram on the right.

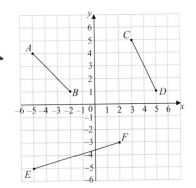

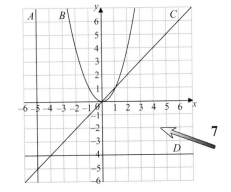

7　Match the graphs shown on the left with the correct equation from the list below.

   $y = x$　　　$x = -5$　　　$y = x^2$　　　$y = -4$

8 Find the gradient of the line passing through the following points.
   a) (0, 0) and (3, 15)
   b) (−4, −5) and (−1, 4)
   c) (−7, 2) and (−4, −1)
   d) (5, −2) and (2, 10)

9 **a)** Write down the coordinates of each of the points A to E.
   b) Find the coordinates of the midpoint of AB.
   c) Find the coordinates of the midpoint of BC.
   d) Write down the equation of the line that passes through points A and E.
   e) Find the gradient of the line BC.

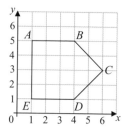

10 Draw each of the following lines on a set of axes.
   a) $x = 1$
   b) $y = -3$
   c) $x = -1$
   d) $y = 5$

11 **a)** Copy and complete the table to show the value of $y = 8 - x$ for values of x from −3 to 3.
   b) Plot the graph of $y = 8 - x$.

x	−3	−2	−1	0	1	2	3
y							
Coordinates							

12 **a)** Copy and complete the table to show the value of $y = 2x + 2$ for values of x from −3 to 3.
   b) Plot the graph of $y = 2x + 2$.
   c) Use your graph to find the value of x when $y = 5$.

x	−3	−2	−1	0	1	2	3
y							
Coordinates							

13 Draw the line $y = 6 - 3x$ for values of x from −1 to 3.

14 The graph on the right shows the curve $y = 3 - x - x^2$. Use the graph to solve the equation $3 - x - x^2 = -2$.

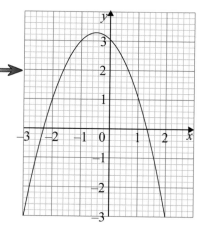

15 **a)** Copy and complete this table to show the value of $y = x^2 + 4x$ for values of x from −4 to 2.

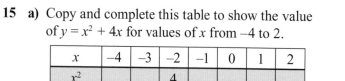

x	−4	−3	−2	−1	0	1	2
x^2			4				
$4x$			−8				
$x^2 + 4x$			−4				

   b) Draw the graph of $y = x^2 + 4x$ for values of x from −4 to 2.
   c) Use your graph to solve the equation $x^2 + 4x = -2$.

Section 13 — Real-Life Graphs

13.1 Interpreting Real-Life Graphs

Graphs can be used to represent real-life situations.
For example, straight-line graphs can be used to convert between different units or currencies.

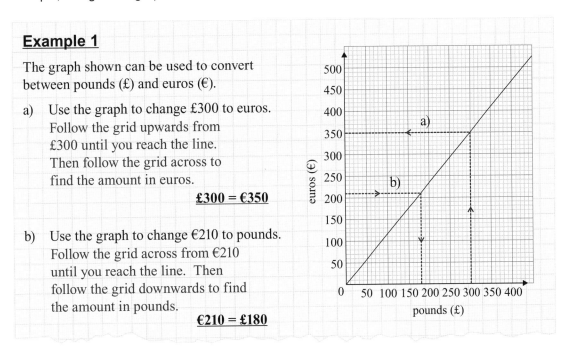

Example 1

The graph shown can be used to convert between pounds (£) and euros (€).

a) Use the graph to change £300 to euros.
Follow the grid upwards from £300 until you reach the line.
Then follow the grid across to find the amount in euros.

£300 = €350

b) Use the graph to change €210 to pounds.
Follow the grid across from €210 until you reach the line. Then follow the grid downwards to find the amount in pounds.

€210 = £180

Exercise 1

The graph on the right can be used to convert between pounds (£) and euros (€).
Use this graph to answer **Questions 1-4**.

1 Use the graph to convert the following amounts from pounds to euros.

   a) £50   **b)** £250   **c)** £110   **d)** £290

2 Use the graph to convert the following amounts from euros to pounds.

   a) €50   **b)** €200   **c)** €360   **d)** €430

3 A dress costs €130. How much is this in pounds?

4 **a)** A TV costs £420 in the UK.
   How much is this in euros?

   b) The price of the TV in France is €470.
   How much is this in pounds?

   c) In which country is the TV cheaper?

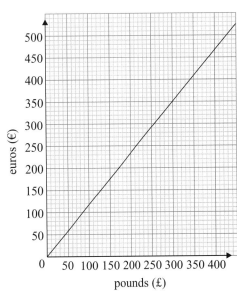

The graph on the right can be used to convert between pounds (£) and Canadian dollars ($). Use this graph to answer **Questions 5-8**.

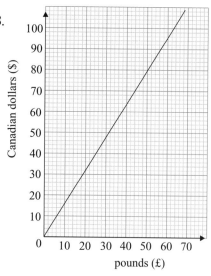

5 Use the graph to convert the following amounts from pounds to Canadian dollars.
  a) £10   **b)** £30   **c)** £44   **d)** £62

6 Use the graph to convert the following amounts from Canadian dollars to pounds.
  a) $10   **b)** $74   **c)** $54   **d)** $40

7 **a)** A shirt costs $58. How much is this in pounds?
  b) I want to buy two shirts. How much will it cost me in pounds?

8 **a)** Convert £40 into Canadian dollars.
  b) Use your answer to convert £80 into Canadian dollars.

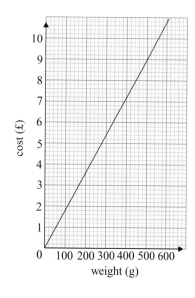

The graph on the left shows the cost of different weights of fudge. Use this graph to answer **Questions 9-12**.

9 Estimate the cost of the following weights of fudge.
  a) 100 g   **b)** 380 g   **c)** 60 g   **d)** 410 g

10 Use the graph to estimate the weight of fudge that could be bought with the following amounts of money.
  a) £5   **b)** £9   **c)** £2.20   **d)** £3.80

11 **a)** Find the cost of 400 g of fudge.
  b) Use your answer to find the cost of 800 g of fudge.

12 How much fudge could I buy for £20?

The graph on the right can be used to convert between kilometres per hour (km/h) and miles per hour (mph). Use this graph to answer **Questions 13-15**.

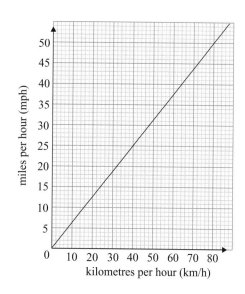

13 **a)** Convert 38 km/h into miles per hour.
  b) Convert 27 mph into km/h.

14 The speed limit on a particular road is 30 mph. A driver travels at 52 km/h. By how many miles per hour is the driver breaking the speed limit?

15 The maximum speed limit in the UK is 70 mph. The maximum speed limit in Spain is 120 km/h. Which country has the higher speed limit, and by how much?

Non-Linear Graphs

Graphs describing real-life situations can be almost any shape.

Example 2

The graph shows the temperature of an oven as it heats up.

a) Describe how the temperature of the oven changes during the first 10 minutes shown on the graph.

b) What is the temperature of the oven after 7 minutes?

c) How long does it take for the temperature to reach 190 °C?

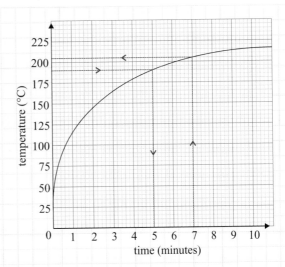

1. The curve is very steep at first, then begins to level out as the temperature increases.

2. Follow the grid upwards from 7 minutes until you reach the curve, then read across to find the temperature.

3. Follow the grid across from 190 °C, then read downwards to find the time.

a) The temperature rises quickly at first, but then rises more slowly as the oven heats up.

b) **205 °C**

c) **5 minutes**

Exercise 2

1 Match each graph below to the most accurate description.

a)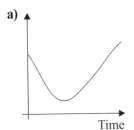

b)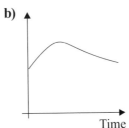

c)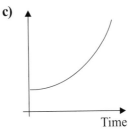

d)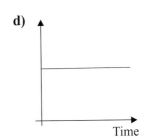

A: The temperature rose quickly, and then fell again gradually.

B: The number of people who needed hospital treatment stayed at the same level all year.

C: The cost of gold went up more and more quickly.

D: The temperature fell overnight, but then climbed quickly again the next morning.

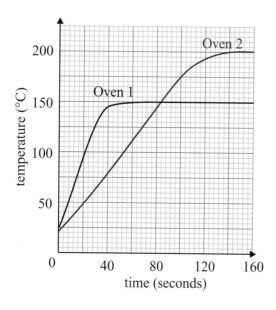

2 The graph on the left shows the temperature in two ovens as they warm up.

  a) Which oven reaches 100 °C more quickly?

  b) Which oven reaches a higher maximum temperature?

  c) Estimate how many seconds it takes Oven 1 to reach its maximum temperature.

  d) Estimate how many seconds it takes Oven 2 to reach its maximum temperature.

  e) (i) After how many seconds are the two ovens at the same temperature?

     (ii) What temperature do they both reach at this time?

3 The graph shows the depth of water in a harbour one day between the times of 08:00 and 20:00.

  a) Describe how the depth of water changed over this time period.

  b) At approximately what time was the depth of water the greatest?

  c) What was the minimum depth of water during this period?

  d) At approximately what times was the water 3 m deep?

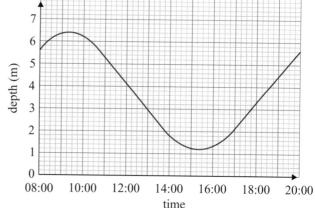

  e) Mike's boat floats when the depth of the water is 1.6 m or over. Estimate the amount of time that his boat was not floating during this period.

4 a) Vase P is 30 cm tall. The depth of water in Vase P as it is filled up with water flowing at a steady rate is shown on the graph on the right. By how much does the depth of water increase:

    (i) between 0 and 5 seconds?

    (ii) between 10 and 15 seconds?

    (iii) between 25 and 30 seconds?

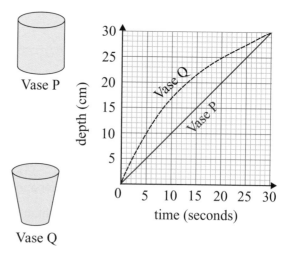

  b) Vase Q is also 30 cm tall. The depth of water in Vase Q is also shown on the graph. By how much does the depth of water increase:

    (i) between 0 and 5 seconds?

    (ii) between 10 and 15 seconds?

    (iii) between 25 and 30 seconds?

  c) Describe the difference between how the depth of water increases in Vase P and Vase Q.

13.2 Drawing Real-Life Graphs

To draw a graph representing a real-life situation, you need some points to plot.

Your graph could be either a **straight line** or a **curve**.
- For a **straight line**, you'll need to plot **at least three** points.
- But if the graph is a **curve**, you'll need **more than three** points.

Example 1

A plumber charges customers a standard fee of £40, plus £30 per hour for all work carried out.

a) Draw a graph to show how the plumber's fee varies with the amount of time the job takes.

b) Use the graph to estimate the amount of time taken to do a job costing £250.

1. Make a table showing the fee for different numbers of hours.
   A 1-hour job will cost £40 + £30 = £70.
   A 2-hour job will cost £40 + (2 × £30) = £100.
   A 3-hour job will cost £40 + (3 × £30) = £130.

a)

Time (hours)	1	2	3	4	5
Fee (£)	70	100	130	160	190

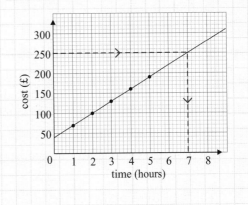

2. Plot the values on a sheet of graph paper and join the points to draw the graph.

   For each extra hour, the fee increases by £30, so this is a straight-line graph.
   This means you only really needed 3 points in your table — but if you're not sure whether it's going to turn out to be a straight line or not, it's always best to plot too many points.

3. Follow the grid across from £250, then read downwards to find the correct time.

b) **7 hours**

Exercise 1

1 The cost of hiring a digger is £40 per day, plus a fixed cost of £20.

   a) Copy and complete the table to show the cost of hiring the digger for different numbers of days.

No. Days	1	2	3	4	5
Cost (£)	60				

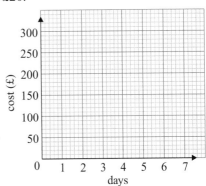

   b) Copy the coordinate grid on the right, then plot the values from your table and draw a line through the points.

   c) Using your graph, find:
      (i) The cost of hiring the digger for 7 days.
      (ii) The number of days the digger was hired for if it cost £260.

2   The instructions for cooking different weights of chicken are as follows:

　　　'**Cook for 35 mins per kg, plus an extra 25 minutes.**'

　　a) Copy and complete the table to show the cooking times for chickens of different weights.

Weight (kg)	1	2	3	4	5
Time (minutes)					

　　b) Draw a set of axes on a sheet of graph paper. Plot the weight on the vertical axis and the time on the horizontal axis. Then plot the values from your table to draw a graph showing the cooking times for different weights of chicken.

$T = 35w + 25$

　　c) A chicken cooks in 110 minutes. What is the weight of the chicken?

3   The cost of a hotel room is £80 per night for the first 3 nights, then £50 per night for every night after that.

　　a) Draw a graph showing how the cost of staying at the hotel varies with the length of stay.

　　b) Use your graph to find how much it would cost to stay at the hotel for 6 nights.

　　c) A guest was charged £340. How many nights did she stay at the hotel?

4   A delivery company charges £6.40 to deliver the first parcel in an order, plus £1.30 for every additional parcel in the order after that.

　　a) Draw a graph showing how the cost of a delivery varies with the number of parcels in the delivery. Plot the number of parcels on the horizontal axis and the cost on the vertical axis.

　　b) Use your graph to find the cost of sending 8 parcels.

　　c) How many parcels did a customer post if she was charged £14.20?

5   This table shows how the fuel efficiency of a car in miles per gallon (mpg) varies with the speed of the car in miles per hour (mph).

Speed (mph)	55	60	65	70	75	80
Fuel Efficiency (mpg)	32.3	30.7	28.9	27.0	24.9	22.7

　　a) Draw a pair of axes with speed on the horizontal axis and fuel efficiency on the vertical axis. Plot the points from the table on your axes and join them up with a smooth curve.

　　b) Use your graph to predict the fuel efficiency of the car when it is travelling at 73 mph.

6   Helena is a baby girl. A health visitor records the weight of Helena every two months. The measurements are shown in the table below.

Age (months)	0	2	4	6	8	10	12	14	16
Weight (kg)	3.2	4.6	5.9	7.0	7.9	8.7	9.3	9.8	10.2

　　a) Draw a graph to show this information. Plot age on the horizontal axis and weight on the vertical axis. Join your points with a smooth curve.

　　b) Keira is 9 months old and has a weight of 9.1 kg. Use your graph to estimate how much heavier Keira is than Helena was at 9 months old.

Section 14 — Angles and 2D Shapes

14.1 Basic Angle Properties

Angles at a point **on a straight line** add up to **180°**.

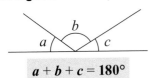

$a + b + c = 180°$

Angles **around a point** add up to **360°**.

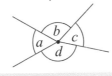

$a + b + c + d = 360°$

Perpendicular lines meet at 90° to form a **right angle** (shown by the little square).

$a + b = 90°$

Angles within a **right angle** add up to **90°**.

Example 1

Find the size of angle a.

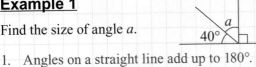

1. Angles on a straight line add up to 180°.
    Use this to form an equation in terms of a.
2. Simplify the equation.
3. Solve the equation to find a.

$40° + a + 90° = 180°$

$a + 130° = 180°$

$a = 180° - 130°$

$\boldsymbol{a = 50°}$

Exercise 1

In **Questions 1-3**, find the missing angles marked with letters.
(The angles aren't drawn accurately, so you shouldn't try to measure them.)

1

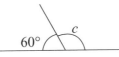

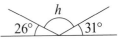

2

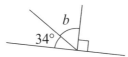

3

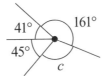

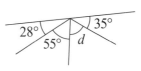

Example 2

Find the value of *a* in the diagram.

1. Angles around a point add up to 360°.
   Use this to form an equation in terms of *a*.
2. Simplify the equation.
3. Then solve your equation to find *a*.

$a + 2a + 80° + 40° + 90° = 360°$

$3a + 210° = 360°$

$3a = 360° - 210° = 150°$

$a = 150 \div 3 = \underline{\mathbf{50°}}$

Exercise 2

The angles in this Exercise aren't drawn accurately, so don't try to measure them.

1 Find the value of each of the letters in the following diagrams.

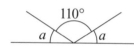

   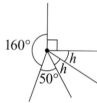

2 Using the diagram on the right, state whether the following are true or false. Give a reason for your answer in each case.

a) *EB* is a straight line

b) *AO* is perpendicular to *EO*

c) *FC* is a straight line

d) the angle *p* = 98°

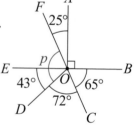

3 Find the value of each of the letters in the following diagrams.

4 Explain why the line *AOB* on the right cannot be a straight line.

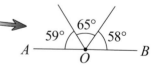

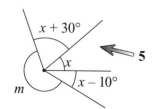

5 a) Given that *x* = 40°, find the sizes of the three angles involving *x* in the diagram.

b) Find the value of *m*.

14.2 Triangles

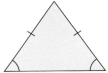

An **isosceles** triangle has 2 equal sides (shown by the 'tick marks'). It also has 2 equal angles.

An **equilateral** triangle has 3 equal sides. It also has 3 equal angles.

The sides and angles of a **scalene** triangle are all different.

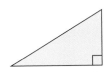

A **right-angled** triangle has 1 right angle.

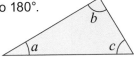

An **acute-angled** triangle has 3 acute angles.

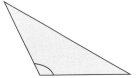

An **obtuse-angled** triangle has 1 obtuse angle.

The angles in **any** triangle add up to 180°.

$a + b + c = 180°$

Example 1

Find the value of x in the triangle shown.

1. The angles in a triangle add up to 180°. Use this to form an equation in terms of x.

$$x + 60° + 90° = 180°$$
$$x + 150° = 180°$$

2. Solve your equation to find x.

$$x = 180° - 150° = \underline{\mathbf{30°}}$$

Exercise 1

1 Describe each of these triangles using the above definitions.

a)
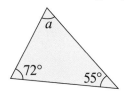

b)
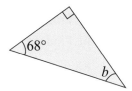

c)

d)

In **Questions 2-7**, the angles aren't drawn accurately, so don't try to measure them.

2 Find the missing angles marked with letters.

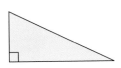

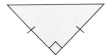

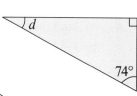

3   Find the missing angles marked with letters.

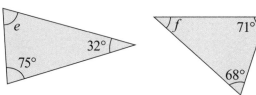

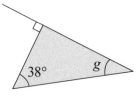

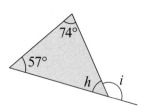

Example 2

Find the value of x in the triangle shown.

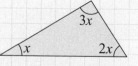

1.   Form an equation in terms of x. $x + 2x + 3x = 180°$
2.   Solve your equation to find x. $6x = 180°$

$$x = 180° \div 6 = \underline{\mathbf{30°}}$$

---

4   Find the values of the letters shown in the following diagrams.

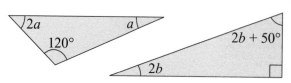

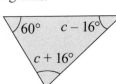

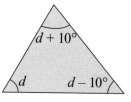

Example 3

Find the values of j and k in the isosceles triangle shown.

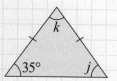

1.   The triangle is isosceles, so angle j is the same size as the angle of 35°. $\underline{\mathbf{j = 35°}}$

2.   Now use the fact that angles in a triangle add up to 180° to form $35° + 35° + k = 180°$
an equation in terms of k. Then solve your equation to find k. $70° + k = 180°$

$$k = 180° - 70° = \underline{\mathbf{110°}}$$

---

5   Find the values of the letters shown in these diagrams.

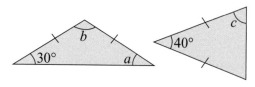

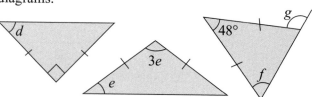

6   **a)** Find the value of x.
   b) Find the value of y.

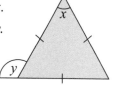

7   **a)** Find the value of p.
   b) Find the value of q.

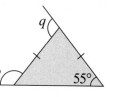

14.3 Parallel and Intersecting Lines

Opposite Angles

When two straight lines **intersect** (or cross), two pairs of
opposite angles are formed. Opposite angles are equal.

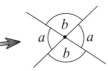

Example 1

Find the values of *a*, *b* and *c*
shown in the diagram.

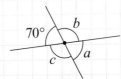

1. *a* and 70° are opposite angles, so they are equal.
2. *b* and the angle marked 70° lie on a straight line,
   so they add up to 180°.
3. *c* and *b* are opposite angles, so they are equal.

$\underline{a = \mathbf{70°}}$

$70° + b = 180°$

$b = 180° - 70° = \underline{\mathbf{110°}}$

$c = b = \underline{\mathbf{110°}}$

Exercise 1

In **Questions 1-4**, the angles aren't drawn accurately, so don't try to measure them.

1 Find the missing angles marked by letters.

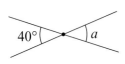

2 The diagram on the right shows a teepee in the shape of an isosceles triangle.

   a) Find the size of angle *v*.

   b) Use your answer to write down the value of *w*.
   Give a reason for your answer.

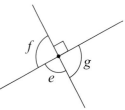

3 Find the missing angles marked by letters.

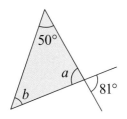
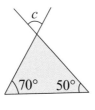
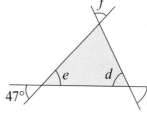
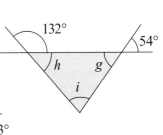

4 The diagram on the right shows two isosceles triangles.
Find the missing angles marked by letters.

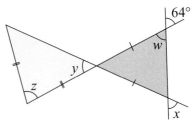

Section 14 — Angles and 2D Shapes **151**

Alternate Angles

When a straight line crosses two parallel lines (shown by the arrows), it forms two pairs of **alternate angles** (in a sort of Z-shape). Alternate angles are equal.

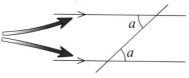 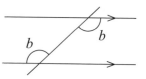

Example 2

Find the values of a, b and c in the diagram.

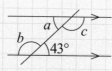

1. a and $43°$ are alternate angles, so they are equal.

   $\underline{\textbf{\textit{a} = 43°}}$

2. b and the angle marked $43°$ lie on a straight line, so they add up to $180°$.

   $43° + b = 180°$

   $b = 180° - 43° = \underline{\textbf{137°}}$

3. c and b are alternate angles, so they are equal.

   $c = b = \underline{\textbf{137°}}$

Exercise 2

In **Questions 1-3**, the angles aren't drawn accurately, so don't try to measure them.

1 Find the missing angles marked by letters.

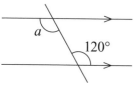 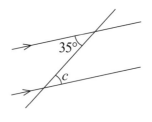 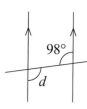

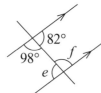 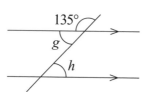 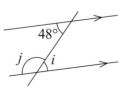

2 The diagram on the right shows a staircase between two parallel floors of a building. The staircase makes an angle of $42°$ with the lower floor.

a) Write down the angle that the staircase makes with the upper floor, marked x on the diagram.

b) Give a reason for your answer.

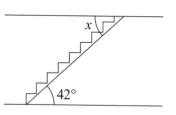

3 Find the missing angles marked by letters.

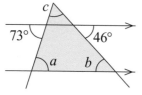 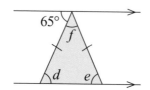 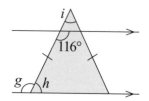

Corresponding Angles and Supplementary Angles

Corresponding angles formed
by parallel lines are equal.

Corresponding angles
form a sort of F-shape.

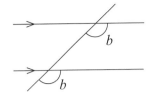

Supplementary angles add up to 180°.
A pair of supplementary angles are
formed when a straight line crosses two
parallel lines, making a kind of C-shape.

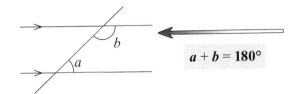

$$a + b = 180°$$

Example 3

Find the values of a, b and c
shown in the diagram.

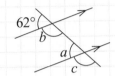

1. a and 62° are corresponding angles, so they are equal. $\underline{a = 62°}$
2. b and the angle marked 62° lie on a straight line,
    so they add up to 180°. (Or you could say a and b are
    supplementary angles, so they add up to 180°.)
    $$62° + b = 180°$$
    $$b = 180° - 62° = \underline{118°}$$
3. c and b are corresponding angles, so they're equal. $c = b = \underline{118°}$

Exercise 3

In **Questions 1-4**, the angles aren't drawn accurately, so don't try to measure them.

1 Find the missing angles marked by letters.

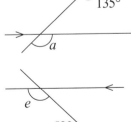

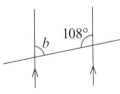

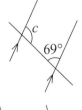

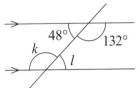

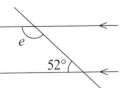

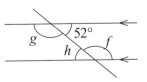

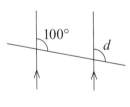

2 Find the missing angles marked by letters.

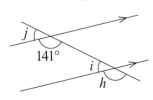

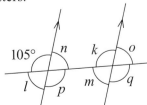

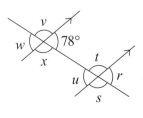

3 Two wooden posts stand vertically on sloped ground. The first post makes an angle of 99° with the downward slope, as shown. Find the angle that the second post makes with the upward slope, labelled *y* on the diagram.

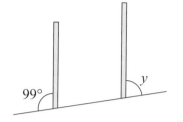

4 Find the missing angles marked by letters.

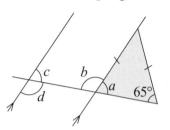 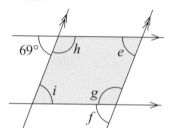 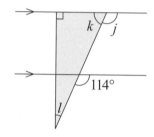

Exercise 4 — Mixed Exercise

In **Questions 1-2**, the angles aren't drawn accurately, so don't try to measure them.

1 Find the missing angles marked by letters. In each case, give a reason for your answer.

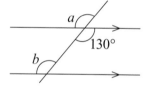 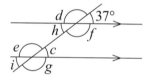 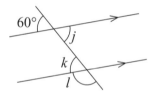

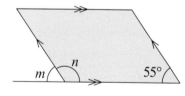 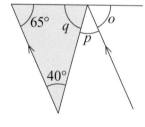 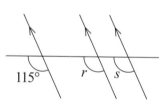

 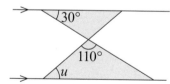 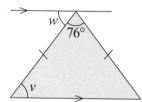

2 The diagram on the right shows some scaffolding. The triangle formed between the two horizontal bars is isosceles.

Find the size of angles *w*, *x*, *y* and *z*, giving a reason for your answer in each case.

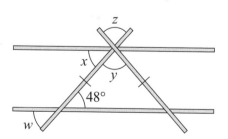

14.4 Quadrilaterals

A **quadrilateral** is a 4-sided shape. The angles in a quadrilateral add up to **360°**.

Example 1

Find the missing angle x in this quadrilateral.

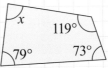

1. The angles in a quadrilateral add up to 360°.
   Use this to write an equation involving x.
2. Then solve your equation to find the value of x.

$79° + 73° + 119° + x = 360°$

$271° + x = 360°$

$x = 360° - 271° = \underline{\mathbf{89°}}$

Exercise 1

1 Find the size of the angles marked by letters in the following quadrilaterals.
(They're not drawn accurately, so don't try to measure them.)

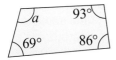 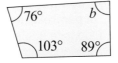 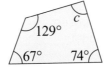 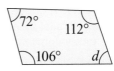 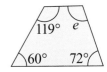

Squares and Rectangles

A **square** is a quadrilateral
with 4 equal sides
and 4 angles of 90°.

A **rectangle** is a quadrilateral with
4 angles of 90° and opposite
sides of the same length.

Exercise 2

1 Copy the diagram below, then add two
more points to form a square. Join the
points to complete the square.

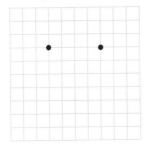

2 Copy the diagram below, then add two
more points to form a rectangle. Join the
points to complete the rectangle.

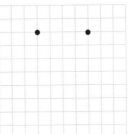

3 **a)** Measure the length of the diagonals on the square on the right. What do you notice?

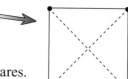

b) At what angle do the two diagonals cross?

c) By measuring diagonals, determine which of the following are squares.

(i)   **(ii)**   **(iii)**

Parallelograms and Rhombuses

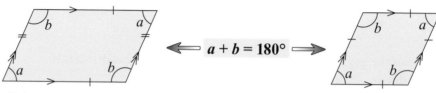

$a + b = 180°$

A **parallelogram** is a quadrilateral with 2 pairs of equal, parallel sides. Opposite angles of a parallelogram are equal. Neighbouring angles add up to 180°.

A **rhombus** is a quadrilateral with 2 pairs of parallel sides, all of the same length. Opposite angles of a rhombus are equal. Neighbouring angles add up to 180°.

Example 2

Find the size of the angles marked with letters in this rhombus.

1. Opposite angles in a rhombus are equal. Use this fact to find angle x.

2. Neighbouring angles in a rhombus add up to 180°. Use this fact to find angle y.

3. Opposite angles in a rhombus are equal, so z is the same size as y.

$x = \mathbf{60°}$

$60° + y = 180°$

$y = 180° - 60° = \underline{\mathbf{120°}}$

$\underline{z = \mathbf{120°}}$

Exercise 3

1 **a)** Copy the diagram on the right. Add one more point and join the points to form a rhombus.

b) On a new grid, plot four points to form a parallelogram.

2 Calculate the size of the angles marked by letters in these quadrilaterals. (They're not drawn accurately, so don't try to measure them.)

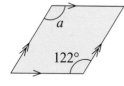   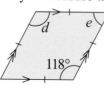 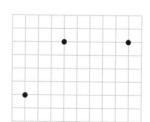 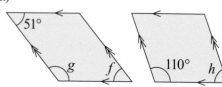

Kites

A **kite** is a quadrilateral with
2 pairs of equal sides and 1 pair of
equal angles in opposite corners.

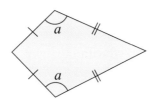

Example 3

Find the size of the angles
marked with letters in this kite.

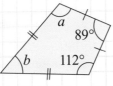

1. a and the 112° angle must be equal.
2. A kite is a quadrilateral, so its angles add up to 360°.
    Use this to write an equation in terms of b.

$\underline{a = 112°}$

$112° + 112° + 89° + b = 360°$

$313° + b = 360°$

$b = 360° - 313° = \underline{47°}$

Exercise 4

1 Which letter goes in each box to complete the sentences about this kite? ➡

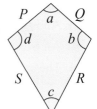

   a) Angle b is the same size as angle ☐

   b) The length of side P is the same as side ☐

   c) The length of side R is the same as side ☐

2 Find the size of the angles marked by letters in these kites.
   (They're not drawn accurately, so don't try to measure them.)

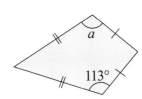 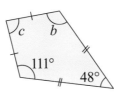 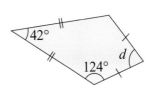 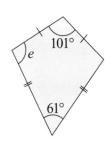

Trapeziums

$a + b = 180°$ $c + d = 180°$

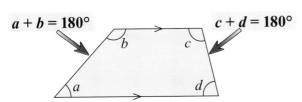

A **trapezium** is a quadrilateral
with 1 pair of parallel sides.

$a + b = 180°$

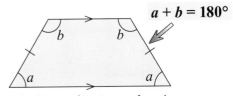

An **isosceles trapezium** is a
trapezium with 2 pairs of equal angles,
and 2 sides of the same length.

Example 4

Find the size of the angles marked with
letters in this isosceles trapezium.

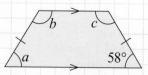

1. This is an isosceles trapezium, so a must equal 58°.

    $a = 58°$

2. Angle c and the angle of 58° must add up to 180°.

    $c + 58° = 180°$
    $c = 180° - 58° = \underline{\mathbf{122°}}$

3. Angles a and b must add up to 180°.
    (Or use the fact that b and c must be equal.)

    $a + b = 180°$
    $b = 180° - a = 180° - 58° = \underline{\mathbf{122°}}$

Exercise 5

1 Choose the correct word from each pair to complete the following sentences.

   a) A trapezium is a quadrilateral with one pair of (**parallel** / **equal**) sides.

   b) An isosceles trapezium has (**one pair** / **two pairs**) of equal angles.

   c) An isosceles trapezium has (**one pair** / **two pairs**) of parallel sides.

   d) An isosceles trapezium has (**one pair** / **two pairs**) of equal sides.

   e) The angles in a trapezium add up to (**180°** / **360°**).

2 Find the size of the angles marked by letters in these trapeziums. (Don't measure them.)

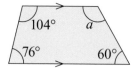
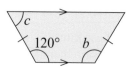
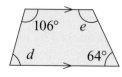
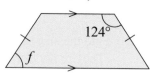

Exercise 6 — Mixed Exercise

1 Match one name from the box to
     each of the quadrilaterals below.

   | square   kite   rectangle   trapezium   parallelogram |

   a) 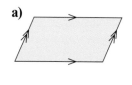 **b)** 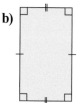 **c)** 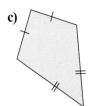 **d)** 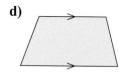 **e)**

2 Write down all the different types of quadrilaterals which satisfy each of the following properties.

   a) 4 equal sides

   b) 4 angles of 90°

   c) 2 pairs of equal sides

   d) 2 pairs of parallel sides

   e) at least 1 pair of parallel sides

   f) exactly 1 pair of parallel sides

3 Find the size of the angles marked by letters in these diagrams. (Don't measure them.)

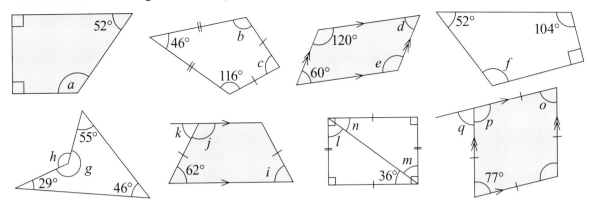

4 A quadrilateral has 40°, 83° and 99° angles. Find the size of the fourth angle.

5 A parallelogram has two angles of 100° each. Find the size of the other two angles.

6 An isosceles trapezium has two angles of 53°. Find the size of the other two angles.

7 A kite has exactly one angle of 50° and exactly one angle of 90°. Find the size of the other two angles.

14.5 Interior and Exterior Angles

A **polygon** is a shape whose sides are all straight.

A **regular polygon** has sides of equal length and angles that are all equal.

Polygons have special names depending on the number of sides they have.
For example: (i) A polygon with 3 sides is a **triangle**. (ii) A polygon with 4 sides is a **quadrilateral**.
 (iii) A polygon with 5 sides is a **pentagon**. (iv) A polygon with 6 sides is a **hexagon**.

Interior Angles

The **interior angles** of a polygon are the angles inside each corner.

The **sum** of a polygons's interior angles depends on the **number of sides** it has.
For example, the interior angles of a shape with 3 sides (a triangle) always add up to 180°.

Example 1

Find the sum of the interior angles of a pentagon.

1. You can find the sum of a shape's interior angles by splitting it up into triangles. So first draw any pentagon — it doesn't have to be regular.

2. Split the pentagon into triangles by drawing lines from one corner to all the others.

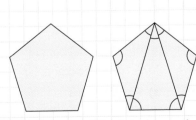

3. Angles in a triangle add up to 180°, and there are 3 triangles.

So the sum of the interior angles of a pentagon is 3 × 180° = **540°**

Exercise 1

1 By dividing each shape into triangles, find the sum of the interior angles of the following.

a)    **b)**    **c)**    **d)**

2 Find the sum of the interior angles of a polygon with:

a) 6 sides   **b)** 10 sides   **c)** 12 sides   **d)** 20 sides

---

Example 2

A pentagon has four interior angles of 100°. Find the size of the fifth angle.

1. The interior angles of a pentagon add up to 540°. Use this fact to write an equation for the size of the missing angle, x.

$100° + 100° + 100° + 100° + x = 540°$

$400° + x = 540°$

2. Solve your equation to find x.

$x = 540° - 400° = \underline{\mathbf{140°}}$

---

3 Sketch the polygon shown on the right.

a) What happens when you try to divide the polygon into triangles by drawing a line from the 65° angle to each of the other corners?

b) Join the corner marked x to each of the other corners to split the shape into triangles.

c) Find the sum of the interior angles of the shape.

d) Find the size of the angle marked x.

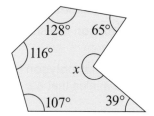

4 Find the size of the angles marked by letters in these polygons.

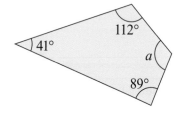   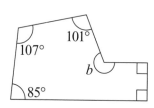   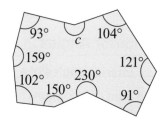

Example 3

Find the size of each of the interior angles of a regular hexagon.

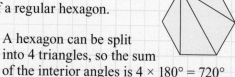

1. Find the sum of the interior angles of a hexagon.

A hexagon can be split into 4 triangles, so the sum of the interior angles is $4 \times 180° = 720°$

2. All the angles in a regular polygon are equal, so divide the sum of the angles by how many there are.

So each interior angle of a regular hexagon is $720° \div 6 = \underline{\mathbf{120°}}$

---

5 A regular heptagon is shown on the right.

   a) Find the sum of the interior angles of a heptagon.

   b) Find the size of each of the interior angles of a regular heptagon.

6 Find the size of each of the interior angles in the following shapes.

   a) Regular octagon
      (8 sides)

   b) Regular nonagon
      (9 sides)
      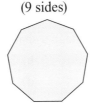

   c) Regular decagon
      (10 sides)
      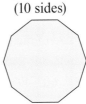

7 Four angles of a pentagon are 110°.

   a) Find the size of the fifth angle.

   b) Is this a regular pentagon? Give a reason for your answer.

Exterior Angles

The **exterior angles** of a polygon are the angles between a side and a line that extends out from one of the neighbouring sides.

The sum of the exterior angles of any polygon is **360°**.

$$a + b + c + d + e = 360°$$

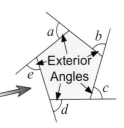

Example 4

Find the size of each of the exterior angles of a regular hexagon.

1. A hexagon has 6 exterior angles.
   Exterior angles always add up to 360°.

2. Divide to find the size of each angle.

   $360° \div 6 = 60°$

   So each exterior angle is **60°**

Exercise 2

1 The diagram on the right shows a regular pentagon with the exterior angles marked on.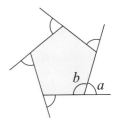

   a) Find a, the size of each of the exterior angles of the pentagon.

   b) Hence find b, the size of each of the interior angles of the pentagon.

2 **a)** Find the size of each of the exterior angles of the following polygons.

   (i) regular heptagon   **(ii)** regular octagon   **(iii)** regular nonagon

   b) Use your answers to part **a)** to find the size of each of the interior angles of these polygons.

3 Find the size of the angles marked by letters in these diagrams.

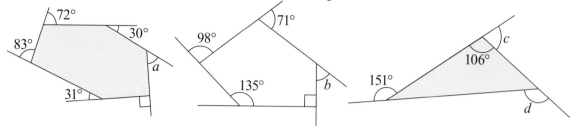

4 Find the size of the unknown exterior angle in a shape whose other exterior angles are:

a) 100°, 68°, 84° and 55°

b) 30°, 68°, 45°, 52°, 75° and 50°

c) 42°, 51°, 60°, 49°, 88° and 35°

d) 19°, 36°, 28°, 57°, 101°, 57 and 22°

Example 5

A regular polygon has exterior angles of 30°.
How many sides does the polygon have? Explain your answer.

1. Divide 360° by the size of the exterior angles to find how many exterior angles the shape has.

2. The number of exterior angles is the same as the number of sides.

Exterior angles of a polygon add up to 360°.
In a regular polygon, all the exterior angles are equal, so there are 360° ÷ 30° = 12 exterior angles.
This means the polygon has **12 sides**.

---

5 A regular polygon has exterior angles of 45°.

a) How many sides does the polygon have? What is the name of this kind of polygon?

b) Sketch the polygon.

c) What is the size of each of the polygon's interior angles?

d) What is the sum of the polygon's interior angles?

6 The exterior angles of some regular polygons are given below.
For each exterior angle, find:

    (i) the number of sides the polygon has,

    (ii) the size of each of the polygon's interior angles,

    (iii) the sum of the polygon's interior angles.

a) 60°   **b)** 90°   **c)** 40°   **d)** 120°   **e)** 10°

f) 9°   **g)** 6°   **h)** 5°   **i)** 4°   **j)** 3°

7 Find the values of the letters in the following diagrams.

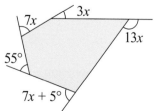 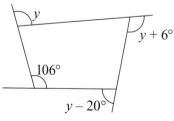 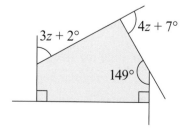

Tessellations

A **tessellation** is a tiling pattern where a shape can be repeated forever with no gaps or overlaps. Not all shapes tessellate — with these, you get gaps or overlaps when you try and arrange them.

Example 6

a) Show how an equilateral triangle tessellates.
You can tile a floor with equilateral triangles with no gaps or overlaps, and the pattern can be repeated forever.

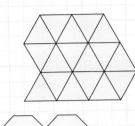

b) Does a regular octagon (8 sides) tessellate?
If you try to tile a floor with regular octagons, you'll always leave gaps, or the octagons will overlap.

A regular octagon **does not tessellate**.

Exercise 3

1 By making a tiling pattern, show whether or not the following shapes tessellate.

a)   b)   c)  d)

2 Show how each of these shapes tessellates by fitting together 6 copies of the shape on a grid.

a) 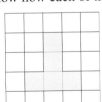 b) 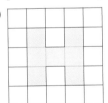 c)   d)

3 Show how each of these shapes tessellates.

a) a trapezium b) a kite c) a rhombus d) a parallelogram

4 Draw a set of axes with x-values from 0 to 8 and y-values from 0 to 6.
For each of the following, draw the shape whose corners are given by the coordinates.
Then show how the shape tessellates by fitting together 6 copies of the shape.

a) (0, 0), (2, 0), (2, 2)
b) (2, 2), (4, 2), (4, 3), (2, 4)
c) (0, 0), (3, 0), (3, 1), (1, 1), (1, 3), (0, 3)
d) (0, 0), (4, 0), (3, 2), (1, 2)

5 Draw **any** quadrilateral. Show how your quadrilateral tessellates.

14.6 Symmetry

Line Symmetry

A **line of symmetry** on a shape is a mirror line, where you can fold the shape so that both halves match up exactly. Each side of the line of symmetry is a **reflection** of the other.

Line of Symmetry

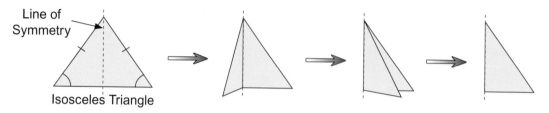

Isosceles Triangle

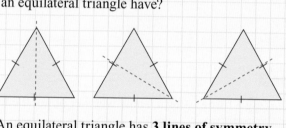

Example 1

How many lines of symmetry does an equilateral triangle have?

An equilateral triangle has three mirror lines, where the shape can be folded perfectly in half.

An equilateral triangle has **3 lines of symmetry**.

Exercise 1

1   Copy each of the shapes below, then draw on any lines of symmetry.
    State the number of lines of symmetry you have drawn for each shape.

a)    b) 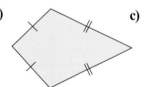   c)    d)

e) 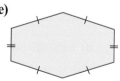   f) 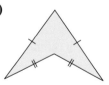   g)    h)

2   Sketch each of the shapes below, then draw on any lines of symmetry.
    State the number of lines of symmetry you have drawn for each shape.

a) rectangle   b) rhombus   c) parallelogram   d) isosceles trapezium

e) regular pentagon   f) regular hexagon g) regular heptagon   h) regular octagon

Rotational Symmetry

The **order of rotational symmetry** of a shape is the number of positions you can rotate (turn) the shape into so that it looks exactly the same.

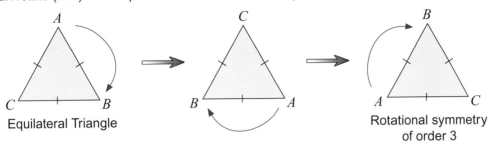

Equilateral Triangle

Rotational symmetry
of order 3

A shape that only looks the same once every complete turn has rotational symmetry of **order 1** (or **no rotational symmetry**).

Example 2

What is the order of rotational symmetry of a rhombus?

There are two orientations
in which a rhombus
looks exactly the same.

180°

A rhombus has **rotational symmetry of order 2**.

Exercise 2

1   Find the order of rotational symmetry of each of the following shapes.

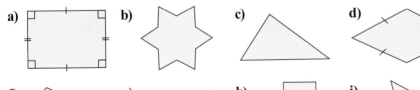

a) **b)** **c)** **d)** **e)**

f) **g)** **h)** **i)** **j)**

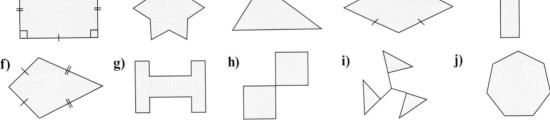

2   Sketch each of the shapes below, then find the order of rotational symmetry for each.

   a) square   **b)** isosceles triangle   **c)** scalene triangle   **d)** isosceles trapezium

   e) regular pentagon   **f)** regular hexagon   **g)** regular octagon   **h)** regular decagon

Exercise 3 — Mixed Exercise

1 For each of the shapes below, find:
  (i) the number of lines of symmetry,
  (ii) the order of rotational symmetry.

a)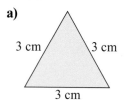

3 cm   3 cm

3 cm

b)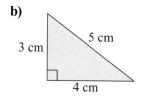

3 cm   5 cm

4 cm

c)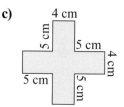

4 cm

5 cm   5 cm

5 cm   4 cm

5 cm

d)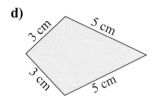

3 cm   5 cm

3 cm   5 cm

2 Decide which of the shapes below matches each of the descriptions.

A 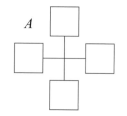   *B* 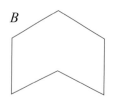   *C*   *D*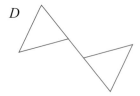

  a) 1 line of symmetry, no rotational symmetry.
  b) 4 lines of symmetry, rotational symmetry of order 4.
  c) No lines of symmetry, rotational symmetry of order 2.
  d) 5 lines of symmetry, rotational symmetry of order 5.

3 Copy the diagram below, then shade one more square to make a pattern with 1 line of symmetry.

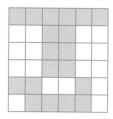

5 Copy the diagram below, then shade one more square to make a pattern with rotational symmetry of order 2.

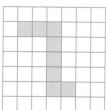

4 Copy the diagram below, then shade two more squares to make a pattern with 2 lines of symmetry.

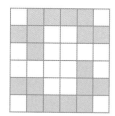

6 Copy the diagram below, then shade two more squares to make a pattern with 4 lines of symmetry and rotational symmetry of order 4.

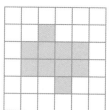

14.7 Angles and 2D Shapes Problems

Exercise 1

For **Questions 1-3**, find the missing angles marked with letters.
(None of the pictures are drawn accurately, so don't measure them.)

1

162° *a*

28° *b*

53° *d* *c* *e*

f *f* *f* *f*

g 115° 59°

h 135° 41°

i *i* *i* *i* *i*

j 31°

58° *m* 75° *l* *k* *n*

2

101° 87° *r*

s 95° 103° *t*

62° *u* *v*

y 102° *w* *x* 71° 95°

3

124° *o*

p 62° *q*

r 108° 85°

4 This question is about shapes *A-G* below.

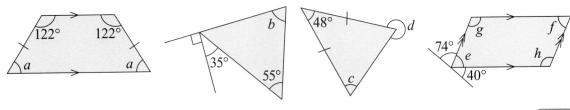

A   *B*   *C*   *D*   *E*   *F*   *G*

a) Which of the shapes are polygons?
b) Which of the shapes are hexagons?
c) Which of the shapes are pentagons?
d) Which of the shapes are quadrilaterals?

5 Find the size of the angles marked with letters.

122° 122° *a* *a*

35° 55° *b*

48° *c* *d*

74° *g* *e* 40° *f* *h*

6 Find the size of the angles marked with letters.

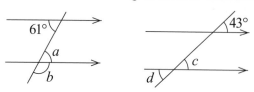

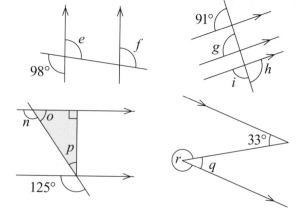

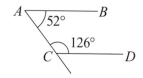

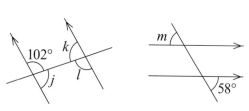

7 Are the lines AB and CD parallel to each other? Explain your answer.

A — 52° — B
C — 126° — D

8 a) Calculate the sum of the interior angles of a hexagon.
   b) Use your answer to find angle x.

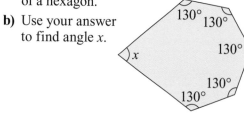

130° 130°
130°
x
130°
130°

9 a) Calculate the sum of the interior angles of a pentagon.
   b) Use your answer to find the size of angle y.

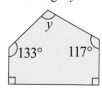

y
133° 117°

10 Find angles w and z.

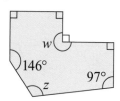

w
146°
z 97°

11 Find angle p in the diagram below.

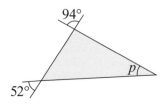

94°
p
52°

12 The diagram below shows a kite and a square.
   a) Write down the value of a.
   b) Use your answer to find the size of angles b and c.

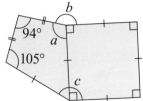

b
94° a
105°
c

13 a) Find x in the diagram below.
   b) Use your answer to find y.

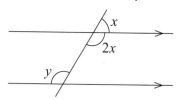

x
$2x$
y

14 Find x and y in the diagram below.

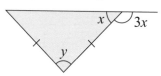

x $3x$
y

Section 15 — Units, Measuring and Estimating

15.1 Reading Scales

Reading Scales

Some marks on a **scale** have a number written next to them. Usually, other marks don't — you have to work out what they represent.

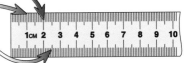

Example 1

Write down the volume of liquid in the beaker on the right.

1. Write down the interval between the numbered units.   10 ml

2. Divide this interval by the number of smaller divisions $10 \div 2 = 5$ ml
    between each number to find what each division represents.
    Here, there are 2 divisions between each number.

3. The amount in the beaker is 20 ml, plus the $20 + 5 = $ **25 ml**
    amount represented by one small division.

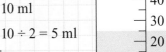

Exercise 1

1   Write down the lengths shown by the arrows on the ruler. Give your answers in centimetres.

a)

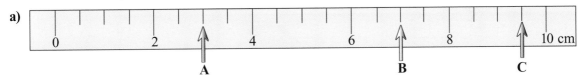

b)

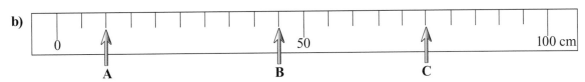

c)

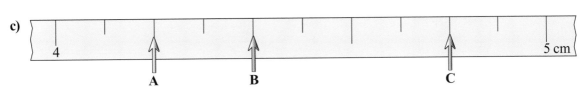

d)

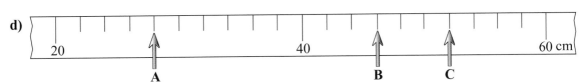

2   Use the fact that 1 cm = 10 mm to write down the length of each of the bugs in mm.

a)
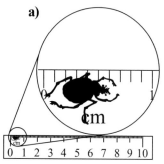

b)
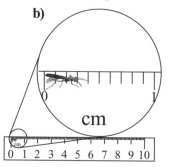

c)
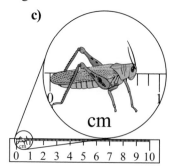

3   How tall is Jules the toy giraffe?

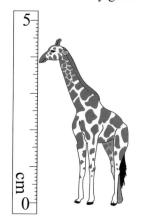

4   For each sunflower, write down how tall it has grown.

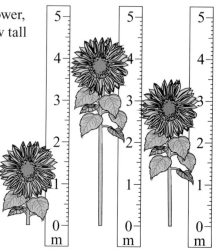

5   Write down the mass shown by the arrow on each scale.

a)

b)

c)

d)

e)

f)

g)

h)

i)

6 Write down the weight of the bananas.

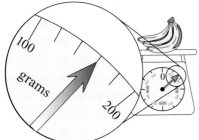

7 Write down the volume of liquid in the bottle.

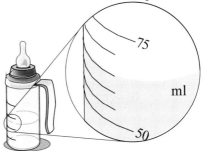

8 Write down the volume of liquid shown in each of these containers.

a)

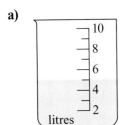

b)

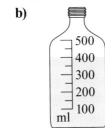

c)

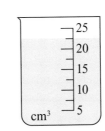

d)

e)

f)

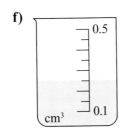

g)

h)

Inaccuracy of Measurements

The **accuracy** of a measurement depends on the device being used to make that measurement.

For example, this ruler measures to the nearest millimetre — so both these bugs seem to be 9 mm long.
But using a more precise piece of equipment, you can see the first bug is actually slightly smaller than the second.

When you measure to the nearest millimetre, anything from 8.5 mm up to 9.5 mm would round to 9 mm. We say that 8.5 mm is the **lower bound** and 9.5 mm is the **upper bound**.

Example 2

The length of a pen is measured and found to be 15 cm, to the nearest 1 cm.
Write down the lower bound and the upper bound for the pen's length.

1. The length has been rounded to the nearest cm.
    The smallest value that would round up to 15 cm is 14.5 cm.   Lower bound = **14.5 cm**
2. The biggest value that would round down to 15 cm is 15.5 cm.   Upper bound = **15.5 cm**

Exercise 2

1 Find the lower and upper bounds for each of these measurements.

  a) A length of 10 cm, which has been measured to the nearest 1 cm.

  b) A mass of 15 g, which has been measured to the nearest 1 g.

  c) A length of 23 km, which has been measured to the nearest 1 km.

  d) A volume of 18 litres, which has been measured to the nearest 1 litre.

  e) A length of 57 mm, which has been measured to the nearest 1 mm.

  f) A volume of 133 ml, which has been measured to the nearest 1 ml.

Example 3

The volume of a teacup is measured and found to be 135 ml, to the nearest 5 ml.
Write down the lower bound and the upper bound for the teacup's volume.

1. The volume has been rounded to the nearest 5 ml.   Lower bound $= 135 - (5 \div 2)$
    Find the lower bound by subtracting <u>half</u> of 5 ml $= \mathbf{132.5\ ml}$
    from 135 ml.

2. Find the upper bound by adding <u>half</u> of 5 ml to 135 ml.   Upper bound $= 135 + (5 \div 2)$

3. So values from 132.5 to 137.5 ml would round to 135 ml, $= \mathbf{137.5\ ml}$
    when measured to the nearest 5 ml.

---

2 Find the lower and upper bounds for each of these measurements.

  a) A length of 175 cm, which has been measured to the nearest 5 cm.

  b) A length of 890 km, which has been measured to the nearest 10 km.

  c) A mass of 230 g, which has been measured to the nearest 5 g.

  d) A volume of 65 litres, which has been measured to the nearest 5 litres.

  e) A volume of 2100 litres, which has been measured to the nearest 100 litres.

  f) A length of 20 m, which has been measured to the nearest 2 m.

3 A pipette contains 5.7 cm³ of liquid, measured to the nearest 0.1 cm³.
What is the greatest amount of liquid that could be in the pipette?

4 A snake is measured to be 10.6 m long to the nearest 0.2 m.
Write down the lower and upper bound for the snake's length.

5 **a)** What temperature is shown on the thermometer on the right?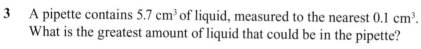

  b) This thermometer is accurate to 5 °C. Tom's tomato plants can only survive outside over 20 °C.
  Is it safe for Tom to put his plants outside?

6 Liz's house has a front door which is 96.5 cm wide.
She wants to buy a table which is given as 95 cm wide, to the nearest 2 cm.
Can she be sure that the table will fit through her door?

7 A set of kitchen scales can measure masses correct to the nearest 10 g.
Janek weighs out 100 g of flour. Work out the lower and upper bounds for the mass of the flour.

8 Tanya and Kyle measure their heights. They both say that they are 170 cm to the nearest 10 cm.
What is the maximum possible difference between their heights?

15.2 Converting Metric Units — Length, Mass and Volume

To convert between metric units, multiply or divide by the correct **conversion factor**.

Length	Mass	Volume
1 cm = 10 mm	1 g = 1000 mg	1 litre (l) = 1000 ml
1 m = 100 cm	1 kg = 1000 g	1 litre = 100 centilitres (cl)
1 km = 1000 m	1 tonne = 1000 kg	1 ml = 1 cm^3

Example 1

a)   Convert 2.5 m into cm.

   1. There are 100 cm in 1 m, so the conversion factor is 100.   1 m = 100 cm

   2. To convert m into cm you need to   So 2.5 m = 2.5 × 100
       multiply by the conversion factor.   = **250 cm**

b)   Convert 2500 m into km.

   1. There are 1000 m in 1 km, so the conversion factor is 1000.   1 km = 1000 m

   2. To convert m into km you need to   So 2500 m = 2500 ÷ 1000
       divide by the conversion factor.   = **2.5 km**

Exercise 1

For **Questions 1-3**, convert each measurement into the units given.

1   **a)** 2 cm into mm   **b)** 3 l into ml   **c)** 4.1 g into mg   **d)** 15 ml into cm^3
       e) 126.7 cm^3 into ml   **f)** 2 km into m   **g)** 2.5 l into cl   **h)** 2.3 tonnes into kg

2   **a)** 400 cm into m   **b)** 3400 m into km   **c)** 50 cm into m   **d)** 3000 g into kg
       e) 2000 ml into l   **f)** 500 ml into l   **g)** 246 kg into tonnes **h)** 500 cl into l

3   **a)** 2 mm into cm   **b)** 3 kg into g   **c)** 12.7 l into ml   **d)** 379 mm into cm
       e) 3000 kg into tonnes   **f)** 400 mg into g   **g)** 123 ml into l   **h)** 51.16 g into kg
       i) 120 cl into l   **j)** 271.65 cm into m **k)** 22.3 mg into g   **l)** 105 cm into m

4   **a)** Convert 1.2 kg to grams.

       b) Use your answer to find how many 30 g servings there are in a 1.2 kg box of cereal.

5   Jane is having a party for 30 guests. Her glasses have a capacity of 400 ml each. If she wants
       everyone to have a glass of juice, how many 2 litres bottles of juice should she buy?

6   **a)** Convert 5 m into cm.

       b) Use your answer to **a)** to convert 5 m into mm.

For **Questions 7-8**, convert each measurement into the units given.

7   **a)** 0.2 km into cm   **b)** 0.6 tonnes into g   **c)** 4 km into cm
       d) 0.231 kg into mg   **e)** 62 m into mm   **f)** 0.0034 km into mm
8   **a)** 1 mm into m   **b)** 3000 mg into kg   **c)** 150 cm^3 into l
       d) 1532 g into tonnes   **e)** 1005 cm into km   **f)** 3023 mg into kg

9 Jack buys 1.2 kg of flour.
How many pizzas can he make if each pizza needs 200 g of flour?

10 A go-kart has a 5 litre petrol tank.
It uses 10 ml of petrol per lap of a 400 m track.

    a) If James fills up the tank, how many laps of the track can he do?

    b) How many km can James travel on each full tank of petrol?

Example 2

Find the total of 0.2 tonnes, 31.8 kg and 1700 g. Give your answer in kg.

1. Convert all the masses to kilograms.	0.2 tonnes = 0.2 × 1000 = 200 kg 1700 g = 1700 ÷ 1000 = 1.7 kg
2. Add the masses together.	200 kg + 31.8 kg + 1.7 kg = **233.5 kg**

Exercise 2

1 Complete each calculation.

    a) 3200 ml + 75.3 l = ⬭ l   **b)** 7.2 tonnes + 340 kg = ⬭ tonnes

    c) 681 cm + 51.2 m = ⬭ cm   **d)** 16.49 km + 6750 m = ⬭ m

    e) 3 kg + 375 g + 0.2 kg = ⬭ kg   **f)** 100 cm + 0.35 m + 12.6 m = ⬭ cm

    g) 300 cm³ + 0.7 l + 250 ml = ⬭ ml   **h)** 7 m + 20 cm + 35 mm = ⬭ cm

    i) 4000 g + 200 kg + 1 tonne = ⬭ kg   **j)** 12.92 km + 170.6 m + 2050 cm = ⬭ m

2 Lucy grows 4.6 kg of potatoes and sells 800 g. What is the mass, in g, of her remaining potatoes?

3 How many metres further is a journey of 3.4 km than a journey of 1800 m?

4 A recipe uses 450 g of flour, 0.2 kg of margarine, 300 g of fruit and 0.1 kg of sugar.
How much more than 1 kg is the total mass of these ingredients? Give your answer in kg.

5 A recycling van collects 3200 g of paper, 15 kg of aluminium, 0.72 tonnes
of glass and 3.2 kg of cardboard. What is the mass of all the recycling in kg?

6 Sharon, Trevor and Elsie get into a cable car while skiing.
Sharon weighs 55.2 kg, Trevor weighs 78.1 kg and Elsie weighs 65.9 kg.
Each person's equipment weighs 9000 g. The cable car is unsafe when carrying
a mass of over a quarter of a tonne. Will Sharon, Trevor and Elsie be safe?

Exercise 3

1 Callum buys 2 tonnes of topsoil for his gardening business.
If he uses 250 kg each day, how long will his supply last?

2 Milly runs a 1500 m fun run, a 100 m sprint and a 13.2 km race.
How many km has she run in total?

3 A café puts two slices of ham into every ham sandwich. A slice of ham weighs 10 g.
If the café expects to sell 500 ham sandwiches, how many 1.5 kg packs of ham should they order?

4 A reservoir contains 600 000 l of water. A stream flowing into it adds 750 000 ml of water a day.

   a) If no water was removed from the reservoir, how many litres
   would the volume of water increase by each day?

   b) The reservoir can only hold 800 000 l of water.
   How many days will it take for the reservoir to start overflowing?

5 **a)** A recipe for lasagne needs 0.7 kg of minced beef, 400 g of tomato sauce, 300 g of cheese sauce,
   0.2 kg of lasagne and 2500 mg of herbs and spices. How many kg do these ingredients weigh?

   b) If 0.2 kg of ingredients will feed one person, how many people can be fed with this recipe?

15.3   Converting Units — Area and Volume

Area

Area is measured in units squared (e.g. m², cm², mm²).

To convert between different units of area, multiply or divide
by the **square** of the 'length' conversion factor.

For example, the conversion factor between cm and mm is 10.
This means the conversion factor between cm² and mm² is $10^2 = 10 \times 10 = 100$.

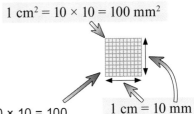

$1 \text{ cm}^2 = 10 \times 10 = 100 \text{ mm}^2$

$1 \text{ cm} = 10 \text{ mm}$

Example 1

Find the area of this rectangle in mm² by:

  a)   first converting its length and width to mm.

     1. Convert the dimensions to mm.   5 cm = 50 mm
                                   3 cm = 30 mm

     2. Multiply to get the area. $50 \times 30 = \textbf{1500 mm}^2$

5 cm

3 cm

  b)   first finding the area in cm², and then using the appropriate conversion factor.

     1. Find the area in cm². $5 \times 3 = 15 \text{ cm}^2$

     2. Find the conversion factor from cm² to mm².   1 cm = 10 mm,
                                             so 1 cm² = 10 × 10 = 100 mm².

     3. Use the conversion factor to convert 15 cm² to mm². $15 \text{ cm}^2 = 15 \times 100 = \textbf{1500 mm}^2$

Example 2

Convert an area of 600 cm² to m².

  1. Work out the conversion factor from cm² to m².   1 m = 100 cm,
                                           so 1 m² = 100 × 100 = 10 000 cm².

  2. Divide by the conversion factor. $600 \text{ cm}^2 = 600 \div 10\,000 = \underline{\textbf{0.06 m}^2}$

Exercise 1

1 Work out the area (in m²) of a field measuring 2 km by 3 km by:
    a) first converting its length and width to m.
    b) first finding the area in km², and then using the appropriate conversion factor.

2 **a)** Calculate the area (in mm²) of a sticker measuring 20 mm by 40 mm.
    b) Convert this area to cm² by using the appropriate conversion factor.

For **Questions 3-4**, convert each area into the units given.

3 **a)** 26 cm² into mm²   **b)** 0.036 km² into m²   **c)** 1.7 cm² into mm²
    d) 1.05 m² into cm²   **e)** 0.07 km² into m²   **f)** 1.2 m² into cm²

4 **a)** 84 mm² into cm²   **b)** 1750 cm² into m²   **c)** 29 000 mm² into cm²
    d) 3 150 000 m² into km²   **e)** 8500 mm² into cm²   **f)** 1700 cm² into m²

5 One bottle of weedkiller can treat an area of 16 m². How many bottles of this weedkiller should Ali buy to treat her lawn measuring 990 cm by 430 cm?

6 Sandeesh wants to carpet two rectangular rooms. One of the rooms measures 1.7 m by 3 m, while the other is 670 cm by 420 cm. How many square metres of carpet will she need?

7 **a)** Convert 8 500 000 mm² to cm².
    b) Use your answer to **a)** to convert 8 500 000 mm² into m².

8 **a)** Convert 0.00065 m² to cm².
    b) Use your answer to **a)** to convert 0.00065 m² into mm².

9 Convert each of these areas into the units given.
    a) 1.2 m² into mm²   **b)** 0.001 km² into cm²   **c)** 60 500 mm² into m²
    d) 673 000 000 cm² into km²   **e)** 50 million mm² into m²   **f)** 0.000005 km² into mm²

Volume

Volume is measured in units cubed (e.g. m³, cm³, mm³).

To convert between different units of volume, multiply or divide by the **cube** of the 'length' conversion factor.

For example, the conversion factor between cm and mm is 10. This means the conversion factor between cm³ and mm³ is 10³ = 10 × 10 × 10 = 1000.

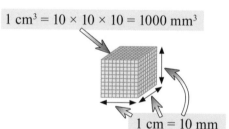

$1 \text{ cm}^3 = 10 \times 10 \times 10 = 1000 \text{ mm}^3$

1 cm = 10 mm

Example 3

Convert a volume of 382 000 cm³ to m³.

1. Work out the conversion factor from cm³ to m³.
    1 m = 100 cm,
    so 1 m³ = 100³ = 100 × 100 × 100 = 1 000 000 cm³.

2. Divide by the conversion factor.
    So 382 000 cm³ = 382 000 ÷ 1 000 000 = **0.382 m³**

Exercise 2

1 Work out the volume (in m³) of the swimming pool shown by:

   a) first converting its length, width and depth to m.

   b) first finding the volume in cm³, and then using
     the appropriate conversion factor.

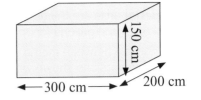

150 cm

←— 300 cm —→ 200 cm

2 Convert each of these volumes into the units given.

   a) 0.001 km³ into m³   **b)** 15 cm³ into mm³   **c)** 0.2 m³ into cm³

   d) 0.055 cm³ into mm³   **e)** 1.2 km³ into m³   **f)** 17.6 m³ into cm³

   g) 0.435 km³ into m³   **h)** 6.7 km³ into m³   **i)** 0.000045 cm³ into mm³

3 Convert each of these volumes into the units given.

   a) 134 000 cm³ into m³   **b)** 16 000 mm³ into cm³   **c)** 3000 cm³ into m³

   d) 453 600 mm³ into cm³   **e)** 150 m³ into km³   **f)** 91.475 mm³ into cm³

   g) 35.9 cm³ into m³   **h)** 131 400 mm³ into cm³   **i)** 17 900 m³ into km³

4 A brand of coffee powder is sold in cuboid packets
with dimensions 20 cm by 25 cm by 10 cm.
A volume of 0.003 m³ of coffee powder has already been used.
What volume (in m³) of coffee powder is left?

5 A carton of apple juice measures 7 cm by 50 mm by 0.17 m,
and is completely full.

   a) Find the volume of the carton in cm³.

   b) Hati fills 7 glasses, each of which has a volume of 20 cm³, with juice.
     How much juice (in cm³) does she use?

   c) How much juice (in mm³) will she have left in the carton?

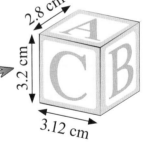

2.8 cm

3.2 cm

3.12 cm

6 How many of these plastic bricks can be made out of 1 m³ of plastic?

7 A box is 10.5 cm long by 5.3 cm wide by 8.67 cm tall.
Find the volume of the box in mm³.

8 A 1 litre bottle of orange concentrate says to dilute 25 cm³ of concentrate
with 0.5 l of water to make one glass of squash.

   a) How many glasses of squash can you get from this bottle?

   b) What is the total volume of one glass of squash in mm³?

9 A swimming pool measures 3 m deep and has a base with area 375 m².

   a) Work out the volume of the swimming pool in m³.

   b) Find the volume of the pool in cm³.

   c) How many litres of water can the pool hold?

10 a) Convert 0.56 m³ to cm³.

   b) Use your answer to **a)** to convert 0.56 m³ into mm³.

15.4 Metric and Imperial Units

Imperial units are things like inches, feet and miles for lengths, pounds and ounces for mass, and pints and gallons for volume.

To convert between metric and imperial units, multiply or divide by the **conversion factors** below. (The conversions shown with a wavy equals sign ($\approx$) are not exact, but are very close.)

Length	Mass	Volume
1 inch $\approx$ 2.5 cm	1 ounce $\approx$ 28 g	1 pint $\approx$ 0.57 litres
1 foot = 12 inches $\approx$ 30 cm	1 pound = 16 ounces $\approx$ 450 g	1 gallon = 8 pints $\approx$ 4.5 litres
1 yard = 3 feet $\approx$ 90 cm	1 stone = 14 pounds $\approx$ 6400 g	
1 mile $\approx$ 1.6 km	1 kg $\approx$ 2.2 pounds	

Example 1

a) Convert 15 miles into km.
   1. 1 mile $\approx$ 1.6 km so the conversion factor is 1.6.   1 mile = 1.6 km.
   2. Multiply 15 miles by the conversion factor.   So 15 miles = 15 × 1.6 = **24 km**

b) Convert 10 km into miles.
   1. Again, the conversion factor is 1.6.   1 mile = 1.6 km.
   2. Divide by the conversion factor.   So 10 km = 10 ÷ 1.6 = **6.25 miles**

Exercise 1

For **Questions 1-2**, convert the measurements into different imperial units using the conversion factors above.

1 **a)** 2 feet into inches   **b)** 4 yards into feet   **c)** 0.5 gallons into pints
   d) 4 stone into pounds   **e)** 9 gallons into pints   **f)** 3600 yards into feet

2 **a)** 32 ounces into pounds   **b)** 56 pounds into stone   **c)** 15 feet into yards
   d) 60 inches into feet   **e)** 32 pints into gallons   **f)** 42 pounds into stone

3 Convert these measurements from imperial units to metric.
   a) 4 inches into cm   **b)** 3 ounces into g   **c)** 2 gallons into l
   d) 10 stone into g   **e)** 5 yards into cm   **f)** 25 miles into km
   g) 2.7 inches into cm   **h)** 4.5 pints into l   **i)** 6.9 feet into cm

4 Convert these measurements from metric units to imperial.
   a) 8 km into miles   **b)** 57 litres into pints   **c)** 12 800 g into stone
   d) 60 cm into feet   **e)** 25 cm into inches   **f)** 16 km into miles
   g) 56 g into ounces   **h)** 7.5 kg into pounds   **i)** 48 km into miles

5 A running track is 400 m long. How many laps of the track make one mile?

6 A large box of juice holds 3 litres.

   a) How many whole pint jugs can be filled from the box?

   b) Approximately how many litres of juice will be left in the box?

7 Marion is on holiday in Spain. Her car measures speed in mph but the Spanish road signs are in km/h. The speed limit is 90 km/h. What is this in mph?

8 A car manual states that the oil in the car's engine must be changed every 5000 miles. Jack has travelled 3500 miles since the last oil change, driving to and from work. He has also been on two holidays in his car in which he travelled 1000 km and 500 km. How many more miles can Jack travel before he should change the oil?

9 **a)** Convert 18 yards into cm.

   b) Use your answer to part **a)** to convert 18 yards into metres.

For **Questions 10-11** convert each measurement into the units given.

10 **a)** 5 pounds into kg   **b)** 11 feet into m   **c)** 1 stone into kg   **d)** 3 gallons into ml

    e) 20 yards into m   **f)** 330 inches into m   **g)** 16 pints into ml   **h)** 25 stone into kg

11 **a)** 800 ml into pints   **b)** 3.2 kg into stone   **c)** 300 m into miles   **d)** 6.4 kg into stone

    e) 1.35 kg into ounces   **f)** 2800 ml into pints   **g)** 10 kg into ounces   **h)** 0.9 m into feet

Example 2

a) Convert 6 pounds and 2 ounces into kg.

   1. Write the whole mass using the same unit (here, ounces).

      1 pound = 16 ounces,
      so 6 pounds = 6 × 16 = 96 ounces.

      This means 6 pounds and 2 ounces
      = 96 + 2 = 98 ounces

   2. Convert this into grams first. Then convert the result into kg.

      98 ounces = 98 × 28 = 2744 g = **2.744 kg**

b) Convert 35 cm into feet and inches.

   1. Convert 35 cm into inches first.

      35 cm = 35 ÷ 2.5 = 14 inches

   2. Work out how many full feet there are in your answer, and how many inches remaining.

      1 foot = 12 inches,
      so 14 inches = 12 inches + 2 inches
               = **1 foot 2 inches**

Exercise 2

1 For each of the following:

   (i) Convert the mass into ounces, using the conversion factor of 1 ounce ≈ 28 g.

   (ii) Write this in pounds and ounces.

   a) 1904 g   **b)** 840 g   **c)** 2688 g   **d)** 4.9 kg   **e)** 0.98 kg

2 Convert each of the following into feet and inches.

   a) 2 m   **b)** 52.5 cm   **c)** 1.5 km   **d)** 0.75 m   **e)** 50 mm

3 A ride at a theme park states you must be 140 cm or over to ride. Maddie is 4 foot 5 inches and Lily is 4 foot 9 inches. Can they both go on the ride?

4   Jamie and Oliver are cooking. They need 1 pound and 12 ounces of meat for their recipe. They see a 750 g packet of meat in the supermarket. Will this be enough?

Exercise 3 — Mixed Exercise

1   State which is the bigger amount in each of the following pairs.
     a) 10 feet or 3.5 m   **b)** 1 stone or 7 kg   **c)** 10 miles or 12 km   **d)** 15 pints or 9 l
     e) 3 pounds or 1.5 kg   **f)** 5 stone or 31 kg   **g)** 160 stone or 1 tonne   **h)** 2 gallons or 10 l

2   Julie fills up her car with 6 gallons of petrol.
     How much will she have to pay if petrol costs £1.33 per litre?

3   Jacob's mother asks him to buy 4 pints of milk.
     The shop only sells milk in 1 litre, 2 litre and 4 litre cartons.
     Which of these amounts is closest to what his mother asked for?

4   Lotte's car travels 55 miles to the gallon of petrol.
     If her petrol tank contains 45 litres, how many miles can she travel?

5   Complete each of these calculations.
     a) 2 pints + 400 ml = ◯ ml   **b)** 7.2 kg + 2 stone = ◯ kg
     c) 681 cm + 12.4 yards = ◯ m   **d)** 16.49 km + 21.5 miles = ◯ km
     e) 3 kg + 1 stone + 1.5 kg = ◯ kg   **f)** 100 cm + 2 yards + 15 feet = ◯ cm
     g) 3 l + 4.5 pints + 250 ml = ◯ ml   **h)** 7 m + 8 inches + 35 mm = ◯ cm

6   The weights of 10 people getting into a lift are shown below.

11 stone 4 pounds	10 stone	7 stone 2 pounds	13 stone 1 pound	15 stone 4 pounds
12 stone	8 stone 9 pounds	10 stone 3 pounds	16 stone	11 stone 6 pounds

     The lift has a weight limit of 1 tonne. Will the total weight of the 10 people exceed this limit?

15.5   Estimating in Real Life

You can **estimate** how big something is by comparing it with something you already know the size of.

For example, the average height of a man is approximately 1.8 m, so something half as tall as an average-height man would be just under a metre tall.

Example 1

Estimate the height of this lamp post.

1. Estimate the height of the man.   Average height of a man ≈ 1.8 m.

2. Estimate how much taller the lamp post is than the man.   The lamp post is roughly twice the height of the man.

3. Estimate the height of the lamp post.   Height of the lamp post ≈ 2 × 1.8 m = **3.6 m**

1.8 m

Example 2

Give sensible units for measuring the height of a room.

When you give a measurement, use units that mean the value isn't too big or too small.

A sensible unit is **metres**.

Most rooms are taller than an average man, but not that much taller — roughly 2 to 3 metres. So it makes sense to measure the height of a room in metres (or possibly cm). You wouldn't use km to measure the height of a room — the number would be very small (0.002 km).

Exercise 1

1 Suggest a sensible metric unit to measure each of the following.

   a) the length of a pencil   **b)** the mass of a tomato   **c)** the height of a house

   d) the length of an ant   **e)** the mass of a bus   **f)** the weight of a baby

   g) the distance from Birmingham to Manchester

2 Estimate each of the following, using sensible units.

   a) the height of your bedroom   **b)** the length of a family car

   c) the height of a football goal   **d)** the arm span of a man

   e) the diameter of a football   **f)** the volume of a bath

For **Questions 3-7** give your answer in sensible units.

3 Estimate the height of this house.

5 Estimate the length and height of the bus.

6 Estimate the height and length of this dinosaur by comparing it with a chicken.

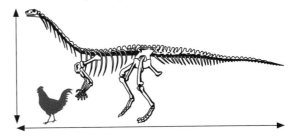

4 Estimate the height of this elephant.

7 Estimate the height of this rhino by comparing it with a domestic cat.

Section 16 — Speed, Distance and Time

16.1 Speed, Distance, Time Calculations

Finding an Object's Speed

Distance, time and (average) speed are connected by the formula: $\textbf{Speed} = \dfrac{\textbf{Distance}}{\textbf{Time}}$

Example 1

A car travels 150 km in 3 hours. What is the average speed of the car?

1. Substitute the distance and time into the formula.
2. The units of speed are a combination of the units of distance (here, km) and time (here, hours).

$\text{Speed} = \dfrac{\text{Distance}}{\text{Time}}$

$= \dfrac{150}{3} = \textbf{50 km/h}$.

Exercise 1

1 Calculate the average speed of each of the following journeys.
   a) distance = 30 km, time = 2 hours
   b) distance = 60 km, time = 3 hours
   c) distance = 150 miles, time = 5 hours
   d) distance = 100 m, time = 25 seconds
   e) distance = 72 000 km, time = 12 hours
   f) distance = 140 miles, time = 4 hours

2 Find the average speed of the following.
   a) a car travelling 80 km in 2 hours
   b) a cyclist travelling 32 km in 2 hours
   c) a cheetah running 100 m in 4 seconds
   d) a snail crawling 50 cm in 500 seconds
   e) a plane flying 1800 miles in 3 hours
   f) a rocket travelling 39 000 m in 5 seconds
   g) an escalator moving 15 m in 10 seconds
   h) a lift travelling 100 m in 80 seconds

3 Find the average speed of the following in km/h.
   You will need to convert the units to kilometres and hours first.
   a) a tractor moving 10 km in 30 minutes
   b) a man walking 1.5 km in 15 minutes
   c) a train travelling 30 000 m in 2.5 hours
   d) a river flowing 2.25 km in 45 minutes
   e) a fish swimming 0.5 km in 12 minutes
   f) a balloon rising 700 m in 3 minutes

Finding Distance and Time

You can rearrange the formula for speed to find distance and time.

$\textbf{Distance} = \textbf{Speed} \times \textbf{Time}$

$\textbf{Time} = \dfrac{\textbf{Distance}}{\textbf{Speed}}$

Example 2

A man runs for 30 minutes with average speed 12 km/h. How far does he run?

1. The speed is in km/h, so convert the time into hours.
2. Substitute the speed and time into the formula.
3. The speed is in km/h, so the distance will be in km.

30 minutes = 0.5 hours

Distance = Speed × Time

$= 12 \times 0.5 = \textbf{6 km}$.

Example 3

A train travels 60 miles at a speed of 100 mph. How many minutes will the journey take?

1. Substitute the distance and speed into the formula. $\text{Time} = \dfrac{\text{Distance}}{\text{Speed}} = \dfrac{60}{100} = 0.6 \text{ hours}$

2. Convert your answer into minutes. $0.6 \text{ hours} = 0.6 \times 60 \text{ minutes}$
   $= \underline{\mathbf{36\ minutes}}$

Exercise 2

1 For each of the following, use the speed and time given to calculate the distance travelled.
   a) speed = 20 km/h, time = 2 hours   b) speed = 25 mph, time = 2 hours
   c) speed = 10 m/s, time = 50 seconds   d) speed = 3 km/h, time = 24 hours
   e) speed = 15 m/s, time = 9 seconds   f) speed = 70 mph, time = 2.5 hours

2 For each of the following, use the speed and distance given to calculate the time taken.
   a) speed = 2 km/h, distance = 4 km   b) speed = 3 m/s, distance = 15 m
   c) speed = 15 m/s, distance = 45 m   d) speed = 60 mph, distance = 150 miles
   e) speed = 18 m/s, distance = 9 m   f) speed = 24 km/h, distance = 6 km

3 Find the distance travelled by a bus moving at 30 mph for 4 hours.

4 A flight to Spain takes 2 hours. The plane travels at an average speed of 490 mph. How far does the plane travel?

5 A dart is thrown with speed 15 m/s. It hits a dartboard 2.4 m away. How long is the dart in the air?

6 A marathon is approximately 42 km long. How long would it take to complete the marathon at an average speed of 8.4 km/h?

7 A train travels at 56 km/h for 5.6 km. How many minutes does the journey take?

8 A girl skates at an average speed of 7.5 mph. How far does she skate in 15 minutes?

Exercise 3 — Mixed Exercise

1 A football is passed between two players 10 m apart. The ball travels for 2.5 seconds. Find the average speed of the ball in m/s.

2 A man swims one length of a pool in 50 seconds. His speed is 0.5 m/s. Find the length of the pool.

3 A car's average speed is 40 mph. How long will it take the car to travel 100 miles?

4 A bobsleigh covers 1400 m in 50 seconds. Find its average speed in m/s.

5 A tree grows at a rate of 90 cm per year. How much taller does it grow in 4.5 years?

6 A tennis ball moves at an average speed of 48 m/s. How long does it take the tennis ball to travel 36 m?

7 A jogger ran for half an hour at an average speed of 8.1 km/h. How far did he run?

8 A tortoise walks 9 m in 3 minutes. Find the tortoise's average speed in m/s.

9 A snail slides 0.8 m in 1 minute 40 seconds. Find the snail's average speed in m/s.

10 A leopard runs 0.25 miles at an average speed of 40 mph. How many seconds does this take the leopard?

16.2   Distance-Time Graphs

Representing a Journey on a Distance-Time Graph

A **distance-time** graph shows how the distance of a moving object from its starting position changes.

Example 1

Danny cycles 5 miles in 20 minutes. He stops and rests for 10 minutes, then returns to his starting point in 30 minutes. Copy the axes on the right and use them to draw a graph of Danny's journey.

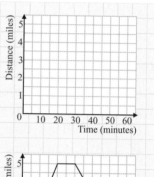

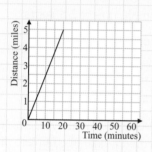

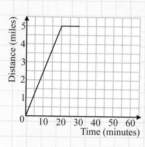

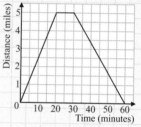

1. The first part of the graph shows 5 miles being covered in 20 minutes.

2. The second part of the graph shows no distance covered during the next 10 minutes.

3. The final part of the graph shows the 5-mile return journey taking 30 minutes.

Exercise 1

1   Adi is a keen cyclist. The following points describe the different stages of one of her bike rides.

   • Adi cycles 30 km in 2 hours.

   • She stops and rests for half an hour.

   • She then cycles a further 40 km in 2.5 hours.

Copy the coordinate grid on the right.

a) Draw a straight line on the grid to represent the first stage of Adi's journey.

b) The second stage of her ride is represented by a horizontal line. Draw this part of the graph.

c) (i) After the third stage of her ride, how far is Adi from her original starting point?

   (ii) Draw the straight line representing the third stage of Adi's ride.

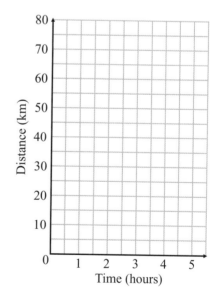

2 The following points describe the different
   stages of one of James's runs.

   - James runs 10 km in 2 hours.
   - He stops to rest for an hour.
   - He then returns to his starting point in 2.5 hours.

   Copy the coordinate grid on the right.

   a) Draw the line representing the first stage of his run.
   b) Draw the line representing his hour of rest.
   c) Draw the line showing his return journey.

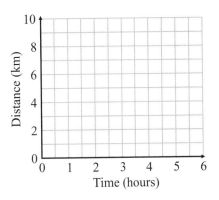

Draw a graph representing each of the journeys described in **Questions 3-6**.

3 Yemi drives 50 km in 1 hour, stops at a service station for half an hour,
   then drives a further 30 km in half an hour.

4 Sandy walks 2 km to the bus stop in 20 minutes. She waits for 10 minutes for a bus to arrive.
   She then travels a further 5 km on the bus in 15 minutes.

5 Harry walks 3 km in 50 minutes to his friend's house. He stays there for 1 hour.
   He then walks back towards home for 30 minutes until he gets to a shop, 1 km from home.
   He stays at the shop for 10 minutes before walking home, which takes a further 15 minutes.

6 Josh and Ron live 3.5 miles apart. Josh walks 1 mile to the bus stop in 20 minutes.
   He waits 10 minutes for the bus, then travels 2 miles in 5 minutes.
   He gets off the bus and walks the rest of the way to Ron's house in 15 minutes.

7 This graph shows a family's car journey. The family left home at 9:00 am.

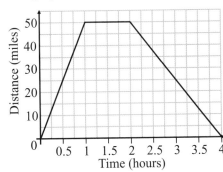

   a) (i) How long did the family travel
              for before stopping?
   (ii) How far had they travelled
           when they stopped?
   b) How long did the family stay at their
          destination before setting off home?
   c) (i) What time did they start back home?
   (ii) How long did the journey home take?

8 Describe the journey that is represented by each of these distance-time graphs.

a)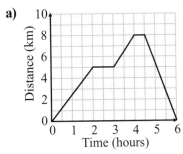

b)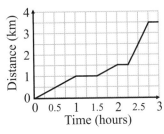

c)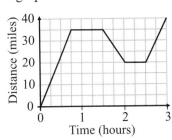

Finding Speed from a Distance-Time Graph

The **gradient** of a distance-time graph gives the **speed** of an object.

The **steeper** the graph, the **faster** the object is moving.
A **horizontal** line means the object is **stationary**.

Example 2

Bill left his house at 8:00 am and walked to a bus stop. He waited 15 minutes for the bus, and then travelled to his hospital appointment. After his appointment, he returned home by taxi. The graph shows Bill's journey.

a) (i) How far is the bus stop from Bill's house?
   (ii) How long (in hours) did it take Bill to walk to the bus stop?
   (iii) How fast (in km/h) did Bill walk to the bus stop?
b) (i) How far did Bill travel on the bus?
   (ii) How long did Bill's bus journey take?
   (iii) What was the average speed of the bus?
c) What was the average speed of the taxi?

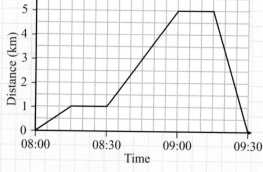

1. You can read distances and times from the graph.
2. If you know the distance something has travelled and how long it took, then you can work out its speed using 'speed = distance (d) ÷ time (t)'.
3. Notice that the faster an object travels, the steeper the graph is for that section of its journey. For example, the 'bus section' of the graph is steeper than the 'walking section'. But the steepest part is the 'taxi section'.

a) (i) **1 km**
   (ii) 15 minutes = **0.25 hours**
   (iii) Speed $= \dfrac{d}{t} = \dfrac{1}{0.25} = $ **4 km/h**
b) (i) **4 km**
   (ii) 30 minutes = **0.5 hours**
   (iii) Speed $= \dfrac{4}{0.5} = $ **8 km/h**
c) Speed $= 5 \div \dfrac{1}{4} = 5 \times 4 = $ **20 km/h**

Exercise 2

1   This graph shows a commuter's journey to work. His journey consisted of two stages of travelling, separated by a break of 30 minutes.

   a) Without carrying out any calculations, state which of the journey's two stages was at a higher speed. Explain your answer.

   b) (i) How far did the commuter travel in stage 1 of his journey (the first 30 minutes)?

   (ii) What was his speed (in km/h) for the first stage?

   c) What was his speed (in km/h) during the second stage of his journey?

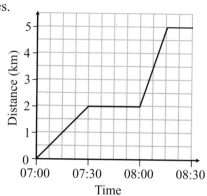

2 The graph shows a hill walker's trek. She stopped for a rest at 12:00 and for lunch at 13:00.

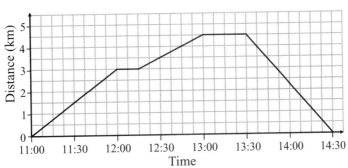

a) Without carrying out any calculations, state the times between which she was walking fastest. Explain your answer.

b) **(i)** For how long did she walk before she first stopped for a rest?

  (ii) How far did she walk during this time?

  (iii) What was her average speed during this first part of her walk?

c) What was her average speed after her rest but before she stopped for lunch?

d) What was her average speed after lunch?

3 Chay is going on a journey. The following points describe his journey.
  • Chay travels 40 km by bus, as shown on the graph.
  • He gets off the bus and then waits half an hour for a train.
  • He gets on the train and travels for a further 1 hour 30 minutes, as shown on the graph.
  • He spends 30 minutes at his destination.
  • He then returns home by taxi at an average speed of 60 km/h.

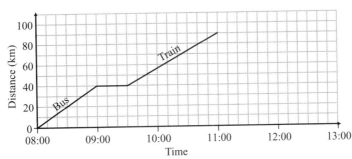

a) Find the average speed Chay travelled:

  (i) by bus.   **(ii)** by train.

b) Copy the above graph, and extend the line to show Chay's 30 minutes at his destination.

c) Find the time it took Chay to travel home by taxi.

d) Show Chay's taxi ride home on your graph.

4 Draw distance-time graphs to show the following journeys.

a) Ash catches a train at 10:00, then travels for 200 miles at an average speed of 100 mph.

b) Corey sets off at 09:00 and drives 120 miles at an average speed of 40 mph.
  After 1 hour at his destination, he drives back to his starting point at an average speed of 60 mph.

Section 17 — Pythagoras, Bearings and Scale Drawings

17.1 Pythagoras' Theorem

In a right-angled triangle, the lengths of the sides are connected by Pythagoras' Theorem: $h^2 = a^2 + b^2$

h is the hypotenuse — the longest side, opposite the right angle.
a and b are the shorter sides.

Example 1

Find the length x on the triangle shown. Give your answer to 2 decimal places.

1. x is the hypotenuse, so substitute x for h and replace a and b with 4 and 7.

    $h^2 = a^2 + b^2$
    $x^2 = 7^2 + 4^2$
    $x^2 = 49 + 16 = 65$
    $x = \sqrt{65} = 8.0622...$

2. Find x.

3. Round your answer and use the correct units.

    So $x = \underline{\textbf{8.06 cm}}$ *(to 2 d.p.)*

Exercise 1

Unless told otherwise, give any non-exact answers to 2 decimal places.

1 Find the length of the hypotenuse in each of the triangles below.

a)

b)
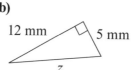

c)
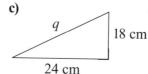

d)
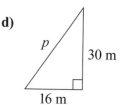

e)
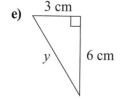

f)
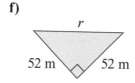

g)
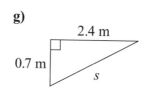

h)
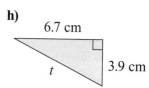

i)
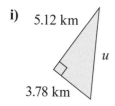

j)
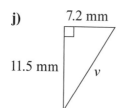

k)
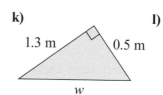

l)

2 Find the length of the longest side of a right-angled triangle if the other sides are 8.7 cm and 6.1 cm in length.

3 Find the length of the hypotenuse of a right-angled triangle if the shorter sides have the following lengths.

   a) $a = 5$ cm, $b = 7$ cm

   b) $a = 4$ cm, $b = 11$ cm

   c) $a = 6.3$ mm, $b = 1.9$ mm

4 In triangle XYZ, angle XYZ is 90°, XY is 4.5 cm and YZ is 4.9 cm. Find the length of XZ.

5 Find the distance PS in the rectangle below.

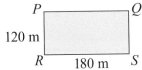

6 A rectangular field is 20 m long and 15 m wide. What is the distance diagonally across the field?

7 I run 540 m south and then 970 m east. What is my final distance from my starting point? Give your answer to the nearest metre.

8 XYZ is an isosceles triangle. M is the mid-point of YZ. Find the length of XY.

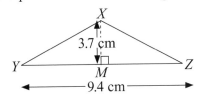

9 The triangle JKL is drawn inside a circle centred on O, as shown. JK and KL have lengths 4.9 cm and 6.8 cm respectively.

   a) Find the length of JL.

   b) Find the radius of the circle.

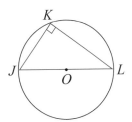

10 Find the length of the line segment AB.

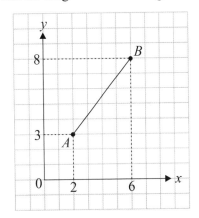

11 A spaghetti jar is in the shape of a cylinder. The jar has radius 6 cm and height 28 cm. What is the length of the longest stick of dried spaghetti that will fit inside the jar?

Example 2

Find the length a on the triangle shown. Give your answer to 2 decimal places.

1. a is one of the shorter sides, so use Pythagoras' formula with $h = 11$ and $b = 7$.

$$h^2 = a^2 + b^2$$
$$11^2 = a^2 + 7^2$$

2. Rearrange to find a.

$$a^2 = 11^2 - 7^2$$
$$a^2 = 121 - 49 = 72$$
$$a = \sqrt{72} = 8.4852...$$

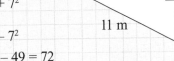

3. Round your answer and use the correct units.

So $a = \underline{\textbf{8.49 m}}$ *(to 2 d.p.)*

Exercise 2

Unless told otherwise, give any non-exact answers to 2 decimal places.

1 Find the lengths of the missing sides in these triangles.

a)
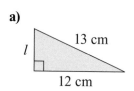
13 cm, 12 cm, l

b)
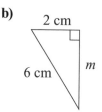
2 cm, 6 cm, m

c)
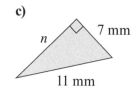
7 mm, n, 11 mm

d)
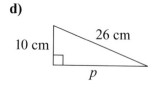
26 cm, 10 cm, p

e)
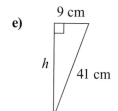
9 cm, h, 41 cm

f)
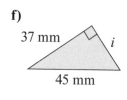
37 mm, i, 45 mm

g)
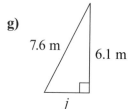
7.6 m, 6.1 m, j

h)
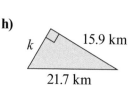
k, 15.9 km, 21.7 km

i)
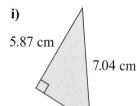
5.87 cm, 7.04 cm, f

j)
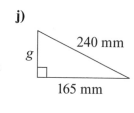
240 mm, g, 165 mm

k)
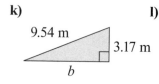
9.54 m, 3.17 m, b

l)
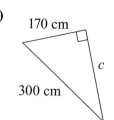
170 cm, c, 300 cm

2 Find the length b in the right-angled triangle if a and h are as follows.

a) $a = 1$ cm, $h = 8$ cm

b) $a = 6$ m, $h = 13$ m

c) $a = 4.1$ mm, $h = 11.3$ mm

d) $a = 17.7$ cm, $h = 22.9$ cm

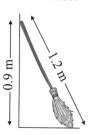

3 The lengths of the longest and shortest sides of a right-angled triangle are 17.3 cm and 6.6 cm. Find the length of the third side.

4 Find the horizontal distance from the bottom of the broom to the base of the wall.

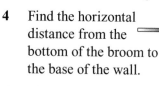
0.9 m, 1.2 m

5 The end of a ladder of length 3.3 m is placed on the ground 0.8 m from the base of a wall. When leant against the wall, how high up the wall does the ladder reach?

6 A slice of toast is in the shape of a right-angled triangle. The hypotenuse of the triangle has length 14 cm, and a shorter side is of length 11 cm. Find the length of the third side.

7 Find the radius of the base of the cone shown below.

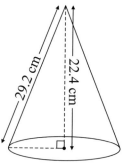
29.2 cm, 22.4 cm

8 A kite gets stuck at the top of a tree. The kite's 15 m string is taut, and its other end is held on the ground, 8.5 m from the base of the tree. Find the height of the tree.

9 Find the vertical height of the tent shown. ⟹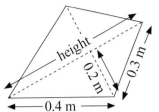

10 A pilot flies 860 km from Lyon to Prague. He then flies 426 km south to Ljubljana, which is directly east of Lyon. Find the distance from Ljubljana to Lyon to the nearest kilometre.

11 Newtown is 88 km northwest of Oldtown. Bigton is 142 km from Newtown, and lies northeast of Oldtown. What is the distance from Bigton to Oldtown? Give your answer to the nearest kilometre.

12 What is the height of the kite below?

Exercise 3 — Mixed Exercise

Unless told otherwise, give any non-exact answers to 2 decimal places.

1 Kevin is mending the battlements on his castle. How long is his ladder?

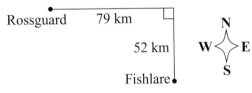

2 What is the shortest distance from Fishlare to Rossguard?

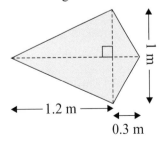

3 Find the length of the diagonals of a square with sides of length 7.7 m.

4 My favourite twig is 43 cm long. Will it fit on a tray 35 cm long and 25 cm wide?

5 A rectangular wooden frame is supported by a diagonal strut from one corner to the opposite corner. The frame measures 2 m by 0.7 m. Find the length of the strut.

6 A boat is rowed 200 m east and then 150 m south. If it was rowed in a straight line instead, how much shorter would the journey be?

7 A delivery company charges extra if a letter has a diagonal length greater than 25 cm. I want to send a letter that measures 205 mm by 155 mm. Will I have to pay extra?

8 Find the length of corrugated iron needed to make a roof for my bike shed, shown below.

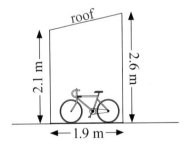

9 I want to put a gold ribbon around the edges of my kite. Ribbon is sold in lengths of 10 cm. What length of ribbon should I buy?

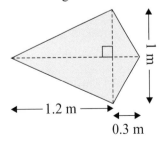

10 An equilateral triangle has sides of length 10 cm. Find the triangle's vertical height.

11 Find the following lengths.

    a) *AB*   **b)** *BC*   **c)** *AC*

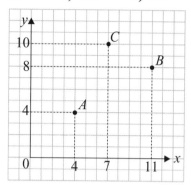

12 The diagram below shows the triangle *DGF*. Find the lengths of *GE* and *GD*.

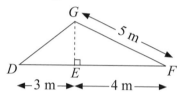

13 The diagram below shows two triangles, *PRS* and *PQS*. Find the lengths of:

    a) *PQ*   **b)** *PR*   **c)** *QR*

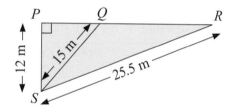

14 A pool is 50 m by 25 m. How many 6 cm goldfish could float head-to-tail in a line across the pool's diagonal?

15 Find the distance between points *P* and *Q* with coordinates (11, 1) and (17, 19) respectively.

16 Is Croughton closer to Dullverston or Marrow? By how far?

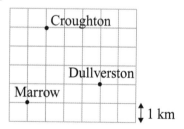

17 Find the height of the symmetrical house shown below.

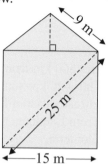

18 Find the side lengths of the rhombus below.

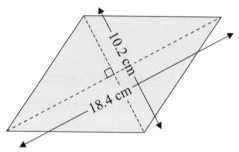

19 Kevin wants to set up a 20 m death-slide from the top of his 5.95 metre-high tower.

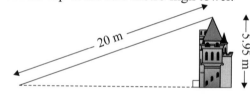

    a) How far from the base of the castle should Kevin anchor the slide?

    b) A safety inspector shortens the slide and anchors it 1.5 m closer to the castle. What is the new length of the slide?

20 The square *PQRS* is drawn inside another square *ABCD*, as shown in the diagram. Find the side length of *ABCD*.

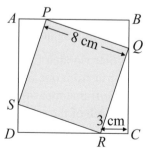

17.2 Scale Drawings

Scales with Units

A scale tells you the relationship between distances on a map or plan and distances in real life.

E.g. A map scale of 1 cm : 100 m means that 1 cm on the map represents an actual distance of 100 m.

Example 1

A plan of a garden is drawn to a scale of 1 cm : 5 m.

a) The distance between two trees is measured on the plan as 3 cm. What is the actual distance between the trees?

b) The actual distance between the garden shed and the pond is measured as 2.5 m. What would the distance between the shed and the pond be on the plan?

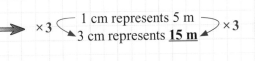

×3 1 cm represents 5 m ×3
3 cm represents **15 m**

÷2 5 m is shown as 1 cm ÷2
2.5 m is shown as **0.5 cm**

Exercise 1

1 A map scale is given as 2 cm : 1 km.

   a) Convert the following distances on the map to actual distances.

   (i) 4 cm   **(ii)** 6 cm   **(iii)** 22 cm   **(iv)** 3 cm   **(v)** 0.5 cm   **(vi)** 0.25 cm

   b) Convert the following actual distances to distances on the map.

   (i) 5 km   **(ii)** 8 km   **(iii)** 14 km   **(iv)** 3.5 km   **(v)** 0.5 km   **(vi)** 0.7 km

2 An atlas uses a scale of 1 cm : 100 km. Find the actual distances represented by the following.

   a) 7 cm   **b)** 1.5 cm   **c)** 0.8 cm   **d)** 6.22 cm   **e)** 3.01 cm   **f)** 43 mm

3 The scale on a map of Europe is 1 cm : 50 km. Find the distance used on the map to represent the following actual distances.

   a) 150 km   **b)** 600 km   **c)** 1000 km   **d)** 25 km   **e)** 10 km   **f)** 15 km

4 The floor plan of a house is drawn to a scale of 1 cm : 2 m. Find the actual dimensions of the rooms if they are shown on the plan as:

   a) 2.7 cm by 1.5 cm   **b)** 3.2 cm by 2.2 cm   **c)** 1.85 cm by 1.4 cm   **d)** 0.9 cm by 1.35 cm

Example 2

The distance between two villages is 12 km. This is represented on a map by a distance of 24 cm. Express the scale of the map in the form 1 cm : n km.

1. Write down the distances you are given as a scale.

2. Divide both sides by 24 to find the scale in the form 1 cm : n km.

24 cm : 12 km

(24 ÷ 24) cm : (12 ÷ 24) km

1 cm : 0.5 km

5 The distance from Madrid to Malaga is shown on a map as 11 cm. The actual distance is 440 km. Express the scale of the map in the form 1 cm : n km.

6 The distance from Thenford to Syresham is 12 km. This is shown on a map as 4 cm.

   a) Express the scale of the map in the form 1 cm : n km.

   b) The same map shows the distance from Chacombe to Badby as 7 cm. What is the actual distance between these two villages?

7 You are asked to draw up the plans for a building using the scale 1 cm : 0.5 m. Find the lengths you should draw on the plan to represent the following actual distances.

   a) 4 m   **b)** 18 m   **c)** 21 m   **d)** 11.8 m

8 A street of length 0.8 km is to be drawn on a map with scale 1 cm : 0.5 km. What length will the street appear on the map?

9 Below is the plan for a kitchen surface.

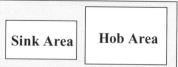

Measure the appropriate lengths on the plan to find the actual dimensions of the following.

   a) The sink area   **b)** The hob area

10 The plan below represents the distances between A, B and C.
The actual distance AB is 150 m.

   a) Measure AB on the plan to find the scale in the form 1 cm : n m.

   b) Use your scale to find:
   (i) the distance AC **(ii)** the distance BC

Scales Without Units

A scale without units (e.g. 1 : 100) means you can use any units.
For example, 1 cm : 100 cm or 1 mm : 100 mm.

> ### Example 3
>
> A map uses a scale of 1 : 200. What is the actual distance between two points which appear 35 cm apart on the map?
>
> 1. Write the scale down using centimetres, to match the distance given in the question.   1 cm : 200 cm
>
> 2. Multiply both sides of the equation by the same number.   1 cm represents 200 cm, so 35 cm represents 35 × 200 = 7000 cm.
>
> 3. Give your answer using sensible units.   So the actual distance is **70 m**.

Exercise 2

1 A map scale is given as 1 : 350.

   a) Convert the following distances on the map to actual distances.

   (i) 2 cm   **(ii)** 7 cm   **(iii)** 22 cm   **(iv)** 9.9 cm   **(v)** 14.5 cm   **(vi)** 25.7 cm

   b) Convert the following actual distances to distances on the map.

   (i) 700 cm   **(ii)** 875 cm   **(iii)** 175 cm   **(iv)** 2.1 m   **(v)** 945 cm   **(vi)** 1.47 m

2 A plan uses the scale 1 : 75. Find the actual distances represented by these lengths on the plan.

   a) 4 cm   **b)** 11 cm   **c)** 5.5 cm   **d)** 7.9 cm   **e)** 24.1 cm   **f)** 17.2 cm

3 Convert these actual distances to the lengths they will appear on a map with scale 1 : 1000.

   a) 300 m   **b)** 1400 m   **c)** 840 m   **d)** 120 m   **e)** 1 km   **f)** 0.43 km

4 Toy furniture is made to a scale of 1 : 40. Find the dimensions of the actual furniture when the toys have the following measurements.

   a) Height of wardrobe: 5 cm

   b) Width of bed: 3.5 cm

   c) Length of table: 3.2 cm

   d) Height of chair: 2.4 cm

5 A road of length 6.7 km is to be drawn on a map. The scale of the map is 1 : 250 000. How long will the road be on the map?

6 A model railway uses a scale of 1 : 500. Use the actual measurements given below to find measurements for the model.

   a) Length of carriage: 20 m

   b) Height of coal tower: 30 m

   c) Length of footbridge: 100 m

   d) Height of signal box: 6 m

7 A map uses the scale 1 : 72. Find the lengths on the map that represent these actual distances.

   a) 5.4 m   **b)** 8.1 m   **c)** 3.24 m

Example 4

The plan of the grounds of a stately home has a scale of 1 : 40 000.
Represent this scale in the form 1 cm : n m.

1. Write the scale down using centimetres to match the left-hand side of 1 cm : n m.

      1 cm : 40 000 cm

2. Convert the right-hand side to metres by dividing by 100.

      1 cm : (40 000 ÷ 100) m

      1 cm : 400 m

---

8 A path of length 4.5 km is shown on a map as a line of length 3 cm.

   a) Express the scale in the form 1 cm : n km.

   b) Express the scale in the form 1 : k.

9 The plan for a school has a scale of 1 : 1500.

   a) Express this scale in the form 1 cm : n m.

   b) The school playground is 60 m in length. Find the corresponding length on the plan.

10 On the plans for a house, 3 cm represents the length of a garden with actual length 18 m.

   a) Find the map scale in the form 1 : n.

   b) On the plan, the width of the garden is 1.2 cm. What is its actual width in metres?

   c) The lounge has a length of 4.5 m. What is the corresponding length on the plan?

11 The grid below shows the main tourist attractions of a major city.

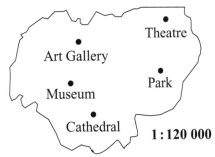

Find the actual distances between:

   a) the museum and the cathedral

   b) the art gallery and the theatre

   c) the cathedral and the park

Example 5

The diagram shows a rough sketch of a garden.
Use the scale 1 : 400 to draw an accurate plan of the garden.

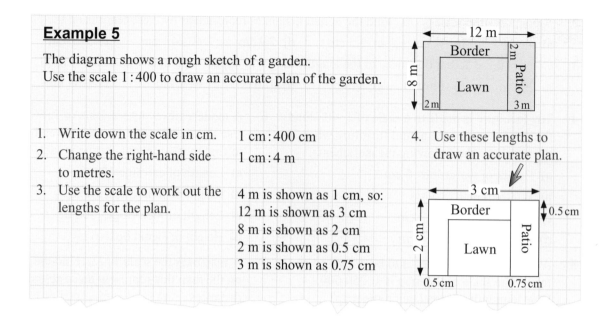

1. Write down the scale in cm. 1 cm : 400 cm
2. Change the right-hand side to metres. 1 cm : 4 m
3. Use the scale to work out the lengths for the plan.

4 m is shown as 1 cm, so:
12 m is shown as 3 cm
8 m is shown as 2 cm
2 m is shown as 0.5 cm
3 m is shown as 0.75 cm

4. Use these lengths to draw an accurate plan.

Exercise 3

1 A sketch of the floor plan for a symmetrical squash court is shown below. Use the scale 1 : 50 to draw an accurate plan of the court.

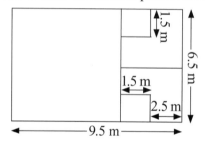

2 Draw an accurate plan of the kitchen shown below using the scale 1 : 20.

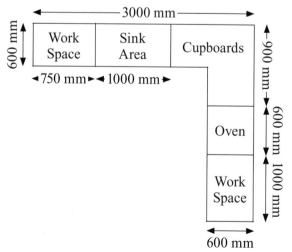

3 Below is a rough sketch of a house extension.

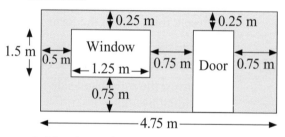

a) Use the scale 1 : 25 to draw an accurate plan for the extension.

b) Find the door's actual width and height.

4 Below is a sketch of a park lake.

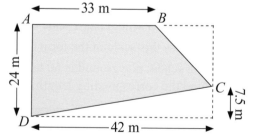

a) Draw an accurate plan of the lake using the scale 1 cm : 3 m.

b) There is a duck house at the intersection of *AC* and *BD*.
Use your plan to find the actual distance from the duck house to point *B*.

17.3　Bearings

A bearing tells you the direction of one point from another.
Bearings are given as three-figure angles, measured clockwise from north.

Example 1

a) Find the bearing of B from A.
b) Find the bearing of C from A.

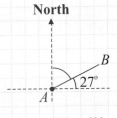

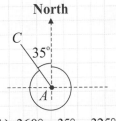

1. Find the clockwise angle from north.

2. Give the bearing as three figures.

a) $90° - 27° = 63°$

So the bearing of
B from A is **063°**.

b) $360° - 35° = 325°$

So the bearing of
C from A is **325°**.

Exercise 1

1 Write these compass directions as bearings.

a) East　　　b) Northeast

c) South　　　d) West

e) Southwest　f) Northwest

2 Find the bearing of B from A in the following.

a) North

b) North

c) North

d) North

e) North

f) North

g) North
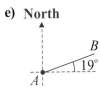

h) North
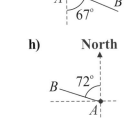

3 A ship travels in a direction which is 25° north of east. Write this as a bearing.

4 Find the angle θ in each of the following using the information given.

a) North
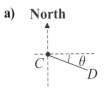

b) North

Bearing of D from C is 111°

Bearing of D from C is 203°

c) North

d) North

Bearing of D from C is 285°

Bearing of D from C is 243°

e) North
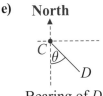

f) North
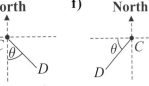

Bearing of D from C is 135°

Bearing of D from C is 222°

5 Leicester is 100 km south of Doncaster. King's Lynn is 100 km east of Leicester.

a) Sketch the layout of the three locations.

b) Find the bearing of King's Lynn from Leicester.

c) Draw a north line through Doncaster. Find the bearings from Doncaster of:

    (i) Leicester   **(ii)** King's Lynn

d) Draw a north line through King's Lynn. Find the bearings from King's Lynn of:

    (i) Leicester   **(ii)** Doncaster

6 Mark a point O and draw in a north line. Use a protractor to help you draw the points **a)** to **f)** with the following bearings from O.

a) 040°   b) 079°   c) 321°

d) 163°   e) 007°   f) 263°

7 Use a protractor to help you find the bearing of the points **a)** to **f)** from X.

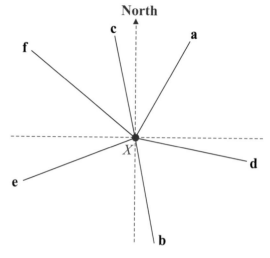

Example 2

The bearing of X from Y is 244°. Find the bearing of Y from X.

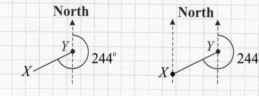 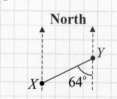

1. Draw a diagram showing what you know.
2. Draw a north line through point X.
3. Find the **alternate angle** to the one you're looking for.
4. Use angle properties to find the bearing.

So the bearing of Y from X is **064°**.

Exercise 2

1 The bearing of B from A is 218°. Find the bearing of A from B.

2 The bearing of D from C is 125°. Find the bearing of C from D.

3 The bearing of F from E is 310°. Find the bearing of E from F.

4 The bearing of *H* from *G* is 023°.
Find the bearing of *G* from *H*.

5 The bearing of *K* from *J* is 101°.
Find the bearing of *J* from *K*.

6 Find the bearing of *N* from *M* given that the bearing of *M* from *N* is:

a) 200°   **b)** 310°   **c)** 080°

d) 117°   **e)** 015°   **f)** 099°

7

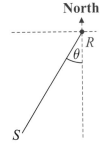

a) Measure the angle θ in the diagram.

b) Write down the bearing of *R* from *S*.

8 The point *Q* lies west of point *P*.

a) Write down the bearing of *Q* from *P*.

b) Write down the bearing of *P* from *Q*.

9 The point *Z* lies southeast of the point *Y*.

a) Write down the bearing of *Z* from *Y*.

b) Find the bearing of *Y* from *Z*.

10

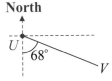

a) Find the bearing of *V* from *U*.

b) Find the bearing of *U* from *V*.

⑪

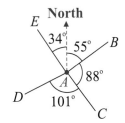

Find the bearing of:

a) *B* from *A*   **b)** *C* from *A*

c) *D* from *A*   **d)** *E* from *A*

e) *A* from *B*   **f)** *A* from *C*

g) *A* from *D*   **h)** *A* from *E*

Example 3

The points *P* and *Q* are a distance of 75 km apart. *Q* lies on a bearing of 055° from *P*. Use the scale 1 cm : 25 km to draw an accurate scale diagram of *P* and *Q*.

1. Draw *P* and a north line through it. Measure the required bearing.

2. Use the scale to work out the distance between the two points.

25 km is shown by 1 cm, so 75 km is shown by 3 cm.

3. Draw *Q* the correct distance and direction from *P*.

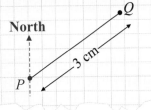

Exercise 3

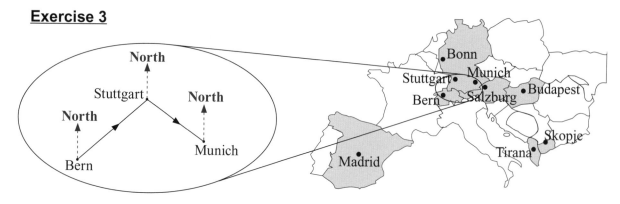

1 Above is a rough map of part of Europe. A pilot flies from Bern to Stuttgart, then on to Munich. This is shown on the enlarged part of the map, which is drawn using a scale of 1 cm : 100 km.

   a) Find the distance and bearings of the following stages of the journey.

      (i) Bern to Stuttgart   **(ii)** Stuttgart to Munich

   b) The pilot returns directly from Munich to Bern. Find the actual distance travelled in this stage.

2 Skopje is 150 km from Tirana, on a bearing of 048°. Draw an accurate scale diagram of Skopje and Tirana using the scale 1 cm : 30 km.

3 Salzburg lies 540 km from Bonn, on a bearing of 125°. Draw an accurate scale diagram of the two locations using the scale 1 cm : 90 km.

4 A pilot flies 2000 km from Budapest to Madrid, on a bearing of 242°. Draw an accurate scale diagram of the journey using the scale 1 : 100 000 000.

5 Use the scale 1 : 22 000 000 to draw an accurate scale diagram of a 880 km journey from Budapest to Bern, on a bearing of 263°.

6 The scale drawing on the right shows three more European cities. The scale of the diagram is 1 : 10 000 000.

   a) Use the diagram to find the following distances.

      (i) *PQ*   **(ii)** *QR*   **(iii)** *PR*

   b) Use a protractor to find the following bearings.

      (i) *Q* from *P*   **(ii)** *R* from *Q*   **(iii)** *P* from *R*

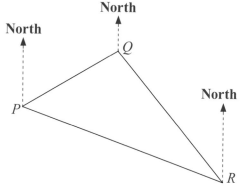

17.4 Pythagoras, Bearings and Scale Drawing Problems

Exercise 1

1 A pilot flies 150 km on a bearing of 090°, then 270 km on a bearing of 180°. Find the direct distance from his start point to his end point. Give your answer to the nearest kilometre.

2 Town *A* is 14 km north of Town *B*, which is 14 km east of Town *C*. Find the following bearings.

   a) Town *B* from Town *A*   **b)** Town *C* from Town *B*   **c)** Town *C* from Town *A*

3

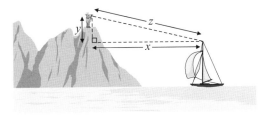

I am standing on a cliff, looking at a boat out at sea, as shown on the scale diagram above. The actual distance represented by the length x is 300 m.

a) Find the diagram's scale in the form $1:n$.

b) Find the actual distance represented by the length y.

c) Use Pythagoras to find the actual distance represented by the length z. Give your answer to the nearest metre.

4 The diagram shows an accurate scale plan of a circular walk. The actual distance from The Knott to Hartsop Village is 3 km.

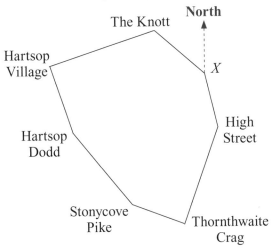

a) Find the scale of the plan in the form $1\,\text{cm}:n\,\text{km}$.

b) Measure the distances on the diagram to find the total length of the walk.

Point X lies between High Street and The Knott. There are two paths leading away from X.

c) What bearing should a walker take at X to ensure they take the correct path to the Knott?

5 A jogger runs 230 m on a bearing of 020°, then 390 m on a bearing of 110°.

a) Use the scale 1 cm : 100 m to draw an accurate scale diagram of the two stages of his run.

b) Find the angle the jogger changes direction by after the first stage of his run.

c) Calculate the direct distance between the start and end points of his run.

6 A boat sails on a bearing of 055° for 2000 m. It then changes course and sails on a bearing of 100° for 1500 m.

a) Draw a scale diagram of the boat's journey. Use the scale 1 cm : 500 m.

The boat returns directly to its starting point. Use your scale diagram to find the following:

b) the direct return distance,

c) the bearing of the return journey.

7 Arran is at the centre of a maze. He makes the following sequence of moves.

Walk 10 m, turn right
Walk 10 m, turn right
Walk 20 m, turn left
Walk 10 m, turn left
Walk 30 m, turn left
Walk 30 m

He is now at the exit of the maze.

a) Using a suitable scale, make a scale drawing of the path that Arran follows to find the exit.

b) Use your drawing to find the direct distance from the centre of the maze to the exit.

8 A pilot flies 950 km from Zurich to Berlin, on a bearing of 030°. He then flies a further 950 km to Budapest on a bearing of 120°.

a) Use Pythagoras to find the direct return distance from Budapest to Zurich to the nearest kilometre.

b) Without drawing a scale diagram, find the bearing of the direct return journey from Budapest to Zurich.

Section 18 — Constructions

18.1   Circles

Radius and Diameter

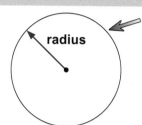

Radius: a line from the centre of a circle to the edge. The circle's centre is the same distance from all points on the edge.

radius

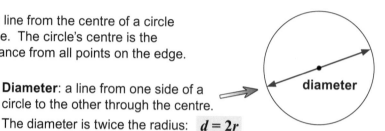

Diameter: a line from one side of a circle to the other through the centre.

The diameter is twice the radius: $d = 2r$

diameter

Example 1

a)   A circle has radius 4 cm. What is its diameter?

b)   A circle has diameter 7 m. What is its radius?

1. Use the formula $d = 2r$.

2. Remember to use the correct units.

a) $d = 2r$
$d = 2 \times 4$
= **8 cm**

b) $7 = 2r$
So $r = 7 \div 2$
= **3.5 m**

Exercise 1

1   Find the diameter of each of the following circles.

a) 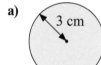 3 cm

b) 2 cm

c) 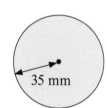 35 mm

d) 28 mm

2   Find the radius of each of the following circles.

a) 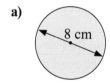 8 cm

b) 10 mm

c) 19 mm

d) 4.8 cm

3   Find the diameter of a circle with radius:

a) 4 cm   b) 6 cm   c) 30 mm   d) 25 m   e) 2.8 m

f) 4.6 mm   g) 3.7 m   h) 49 mm   i) 55 m   j) 4.2 mm

4   Find the radius of a circle with diameter:

a) 2 cm   b) 12 cm   c) 14 m   d) 28 mm   e) 1.4 cm

f) 2.8 m   g) 57 mm   h) 4.3 cm   i) 0.8 m   j) 0.02 cm

5   Use a compass to draw a circle with:

a) a radius of 4 cm   b) a radius of 5 cm   c) a diameter of 80 mm

d) a diameter of 6 cm   e) a diameter of 7 cm   f) a diameter of 23 mm

More Parts of Circles

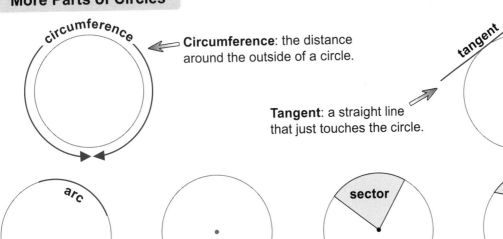

Circumference: the distance around the outside of a circle.

Tangent: a straight line that just touches the circle.

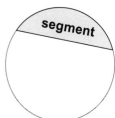

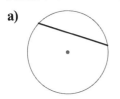

Arc: a part of the circumference.

Chord: a line between two points on the circle **not** through the centre.

Sector: an area of a circle like a "slice of pie".

Segment: the area of a circle between an arc and a chord.

Exercise 2

1   Name the feature highlighted in each diagram below.

a)   **b)**   **c)**   **d)**

e)   **f)**   **g)**   **h)**

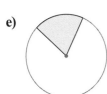
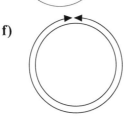
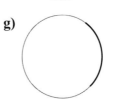
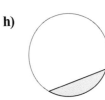

2   What do the labels *A-F* show in the diagrams below?

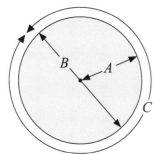
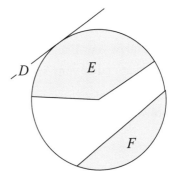

3   Draw a circle. Then draw and label the following features.

a) a chord   **b)** an arc   **c)** a tangent   **d)** a diameter

For this topic, you'll need to know how to use a **ruler** to measure lengths...

...and a **protractor** to measure angles.

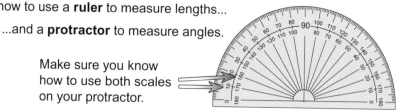

Make sure you know
how to use both scales
on your protractor.

Example 1

Measure the size of angle *a*.

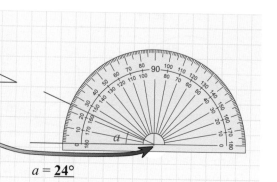

1.   Put the protractor's cross exactly
     where the two lines meet.

2.   Use the correct scale — this is an acute angle,
     so use the scale showing angles less than 90°.

$a = \underline{\mathbf{24°}}$

Exercise 1

1   In each diagram below, measure the size of the angle and the length of the lines.

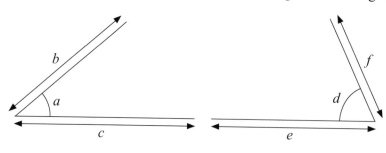

2   Draw a line 6 cm long.

   a) On one end of your line, draw an angle of 70°.

   b) On the other end of your line, draw an angle of 30°.

3   Draw a line 8.5 cm long.

   a) On one end of your line, draw an angle of 130°.

   b) On the other end of your line, draw an angle of 170°.

4   Measure all the angles in these triangles.
    Make sure your answers add up to 180°.

   a)

   b)

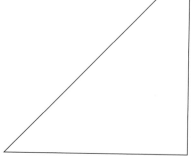

Example 2

Draw triangle ABC, where side AB is 4 cm, angle BAC is 55°, and angle ABC is 35°.

1. Draw and label the side you know the length of.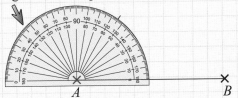

2. Use your protractor to draw the first angle.
   Angle BAC is at point A.

3. Draw the second angle, and complete the triangle.

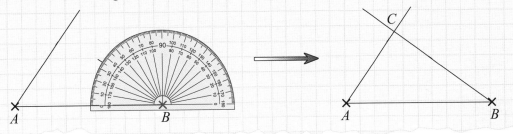

Exercise 2

1 Draw the following triangles accurately, then measure the lengths marked l.

a)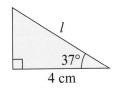

b)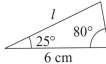

c)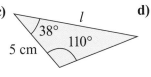

d)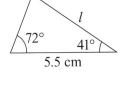

2 a) Draw each of the triangles ABC described below.

   (i) $AB = 4$ cm, angle $BAC = 55°$, angle $CBA = 35°$.

   (ii) $AB = 8$ cm, angle $BAC = 22°$, angle $CBA = 107°$.

   (iii) $AB = 6.5$ cm, angle $BAC = 65°$, angle $CBA = 30°$.

   (iv) $AB = 7.2$ cm, angle $BAC = 120°$, angle $CBA = 28°$.

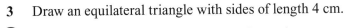

b) Measure the length of side BC in each of your triangles in part **a)**.

3 Draw an equilateral triangle with sides of length 4 cm.

4 Alec is standing 5 km directly west of Brenda.
At noon, Alec starts to walk northeast, while Brenda
starts to walk at the same speed northwest.

By carefully drawing their paths on a scale drawing
using 1 cm to represent 1 km, find how far from their
starting points they eventually meet.

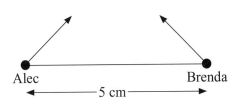

Example 3

Draw triangle *ABC*, where *AB* is 4 cm, *BC* is 4 cm, and angle *ABC* is 25°.

1. Draw and label a side you know the length of.
2. Use your protractor to draw the angle you know.
   Point *C* is 4 cm from *B* along this line.

3. Complete the triangle by drawing the line *AC*.

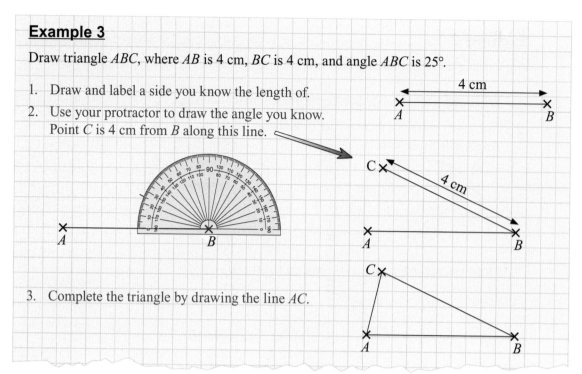

Exercise 3

1 Draw the following triangles accurately, then measure the lengths marked *l*.

a) 5 cm, 12 cm, *l*

b) 7 cm, 6 cm, 50°, *l*

c) 4 cm, 4.5 cm, 70°, *l*

d) 69 mm, 61 mm, 115°, *l*

2 a) Draw each of the triangles *ABC* described below.
   (i) *AB* = 6 cm, *BC* = 7 cm, angle *ABC* = 40°.
   (ii) *AB* = 4 cm, *BC* = 3 cm, angle *ABC* = 110°.
   (iii) *AB* = 65 mm, *BC* = 53 mm, angle *ABC* = 20°.
   (iv) *AB* = 45 mm, *BC* = 45 mm, angle *ABC* = 45°.

b) Measure the length of side *AC* in each of your triangles in part **a)**.

3 Draw an isosceles triangle with an angle of 50° between its two 5 cm long sides.

4 A rhombus *PQRS* has sides of length 5 cm and two angles of 60°.
   a) Draw the side *SR* accurately.
   b) Draw accurately **(i)** the angle *PSR*, which measures 60° and **(ii)** side *PS*.
   c) Angles *SPQ* and *QRS* are equal.
      By considering the angles in a quadrilateral, find the size of angles *SPQ* and *QRS*.
   d) Complete your accurate drawing of the rhombus.

5 a) Draw a rhombus with sides measuring 6 cm and two angles of 40°.
   b) Draw a rhombus with sides measuring 4.5 cm and two angles of 110°.

Example 4

Draw triangle *ABC*, where *AB* is 3 cm, *BC* is 2.5 cm, and *AC* is 2 cm.

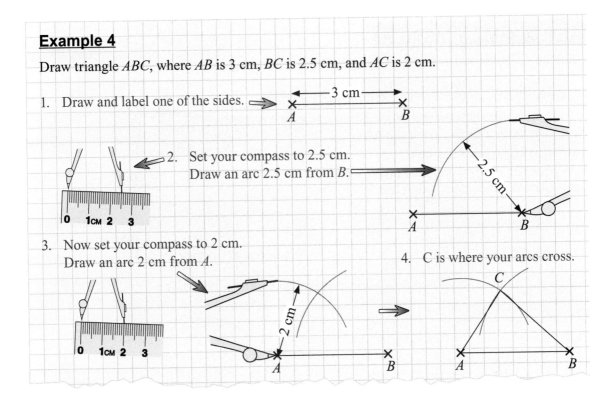

1. Draw and label one of the sides.

2. Set your compass to 2.5 cm.
    Draw an arc 2.5 cm from *B*.

3. Now set your compass to 2 cm.
    Draw an arc 2 cm from *A*.

4. *C* is where your arcs cross.

Exercise 4

1 These triangles are not drawn accurately. Draw them accurately using the measurements given.

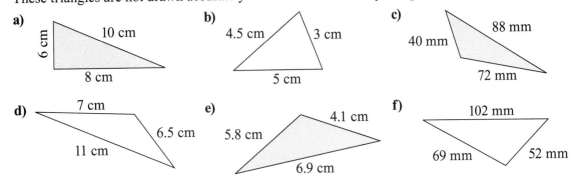

a)
6 cm
10 cm
8 cm

b)
4.5 cm
3 cm
5 cm

c)
88 mm
40 mm
72 mm

d)
7 cm
6.5 cm
11 cm

e)
5.8 cm
4.1 cm
6.9 cm

f)
102 mm
69 mm
52 mm

2 Draw each of the triangles *ABC* described below.

   a) *AB* is 5 cm, *BC* is 6 cm, *AC* is 7 cm.

   b) *AB* is 4 cm, *BC* is 7 cm, *AC* is 9 cm.

   c) *AB* is 8 cm, *BC* is 8 cm, *AC* is 4 cm.

   d) *AB* is 4.6 cm, *BC* is 5.4 cm, *AC* is 8.4 cm.

3 Draw an isosceles triangle with two sides of length 5 cm and a side of length 7 cm.

4 Using a scale of 1 cm : 10 miles, draw a map showing the layout of the following three towns.
(All distances are 'as the crow flies'.)

   • Weymouth is 54 miles from Exeter.

   • Exeter is 47 miles from Yeovil.

   • Yeovil is 27 miles from Weymouth.

18.3 Constructions

For the constructions in this topic, the only things you can use are a **ruler** and **compass**.

Constructing a Perpendicular Bisector

The **perpendicular bisector** of a line between points A and B:
- is at right angles to the line AB
- cuts the line AB in half.

All points on the perpendicular bisector are
the same distance from both A and B.

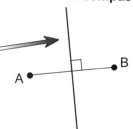

Example 1

Draw a line *AB* 3 cm long. Construct its perpendicular bisector using a ruler and compass only.

1. Draw points *A* and *B* 3 cm apart. Join them with the line *AB*.

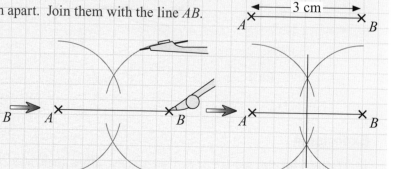

2. Place compass point at *A*, with the radius more than half of the length *AB*. Draw two arcs as shown.

3. Keep the radius the same and put the compass point at *B*. Draw two more arcs.

4. Use a ruler to draw a straight line through the points where the arcs meet. This is the perpendicular bisector.

Exercise 1

1 Draw a horizontal line *PQ* 5 cm long.
Construct its perpendicular bisector using a ruler and compass only.

2 Draw a vertical line *XY* 9 cm long.
Construct its perpendicular bisector using a ruler and compass only.

3 Draw a line *AB* 7 cm long.
Construct its perpendicular bisector using a ruler and compass only.

4 a) Draw a line *AB* 6 cm long. Construct the perpendicular bisector of *AB*.
   b) Draw the rhombus *ACBD* with diagonals 6 cm and 8 cm.

5 a) Draw a circle with radius 5 cm, and draw <u>any</u> two chords.
   Label your chords *AB* and *CD*.
   b) Construct the perpendicular bisector of chord *AB*.
   c) Construct the perpendicular bisector of chord *CD*.
   d) Where do the two perpendicular bisectors meet?

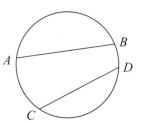

Constructing an Angle Bisector

An **angle bisector** cuts an angle in half.

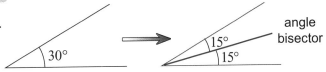

angle
bisector

Example 2

Draw an angle of 60° using a protractor.
Construct the angle bisector using only a ruler and compass.

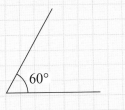

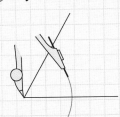

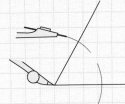

1. Place the point of the compass on the angle...

2. ...and draw arcs crossing both lines...

3. ...using the same radius.

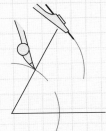

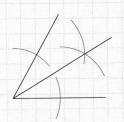

4. Now place the point of the compass where your arcs cross the lines, and draw two more arcs — using the same radius.

5. Draw the angle bisector.

Exercise 2

1 Draw the following angles using a protractor.
For each angle, construct the angle bisector using a ruler and compass.

a) 100°   b) 140°   c) 96°   d) 44°

e) 50°   f) 70°   g) 20°   h) 65°

Check each of your angle bisectors with a protractor.

2 a) Draw any triangle. Use a ruler to make sure all the sides are straight.

b) Construct the bisectors of each of the angles.
What do you notice about these bisectors?

3 a) Use a protractor to draw an angle ABC of 110°, with $AB = BC = 5$ cm.
Construct the bisector of angle ABC.

b) Mark point D on your drawing, where D is the point on the angle bisector with $BD = 8$ cm.
What kind of quadrilateral is $ABCD$?

Constructing a Perpendicular from a Point to a Line

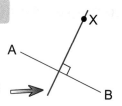

The **perpendicular** from a point to a line:
- passes through the point, and
- meets the line at 90°.

perpendicular from the ➡ point X to the line AB

Example 3

Construct the perpendicular from the point X to the line AB using only a ruler and compass.

X •

A ———————— B

1. Draw an arc centred on X cutting the line twice.

2. Draw an arc centred on one of the points where your arc meets the line.

3. Do the same for the other point, keeping the radius the same.

4. Draw the perpendicular to where the arcs cross.

Exercise 3

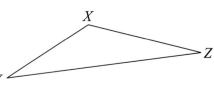

1 Use a ruler to draw a triangle like the one on the right. Construct the perpendicular from X to the line YZ.

2 Draw three points not on a straight line.
Label your points P, Q and R. Draw a long straight line passing through your points P and Q. Construct the perpendicular from R to this line.

3 **a)** On squared paper draw axes with x-values from 0 to 10 and y-values from 0 to 10.

  b) Plot the points $A(1, 2)$, $B(9, 1)$ and $C(6, 8)$.

  c) Construct the perpendicular from point C to the line AB.

4 **a)** Draw any triangle. Use a ruler to make sure all the sides are straight.

  b) Construct a perpendicular from each of the triangle's corners to the opposite side. What do you notice about these lines?

5 **a)** Construct triangle DEF, where $DE = 5$ cm, $DF = 6$ cm and angle $FDE = 55°$.

  b) Construct the perpendicular from F to DE. Label the point where the perpendicular meets DE as point G.

  c) Measure the length FG. Use your result to work out the area of the triangle to 1 decimal place.

Constructing an Angle of 60°

You'd need to construct an angle of 60° to draw an accurate equilateral triangle.

60°

Example 4

Draw a line AB and construct an angle of 60° at A.

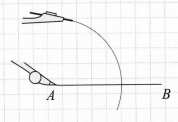 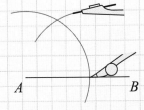 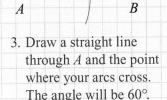

1. Place the compass point on A and draw a long arc that crosses the line AB.

2. Place the compass point where the arc meets the line, and draw another arc of the same radius.

3. Draw a straight line through A and the point where your arcs cross. The angle will be 60°.

Exercise 4

1   Draw a line AB measuring 5 cm. Construct an angle of 60° at A.

2   a) Draw a line measuring 6 cm.
    b) Construct an angle of 60° at each end of the line. Join your lines to form a triangle.
    c) By measuring the lengths of the sides, check that your triangle is equilateral.

Constructing an Angle of 30°

Construct an angle of 30° by bisecting an angle of 60°.

30°

Example 5

Draw a line AB and construct an angle of 30° at A.

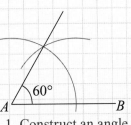 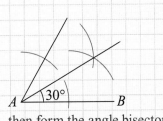

1. Construct an angle of 60° at A...

2. ...then form the angle bisector to make an angle of 30°.

Exercise 5

1   Draw a line AB measuring 6 cm. Construct an angle of 30° at A.

2   a) Construct the triangle ABC where $AB = 7$ cm, angle $CAB = 60°$ and angle $CBA = 30°$.
    b) Check that angle ACB is a right angle using a protractor.

3   Construct an isosceles triangle PQR where $PQ = 8$ cm and the angles RPQ and RQP are both 30°.

Constructing an Angle of 90°

Remember, an angle of 90° is called a right angle.

90°

Example 6

Construct an angle of 90°.

1. Draw a straight line, and mark the point where you want to form the right angle.

2. Draw arcs of the same radius on either side of your point.

3. Increase the radius of your compass, and draw two arcs of the same radius — one arc centred on each of the intersections.

4. Draw a straight line to complete the right angle.

Exercise 6

1 a) Draw a straight line, and mark a point roughly halfway along it. Label the point X.
   b) Construct a right angle at X using only a ruler and compass.

2 Using a ruler and compass only, construct a rectangle with sides of length 5 cm and 7 cm.

Constructing an Angle of 45°

Construct an angle of 45° by bisecting an angle of 90°.

45°

Example 7

Construct an angle of 45°.

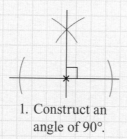

1. Construct an angle of 90°.

2. ...then form the angle bisector to make an angle of 45°.

Exercise 7

1 a) Draw a straight line, and mark a point roughly halfway along it. Label the point X.
   b) Construct an angle of 45° at X using only a ruler and compass.

2 Construct an isosceles triangle ABC where AB = 8 cm and the angles CAB and CBA are both 45°.

Constructing Parallel Lines

Construct parallel lines by making two angles of 90°.

Example 8

Construct a line parallel to AB through the point P.

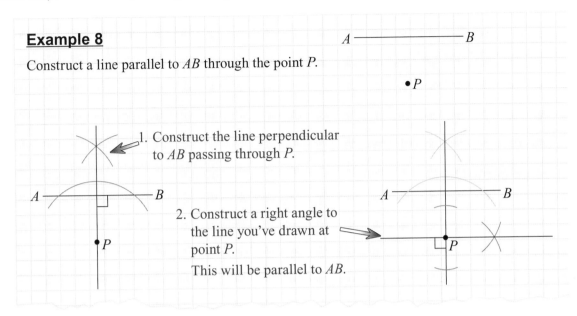

1. Construct the line perpendicular to AB passing through P.

2. Construct a right angle to the line you've drawn at point P.
This will be parallel to AB.

Exercise 8

1 Draw a line *AB*, and mark a point *P* approximately 4 cm from your line. Construct a line parallel to *AB* through the point *P*.

2 Draw two straight lines that cross each other at a single point. By adding two parallel lines, construct a parallelogram.

3 Draw a line *AB* 10 cm long.

   a) Construct angles of 60° at points *A* and *B*, as shown.

   b) Mark point *C* on the line 3 cm from *B*.

   c) By drawing a line parallel to *AB*, complete the trapezium *ABCD*.

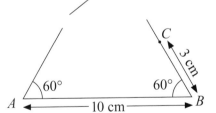

Exercise 9 — Mixed Exercise

1 Draw a line *AB* 8 cm long.

   a) Construct an angle of 60° at *A*.

   b) Complete the construction of a rhombus *ABCD* with sides of length 8 cm.

2 **a)** Construct an equilateral triangle with sides of 5.8 cm.

   b) Construct a line through one of the vertices that is parallel to the opposite side.

3 **a)** Construct the triangle *ABC* with *AB* = 7.4 cm, angle *CAB* = 60° and angle *ABC* = 45°.

   b) Calculate the size of angle *ACB*.
Check the angle in your drawing using a protractor.

4 Using a ruler and compass only, construct an angle of 15°.

18.4 Loci

A **locus** (plural = 'loci') is a set of points which satisfy a particular condition.

The locus of points 1 cm from a point P is a **circle** with radius 1 cm centred on P.

The locus of points 1 cm from a line AB is a 'sausage shape'.

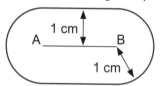

The locus of points **equidistant** (the same distance) from points A and B is the **perpendicular bisector** of AB.

The locus of points equidistant from two lines is their **angle bisector**.

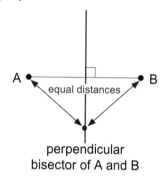

perpendicular bisector of A and B

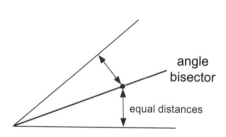

angle bisector

equal distances

Example 1

Construct the locus of points that satisfy all the following conditions:
(i)   inside rectangle *ABCD*,
(ii) more than 2 cm from point *A*,
(iii) less than 1 cm from side *CD*.

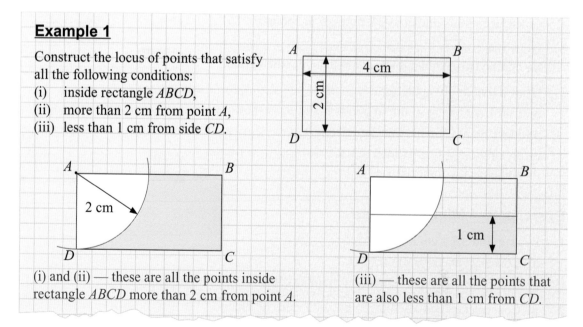

(i) and (ii) — these are all the points inside rectangle *ABCD* more than 2 cm from point *A*.

(iii) — these are all the points that are also less than 1 cm from *CD*.

Exercise 1

1   Draw a 7 cm long line *AB*. Construct the locus of all the points 2 cm from the line.

2   **a)** Mark a point *X* on your page. Draw the locus of all points which are 3 cm from *X*.
    b) Shade the locus of all points that are less than 3 cm from *X*.

3 Mark two points A and B on your page 6 cm apart.
Construct the locus of all points which are equidistant from A and B.

4 Draw two lines that meet at an angle of 50°.
Construct the locus of all points which are equidistant from the two lines.

5 Draw a line AB 6 cm long. Draw the locus of all points which are 3 cm from AB.

6 a) Mark points P and Q on your page 5 cm apart.

b) Draw the locus of points which are 3 cm from P.

c) Draw the locus of points which are 4 cm from Q.

d) Show clearly which points are both 3 cm from P and 4 cm from Q.

7 a) Draw axes on squared paper with x- and y-values from 0 to 10.
Plot the points $P(2, 7)$ and $Q(10, 3)$.

b) Construct the locus of points which are equidistant from P and Q.

8 a) Construct a triangle with sides 4 cm, 5 cm and 6 cm.

b) Draw the locus of all points which are exactly 1 cm from any of the triangle's sides.

9 a) Construct an isosceles triangle DEF with $DE = EF = 5$ cm and $DF = 3$ cm.

b) Draw the locus of points which are equidistant from D and F and less than 2 cm from E.

Exercise 2

1 A ship sails so that it is always the same distance from a port P and a lighthouse L. The lighthouse and the port are 3 km apart.

a) Draw a scale diagram showing the port and lighthouse. Use a scale of 1 cm : 1 km.

b) Show the path of the ship on your diagram.

2 Some students are doing a treasure hunt. They know the treasure is:
- located in a square region $ABCD$, which measures 10 m × 10 m
- the same distance from AB as from AD
- 7 m from corner C.

Draw a scale diagram to show the location of the treasure. Use a scale of 1 cm : 1 m.

3 Two edges of a field meet at an angle of 80°. A bonfire has to be the same distance from each edge and 3 m from the corner.

Copy and complete the diagram below to show the position of the fire.

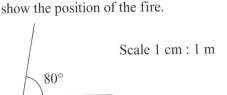

Scale 1 cm : 1 m

80°

4 Two camels set off at the same time from towns A and B, located 50 miles apart in the desert.

a) Draw a scale diagram showing towns A and B. Use a scale of 1 cm : 10 miles.

b) If a camel can walk up to 40 miles in a day, show on your diagram the region where the camels could possibly meet each other after walking for one day.

5 A walled rectangular yard has length 4 m and width 2 m. A dog is secured by a lead of length 1 m to a post in the corner of the yard.

a) Show on an accurate scale drawing the area in which the dog can move. Use the scale 1 cm : 1 m.

b) The post is replaced with a 3 m rail mounted horizontally along one of the long walls, with one end in the corner.

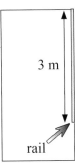

3 m

rail

If the end of the lead attached to the rail is free to slide, show the area in which the dog can move.

Section 19 — Area and Perimeter

19.1   Rectangles and Triangles

Perimeter

Perimeter (P) is the distance around the outside of a shape.

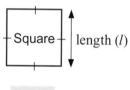

Square + length (l)

$P = 4l$

Rectangle   width (w)

←length (l)→

$P = 2l + 2w$

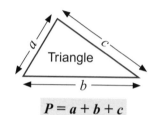

Triangle

$P = a + b + c$

Example 1

Find the perimeter of
each of these shapes:

a)
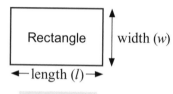
5 cm
3 cm

b)
4.1 m
6.2 m
8.3 m

1. Write down the formula for perimeter.
2. Substitute in the lengths of the sides.

$P = 2l + 2w$
$= (2 \times 5) + (2 \times 3)$
$= 10 + 6$
$= \underline{\textbf{16 cm}}$

$P = a + b + c$
$= 4.1 + 8.3 + 6.2$
$= \underline{\textbf{18.6 m}}$

Exercise 1

1   Find the perimeters of the shapes below.

a)
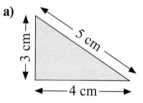
3 cm
5 cm
4 cm

b)

3 m
11 m

c)
5 cm

d)
6 cm
4 cm

e)
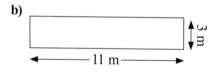
18 m
14 m   11 m

f)
30 mm
15 mm

g)
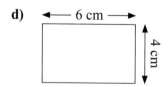
4.2 cm

h)
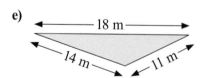
5.2 mm
13.8 mm
12.8 mm

i)
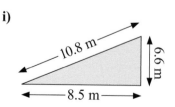
10.8 m
6.6 m
8.5 m

Area

Area (A) is the amount of space inside a shape.

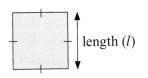 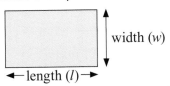 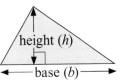

Area = (side length)²   **Area = length × width**   **Area = ½ × base × perpendicular height**

$A = l^2$ $A = lw$ $A = \frac{1}{2}bh$

Example 2

Find the area of each of these shapes:

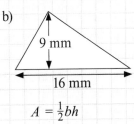

a) 3.2 m

b) 9 mm, 16 mm

1. Write down the formula for area. $A = l^2$ $A = \frac{1}{2}bh$

2. Substitute in the lengths needed. $= 3.2^2$ $= \frac{1}{2} \times 16 \times 9$

3. It's an area, so use 'squared' units. $= \underline{\mathbf{10.24\ m^2}}$ $= \underline{\mathbf{72\ mm^2}}$

Exercise 2

1   Find the areas of the shapes below.

a)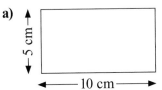

b)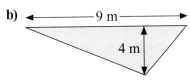

c)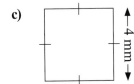

d)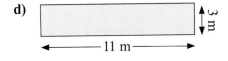

e)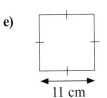

f)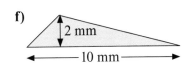

g)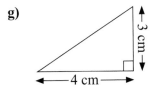

h)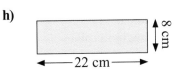

i)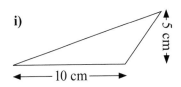

Exercise 3 — Mixed Exercise

1 For each shape below, find: **(i)** its perimeter, **(ii)** its area.

a)
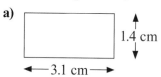
1.4 cm
3.1 cm

b)
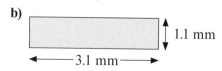
1.1 mm
3.1 mm

c)
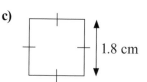
1.8 cm

2 For each shape described below, find: **(i)** its perimeter, **(ii)** its area.

a) a square with sides of length 4 cm.

b) a rectangle of width 6 m and length 8 m.

c) a rectangle 23 mm long and 15 mm wide.

d) a square with 17 m sides.

e) a rectangle 22.2 m long and 4.3 m wide.

f) a rectangle of length 9 mm and width 2.4 mm.

3 For each of the triangles below, find: **(i)** its perimeter, **(ii)** its area.

a)
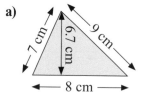
7 cm, 6.7 cm, 9 cm, 8 cm

b)
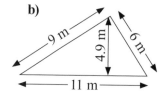
9 m, 4.9 m, 6 m, 11 m

c)
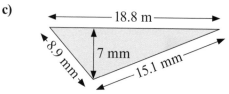
18.8 m, 8.9 mm, 7 mm, 15.1 mm

d)
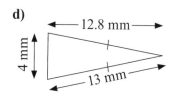
12.8 mm, 4 mm, 13 mm

e)
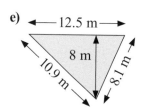
12.5 m, 8 m, 10.9 m, 8.1 m

f)
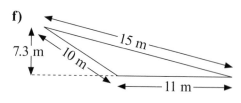
15 m, 7.3 m, 10 m, 11 m

4 Barbie has a rectangular lawn 23.5 m long by 17.3 m wide. She is going to mow the lawn and then put edging around the outside.

a) What area will Barbie have to mow (to the nearest m²)?

b) How much lawn edging will she need?

5 The police need to cordon off and then search a rectangular crime scene measuring 2.1 m by 2.8 m.

a) What area do the police need to search?

b) What is the perimeter of the crime scene?

6 A rectangular garden 24 m long and 5.4 m wide is to be re-turfed. Turf is bought in rolls that are 60 cm wide and 8 m long.
How many rolls of turf are needed to cover the garden?

7 A rectangular floor measures 9 m by 7.5 m. It is to be tiled using square tiles with sides of length 0.5 m.

0.5 m
0.5 m

a) What is the area of the floor?

b) What is the area of one of the tiles?

c) How many tiles will be needed to cover the floor?

8 Ali bakes the cake shown below.

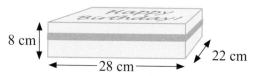
8 cm
28 cm
22 cm

a) What length of ribbon is needed to go around the outside of the cake?

b) If the top and the four sides are to be iced, what area of icing will be needed?

A composite shape is one that's made out of simpler shapes joined together.

Example 3

Find this shape's: a) perimeter, b) area.

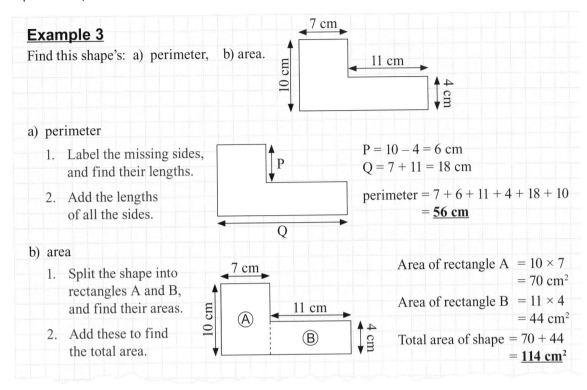

a) perimeter

1. Label the missing sides, and find their lengths.

2. Add the lengths of all the sides.

$P = 10 - 4 = 6$ cm
$Q = 7 + 11 = 18$ cm

perimeter $= 7 + 6 + 11 + 4 + 18 + 10$
$= \underline{\mathbf{56 \ cm}}$

b) area

1. Split the shape into rectangles A and B, and find their areas.

2. Add these to find the total area.

Area of rectangle A $= 10 \times 7$
$= 70$ cm²
Area of rectangle B $= 11 \times 4$
$= 44$ cm²
Total area of shape $= 70 + 44$
$= \underline{\mathbf{114 \ cm^2}}$

Exercise 4

1 Find the area of each shape below.

a)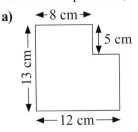

b)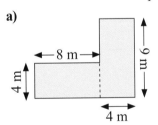

c)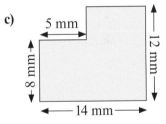

2 For each shape below, find: **(i)** its perimeter, **(ii)** its area.

a)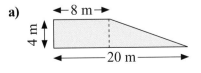

b)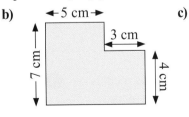

c)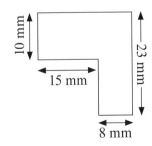

3 Find the area of the shapes below by splitting them into a rectangle and a triangle.

a)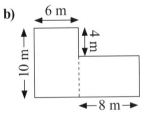

b)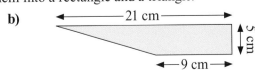

19.2 Other Quadrilaterals

Parallelograms

Parallelograms have two pairs of parallel sides, with opposite sides being the same length. Parallel sides are shown with matching arrows.

The **area** of a parallelogram is given by the formula: $A = bh$

Here, h is the perpendicular height — it's measured at right angles to the base.

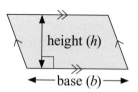

Example 1

Find the area of the parallelogram on the right.

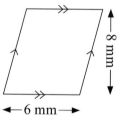

1. Write down the formula for the area of a parallelogram. $A = bh$
2. Substitute in the values for b and h. $= 8 \times 3$
3. Use 'squared' units — here, it's cm². $= \underline{\textbf{24 cm}^2}$

Exercise 1

1 Find the area of each parallelogram below.

a)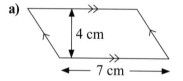

b)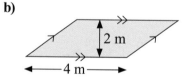

c)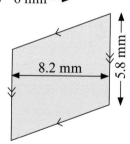

d)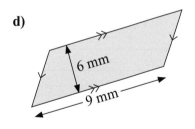

e)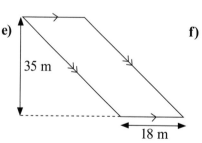

f)

2 The logo of a company that designs rockets consists of two identical parallelograms. Find the total area of the logo.

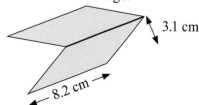

3 Without doing any calculations, explain which of the shapes below has the larger area.

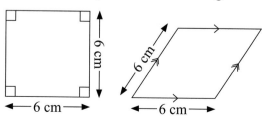

Trapeziums

The shape on the right is a trapezium. It has one pair of parallel sides.

The **area** of a trapezium is given by the formula:

$$A = \frac{1}{2}(a + b) \times h$$

Remember, a and b are the parallel sides, and h is the perpendicular height.

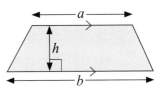

Example 2

Find the area of the trapezium on the right.

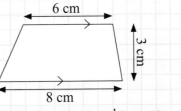

1. Write down the formula for the area of a trapezium.

2. Substitute in the values for a, b and h.

3. Use 'squared' units — here, it's cm².

$$A = \frac{1}{2}(a + b) \times h$$
$$= \frac{1}{2}(6 + 8) \times 3$$
$$= \frac{1}{2} \times 14 \times 3$$
$$= 7 \times 3 = \underline{\mathbf{21 \ cm^2}}$$

Exercise 2

1 Find the area of each trapezium below.

a)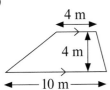

b)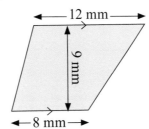

c)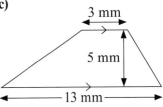

d)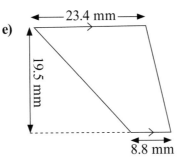

e)

f)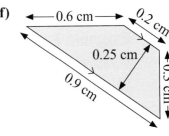

2 The picture below shows the end of a barn. Find its total area.

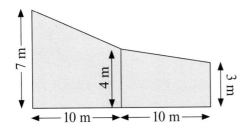

3 What can you say about the area of these two shapes? Explain your answer.

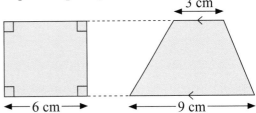

Exercise 3 — Mixed Exercise

1 Find the area of each shape below.

a)
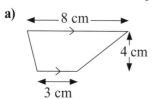

b)
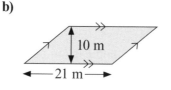

c)
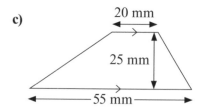

d)
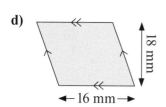

e)
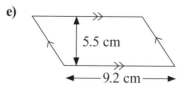

f)
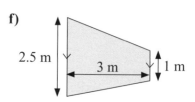

2 The picture below shows part of a tiled wall. All the tiles are parallelograms.

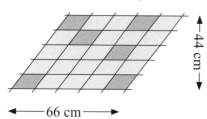

Find the area of one tile.

3 The flag below is in the shape of a trapezium. The coloured strips along the top and bottom edges are parallelograms.

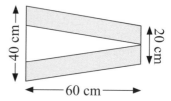

a) Find the total area of the flag.

b) Find the total area of the coloured strips.

Composite Shapes involving Parallelograms and Trapeziums

The area of a composite shape can be found by adding or subtracting the areas of simpler shapes.

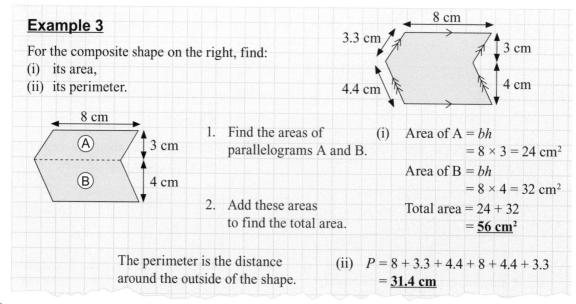

Example 3

For the composite shape on the right, find:
(i) its area,
(ii) its perimeter.

1. Find the areas of parallelograms A and B.

(i) Area of A = bh
     $= 8 \times 3 = 24$ cm²

Area of B = bh
     $= 8 \times 4 = 32$ cm²

2. Add these areas to find the total area.

Total area = 24 + 32
     = **56 cm²**

The perimeter is the distance around the outside of the shape.

(ii) $P = 8 + 3.3 + 4.4 + 8 + 4.4 + 3.3$
     = **31.4 cm**

Example 4

Find the area of the shape on the right.

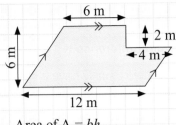

1. Form a parallelogram (A) by adding a trapezium (B) to the corner of the original shape.

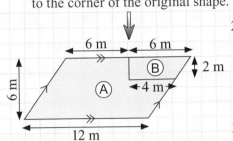

2. Find the areas of parallelogram A and trapezium B.

Area of A = bh

= 12 × 6 = <u>72 m²</u>

Area of B = $\frac{1}{2}(a + b) \times h$

= $\frac{1}{2}(6 + 4) \times 2$ = <u>10 m²</u>

3. Subtract to find the original shape's area.

Total area = 72 – 10 = **<u>62 m²</u>**

Exercise 4

1 Find each shaded area below.

a)

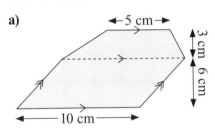

b)

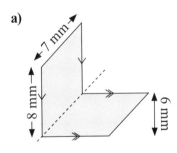

2 For each shape below, find: **(i)** the area, **(ii)** the perimeter. The dotted lines show lines of symmetry.

a)

b)

c)

d)

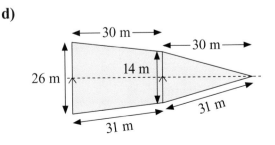

19.3 Circumference of a Circle

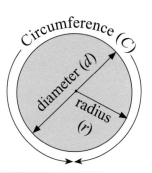

The **circumference** (C) of a circle is given by the formula: $C = \pi d$

Calculators usually have a special button for the number π.
If your calculator doesn't have a button for π, use the value 3.142.

Remember, the diameter (d) of a circle is always twice as long as the radius (r): $d = 2r$

Example 1

Find the circumference of the circle shown. Give your answer to 1 decimal place.

1. Write down the diameter.	$d = 8$ cm
2. Use the formula $C = \pi d$.	$C = \pi d$
	$C = 3.142 \times 8$
	$C = 25.136$
3. Round your answer. And use the correct units.	$C = \underline{\textbf{25.1 cm}}$ *(to 1 d.p.)*

Example 2

Find the circumference of a circle which has radius 6 m. Give your answer to 1 decimal place.

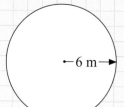

1. Use $d = 2r$ to find the diameter.	$d = 2r$
	$d = 2 \times 6$
	$d = 12$ m
2. Use the formula $C = \pi d$ to find the circumference.	$C = \pi d$
	$C = \pi \times 12$
	$C = \underline{\textbf{37.7 m}}$ *(to 1 d.p.)*

Exercise 1

1 Find the circumference of each circle. Give your answers to 1 decimal place.

a)

8 cm

b)

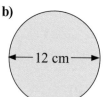
12 cm

c)

2 cm

d)

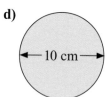
10 cm

e)

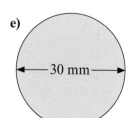
30 mm

f)

5 mm

g)

7 m

h)

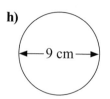
9 cm

2 For each circle below, write down the diameter and then find its circumference.
Give your answers to 1 decimal place.

a)
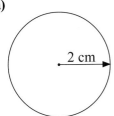
2 cm

b)

1.5 mm

c)

2.5 cm

d)
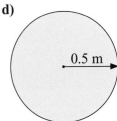
0.5 m

e)

1.7 cm

f)

1.3 mm

g)

2.6 m

h)
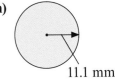
11.1 mm

3 Find the circumference of the circles with the diameter (*d*) or radius (*r*) given below.
Give your answers to 1 decimal place.

a) *d* = 4 cm   **b)** *d* = 8 mm   **c)** *d* = 9 m   **d)** *d* = 6 cm

e) *r* = 11 m   **f)** *r* = 22 cm   **g)** *r* = 14 km   **h)** *r* = 35 mm

i) *d* = 2.5 m   **j)** *r* = 1.9 cm   **k)** *r* = 0.1 km   **l)** *d* = 6.3 mm

---

Example 3

The shape on the right consists of a semicircle on top of a rectangle.
Find the perimeter of the shape.

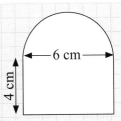

1. Find the curved length.
    This is half the circumference
    of a circle with diameter 6 cm.

    Curved length = $\pi d \div 2$
    $= \pi \times 6 \div 2$
    $= 9.42$ cm *(to 2 d.p.)*

2. Find the total length of
    the straight sides.

    Total of straight sides = 4 + 6 + 4
    $= 14$ cm

3. Add the two parts.

    Total length = curved length + straight length
    $= 9.42 + 14$
    $= \underline{\mathbf{23.4\ cm}}$ *(to 1 d.p.)*

Exercise 2

1 Find the perimeter of each shape below. Give your answers to 1 decimal place.

a)
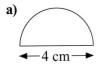
4 cm

b)

26 mm

c)

2 m

d)

7 cm

2 Find the perimeter of each shape below. Give your answers to 1 decimal place.

a)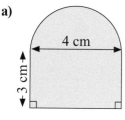
4 cm
3 cm

b)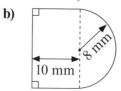
8 mm
10 mm

c)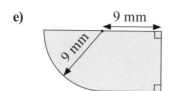
5 cm
4 cm
4 cm

d)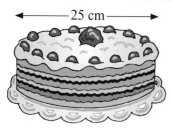
9 mm

e)
9 mm
9 mm

f)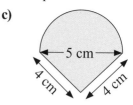
3 cm
2 cm

Exercise 3

In the following questions, give your answers to 1 decimal place unless the question tells you otherwise.

1 What is the circumference of a circular flower bed with a diameter of 3 m?

2 A circular table mat has a radius of 10 cm. What is the circumference of the mat?

3 Find the circumference of this circular cake.

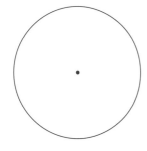
← 25 cm →

4 An archaeologist plans to excavate a circular burial mound with radius 23 m. What is the circumference of the mound?

5 A circular pond has a diameter of 84 cm. What is the circumference of the pond to the nearest cm?

6 Measure the diameter of the circle below, and then calculate its circumference.

7 A volcanic crater has a radius of 5.7 km. Kate and William walked all the way around the outside. How far did they walk?

8 A craftsman makes a circular table with a radius of 55 cm.

  a) What is the circumference of the table?

  b) A customer orders a smaller circular table with a diameter only half as big. Find the circumference of the smaller table.

9 A lake is in the shape of a quarter-circle, as shown. How long would a footpath around the lake be?

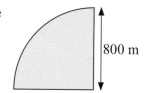
800 m

10 A running track consists of two semicircles of radius 80 m, joined together by two straight sections, each with length 100 m. Calculate the length of the running track.

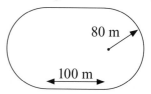
80 m
100 m

11 Alec used wooden fencing to build a semicircular sheep pen, with a wall forming the straight side. If the radius of the semicircle is 16 m, how many metres of fencing did Alec have to use?

12 A window consists of a rectangle 1.5 m wide and 2.1 m high with a semicircle on top. Calculate the perimeter of the window.

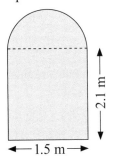

13 A company's logo consists of a rectangle measuring 5 cm by 3 cm, with a semicircle on each side.

Calculate the length of the logo's perimeter to 1 decimal place.

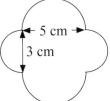

19.4   Area of a Circle

Area = A

The area (A) of a circle is given by the formula: $A = \pi r^2$

Example 1

Find the area of the circle below. Give your answer to 1 decimal place.

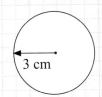
3 cm

1. Write down the radius.

$r = 3$

2. Use the formula $A = \pi r^2$. (Remember: $r^2 = r \times r$)

$A = \pi r^2$
$= \pi \times 3 \times 3$
$= 28.274...$

3. Round your answer. And use 'squared' units — here, it's cm^2.

$A = \underline{\mathbf{28.3\ cm^2}}$ *(to 1 d.p.)*

Exercise 1

In the following questions, give your answers to 1 decimal place unless told otherwise.

1 Find the area of each circle.

a)

2 cm

b)

10 mm

c)

3 m

d)
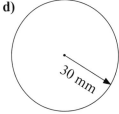
30 mm

2 Write down the radius of each circle, and then find its area.

a)
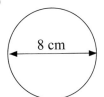
8 cm

b)
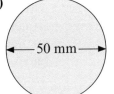
50 mm

c)

7 m

d)

12 mm

3 Find the areas of the circles with the diameter (d) or radius (r) given below.
Give your answers to 1 decimal place.

a) $r = 6$ mm   b) $r = 5$ cm   c) $r = 4$ m   d) $r = 6.5$ cm

e) $d = 8.5$ mm   f) $d = 3.5$ m   g) $d = 12$ km   h) $d = 22$ cm

i) $r = 1.3$ m   j) $d = 44$ mm   k) $d = 1.2$ mm   l) $r = 1.05$ m

4 What is the area of a circular rug whose radius is 3.5 m?

5 What is the area of the following badge?

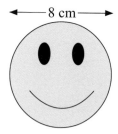

←——— 8 cm ———→

6 A drinks coaster has a diameter of 13 cm. What is its area?

7 A circular pond has diameter 7.2 m. What is its area?

8 What is the area of a circular reservoir of radius 0.8 km?

9 Find the coloured area in the diagram below.

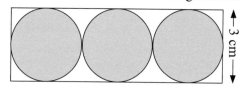

10 a) A 2p coin has a radius of 1.3 cm. What is its area?

b) A 5p coin has a diameter of 1.8 cm. Which has the greater area: a 2p coin or two 5p coins?

11 Which of these shapes has the greater area?

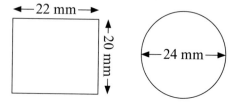

12 Find the area of the semicircle below.

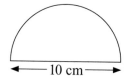

←——— 10 cm ———→

13 What is the area of this quarter-circle?

Example 2

Find the total area of the shape on the right.

3 cm

2 cm

1. Divide the shape into a rectangle and a semicircle.

2. Find the area of the rectangle.   Area of rectangle $= 3 \times 2$
$\qquad\qquad\qquad\qquad\qquad\qquad\qquad\quad = 6$ cm^2

3. Find the area of the semicircle. (Since its diameter is 2 cm, its radius must be 1 cm.)
   Area of semicircle $=$ (area of circle of radius 1 cm) $\div 2$
$\qquad\qquad\qquad\qquad\quad = (\pi r^2) \div 2$
$\qquad\qquad\qquad\qquad\quad = (\pi \times 1^2) \div 2$
$\qquad\qquad\qquad\qquad\quad = 1.6$ cm^2 *(to 1 d.p.)*

4. Add the two areas.   Total area $=$ area of rectangle $+$ area of semicircle
$\qquad\qquad\qquad\qquad\qquad\quad = 6 + 1.6$
$\qquad\qquad\qquad\qquad\qquad\quad = \underline{\textbf{7.6 cm}^2}$ *(to 1 d.p.)*

Exercise 2

1 Find the area of each shape below. Give your answers to 1 decimal place.

a)

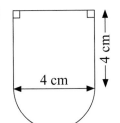
7 cm

b)

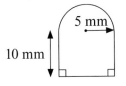
5 mm
10 mm

c)

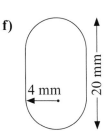
5 cm
2 cm

d)

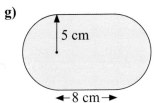
4 cm
4 cm

e)

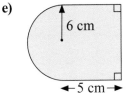
6 cm
5 cm

f)

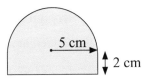
4 mm
20 mm

g)

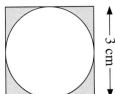
5 cm
8 cm

h)

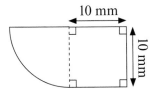
10 mm
10 mm

i)

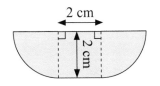
2 cm
2 cm

2 A flower bed is in the shape of a semicircle of radius 2.5 m. What is its area?

3 A church window is in the shape of a rectangle 1 m wide and 2 m high, with a semicircle on top. What is its area?

4 A cookie cutter is in the shape of a quarter circle of radius 6 cm. What is the area of each biscuit made with the cutter?

5 Find the area of the sports field below.

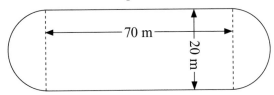
70 m
20 m

6 Find the coloured area in the diagram below.

3 cm

7 A circular pond of diameter 4 m is surrounded by a path 1 m wide, as shown below. What is the area of the path?

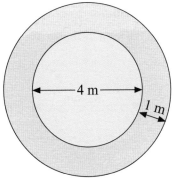
4 m
1 m

8 Timi made an apron from a rectangle of material 50 cm wide and 80 cm high. She cut out a quarter circle of radius 15 cm from the top two corners.

a) What area did Timi cut away?

b) What was the area of the finished apron?

19.5 Area and Perimeter Problems

Exercise 1

Where necessary, give your answers to 1 decimal place.

1 Find the shaded area in each of the following.

All 4 parallelograms are identical.

a)

1 m
1.5 m
4 m
1.5 m
6 m

b)

20 mm
50 mm
40 mm

c)

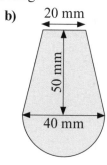

6 mm
9 mm

2 Find the perimeter and area of the following shapes. Give your answers to 1 decimal place.

a)

1 cm
1 cm

Curved sections are semicircles.

b)

80 m
80 m
80 m

c)

1 cm   6 cm
1 cm
1 cm

Curved sections are quarter-circles.

3 A circular gasket is a ring of material with a hole in the centre.

a) Find the area of the gasket below.

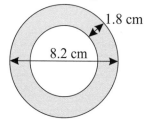

1.8 cm
8.2 cm

b) A different circular gasket has a diameter of 10.1 cm. The hole in the centre has a radius of 3.8 cm. Find the area of the gasket.

4 A circular tower has a radius of 8 m, and is surrounded by a moat that is 16 m wide.

What is the area of the moat's surface?

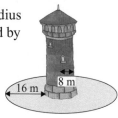

16 m   8 m

5 Raheel assembled the four pieces of wood shown below to make a photo frame. Each piece of wood is in the shape of a trapezium. Find the total area of wood.

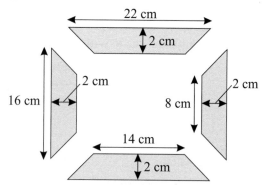

22 cm
2 cm
2 cm
2 cm
16 cm
8 cm
14 cm
2 cm

6 What can you say about the areas of these two shapes? Explain your answer.

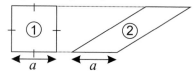

① ②
a a

Example 1

What is the diameter of a circle which has circumference 26 cm?

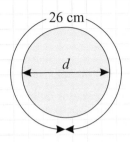

1. Write down the formula linking the diameter and circumference. $C = \pi d$

2. Substitute in the numbers from the question. $26 = \pi \times d$
$$d = \frac{26}{\pi}$$

3. Rearrange to find the diameter. And remember the units. $d = \textbf{8.28 cm}$ *(to 2 d.p.)*

Exercise 2

Where necessary, give your answers to 1 decimal place.

1 The circumference of a circle is 128 m. What is its diameter?

2 The circumference of a circle is 45 cm. What is its diameter?

3 The circumference of a circle is 18.9 cm. What is its radius?

4 A tree measures 29 feet around its base. What is its diameter?

5 Jo walked all the way round a circular lake, a distance of 16 km. Find the lake's diameter.

 6 Fifty people stand in a circle with their arms stretched out so their fingertips just touch. The average fingertip-to-fingertip distance is measured as 1.6 m.

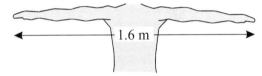

What is the diameter of the circle made by the 50 people?

Example 2

What is the radius of a circle which has area 50 m²?

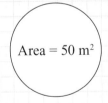

Area = 50 m²

1. Write down the formula linking the radius and area. $A = \pi r^2$

2. Substitute in the numbers from the question. $50 = \pi \times r^2$

3. Rearrange to find r^2. $r^2 = 50 \div \pi = 15.915$

4. Take the square root ($\sqrt{}$) to find r. $r = \sqrt{15.915}$
$= \textbf{4.0 m}$ *(to 1 d.p.)*

Exercise 3

Where necessary, give your answers to 1 decimal place.

1 The area of a circle is 75 cm². What is its radius?

2 What's the radius of a circle with area 29 m²?

3 A park's population of frogs lives in a circular pond covering an area of 125 m². What is the radius of the pond?

4 A circular pool for sailing model yachts is to be built. Each model yacht will need 20 m² of water.

What is the smallest possible diameter of the pool if it must be able to accommodate at least 12 yachts?

Section 20 — 3D Shapes

20.1 Nets

Faces, Vertices and Edges

You need to know how to describe the different parts of a three-dimensional (3D) object.

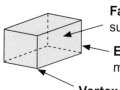

Face: one of the flat surfaces of a 3D object.

Edge: where two faces (or surfaces) meet — edges are usually straight.

Vertex (plural = 'vertices'): a corner.

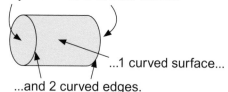

A cylinder has 2 circular faces...

...1 curved surface...

...and 2 curved edges.

Example 1

How many faces, vertices and edges does a cube have?

1. Count the number of flat surfaces.

2. Count the number of corners.

3. Count how many places two faces meet.

So a cube has **6 faces**, **8 vertices** and **12 edges**.

Prisms

A **prism** is a 3D shape which has a **constant cross-section** — this means it's the "same all the way through".

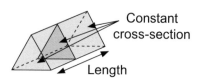

Constant cross-section

Length

Exercise 1

1 Write down the number of faces, vertices and edges in the following 3D shapes.

a) Cuboid   **b)** Triangular Prism   **c)** Tetrahedron   **d)** Square-based Pyramid

  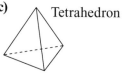

2 Name the 3D shapes described below.

  a) 6 identical faces, 8 vertices and 12 edges   **b)** 2 parallel triangular faces, 3 rectangular faces

  c) 4 triangular faces, 6 edges   **d)** 1 square face, 4 identical triangular faces

  e) 2 circular faces, 1 curved surface and 2 curved edges

3 Which of the following 3D shapes are prisms?

A B C D E

A net of a 3D object is a 2D (two-dimensional, or 'flat') shape that can be folded to make the 3D object.

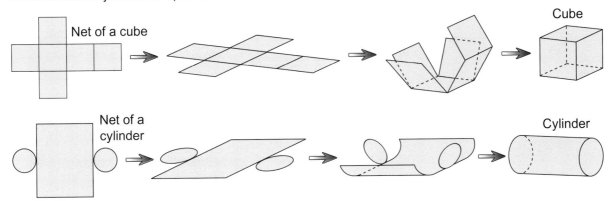

Net of a cube

Cube

Net of a cylinder

Cylinder

Example 2

How many a) triangles and b) rectangles are there in the net of a triangular prism?

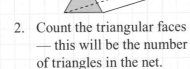

1. Sketch a triangular prism.

2. Count the triangular faces — this will be the number of triangles in the net.

3. Count the rectangular faces — this will be the number of rectangles in the net.

So the net will have a) **2 triangles** and b) **3 rectangles**.

Exercise 2

1 State how many **(i)** squares and **(ii)** triangles there will be in the nets of the following.

a) tetrahedron   **b)** cube

c) square-based pyramid

2 How many faces will the 3D shape with this net have?

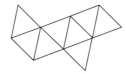

3 Is the net on the right the net of a cuboid? Explain your answer.

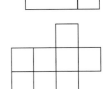

4 Is the net on the right the net of a cube? Explain your answer.

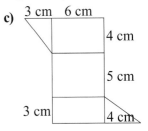

5 Name and sketch the 3D objects with the following nets. Mark the edge lengths on your sketches.

a)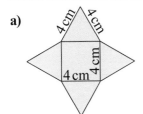

b)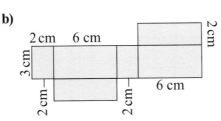

c)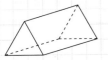

3 cm   6 cm

4 cm

5 cm

3 cm

4 cm

6 How many rectangles with the following dimensions will the net of this cuboid have?

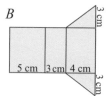

a) 2 cm × 3 cm   b) 2 cm × 4 cm

c) 3 cm × 4 cm   d) 2 cm × 2 cm

7 How many rectangles with the following dimensions will the net of this triangular prism have?

a) 4 cm × 6 cm   b) 5 cm × 6 cm

c) 3 cm × 6 cm   d) 3 cm × 4 cm

8 Which of the nets *A*, *B* or *C* is the net of the triangular prism shown below?

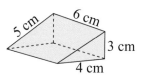

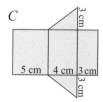

Example 3

Draw a net for a cuboid with dimensions 2 cm × 2 cm × 3 cm.
Label the net with its dimensions.

1. Sketch the cuboid.

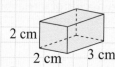

2. Draw it 'unfolded' — there could be several ways of doing this.

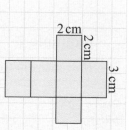

Example 4

Draw a net for a cylinder with length 6 cm and radius 1 cm.
Label the net with its dimensions.

1. Sketch the cylinder.

2. Draw it 'unfolded'.

3. Find the missing length, *l*, of the rectangle — it's equal to the circumference of the circle.

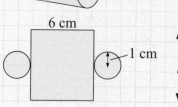

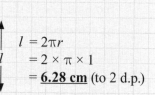

$$l = 2\pi r$$
$$= 2 \times \pi \times 1$$
$$= \mathbf{6.28\ cm}\ (\text{to 2 d.p.})$$

Exercise 3

1 Copy and complete the unfinished nets of the objects shown below.

a)

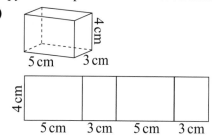

b)

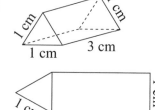

2 Draw a net of each of the following objects. Label each net with its dimensions.

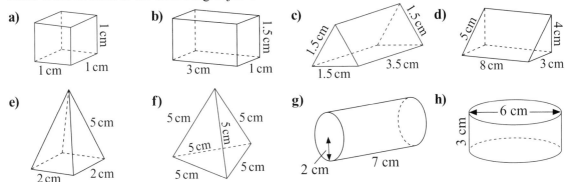

a) 1 cm, 1 cm, 1 cm
b) 3 cm, 1.5 cm, 1 cm
c) 1.5 cm, 1.5 cm, 1.5 cm, 3.5 cm
d) 5 cm, 4 cm, 8 cm, 3 cm
e) 5 cm, 2 cm, 2 cm
f) 5 cm, 5 cm, 5 cm, 5 cm, 5 cm
g) 2 cm, 7 cm
h) 6 cm, 3 cm

3 Draw a net of each of the following objects. Label each net with its dimensions.

a) a cube with 2 cm edges

b) a 1.5 cm × 2 cm × 2.5 cm cuboid

c) a tetrahedron with 3.5 cm edges

d) a cylinder of length 4 cm and radius 2.5 cm

e) a prism of length 3 cm whose cross-section is an equilateral triangle of side 2 cm

f) a pyramid with square base of side 5 cm and slanted edge of length 4 cm

20.2   Plans and Elevations

Plans and elevations are two-dimensional (flat) pictures of three-dimensional objects, viewed from particular directions. The view looking vertically downwards from above is the **plan**. The views looking horizontally from the front and side are called the **front** and **side elevations**.

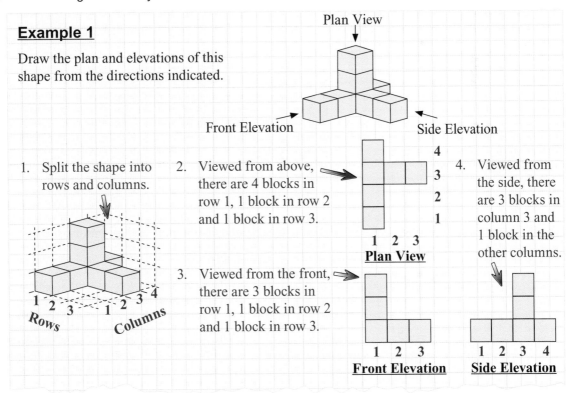

Example 1

Draw the plan and elevations of this shape from the directions indicated.

1. Split the shape into rows and columns.

2. Viewed from above, there are 4 blocks in row 1, 1 block in row 2 and 1 block in row 3.

3. Viewed from the front, there are 3 blocks in row 1, 1 block in row 2 and 1 block in row 3.

4. Viewed from the side, there are 3 blocks in column 3 and 1 block in the other columns.

Exercise 1

1   Below are the front and side elevations of the given objects. Draw the plan view for each.

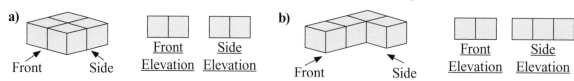

2   Below are the plan view and front elevation of the given objects. Draw the side elevation for each.

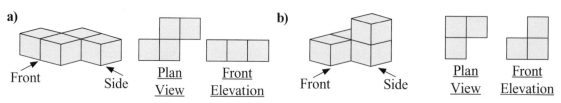

3   For each of the following, draw: **(i)**   the plan view,
                                          (ii) the front and side elevations, using the directions shown in **a)**.

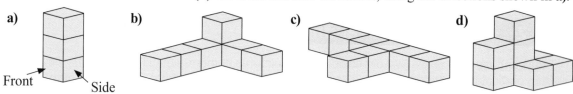

4   Which of the solid objects *A*, *B* or *C* below corresponds to the plan and elevations shown?

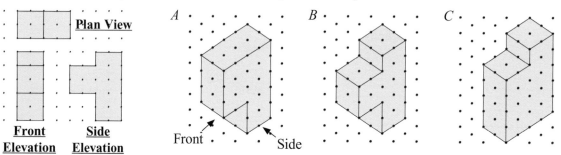

5   Which of the solid objects *P*, *Q* or *R* below corresponds to the plan and elevations shown?

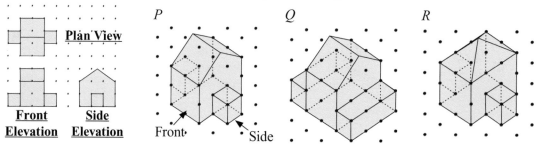

6 Use a square grid to draw: **(i)** the plan view,
                                (ii) the front and side elevations, using the directions shown in **a)**.
(The distance between neighbouring dots is 1 cm.)

a)
Front   Side

b)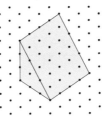

c)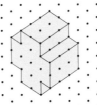

d)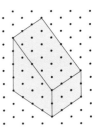

e)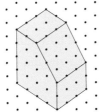

f)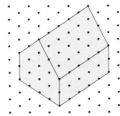

g)

h)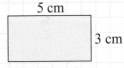

Example 2

Draw the plan and elevations of this cuboid.
Label the plan and elevations with their dimensions.

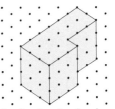
3 cm

Front   1 cm   5 cm   Side

1. Viewed from above, the cuboid
   appears as a 5 cm × 1 cm rectangle.

2. Viewed from the front, the cuboid
   appears as a 1 cm × 3 cm rectangle.

3. Viewed from the side, the cuboid
   appears as a 5 cm × 3 cm rectangle.

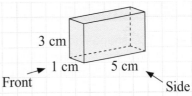

Plan View   5 cm   1 cm

1 cm   5 cm

3 cm   3 cm

Front Elevation   **Side Elevation**

Exercise 2

1 For each of the following, draw the plan, front elevation and side elevation from the directions
indicated in part **a)**. Label the plan and elevations with their dimensions.

a)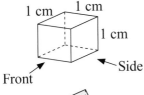
1 cm   1 cm   1 cm
Front   Side

b)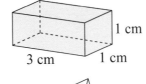
1 cm
3 cm   1 cm

c)
5 cm
2 cm   2 cm

d)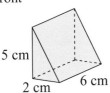
5 cm
2 cm   6 cm

e)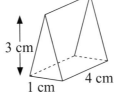
3 cm
1 cm   4 cm

f)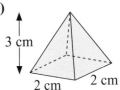
3 cm
2 cm   2 cm

2 For each of the following, draw the plan, front elevation and side elevation from the directions indicated in part **a)**. Label the plan and elevations with their dimensions.

a)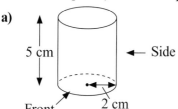

b)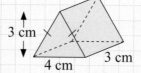

c)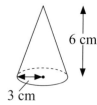

3 Draw the plan, front elevation and side elevation for each of the following. Label the plan and elevations with their dimensions.

a) a cube of side 2 cm

b) a 2 cm × 1 cm × 5 cm cuboid

c) a cylinder of radius 3 cm and length 4 cm

d) a cone of height 4 cm and base radius 1 cm

e) a 4 cm long prism whose cross-section is an isosceles triangle of height 5 cm and base 3 cm

f) a pyramid of height 5 cm whose base is a square of side 3 cm

20.3 Isometric Drawings

Pictures of 3D shapes drawn on a grid of dots or lines arranged in a pattern of equilateral triangles are called **isometric drawings**.

Example 1

Draw this triangular prism on isometric paper.

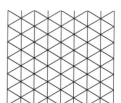

1. Vertical lines stay vertical on isometric drawings, while horizontal lines appear at an angle. Draw the vertical height (3 cm) and base width (4 cm) of the triangular face, then complete the triangle.

2. Draw the 3 cm edges of the prism.

3. Complete the drawing by adding in the final edge.

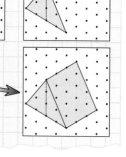

Exercise 1

1 Draw the following cuboids on isometric paper.

a)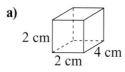

b)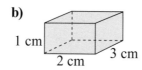

c)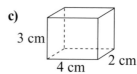

d)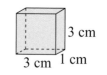

2 Draw the following triangular prisms on isometric paper.

a)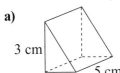
3 cm
2 cm 5 cm

b)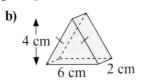
4 cm
6 cm 2 cm

c)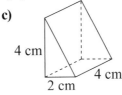
4 cm
2 cm 4 cm

d)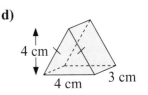
4 cm
4 cm 3 cm

3 Draw the following 3D objects on isometric paper.

a) a cube with 2 cm edges **b)** a cube with 3 cm edges

c) a 2 cm × 2 cm × 3 cm cuboid **d)** a 1 cm × 2 cm × 4 cm cuboid

e) a prism of length 3 cm whose
cross-section is a right-angled triangle
of base 3 cm and vertical height 2 cm

f) a prism of length 2 cm whose
cross-section is an isosceles triangle
of base 4 cm and vertical height 4 cm

4 Draw the following prisms on isometric paper.

a)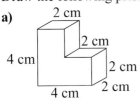
2 cm
2 cm
4 cm
2 cm
4 cm 2 cm

b)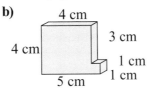
4 cm
4 cm
3 cm
1 cm
5 cm 1 cm

c)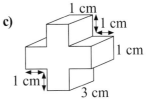
1 cm
1 cm
1 cm
1 cm
3 cm

d)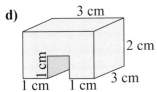
3 cm
2 cm
1 cm
1 cm 1 cm 3 cm

e)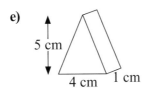
5 cm
4 cm 1 cm

f)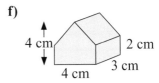
4 cm
2 cm
4 cm 3 cm

Example 2

The diagram shows the plan and front
and side elevations of a prism.
Draw the prism on isometric paper.

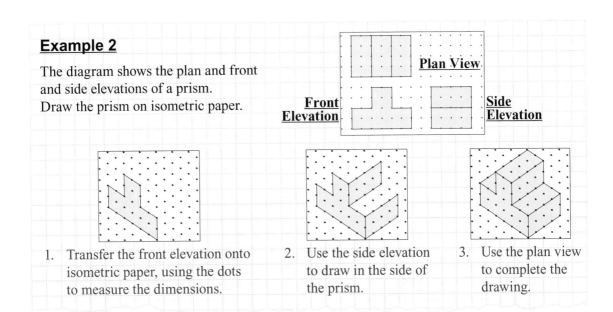

Plan View
Front Elevation
Side Elevation

1. Transfer the front elevation onto
   isometric paper, using the dots
   to measure the dimensions.

2. Use the side elevation
   to draw in the side of
   the prism.

3. Use the plan view
   to complete the
   drawing.

Exercise 2

1   The following diagrams show the constant cross-section of prisms of length 3 cm.
     Draw each prism on isometric paper.

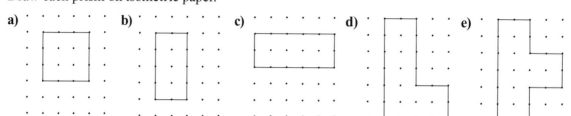

a)   b)   c)   d)   e)

2   The following diagrams show the constant cross-section of prisms of length 2 cm.
     Draw each prism on isometric paper.

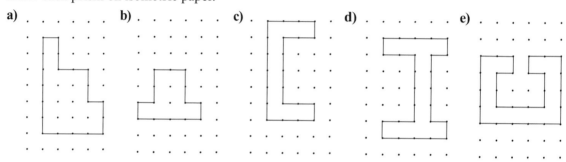

a)   b)   c)   d)   e)

3   The following diagrams show the plan, and front and side elevations of different 3D objects.
     Draw each object on isometric paper.

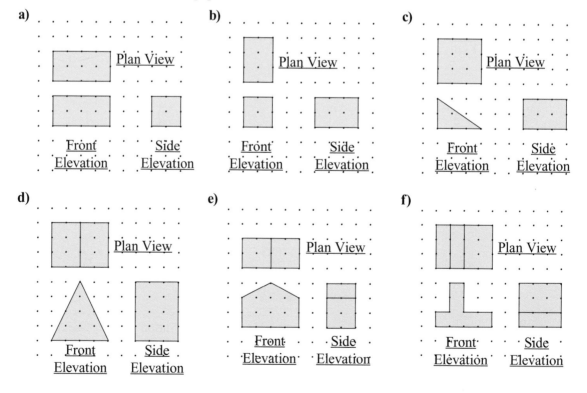

a)   b)   c)

d)   e)   f)

20.4 Volume

Volume of a Cuboid

The volume of a cuboid is given by the following formula.

$$\text{Volume} = \text{Length} \times \text{Width} \times \text{Height}$$

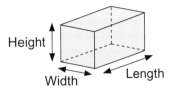

Height
Width
Length

Example 1

Find the volume of the cuboid shown.

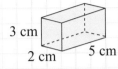

3 cm
2 cm
5 cm

1. Substitute the values of the length, width and height of the cuboid into the equation.
2. Give your answer with correct units.

Volume = Length × Width × Height
= 5 × 2 × 3 = **30 cm³**

Exercise 1

1

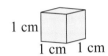

1 cm
1 cm   1 cm

a) Find the volume of the cube shown above.

b) The following shapes are made up of cubes with edges of length 1 cm. Find the volumes of the shapes.

(i)   **(ii)**   **(iii)**   **(iv)**

2 Find the volumes of the following cuboids.

a)

1 cm
5 cm   6 cm

b)

1 m
2 m   5 m

c)

7 cm
2 cm   2 cm

d)

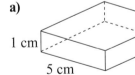

6 mm
2 mm   7 mm

e)

9 cm   1.5 cm
2 cm

f)

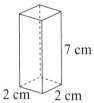

4 m
4 m   4 m

3 Find the volumes of the cuboids with the following dimensions.

a) 1 cm × 2 cm × 3 cm   **b)** 3 cm × 2 cm × 4 cm   **c)** 5 m × 2 m × 7 m

d) 20 cm × 10 cm × 8 cm   **e)** 2.5 cm × 3.0 cm × 4.2 cm   **f)** 18 m × 14 m × 3 m

g) 2 mm × 13 mm × 5 mm   **h)** 1.8 mm × 3.2 mm × 6.1 mm   **i)** 9.1 cm × 2.9 cm × 7.6 cm

4 Find the volume of a cube whose edges are 3.2 mm long.

5 Box *A* measures 1 m × 0.3 m × 2.4 m. Box *B* measures 2 m × 0.3 m × 1.1 m. By how much do their volumes differ?

6 Will 3.5 m³ of sand fit in a cuboid-shaped box with dimensions 1.7 m × 1.8 m × 0.9 m?

7 A cereal box is 9 cm long, 23 cm wide and 32 cm high. The box is half full of cereal. What is the volume of cereal in the box?

8 Split the following 3D objects into cuboids to find their volumes.

a)
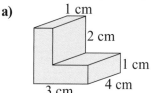
1 cm
2 cm
1 cm
3 cm
4 cm

b)
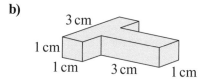
3 cm
1 cm
1 cm   3 cm   1 cm

9 A matchbox is 5 cm long and 3 cm wide. The volume of the matchbox is 18 cm³. What is its height?

10 A bath can be modelled as a cuboid with dimensions 1.5 m × 0.5 m × 0.6 m, as shown.

a) What is the maximum volume of water that the bath will hold?

b) Find the volume of water needed to fill the bath to a height of 0.3 m.

c) Find the height of the water in the bath if the volume of water in the bath is 0.3 m³.

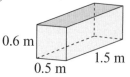
0.6 m
0.5 m
1.5 m

Volume of a Prism

The volume of a prism is given by the following formula.

$$\textbf{Volume = Area of Cross-Section} \times \textbf{Length}$$

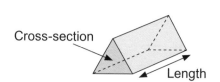
Cross-section
Length

Example 2

Find the volume of each of the shapes on the right.

a)
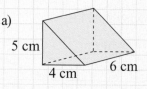
5 cm
4 cm   6 cm

b)
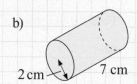
2 cm   7 cm

1. Find the area of the cross-section.

2. Substitute the values of the cross-sectional area and length into the volume formula.

3. Give your answer with correct units.

a) Area of Cross-section $= \frac{1}{2} \times$ base × height

$= \frac{1}{2} \times 4 \times 5 = 10$ cm²

Volume = Area of Cross-section × Length

$= 10 \times 6 = \underline{\textbf{60 cm}^3}$

b) Area of Cross-section $= \pi r^2$

$= \pi \times 2^2 = 12.57$ cm²

Volume = Area of Cross-section × Length

$= 12.57 \times 7 = \underline{\textbf{88.0 cm}^3}$ *(to 1 d.p.)*

Exercise 2

1 Find the volumes of the prisms with the following cross-sectional areas and lengths.

    a) area = 2 cm², length = 3 cm   **b)** area = 6 cm², length = 9 cm

    c) area = 1.5 m², length = 6 m   **d)** area = 3.5 cm², length = 3.5 cm

    e) area = 9.25 mm², length = 1.75 mm   **f)** area = 11.6 mm², length = 9.1 mm

2 Find the volumes of the following prisms.

    a)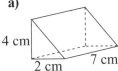
    b)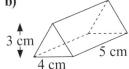
    c)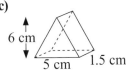
    d)

3 The following diagrams show the cross-sections of prisms of the length shown.
    Find the volume of each prism. The grid spacing is 1 cm.

    a) Length = 2 cm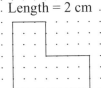
    b) Length = 3 cm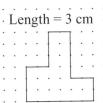
    c) Length = 1.2 cm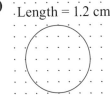
    d) Length = 4.6 cm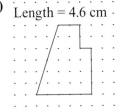

4 Find the volumes of the following prisms.

    a) a triangular prism of base 13 cm, vertical height 12 cm and length 8 cm

    b) a triangular prism of base 4.2 m, vertical height 1.3 m and length 3.1 m

    c) a cylinder of radius 4 m and length 18 m

    d) a cylinder of radius 6 mm and length 2.5 mm

    e) a prism with parallelogram cross-section of base 3 m and vertical height 4.2 m, and length 1.5 m

5 By first calculating their cross-sectional areas, find the volumes of the following prisms.

    a)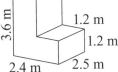
    b)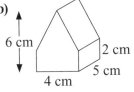
    c)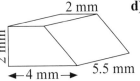
    d)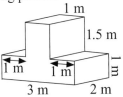

6 The following diagrams show prisms drawn on isometric paper with grid spacing 1 cm.
    Find the volume of each prism.

    a)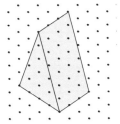
    b)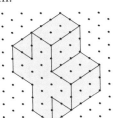
    c)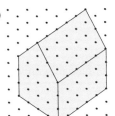
    d)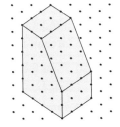

Find the surface area of a 3D shape by adding together the areas of all its faces.

Example 1

Find the surface area of the cuboid shown.

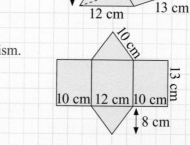

1. Find the area of each face of the shape.

2 faces of area 8 × 5 = 40 cm²
2 faces of area 8 × 3 = 24 cm²
2 faces of area 5 × 3 = 15 cm²

2. Add together the areas of the faces.

So the total surface area is
(2 × 40) + (2 × 24) + (2 × 15) = 80 + 48 + 30

3. Give your answer with correct units.

= **158 cm²**

Example 2

Find this prism's surface area by considering its net.

1. Draw the net of the triangular prism.

2. Find the area of each face.

Area of 1 triangular face = ½ × 12 × 8 = 48 cm²

Area of 'base' rectangle = 12 × 13 = 156 cm²

3. Add the different areas to find the total surface area.

Area of 'slanted' rectangle = 10 × 13 = 130 cm²

Total surface area of triangular prism

4. Give your answer with correct units.

= (2 × 48) + 156 + (2 × 130) = **512 cm²**.

Exercise 1

1 A cube has 6 faces, each of area 2 cm².
Find the total surface area of the cube.

2 a) Find the area of one face of the cube shown.

b) Find the total surface area of the cube.

3 a) Find the area of one face of a cube with edges of length 2 m.

b) Find the total surface area of the cube.

4

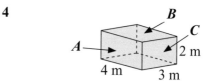

a) Find the area of face **A** of the cuboid shown.

b) Find the area of face **B**.

c) Find the area of face **C**.

d) Find the total surface area of the cuboid.

5 Find the surface area of the following prisms.

a)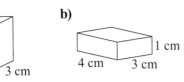
3 cm, 3 cm, 3 cm

b)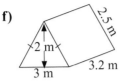
1 cm, 4 cm, 3 cm

c)
4 m, 1 m, 1.5 m

d)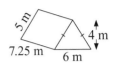
2.5 m, 2.5 m, 4.5 m

e)
13 mm, 12 mm, 5 mm, 11 mm

f)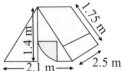
2.5 m, 2 m, 3 m, 3.2 m

g)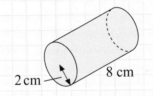
0.5 m, 0.3 m, 0.9 m, 0.4 m

h)
5 m, 7.25 m, 6 m, 4 m

6 Find the surface area of the following prisms.
  a) a cube with edges of length 5 m
  b) a cube with edges of length 6 mm
  c) a 1.5 m × 2 m × 6 m cuboid
  d) a 7.5 m × 0.5 m × 8 m cuboid
  e) a prism of length 2.5 m whose cross-section
    is an isosceles triangle of height
    4 m, slant edge 5 m and base 6 m

7 The local boy scouts
are waterproofing
their tent, shown.
1.4 m, 1.75 m, 2.1 m, 2.5 m

  a) Find the surface
    area of the outside of the tent.

  b) How many tins of waterproofing
    spray will they need to buy to cover
    the outside of their tent if each tin
    covers an area of 4 m²?

Example 3

Find this cylinder's surface
area by considering its net.

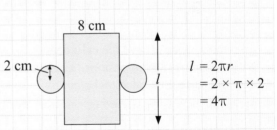
2 cm, 8 cm

1. Draw the net of the cylinder.

2. Find the missing length, l, of the
   rectangle — it's equal to the
   circumference of the circle.

8 cm
2 cm
l

$l = 2\pi r$
$= 2 \times \pi \times 2$
$= 4\pi$

3. Find the area of each face.

Area of circle $= \pi r^2 = \pi \times 2^2 = 4\pi$
$= 12.566$ cm²

Area of rectangle $= 8 \times 4\pi$
$= 100.531$ cm²

4. Add together the individual areas.
5. Give your answer with correct units.

So total surface area $= (2 \times 12.566) + 100.531$
$= \underline{\textbf{125.7 cm}^2}$ *(to 1 d.p.)*

Exercise 2

Round any inexact answers to 2 decimal places unless told otherwise.

1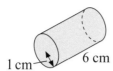

    a) Draw the net of the cylinder shown above.

    b) Find the area of each surface of the cylinder.

    c) Find the surface area of the cylinder, correct to 1 decimal place.

2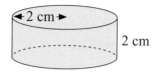

    a) Draw the net of the cylinder shown above.

    b) Find the area of each surface of the cylinder.

    c) Find the surface area of the cylinder, correct to 1 decimal place.

3 Find the surface area of the following cylinders.

    a)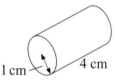

    b)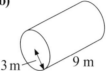

    c)

    d)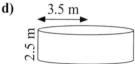

    e)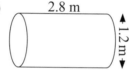

    f)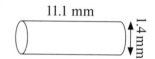

    g)

    h)

4 Find the surface area of the cylinders with the following dimensions. Give your answers correct to 1 decimal place.

    a) radius = 2 m, length = 7 m

    b) radius = 7.5 mm, length = 2.5 mm

    c) radius = 12.2 cm, length = 9.9 cm

    d) diameter = 22.1 m, length = 11.1 m

    e) diameter = 0.8 m, length = 0.6 m

5 Ian is painting his cylindrical gas tank. The tank has radius 0.8 m and length 3 m. He uses tins of paint which cover an area of 14 m².

    a) What is the surface area of the tank?

    b) How many tins of paint will Ian need?

6 A cylindrical metal pipe has radius 2.2 m and length 7.1 m. The ends of the pipe are open.

    a) Find the curved surface area of the outside of the pipe.

    b) A system of pipes consists of 9 of the pipes described above. What area of metal is required to build the system of pipes? Give your answer correct to 1 decimal place.

7 The diagram shows a cylindrical bin which is closed at one end and open at the other. Find the total surface area of the outside of the bin.

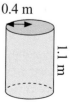

Exercise 3 — Mixed Exercise

Give any inexact answers correct to 2 decimal places unless told otherwise.

1 The diagram on the right shows part of a net of a triangular prism of width 6 cm, vertical height 4 cm, and length 3 cm.

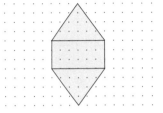

   a) Copy the diagram. After measuring an appropriate length, add the remaining faces to the net.

   b) Use the net to find the surface area of the triangular prism.

2 A cylindrical disc has a radius of 4 cm and a height of 0.5 cm.

   a) Find the surface area of the disc.

   b) Find the surface area of a stack of 10 discs, assuming there are no gaps between each disc.

3 The following shapes are drawn on isometric paper with grid spacing 1 cm. Find the surface area of each shape.

a)   **b)**   **c)**   **d)**

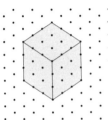 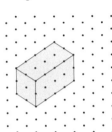 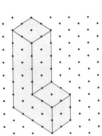 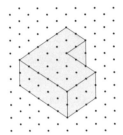

4 **a)** Use Pythagoras' formula $h^2 = a^2 + b^2$ to find the vertical height, b, of the triangular prism shown.

   b) Draw a net of the prism.

   c) Find the surface area of the prism.

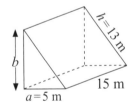

5 The diagram on the right shows a conservatory in the form of a prism, made up of three glass walls and a glass roof.

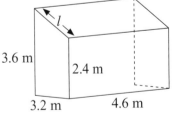

   a) Make an accurate scale drawing of a side elevation of the conservatory. Use the scale 1 cm : 1 m.

   b) Use your drawing to find the actual length marked l in the diagram. Give your answer to the nearest tenth of a metre.

   c) Calculate the total surface area of the outside of the conservatory. Give your answer to the nearest square metre.

A window cleaner charges £5 plus £0.50 per square metre (rounded up to the next whole number of m²) to clean windows.

   d) How much would it cost to have the outside of the conservatory cleaned?

   e) How much would it cost to have the inside of the conservatory cleaned as well as the outside?

20.6 3D Shapes Problems

Exercise 1

Where appropriate, give your answers to these questions to 2 decimal places.

1

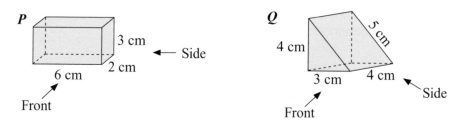

For each of the shapes **P** and **Q** above, complete the following.

a) Draw a net of the shape.

b) Draw the plan, and front and side elevations of the shape from the directions indicated.

c) Draw the shape on isometric paper.

d) Calculate the shape's volume.

e) Calculate the shape's surface area.

2 **a)** Draw an accurate net of a cylinder of length 3 cm and radius 1.5 cm. Label your diagram with the net's dimensions.

    b) Use the net to find the cylinder's surface area.

3 24 cubes with edges of length 8 cm fit exactly in a tray of depth 8 cm, as shown.

    a) Find the volume of one cube.

    b) Find the volume of the tray.

4 **a)** Sketch the 3D shape with the net shown.

    b) Use isometric paper to accurately draw the shape.

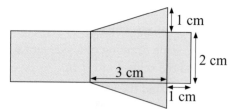

5 **a)** Draw an accurate, full-sized net of the triangular prism shown.

    b) Measure the appropriate length on your drawing to find the vertical height, h, of the prism.

    c) Draw the plan, and front and side elevations of the prism.

    d) Draw the triangular prism on isometric paper.

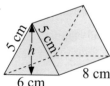

6 Karl is making jam for the summer fete. His jam pan is cylindrical with radius 20 cm.
The jam in his pan is 18 cm deep.

  a) Find the volume of jam in Karl's pan to the nearest cm^3.

Jam jars are cylindrical with radius 3 cm and can be filled to a depth of 10 cm.

  b) Find the volume of one jar to the nearest cm^3.

  c) How many jars can Karl fill with the amount of jam he has made?

7 A cube has a total surface area of 54 cm^2.

  a) Find the area of one face of the cube.

  b) Find the length of the edges of the cube.

  c) Find the cube's volume.

  d) Draw the cube on isometric paper.

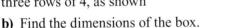

8 Beans are sold in cylindrical tins of diameter 7.4 cm and height 11 cm.

  a) Find the volume of one tin.

The tins are stored in boxes which hold 12 tins in three rows of 4, as shown

  b) Find the dimensions of the box.

  c) Find the volume of the box.

  d) Calculate the volume of the box that is not taken up by tins when it is fully packed. Give your answer correct to 1 decimal place.

9 Toilet paper is sold in cylindrical rolls of diameter 12 cm and height 11 cm.
The card tube at the centre of the roll is 5 cm in diameter.

  a) Find the total volume of one roll of toilet paper, including the card tube.

  b) Find the volume of the card tube.

  c) Hence find the volume of the paper. Give your answer correct to 1 decimal place.

Each rectangular sheet of paper measures 11 cm × 13 cm and is 0.03 cm thick.

  d) Find the volume of one sheet of paper.

  e) Hence find the number of sheets of paper in one roll, to the nearest sheet.

10 A cylinder of diameter 25 mm has volume 7854 mm^3.

  a) Find the length of the cylinder.

  b) Find the surface area of the cylinder to the nearest mm^2.

The cylinder is enclosed in a cuboid, as shown.

  c) Find the volume of the cuboid to the nearest mm^3.

  d) Find the volume of the empty space between the cylinder and the cuboid to the nearest mm^3.

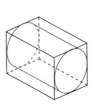

Section 21 — Transformations

21.1 Reflection

When an object is **reflected** in a line, its size, shape and distance from the line all stay the same.

Example 1

Copy the first diagram below, then reflect the shape in the mirror line.

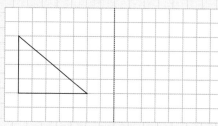 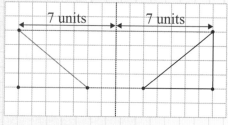

1. Reflect one corner at a time.
2. The image of each point is the same distance from the mirror line as the original.
3. Join up the corners to create the image.

Exercise 1

1 Copy the diagrams below, and reflect each of the shapes in the mirror line.

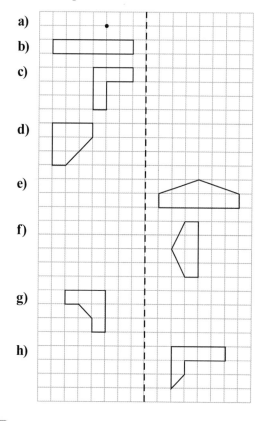

2 Copy the diagrams below, and reflect each of the shapes in the mirror line.

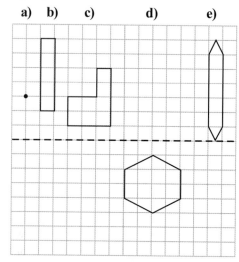

3 Copy the diagram, and reflect the shape in the mirror line.

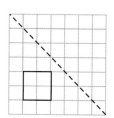

Example 2

a) Copy the axes shown, then reflect the shape *ABCDE* in the *y*-axis.

b) Label the image points A_1, B_1, C_1, D_1 and E_1 with their coordinates.

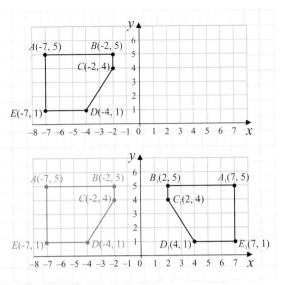

1. This time, the *y*-axis is the mirror line.

2. Reflect the shape — one point at a time.

3. Write down the coordinates of each of the image points.

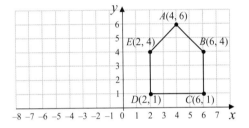

Exercise 2

1 a) Copy the diagram on the right, and reflect the shape in the *y*-axis.

b) Label the image points A_1, B_1, C_1, D_1 and E_1 with their coordinates.

c) Describe a rule connecting the coordinates of *A*, *B*, *C*, *D* and *E* and the coordinates of A_1, B_1, C_1, D_1 and E_1.

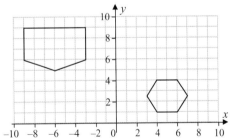

2 Copy each of the diagrams below, and reflect the shapes in the *y*-axis.

a)

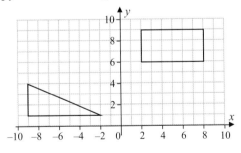

b)

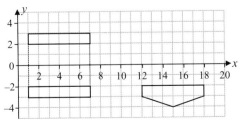

3 a) Copy each of the diagrams below, and reflect the shapes in the *x*-axis. The first shape has been done for you.

(i)

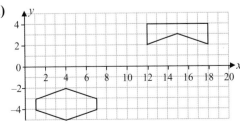

(ii)

b) Describe a rule connecting the coordinates of a point and its reflection in the *x*-axis.

4 The following points are reflected in the x-axis. Find the coordinates of the image points.

a) (1, 2) b) (3, 0) c) (−2, 4) d) (−1, −3) e) (−2, −2)

5 The following points are reflected in the y-axis. Find the coordinates of the image points.

a) (4, 5) b) (7, 2) c) (−1, 3) d) (−3, −1) e) (−4, −8)

6 Copy the diagram shown on the right.

a) Reflect shape P in the y-axis. Label the image Q.

b) Reflect shape P in the x-axis. Label the image R.

c) Reflect shape Q in the x-axis. Label the image S.

d) In which line would you reflect shape R to get shape S?

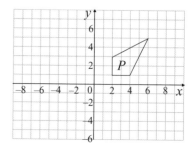

Example 3

Copy the diagram shown, then reflect the shape in the line $x = 5$.

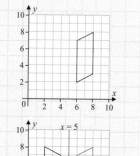

1. Draw in the mirror line, $x = 5$.

2. Reflect the shape in the line as usual, one point at a time. The image of each point should be the same distance from the mirror line as the original point.

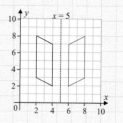

Exercise 3

1 Copy the diagram shown on the right.

a) Reflect shape A in the line $x = 2$. Label the image A_1.

b) Reflect shape B in the line $x = -1$. Label the image B_1.

c) Reflect shape C in the line $x = 1$. Label the image C_1.

d) Complete the following: *Shape B_1 is the reflection of shape A using the mirror line y =* ☐

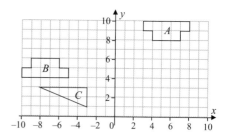

2 Copy the diagram shown on the right.

a) Reflect shape A in the line $y = 6$. Label the image A_1.

b) Reflect shape B in the line $y = 4$. Label the image B_1.

c) Reflect shape C in the line $y = 5$. Label the image C_1.

d) Reflect shape D in the line $y = 3$. Label the image D_1.

e) Shape C_1 is the reflection of shape B in which mirror line?

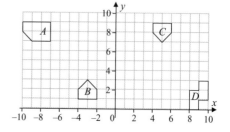

Example 4

Copy the diagram below, then reflect the shape in the line $y = x$.

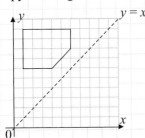 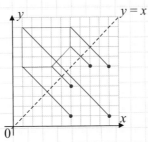 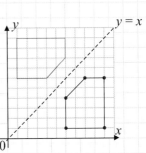

1. Reflect each corner in the mirror line. The image should be the same distance from the mirror as the point, and the line joining a point to its image should be perpendicular to the mirror line.

2. Join up the vertices to create the image.

Exercise 4

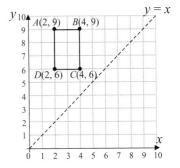

1 **a)** Copy the diagram on the right, and reflect the shape $ABCD$ in the line $y = x$.

b) Label the image points A_1, B_1, C_1 and D_1 with their coordinates.

c) Describe a rule connecting the coordinates of a point and the coordinates of its image after reflection in the line $y = x$.

2 Copy each of the diagrams below, and reflect the shapes in the line $y = x$.

a)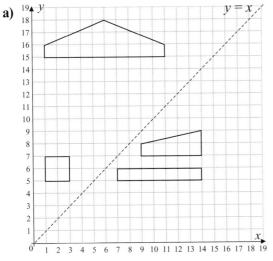

b)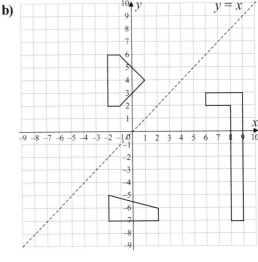

3 The points with the following coordinates are reflected in the line $y = x$. Find the coordinates of the reflections.

a) $(1, 2)$ **b)** $(3, 0)$ **c)** $(-2, 4)$ **d)** $(-1, -3)$ **e)** $(-2, -2)$

21.2 Rotation

When an object is **rotated** about a point, its size, shape and distance from the point all stay the same.
You need three pieces of information to describe a rotation:
   (i) the **centre** of rotation   (ii) the **direction** of rotation   (iii) the **angle** of rotation
(But a rotation of 180° is the same in both directions, so you don't need to state the direction.)

Remember, $90° = \frac{1}{4}$ turn, $180° = \frac{1}{2}$ turn, $270° = \frac{3}{4}$ turn.

Example 1

Copy the first diagram below, then rotate the shape 180° about point *P*.

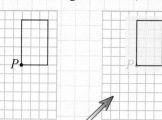 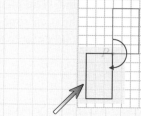 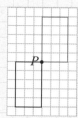

1. Draw the shape on a piece of tracing paper. (Or imagine a drawing of it.)

2. Rotate the tracing paper half a turn about *P*, the centre of rotation. ('About *P*' means *P* doesn't move.)

3. Draw the image in its new position.

Exercise 1

1 Copy the diagrams below, then rotate the shapes 180° about *P*.

a) 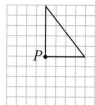   b)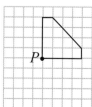

2 Copy the diagrams below, then rotate the shapes 90° clockwise about *P*.

a) 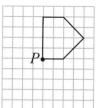   b)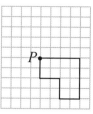

Example 2

Copy the first diagram below, then rotate the shape 90° clockwise about point *P*.

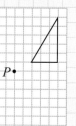 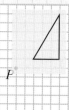 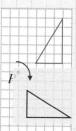 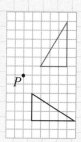

1. This time the centre of rotation is not a point on the shape.

2. Draw the shape on a piece of tracing paper. (Or imagine a drawing of it.)

3. Rotate the tracing paper 90° clockwise about *P*.

4. Draw the image.

3   Copy the diagrams below, then rotate the shapes 90° anticlockwise about *P*.

a) 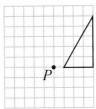   b) 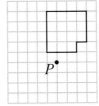   c) 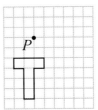   d)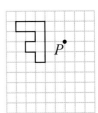

4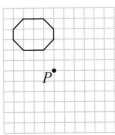

Copy the diagram above, then rotate the shape by the following angles about *P*.

a) 90° clockwise   **b)** 270° clockwise

7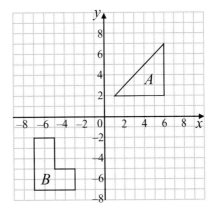

Copy the diagram above, then complete the following.

a) Rotate *A* 90° clockwise about the origin.

b) Rotate *B* 270° anticlockwise about the origin.

5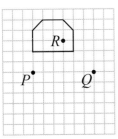

On separate copies of the diagram above, rotate the shape as follows.

a) 90° clockwise about *P*

b) 270° clockwise about *Q*

c) 180° about *R*

8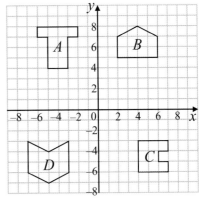

Copy the diagram above, then complete the following.

a) Rotate *A* 90° clockwise about (–8, 5).

b) Rotate *B* 90° clockwise about (1, 4).

c) Rotate *C* 90° clockwise about (8, –4).

d) Rotate *D* 180° about (–2, –5).

6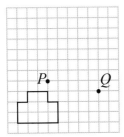

Copy the diagram above, then rotate the shape as follows.

a) 90° anticlockwise about *P*.

b) 90° clockwise about *Q*.

9

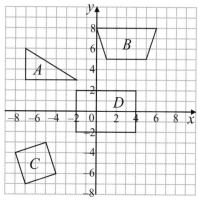

Copy the diagram above, then complete the following.

a) Rotate A 180° about (–5, 6).

b) Rotate B 90° anticlockwise about (5, 9).

c) Rotate C 180° about (–3, –5).

d) Rotate D 180° about (3, –1).

10 The point X has coordinates (4, 2).

    a) Plot X on a pair of axes.

    b) Rotate X 180° about the origin. Label the image Y.

    c) Write down the coordinates of Y.

11 The triangle ABC has vertices A(–2, 1), B(–2, 6) and C(4, 1).

    a) Draw the triangle on a pair of axes.

    b) Rotate the triangle 90° anticlockwise about (5, 4). Label the image $A_1 B_1 C_1$.

    c) Write down the coordinates of A_1, B_1 and C_1.

12 The triangle DEF has coordinates D(–2, –2), E(–2, 5) and F(3, 5). DEF is rotated 180° about (2, 0) to create the image $D_1 E_1 F_1$. Find the coordinates of D_1, E_1 and F_1.

Example 3

Describe fully the rotation that transforms shape A to shape B.

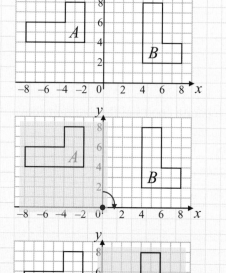

1. The shape looks like it has been rotated clockwise by 90°.

2. Rotate the shape 90° clockwise about different points until you get the correct image — tracing paper will help if you have some.

3. Write down the centre, direction and angle of rotation.

So A is transformed to B by a rotation of **90° clockwise** (or **270° anticlockwise**) about **the origin**.

Exercise 2

1

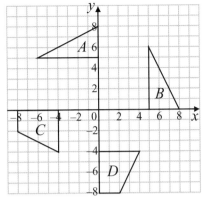

a) Describe fully the rotation that transforms shape *A* to shape *B*.

b) Describe fully the rotation that transforms shape *C* to shape *D*.

3

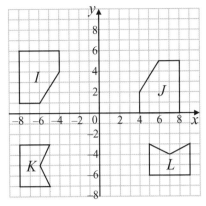

a) Describe fully the rotation that transforms shape *I* to shape *J*.

b) Describe fully the rotation that transforms shape *K* to shape *L*.

2

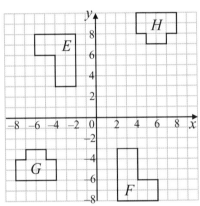

a) Describe fully the rotation that transforms shape *E* to shape *F*.

b) Describe fully the rotation that transforms shape *G* to shape *H*.

4

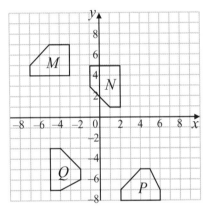

a) Describe fully the rotation that transforms shape *M* to shape *N*.

b) Describe fully the rotation that transforms shape *P* to shape *Q*.

5 a) Describe fully the rotation that transforms shape *R* to shape *S*.

b) Describe fully the rotation that transforms shape *R* to shape *T*.

c) Describe fully the rotation that transforms shape *S* to shape *T*.

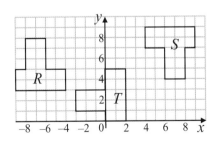

6 The triangle *UVW* has vertices *U*(1, 1), *V*(3, 5) and *W*(–1, 3).
The triangle *XYZ* has vertices *X*(–2, 4), *Y*(–6, 6) and *Z*(–4, 2).

a) Draw the two triangles on a pair of axes.

b) Describe fully the rotation that transforms *UVW* to *XYZ*.

21.3 Translations

When an object is **translated**, its size and shape stay the same, but its position changes.

A translation can be described by the vector $\begin{pmatrix} a \\ b \end{pmatrix}$ — where the shape moves a units right and b units up.

Example 1

Copy the diagram below, then translate the shape by the vector $\begin{pmatrix} 5 \\ -3 \end{pmatrix}$.

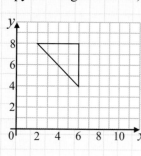

$\begin{pmatrix} 5 \\ -3 \end{pmatrix}$ is a translation of:

(i) 5 units to the right,

(ii) 3 units down (which is the same as –3 units up).

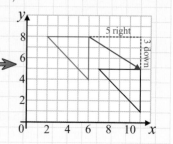

Exercise 1

1 Write down in words the translations described by the following vectors.

a) $\begin{pmatrix} 1 \\ 1 \end{pmatrix}$
b) $\begin{pmatrix} 2 \\ 0 \end{pmatrix}$
c) $\begin{pmatrix} 3 \\ -1 \end{pmatrix}$
d) $\begin{pmatrix} -2 \\ 6 \end{pmatrix}$
e) $\begin{pmatrix} -3 \\ -2 \end{pmatrix}$
f) $\begin{pmatrix} -5 \\ 0 \end{pmatrix}$

2 Copy the diagrams below, then translate each shape by the vector written next to it.

a)

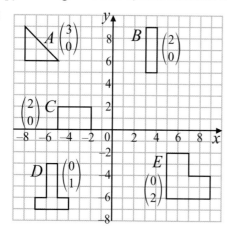

b)

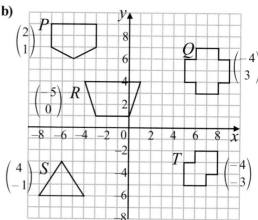

3 **a)** Copy the diagram on the right, then translate the triangle ABC by the vector $\begin{pmatrix} -10 \\ -1 \end{pmatrix}$. Label the image $A_1B_1C_1$.

b) Label A_1, B_1 and C_1 with their coordinates.

c) Describe a rule connecting the coordinates of A, B and C and the coordinates of A_1, B_1 and C_1.

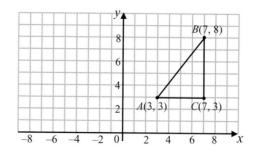

Example 2

Find the coordinates of the point $(2, -5)$ after it has been translated by $\begin{pmatrix} 6 \\ -4 \end{pmatrix}$.

The x-coordinate increases by 6, while the y-coordinate decreases by 4.

$(2 + 6, -5 - 4) = \underline{\mathbf{(8, -9)}}$

---

4 Find the coordinates of the image of the point $(3, -4)$ after it has been translated by:

a) $\begin{pmatrix} 0 \\ 1 \end{pmatrix}$ **b)** $\begin{pmatrix} 3 \\ 0 \end{pmatrix}$ **c)** $\begin{pmatrix} 4 \\ -2 \end{pmatrix}$ **d)** $\begin{pmatrix} -1 \\ -5 \end{pmatrix}$ **e)** $\begin{pmatrix} -3 \\ 5 \end{pmatrix}$ **f)** $\begin{pmatrix} 2 \\ -2 \end{pmatrix}$

5 Find the coordinates of the following points after they have been translated by $\begin{pmatrix} -3 \\ 4 \end{pmatrix}$.

a) $(1, 0)$ **b)** $(2, 5)$ **c)** $(-3, 1)$ **d)** $(6, -2)$ **e)** $(-2, -7)$ **f)** $(-4, 4)$

6 The triangle DEF has corners $D(1, 1)$, $E(3, -2)$ and $F(4, 0)$. After the translation $\begin{pmatrix} -2 \\ 2 \end{pmatrix}$, the image of DEF is $D_1E_1F_1$. Find the coordinates of D_1, E_1 and F_1.

7 The quadrilateral $PQRS$ has corners $P(0, 0)$, $Q(4, 1)$, $R(2, 3)$, $S(-1, 2)$. After the translation $\begin{pmatrix} -3 \\ -4 \end{pmatrix}$, the image of $PQRS$ is $P_1Q_1R_1S_1$. Find the coordinates of P_1, Q_1, R_1 and S_1.

Example 3

Describe fully the translation that maps A onto B.

1. Count how many units horizontally and vertically the shape has moved.

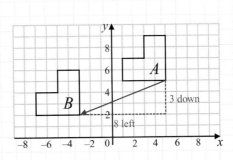

2. Giving the translation vector is a way to describe it fully.

The image is 8 units to the left and 3 units down, so the translation is described by the vector $\begin{pmatrix} -8 \\ -3 \end{pmatrix}$.

Exercise 2

1 Write the following translations in vector form.

a) 1 unit to the right, 2 units up   **b)** 1 unit to the right, 2 units down

c) 2 units to the left   **d)** 3 units down

e) 4 units to the left, 3 units down   **f)** 6 units to the right, 7 units up

g) 5 units to the left, 2 units up   **h)** 6 units up

2

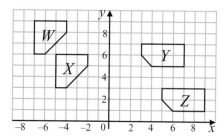

a) Write down in words the translation that maps *W* onto *X*.

b) Write the vector describing the translation that maps *W* onto *X*.

c) Describe fully the translation that maps *Y* onto *Z*.

3

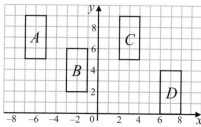

Describe fully the translation that maps:

a) *A* to *B*   b) *A* to *C*   c) *C* to *B*

d) *C* to *D*   e) *D* to *A*   f) *D* to *B*

4

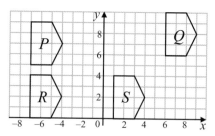

Describe fully the translation that maps:

a) *P* to *R*   b) *R* to *S*   c) *P* to *Q*

d) *S* to *R*   e) *Q* to *R*   f) *S* to *P*

5 The triangle *DEF* has vertices *D*(–3, –2), *E*(1, –1) and *F*(0, 2). The triangle *GHI* has vertices *G*(0, 2), *H*(4, 3) and *I*(3, 6).

a) Sketch triangles *DEF* and *GHI*.

b) Describe fully the translation that maps *DEF* onto *GHI*.

6 The triangle *JKL* has vertices *J*(1, 0), *K*(–2, 4) and *L*(–4, 7). The triangle *MNP* has vertices *M*(0, 2), *N*(–3, 6) and *P*(–5, 9).

a) Describe fully the translation that maps *JKL* onto *MNP*.

b) Describe fully the translation that maps *MNP* onto *JKL*.

Example 4

Shape *B* is the image of shape *A* after the translation $\begin{pmatrix} 7 \\ -3 \end{pmatrix}$.

Draw shape *A*.

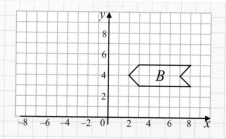

1. Find the vector that maps *B* onto *A* — it's the negative of the vector that maps *A* to *B*. ⟹ *A* to *B* is given by $\begin{pmatrix} 7 \\ -3 \end{pmatrix}$.
So *B* to *A* must be given by $\begin{pmatrix} -7 \\ 3 \end{pmatrix}$.

2. So shape *A* must be 7 units to the left and 3 units up from shape *B*. ⟹

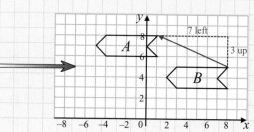

Exercise 3

1 This question is about the diagram on the right.

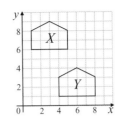

   a) Describe fully the transformation that maps X onto Y.

   b) Describe fully the transformation that maps Y onto X.

   c) What do you notice about your answers to **a)** and **b)**?

2 Shape Z is the image of shape W after the translation $\begin{pmatrix} 1 \\ -4 \end{pmatrix}$.
   Write down the translation that maps Z onto W.

3

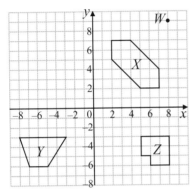

   Copy the diagram on the left.

   a) W is the image of A after the translation $\begin{pmatrix} 0 \\ 2 \end{pmatrix}$. Draw A.

   b) Draw B, given that X is the image of B after the translation $\begin{pmatrix} 5 \\ 0 \end{pmatrix}$.

   c) Y is the image of C after the translation $\begin{pmatrix} -1 \\ -5 \end{pmatrix}$. Draw C.

   d) Draw D, given that Z is the image of D after the translation $\begin{pmatrix} 3 \\ 2 \end{pmatrix}$.

4 The triangle PQR has vertices $P(-1, 0)$, $Q(-4, 4)$ and $R(3, 2)$. PQR is the image of the triangle
   DEF after the translation $\begin{pmatrix} -1 \\ 4 \end{pmatrix}$. Find the coordinates of D, E and F.

21.4 Enlargements

Scale Factors

When an object is **enlarged**, its shape stays the same, but its size changes (and can be either bigger or smaller). The **scale factor** of an enlargement tells you how much the size changes.

Example 1

Copy the diagram on the right, then enlarge the shape anywhere on the grid by scale factor 2.

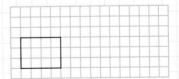

1. Find the dimensions of the shape you're enlarging.

2. Multiply these by the scale factor to find the dimensions of the image.

3. Draw the image using the dimensions you've found.

The original shape is 4 units wide and 3 units tall. So the enlargement will be $4 \times 2 = 8$ units wide and $3 \times 2 = 6$ units tall.

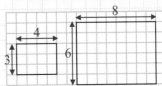

Exercise 1

1 Copy the diagram below, then enlarge the shapes by scale factor 2.

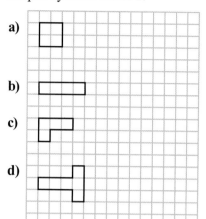

a)

b)

c)

d)

2 Copy the diagram below, then enlarge the shapes by scale factor 3.

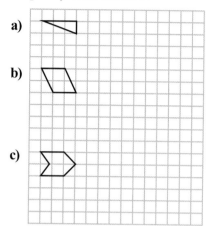

a)

b)

c)

3 Sketch the following shapes after they have been enlarged by scale factor 5.

 a) 1 cm, 1 cm

b) 2 cm, 1 cm

c) 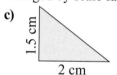 1.5 cm, 2 cm

d) 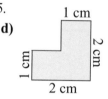 1 cm, 1 cm, 2 cm, 2 cm

---

Example 2

Copy the diagram on the right, then enlarge the shape anywhere on the grid by scale factor $\frac{1}{2}$.

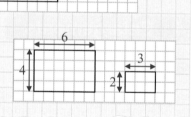

1. Again, multiply the dimensions of the shape by the scale factor: $6 \times \frac{1}{2} = 3$ and $4 \times \frac{1}{2} = 2$.
2. Draw the image using the new dimensions — this time, the image will be smaller than the original.

6, 4, 3, 2

Exercise 2

1 Copy the diagram below, then enlarge the shapes by scale factor $\frac{1}{2}$.

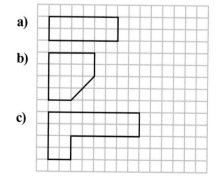

a)

b)

c)

2 Copy the diagram below, then enlarge the shapes by scale factor $\frac{1}{3}$.

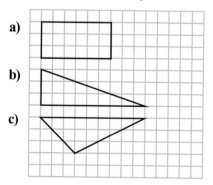

a)

b)

c)

3   A square with sides of length 16 cm is enlarged by scale factor $\frac{1}{4}$. How long are the square's sides after the enlargement?

4   A 15 cm × 35 cm rectangle is enlarged by scale factor $\frac{1}{5}$. What are the dimensions of the rectangle after the enlargement?

Centres of Enlargement

The **centre of enlargement** tells you where the enlargement is measured from.

Example 3

Copy the first diagram below, then enlarge the shape by scale factor 2 with centre of enlargement (2, 2).

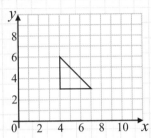 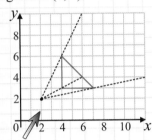 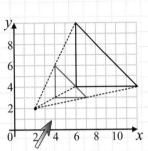

1. Draw a line from (2, 2) through each corner of the shape. Continue each line until it is twice as far away from (2, 2) as the original corner.

2. Join up the ends of the lines to create the image.

Exercise 3

1   Copy each of the following diagrams, then enlarge each shape by scale factor 2 with centre of enlargement (0, 0).

a) 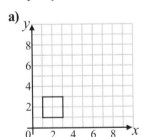   **b)** 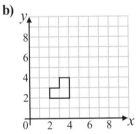   **c)** 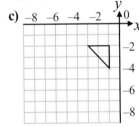   **d)**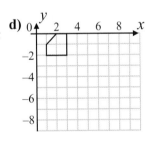

2   Copy the diagram on the right.

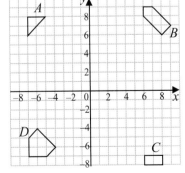

     a) Enlarge A by scale factor 2 with centre of enlargement (−8, 9).

     b) Enlarge B by scale factor 2 with centre of enlargement (9, 9).

     c) Enlarge C by scale factor 3 with centre of enlargement (9, −8).

     d) Enlarge D by scale factor 4 with centre of enlargement (−8, −8).

3   The triangle PQR has corners at $P(1, 1)$, $Q(1, 4)$ and $R(4, 2)$.

     a) Draw PQR on a pair of axes.

     b) Enlarge PQR by scale factor 2 with centre of enlargement (−1, 1).

4

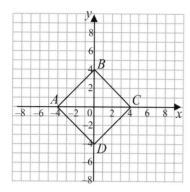

The square $ABCD$ is shown on the left. $A_1B_1C_1D_1$ is the image of $ABCD$ after it has been enlarged by scale factor 2 with centre of enlargement $(0, 0)$.

a) Find the distance of each of the following corners from $(0, 0)$.
   (i) A **(ii)** B **(iii)** C **(iv)** D

b) What will the distance of the following corners be from $(0, 0)$?
   (i) A_1 **(ii)** B_1 **(iii)** C_1 **(iv)** D_1

c) Copy the diagram and draw a line from $(0, 0)$ through each corner of $ABCD$. Mark the points A_1, B_1, C_1 and D_1 on these lines. Join up the points A_1, B_1, C_1 and D_1 to draw $A_1B_1C_1D_1$.

5 Copy the diagram on the right, then enlarge each shape by scale factor 2, using the centre of enlargement marked inside the shape.

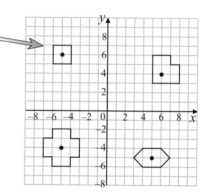

6 The shape $WXYZ$ has corners at $W(0, 0)$, $X(1, 3)$, $Y(3, 3)$ and $Z(4, 0)$.

a) Draw $WXYZ$ on a pair of axes.

b) Enlarge $WXYZ$ by scale factor 3 with centre of enlargement $(2, 2)$.

7

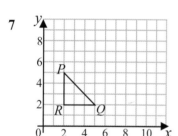

The triangle PQR is shown on the left. $P_1Q_1R_1$ is the image of PQR after it has been enlarged by scale factor 2 with centre of enlargement $(2, 2)$.

a) Find the distance of each of the following corners from $(2, 2)$.
   (i) P **(ii)** Q **(iii)** R

b) What will the distance of the following corners be from $(2, 2)$?
   (i) P_1 **(ii)** Q_1 **(iii)** R_1

c) Copy the diagram and draw a line from the point $(2, 2)$ through P and Q. Mark the points P_1, Q_1 and R_1 on your diagram. Join up the points P_1, Q_1 and R_1 to draw $P_1Q_1R_1$.

8 Copy the diagram on the right, then enlarge each shape by scale factor 2, using the centre of enlargement marked on the shape's corner.

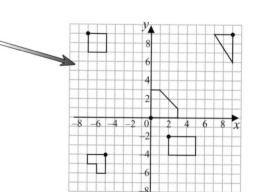

9 The shape $KLMN$ has corners at $K(3, 4)$, $L(3, 6)$, $M(5, 6)$ and $N(5, 5)$.

a) Draw $KLMN$ on a pair of axes.

b) Enlarge $KLMN$ by scale factor 3 with centre of enlargement $(3, 6)$. Label the shape $K_1L_1M_1N_1$.

c) Enlarge $KLMN$ by scale factor 2 with centre of enlargement $(5, 6)$. Label the shape $K_2L_2M_2N_2$.

Example 4

Copy the first diagram below, then enlarge the shape
by scale factor $\frac{1}{2}$ with centre of enlargement (2, 7).

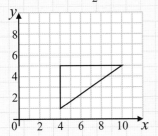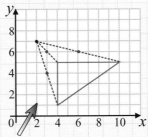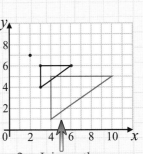

1. Draw lines from (2, 7) to each corner. The image points will lie
    $\frac{1}{2}$ as far from the centre of enlargement as the original corner.

2. Join up the
    image points.

Exercise 4

1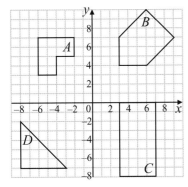

Copy the diagram on the left.

a) Enlarge A by scale factor $\frac{1}{2}$ with centre of enlargement (−8, 9).

b) Enlarge B by scale factor $\frac{1}{3}$ with centre of enlargement (0, 1).

c) Enlarge C by scale factor $\frac{1}{4}$ with centre of enlargement (−1, −8).

d) Enlarge D by scale factor $\frac{1}{5}$ with centre of enlargement (2, 3).

2 Copy the diagram on the right.

a) Enlarge A by scale factor $\frac{1}{2}$ with centre of enlargement (−4, 5).

b) Enlarge B by scale factor $\frac{1}{3}$ with centre of enlargement (7, 7).

c) Enlarge C by scale factor $\frac{1}{4}$ with centre of enlargement (6, −4).

d) Enlarge D by scale factor $\frac{1}{5}$ with centre of enlargement (−3, −2).

Example 5

Describe the enlargement that maps shape X onto shape Y.

1. Pick any side of the shape, and see
    how many times bigger this side
    is on the image than the original.
    This is the scale factor.

2. Draw a line from each corner on the
    image through the corresponding
    corner on the original shape.
    The point where these lines meet is
    the centre of enlargement.

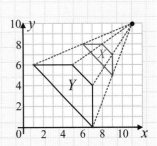

An enlargement by scale factor **2**, centre **(11, 10)**.

Exercise 5

1 For each of the following, describe the enlargement that maps shape *A* onto shape *B*.

a) 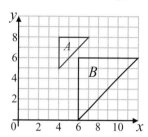 **b)** 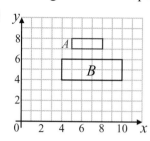 **c)**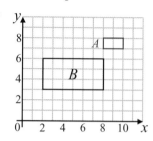

2 For each of the following, describe the enlargement that maps shape *A* onto shape *B*.

a) 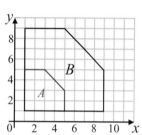 **b)** 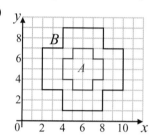 **c)**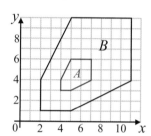

Perimeter, Area and Volume

When a 2D shape is enlarged, **lengths** (such as the lengths of sides, or the shape's **perimeter**) are multiplied by the scale factor. But the shape's **area** is multiplied by the **square of the scale factor**.
When a 3D object is enlarged, its **volume** is multiplied by the **scale factor cubed**.

Example 6

Find the perimeter of this triangle after it has been enlarged by scale factor 4.

1. Find the perimeter of the original triangle.

   Perimeter = 3 + 4 + 5 = 12 cm

2. The perimeter of the enlarged triangle will be 12 + 16 + 20 = 48 cm. This is the same as the original perimeter multiplied by the scale factor.

   Perimeter after enlargement = 12 × 4 = 48

3. Give your answer with the correct units.

   So the perimeter of the image is **48 cm**.

Exercise 6

1 The rectangle *WXYZ* has vertices *W*(1, 1), *X*(1, 2), *Y*(4, 2) and *Z*(4, 1).
   a) Draw *WXYZ* on a pair of axes, and find the perimeter of *WXYZ*.
   b) Enlarge *WXYZ* by scale factor 2 with centre of enlargement (0, 0). Label the image $W_1X_1Y_1Z_1$.
   c) Find the perimeter of $W_1X_1Y_1Z_1$.

2 The shapes below are enlarged by the given scale factor. Find the perimeter of each image.
   a) a square of side 3 cm; scale factor 3   **b)** a 2 m × 8 m rectangle; scale factor 5
   c) a triangle with sides of length 5 m, 12 m and 13 m; scale factor 6

Example 7

Find the area of this rectangle after it has been enlarged by scale factor 3.

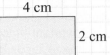

4 cm

2 cm

1. Find the area of the original rectangle.

Area = 4 × 2 = 8 cm²

2. The image will have sides of length 12 cm and 6 cm. So the area of the image will be 12 × 6 = 72 cm², the same as the original area multiplied by the square of the scale factor.

Area after enlargement = 8 × 3² = 8 × 9 = 72

3. Give your answer with the correct units.

So the area of the image is **72 cm²**.

3 The square $ABCD$ has vertices $A(0, 0)$, $B(0, 3)$, $C(3, 3)$ and $D(3, 0)$.

a) Draw $ABCD$ on a pair of axes, and find the area of $ABCD$ in square units.

b) Enlarge $ABCD$ by scale factor 2 with centre of enlargement $(0, 0)$. Label the image $A_1B_1C_1D_1$.

c) Find the area of $A_1B_1C_1D_1$ in square units.

4 The shapes below are enlarged with the given scale factors. Find the area of each image.

a) a shape with area 4 cm²; scale factor 2

b) a square of side 2 cm; scale factor 3

c) a 5 m × 3 m rectangle; scale factor 3

d) a triangle with base 5 cm and vertical height 1 cm; scale factor 4

Example 8

Find the volume of this cube after it has been enlarged by scale factor 4.

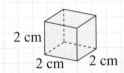

2 cm

2 cm 2 cm

1. Find the volume of the original cube.

Volume = 2 × 2 × 2 = 8 cm³

2. The volume of the enlarged cube will be 8 × 8 × 8 = 512 cm³. This is the same as the original volume multiplied by the scale factor cubed.

Volume after enlargement = 8 × 4³ = 8 × 64 = 512

3. Give your answer with the correct units.

So the volume of the cube after it has been enlarged is **512 cm³**.

5 A cuboid has dimensions 1 cm × 4 cm × 3 cm.

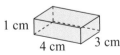

1 cm

4 cm 3 cm

a) Find the volume of the cuboid.

The cuboid is enlarged by scale factor 2.

b) Sketch the image of the cuboid, labelling the edges with their dimensions.

c) Find the volume of the cuboid's image.

6 The objects below are enlarged with the given scale factors. Find the volume of each image.

a) an object with volume 5 cm³; scale factor 2

b) an object with volume 1 cm³; scale factor 4

c) a cube of edge 1 cm; scale factor 3

d) a cube of edge 3 m; scale factor 2

e) a 2 m × 2 m × 1 m cuboid; scale factor 5

21.5   Combinations of Transformations

Transformations can be **combined** (performed one after another). But the **order** in which you combine them is important — for example, a reflection followed by a rotation won't necessarily give the same result as the rotation followed by the reflection.

Example 1

Copy the first diagram below and then: (i) reflect the shape in the line $x = 1$,
(ii) rotate the image 90° anticlockwise about the origin.

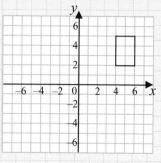   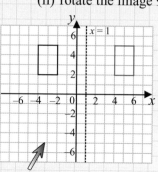   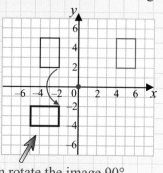

1. First reflect the shape
    in the line $x = 1$.

2. Then rotate the image 90°
    anticlockwise about the origin.

Example 2

Copy the first diagram below and then: (i) rotate the shape 90° anticlockwise about the origin,
(ii) reflect the image in the line $x = 1$.

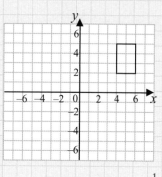   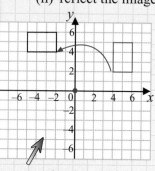   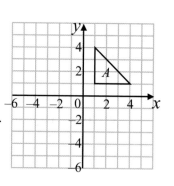

1. First rotate the shape 90°
    anticlockwise about the origin.

2. Then reflect the image
    in the line $x = 1$.

Exercise 1

1   Copy the diagram on the right.

   a) (i)   Reflect shape A in the line $y = -1$.

   (ii)   Rotate the image 90° clockwise about the origin.
   Label the final image A_1.

   b) (i)   Now rotate the **original** shape A 90° clockwise about the origin.

   (ii)   Reflect this new image in the line $y = -1$.
   Label the final image A_2.

2 Copy the diagram on the right.

   a) (i) Translate A by $\begin{pmatrix} 0 \\ -2 \end{pmatrix}$.

      (ii) Enlarge the image by scale factor 3 with centre of enlargement $(9, -7)$. Label the final image A_1.

   b) (i) Translate B by $\begin{pmatrix} -2 \\ -1 \end{pmatrix}$.

      (ii) Reflect the image in the y-axis. Label the final image B_1.

   c) (i) Rotate C 90° clockwise about $(-5, -5)$.

      (ii) Translate the image by $\begin{pmatrix} 3 \\ -1 \end{pmatrix}$. Label the final image C_1.

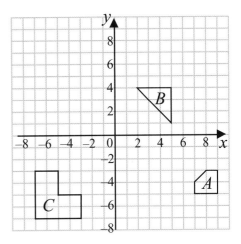

3 Copy the diagram on the right.

   a) (i) Enlarge A by scale factor 3 with centre of enlargement $(9, -7)$.

      (ii) Translate the image by $\begin{pmatrix} 0 \\ -2 \end{pmatrix}$. Label the final image A_2.

   b) (i) Reflect B in the y-axis.

      (ii) Translate the image by $\begin{pmatrix} -2 \\ -1 \end{pmatrix}$. Label the final image B_2.

   c) (i) Translate C by $\begin{pmatrix} 3 \\ -1 \end{pmatrix}$.

      (ii) Rotate the image 90° clockwise about $(-5, -5)$. Label the final image C_2.

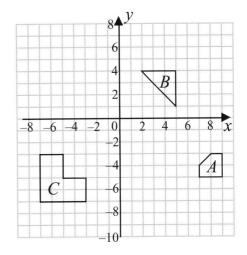

4 **a)** Triangle DEF has corners at $D(-3, -2)$, $E(0, -2)$ and $F(-1, 3)$. Draw DEF on a pair of axes.

   b) (i) Reflect DEF in the line $x = 1$. Label the image $D_1E_1F_1$.

     (ii) Rotate $D_1E_1F_1$ 90° clockwise about $(7, 1)$. Label the image $D_2E_2F_2$.

   c) (i) Rotate the original shape DEF 90° clockwise about $(7, 1)$. Label the image $D_3E_3F_3$.

     (ii) Reflect $D_3E_3F_3$ in the line $x = 1$. Label the image $D_4E_4F_4$.

5 **a)** Triangle PQR has corners at $P(0, 0)$, $Q(4, 2)$ and $R(4, 0)$. Draw PQR on a pair of axes.

   b) (i) Rotate PQR 90° clockwise about the point $(4, 2)$. Label the image $P_1Q_1R_1$.

     (ii) Enlarge $P_1Q_1R_1$ using a scale factor 1.5 and centre of enlargement $(2, 6)$. Label the image $P_2Q_2R_2$.

   c) (i) Enlarge the original shape PQR using a scale factor 1.5 and centre of enlargement $(2, 6)$. Label the image $P_3Q_3R_3$.

     (ii) Rotate $P_3Q_3R_3$ 90° clockwise about the point $(4, 2)$. Label the image $P_4Q_4R_4$.

Example 3

Draw triangle ABC, which has its corners at $A(2, 2)$, $B(6, 5)$ and $C(6, 2)$.

a) Rotate ABC 180° about the point (1, 1), then translate the image by $\binom{-2}{-2}$. Label the image $A_1B_1C_1$.

b) Find a **single** rotation that transforms triangle ABC onto the image $A_1B_1C_1$.

a)
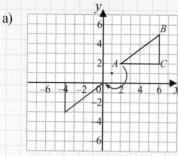

Rotate ABC 180° about (1, 1)...

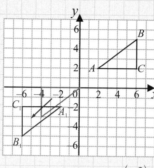

... then translate by $\binom{-2}{-2}$.

b)
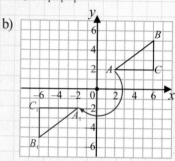

A rotation of 180° about the origin maps ABC onto $A_1B_1C_1$.

Exercise 2

1 Copy the diagram below.

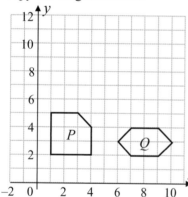

a) (i) Rotate shape P 180° about (4, 5).

   (ii) Translate the image by $\binom{2}{2}$. Label the final image P_1.

b) Rotate shape P 180° about (5, 6). Label the final image P_2.

c) (i) Rotate shape Q 180° about (4, 5).

   (ii) Translate the image by $\binom{2}{2}$. Label the final image Q_1.

d) Rotate shape Q 180° about (5, 6). Label the final image Q_2.

e) What do you notice about images P_1 and P_2 and about images Q_1 and Q_2?

2 Triangle ABC has its corners at $A(2, 1)$, $B(6, 4)$ and $C(6, 1)$.

  a) Draw triangle ABC on a pair of axes, where both the x- and y-axes are labelled from −6 to 6.

  b) Reflect ABC in the y-axis. Label the image $A_1B_1C_1$.

  c) Reflect the image $A_1B_1C_1$ in the x-axis. Label the image $A_2B_2C_2$.

  d) Find a **single** rotation that transforms triangle ABC onto the image $A_2B_2C_2$.

3 Draw triangle PQR with corners at $P(2, 3)$, $Q(4, 3)$ and $R(4, 4)$.

  a) Rotate PQR 90° clockwise about the point (2, 3). Label the image $P_1Q_1R_1$.

  b) Translate $P_1Q_1R_1$ by $\binom{1}{-5}$. Label the new image $P_2Q_2R_2$.

  c) Describe a **single** transformation that transforms triangle PQR onto the image $P_2Q_2R_2$.

4 By considering triangle STU with corners at $S(1, 1)$, $T(3, 1)$ and $U(1, 2)$, find the single transformation equivalent to a rotation of 180° about the origin, followed by a translation by $\binom{6}{2}$.

21.6 Congruence and Similarity

Congruence

Two shapes are **congruent** if they are exactly the **same shape** and **size**.
The images of rotated and reflected shapes are congruent to the original shapes.

Example 1

Which two of the shapes *A*, *B* and *C* are congruent?

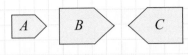

Compare each shape to see if they are the same
shape and size. Tracing paper may help with this.

1.   *A* and *B* are different sizes.
2.   *A* and *C* are different sizes.
3.   *B* and *C* are the same size and shape, just in
     different orientations.

The two congruent
shapes are ***B* and *C***.

Exercise 1

1   Write down the letters of the congruent pairs of shapes shown in the box below.
For example, *A* is congruent to *G*.

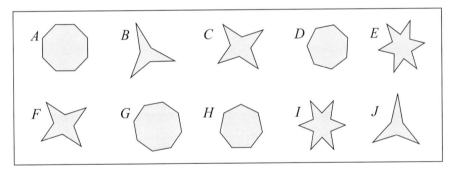

2   For each of the following, decide which shape is **not** congruent to the others.

a)

b)

c)

d)

e)

f)

Section 21 — Transformations

Similarity

Two shapes are **similar** if they are exactly the **same shape**, but they can be **different sizes**. The image of a shape after it has been enlarged is similar to the original shape.

Example 2

Which two of the shapes *P*, *Q* and *R* are similar?

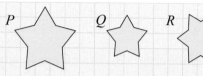

1. Compare *P* and *Q* — they are the same shape, but different sizes.
2. Compare *P* and *R* — they are different shapes.
3. Compare *Q* and *R* — they are different shapes.

The two similar shapes are ***P* and *Q***.

Exercise 2

1 Write down the letters of the similar shapes shown in the box below.
For example, *A*, *C* and *F* are similar.

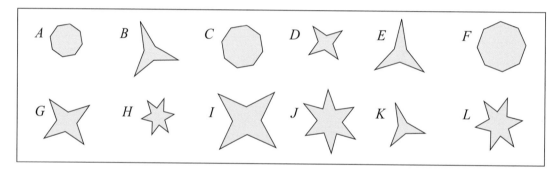

2 For each of the following, decide which two shapes are similar.

a)

b)

c)

d)

e)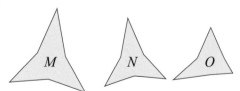

f)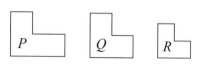

Similar Triangles

Two triangles are similar if they satisfy **any** of the following conditions.
And if two triangles *are* similar, then **all** of the conditions are true.

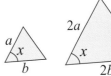

The angles in one triangle
are the same as the angles
in the other triangle.

All corresponding sides
of the two triangles are
in the same ratio.

Two sides of the triangles are in the
same ratio, and the angle between
them is the same for both triangles.

Example 3

Are these two triangles similar?
Give a reason for your answer.

 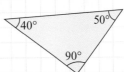

Look to see whether the triangles satisfy
any of the conditions for similarity. The
orientation of the triangles doesn't matter.

The angles in one triangle are the
same as the angles in the other triangle.

So the triangles **are similar**.

Example 4

Explain why these two
triangles are similar.

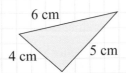 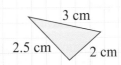

Look to see which condition for similarity
the triangles satisfy. Again, the orientation
of the triangles doesn't matter.

All the sides in the first triangle are twice the
length of those in the second triangle.
So **corresponding sides are in the same ratio**.

Exercise 3

1   Explain why each of the following pairs of triangles are similar.

a)

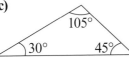

b)

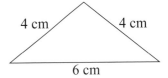

c)

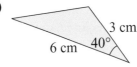

d)

2   Decide whether each of the following pairs of triangles are similar.

a)
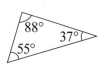 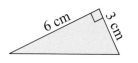

b)
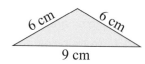

c)
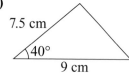

d)
 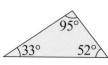 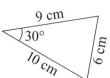 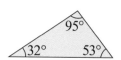

e)
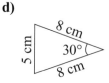

f)
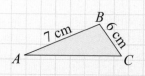 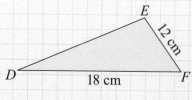

Example 5

Triangles *ABC* and *DEF* are similar.
Find the lengths of *DE* and *AC*.

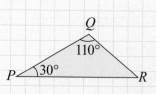 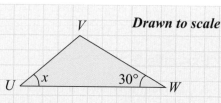

1. The triangles are similar, so the side lengths must be in the
    same ratio from one triangle to the other.

2. Compare the lengths of corresponding sides to find the ratio.

3. Use this ratio to find the missing side lengths.

4. Give your answers with the correct units.

$EF = 2 \times BC$
So $DE = 2 \times AB$
$= 2 \times 7 = \underline{\textbf{14 cm}}$
And $DF = 2 \times AC$
So $AC = DF \div 2$
$= 18 \div 2 = \underline{\textbf{9 cm}}$

Example 6

Triangles *PQR* and *UVW*
are similar. Find angle *x*.

Drawn to scale

1. Find the missing angle in triangle *PQR*.

    Angle $QRP = 180° - (110° + 30°)$
    $= 40°$

2. Work out which angles in the
    triangles correspond to each other.

    The diagrams are drawn to scale, so the
    obtuse angle *PQR* corresponds to angle *UVW*.
    And angle *QPR* corresponds to angle *VWU*.

3. Use the properties of similar triangles to
    determine the required angle.

    So angle *QRP* must correspond to
    angle *VUW*, which means $\underline{x = 40°}$

Exercise 4

1 The triangles in each pair below are similar.

a) (i) Write down the value of x.

(ii) Find the value of y.

b) Find the value of z.

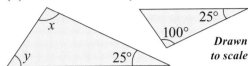
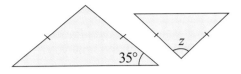

Drawn to scale

In **Questions 2-6**, the lines marked with arrows are parallel.

2 The diagram shows two similar triangles, ABC and ADE.

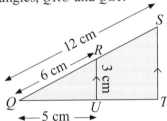

a) State which angle in triangle ABC corresponds to:

(i) angle ADE

(ii) angle AED

(iii) angle DAE

b) Find the ratio of the length of AB to the length of AD.

c) Find the length of: **(i)** AE **(ii)** BC

3 The diagram shows two similar triangles, QRU and QST.

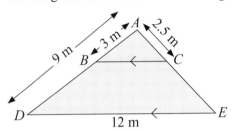

a) Find the length of ST.

b) Find the length of QT.

c) Find the length of UT.

5 Triangles XRQ and XYZ are similar.

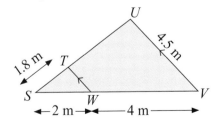

a) State the size of angle QXR. Explain your answer.

b) Use alternate angles to state which angle in triangle XRQ is equal to angle XYZ.

c) Find the ratio of the length of RX to the length of YX.

d) Use your answers to find the length of:

(i) YZ **(ii)** XQ

4 The diagram shows two similar triangles, STW and SUV.

a) Find the length of TW.

b) Find the length of SU.

c) Find the length of TU.

6 Find the missing angles and lengths marked a-f in the diagram below.

Section 22 — Collecting Data

22.1 Using Different Types of Data

The first stage in the data-handling cycle is to decide **what data** you need to collect and **how** you're going to get it.

Primary data is data you **collect yourself**, e.g. by doing a survey or experiment. **Secondary data** is data that has been **collected by someone else**. You can get secondary data from things like newspapers or the internet.

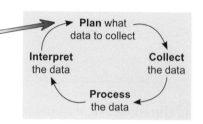

Example 1

Marya wants to know if there's a link between area and population in 10 African countries.

a) What pieces of data does Marya need to find? This is the information she needs to answer her question. ⟹ The **areas and populations** of the 10 countries she's interested in.

b) Where could Marya get the data from? ⟹ E.g. she could find it on the **internet**.

c) Is Marya's data primary or secondary data? The data has been collected by someone else, so... ⟹ It's **secondary** data.

Example 2

Jon wants to test whether a six-sided dice has an equal chance of landing on each of its sides. Explain how he could collect data for the test. Is his data primary or secondary data?

1. Jon needs to do an experiment. ⟹ He could roll the dice lots of times and record how many times it lands on each side using a tally chart.

2. He collects the data himself, so... ⟹ His data is **primary** data.

Exercise 1

Will the data collected in **Questions 1-4** be primary or secondary data?

1 Megan and Jane want to find out the types of music that students like.
   a) Megan plans to send a questionnaire to students from her college.
   b) Jane plans to use the results of an online music survey on the college's website.

2 James plans to interview people as they leave a supermarket to find out how often they shop there.

3 Faheem is going to use the data on election results that appeared in his local newspaper.

4 Nancy is going to time how long it takes her friends to run 100 metres.

For each investigation in **Questions 5-9**:
  a) Describe what data is needed and suggest a suitable method for collecting it.
  b) Say whether the data will be primary or secondary data.

5   Nikita wants to know what the girls in her class think about school dinners.

6   Dan wants to find the most common colour of car passing his house in a 30-minute interval.

7   Anne wants to compare the daily rainfall in London and Manchester last August.

8   Rohan wants to test his theory that the boys in his class can throw a ball further than the girls.

9   Jim wants to find out how the temperature in his garden at 10 am each morning compares with the temperature recorded by the Met Office for his local area.

Discrete and Continuous Data

Data can be **qualitative** (in the form of **words**), or **quantitative** (**numbers**).

Quantitative data can be **discrete** or **continuous**. **Discrete data** can only take certain values (usually whole numbers). It's often things you can count, e.g. the number of goals scored in a football match. **Continuous data** can take any value in a range. It's always measured, e.g. the height or weight of something.

Example 3

Say whether the following data is qualitative, discrete or continuous.

a)   The hometowns of 10 people.
     This data is in the form of words, so... ⟹ It's **qualitative** data.

b)   The weights of the bags of potatoes on sale in a greengrocer's.
     This data is numerical and has to be measured, so... ⟹ It's **continuous** data.

c)   The number of students in each class at a school.
     This data is numerical and can be counted, so... ⟹ It's **discrete** data.

Exercise 2

Will the data in **Questions 1-10** be qualitative, discrete or continuous?

1   The number of words in your favourite song.

2   Your favourite food.

3   The numbers of pets in 20 households.

4   The sizes of the crowds at 10 rugby matches.

5   The heights of 100 tomato plants.

6   The time it takes Matt to walk to school.

7   The nationalities of the people in a park.

8   The lengths of 30 worms.

9   The distances of planets from the Sun.

10   The hair colours of 50 people.

11   Gemma thinks there is a link between the average number of chocolate bars eaten each week by pupils in her class and how fast they can run 100 metres.

   a) Describe two sets of data Gemma should collect to investigate this link.

   b) Describe suitable methods for collecting the data.

   c) Say whether each set of data is discrete data or continuous data.

   d) Say whether each set of data is primary data or secondary data.

22.2 Data-Collection Sheets and Questionnaires

Data-Collection Sheets

Data-collection sheets vary with the type of data being collected. Simple **tally charts** can be used to record data as you collect it. If there's a **large range** of data values, you need to **group** them into classes. If **two variables** are being recorded, you can use a **two-way table**.

Example 1

A restaurant manager asks 50 customers to choose their favourite way to eat potatoes from the following four options: boiled, mashed, baked and roast.

Design a tally chart that could be used to record the data.

Column for
data names...

Potato type	Tally	Frequency
Boiled		
Mashed		
Baked		
Roast		

...with a row
for every
possible answer

Frequency column
for adding up the
tally marks

Tally column with plenty of space to record the marks

Exercise 1

1 Give **two** things that are wrong with each of the following tally charts.

a) Chart for recording the colours
of cars in a car park.

Car colour	Frequency
Red	
Black	
Blue	
Silver	

b) Chart for recording the number of goals
scored by a football team in each match.

No. of goals	Tally	Frequency
0		
1		
2		
3		

2 Design a tally chart that could be used to record the answers to each of the questions below. In each case, all the possible answers are listed.

a) Which of these types of TV programme would you prefer to watch?
Choose from: drama, news, sit-com, reality.

b) How many times a week do you go to the supermarket? Choose from: 0, 1, 2, 3, more than 3.

c) Where did you go for your last holiday? Choose from: UK, Europe, USA, Asia, other.

d) How many breeds of cow can you name? Choose from: 0, 1, 2, 3, 4, 5, more than 5.

3 Design a tally chart that could be used to record the answers to each of these questions.

a) How many brothers and sisters do you have in total?

b) What's the main method of transport you use to get to work?

c) What's your favourite type of fruit?

d) How many days were there in the month you were born?

Example 2

A group of students take a test. The tests are marked and given a score out of 50. Design a tally chart to record the students' scores. (You can assume that all scores are whole numbers.)

1. This is discrete data, but a large range of scores are possible, so group them into a sensible number of classes.

2. Make sure the classes cover all possible scores between 0 and 50.

3. Make sure the classes don't overlap — each score should only be able to go into one class.

Test Score	Tally	Frequency
0 – 10		
11 – 20		
21 – 30		
31 – 40		
41 – 50		

Example 3

An assault course is designed to take about 10 minutes to complete.
Design a tally chart that could be used to record the times taken by a group of people.

1. The data is continuous, so describe the classes using inequalities.

2. Make sure there are no gaps between classes and that classes don't overlap.

3. Leave the last class open-ended to make sure all possible times are covered.

Time (t mins)	Tally	Frequency
$0 < t \le 5$		
$5 < t \le 10$		
$10 < t \le 15$		
$15 < t \le 20$		
$t > 20$		

Exercise 2

1 Give **two** things that are wrong with each of these tally charts and design an improved version.

a) Chart for recording the number of times people went to the cinema last year.

No. of cinema trips	Tally	Frequency
1 – 10		
10 – 20		
20 – 30		
30 – 40		
40 or more		

b) Chart for recording the number of people watching a band play at each venue on their tour (max. venue capacity = 25 000).

No. of people	Tally	Frequency
0 – 5000		
6000 – 10 000		
11 000 – 15 000		
16 000 – 20 000		

c) Chart for recording the length of time people can hop on one leg for.

Time (t mins)	Tally	Frequency
$t \le 5$		
$t \ge 5$		

d) Chart for recording weights of pumpkins.

Weight (w kg)	Tally	Frequency
$w < 3$		
$3 < w < 3.5$		
$3.5 < w < 4$		

2 Write down five classes that could be used in a tally chart for recording each set of data below.

 a) The heights of 50 plants, which range from 5 cm to 27 cm.

 b) The number of quiz questions, out of a total of 20, answered correctly by some quiz teams.

 c) The weights of 30 bags of apples, where each bag should weigh roughly 200 g.

 d) The volumes of tea in 50 cups of tea as they're served in a cafe. Each cup can hold 300 ml.

3 Design a tally chart that could be used to record the following data.

 a) The average lengths of time 100 people spend watching TV each week.

 b) The numbers of pairs of socks owned by 50 students.

 c) The lengths of 20 people's feet.

 d) The distances that 30 people travel to get to work and back each day.

Example 4

Raymond is investigating how fast the players at a tennis club can serve.
He's interested in whether being right-handed or left-handed has any effect on average speed.

Design a two-way table he could use to record the data he needs.

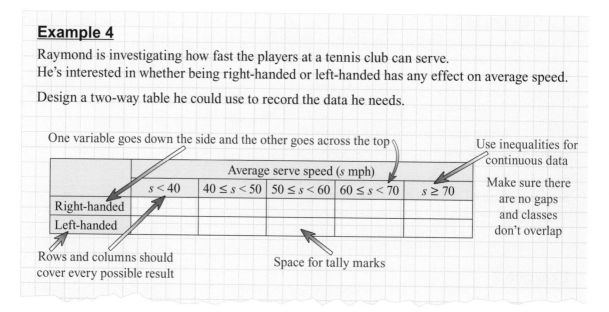

One variable goes down the side and the other goes across the top

Use inequalities for continuous data

		Average serve speed (*s* mph)			
	$s < 40$	$40 \leq s < 50$	$50 \leq s < 60$	$60 \leq s < 70$	$s \geq 70$
Right-handed					
Left-handed					

Make sure there are no gaps and classes don't overlap

Rows and columns should cover every possible result

Space for tally marks

Exercise 3

1 This table has been designed to record the hair colour and age (in whole years) of 100 adults.

 a) Give three criticisms of the table.

 b) Design an improved version of the table.

	Age in whole years					
	0 – 15	15 – 30	30 – 45	45 – 60	60 – 75	75 or older
Blonde						
Light brown						
Dark brown						

2 Design two-way tables that could be used to record the following data.

 a) The favourite flavour of crisps of the boys and girls in a class.
 Choose from the flavours: plain, salt and vinegar, cheese and onion, prawn cocktail, other.

 b) The favourite season of the year of 50 men and 50 women.

 c) The type of music adults and children prefer listening to out of pop, classical and rock.

 d) The average length of time spent doing homework each evening by pupils in each of the school years 7-11. Assume no one spends more than an average of 4 hours an evening on homework.

3 For each investigation below, design a two-way table for recording the data.

   a) Hoi Wan is going to ask 50 adults if they prefer cats or dogs.
   She wants to find out if it's true that men prefer dogs and women prefer cats.

   b) Nathan wants to find out whether children watch more TV on average each day than adults.

   c) Felicity is investigating whether pupils in different school years use different methods of transport to get to school.

   d) Chloe is going to ask people how tall they are and how many portions of fruit they eat on average each week.

Exercise 4

For each investigation below, design a data-collection sheet to record the data.

1 Camilla plans to count the number of people in each of 50 cars driving into a car park.

2 Theo is going to ask 100 people to rate his new hairstyle from 1 to 5.
   He's interested in whether children give him higher scores than adults.

3 Greg is investigating how much pocket money everyone in his class gets.

4 Simran wants to test her theory that people who play a lot of sport don't watch much TV.

Questionnaires

Questionnaires need to be **easy to use** — e.g. the questions should be clear and easy to answer accurately. It's also important to design the questions so that the answers will be **easy to analyse** and will give relevant and unbiased information.

Example 5

John and Carly are both investigating how people spend their pocket money.

John's questionnaire includes the following question. | *How much do you spend on sweets?* |

Carly's questionnaire includes this question:

| *How much money do you spend on sweets each week on average?* |
| **None** ☐   **Less than £1** ☐   **£1–£2** ☐   **More than £2** ☐ |

Explain why Carly's question is better than John's question.

   1. Look at how easy the questions are to answer.
       Carly's question is **easier to answer** because she's given a **specific time span** and a **range of options** to tick.

   2. Look at how easy the answers will be to analyse.
       It will be **easier to analyse** Carly's data because there are **only 4 options** to choose from, whereas the answers to John's question could all be different.

Example 6   Give two criticisms of the following question.

> **How many hours of TV do you watch each day on average?**
> 0–1 ☐   1–2 ☐   2–3 ☐   3–4 ☐

Look closely at the tick boxes.
The **tick boxes overlap** — e.g. if you watch 1 hour of TV, you don't know whether to tick the first or second box. And the **boxes don't cover all possible options**.

Example 7

The following questions are from a questionnaire. Give one criticism of each question.

a) **How old are you?**

Think about the people answering the question.
This could be a **sensitive question**, so it would be better to have a range of options to tick.

b) **Do you agree that it's important to follow the latest fashions?**

Think about whether the question is fair or biased.
This is a **leading question**. It encourages people to give a certain opinion, so the results might be **biased**.

Exercise 5

Give one criticism of each of the following questions.

1 How often do you go to the cinema?

2 Do you agree that the best superhero is *Super-Invisible-Wonder-Penguin*?

3 How much do you weigh?

4 Do you like rock music better than pop?

5 How much do you earn each month?

6 How many pets does your family have?
1 ☐   2 ☐   3 ☐   More than 3 ☐

7 Tick your favourite flavour of ice cream.
Vanilla ☐   Chocolate ☐
Strawberry ☐   Toffee ☐

8 How tall are you?   150 cm or less ☐
150–180 cm ☐   180 cm or more ☐

9 Here are questions from Amber and Jay's questionnaires about how much sport people play. Say whose question is better and give two reasons why.

Amber: How much sport do you play?

Jay: How many times a week do you play sport on average? Tick one box.
None ☐   One ☐   Two ☐   Three ☐   More than three ☐

Exercise 6

Write an improved version of each of the questions below.

1   How much time do you spend reading each week on average?

   0–1 hours ☐   1–2 hours ☐   2–3 hours ☐   3–4 hours ☐   4 or more hours ☐

2   What's your favourite type of TV programme? Tick one box.

   Comedy ☐   Soap ☐   Reality ☐   Sport ☐

3   Which type of film do you prefer — horror or thriller?   Horror ☐   Thriller ☐

4   Do you agree that the gym should open a new tennis court rather than a new squash court?

Exercise 7

Write a question to find out each of the following pieces of information. Use suitable tick boxes.

1   The main means of transport people use to get to school.

2   The amount of time people spend doing household chores.

3   How often the members of a gym use the facilities.

4   Which days of the week people usually shop at the supermarket (allow more than one day).

5   What the people who attend a dance class think of the length of the class.

22.3   Sampling and Bias

The group of people or things you want to find out about is called the **population**. Usually, it's quicker, cheaper and more practical to collect data from a **sample** of the population, rather than the whole thing.

Different samples will give different results, but the **bigger** the sample, the more reliable they should be.

Example 1

Michael and Tina have written a questionnaire to find out what students at their college think about public transport. Michael gives the questionnaire to 10 students and Tina gives the questionnaire to 50 students. Michael concludes that 50% of students are happy with public transport, whereas Tina concludes that only 30% are happy.

a)   Why have Michael and Tina only given the questionnaire to some of the students?
     Think about the advantages of sampling...
        E.g. there are fewer copies to print, so **print costs will be lower**.
        Also, it will take them **much less time** to collect and analyse the results.

b)   Whose results are likely to be more reliable? Explain your answer.
     Think about the size of the sample...
        Tina's results are likely to be more reliable because she has used a **bigger sample**.

Exercise 1

1   Jenny wants to know how long it takes the pupils in Year 7 to type out a poem. She plans to time a sample of 30 out of the 216 Year 7 pupils. Give two advantages for Jenny of using a sample.

2   A supermarket chain wants to know what people in a town think of their plan to build a new supermarket there. They've hired a team of researchers to interview a sample of 500 people. Give one reason why they wouldn't want to interview everyone in the town.

3   Jim is testing a box of matches to see how long they burn for. He does this by lighting 10 of the matches. Explain why Jim doesn't test all the matches.

4   An audience of 1000 people are watching a musical. Kelly wants to know what they think about it and plans to interview 5 of the audience afterwards. What's wrong with Kelly's plan?

5   Melissa and Karen are doing an experiment to see if a coin is fair. They each toss the coin 100 times and record the number of heads. 52% of Melissa's tosses are heads and 47% of Karen's tosses are heads. Explain why Melissa and Karen get different results.

6   Alfie and Lisa want to find out what the most popular flavour of ice cream is. Alfie asks 30 people and finds that 'chocolate' is the most popular. Lisa asks 15 people and finds that it's 'strawberry'. Based on this information, what would you say is the most popular flavour? Explain your answer.

7   Jack, Nikhil and Daisy bake a batch of 200 cupcakes to sell on their market stall. Jack thinks they should taste one cake to check the quality is OK. Nikhil thinks they should taste 10 cakes and Daisy thinks they should taste 50 cakes. Say who you agree with and explain why.

Choosing a Fair Sample

When you're choosing a sample, it's important to make sure that it **fairly represents** the **population**.
If it's **biased**, the data you get will be different from the data you'd get if you asked everyone.

To **avoid bias**, you need to choose the items or people to include in your sample carefully.
If possible, it's a good idea to select your sample at **random** — which means that everything or everyone in the population has an equal chance of being selected.

Example 2

Gina plans to sample 50 shoppers at a supermarket to see what they think about the supermarket's decision to close earlier in the evenings. She decides to stand outside the supermarket on a Wednesday morning and ask the first 50 people she sees leaving the shop.

a)   Explain why this will give her a biased sample.

Think about when she selects the sample...

E.g. Gina is only asking people who are free to shop on a Wednesday morning, so she's excluding all the shoppers who are at work or school. She's also excluding people who only shop in the evening, who will probably be more affected by the earlier closing.

b)   Suggest how Gina could choose a fairer sample.

Think about how she could include more groups of shoppers...

E.g. Gina should ask people on different days of the week and at different times of day.

Exercise 2

Explain why the following methods of selecting a sample will each result in a biased sample.

1   Barry wants to know what people at his college think about a particular film, so he asks 10 of his friends for their opinions.

2   A school cook wants to know whether the pupils want all school dinners to be vegetarian. He asks all the members of the school's animal rights group.

3   A library needs to reduce its opening hours. The librarian asks 20 people on a Monday morning whether the library should close on a Monday or a Friday.

4   A market research company wants to find out about people's working hours. They select 100 home telephone numbers and call them at 2 pm one afternoon.

Example 3

Adam wants to choose 20 of the 89 members of his choir to fill in a questionnaire.
Explain how he could select a random sample.

Everyone should have the same chance of being chosen,
so he needs to start with a list of everyone in the population...

1. First, he should make a list of all the people in the choir and assign everyone a number.
2. Then he could use a calculator or computer to generate 20 random numbers.
3. Finally, he needs to match these numbers to the people on the list to create the sample.

Exercise 3

1   A dentist wants his patients to test a new type of toothbrush.
How could he select a random sample of 20 of his adult patients?

2   A head teacher wants to know what pupils in Year 7 think about after-school clubs.
Explain how he could select a random sample of 50 Year 7 pupils.

3   The manager of a health club wants to survey a random sample of 40 female members.
Explain how she could do this.

Exercise 4

1   George and Stuart want to find out which football team is most popular at their school.
George asks a random selection of 30 pupils and Stuart asks the first 5 pupils he sees at lunchtime.
Give two reasons why George's sample will be more representative of the whole school.

2   Seema wants to find out about the religious beliefs of people in her street, so she stands outside her house on a Sunday morning and interviews the first 20 people she sees. Explain why her sample will be biased, and suggest a better method for selecting her sample.

3   A company has 5 branches across the country. Describe how the management team could select a representative sample of 100 employees to question about pay and working conditions.

4   A factory makes hundreds of the same component each day. Describe how a representative sample of 50 components could be tested each day to make sure the machinery is working properly.

Section 23 — Analysing Data

23.1   Using Lists and Tables

Tally Charts and Frequency Tables

The **frequency** of a data value is the number of times it occurs in a data set.

Sometimes data values are put into **groups** (e.g. values from 0 to 5, values from 6 to 10, and so on). **Grouped frequency tables** can make complex data sets easier to understand, but they don't show the exact data values.

Example 1

A mathematics test is marked out of 40. Here are the marks for 20 students.

| 10 | 18 | 28 | 38 | 40 | 40 | 29 | 11 | 13 | 16 |
| 18 | 20 | 31 | 40 | 27 | 25 | 22 | 40 | 9 | 34 |

a)   Complete the grouped frequency table to show the marks.
1. Add a tally mark (|) in the Tally column for every test score. Write the tally marks in groups of 5, with the fifth tally mark across the others to make a '5-bar gate'.
2. Find each frequency by counting the tally marks.

Mark	Tally	Frequency
0-10	||	2
11-20	ĦĦ		6
21-30	ĦĦ	5
31-40	ĦĦ ||	7

b)   The pass mark for this test was 21 out of 40.
How many students passed the test?
Add the frequencies for the bottom two rows. $5 + 7 = \underline{\textbf{12}}$

Exercise 1

1   Ben asks a group of people what type of music they like most. Here are their responses.

| Pop | R&B | Rock | Indie | Pop | R&B | Indie | Pop | Jazz | Pop |
| Pop | Rock | Pop | Pop | Jazz | Pop | Pop | Classical | Indie | Rock |

a)   Copy and complete the frequency table on the right.

b)   Use your table to answer the following.

   (i)   How many people like classical music most?

   (ii)   What is the most popular type of music?

   (iii) How many people does Ben ask?

Type of Music	Tally	Frequency
Classical		
Indie		
Pop		
Rock		
Other		

2   The weights (in g) of 16 bananas from a bunch are shown below.

| 118 | 119 | 117 | 120 | 122 | 121 | 117 | 120 |
| 120 | 119 | 117 | 120 | 121 | 121 | 118 | 121 |

a)   Copy and complete the frequency table on the right.

b)   Use your table to find the most common weight(s) for a banana in this bunch.

Weight (g)	Tally	Frequency
117		
118		
119		
120		
121		
122		

3 Here are the ages of 50 guests at a party.

30	56	4	18	19	35	65	79	54	54
45	32	36	39	26	27	1	3	51	56
19	23	9	11	23	45	41	48	23	32
39	43	44	5	77	61	62	78	39	47
52	56	1	2	80	21	48	54	55	78

a) Copy and complete this grouped frequency table. Continue using groups of 10 years for the rest of the table.

b) Use your table to find which of these age groups is the most common.

Age (years)	Tally	Frequency
0-9		
10-19		
20-29		

4 A mathematics test is marked out of 100. The marks for 50 students are in the box on the right.

20	90	64	35	44	62	29	30	68	69
73	88	80	45	55	61	39	29	47	91
38	65	66	42	81	92	99	33	81	88
45	56	65	65	78	91	95	36	56	27
65	98	39	79	81	82	31	31	98	92

a) Complete this grouped frequency table to show the students' marks.

b) The pass mark for this test was 60 out of 100. Use your table to find how many students passed the test.

c) Could you use your table to find out how many students had passed the test if the pass mark was reduced to 55 out of 100? Explain your answer.

Mark	
20-29	
30-39	
40-49	

23.2 Averages and Range

Averages: Mean, Median and Mode

An **average** is a way of representing the value of a whole set of data using just one number. The **mode**, **median** and **mean** are three different types of average.

> **mode** (or **modal value**) = the **most common** value
>
> **median** = **middle value** once the items have been put **in order** from smallest to largest
>
> **mean** = the **total** of all the values ÷ the **number** of values

Example 1

Find the mode of these numbers: 3   7   4   8   3

The mode is the most common number.   Mode = **3**

Exercise 1

1 Find the mode of the following sets of data.

a) 8, 5, 3, 8, 4

b) 6, 9, 2, 7, 7, 6, 5, 9, 6

c) 16, 8, 12, 13, 13, 8, 8, 17

2   Nine students score the following marks on a test: 34   67   86   58   51   52   71   65   58
Find the mode.

3   The times (to the nearest second) of nine athletes running the 400 m hurdles are:
78   78   84   81   90   79   84   78   95
Find the modal time.

4   Find the modal value of the following: red, yellow, red, black, orange, purple, red, green, black

---

Example 2

a)   Find the median of these numbers: 3   7   4   8   3

   1. Put the numbers in order first.   From smallest to largest, the numbers are: 3   3   4   7   8

   2. If there's an odd number of values, then there will be just one value in the middle.   The median is the value in the middle, so the median = **4**

b)   The number 5 is added to the list. Find the new median.

   1. If there's an even number of values, then there are two values in the middle.   From smallest to largest, the list is now: 3   3   4   5   7   8

   2. The median will be halfway between the two middle numbers. Find it by adding them together and dividing by 2.   The two middle values are 4 and 5, so the median = $\frac{4+5}{2}$ = **4.5**

Exercise 2

1   Find the median of the following sets of data.

   a) 8, 5, 3, 8, 4   **b)** 6, 9, 2, 7, 7, 6, 5, 9, 6   **c)** 16, 18, 12, 13, 13, 8, 8, 17

2   Find the median of the following sets of data.

   a) 1.5, 2.7, 3.8, 4.8, 5.6   **b)** 15, 16, 22, 17   **c)** 3, 3, 3, 3, 3, 3, 3, 4

3   Nine students score the following marks on a test: 34   67   86   58   51   52   71   65   58
Find the median mark.

4   The times (to the nearest second) of nine athletes running the 400 m hurdles are:
78   78   84   81   90   79   84   78   95
Find the median time.

5   The median of the following data set is 7, but one value is missing.   6, 5, ?, 9, 10
What is the missing value?

6   The median of the following data set is 16.7, but one value is missing.   16.5, 16.9, 15.8, 14.3, 18.9, ?
What is the smallest that the missing number could be?

Example 3

Find the mean of these numbers: 3   7   4   8   3

1. Find the total of the values.

    The total is $3 + 7 + 4 + 8 + 3 = 25$.

2. Divide the total by the number of values.

    So the mean $= 25 \div 5 = \underline{5}$

Exercise 3

1 Find the mean of the following sets of data.

   a) 8, 5, 3, 8, 4   **b)** 6, 9, 2, 7, 7, 6, 5, 9, 6   **c)** 16, 18, 12, 13, 13, 8, 8, 17

2 Find the mean of the following sets of data.

   a) 1.5, 2.7, 3.8, 4.8, 5.6   **b)** 15.85, 16.96, 22.04, 17.45   **c)** 3, 3, 3, 3, 3, 3, 3, 4

3 Nine students score the following marks on a test: 34   67   86   58   51   52   71   65   58
   Find the mean.

4 The times (to the nearest second) of nine athletes running the 400 m hurdles are:
   78   78   84   81   90   79   84   78   95
   Find the mean time.

5 Find the mean, median and mode for each of the following two sets of data.

   a) 1, 2, 2, 2, 3, 3, 5, 8   **b)** 1, 2, 3, 3, 3, 3, 4, 5

6 If the mean of the following data set is 7, find the missing value. $\boxed{6, 5, 8, 8, 5, ?}$

7 If the mean of the following data set is 16.3, find the missing value. $\boxed{16.6, 16.9, 15.8, 14.3, 18.9, ?}$

The Range

The **range** tells you how spread out your values are: **range = largest** value **– smallest** value

Example 4

Find the range of these numbers: 3   7   4   8   3

Subtract the lowest value from the highest.   Range $= 8 - 3 = \underline{5}$

Exercise 4

1 Find the range of the following sets of data.

   a) 8, 5, 3, 8, 4   **b)** 6, 9, 2, 7, 7, 6, 5, 9, 6   **c)** 16, 8, 12, 13, 13, 8, 8, 17

2 Find the range of the following sets of data.

   a) 1.5, 2.7, 3.8, 4.8, 5.6   **b)** 15.85, 16.96, 22.04, 17.45   **c)** 3, 3, 3, 3, 3, 3, 3, 4

3 Nine students score the following marks on a test: 34   67   86   58   51   52   71   65   58
   Find the range of the marks.

4 The times (to the nearest second) of nine athletes running the 400 m hurdles are:
   78   78   84   81   90   79   84   78   95
   Find the range of these times.

5 The range of the following data set is 6. $\boxed{6, 5, 8, 8, 5, ?}$
   What are the two possible values for the missing number?

Finding Averages and the Range from a Frequency Table

Example 5

This frequency table shows the number of mobile phones owned by a group of people.

Number of mobile phones	0	1	2	3
Frequency	4	9	5	2

a) Find the modal number of phones owned.
This is the number with the highest frequency.   Modal number of phones owned = **1**

b) What is the median number of mobile phones owned?
1. The frequencies tell you that the list of all the individual data values would be:
0, 0, 0, 0, 1, 1, 1, 1, 1, 1, 1, 1, 1, 2, 2, 2, 2, 2, 3, 3

2. There are 20 values, so the median is halfway between the 10th and the 11th values. Both these values are 1.

$$\text{Median} = \frac{10\text{th value} + 11\text{th value}}{2} = \frac{1 + 1}{2} = \underline{1}$$

c) What is the range of mobile phones owned? Range = largest value − smallest value
= 3 − 0 = **3**

Example 6

This frequency table shows the number of mobile phones owned by a group of people.

Number of mobile phones	0	1	2	3
Frequency	4	9	5	2

a) How many people were in the group altogether?
This is the total of the frequencies.   Total number of people = 4 + 9 + 5 + 2 = **20**

b) What is the total number of mobile phones owned by this group of people?
You could use the list of values, like in the previous example. But there's another way.

1. First multiply the number of mobile phones by its frequency.

Number of mobile phones	0	1	2	3
Frequency	4	9	5	2
Phones × frequency	0	9	10	6

2. Then add the results together.   Total number of mobile phones = 0 + 9 + 10 + 6 = **25**

c) Find the mean number of mobile phones owned by each person.
Divide the total number of phones by the number of people.

$$\text{Mean of mobile phones owned} = \frac{\text{Total number of mobile phones}}{\text{Total number of people}} = \frac{25}{20} = \underline{\textbf{1.25 phones}}$$

Exercise 5

1 This frequency table shows the number of pets the students in a class have.

Number of pets	0	1	2	3	4
Frequency	5	8	7	5	2

a) What is the modal number of pets owned?
b) What is the median number of pets owned?
c) How many students had: **(i)** no pets?   **(ii)** 1 pet?   **(iii)** 2 pets?   **(iv)** 3 pets?   **(v)** 4 pets?
d) Use your answer to c) to find the total number of pets owned by the students.
e) How many students are in the class altogether?
f) Use your answers to d) and e) to find the mean number of pets owned by each student.

2 The table shows the number of people living in each of 30 houses.

Number of people	1	2	3	4	5
Frequency	4	6	7	10	3

a) Write down the modal number of people living in a house.

b) Find the median number of people living in a house.

c) Calculate the mean number of people living in a house.

d) Work out the range of the data.

3 During June, a student wrote down the temperature in his garden in degrees Celsius (°C) every day at noon, as shown in the table.

a) Find the median noon temperature.

b) Find the mean noon temperature (correct to 1 decimal place).

c) The average noon temperature in June in the UK is approximately 18.5 °C. What does this suggest about these results?

Temperature (°C)	Frequency
16	4
17	9
18	2
19	5
20	4
21	6

Finding Averages from a Grouped Frequency Table

If your data is **grouped**, then you can only **estimate** the mean using the **midpoint** of each group. For the median, you can only say **which group** it lies in — not the exact value. And instead of a mode, you can only find a **modal group**.

Example 7

The test results of 20 people are shown in this grouped frequency table.

Marks scored	0-5	6-10	11-15	16-20	21-25	26-30
Frequency	2	3	6	4	4	1

a) Write down the modal group.
The modal group is the one with the highest frequency.   Modal group is **11-15**.

b) Which group contains the median?
Both the 10th and 11th values are in the group for 11-15 marks. So the median must lie in that group too.

There are 20 values, so the median lies halfway between the 10th and 11th values. This means the median is in the group **11-15**.

c) Find an estimate for the mean.
Find the midpoint for each group by adding together the highest and lowest values that could go in the group, and then dividing by 2.

Marks scored	0-5	6-10	11-15	16-20	21-25	26-30
Frequency	2	3	6	4	4	1
Midpoint of group	$\frac{0+5}{2}=2.5$	$\frac{6+10}{2}=8$	$\frac{11+15}{2}=13$	$\frac{16+20}{2}=18$	$\frac{21+25}{2}=23$	$\frac{26+30}{2}=28$

Now find the mean as before, using the midpoints instead of the actual data values.

Frequency × midpoint	$2 \times 2.5 = 5$	$3 \times 8 = 24$	$6 \times 13 = 78$	$4 \times 18 = 72$	$4 \times 23 = 92$	$1 \times 28 = 28$

Divide the total of this new row by the total of the frequencies.

$$\text{Mean} = \frac{5 + 24 + 78 + 72 + 92 + 28}{2 + 3 + 6 + 4 + 4 + 1} = \frac{299}{20} = \textbf{14.95}$$

Exercise 6

1 The test results of 25 people are shown in this grouped frequency table.

Marks scored	1-5	6-10	11-15	16-20
Frequency	4	5	7	9

   a) Write down the modal group.
   b) Which group contains the median?
   c) Find an estimate for the mean.

2 The table on the right shows some information about the weights (measured to the nearest gram) of some tangerines in a supermarket.

   Find an estimate for the mean to 1 decimal place.

Weight in grams	Frequency
0-20	1
21-40	6
41-60	9
61-80	24

3 Troy collected some information about the number of hours (to the nearest whole hour) students spent watching television over a week.

   a) Write down the modal group.
   b) Which group contains the median?
   c) Find an estimate for the mean to 1 decimal place.

Time in hours	Frequency
0-5	3
6-10	8
11-15	11
16-20	4

Exercise 7 — Mixed Exercise

1 The heights of some sunflowers (to the nearest cm) are shown below.
   132   142   126   142   159   127   148   128
   a) Find: (i) the mean,   (ii) the median,   (iii) the mode.
   b) Find the range.

2 The prices (in £) charged by a selection of stores for the same item are shown below.
   5.00   4.21   4.97   5.00   5.00   5.29   5.05   5.50   5.79   5.00   5.40
   5.20   5.10   5.06   4.50   4.50   5.50   4.50   5.00   5.00   5.50   4.82
   a) Find: (i) the mean,   (ii) the median,   (iii) the mode.
   b) Find the range.

3 The lengths (in cm) of some blades of grass are:
   6.5   7.8   4.3   8.5   4.3   5.9   6.2   9.0   5.7   6.7
   a) Find: (i) the mean,   (ii) the median,   (iii) the mode.
   b) Find the range.

4 This table shows how many customers bought different numbers of cakes from a bakery one day.
   a) Write down the modal number of cakes bought.
   b) Work out the number of customers served.
   c) Find the median number of cakes bought.
   d) (i)   Calculate the total number of cakes bought.
      (ii) Work out the mean number of cakes bought.
   e) Work out the range of the number of cakes bought.

Number of cakes bought	Frequency
0	8
1	6
2	4
3	2

5 This table shows the number of goals scored one week by 18 teams in the premier division.

Number of goals	0	1	2	3	4	5
Number of teams	1	3	4	5	3	2

    a) Find the median number of goals.

    b) Find the mean number of goals. Give your answer to 1 decimal place.

    c) Write down the mode.

    d) The mean, median and modal numbers of goals scored in the same week of the previous year were all 2. How do these results compare?

6 This table shows the heights (in metres) of 20 people, measured to the nearest centimetre.

Height in metres	Frequency
1.51-1.60	2
1.61-1.70	9
1.71-1.80	7
1.81-1.90	2

    a) Write down the modal group.

    b) Which group contains the median?

    c) Find an estimate for the mean.

23.3 Two-Way Tables

A **two-way table** shows two variables at the same time.

Example 1

This table shows how students in a class travel to school.

	Walk	Bus	Car	Total
Boys	8	7		19
Girls	6		2	
Total		12		

    a) Complete the table.
       Add entries to find row/column totals.
       Subtract from row/column totals to find other entries.

	Walk	Bus	Car	Total
Boys	8	7	$19 - 8 - 7 = \underline{\textbf{4}}$	19
Girls	6	$12 - 7 = \underline{\textbf{5}}$	2	$6 + 5 + 2 = \underline{\textbf{13}}$
Total	$8 + 6 = \underline{\textbf{14}}$	12	$4 + 2 = \underline{\textbf{6}}$	$19 + 13 = \underline{\textbf{32}}$

    b) How many girls take the bus to school?
       Find the entry in the Bus column and the Girls row.   **<u>5</u>**

    c) How many students walk to school?
       This is the total of the Walk column.   **<u>14</u>**

    d) What percentage of students take the bus to school? $\frac{12}{32} = 0.375 = \underline{\textbf{37.5\%}}$
       Divide the total of the Bus column by the overall total.

Exercise 1

1 Copy and complete these two-way tables, showing how groups of students travel to school.

  a)

	Walk	Car	Total
Boys	12	6	
Girls	16	3	
Total			

  b)

	Walk	Car	Total
Boys	16		25
Girls		4	
Total	34		

  c)

	Walk	Bus	Car	Total
Boys	9	5	3	
Girls	5	8	6	
Total				

  d)

	Walk	Bus	Car	Total
Boys			8	
Girls	11		4	30
Total	21			60

2 This two-way table shows how many male and female language students from a university Languages department went to study in Germany, France or Spain.

	Germany	France	Spain	Total
Male	16	7	12	
Female	18	4	16	
Total				

a) Copy the table and fill in the entries in the final row and final column.

b) How many female students went to France?

c) How many male students went to Germany?

d) How many students in total went to Spain?

e) How many female students went to either Germany, France or Spain to study?

f) What was the total number of students from this department that went to either Germany, France or Spain to study?

3 This two-way table gives information about some students' favourite type of snack.

a) Copy and complete the two-way table.

b) How many students preferred crisps?

c) How many females preferred jellies?

d) What percentage of males preferred chocolate?

	Chocolate	Crisps	Jellies	Total
Male	3			
Female		7	2	
Total	6	12		30

4 This two-way table gives information about the colours of the vehicles in a car park.

a) Copy and complete the two-way table.

b) How many motorbikes were blue?

c) How many vans were there?

d) What percentage of vehicles were:
    (i) cars?   **(ii)** vans?   **(iii)** red?

	Red	Black	Blue	White	Total
Cars	8	7	4		22
Vans		2	1	10	
Motorbikes	2	1		2	
Total	12		6		

23.4   Bar Charts, Pictograms and Histograms

Bar Charts

Bar charts show how many items fall into different categories.
A **dual bar chart** shows the same categories for two different people or things.

Example 1

The eye colour of 50 students is shown in the frequency table below.

Eye colour	Blue	Brown	Green	Other
Frequency	15	19	10	6

Draw a bar chart to display this information.
Draw a bar of equal width for each eye colour, with a space between each bar.

Exercise 1

1 Arthur asked some students in the canteen which meal they had bought at lunchtime.
His results are in the table below. Draw a bar chart to show this information.

Meal	Pie & Chips	Pasta	Baked potato	Baguette	Salad
Frequency	11	3	7	10	4

2 Some people at a bus stop were asked which bus they were waiting for.
Their responses are shown in this frequency table.

Bus	Number 7	Number 23	Coastlander	X94	12a
Frequency	6	5	2	3	2

Draw a bar chart to show this information.

3 One morning a coffee shop recorded the first 100 drinks that were ordered.
Their results are in the frequency table below. Draw a bar chart to show this information.

Drink	Espresso	Latte	Cappuccino	Mocha	Tea	Other
Frequency	23	19	12	15	22	9

Example 2

Manpreet and Parminder recorded how many TV programmes they watched each day for a week. Their results are in the table below. Draw a dual bar chart to display this information.

Day	Mon	Tues	Wed	Thur	Fri	Sat	Sun
Number of programmes watched by Manpreet	1	2	4	2	3	7	4
Number of programmes watched by Parminder	2	1	0	2	3	4	0

1. Each day will have two bars — one for Manpreet and one for Parminder.

2. Use different colours or shades for Manpreet and Parminder's bars — and include a key to show which is which.

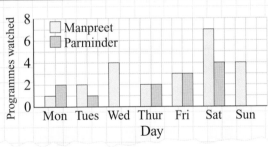

4 The number of rainy days each season in Plymouth and Aberdeen is shown in the table.

Season	Spring	Summer	Autumn	Winter
Rainy days (Plymouth)	38	40	48	52
Rainy days (Aberdeen)	45	47	53	53

Draw a dual bar chart to show this information.
Use different coloured bars for Plymouth and Aberdeen.

5 The people in an office were asked how many cups of tea they drank each morning and afternoon.
The results are in this table.

Name	Nigel	Ali	Raul	Kate	Ailsa	Jan
Cups (Morning)	3	2	1	3	0	2
Cups (Afternoon)	2	1	4	3	0	2

Draw a dual bar chart to show this information.
Use different coloured bars for 'morning' and 'afternoon'.

Pictograms

A **pictogram** uses symbols to represent a certain number of items.

Example 3

This table shows the number of TVs in four secondary schools.

School	Long Beck	Tudor Hall	Alderbrook	Lode Heath
TVs	20	10	8	13

Using the symbol ▢ to represent 4 TVs, draw a pictogram to show this information.

1. Work out how many symbols you need to draw for each school.
   For example, for Tudor Hall:

   $\times 2.5 \Big\{ \begin{array}{l} 4 \text{ TVs} = \boxed{} \\ 10 \text{ TVs} = \boxed{}\boxed{}\textsf{C} \end{array} \Big\} \times 2.5$

Long Beck	▢ ▢ ▢ ▢ ▢
Tudor Hall	▢ ▢ C
Alderbrook	▢ ▢
Lode Heath	▢ ▢ ▢ ⌐

2. Include a key to show what one symbol represents. ⟶ Key: ▢ represents 4 TVs.

Exercise 2

1 Members of a hockey club were asked which activity they would like to do on a team day out. The results are in this frequency table.

Activity	Theme Park	Bowling	Cinema	Boat Trip
Frequency	14	10	5	3

Draw a pictogram to show this information. Represent 2 club members using the symbol: 🧍

2 The incomplete pictogram on the right shows the number of packets of sweets a shop sold on Monday, Tuesday and Wednesday.

a) How many packets of sweets were sold on:

   (i) Tuesday?   **(ii)** Wednesday?

b) Copy the pictogram, and use the information below to complete it.

   • On Thursday the shop sold 20 packets.
   • On Friday they sold 50 packets.
   • On Saturday they sold 65 packets.
   • On Sunday the shop was closed.

Monday	▷▢◁▷▢◁▷▢◁
Tuesday	▷▢◁▷▢◁
Wednesday	▷▢◁▷C
Thursday	
Friday	
Saturday	
Sunday	
Key: ▷▢◁ represents 20 packets of sweets	

3 This pictogram shows the number of letters that were delivered to each of the 6 houses in a street one week.

a) How many letters were delivered to Number 4?

b) Which house received fewest letters during the week?

c) How many letters in total were delivered to the 6 houses?

Key: ✉ represents 4 letters

Number 1	◣
Number 2	✉ ⌐
Number 3	✉ ✉ ✉
Number 4	✉ ✉ ◣
Number 5	✉
Number 6	✉ ◣

Histograms and Frequency Polygons

Histograms and **frequency polygons** are similar to bar charts, but they're used to show **continuous** data (data that is measured rather than counted). So instead of a label under each bar, there's a continuous scale on the horizontal axis, divided into a number of **classes**.

Example 4

This frequency table shows some information about the height of 30 adults.
Draw a histogram to represent this information.

Height (h) in cm	Frequency
$155 \leq h < 160$	1
$160 \leq h < 165$	3
$165 \leq h < 170$	3
$170 \leq h < 175$	4
$175 \leq h < 180$	9
$180 \leq h < 185$	7
$185 \leq h < 190$	1
$190 \leq h < 195$	1
$195 \leq h < 200$	1

1. The class interval "$155 \leq h < 160$" means h is greater than or equal to 155, but less than 160.
   So draw a bar of height 1 between 155 and 160 on the horizontal axis.

2. Draw bars for each of the other class intervals in the same way.

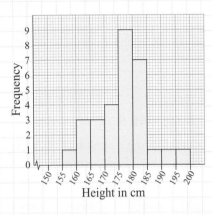

Exercise 3

1 The grouped frequency table on the right shows some information about the weight (w) in kg of 22 pigs on a farm.

Draw a histogram to represent this information.

Weight (w) in kg	Frequency
$10 \leq w < 20$	5
$20 \leq w < 30$	7
$30 \leq w < 40$	8
$40 \leq w < 50$	2

2 Participants in a circus skills workshop were asked to juggle 3 balls for as long as possible without dropping them.

The frequency table on the right shows some information about how long they were able to do this for.

Draw a histogram to represent this information.

Time (t) in seconds	Frequency
$0 \leq t < 4$	19
$4 \leq t < 8$	12
$8 \leq t < 12$	7
$12 \leq t < 16$	3
$16 \leq t < 20$	1

3 Some students were asked the length of their journey to university. This histogram shows their responses.

a) How many students had a journey of 5 km or less?

b) How many students had a journey of 6 km or longer?

c) What is the modal class of this data?

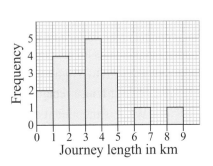

Example 5

Ameen recorded the speed of the cars that passed outside his house one day.
The results are shown in the grouped frequency table below.

Draw a frequency polygon to represent this information.

Speed (s) in mph	Frequency
$25 \leq s < 30$	1
$30 \leq s < 35$	5
$35 \leq s < 40$	12
$40 \leq s < 45$	16
$45 \leq s < 50$	9
$50 \leq s < 55$	2

1. Find the midpoint of each interval by adding the endpoints, and dividing by 2. So the first midpoint is
$$\frac{25 + 30}{2} = 27.5$$

2. Then plot the frequency at each of these midpoints.

3. Join your points with a line.

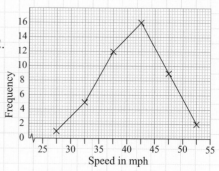

Exercise 4

1 During a cooking competition some chefs were asked to cut a 120 g portion of fish without weighing it.

The frequency table on the right shows the results.

Draw a frequency polygon to represent this information.

Weight (w) in g	Frequency
$80 \leq w < 90$	2
$90 \leq w < 100$	1
$100 \leq w < 110$	11
$110 \leq w < 120$	13
$120 \leq w < 130$	9
$130 \leq w < 140$	4

Floor area (a) in thousands of square feet	Frequency
$9 \leq a < 13$	3
$13 \leq a < 14$	7
$14 \leq a < 15$	5
$15 \leq a < 16$	2

2 Some students recorded the total floor area of local supermarkets for a project.
Their results are shown in the table.

Draw a frequency polygon to show this information.

3 Emma recorded the number of hours of sunshine each day in February, using class widths of 0.5 hours. The frequency polygon on the right shows her results.

a) How many days fell into the class for 1 to 1.5 hours of sunshine?

b) What is the modal class for this data?

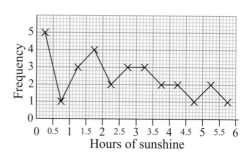

4 An airline recorded the delay in minutes of all of its flights one day, using class intervals 5 minutes wide. Their results are shown in this frequency polygon.

a) How many flights had a delay that was 40 minutes or longer?

b) What is the modal class for this data?

c) In total, how many flights did this airline have that day?

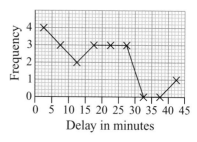

23.5   Stem and Leaf Diagrams

Building Stem and Leaf Diagrams

Stem and leaf diagrams are a bit like bar charts, but the bars are made out of the actual data.
A stem and leaf diagram always needs a **key** to show someone how to read it.

Example 1

Here are the marks scored by pupils in a class test.
56, 52, 82, 65, 76, 82, 57, 63, 69, 73, 58, 81, 73, 52, 73, 71, 67, 59, 63

a) Use this data to build an ordered stem and leaf diagram.
   1. Write down the 'stems' — here use the first digit of the marks. ⟹

```
5 |
6 |
7 |
8 |
```

```
5 | 6 2 7 8 2 9
6 | 5 3 9 7 3        ⟸  2.  Next, make a 'leaf' for each data value by
7 | 6 3 3 3 1             adding the second digit to the correct stem.
8 | 2 2 1
```

   3. Put the leaves in each row in order
      — from lowest to highest.
   4. Always include a key. ⟹ Key: 2 | 1 means 21

```
5 | 2 2 6 7 8 9
6 | 3 3 5 7 9
7 | 1 3 3 3 6
8 | 1 2 2
```

b) Use your stem and leaf diagram to write the data in order from lowest to highest.
   Read across the diagram from left to right, using the key to write the numbers in full.
   52, 52, 56, 57, 58, 59, 63, 63, 65, 67, 69, 71, 73, 73, 73, 76, 81, 82, 82

Exercise 1

1   Use the data sets below to make ordered stem and leaf diagrams.
   a) 41, 48, 51, 54, 59, 65, 65, 69, 74, 80, 86, 89
   b) 12, 15, 26, 15, 39, 24, 41, 41, 27, 17, 36, 31
   c) 46, 87, 42, 94, 67, 54, 59, 63, 83, 71, 66, 74

2   Only some of the values from the data sets have been added to the stem and leaf diagrams below.
   Copy and complete the diagrams by adding the rest of the data values. Use the keys to help.

   a)
```
3 | 1
4 | 0 4
5 | 3 7 9
6 | 0
7 | 7
```
   Key: 3 | 1 means 3.1

3.1	4.0	4.4	5.3
5.7	5.9	6.0	7.7
3.4	4.9	5.4	5.1
6.1	5.7	7.1	4.4

   b)
```
20 | 3 5
30 | 1
40 | 2 9
50 | 0
60 | 6 8
```
   Key: 20 | 1 means 201

203	205	301	402
409	500	606	608
304	409	404	501
403	601	503	402

3   The amount of rainfall in cm over Morecambe Bay was recorded every week for 16 weeks.
   The measurements are shown below. Use this data to make an ordered stem and leaf diagram.

   | 0.0 | 3.8 | 3.6 | 0.1 | 2.7 | 0.6 | 0.3 | 1.1 |
   | 2.0 | 1.3 | 0.0 | 1.6 | 4.1 | 0.0 | 2.5 | 3.1 |

4 Write out the data values from these stem and leaf diagrams in order, from lowest to highest.

a)
```
5 | 1 8
6 | 3 7 7
7 | 3 4 6 8 8
8 | 2 7 7
9 | 1 3
```
Key: 5 | 1 means 51

b)
```
21 | 1 3 3 5 8
22 | 2 4 4
23 | 1 9
24 | 2
25 | 1 3 5 9
```
Key: 21 | 1 means 211

Using Stem and Leaf Diagrams

You can find the mode, median and range from a stem and leaf diagram.
You can also quickly see how many values fall between certain limits — 'between 2 and 8', for example.

Example 2

The stem and leaf diagram below shows the number of seconds 19 children took to open a jar of jam. Use it to find:
a) the mode of the data   b) the median of the data   c) the range of the data

```
0 | 6 8 8
1 | 0 2 4 4 4 5 5 7
2 | 0 4 5 6 6 7
3 | 1 3
```
Key: 2 | 1 means 21 seconds

1. Find the mode by looking for the number that repeats most often in one of the rows — here, there are three 4's in the second row. Use the key to work out what it represents.   a) **14 seconds**

2. There are 19 data values, so the median is the 10th value. Count along the 'leaves' to find it, starting with the first row.   b) **15 seconds**

3. Find the range by subtracting the first number from the last.   c) $33 - 6 =$ **27 seconds**

Exercise 2

1 Use the stem and leaf diagram on the right to find:
   a) the mode of the data
   b) the median of the data
   c) the range of the data

```
0 | 5 8
1 | 2 3 7 9
2 | 0 1 3 9
3 | 2 2 2
```
Key: 2 | 1 means 21

2 Use this diagram showing 12 pupils' test marks to find:
   a) the median mark
   b) the number of marks above 60
   c) the number of marks between 53 and 63

```
5 | 2 5 5 7 8
6 | 1 1 8 9
7 | 1 7 7
```
Key: 2 | 1 means 21

3 The times in seconds that 16 people took to run a 100 m race are shown in the box.
   a) Use these times to create an ordered stem and leaf diagram.
   b) Find the mode of the times.
   c) Find the range of the times.
   d) To qualify for the final, a contestant had to finish in under 13 seconds. How many of those who took part qualified?

10.2	13.1	13.9	14.2
17.3	11.7	11.4	12.9
15.4	13.6	13.9	10.6
12.8	13.9	12.4	13.3

Back-to-Back Stem and Leaf Diagrams

Back-to-back stem and leaf diagrams can be used to compare two sets of data alongside each other. One set of data is read as usual, while the other is read "backwards".

Example 3

14 girls and 14 boys completed a puzzle. The time in seconds it took each pupil to finish was recorded. Here are the results:

Girls: 23, 42, 34, 28, 25, 42, 25, 28, 31, 38, 37, 29, 44, 32
Boys: 33, 29, 14, 19, 54, 49, 51, 17, 56, 38, 32, 27, 14, 51

a) Use the data to make an ordered back-to-back stem and leaf diagram.

1. Use the same stems to build two stem and leaf diagrams. For one graph, the leaves will be on the right as usual. For the other graph, the leaves will be on the left. Your key needs to explain how to read both sides.

girls		boys
	1	4 4 7 9
9 8 8 5 5 3	2	7 9
8 7 4 2 1	3	2 3 8
4 2 2	4	9
	5	1 1 4 6

2. For girls, the stem is on the right.

Key: 1 | 2 for girls means 21
     1 | 2 for boys means 12

3. For boys, the stem is on the left.

b) Describe the shape of the diagram. What conclusions can you draw from this?
Look at the shapes of the two sides of the diagram and describe how they're different.
Boys did the 4 fastest times, but also the 5 slowest. This shows they found the puzzle either very easy or very hard. All of the girls' times are in the three middle rows. This shows the girls' times are more consistent.

Exercise 3

1 Use these two data sets to make an ordered back-to-back stem and leaf diagram.

Set 1: [12, 18, 29, 24, 28, 33, 38, 37, 32, 41, 48]   Set 2: [13, 19, 13, 15, 18, 23, 22, 25, 27, 22, 32]

2 Ed measured the heart rates (in beats per minute, bpm) of 15 people at rest, and then again after they'd exercised.

Key: 7 | 6 at rest means 67 bpm
     7 | 6 after exercise means 76 bpm

a) Calculate the median of:
   (i) the 'at rest' data
   (ii) the 'after exercise' data

heart rate at rest		heart rate after exercise
8 7 6 4 3 2 2	6	5 8 8 9
9 8 6 3 2 2	7	4 5 7 7 8
4 1	8	5 6 7
	9	1 3 7

b) What conclusions can you draw from your answers to **a)**?

3 The data on the right shows daily temperatures (in °C) in Dundee and in London during the same period.

Dundee	12	19	6	7	23	4
	3	1	15	5	2	3

a) Plot a back-to-back stem and leaf diagram to show the data.

London	4	9	18	7	24	12
	13	12	15	21	11	16

b) Use your answer to **a)** to describe one of the main differences between the two sets of data.

23.6   Pie Charts

In a **pie chart**, the size of the **angle** of each sector represents the **frequency** of a data value.

Example 1

Jack asked everyone in his class to name their favourite colour. The frequency table on the right shows his results.

Colour	Red	Green	Blue	Pink
Frequency	12	7	5	6

Draw a pie chart to show his results.

1. Calculate the total frequency.
    This is the number of people in Jack's class. → Total frequency = 12 + 7 + 5 + 6 = 30

2. Divide 360° by the total frequency to find the number of degrees needed to represent each person. → Each person represented by 360° ÷ 30 = 12°

3. Multiply each frequency by the number of degrees for one person.

Colour	Red	Green	Blue	Pink
Frequency	12	7	5	6
Angle	144°	84°	60°	72°

This tells you the angle for each colour.
(These should add up to 360°.
Here: 144° + 84° + 60° + 72° = 360°)

4. Draw a pie chart — the sizes of the sectors are the angles you've just calculated.

Exercise 1

1   Albert recorded the colours of cars that passed his school. His results are shown in the table on the right.

Colour	Black	Silver	Red	Other
Frequency	25	17	8	10

   a) Find the total number of cars Albert recorded.

   b) Find how many degrees represent one car.

   c) Calculate the angle needed to represent each colour.

   d) Draw a pie chart to illustrate this data.

2   Becky asked her friends which football team they support. Their answers are shown in the table below.

Team	Carlisle United	Kendal Town	Millom Reds	Bristol
Frequency	13	9	8	6

   a) Find the total frequency.

   b) Calculate the angle needed to represent each of the four football teams.

   c) Draw a pie chart showing Becky's results.

3   Clive carried out a survey to find
    how many brothers or sisters the
    pupils in his school have.
    His results are in the frequency
    table on the right.
    Draw a pie chart to display Clive's results.

Number of brothers or sisters	1	2	3	4 or more
Frequency	67	24	19	10

4   Daisy asked a group of people where they went on holiday last year.
    Her results are in the table below. Draw a pie chart to show her data.

Holiday destination	UK	Europe	USA	Other	Did not go on holiday
Frequency	22	31	8	11	18

5   Vicky asked people entering a sports centre what activity they were going to do.

    • 33 were going to play squash   • 52 were going to use the gym
    • 21 were going swimming   • 14 had come to play table tennis.

    Draw a pie chart to show this data.

6   Mina recorded the favourite
    flavour of crisps of each of
    the pupils at her school.

Flavour	Plain	Salt and Vinegar	Cheese and Onion	Other
Frequency	18	13	10	7

    a) Calculate the
       total frequency.

    b) Calculate the size of the angle needed to represent each flavour in a pie chart.

    c) Draw a pie chart to represent Mina's data.

7   Peter surveyed his friends to find out how
    they travelled to school. He recorded the
    results in the table on the right.

Method of transport	Walking	Bus	Car	Bike
Frequency	36	16	12	16

    Draw a pie chart to represent Peter's data.

8   Oliver recorded the types of vehicle he saw on a busy road using the tally chart below.
    Show Oliver's data in a pie chart.

Car	Van	Lorry	Bicycle	Other
ЖЖ ЖЖ ЖЖ ЖЖ ЖЖ ЖЖ ЖЖ ЖЖ ЖЖ ЖЖ ЖЖ ЖЖ ЖЖ ЖЖ III	ЖЖ ЖЖ ЖЖ ЖЖ II	ЖЖ ЖЖ ЖЖ ЖЖ ЖЖ ЖЖ ЖЖ II	ЖЖ ЖЖ ЖЖ IIII	ЖЖ IIII

9   Basil used a questionnaire to find out which subject pupils at his school enjoyed the most.
    His data is shown in the frequency table below. Show this data in a pie chart.

Subject	Maths	Art	PE	English	Science	Other
Frequency	348	297	195	87	108	45

Interpreting Pie Charts

Pie charts let you compare the frequencies of different items, and say which ones occurred more often, and which ones occurred less often. However, pie charts **don't** show the frequencies themselves.

To work out the frequencies from a pie chart, you need to know the sizes of the **angles** of the sectors.

Example 2

A headteacher carries out a survey to find out how pupils travel to school. The pie chart on the right shows the results of the survey.

a) What is the most popular way to travel to school?
   The most popular way to travel is the one
   represented by the largest sector.   **Walking**

b) Which method of transport is twice as common as cycling?
   Cycling is represented by a sector with an angle of 45°.
   Travelling by car is represented by a sector with an angle of 90°.   **Travelling by car**

c) 280 pupils walk to school. How many pupils took part in the survey altogether?
   1. The 280 pupils who walk are   140° represents 280 pupils
      represented by an angle of 140°.   So 1° represents 280 ÷ 140 = 2 pupils.
   2. Use this to work out how many   This means 360° represents 360 × 2 = **720 pupils**.
      pupils the whole pie chart represents.

d) How many pupils cycle to school?
   1. You already know what 1° of the
      pie chart represents.   1° represents 2 pupils.
   2. Multiply this by the 'Cycle' sector angle   So 45° represents **90 pupils**.
      to find how many pupils cycle to school.

Exercise 2

1 Match pie charts *P*, *Q*, *R* and *S* to the correct data set.

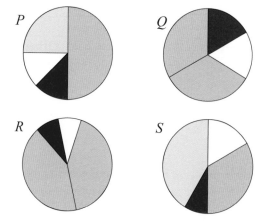

Data Set 1	A	B	C	D
Frequency	10	10	5	5

Data Set 2	A	B	C	D
Frequency	24	12	6	6

Data Set 3	A	B	C	D
Frequency	25	20	10	5

Data Set 4	A	B	C	D
Frequency	25	25	5	5

2 The pie chart on the right shows the proportions of pupils in a school owning different types of pet.

a) What fraction of the pupils own a dog?

b) Which pet is owned by more pupils, rabbits or hamsters?

c) 5 pupils own a cat. How many pupils are shown in the pie chart altogether?

d) How many pupils own a rabbit?

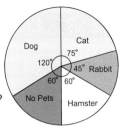

3 Jennifer asked pupils in her school to name their favourite type of pizza. The pie chart on the right shows the results.

a) Which was the most popular type of pizza?

b) What fraction of the pupils said cheese and tomato was their favourite type of pizza?

c) 17 pupils said that vegetable was their favourite type of pizza. Calculate the total number of pupils that Jennifer asked.

d) Use your answer to part **c)** to calculate the number of pupils that said spicy chicken was their favourite type of pizza.

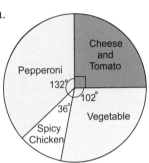

4 Andy and Beth record the number of homework tasks they are set in their Maths, English and Science lessons during one term.

Their data is displayed in the pie charts on the right.

a) Andy says: "Half of all the homework tasks I recorded were for Maths." Is he correct?

b) Beth says: "I got the same number of Maths tasks and English tasks." Is she correct?

c) Do the pie charts tell you who spent more time on their English homework? Explain your answer.

5 A librarian carried out a survey of the ages of people using the library. The results are shown in the pie chart on the right.

a) Which age group used the library most?

b) What fraction of the library users were aged 11-16?

c) There were 18 people aged 17-29 who took part in the survey. How many people took part in the survey altogether?

d) How many of the people in the survey were:

   (i) Under 11?   **(ii)** 11-16?

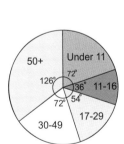

Leaflets were handed out to persuade more young people to use the library. Another survey was then carried out to find the ages of library users. The results are shown in the pie chart on the right.

e) The second survey was smaller than the original one. If 6 people aged 17-29 took part in this second survey, how many people took part altogether?

f) How many people who took part in the new survey were aged 16 or under?

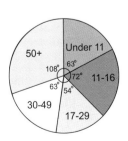

23.7 Line Graphs

Line graphs are useful for showing how a quantity (such as temperature, or the price of something) changes over time. They're also good for comparing two or more sets of data.

Example 1

This line graph shows the monthly rainfall recorded by a rain gauge in Jack's garden last year.

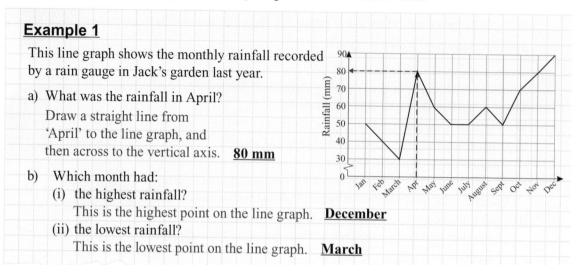

a) What was the rainfall in April?
Draw a straight line from 'April' to the line graph, and then across to the vertical axis. **80 mm**

b) Which month had:
  (i) the highest rainfall?
     This is the highest point on the line graph. **December**
  (ii) the lowest rainfall?
     This is the lowest point on the line graph. **March**

Exercise 1

1 This graph shows the number of customers in a shop, recorded every 30 minutes between 07:00 and 19:00 one day.

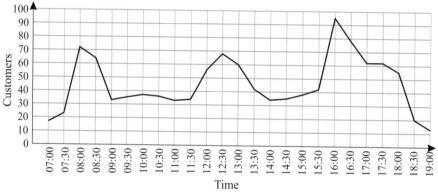

At which time did the shop have:

a) most customers?   **b)** fewest customers?

2 The graph on the right shows how the value of a car changes in the years after it is made.
The car's value in year 0 is its price when brand new.

a) How much did the car cost when it was new?

b) How much was the car worth after one year?

c) What was the car worth after 5 years?

d) How long did it take for the value of the car to fall to half its original value?

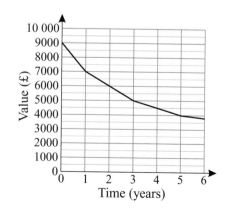

Example 2

The table below shows the height of two chilli plants at various times after planting. Plot the data as line graphs on the same axes to compare the growth of the two plants.

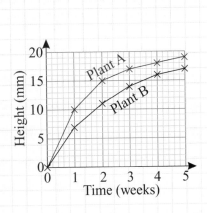

Weeks since planting	0	1	2	3	4	5
Height of Plant A (mm)	0	10	15	17	18	19
Height of Plant B (mm)	0	7	11	14	16	17

1. Plot the points in the data table on sensible axes.
2. For each graph, join up the points with straight lines.

Exercise 2

1 Copy and complete the line graph to show the maximum temperature in London during one week. Use the data in the table below.

Day	Mon	Tues	Wed	Thu	Fri	Sat	Sun
Temp (°C)	17	16	20	19.5	18	20	21

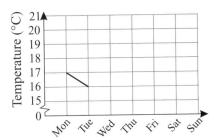

2 This table shows the amount of gas used (in m³) by a family over a period of three years.

Season	Spring	Summer	Autumn	Winter
2008	198	63	159	285
2009	201	76	161	297
2010	183	74	149	269

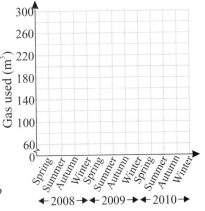

a) Copy the axes on the right, and draw a graph to show how the amount of gas used varied over the three years.

b) Describe the main features of your graph. What does this tell you about the way this family uses gas?

3 The table below shows the percentage of students in a school between 2000 and 2010 that owned mobile phones.

Year	2000	2001	2002	2003	2004	2005	2006	2007	2008	2009	2010
%	9	14	26	40	43	46	63	77	85	93	94

a) Draw a line graph to show how the percentage of people who owned mobile phones changed between 2000 and 2010.

b) Describe the main features of your graph. What does this tell you about how the percentage of students owning mobile phones changed between 2000 and 2010?

4 This table shows the highest temperature recorded in
London and Sydney each month during one year.

Month	Jan	Feb	Mar	Apr	May	Jun	Jul	Aug	Sep	Oct	Nov	Dec
London	7	8	11	13	17	20	23	22	19	15	11	8
Sydney	26	27	25	22	20	17	16	18	19	22	24	25

a) Draw a line graph to show the highest monthly temperature in London during the year.

b) On the same axes, draw a line graph to show the highest monthly temperature in
Sydney during the year.

c) Describe the shapes of your two lines. What does this tell you about the way the
temperature changes in the two cities during the year?

23.8   Scatter Graphs

Drawing Scatter Graphs

A **scatter graph** shows two variables plotted against each other.
These variables are often the results from a survey or an experiment.

Example 1

Jeremy measured the height and shoe size of 10 people.
Use his results to plot a scatter graph of shoe size against height in cm.

Height (cm)	165	159	173	186	176	172	181	169	179	194
Shoe size	6	5	8	9	8.5	7	8	6	8	11

1. Draw and label your axes.
    Here, height has been plotted
    along the horizontal axis and
    shoe size up the vertical axis.

2. Plot each point carefully.

3. Don't join the points up on a
    scatter graph.

Exercise 1

1 The scatter graph on the right shows the number of flags
a shop sold each day of a football tournament.

a) How many flags were sold on the
3rd day of the tournament?

b) On which day of the tournament were most flags sold?

c) On how many days did the shop sell 7 flags?

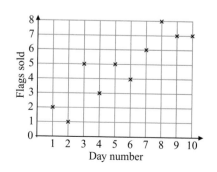

2 The outside temperature and the number of ice creams sold in a cafe were recorded for six days. The results are shown in the table below.

Temp (°C)	28	25	26	21	23	29
Ice creams sold	30	22	27	5	13	33

Copy the axes on the right, then use the data from the table to plot the scatter graph.

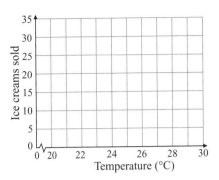

3 Ten children of different ages were asked how many baby teeth they still had. Use the results below to plot a scatter graph. Plot age on the horizontal axis and the number of baby teeth on the vertical axis.

Age (years)	5	6	8	7	9	7	10	6	8	9
Baby teeth	20	17	11	15	7	17	5	19	13	8

Correlations and Lines of Best Fit

Two variables are **correlated** if they are related to each other.
- A **positive correlation** means that the variables increase and decrease together.
- A **negative correlation** means that as one variable increases, the other decreases.

Correlations are easy to see on a scatter graph.
If two variables are correlated, then you can draw a **line of best fit** on their scatter graph.
This is a straight line that passes close to most of the points.

Example 2
Do the following graphs show a positive correlation, a negative correlation or no correlation?

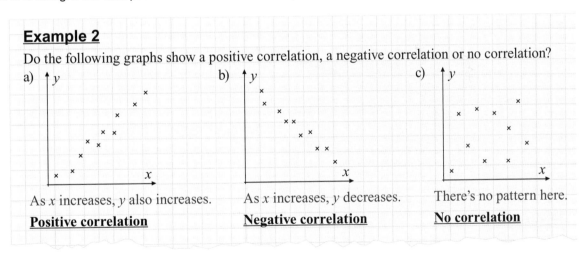

a) As x increases, y also increases. **Positive correlation**

b) As x increases, y decreases. **Negative correlation**

c) There's no pattern here. **No correlation**

Exercise 2

1 Do the following scatter graphs show a positive correlation, a negative correlation or no correlation?

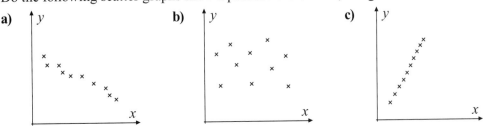

2 Are the following pairs of variables likely to show positive correlation, negative correlation or no correlation? Explain your answers.

    a) Outside temperature and ice cream sales   **b)** Outside temperature and hot chocolate sales

    c) Outside temperature and bread sales   **d)** Age of a child and his or her height

    e) Speed limit in a street and the average speed of cars as they drive down that street

---

Example 3

The scatter graph on the right shows the marks a class of pupils achieved in a Maths test plotted against the marks they achieved in an English test.

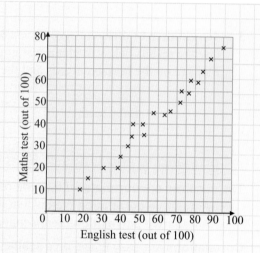

1   **a)** Draw a line of best fit on the graph.

    b) Jimmy was ill on the day of the Maths test. If he scored 75 in his English test, predict what his Maths mark would have been.

    c) Elena was ill on the day of the English test. If she scored 35 on her Maths test, predict what her English result would have been.

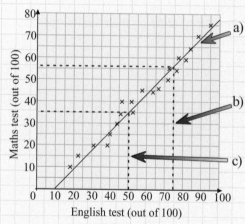

a) The marks are positively correlated, so you can draw a line passing close to all the points. It doesn't have to actually go through any of the points or the origin.

b) Draw a line up from 75 on the 'English' axis to the line of best fit, then across to the 'Maths' axis. Predicted Maths mark for Jimmy = **56**

c) Draw a line across from 35 on the 'Maths' axis to the line of best fit, and then down. Predicted English mark for Elena = **51**

Exercise 3

1 Could a line of best fit be drawn on each of these graphs? Explain your answers.

  a)

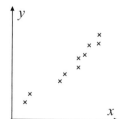

  b)

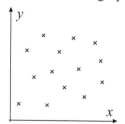

  c)

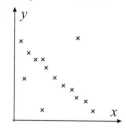

2 Pupils in a class were asked how many hours at the weekend they spent doing homework and watching television. The results are shown on this scatter graph.

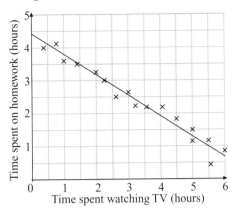

a) Describe the correlation between time spent watching TV and time spent doing homework.

b) Use the line of best fit to predict how long a pupil spends on homework if they watch 5.5 hours of TV at the weekend.

c) Amelia did 3.5 hours of homework at the weekend. Predict how many hours she spent watching TV.

3 The graph on the right shows the height of various types of tree plotted against the width of their trunks.

a) Describe the correlation between the width of the trunks and the height of the trees.

b) Use the graph to predict the width of a tree's trunk if it is 13 m tall.

c) A tree has grown into power lines, meaning that measuring its height would be dangerous. If the trunk is 100 cm wide, predict the tree's height.

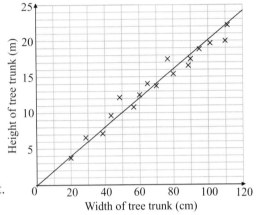

4 Anton wants to buy a particular model of car. The table below shows the cost of several of these cars that are for sale, as well as their mileage.

Mileage	5000	20 000	10 000	12 000	5000	25 000	27 000
Cost (£)	3500	2000	3000	2500	3900	1000	500

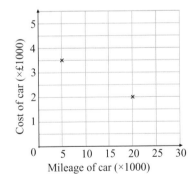

a) The first two points have already been plotted on the scatter graph on the right. Copy and complete the graph.

b) Draw a line of best fit through your points.

c) Thelma has seen a car of this model with a mileage of 15 000. Predict the cost of this car.

5 The outside temperature and the number of drinks sold by two vending machines were recorded over a 10-day period.

The results are shown in these tables.

Temperature (°C)	14	29	23	19	22	31	33	18	27	21
Drinks sold from Machine 1	6	24	16	13	15	28	31	13	22	14

Temperature (°C)	14	29	23	19	22	31	33	18	27	21
Drinks sold from Machine 2	7	25	18	15	17	32	35	14	24	17

For each machine:

a) Draw a scatter graph to represent the data.

b) Draw a line of best fit.

c) Predict the number of drinks that would be sold if the outside temperature was 25 °C.

Section 24 — Probability

24.1 Probability — The Basics

Probability is all about **how likely** events are to happen. The probability of any event happening is between **impossible** (definitely won't happen) and **certain** (definitely will happen). So events can be put on a **probability scale** like this.

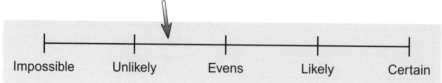

Impossible   Unlikely   Evens   Likely   Certain

Example 1

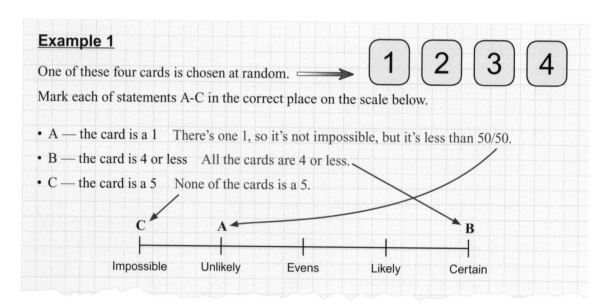

One of these four cards is chosen at random. ⟹ | 1 | 2 | 3 | 4 |

Mark each of statements A-C in the correct place on the scale below.

- A — the card is a 1   There's one 1, so it's not impossible, but it's less than 50/50.
- B — the card is 4 or less   All the cards are 4 or less.
- C — the card is a 5   None of the cards is a 5.

C   A   B

Impossible   Unlikely   Evens   Likely   Certain

Exercise 1

1   For each of these pairs of events A and B, say which is **more likely**.

   a) If you spin a spinner with eight sections numbered 1-8...
     A: spinning less than 2   B: spinning more than 2

   b) If you pick a card at random from a standard pack of cards...
     A: picking a 10   B: picking a spade

   c) If you look up what day of the week it was when you were born...
     A: the day begins with S   B: the day begins with F

2   Put the following statements in order, from least likely to most likely.

   1. You roll a fair, six-sided dice and get an even number.

   2. You will win the 100 metres race at the next Olympics.

   3. You will be a year older on your next birthday than on your last birthday.

   4. It will rain in the UK at least once in the next 30 days.

3 Choose from the words: *impossible*, *unlikely*, *evens*, *likely* and *certain* to describe the following.

   a) Tossing a coin and getting tails.   **b)** Rolling a '9' on a normal six-sided dice.

   c) A person growing to be 10 metres tall.   **d)** Rolling an even number on a fair dice.

   e) Rolling 1 or more on a normal dice.   **f)** Spinning '6' on a spinner labelled 5, 6, 7, 8.

   g) Picking a red card from a standard pack of cards.

   h) Spinning 2 or more on a spinner labelled 1-4.

4 This scale shows the probabilities of four events — A, B, C and D.
   Match each event to the correct description.

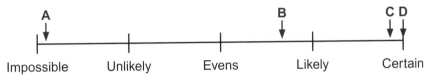

   a) It will rain in the UK at least once in December.

   b) You roll a fair, six-sided dice and get a number from 1 to 6.

   c) You spin purple on a fair, three-sided spinner with one red section and two purple sections.

   d) Britain will be top of the medals table at each of the next three Olympics.

5 One card is picked at random from eight cards numbered 1 to 8.

   Make a copy of this probability scale and add arrows to show the probability of each
   of the events described below. Each arrow should match one of the words.

   a) The card is less than 9.   **b)** The card is an odd number.

   c) The card is greater than 2.   **d)** The card is greater than or equal to 7.

   e) The card is 6 or less.   **f)** The card is a zero.

6 These eight cards are placed face down on a table and one is selected at random.

   a) Which letter is twice as likely to be on the selected card as the letter P?

   b) Which letter is three times as likely to be on the selected card as the letter E?

   c) The three arrows below show the probability of selecting each of the letters P, A, R, L and E.
   Match each letter to one of the arrows. (You can use each arrow for more than one letter.)

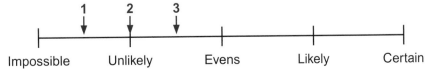

Writing Probabilities as Numbers

All probabilities can be written as a number between **0 and 1**. An event that's **impossible** has a probability of **0** and an event that's **certain** has a probability of **1**.

So, using **fractions**, the probability scale looks like this: ⟹

You can also write probabilities as **decimals** or **percentages**.

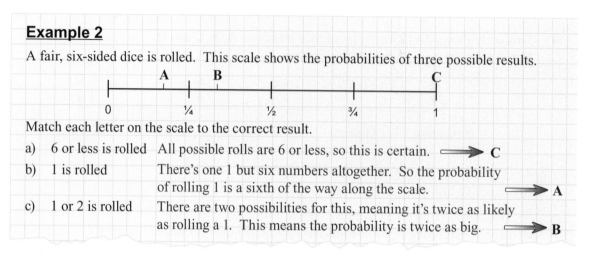

Example 2

A fair, six-sided dice is rolled. This scale shows the probabilities of three possible results.

Match each letter on the scale to the correct result.

a) 6 or less is rolled   All possible rolls are 6 or less, so this is certain. ⟹ **C**

b) 1 is rolled   There's one 1 but six numbers altogether. So the probability of rolling 1 is a sixth of the way along the scale. ⟹ **A**

c) 1 or 2 is rolled   There are two possibilities for this, meaning it's twice as likely as rolling a 1. This means the probability is twice as big. ⟹ **B**

Exercise 2

1 Match each letter on this scale to the correct probability.

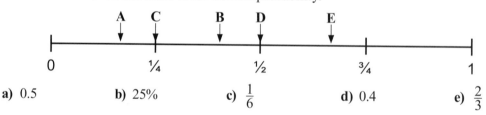

a) 0.5   **b)** 25%   **c)** $\frac{1}{6}$ **d)** 0.4   **e)** $\frac{2}{3}$

2 Match each letter on this probability scale to one of the events below.

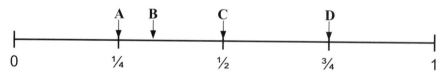

a) Rolling an odd number on a fair dice.

b) Selecting a card at random from a pack of 52 cards and getting a diamond.

c) Selecting a card at random from a pack of 52 cards and not getting a diamond.

d) Spinning blue on a fair, three-sided spinner with 1 blue section and 2 orange sections.

3 Draw a probability scale from 0 to 1 and mark on the probabilities of the events below.

a) Tossing a fair coin and getting heads or tails.

b) Rolling a fair, six-sided dice and getting a 4, 5 or 6.

c) Selecting one card at random from cards numbered 1 to 10, and getting:

   (i) the number 7,   **(ii)** either the number 9 or the number 10.

24.2 Calculating Probabilities

The **probability** of something happening depends on the **total number of possible outcomes** — that's just the total number of different things that could possibly happen. When **all** the possible outcomes are **equally likely**, you can work out probabilities using this formula:

$$\text{Probability of event} = \frac{\text{number of ways event can happen}}{\text{total number of possible outcomes}}$$

Example 1

A box contains 20 coloured counters, numbered 1 to 20.
11 of the counters are blue, 7 of the counters are purple and 2 of the counters are yellow.
If one counter is selected at random, work out the following probabilities.

a) The counter is the number 12.

1. Find the total number of outcomes — there are 20 counters, so... ⟹ Total outcomes = 20

2. Count the number of outcomes that are 12. There's 1 counter numbered 12, so... ⟶ There's 1 way of getting 12.

3. Put the numbers into the formula. Probability of number 12 = $\frac{1}{20}$

b) The counter is yellow.

1. Count the number of outcomes that are yellow. There are 2 yellow counters, so... ⟹ There are 2 ways of getting yellow.

2. Put the numbers into the formula. (You already know there are 20 outcomes in total.) Probability of yellow counter = $\frac{2}{20} = \frac{1}{10}$

3. Don't forget to cancel fractions where possible.

c) The counter is either blue or yellow.
Count how many counters are either blue or yellow, and then divide by 20.

13 counters are either blue or yellow.

Probability of selecting either blue or yellow = $\frac{13}{20}$

Exercise 1

1 State the total number of possible outcomes in each of the following situations.
   a) A coin is tossed.
   b) One card is selected from a pack of 52.
   c) A ten-sided dice is rolled.
   d) A fair spinner with 8 sections is spun.
   e) One day of the week is chosen at random.
   f) One day of the year is chosen at random.

2 This fair spinner is spun once.
   a) How many possible outcomes are there?
   b) What is the probability of spinning a 1?
   c) What is the probability of spinning a 3?

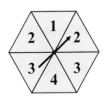

3 Calculate the probability of rolling a fair, six-sided dice and getting each of the following.

    a) 6   **b)** 2   **c)** 7

    d) 4 or 5   **e)** a multiple of 3   **f)** a factor of 6

4 Nine cards numbered 1 to 9 are face down on a table. If one of the cards is selected at random, find the probability of selecting each of the following.

    a) card 4   **b)** card 1 or 2   **c)** an even number   **d)** a number less than 6

5 A fair spinner has 12 equal sections. 5 are yellow, 3 are green and the rest are purple. Find the probability that the spinner lands on the following colours.

    a) green   **b)** purple   **c)** yellow or green   **d)** not green

6 A bag contains some coloured balls — 2 black, 4 blue, 2 green, 3 red, 2 yellow, 1 orange, 1 brown and 1 purple. If a ball is selected at random, find the probabilities of getting the following colours.

    a) green   **b)** red   **c)** orange   **d)** black

    e) blue or green   **f)** red, green or brown   **g)** not purple   **h)** white

7 A pack of 52 playing cards is shuffled and one card is selected at random. Find the probability of selecting each of the following.

    a) a club   **b)** an ace   **c)** a red card

    d) the two of hearts   **e)** not a spade   **f)** a 4 or a 5

8 For each of the following, draw a copy of this spinner and then number the sections to fit the rule.

    a) The probability of getting 2 is $\frac{3}{8}$.

    b) The probability of getting 3 is $\frac{1}{2}$.

    c) The probability of getting 5 and the probability of getting 6 are both $\frac{1}{4}$.

Exercise 2

1 John was born in 1996 (a leap year). A friend tries to guess John's birthday. What is the probability that he guesses:

    a) the correct month?   **b)** the exact date?

2 Diane has 20 different pairs of socks. She picks 1 sock at random. If she then picks another sock at random from the remaining socks, what is the probability that the 2 socks make a pair?

3 A box of chocolates contains 8 caramels, 6 truffles and 4 pralines. Half of each type of chocolate are coated in milk chocolate and half are coated in white chocolate. All the chocolates are individually wrapped in identical paper.

Chelsea selects a chocolate at random. She doesn't like pralines or white chocolate.

    a) What is the probability that she gets a white-chocolate-coated praline?

    b) (i) How many chocolates are <u>neither</u> praline <u>nor</u> coated in white chocolate?

        (ii) What is the probability that Chelsea gets a chocolate she likes?

4   At a summer fair, 100 raffle tickets are sold. Each ticket is bought by a different person.
The winning number is drawn at random.

    a) What is the probability that the first person to buy a ticket wins the first prize to be drawn?

    b) What is the probability that the last person to buy a ticket wins the first prize to be drawn?

5   Explain why the following statement is false.

> *"When a football team plays a match there are 3 possible outcomes for the team — win, draw and lose. So the probability that they win the match is always $\frac{1}{3}$."*

Mutually Exclusive Events

Events that can't happen at the same time are called **mutually exclusive**.
For example, rolling a 1 and rolling a 3 in the same dice roll are mutually exclusive events.

- The probabilities of mutually exclusive events covering **all possible outcomes** always **add up to 1**.
- The probability of something happening and the probability of that thing **not** happening must always add up to 1, because these are mutually exclusive events. This means:

> Probability something <u>doesn't</u> happen = 1 – Probability it <u>does</u> happen

Example 2

Jim gets the train to work every day. The probability that his train is late on any day is 0.05.

    a)   Explain whether the events 'train is late' and 'train is not late' are mutually exclusive.

        The train can't be both late and not late, so the events **are mutually exclusive**.

    b)   Work out the probability that Jim's train is not late.

        The train is either late or not late, so... ⟶ Probability = 1 – 0.05 = **0.95**

Exercise 3

1   A fair, six-sided dice is rolled. Here are three possible events:

    A — a 5 is rolled,   **B — a number less than 3 is rolled,**   **C — an odd number is rolled**

    Say whether these pairs of events are mutually exclusive.

    a) A and B   **b)** A and C   **c)** B and C

2   Charlie chooses one month of the year at random. Here are four possible events.

    A — the name begins with J   **B — the name begins with M**
    C — the name ends in Y   **D — it's one of the first four months**

    Say whether these pairs of events are mutually exclusive.

    a) A and B   **b)** A and C   **c)** A and D

    d) B and C   **e)** B and D   **f)** C and D

3 The probability that Jake's school bus is late is 0.2. What is the probability that it's not late?

4 The probability that it will snow in a particular Canadian town on a particular day is $\frac{5}{8}$. What is the probability that it won't snow there on that day?

5 The probability that Clara wins a raffle prize is 25%. Find the probability that she doesn't win a prize.

6 Gary and Phil have worked out that the probability that Gary beats Phil at tennis is 0.45. Find the probability that Phil beats Gary at tennis.

7 If the probability that Jed doesn't finish a crossword is 0.74, what's the probability he does finish it?

8 In a class, the probability that a randomly selected pupil is a boy is 0.45, and the probability that the pupil has blonde hair is 0.2. Find the probability that a randomly selected pupil:

   a) is a girl   **b)** doesn't have blonde hair

Example 3

A bag contains red, green, blue and white counters.
The table opposite shows the probabilities of randomly selecting a red, green or white counter.

Colour	Red	Green	Blue	White
Probability	0.2	0.1		0.5

Work out the probability of selecting a blue counter.

These are mutually exclusive events, so the probabilities must add up to 1. This means the probability of selecting blue is 1 minus the other 3 probabilities added together.

Probability $= 1 - (0.2 + 0.1 + 0.5)$
$= 1 - 0.8 = \mathbf{\underline{0.2}}$

Exercise 4

1 This table shows the probabilities of winning the four possible prizes in a lucky dip.

Find the missing probability.

Prize	Lollipop	Pen	Cuddly toy	Gift voucher
Probability	0.4	0.1		0.2

2 This table shows the probabilities of getting each of the five possible colours on a spinner.

   a) Find the missing probability.

   b) Find the probability of spinning 'not pink'.

Colour	Red	Blue	Green	Pink	Black
Probability		0.2	0.1	0.1	0.3

3 When two football teams play each other the probability that Team A wins is 0.4 and the probability that Team B wins is 0.15. What is the probability that the match is a draw?

4 A bag contains some equal-sized discs. The discs are either yellow, orange or red. If Jack takes out one disc without looking, the probability it's yellow is $\frac{1}{4}$ and the probability it's orange is $\frac{3}{8}$. Work out the probability that Jack takes a red disc.

5 One counter is selected at random from a box containing blue, green and red counters. The probability that it's a blue counter is 0.5 and the probability that it's a green counter is 0.4. If there are 4 red counters in the box, how many counters are there altogether?

Exercise 5 — Mixed Exercise

1 This table shows the number of sweets of various colours in a bag.

Yellow	Orange	Red
6	4	5

   a) If one sweet is chosen at random, find the probability that the sweet:

      (i) is yellow   **(ii)** is red   **(iii)** is not red

   b) Three white sweets are added to the bag. Find the probability that a randomly selected sweet:

      (i) is red   **(ii)** is not red   **(iii)** is not yellow

2 A game of chance involves spinning the pointer on this circular disc.

   a) What is the probability that the pointer stops on A?

   b) What is the probability that the pointer doesn't stop on C?

3 A fair, six-sided dice is rolled.

   a) What is the probability of rolling an even number?

   b) What is the probability of rolling a multiple of 3?

   c) Explain why your answers to parts **a)** and **b)** don't add up to 1.

24.3   Listing Outcomes

When **two things** are happening at once (for example, tossing a coin and rolling a dice) it's much easier to work out probabilities if you **list all the possible outcomes** in a logical way.

Example 1

Anne has three tickets for a theme park. She chooses two friends at random to go with her. She chooses one girl from Belinda, Claire and Dee, and one boy from Fred and Greg.

   a) List all the possible combinations of friends she could choose.

      1. Make a simple two-column table — 1 column for the girls and 1 for the boys.

      2. Write in the first girl and then fill in all the possibilities for the boys.

      3. Repeat for the other 2 girls.

      4. Each row of the table is a possible outcome.

Girls	Boys
Belinda	Fred
Belinda	Greg
Claire	Fred
Claire	Greg
Dee	Fred
Dee	Greg

   b) What is the probability that Anne chooses Claire to go with her?

      1. Count the number of rows that Claire's name appears in.   There are 2 outcomes that include Claire.

      2. The total number of rows is the total number of outcomes.   And there are 6 possible outcomes in total.

      3. Divide the two numbers to find the probability.   So probability $= \frac{2}{6}$ or $\frac{1}{3}$

Exercise 1

1 Use a two-column table to list all the possible outcomes when:

    a) two coins are tossed   **b)** a six-sided dice is rolled and a coin is tossed

2 A bag contains two balls — one green and one blue. One ball is selected at random, then replaced before a second ball is selected at random. List all the possible combinations of colours.

3 A spinner has three equal sections coloured blue, purple and orange.
List all the possible outcomes if this spinner is spun twice.

4 A burger bar offers the meal deal shown here.

    a) List all the different combinations available.

    Jana picks one combination at random.

    b) What is the probability she chooses a veggie burger and cola?

    c) What is the probability she chooses a cheeseburger?

> **Choose 1 burger and 1 drink**
>
> | *Burgers* | *Drinks* |
> |---|---|
> | Hamburger | Cola |
> | Cheeseburger | Lemonade |
> | Veggie burger | Coffee |

5 The spinner on the right is spun twice.

    a) Copy and complete the table to list all the possible combinations of scores.

    b) What is the probability of spinning 3 on each spin?

    c) What is the probability of getting a total of 3 or less over two spins?

1st spin	2nd spin
1	1
1	2

6 **a)** A coin is tossed three times. List all the possible outcomes.

    b) Work out the probability of getting:

        (i) three tails   **(ii)** one head and two tails

Using Two-Way Tables

If there are lots of possible outcomes from **two experiments**,
you can use a **two-way table** to record them all.

Example 2

A white four-sided dice and a blue four-sided dice, both numbered 1-4, are rolled together.

a) Draw a two-way table to show all the possible total scores.

    1. Put the outcomes for one dice across the top and those for the other dice down the side.

    2. Fill in each square with the score for the row and the score for the column added together.

		White dice			
		1	2	3	4
Blue dice	1	2	3	4	5
	2	3	4	5	6
	3	4	5	6	7
	4	5	6	7	8

b) What is the probability of scoring a total of 4?

    1. Count how many times a total of 4 appears in the table.

    2. Then divide by the total number of outcomes.

3 of the outcomes are 4 and there are 16 outcomes in total.

So probability $= \dfrac{3}{16}$

Exercise 2

1 Copy and complete each of the tables below to show all the possible outcomes.

a) A coin is tossed and a six-sided dice is rolled.

	1	2	3	4	5	6
H	H1	H2				
T						T6

b) A spinner with 3 equal sections, coloured red, white and blue, is spun twice.

	Red	White	Blue
Red	RR		
White			
Blue			

2 Two six-sided dice are rolled.

a) Copy and complete this table to show all the possible total scores.

b) How many possible outcomes are there?

c) Find the probability of each of the following total scores.

    (i) 6   **(ii)** 12   **(iii)** 1

    (iv) less than 8   **(v)** more than 8   **(vi)** an even number

	1	2	3	4	5	6
1						
2						
3						
4						
5						
6						

3 A bag contains 3 balls — 1 blue, 1 green and 1 yellow.
A second bag contains 4 balls — 1 blue, 2 green and 1 yellow.
One ball is taken at random from each bag.

a) Copy and complete this table to show all the possible outcomes.

b) Find the probability of selecting:

    (i) 2 blue balls   **(ii)** 2 green balls

    (iii) 2 balls the same colour   **(iv)** at least 1 yellow ball

	B	G	G	Y
B				
G				
Y				

Exercise 3

1 Tom rolls a six-sided dice and spins a spinner with four equal sections labelled A, B, C and D.

a) Draw a two-way table to show all the possible outcomes.

b) Find the probability that Tom gets each of the following.

    (i) 6 and A   **(ii)** C and 5   **(iii)** B and less than 3

    (iv) an odd number and B   **(v)** C and an even number   **(vi)** A or B and more than 4

2 Hayley and Asha are playing a game. In each round they both spin a spinner with five equal sections labelled 1 to 5.

a) Copy and complete this two-way table to show all the possible outcomes for the girls' spins.

b) What is the probability that Hayley gets a higher score than Asha in a round?

c) What is the probability that Asha scores 5 and Hayley scores less than 5 in a round?

Hayley's score (1st number)	Asha's score (2nd number)				
	1	2	3	4	5
1	1, 1	1, 2			
2	2, 1				
3	3, 1				
4					
5					

24.4 Probability from Experiments

Estimating Probabilities

You can **estimate** probabilities using the results of an experiment or what you know has already happened. Your estimate is called an **experimental probability** (or a **relative frequency**). Work out experimental probability using this formula:

$$\text{Experimental probability} = \frac{\text{Number of times the result has happened}}{\text{Number of times the experiment has been carried out}}$$

The **more times** you do the experiment, the **more accurate** the estimate should be.

Example 1

A biased dice is rolled 100 times. Here are the results.

Score	1	2	3	4	5	6
Frequency	11	14	27	15	17	16

a) Estimate the probability of rolling a 1.
   1. Find the number of times 1 was rolled.
   2. Divide by the total number of rolls.

1 was rolled 11 times.
So probability = $\frac{11}{100}$

b) Estimate the probability of rolling a 3.
   1. Find the number of times 3 was rolled.
   2. Divide by the total number of rolls.

3 was rolled 27 times.
So probability = $\frac{27}{100}$

Exercise 1

1 Ken wants to estimate the probability that a drawing pin lands with its point up when it's dropped. He drops the drawing pin 50 times and finds that it lands with its point up 17 times.

   a) Use these results to estimate the probability that the drawing pin lands with its point up.

   b) Estimate the probability that the drawing pin lands with its point down.

2 A spinner with four sections is spun 100 times. The results are shown in the table below.

   a) Find the relative frequency of each colour.

   b) Sam uses these relative frequencies to estimate the probability of spinning each colour. How could these estimates be made more accurate?

Colour	Red	Green	Yellow	Blue
Frequency	49	34	8	9

3 Stacy rolls a six-sided dice 50 times, and 2 comes up 13 times.
   Jason rolls the same dice 100 times, and 2 comes up 18 times.

   a) Use Stacy's results to estimate the probability of rolling a 2 on this dice.

   b) Use Jason's results to estimate the probability of rolling a 2 on this dice.

   c) Explain whose estimate should be more accurate.

4 Jamal records the colours of the cars passing his school.

   a) Find the relative frequency (as a decimal) of:
      (i) silver   **(ii)** red

   b) Estimate the probability that the next car passing Jamal's school will not be silver, black, red or blue.

Colour	Silver	Black	Red	Blue	Other
Frequency	452	124	237	98	89

5   Sue wants to know how likely it is that her school bus will arrive on time.
     She keeps a record for 6 weeks and finds that the bus is on time 25 times out of 30 days.
     Estimate the probability that the next time Sue gets the bus, it will arrive on time.

6   Jack and his dad have played golf against each other 15 times.
     Jack has won 8 times, and there have been no draws.
     a) Estimate the probability that Jack will win the next time they play.
     b) Estimate the probability that Jack's dad will win the next time they play.

7   George has burnt 12 of the last 20 cakes he's baked.
     Estimate the probability that the next cake he bakes won't be burnt.

8   Lilia wants to estimate the probability that the football team she supports will win a match.
     Describe how she could do this.

Expected Frequency

You can **estimate** the **number of times** an event will happen by working out its **expected frequency**.

> Expected frequency of an event = probability of the event × number of trials

Here, 'trial' just means an action that could lead to the event happening
— for example, a toss of a coin or a spin of a dice.

Example 2

The probability that a biased dice lands on 1 is 0.3.
How many times would you expect to roll a 1 if you rolled the dice 50 times?

Multiply the probability of rolling a 1 by the number of rolls. $\implies$ 0.3 × 50 = **15 times**

Exercise 2

1   The probability that a biased dice lands on 4 is 0.75.
     How many times would you expect the dice to land on 4 if it's rolled:
     a) 20 times?   **b)** 60 times?   **c)** 100 times?   **d)** 1000 times?

2   A fair, six-sided dice is rolled 120 times. How many times would you expect to roll:
     a) a 5?   **b)** a 6?   **c)** an even number?   **d)** higher than 1?

3   This spinner on the right has 3 equal sections.
     How many times would you expect to spin 'penguin' in:
     a) 60 spins?   **b)** 300 spins?   **c)** 480 spins?

4   60% of the people who buy bread from a bakery buy brown bread. If 20 people buy bread
     from the bakery tomorrow, how many of them would you expect to buy brown bread?

Fair or Biased?

Things like dice and spinners are **fair** if they have the same chance of landing on each side or section.

To decide whether something is fair or biased, you need to do an experiment. Then you can compare the **theoretical probability** of each outcome with the **relative frequency** from your experiment.

For example, if you rolled a six-sided dice 100 times, you'd expect it to land on 6 about $\frac{1}{6}$ of the time. But if $\frac{1}{2}$ of the rolls were 6, you'd say the dice was **biased**.

Or you can compare the **frequency** of each outcome in your experiment with the **expected frequency**.

For example, if in 100 trials the expected frequency was 17, but the actual frequency was 50, then you'd say the dice was biased.

Example 3

Amir thinks his dice is biased. He rolls it 60 times and records the results shown in this table.

Score	1	2	3	4	5	6
Frequency	12	3	9	10	14	12

a) Work out the relative frequencies of each score.
  1. For each score, work out frequency ÷ total number of rolls.
  2. Write the probabilities as decimals so they're easier to compare.

1: $\frac{12}{60}$ = **0.2**   2: $\frac{3}{60}$ = **0.05**

3: $\frac{9}{60}$ = **0.15**   4: $\frac{10}{60}$ = **0.17**

5: $\frac{14}{60}$ = **0.23**   6: $\frac{12}{60}$ = **0.2**

b) Do you think the dice is fair or biased? Explain your answer.

Compare the relative frequencies to the theoretical probability of $\frac{1}{6}$ = 0.17 for each score.

The relative frequency of a score of 2 is very different from the theoretical probability, so the experiment suggests that the dice is **biased**.

Exercise 3 — Mixed Exercise

1   A spinner has four sections coloured blue, green, white and pink. This table shows the results when the spinner is spun 100 times.

Colour	Blue	Green	White	Pink
Frequency	22	21	18	39

  a) Work out the relative frequencies of the four colours.

  b) Write down the theoretical probability of getting each of the colours, assuming the spinner is fair.

  c) Explain whether you think the spinner is fair or biased.

2   A six-sided dice is rolled 120 times and 4 comes up 32 times.

  a) How many times would you expect 4 to come up in 120 rolls if the dice is fair?

  b) Use your answer to part **a)** to explain whether you think the dice is fair or biased.

  c) Explain how you could find a more accurate estimate for the probability of rolling a 4.

3   Three friends each toss a coin and record the number of heads they get. The table on the right shows their results.

  a) Copy and complete the table.

  b) Explain whose results should be the most accurate.

  c) Explain whether you think the coin is fair or biased.

	Amy	Steve	Hal
No. of tosses	20	60	100
No. of heads	12	33	49
Relative frequency of heads			

Answers

and

Index

Answers

Section 1 — Non-Calculator Arithmetic

1.1 Negative Numbers

Page 1   Exercise 1

1. a) −1   b) 4   c) −1   d) −4
   e) 4   f) −8   g) −11   h) −4
   i) 3   j) −11   k) 5   l) −8

2. a) −2   b) 1   c) 0   d) 5
   e) −12   f) −9   g) 15   h) 0

3. a) −4 °C   b) 3 °C   4 a) 9 °C   b) 3 °C

5. −1 °C   6   5 °C

Page 2   Exercise 2

1. a) 6   b) 2   c) −9   d) −4
   e) −10   f) 0   g) 7   h) 10
   i) −10   j) 6   k) −9   l) 13

2. a) −6   b) −4   c) 5   d) 9
   e) 8   f) −4   g) 20   h) −20

3. a) 11   b) 4   c) 12   d) 7

4. a) $-3 + (-2) = -5$ b) $5 - (-5) = 10$
   c) $11 + (-7) = 4$ d) $-8 - (-2) = -6$

Page 3   Exercise 3

1. a) −12   b) 5   c) −3   d) −16
   e) −1   f) −5   g) −54   h) 88
   i) 12   j) −7   k) 21   l) 9
   m) −6   n) 9   o) −18   p) 8
   q) 36   r) −42   s) −5   t) −24

2. a) $-3 \times 2 = -6$ b) $-14 \div 7 = -2$
   c) $-4 \times 4 = -16$ d) $10 \div (-2) = -5$
   e) $-8 \times 3 = -24$ f) $-18 \div (-6) = 3$
   g) $-12 \times (-3) = 36$ h) $-77 \div 11 = -7$

3. a) −6   b) −4   c) 1   d) 10
   e) 15   f) −90   g) −14   h) 72
   i) 50   j) 40   k) 45   l) −1

1.2 Whole Number Arithmetic

Page 3   Exercise 1

1. a) 79   b) 83   c) 219   d) 421

2. a) 63   b) 46   c) 146   d) 46

3. a) 93   b) 568   c) 1021   d) 902
   e) 112   f) 208   g) 495   h) 179
   i) 2754   j) 2654   k) 2618   l) 2768

4. a) 366   b) 816   c) 358   d) 557
   e) 249   f) 917   g) 1636   h) 757

5. 155   6 £1922   7 588

Page 5   Exercise 2

1. a) 520   b) 187   c) 156   d) 384
   e) 703   f) 645   g) 1696   h) 2088

   i) 4288   j) 3479   k) 6688   l) 9114
   m) 4752   n) 6794   o) 8428   p) 6723

2. a) 2600   b) 3420   c) 8875   d) 11 664
   e) 7595   f) 18 349   g) 25 767   h) 17 015
   i) 22 754   j) 34 362   k) 28 105   l) 42 032

3. 1104   4 £396   5 £12 636

6. 3220 tonnes   7 13 600 matches

8. a) 26 940   b) 56 775   c) 77 049   d) 236 208
   e) 63 000   f) 41 174   g) 110 166   h) 85 994

Page 6   Exercise 3

1. a) 51   b) 34   c) 67   d) 452
   e) 328   f) 225   g) 560   h) 622

2. a) $72\frac{1}{5}$ b) $1737\frac{2}{3}$ c) $839\frac{3}{5}$ d) $512\frac{1}{9}$
   e) $42\frac{6}{7}$ f) $74\frac{5}{9}$ g) $424\frac{1}{6}$ h) $334\frac{1}{4}$ or $334\frac{2}{8}$

3. a) 28   b) 32   c) 41   d) 48
   e) 206   f) 201   g) 401   h) 256
   i) 311   j) 269   k) 310   l) 352

4. a) 21   b) $26\frac{7}{16}$ or $26\frac{14}{32}$ c) $33\frac{6}{7}$ or $33\frac{18}{21}$
   d) 36   e) 38   f) 61
   g) 58   h) $47\frac{1}{33}$ i) $396\frac{1}{6}$ or $396\frac{3}{18}$
   j) $268\frac{18}{25}$ k) $268\frac{15}{31}$ l) $194\frac{3}{44}$

5. 12 stamps, 8 pence change.

6. 28 people   7 225 boxes   8 £347

9. a) £432   b) £2053   10 1256 people

1.3 Decimals

Page 7   Exercise 1

1. $\frac{7}{100}$ 2 $\frac{3}{10}$ 3 $\frac{8}{1000}$ 4 $\frac{1}{10\,000}$

5. 2   6 $\frac{6}{1000}$

7. a) 0.1   b) 0.02   c) 0.005   d) 0.7
   e) 0.07   f) 0.001   g) 0.09   h) 0.8

Page 8   Exercise 2

1. a) 0.31   b) 0.21   c) 0.09   d) 0.472
   e) 8.3   f) 0.05   g) 0.1   h) 0.11
   i) 3.7   j) 7.19   k) 12.1   l) 18.07

2. a) 0.02, 0.15, 0.2   b) 0.16, 0.51, 0.61
   c) 0.559, 0.59, 0.591   d) 0.03, 0.035, 0.04
   e) 0.007, 0.017, 0.07, 0.7   f) 0.41, 1.14, 1.4, 1.41
   g) 0.09, 0.75, 2.03, 2.3   h) 0.078, 0.708, 0.78, 0.782
   i) 0.09, 0.1, 0.101, 0.11   j) 0.61, 1.09, 1.6, 1.66
   k) 0.3, 0.31, 3.01, 3.1   l) 4.05, 4.5, 5.04, 5.4

3. a) −1.5, 1.05, 1.5, 1.55   b) −6, −0.6, 0.6, 6.1
   c) −0.1, −0.09, −0.01, 0.1   d) −5, −0.55, −0.5, −0.45
   e) −7.1, −7.07, −7, 0.007
   f) −0.095, −0.09, −0.05, 0.9

1.4 Adding and Subtracting Decimals

Page 9   Exercise 1

1 a) 6.9   b) 11.7   c) 19.9   d) 6.6
   e) 1.1   f) 12.1   g) 18.3   h) 10.1

2 a) 5.3   b) 5.7   c) 9.3   d) 1.6
   e) 3.22   f) 1.86   g) 2.5   h) 6.6

3 a) 18.23   b) 1.829   c) 92.192   d) 7.394
   e) 6.291   f) 14.879   g) 17.381   h) 24.002
   i) 12.679   j) 1.908   k) 1.011   l) 25.579

4 a) 17.13   b) 1.18   c) 6.215   d) 64.96
   e) 63.19   f) 11.14   g) 6.441   h) 0.876
   i) 3.394   j) 2.08   k) 9.31   l) 0.261

5 a) 13.35   b) 12.2   c) 9.62   d) 2.65
   e) 2.15   f) 2.78   g) 0.48   h) 5.95
   i) 12.72   j) 2.08   k) 1.18   l) 2.31
   m) 3.21   n) 15.02   o) 11.85   p) 23.67

6 a) 0.9   b) 4.49   c) 6.972   d) 6.547

7 a) 3.8   b) 9.7   c) 20.04   d) 22.49
   e) 44.92   f) 4.2   g) 4.8   h) 18.3

8 a) 8.494   b) 11.45   c) 17.14   d) 22.12
   e) 7.983   f) 22.97   g) 16.652   h) 1.082

9 a)
```
    7 . 6 1
  + 0 . 6 0
  ─────────
    8 . 2 1
```
   b)
```
    5 . 9 8
  + 0 . 4 2
  ─────────
    6 . 4 0
```
   c)
```
    6 . 7 5
  + 2 . 4 8
  ─────────
    9 . 2 3
```
   d)
```
    5 . 4 3
  − 2 . 1 2
  ─────────
    3 . 3 1
```

Page 11   Exercise 2

1 6.9 km   2 £49.50   3 1.25 m
4 £51.50   5 £83.21   6 14.85 seconds

1.5 Multiplying and Dividing Decimals

Page 12   Exercise 1

1 a) 9.2   b) 141   c) 725   d) 2.3
   e) 19   f) 1460   g) 6070   h) 990
   i) 130.4   j) 7800   k) 0.6   l) 230

2 a) 2.59   b) 8.615   c) 38.17   d) 0.5491
   e) 9.015   f) 0.63   g) 0.0051   h) 0.0094
   i) 0.008   j) 0.0232   k) 6.012   l) 0.017

Page 12   Exercise 2

1 a) 3141.6   b) 31.416   c) 0.31416   d) 0.031416
2 a) 477.19   b) 4.7719   c) 0.47719   d) 0.047719
3 a) 126   b) (i) 12.6 (ii) 1.26   (iii) 0.0126
4 a) 253   b) (i) 2.53 (ii) 0.253   (iii) 0.0253
5 a) 53.6   b) 19.2   c) 26.4   d) 44.8
   e) 5.85   f) 19.4   g) 10.8   h) 46.5
6 a) 0.18   b) 0.72   c) 0.006   d) 0.002
   e) 0.04   f) 0.006   g) 0.0008   h) 0.000042
7 a) 1.26   b) 1.4   c) 4.05   d) 0.66

---

   e) 1.08   f) 0.153   g) 0.064   h) 0.0656
   i) 0.366   j) 0.0066   k) 0.468   l) 0.0094

8 a) 13.23   b) 3.22   c) 4.05   d) 4.32
   e) 32.37   f) 59.34   g) 0.528   h) 1.173
   i) 0.0624   j) 0.2688   k) 0.01769   l) 0.000578

Page 13   Exercise 3

1 a) 25.648
   b) (i) 256.48   (ii) 2564.8   (iii) 25 648

2 a) 124   b) 420   c) 363   d) 884.8
   e) 122   f) 402.8   g) 6108   h) 4515
   i) 370.08   j) 24   k) 855.75   l) 606.06

Page 14   Exercise 4

1 a) 2.7   b) 3.2   c) 1.54   d) 0.53
   e) 1.03   f) 0.45   g) 14.1   h) 0.231

2 a) 2.13   b) 0.0102   c) 28.2   d) 0.34
   e) 0.535   f) 1.724   g) 2.85   h) 0.009
   i) 0.168   j) 7.05   k) 0.3125   l) 44.55
   m) 0.7025   n) 0.0104   o) 1.5075   p) 0.6122

3 a) 64 ÷ 4   b) 16
4 a) 38.4 ÷ 12   b) 3.2
5 a) 3800 ÷ 8   b) 475

6 a) 32   b) 7.8   c) 2.08   d) 44
   e) 8.85   f) 9.435   g) 11.5   h) 0.55

7 a) 752   b) 821   c) 0.4   d) 5.14
   e) 13.5   f) 255.5   g) 5.04   h) 0.65

8 a) 90   b) 780   c) 1500   d) 7200

9 a) 30   b) 355   c) 700   d) 270
   e) 220   f) 5.93   g) 219   h) 40.03
   i) 2880   j) 0.02   k) 0.0125   l) 1.2

10 a) 0.73 ÷ 5   b) 0.146
11 a) 0.0241 ÷ 4   b) 0.006025
12 a) 0.152   b) 0.0082   c) 0.0444
   d) 0.004574   e) 0.0283   f) 0.005618
   g) 0.1168   h) 0.0022

1.6 Order of Operations

Page 16   Exercise 1

1 a) 8   b) 1   c) 17   d) 16
   e) 8   f) 9   g) 22   h) 33

2 a) 28   b) 15   c) 10   d) 26
   e) 7   f) 25   g) 6   h) 10
   i) 42   j) 6   k) 11   l) 21

3 a) 17   b) 26   c) 3   d) 5
   e) 14   f) 3   g) 2   h) 13

4 a) $9 \times (7 - 5) = 18$ b) $(18 - 6) \div 3 = 4$
   c) $21 \div (4 + 3) = 3$ d) $(5 + 2) \times (6 - 2) = 28$
   e) $(13 - 5) \times (13 - 1) = 96$ f) $(6 + 8 - 7) \times 5 = 35$

5 a) $6 + 7 \times 2 = 20$ b) $16 - 6 \div 3 = 14$
   c) $11 \times 3 + 5 = 38$ d) $5 + 16 \div 2 = 13$
   e) $3 \times 6 - 9 = 9$
   f) $18 - 4 - 6 = 8$ <u>or</u> $18 - (4 + 6) = 8$

Answers   327

g) $8 \div 2 + 6 = 10$ <u>or</u> $8 \times 2 - 6 = 10$
h) $(35 - 7) \times 2 = 56$ **i)** $(3 + 7) \times 4 = 40$
j) $13 - 4 + 1 = 10$ <u>or</u> $13 - (4 - 1) = 10$
k) $14 \div (6 + 8) = 1$ **l)** $45 \div (6 + 3) = 5$

Page 16 Exercise 2

1 a) 3   **b)** 4   **c)** 2   **d)** 1

e) 2   **f)** 2   **g)** 4   **h)** $\frac{9}{2}$

i) $\frac{3}{5}$ **j)** $\frac{2}{3}$ **k)** 3   **l)** 1

1.7 Non-Calculator Arithmetic Problems

Page 17 Exercise 1

1 a) 3   **b)** –21   **c)** –13   **d)** –16
e) 8   **f)** 40   **g)** –6   **h)** –14

2 –11 °C   **3** 860 °C   **4** 450 tins

5 95 tickets   **6** £728   **7** 9 coaches

8 a) –4.76   **b)** 3.78   **c)** 24.74   **d)** 7.43

9 a) 0.034   **b)** 34.8   **c)** –10.83   **d)** –2155

10 a) –0.102   **b)** –0.738   **c)** 0.4   **d)** 0.036

11 £1.46   **12** 8.8 pints   **13** £60.75

14 £137.62   **15** £66.75   **16** £27.65

17 a) 3.7128   **b)** 0.37128   **c)** 37.128   **d)** 371.28

18 £2.95   **19** 34 pieces

20 a) –13   **b)** –4   **c)** –2   **d)** 0.3
e) 0   **f)** 0.08   **g)** –9.6   **h)** 3.2

Section 2 — Approximations

2.1 Rounding — Whole Numbers

Page 18 Exercise 1

1 14.1, 14.02, 13.7, 14.09, 14.4999, 13.901

2 a) 10   **b)** 8   **c)** 12   **d)** 8   **e)** 40
f) 8   **g)** 46   **h)** 1   **i)** 117   **j)** 663

3 a) 12   **b)** 7   **c)** 25   **d)** 46   **e)** 11

4 a) 30   **b)** 30   **c)** 80   **d)** 70   **e)** 50
f) 60   **g)** 50   **h)** 490   **i)** 660   **j)** 187 520

5 a) 200   **b)** 600   **c)** 700   **d)** 400
e) 500   **f)** 5700   **g)** 6300   **h)** 4700
i) 2400   **j)** 12 300

6 a) 3000   **b)** 9000   **c)** 7000   **d)** 10 000
e) 9000   **f)** 2000   **g)** 4000   **h)** 0
i) 3000   **j)** 57 000

7 a) (i) 18   **(ii)** 20   **b) (i)** 16   **(ii)** 20
c) (i) 202   **(ii)** 200   **d) (i)** 1   **(ii)** 0

Page 19 Exercise 2

1 380   **2** 420

3 301 000 km²

4 a) 7452   **b) (i)** 7450 **(ii)** 7500   **(iii)** 7000

5 391 000 000 miles

6 a) 674   **b)** 665   **7** 1649

2.2 Rounding — Decimal Places

Page 20 Exercise 1

1 0.41, 0.405, 0.35, 0.4295, 0.4124

2 a) 0.2   **b)** 0.7   **c)** 2.7   **d)** 7.1
e) 13.6   **f)** 1.3   **g)** 72.4   **h)** 8.4
i) 0.0   **j)** 5.6   **k)** 1.9   **l)** 4.7

Page 20 Exercise 2

1 0.345, 0.3493, 0.3509, 0.3498, 0.3545

2 a) 4.57   **b)** 0.04   **c)** 6.26   **d)** 0.35
e) 3.10   **f)** 23.75   **g)** 0.34   **h)** 0.67
i) 0.08   **j)** 10.30   **k)** 1.17   **l)** 0.09

3 a) 0.967   **b)** 0.255   **c)** 2.437   **d)** 6.533
e) 0.031   **f)** 3.638   **g)** 5.684   **h)** 3.269
i) 0.009   **j)** 13.685   **k)** 5.855   **l)** 4.570

4 a) 0.13   **b)** 0.7   **c)** 5.732   **d)** 0.001
e) 21.35   **f)** 0.3   **g)** 0.40   **h)** 3.30
i) 0.01   **j)** 3.260   **k)** 11.400   **l)** 29.54
m) 6.00   **n)** 0.0046

5 0.04 kg   **6** 1.2 metres   **7** 2.458 km   **8** 0.395

2.3 Rounding — Significant Figures

Page 21 Exercise 1

1 a) 500   **b)** 30   **c)** 7000   **d)** 900
e) 4000   **f)** 80 000   **g)** 100 000 **h)** 1000

2 a) 740   **b)** 6600   **c)** 7100   **d)** 2600
e) 12   **f)** 670   **g)** 140 000 **h)** 970

3 a) 4760   **b)** 46.9   **c)** 5070   **d)** 595
e) 35 700   **f)** 694 000 **g)** 80.6   **h)** 925 000

4 a) 50   **b)** 5690   **c)** 7   **d)** 360
e) 6500   **f)** 757 000 **g)** 100   **h)** 380
i) 79 000   **j)** 600 000 **k)** 600   **l)** 4 570 000

5 1200 km/h   **6** 121 000 km   **7** 260 cm

8 Austria: 84 000 km²   Greece: 130 000 km²
Italy: 300 000 km²   Luxembourg: 2600 km²
Sweden: 450 000 km²

Page 22 Exercise 2

1 a) 0.07   **b)** 0.3   **c)** 0.0006   **d)** 0.02
e) 0.5   **f)** 0.0008   **g)** 0.1   **h)** 0.008

2 a) 0.0038   **b)** 0.026   **c)** 0.00018 **d)** 0.087
e) 3600   **f)** 0.56   **g)** 0.00070 **h)** 170 000

3 a) 0.579   **b)** 0.0852   **c)** 0.107   **d)** 0.000418
e) 147   **f)** 34.7   **g)** 0.00845 **h)** 0.438

4 a) 0.005   **b)** 0.19   **c)** 0.00439
d) 0.006   **e)** 0.0096   **f)** 0.000604
g) 1600   **h)** 2000   **i)** 0.579
j) 0.03   **k)** 0.03487   **l)** 0.050
m) 0.360   **n)** 0.1   **o)** 0.069

5 Common vole: 0.028 kg   Gerbil: 0.15 kg
Meerkat: 0.78 kg   Red squirrel: 0.20 kg
Shrew: 0.0061 kg

6 0.09 kg/m³

2.4 Estimating Answers

Page 23　　Exercise 1

1. **a)** 600 **b)** 1200 **c)** 500
   d) 0.2 **e)** 900 **f)** 700

2. **a)** 800 **b)** 360 **c)** 200
   d) 1600 **e)** 6000 **f)** 5400
   g) 32 000 **h)** 4500 **i)** 21 000

3. **a)** 1800
   b) Yes; the answer on the calculator is approximately 10 times the estimate from part **a)**.

4. **a)** C: 11.088 **b)** B: 1685.1 **c)** B: 1222.2
   d) A: 8.2 **e)** C: 13.5

5. **a)** 4 **b)** 3 **c)** 6 **d)** 4
   e) 3 **f)** 8 **g)** 10 **h)** 5
   i) 20 **j)** 40 **k)** 80 **l)** 3

6. **a)** 59.2 **b)** 62.55 **c)** 147.96 **d)** 198.85
   e) 496.8 **f)** 42.68 **g)** 7.426 **h)** 21.42
   i) 8.225 **j)** 164.4 **k)** 410.4 **l)** 78.75

7. £6.00 **8** £100 **9** £280

10. **a)** £70 000 **b)** £1 400 000

11. £20 **12** 360 000

Section 3 — Powers and Roots

3.1 Squares and Cubes

Page 25　　Exercise 1

1.

x	1	2	3	4	5
x^2	1	4	9	16	25

x	6	7	8	9	10
x^2	36	49	64	81	100

2. **a)** 121 **b)** 144 **c)** 225 **d)** 400 **e)** 900

3. **a)** 16 **b)** 0.01 **c)** 100 **d)** 0.09 **e)** 0.64
   f) 0.36 **g)** 9 **h)** 0.04 **i)** 0.16 **j)** 225

4.

x	1	2	3	4	5
x^3	1	8	27	64	125

5. **a)** 216 **b)** 1000 **c)** 1331 **d)** 8000 **e)** 27 000

6. **a)** −27 **b)** −125 **c)** −1000 **d)** 0.064
   e) 0.125 **f)** −0.125 **g)** −216 **h)** −0.027
   i) −0.512 **j)** −1728

7. **a)** 4 **b)** −8 **c)** 0.01 **d)** 64 **e)** 64

Page 26　　Exercise 2

1.

x	1	4	9	16
$\sqrt{x}$	1	2	3	4
$-\sqrt{x}$	−1	−2	−3	−4

x	25	36	100
$\sqrt{x}$	5	6	10
$-\sqrt{x}$	−5	−6	−10

2. **a)** 7 **b)** −7 **c)** 9 **d)** −9
   e) 11 **f)** 13 **g)** −12 **h)** 20

3. **a)** 8, −8 **b)** 11, −11 **c)** 13, −13 **d)** 100, −100
   e) 14, −14

Page 26　　Exercise 3

1.

x	1	8	27	1000
$\sqrt[3]{x}$	1	2	3	10

x	−1	−8	−27	−1000
$\sqrt[3]{x}$	−1	−2	−3	−10

2. **a)** 4 **b)** 5 **c)** 11 **d)** −4
   e) −5 **f)** 8 **g)** 6 **h)** −9

Page 27　　Exercise 4 — Mixed Exercise

1. **a)** 256 **b)** 1728 **c)** 9 **d)** 100
   e) −7 **f)** 169 **g)** 3375 **h)** −100

2. **a)** 19.683 **b)** 3.61 **c)** 3.16 (to 2 d.p.)
   d) 4.31 (to 2 d.p.) **e)** 0.01 **f)** 0.001
   g) 0.001 **h)** −0.01

3. **a)** 5^2 **b)** $\sqrt{0.5}$ **c)** $\sqrt{27}$
   d) 5^3 **e)** 0.5^2 **f)** $\sqrt{200}$
   g) 100^2 **h)** $\sqrt{1000}$ **i)** 4^3

3.2 Indices

Page 27　　Exercise 1

1. **a)** 3^2 **b)** 2^3 **c)** 7^5
   d) 9^6 **e)** 12^4 **f)** 17^3

2. **a)** 16 **b)** 32 **c)** 81 **d)** 4096
   e) 1296 **f)** 4913 **g)** 3125 **h)** 243

3. **a) (i)** 100 **(ii)** 1000
   (iii) 10 000 **(iv)** 100 000
   (v) 1 000 000 **(vi)** 10 000 000
   (vii) 100 000 000 **(viii)** 1 000 000 000
   b) (i) "10^{15} can be written as a '1' followed by 15 zeros."
   (ii) "10^n can be written as a '1' followed by n zeros."

4. **a)** 10^2 **b)** 10^3 **c)** 10^4 **d)** 10^5
   e) 10^6 **f)** 10^7 **g)** 10^9 **h)** 10^{12}

5. **a)** 17 **b)** 35 **c)** 65 **d)** 61
   e) 964 **f)** 1064 **g)** 118 **h)** 9657
   i) 0 **j)** 100 128

6. **a)** 1 **b)** −11 **c)** −36 **d)** 768
   e) 5000 **f)** 40 **g)** 69 **h)** 1 000 128
   i) 2592 **j)** 20 903 **k)** 512 **l)** 10 000 000
   m) 64 **n)** 745 **o)** 0.1296

7. **a)** 27 **b)** 1 **c)** 16 **d)** 81
   e) 81 **f)** 100 000 **g)** 1247 **h)** 100 002
   i) 1944 **j)** 1 000 000 000 000

Page 28　　Exercise 2

1. **a)** h^4 **b)** t^5 **c)** s^7
   d) k^6 **e)** y^4 **f)** m^5

2 **a)** $a^2 \times b^3$ **b)** $k^4 \times f^3$ **c)** $m^4 \times n^2$
    d) $s^4 \times t$ **e)** $w^3 \times v^3$ **f)** $p^2 \times q^5$

3 **a)** 100   **b)** 200   **c)** 500
    d) 800   **e)** 2000   **f)** 10 000

3.3 Laws of Indices

Page 29   Exercise 1

1 **a)** 3^8 **b)** 10^{10} **c)** 4^{11} **d)** 7^7 **e)** 2^{13}

2 **a)** 6^3 **b)** 8^3 **c)** 5^5 **d)** 6^2 **e)** 2^7

3 **a)** 4^9 **b)** 11^{10} **c)** 100^{69} **d)** 14^{28} **e)** 9^{88}

4 **a)** 4^{16} **b)** 12^4 **c)** 8^{11} **d)** 6^{32} **e)** 3^{48}
    f) 7^5 **g)** 4^8 **h)** 11^{18} **i)** 8^4 **j)** 15^{26}
    k) 129^7 **l)** 72^6 **m)** 145^{18} **n)** 188^{12} **o)** 20^{12}

5 **a)** 9   **b)** 2   **c)** 40   **d)** 4
    e) 3   **f)** 13   **g)** 7   **h)** 6
    i) 7   **j)** 5   **k)** 8   **l)** 7

6 **a)** a^{10} **b)** e^9 **c)** c^{20} **d)** b^3 **e)** m^{48}
    f) y^6 **g)** h^{19} **h)** g^{12} **i)** k^{18} **j)** b^3

7 **a)** 5   **b)** 2   **c)** 6   **d)** 7
    e) 8   **f)** 8   **g)** 3   **h)** 5

Page 30   Exercise 2

1 **a)** 3^{14} **b)** 5^{13} **c)** 8^{17} **d)** 9^{35}
    e) 7^2 **f)** 8   **g)** 12^{12} **h)** 4^{14}

2 **a)** 3^3 **b)** 8^4 **c)** 2^7 **d)** 4
    e) 7^4 **f)** 5^5 **g)** 10^5 **h)** 8^7

3 **a)** 6^{15} **b)** 2^3 **c)** 8^7 **d)** 5^6

4 $\dfrac{4^4 \div 4^3}{4}, \dfrac{5^5 \times 5^9}{(5^2)^7}$

5 **a)** a^7 **b)** z^7 **c)** m^{15} **d)** p^{12}

6 **a)** r^3 **b)** s^5 **c)** y^5 **d)** t^7

Section 4 — Factors and Multiples

4.1 Multiples

Page 31   Exercise 1

1 **a)** 4, 8, 12, 16, 20   **b)** 10, 20, 30, 40, 50
    c) 3, 6, 9, 12, 15   **d)** 6, 12, 18, 24, 30
    e) 7, 14, 21, 28, 35

2 **a)** 9, 12, 15, 18, 21   **b)** 8, 12, 16, 20
    c) 5, 15, 20

3 **a)** 16   **b)** 27, 36, 45   **c)** 30

4 **a)** 10, 20, 30, 40, 50, 60, 70, 80, 90, 100
    b) 15, 30, 45, 60, 75, 90, 105   **c)** 30, 60, 90

5 **a)** 21, 24, 27, 30, 33   **b)** 20, 24, 28, 32
    c) 24

6 30   **7** 40, 80

Page 32   Exercise 2

1 **a)** 12   **b)** 15   **c)** 24   **d)** 10
    e) 42   **f)** 36   **g)** 30   **h)** 60

2 **a)** 24   **b)** 30   **c)** 30
    d) 36   **e)** 70   **f)** 90

Page 32   Exercise 3

1 **a)** 8, 16, 24, 32, 40, 48, 56, 64, 72, 80
    b) 12, 24, 36, 48, 60, 72, 84, 96, 108, 120
    c) After 24 minutes

2 20 days   **3** 35 sweets

4.2 Factors

Page 33   Exercise 1

1 **a)** 1, 4, 8   **b)** 1, 3   **c)** 1, 3, 7
    d) 1, 4, 8, 20   **e)** 1, 4, 7   **f)** 1

2 **a)** 2, 3, 6   **b)** 2, 3, 6, 12   **c)** 2, 3, 5, 6, 15
    d) 2, 3, 6, 12   **e)** 2, 5   **f)** 3, 5, 15

3 **a)** 1, 2, 5, 10   **b)** 1, 2, 4
    c) 1, 13   **d)** 1, 2, 4, 5, 10, 20
    e) 1, 5, 25   **f)** 1, 2, 3, 4, 6, 8, 12, 24
    g) 1, 5, 7, 35   **h)** 1, 2, 4, 8, 16, 32
    i) 1, 2, 4, 5, 8, 10, 20, 40
    j) 1, 2, 5, 10, 25, 50
    k) 1, 3, 9   **l)** 1, 3, 5, 15
    m) 1, 2, 3, 4, 6, 9, 12, 18, 36
    n) 1, 7, 49   **o)** 1, 2, 3, 4, 6, 8, 12, 16, 24, 48

4 **a)** 1   **b)** 1, 2   **c)** 1, 5   **d)** 1, 2, 5, 10

5 **a)** 1, 3, 5, 15   **b)** 1, 3, 7, 21   **c)** 1, 3

6 **a)** 1, 5   **b)** 1, 3   **c)** 1, 3, 5, 15
    d) 1, 2, 5, 10   **e)** 1, 5, 25

7 **a)** 1, 5   **b)** 1, 2   **c)** 1, 5   **d)** 1

Page 34   Exercise 2

1 **a)** 1, 2, 4   **b)** 4

2 **a)** 1, 2, 5, 10   **b)** 10

3 **a)** 4   **b)** 8   **c)** 6   **d)** 12
    e) 1   **f)** 12   **g)** 7   **h)** 7

4 **a)** 1   **b)** 1   **c)** 1

5 **a)** 2   **b)** 3   **c)** 6
    d) 18   **e)** 12   **f)** 25

Page 35   Exercise 3 — Mixed Exercise

1 **a) (i)** 1   **(ii)** 3   **(iii)** 5   **(iv)** 4
    b) (i) 45   **(ii)** 36   **(iii)** 30   **(iv)** 60

2 **a)** 18
    b) No, because 5 isn't a factor of 36 (or 36 isn't a multiple of 5).
    c) 9 ways:
       1 pile of 36 sweets;   2 piles of 18 sweets
       3 piles of 12 sweets;   4 piles of 9 sweets
       6 piles of 6 sweets;   9 piles of 4 sweets
       12 piles of 3 sweets;   18 piles of 2 sweets
       36 piles of 1 sweet

3 6 ways
    1 packet of 12 cakes;   2 packets of 6 cakes
    3 packets of 4 cakes;   4 packets of 3 cakes
    6 packets of 2 cakes;   12 packets of 1 cake

4 9 ways
1 row of 100 chairs;   2 rows of 50 chairs
4 rows of 25 chairs;   5 rows of 20 chairs
10 rows of 10 chairs;   20 rows of 5 chairs
25 rows of 4 chairs;   50 rows of 2 chairs
100 rows of 1 chair

5   **a)** 100, 120, 140   **b)** 120, 150   **c)** 120

6   150   **7**   280

4.3 Prime Numbers

Page 36   Exercise 1

1   **a)** 15   **b)** 3, 5

2   **a)** 33, 35, 39
    b) $33 = 3 \times 11$, so 3 and 11 are factors
       $35 = 5 \times 7$, so 5 and 7 are factors
       $39 = 3 \times 13$, so 3 and 13 are factors

3   5, 47 and 59

4   **a)** 2, 3, 5, 7   **b)** 23, 29

5   **a) (i)** 2   **(ii)** 2 or 7
      (iii) 2 or 17   **(iv)** 2 or 37
    b) Because 2 will always be a factor.

6   They all end in zero, so 10 is a factor of all of them.
    Or: They are all even, so 2 is a factor of all of them.

Page 36   Exercise 2

1   **a) (i)**   **(ii)**

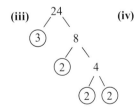

    b) (i) $14 = 2 \times 7$ **(ii)** $33 = 11 \times 3$
      (iii) $10 = 2 \times 5$ **(iv)** $25 = 5^2$

2   **a)** $15 = 3 \times 5$ **b)** $21 = 3 \times 7$ **c)** $22 = 2 \times 11$
    d) $35 = 5 \times 7$ **e)** $39 = 3 \times 13$

3   **a) (i)**   **(ii)**

    (iii)   **(iv)**

    b) (i) $30 = 2 \times 3 \times 5$ **(ii)** $44 = 2^2 \times 11$
      (iii) $24 = 2^3 \times 3$ **(iv)** $72 = 2^3 \times 3^2$

4   **a) (i)**

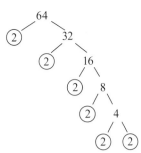

    (ii)

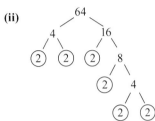

    (iii)

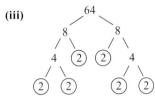

    b) $64 = 2^6$. The prime factors are the same whichever
      factor tree you use.

5   **a)** $42 = 2 \times 3 \times 7$ **b)** $66 = 2 \times 3 \times 11$
    c) $70 = 2 \times 5 \times 7$ **d)** $190 = 2 \times 5 \times 19$
    e) $210 = 2 \times 3 \times 5 \times 7$

6   **a)** $18 = 2 \times 3^2$ **b)** $50 = 2 \times 5^2$
    c) $36 = 2^2 \times 3^2$ **d)** $150 = 2 \times 3 \times 5^2$
    e) $32 = 2^5$

7   **a)** $8 = 2^3$ **b)** $6 = 2 \times 3$
    c) $28 = 2^2 \times 7$ **d)** $27 = 3^3$
    e) $16 = 2^4$ **f)** $60 = 2^2 \times 3 \times 5$
    g) $40 = 2^3 \times 5$ **h)** $98 = 2 \times 7^2$
    i) $24 = 2^3 \times 3$ **j)** $128 = 2^7$
    k) $168 = 2^3 \times 3 \times 7$ **l)** $225 = 3^2 \times 5^2$
    m) $325 = 5^2 \times 13$ **n)** $1000 = 2^3 \times 5^3$
    o) $46 = 2 \times 23$

8   **a)** $75 = 3 \times 5^2$
    b) 3. This is because $75 \times 3 = 3^2 \times 5^2$ — which is a
      square number because 3 and 5 are both raised to
      an even power (2).

Section 5 — Fractions

5.1 Equivalent Fractions

Page 38   Exercise 1

1   **a)** 2, 3, 4   **b)** $\frac{2}{4}$, $\frac{3}{6}$, $\frac{4}{8}$

2 $\frac{2}{6}$, $\frac{3}{9}$, $\frac{4}{12}$

3   **a)** 2   **b)** 3   **c)** 12   **d)** 3
    e) 25   **f)** 18   **g)** 60   **h)** 90

4 **a)** 3 **b)** 5 **c)** 2 **d)** 3
 e) 5 **f)** 27 **g)** 16 **h)** 11

Page 39   Exercise 2

1 **a)** 2 **b)** $\frac{1}{5}$

c) Yes. There are no further common factors of the numerator and denominator.

2 **a)** 5

b) **i)** $\frac{9}{15}$

ii) No. It can be simplified further by dividing numerator and denominator by 3, to get $\frac{3}{5}$

3 **a)** $\frac{1}{3}$ **b)** $\frac{1}{4}$ **c)** $\frac{1}{2}$ **d)** $\frac{1}{8}$
 e) $\frac{1}{5}$ **f)** $\frac{5}{12}$ **g)** $\frac{3}{4}$ **h)** $\frac{4}{5}$
 i) $\frac{3}{5}$ **j)** $\frac{3}{8}$ **k)** $\frac{3}{4}$ **l)** $\frac{1}{4}$

4 **a)** $\frac{1}{3}, \frac{1}{4}, \frac{1}{3} - \frac{5}{20}$ **b)** $\frac{3}{4}, \frac{3}{5}, \frac{3}{5} - \frac{6}{8}$
 c) $\frac{2}{9}, \frac{2}{11}, \frac{2}{9} - \frac{6}{33}$ **d)** $\frac{3}{4}, \frac{3}{4}, \frac{3}{5} - \frac{24}{40}$

5 **a)** $\frac{7}{10}$ **b)** $\frac{35}{46}$ **c)** $\frac{17}{29}$ **d)** $\frac{49}{166}$

5.2 Mixed Numbers

Page 40   Exercise 1

1 **a)** $\frac{6}{3}$ **b)** $\frac{12}{4}$

2 **a)** $\frac{12}{6}$ **b)** $\frac{25}{5}$ **c)** $\frac{30}{5}$ **d)** $\frac{65}{5}$

3 **a)** 12 **b)** $\frac{13}{3}$

4 **a)** 15 **b)** $\frac{17}{5}$

5 **a)** $\frac{4}{3}$ **b)** $\frac{9}{7}$ **c)** $\frac{5}{2}$ **d)** $\frac{25}{7}$

6 **a)** $\frac{9}{5}$ **b)** $\frac{17}{12}$ **c)** $\frac{29}{10}$ **d)** $\frac{53}{10}$
 e) $\frac{19}{4}$ **f)** $\frac{59}{6}$ **g)** $\frac{62}{5}$ **h)** $\frac{110}{7}$
 i) $\frac{41}{6}$ **j)** $\frac{28}{9}$ **k)** $\frac{103}{10}$ **l)** $\frac{23}{3}$

Page 41   Exercise 2

1 **a)** 7 **b)** 2 **c)** 9 **d)** 6

2 **a)** 4 **b)** $1\frac{4}{7}$

3 **a)** 15 **b)** $5\frac{2}{3}$

4 **a)** $1\frac{2}{3}$ **b)** $1\frac{4}{5}$ **c)** $1\frac{7}{10}$ **d)** $1\frac{5}{7}$ **e)** $1\frac{2}{11}$
 f) $2\frac{1}{4}$ **g)** $2\frac{1}{6}$ **h)** $3\frac{1}{5}$ **i)** $2\frac{2}{9}$ **j)** $3\frac{2}{3}$

5 **a)** $\frac{13}{2}$ **b)** $6\frac{1}{2}$

6 **a)** $1\frac{1}{2}$ **b)** $2\frac{1}{2}$ **c)** $3\frac{1}{3}$ **d)** $4\frac{1}{2}$ **e)** $1\frac{1}{3}$
 f) $1\frac{2}{5}$ **g)** $2\frac{1}{4}$ **h)** $4\frac{1}{4}$ **i)** $5\frac{2}{3}$ **j)** $12\frac{1}{4}$

7 **a)** $\frac{5}{2}$ **b)** $3\frac{1}{2}$ **c)** $\frac{15}{4}$ **d)** $\frac{11}{3}$

5.3 Ordering Fractions

Page 42   Exercise 1

1 **a)** $\frac{2}{6}, \frac{1}{6}$ **b)** $\frac{2}{10}, \frac{3}{10}$ **c)** $\frac{4}{16}, \frac{5}{16}$
 d) $\frac{8}{20}, \frac{7}{20}$ **e)** $\frac{3}{8}, \frac{2}{8}$ **f)** $\frac{1}{12}, \frac{8}{12}$
 g) $\frac{5}{18}, \frac{4}{18}$ **h)** $\frac{8}{28}, \frac{5}{28}$

2 **a)** $\frac{5}{10}, \frac{2}{10}$ **b)** $\frac{4}{12}, \frac{3}{12}$ **c)** $\frac{10}{70}, \frac{7}{70}$
 d) $\frac{7}{21}, \frac{3}{21}$ **e)** $\frac{5}{40}, \frac{16}{40}$ **f)** $\frac{3}{12}, \frac{1}{12}$
 g) $\frac{2}{12}, \frac{3}{12}$ **h)** $\frac{3}{24}, \frac{4}{24}$

3 **a)** $\frac{2}{9}, \frac{3}{9}$ **b)** $\frac{8}{12}, \frac{9}{12}$ **c)** $\frac{35}{42}, \frac{6}{42}$
 d) $\frac{4}{18}, \frac{9}{18}$ **e)** $\frac{15}{40}, \frac{32}{40}$ **f)** $\frac{10}{12}, \frac{7}{12}$
 g) $\frac{35}{40}, \frac{12}{40}$ **h)** $\frac{18}{45}, \frac{20}{45}$

4 **a)** $\frac{18}{24}, \frac{15}{24}, \frac{14}{24}$ **b)** $\frac{4}{20}, \frac{14}{20}, \frac{9}{20}$ **c)** $\frac{6}{42}, \frac{8}{42}, \frac{15}{42}$
 d) $\frac{12}{24}, \frac{9}{24}, \frac{16}{24}$ **e)** $\frac{24}{60}, \frac{25}{60}, \frac{22}{60}$ **f)** $\frac{5}{40}, \frac{14}{40}, \frac{24}{40}$
 g) $\frac{28}{42}, \frac{30}{42}, \frac{35}{42}$ **h)** $\frac{100}{360}, \frac{105}{360}, \frac{132}{360}$

Page 43   Exercise 2

1 **a)** $\frac{5}{6}, \frac{4}{6}$ **b)** $\frac{5}{6}$

2 **a)** $\frac{16}{40}, \frac{15}{40}$ **b)** $\frac{2}{5}$

3 **a)** $\frac{5}{8}$ **b)** $\frac{7}{10}$ **c)** $\frac{9}{14}$ **d)** $\frac{2}{3}$
 e) $\frac{5}{6}$ **f)** $\frac{2}{3}$ **g)** $\frac{3}{4}$ **h)** $\frac{3}{4}$

4 **a)** $\frac{15}{45}, \frac{12}{45}, \frac{10}{45}$ **b)** $\frac{2}{9}, \frac{4}{15}, \frac{1}{3}$

5 **a)** $\frac{7}{16}, \frac{1}{2}, \frac{5}{8}$ **b)** $\frac{3}{10}, \frac{7}{20}, \frac{2}{5}$ **c)** $\frac{7}{12}, \frac{5}{8}, \frac{3}{4}$
 d) $\frac{19}{24}, \frac{5}{6}, \frac{11}{12}$

6 **a)** $\frac{5}{12}, \frac{4}{9}, \frac{2}{3}$ **b)** $\frac{4}{5}, \frac{9}{10}, \frac{11}{12}$ **c)** $\frac{5}{22}, \frac{1}{4}, \frac{3}{11}$
 d) $\frac{7}{9}, \frac{4}{5}, \frac{13}{15}$

7 **a)** $\frac{13}{16}, \frac{5}{6}, \frac{7}{8}$ **b)** $\frac{7}{27}, \frac{4}{15}, \frac{13}{45}$ **c)** $\frac{5}{16}, \frac{7}{20}, \frac{9}{25}$
 d) $\frac{4}{15}, \frac{11}{36}, \frac{9}{24}$

8 Ben   **9** Charlene

5.4 Adding and Subtracting Fractions

Page 44   Exercise 1

1 **a)** $\frac{2}{3}$ **b)** $\frac{2}{5}$ **c)** $\frac{2}{11}$ **d)** $\frac{2}{5}$
 e) $\frac{1}{2}$ **f)** $\frac{2}{3}$ **g)** $\frac{1}{2}$ **h)** $\frac{3}{8}$

2 **a)** $1\frac{1}{2}$ **b)** $1\frac{1}{2}$ **c)** $1\frac{3}{5}$ **d)** $1\frac{1}{5}$
 e) $1\frac{9}{11}$ **f)** $2\frac{1}{7}$ **g)** $1\frac{4}{15}$ **h)** $1\frac{9}{20}$

3 **a)** $\frac{2}{4}$ and $\frac{1}{4}$ **b)** $\frac{3}{4}$

4 a) $\frac{7}{10}$ b) $\frac{5}{8}$ c) $\frac{2}{3}$ d) $\frac{1}{2}$
   e) $\frac{1}{9}$ f) $\frac{3}{8}$ g) $\frac{3}{10}$ h) $\frac{1}{18}$

5 a) $\frac{27}{30}$ and $\frac{25}{30}$ b) $\frac{1}{15}$

6 a) $\frac{8}{15}$ b) $\frac{1}{15}$ c) $1\frac{1}{10}$ d) $\frac{5}{12}$
   e) $1\frac{7}{15}$ f) $1\frac{11}{15}$ g) $1\frac{5}{28}$ h) $1\frac{32}{99}$
   i) $\frac{31}{120}$ j) $1\frac{29}{63}$ k) $1\frac{16}{35}$ l) $1\frac{43}{80}$

7 a) $1\frac{5}{18}$ b) $\frac{7}{16}$ c) $\frac{3}{7}$ d) $1\frac{3}{4}$

Page 45 Exercise 2

1 $\frac{5}{9}$ **2** $\frac{2}{7}$ **3** $\frac{1}{2}$ **4** $\frac{7}{20}$ **5** $\frac{3}{10}$

Page 46 Exercise 3

1 a) $\frac{9}{5}$ b) $2\frac{2}{5}$

2 a) 2 b) $3\frac{1}{4}$ c) $3\frac{3}{5}$
   d) 3 e) $\frac{6}{7}$ f) $1\frac{2}{3}$

3 a) (i) $\frac{11}{5}$ (ii) $\frac{8}{5}$ b) $\frac{3}{5}$

4 a) $3\frac{4}{5}$ b) $1\frac{1}{2}$ c) $6\frac{1}{11}$
   d) $2\frac{3}{5}$ e) 5 f) $5\frac{1}{2}$

5 a) (i) $\frac{11}{4}$ (ii) $\frac{3}{2}$
   b) (i) $\frac{11}{4}$ (ii) $\frac{6}{4}$ c) $4\frac{1}{4}$

6 a) $3\frac{7}{10}$ b) $2\frac{8}{9}$ c) $5\frac{1}{4}$ d) $6\frac{3}{8}$
   e) $1\frac{5}{8}$ f) $1\frac{7}{12}$ g) $2\frac{5}{14}$ h) $5\frac{17}{18}$

7 a) (i) $\frac{7}{6}$ (ii) $\frac{25}{8}$
   b) (i) $\frac{28}{24}$ (ii) $\frac{75}{24}$ c) $4\frac{7}{24}$

8 a) $2\frac{7}{20}$ b) $3\frac{7}{24}$ c) $5\frac{22}{35}$ d) $5\frac{19}{30}$
   e) $3\frac{1}{28}$ f) $1\frac{28}{45}$ g) $\frac{11}{28}$ h) $6\frac{4}{33}$
   i) $8\frac{59}{60}$ j) $3\frac{11}{72}$ k) $5\frac{8}{63}$ l) $3\frac{17}{30}$

5.5 Multiplying and Dividing Fractions

Page 47 Exercise 1

1 a) 2 b) 2 c) 3 d) 15
   e) 3 f) 5 g) 4 h) 7
   i) 13 j) 6 k) 8 l) 8

2 a) $4\frac{1}{2}$ b) $2\frac{1}{2}$ c) $8\frac{1}{2}$ d) $2\frac{1}{2}$
   e) $3\frac{1}{5}$ f) $5\frac{1}{4}$ g) $9\frac{3}{4}$ h) $5\frac{4}{5}$
   i) $3\frac{1}{3}$ j) $2\frac{2}{9}$ k) $4\frac{1}{6}$ l) $13\frac{1}{3}$

Page 48 Exercise 2

1 a) 8 b) 21 c) 12 d) 18
   e) 25 f) 14 g) 15 h) 36
   i) 4 j) 20 k) 28 l) 56

2 a) $11\frac{1}{4}$ b) $8\frac{4}{5}$ c) $12\frac{3}{5}$ d) $22\frac{4}{5}$
   e) $13\frac{5}{7}$ f) $22\frac{1}{2}$ g) $21\frac{1}{3}$ h) $27\frac{1}{5}$

   i) $17\frac{7}{9}$ j) $18\frac{3}{4}$ k) $19\frac{7}{11}$ l) $38\frac{3}{4}$

3 a) 27 b) 22 c) 24 d) 30
   e) 15 f) 9 g) $27\frac{1}{2}$ h) $26\frac{1}{4}$

Page 49 Exercise 3

1 a) $\frac{1}{18}$ b) $\frac{2}{15}$ c) $\frac{3}{28}$ d) $\frac{3}{25}$
   e) $\frac{5}{24}$ f) $\frac{8}{35}$ g) $\frac{10}{49}$ h) $\frac{21}{80}$

2 a) $\frac{1}{6}$ b) $\frac{1}{10}$ c) $\frac{1}{9}$ d) $\frac{5}{16}$
   e) $\frac{3}{14}$ f) $\frac{3}{8}$ g) $\frac{3}{4}$ h) $\frac{1}{4}$

3 a) $\frac{10}{7}$ b) $\frac{20}{21}$

4 a) $\frac{1}{2}$ b) $1\frac{13}{20}$ c) $1\frac{2}{9}$ d) $1\frac{1}{2}$
   e) $\frac{10}{21}$ f) $\frac{23}{48}$ g) $3\frac{17}{25}$ h) $\frac{11}{12}$

5 a) $\frac{17}{5}$ b) $\frac{3}{2}$ c) $5\frac{1}{10}$

6 a) $1\frac{1}{2}$ b) 4 c) $2\frac{26}{27}$ d) $2\frac{4}{5}$
   e) $7\frac{29}{42}$ f) $6\frac{11}{24}$ g) $6\frac{2}{63}$ h) $16\frac{29}{60}$

Page 50 Exercise 4

1 a) 3 b) 7 c) $\frac{5}{4}$ d) $\frac{8}{5}$
   e) $\frac{27}{12}$ f) $\frac{10}{9}$ g) $\frac{19}{6}$ h) $\frac{107}{84}$

2 a) $\frac{1}{5}$ b) $\frac{1}{12}$ c) $\frac{1}{9}$ d) $\frac{1}{27}$

3 a) $\frac{5}{4}$ b) $\frac{4}{5}$

4 a) $\frac{5}{8}$ b) $\frac{7}{15}$ c) $\frac{9}{13}$ d) $\frac{4}{11}$
   e) $\frac{12}{23}$ f) $\frac{4}{13}$ g) $\frac{3}{17}$ h) $\frac{7}{30}$

Page 51 Exercise 5

1 a) $\frac{3}{10}$ b) $\frac{5}{12}$ c) $\frac{7}{12}$ d) $\frac{14}{15}$
   e) $\frac{25}{48}$ f) $\frac{12}{35}$ g) $\frac{15}{16}$ h) $\frac{49}{50}$

2 a) $\frac{4}{9}$ b) $\frac{1}{2}$ c) $\frac{4}{7}$ d) $1\frac{1}{2}$
   e) $\frac{11}{24}$ f) $1\frac{1}{3}$ g) $1\frac{1}{3}$ h) $\frac{10}{11}$

3 a) 2 b) 3 c) 5 d) $4\frac{4}{7}$
   e) $\frac{1}{6}$ f) $\frac{2}{15}$ g) $\frac{1}{16}$ h) $\frac{1}{14}$

4 a) $\frac{7}{4}$ b) $\frac{4}{7}$ c) $\frac{8}{35}$

5 a) $\frac{3}{8}$ b) $\frac{5}{9}$ c) $\frac{17}{21}$ d) $\frac{20}{27}$
   e) $3\frac{1}{8}$ f) $1\frac{1}{15}$ g) $2\frac{4}{7}$ h) $\frac{20}{21}$

6 a) $\frac{7}{3}$ and $\frac{9}{5}$ b) $\frac{5}{9}$ c) $1\frac{8}{27}$

7 a) $3\frac{1}{3}$ b) $7\frac{1}{2}$ c) $4\frac{2}{3}$ d) $4\frac{4}{5}$
   e) $\frac{10}{51}$ f) $\frac{9}{28}$ g) $\frac{8}{49}$ h) $\frac{5}{18}$
   i) $1\frac{1}{24}$ j) $2\frac{2}{15}$ k) $2\frac{1}{14}$ l) $1\frac{47}{63}$
   m) $4\frac{1}{14}$ n) $2\frac{18}{23}$ o) $2\frac{6}{7}$ p) $1\frac{27}{50}$

5.6 Fractions and Decimals

Page 52   Exercise 1

1   a) Terminating   b) Terminating
    c) Recurring   d) Terminating
    e) Recurring   f) Terminating
    g) Recurring   h) Terminating
    i) Terminating   j) Recurring
    k) Terminating   l) Recurring

2   a) 0.75   b) 0.8   c) 0.625   d) 0.35
    e) 0.4375   f) 0.15625   g) 0.175   h) 0.46
    i) 0.88   j) 0.828125   k) 0.658   l) 0.7578125

3   a) 1.6   b) 2.125   c) 6.35   d) 2.37
    e) 4.719   f) 5.76   g) 7.34375   h) 8.4375

4   a) $0.\dot{3}$ b) $0.1\dot{8}$ c) $0.8\dot{3}$ d) $0.\dot{4}$

5   a) $\frac{1}{4}, \frac{3}{10}, \frac{7}{16}$ b) $\frac{5}{6}, \frac{17}{20}, \frac{7}{8}$ c) $\frac{9}{25}, \frac{3}{8}, \frac{4}{10}$

6   a) $0.60\dot{3}$ b) $0.123\dot{4}$ c) $0.2\dot{6}$ d) $0.\dot{1}23\dot{4}$

Page 54   Exercise 2

1   a) 0.9   b) 0.2   c) 0.3   d) 0.8

2   a) 0.91   b) 0.42   c) 0.99   d) 0.08

3   a) 0.007   b) 0.201   c) 0.041   d) 0.027

4   a) 0.52   b) 0.6   c) 0.635   d) 0.34
    e) 0.086   f) 0.46   g) 0.9   h) 0.492

5   a) 65   b) 0.65

6   a) $\frac{32}{100}$ b) 0.32

7   a) 0.2   b) 0.3   c) 0.9   d) 0.6

8   a) 0.34   b) 0.88   c) 0.86   d) 0.32

9   a) 0.002   b) 0.132   c) 0.515   d) 0.102

10 a) 0.4   b) 0.48   c) 0.666   d) 0.48
    e) 0.09   f) 0.86   g) 0.35   h) 0.615

Page 55   Exercise 3

1   0.3125   2   0.375

3   a) 0.25   b) 0.75   c) 0.05   d) 0.025
    e) 0.0625   f) 0.875   g) 0.175   h) 0.1625

Page 55   Exercise 4

1   a) $\frac{7}{10}$ b) $\frac{9}{10}$ c) $\frac{1}{10}$ d) $\frac{2}{5}$

2   a) $\frac{93}{100}$ b) $\frac{7}{100}$ c) $\frac{23}{100}$ d) $\frac{47}{100}$

3   a) $\frac{1}{250}$ b) $\frac{801}{1000}$ c) $\frac{983}{1000}$ d) $\frac{49}{500}$

4   a) $\frac{3}{5}$ b) $\frac{3}{25}$ c) $\frac{59}{250}$ d) $\frac{7}{20}$
    e) $\frac{1}{20}$ f) $\frac{21}{250}$ g) $\frac{6}{25}$ h) $\frac{7}{40}$
    i) $\frac{7}{500}$ j) $\frac{2}{25}$ k) $\frac{1}{8}$ l) $\frac{3}{8}$

Page 56   Exercise 5

1   a) $0.5\dot{4}$

2   a) $0.\dot{3}$ b) $0.\dot{1}$ c) $0.08\dot{3}$ d) $0.\dot{4}$
    e) $0.1\dot{6}$ f) $0.0\dot{9}$ g) $0.\dot{6}$ h) $0.3\dot{6}$

i) $0.4\dot{6}$ j) $0.8\dot{3}$ k) $0.2\dot{6}$ l) $0.\dot{7}$

3   a) $0.3\dot{6}$ b) $0.6\dot{2}$ c) $0.5\dot{2}$ d) $0.24\dot{5}$

4   a) (i) $0.\dot{1}4285\dot{7}$ (ii) $0.\dot{2}8571\dot{4}$ (iii) $0.\dot{4}2857\dot{1}$
       (iv) $0.\dot{5}7142\dot{8}$ (v) $0.\dot{7}1428\dot{5}$
    b) The same pattern of 6 numbers in each.
    c) $0.\dot{8}5714\dot{2}$

5.7 Fractions Problems

Page 57   Exercise 1

1   $\frac{18}{27}, \frac{40}{60}, \frac{12}{18}$ 2 $\frac{10}{8}, \frac{25}{20}$

3   a) 0.35   b) 0.084   c) 0.075   d) 0.875

4   $\frac{2}{3}, \frac{11}{16}, \frac{3}{4}, \frac{5}{6}$

5   a) 0.39, 0.35, 0.32, 0.3
    b) $\frac{3}{10}, \frac{8}{25}, \frac{7}{20}, \frac{39}{100}$

6

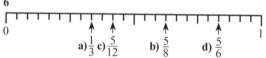

7   a) $1\frac{8}{21}$ b) $\frac{11}{72}$ c) $1\frac{1}{10}$ d) $\frac{11}{40}$

8   a) $\frac{7}{22}$ b) $1\frac{2}{7}$ c) $\frac{3}{7}$ d) $\frac{8}{9}$

9   a) $5\frac{21}{40}$ b) $\frac{17}{40}$ c) $7\frac{13}{20}$ d) $2\frac{1}{8}$

10 a) $2\frac{13}{18}$ b) $2\frac{1}{2}$ c) $24\frac{1}{16}$ d) $4\frac{2}{5}$

11 $4\frac{13}{16}$ inches

12 a) $\frac{7}{12}$ b) $\frac{23}{30}$ c) $\frac{3}{5}$ d) $-\frac{3}{16}$
    e) $1\frac{4}{5}$ f) $1\frac{7}{20}$ g) $-8\frac{5}{6}$ h) $2\frac{47}{56}$

13 a) (i) $2\frac{1}{2}$ (ii) 3   (iii) $1\frac{1}{4}$
    b) The answer is always 1.

14 a) $\frac{1}{6}, \frac{2}{7}, \frac{1}{3}, \frac{4}{5}$
    b) $6, 3\frac{1}{2}, 3, 1\frac{1}{4}$ (in the order from **a**))
    c) $6, 3\frac{1}{2}, 3, 1\frac{1}{4}$
       They are in the same order as the fractions in
       a), because the smaller a fraction, the larger its
       reciprocal.

15 a) Terminating   b) Recurring   c) Recurring
    d) Recurring   e) Terminating

16 $\frac{5}{6}$ and $\frac{2}{9}$ 17 a) $10\frac{9}{20}$ cm   b) $5\frac{17}{20}$ cm²

18 a) $\frac{2}{5}$ b) $\frac{1}{10}$

19 10
    (The cat will eat $9\frac{1}{3}$ tins, but you can't buy $\frac{1}{3}$ of a tin.)

20 16 questions

21 a) $\frac{4}{15}$ b) 20 red, 24 blue and 16 yellow.

22 $\frac{11}{15}$

23 a) 40   b) $\frac{4}{5}$ c) 80

24 a) $\frac{7}{10}$ **b)** $\frac{5}{12}$ **c)** $\frac{41}{42}$

Section 6 — Ratio and Proportion

6.1   Ratios and Simplifying

Page 59   Exercise 1

1 $3:1$ **2** $1:3$ **3** $1:6$ **4** $17:14$

5 $23:15$ **6** $2:6=1:3$ **7** $4:2=2:1$

8   **a)** $1:4$ **b)** $1:3$ **c)** $4:1$ **d)** $2:3$
       e) $4:1$ **f)** $5:2$ **g)** $1:4$ **h)** $5:3$
       i) $4:3$ **j)** $25:3$ **k)** $2:3$ **l)** $3:5$
       m) $11:1$ **n)** $2:5$ **o)** $2:3$ **p)** $4:3$
       q) $1:4$ **r)** $5:2$ **s)** $3:7$ **t)** $11:3$

9   **a)** $3:1:2$ **b)** $5:4:1$ **c)** $7:5:1$ **d)** $6:3:5$
       e) $2:1:5$ **f)** $6:2:5$ **g)** $2:3:10$ **h)** $3:7:6$
       i) $3:8:4$ **j)** $9:10:18$

10 $3:1$ **11** $4:3$ **12** $2:7$ **13** $6:5$ **14** $13:8$

Page 60   Exercise 2

1   **a)** $1:10$ **b)** $1:2$ **c)** $1:100$ **d)** $2:1$
       e) $2:5$ **f)** $3:20$ **g)** $3:10$ **h)** $2:7$

2   **a)** $20:3$
       b) $3:13$ (using weeks) or $84:365$ (using days)
       c) $4:55$ **d)** $3:100$ **e)** $15:2$
       f) $5:3$ **g)** $1:20$ **h)** $5:2$

3 $1:20$ **4** $1:40$ **5** $1:9$

6 $3:14$ **7** $4:11$ **8** $2:5$

Page 61   Exercise 3

1   **a)** $1:3$ **b)** $1:5$ **c)** $1:4$ **d)** $1:4$
       e) $1:3.5$ **f)** $1:6.5$ **g)** $1:3.25$ **h)** $1:0.5$
       i) $1:0.3$ **j)** $1:3.5$ **k)** $1:0.625$ **l)** $1:1.8$

2   **a)** $1:5$ **b)** $1:50$ **c)** $1:4$ **d)** $1:40$
       e) $1:80$ **f)** $1:40$ **g)** $1:12.5$ **h)** $1:0.2$

3 $1:8$ **4** $1:3$ **5** $1:20$ **6** $1:40\,000$

7   1.25 parts   **8** £1 : 8.5 krone   **9** $1:2$

6.2   Using Ratios

Page 62   Exercise 1

1   12   **2**   2   **3**   18   **4**   9

5   189   **6**   750   **7**   50 g   **8**   35 cm

9   £56   **10** 1.98 m   **11** 1500 ml

12 9 slices of courgette, 12 slices of goat's cheese

13 Lizzy is 165 cm, Dave is 185 cm

14 Max – 30 minutes, Maisie – 20 minutes

15 7   **16** 12   **17** 4   **18** 9 minutes

Page 63   Exercise 2

1 $\frac{1}{4}$ **2** $\frac{3}{5}$ **3** $\frac{4}{7}$ **4** $\frac{1}{3}$

5 $\frac{4}{13}$ **6** $\frac{7}{20}$ **7** $\frac{7}{14}=\frac{1}{2}$ **8** $\frac{1}{10}$

9 $\frac{5}{35}=\frac{1}{7}$ **10 a)** $\frac{5}{10}=\frac{1}{2}$ **b)** $\frac{3}{10}$

11 a) $\frac{11}{22}=\frac{1}{2}$ **b)** $\frac{3}{22}$ **c)** $\frac{14}{22}=\frac{7}{11}$

Page 64   Exercise 3

1 $1:2$ **2** $1:7$ **3** $3:7$ **4** $7:5$ **5** $16:3$

6 $1:5:2$ **7** $3:1$ **8** $3:1$ **9** $3:4:1$

6.3   Dividing in a Given Ratio

Page 65   Exercise 1

1   **a)** £32 and £16   **b)** £12 and £36
       c) £40 and £8   **d)** £28 and £20

2   **a)** 72 kg and 18 kg   **b)** 70 kg and 20 kg
       c) 48 kg and 42 kg   **d)** 36 kg and 54 kg

3   **a)** 7 m and 49 m   **b)** 28 m and 28 m
       c) 40 m and 16 m   **d)** 44 m and 12 m

4   **a)** 100 ml and 900 ml   **b)** 500 ml and 500 ml
       c) 150 ml and 850 ml   **d)** 570 ml and 430 ml

5   **a)** 24 cm, 36 cm and 12 cm
       b) 16 cm, 16 cm and 40 cm
       c) 30 cm, 18 cm and 24 cm
       d) 28 cm, 24 cm and 20 cm

6   **a)** £15, £60 and £75   **b)** £45, £15 and £90
       c) £60, £70 and £20   **d)** £65, £55 and £30

7   **a)** £10   **b)** 198 g   **c)** 10 kg   **d)** 500 ml

8   **a)** £22.50   **b)** 21.6 g   **c)** 75 kg   **d)** 15 000 ml

Page 66   Exercise 2

1   Kat – 18, Lindsay – 12

2   12 sandwiches and 20 sandwiches

3   72 men and 40 women

4   Lauren – £640, Cara – £560

5   Yellow – 24 litres, red – 18 litres

6   20   **7** 525   **8** £3420

Page 66   Exercise 3

1   Nicky – 8, Jacinta – 16, Charlie – 12

2   £1500, £2500 and £2000

3   Gemma – 155 cm, Alisha – 160 cm,
       Omar – 175 cm

4   Raspberries – 150 g, strawberries – 225 g,
       redcurrants – 75 g

5   £25   **6** 40   **7** 14

8   72°, 144°, 36° and 108°

9   Length = 30 cm, width = 6 cm

6.4   Proportion

Page 67   Exercise 1

1   **a)** £70   **b)** £175   **c)** £700

2   **a)** €11.40   **b)** €22.80   **c)** €114   **d)** €969

3 £54   4 £378   5 £880   6 3 kg

7 3.75 l   8 £12.96   9 917 Japanese yen

10 a) £13.50   b) £63   c) £270

11 £80   12 £13.86

Page 68   Exercise 2

1 a) 3 books   b) 8 books   c) 25 books

2 a) £8.77   b) £87.72   c) £219.30

3 3.75 kg   4 £39.47   5 4 DVDs

6 13 builders   7 20 people   8 £6.16   9 5 kilos

Page 68   Exercise 3

1 a) 52 minutes   b) 20 km

2 a) 357 km   b) 56 l

3 a) 73.50 Swiss francs   b) £20

6.5 Ratio and Proportion Problems

Page 69   Exercise 1

1 a) $2:5$ b) $1:2.5$ c) $0.4:1$

2 a) $2:5$ b) $\frac{18}{63} = \frac{2}{7}$

3 a) $\frac{8}{9}$ b) 56

4 36 purple cards

5 a) 80 g   b) 392 g   c) 6 cupcakes

6 £96   7 £90

8 a) 5200 rand   b) £122.45

9 30 cm   10 15 books   11 Caroline's is stronger

Section 7 — Percentages

7.1 Percentages

Page 70   Exercise 1

1 a) 40%   b) 47%   c) 61%   d) 89%

2 a) 13%   b) 27%   c) 76%   d) 99%

3 13%   4 a) $\frac{46}{100}$ b) 46%

5 a) $\frac{12}{25}$ b) $\frac{48}{100}$ c) 48%

6 a) $\frac{45}{300}$ b) $\frac{15}{100}$ c) 15%

7 a) 44%   b) 66%   c) 15%   d) 80%
   e) 6%   f) 33%   g) 25%   h) 89%

8 a) 25%   b) 60%   c) 60%   d) 20%
   e) 60%   f) 70%   g) 84%   h) 75%
   i) 40%   j) 20%   k) 40%   l) 30%

9 a) 75%   b) 25%

10 40%   11 40%

Page 72   Exercise 2

1 a) 62.5% b) 85%   c) 12.2% d) 41%
   e) 68.8% f) 28%   g) 38%   h) 40.4%

2 60%   3 45%   4 95%

5 a) 55%   b) 32.5% c) 12.5% d) 8%
   e) 37.5% f) 82.5% g) 32.4% h) 3.5%

6 a) 98%   b) 15%   7 18.5%   8 30%

Page 73   Exercise 3

1 a) 12   b) 41   c) 7.5   d) 9
   e) 20   f) 30   g) 9   h) 27

2 a) 12   b) 36

3 a) 12
   b) (i) 6   (ii) 24   (iii) 30   (iv) 48

4 a) 9   b) 15   c) 7   d) 13
   e) 27   f) 60   g) 77   h) 56
   i) 33   j) 119   k) 225   l) 78

5 £59.50   6 4.95 m   7 £1330

Page 73   Exercise 4

1 a) 34   b) 0.99   c) 6.3   d) 73.8
   e) 217.6 f) 77.7   g) 485.85 h) 584.73
   i) 420.67 j) 674.86 k) 699.79 l) 874.56

2 8.16 kg   3 119.35 km   4 15   5 £28.56

6 46% of £28 is larger by 34p

7 1584 ml (or 1.584 litres)

7.2 Percentage Increase and Decrease

Page 74   Exercise 1

1 a) 180   b) 540

2 a) 36   b) 156

3 a) 16   b) 144

4 a) 16.8   b) 67.2

5 a) 99   b) 45   c) 75   d) 140
   e) 324   f) 176   g) 210   h) 32.5
   i) 19.8   j) 552   k) 203   l) 185

6 a) 30   b) 49.5   c) 18   d) 12
   e) 17.5   f) 60   g) 48   h) 75
   i) 3.3   j) 67.5   k) 91   l) 442

7 a) 543.9   b) 117.16 c) 75.35   d) 143.29
   e) 177.92 f) 570.84 g) 1614.06 h) 1346.97

8 a) 70.84   b) 28.44   c) 71.34   d) 57.57
   e) 117.18 f) 118.94 g) 199.95 h) 75.87

Page 75   Exercise 2

1 £241.50   2 £28 175   3 247 acres

4 £10.50   5 £582   6 2040

7 £921.85   8 £339.45   9 £713.73

10 £71.19   11 60 inches

12 a) £867.75   b) £798.33   13 £31 291.40

Page 76   Exercise 3

1 a) £380   b) £385   c) Mary, by £5.

2 a) £9900 b) £10 540 c) The van, by £640

3 Jason, by 1.2 gallons.   4 Raj, by £250.

5 House A, by £4650. **6** Electricity, by £97.92.

7 Meristock, by 24 264 people (accept 24 265).

Page 77   Exercise 4

1 a) 20% **b)** 10% **c)** 15%

2 a) 20% **b)** 12% **c)** 8%

3 a) 27 **b)** $\frac{27}{45}$ **c)** 60%

4 a) 12 kg **b)** 15%

5 8% **6** 25% **7** 40% **8** 14%

9 12% **10** 60% **11** 2%

12 a) 32% **b)** 50% **c)** 66%

7.3 Percentages, Fractions and Decimals

Page 79   Exercise 1

1 a) (i) 50% **(ii)** 0.5 **(iii)** $\frac{1}{2}$

   b) (i) 25% **(ii)** 0.25 **(iii)** $\frac{1}{4}$

   c) (i) 10% **(ii)** 0.1 **(iii)** $\frac{1}{10}$

   d) (i) 20% **(ii)** 0.2 **(iii)** $\frac{1}{5}$

2 a) $\frac{15}{100}$ **b) (i)** 15% **(ii)** 0.15

3 a) $0.\dot{4}\dot{5}$ **b)** $45.\dot{4}\dot{5}\%$

4 a) (i) 0.75 **(ii)** $\frac{3}{4}$ **b) (i)** 0.3 **(ii)** $\frac{3}{10}$

   c) (i) 0.4 **(ii)** $\frac{2}{5}$ **d) (i)** 0.65 **(ii)** $\frac{13}{20}$

   e) (i) 0.85 **(ii)** $\frac{17}{20}$ **f) (i)** 0.95 **(ii)** $\frac{19}{20}$

   g) (i) 0.24 **(ii)** $\frac{6}{25}$ **h) (i)** 0.32 **(ii)** $\frac{8}{25}$

   i) (i) 0.48 **(ii)** $\frac{12}{25}$ **j) (i)** 0.12 **(ii)** $\frac{3}{25}$

   k) (i) 0.02 **(ii)** $\frac{1}{50}$ **l) (i)** 0.06 **(ii)** $\frac{3}{50}$

   m)(i) 0.05 **(ii)** $\frac{1}{20}$ **n) (i)** 0.13 **(ii)** $\frac{13}{100}$

   o) (i) 0.96 **(ii)** $\frac{24}{25}$ **p) (i)** 0.74 **(ii)** $\frac{37}{50}$

5 a) (i) 0.79 **(ii)** 79% **b) (i)** 0.43 **(ii)** 43%

   c) (i) 0.3 **(ii)** 30% **d) (i)** 0.7 **(ii)** 70%

   e) (i) 0.5 **(ii)** 50% **f) (i)** 0.2 **(ii)** 20%

   g) (i) 0.4 **(ii)** 40% **h) (i)** 0.8 **(ii)** 80%

   i) (i) 0.75 **(ii)** 75% **j) (i)** 0.875 **(ii)** 87.5%

   k) (i) $0.\dot{3}$ **(ii)** $33.\dot{3}\%$ **l) (i)** $0.\dot{1}$ **(ii)** $11.\dot{1}\%$

   m)(i) $0.1\dot{3}$ **(ii)** $13.\dot{3}\%$ **n) (i)** $0.\dot{6}\dot{3}$ **(ii)** $63.\dot{6}\dot{3}\%$

   o) (i) $0.1\dot{6}$ **(ii)** $16.\dot{6}\%$ **p) (i)** 0.16 **(ii)** 16%

6 a) (i) 35% **(ii)** $\frac{7}{20}$ **b) (i)** 86% **(ii)** $\frac{43}{50}$

   c) (i) 70% **(ii)** $\frac{7}{10}$ **d) (i)** 52% **(ii)** $\frac{13}{25}$

   e) (i) 60% **(ii)** $\frac{3}{5}$ **f) (i)** 48% **(ii)** $\frac{12}{25}$

   g) (i) 5% **(ii)** $\frac{1}{20}$ **h) (i)** 72% **(ii)** $\frac{18}{25}$

   i) (i) 36% **(ii)** $\frac{9}{25}$ **j) (i)** 40% **(ii)** $\frac{2}{5}$

   k) (i) 1% **(ii)** $\frac{1}{100}$ **l) (i)** 68% **(ii)** $\frac{17}{25}$

   m)(i) 14% **(ii)** $\frac{7}{50}$ **n) (i)** 13% **(ii)** $\frac{13}{100}$

   o) (i) 12.5% **(ii)** $\frac{1}{8}$ **p) (i)** 32.5% **(ii)** $\frac{13}{40}$

7 0.86 **8** 0.08 **9** 60%

10 $\frac{9}{25}$ **11** 68%

Page 80   Exercise 2

1 a) 0.24 **b)** 0.2 **c)** $\frac{1}{5}$, 24%, 0.25

2 a) 0.35 **b)** 68% **c)** 0.4 **d)** 90%

   e) $\frac{21}{100}$ **f)** $\frac{7}{10}$ **g)** $\frac{3}{4}$ **h)** $\frac{3}{5}$

3 a) 40% **b)** 20% **c)** 1.25% **d)** $\frac{4}{9}$

   e) 8% **f)** 0.615 **g)** $\frac{22}{50}$ **h)** $\frac{4}{24}$

4 a) 25%, $\frac{2}{5}$, 0.42 **b)** 45%, $\frac{1}{2}$, 0.505

   c) 0.2%, 0.15, $\frac{1}{5}$ **d)** 0.37, $\frac{3}{8}$, 38%

   e) 0.2, 22%, $\frac{2}{9}$ **f)** 0.7%, 0.07, $\frac{7}{10}$

   g) 11%, 0.111, $\frac{1}{9}$ **h)** 12.5%, 0.13, $\frac{3}{20}$

   i) $\frac{9}{40}$, 23%, 0.25 **j)** 0.5%, 0.02, $\frac{1}{20}$

   k) 2.5%, $\frac{1}{25}$, 0.4 **l)** 0.06%, 0.006, $\frac{3}{50}$

5 Shop B. **6** No. **7** Oliver. **8** Team X.

Page 81   Exercise 3

1 a) 20% **b)** 30%

2 a) 40% **b)** 12% **c)** 33%

3 51% **4** 21% **5** 20% **6** 20%

7 40% **8** 8% **9** 25%

7.4 Percentages Problems

Page 82   Exercise 1

1 10% **2 a)** £56 **b)** £104

3 607.5 g **4** 3.36 kg **5** £0

6 a) (i) $\frac{1}{5}$ **(ii)** 20% **(iii)** 0.2

   b) (i) $\frac{4}{5}$ **(ii)** 80% **(iii)** 0.8

   c) (i) $\frac{12}{25}$ **(ii)** 48% **(iii)** 0.48

   d) (i) $\frac{8}{25}$ **(ii)** 32% **(iii)** 0.32

7 £259.88 **8** £3526.25

9 a) 13 500 **b)** 14 580

10 6%, $\frac{2}{33}$, 0.061 **11** Kelly.

12 Shop B, by £16.10 **13 a)** 76.5% **b)** 294 525

Section 8 — Algebraic Expressions

8.1 Collecting Like Terms

Page 83   **Exercise 1**

1   a) $4b$ b) $3a$ c) $6x$
   d) $14p$ e) $14s$ f) $20n$

2   a) $6y$ b) $12z$ c) $4p$
   d) $5m$ e) $4y$ f) 0
   g) $-4q$ h) $5m$ i) $-y$

3   a) $3c + 2d$ b) $a + 2b$ c) $3x + y$
   d) $4m + 2n$ e) $8x + 2y$ f) $11a + 7b$
   g) $7p + 4q$ h) $3a + 7b$ i) $3b + 3c$

4   a) $3c + 11$ b) $-3x + 2$ c) $-4y + 5$
   d) $-9m + 21$ e) $3x + 10$ f) $21a + 10$

5   a) $5x + y + 12$ b) $-4a + 3b - 8$ c) $7x + 6y - 3$
   d) $5m + 2n + 4$ e) $8x - 3$ f) $21a + 7b + 7$

6   a) $14p + 7q - 4$ b) $7a - 2b + 9$
   c) $8b + 3c + 7$ d) $-13x + 13y + 2z - 5$
   e) $-11m - 5n - 1$ f) $4p + 4q - 20r - 9$

7   a) $x^2 + 5x + 5$ b) $x^2 + 7x - 2$
   c) $2x^2 + 6x + 4$ d) $3x^2 + x$
   e) $3p^2 - 2p$ f) $7p^2 + 2q$
   g) $7p^2 + pq + 3$ h) $p^2 + 4p - 2q - pq$
   i) $2b^2 + 12b + 7$

8   a) $2x^2 + 4ab - cd + 2xy$ b) $p^2 + 2pq + q^2$
   c) $b^2 + 4ab + 3b$
   d) $b^2 + 6abc + 2ab - 3bc + 5b$

8.2 Expanding Brackets

Page 85   **Exercise 1**

1   a) $2a + 10$ b) $4b + 12$ c) $5d + 35$
   d) $3p + 12$ e) $4x + 32$ f) $30 - 6r$
   g) $14 + 2y$ h) $8h - 16$ i) $9q - 27$
   j) $2t + 12$ k) $4b - 16$ l) $3k + 18$
   m) $15 + 3p$ n) $42 + 7g$ o) $15 - 5y$
   p) $8a - 8b$

2   a) $xy + 5x$ b) $pq + 2p$ c) $ab + 4a$
   d) $mp + 8m$ e) $pq - 4q$ f) $5s - st$
   g) $5y + xy$ h) $n^2 - 7n$ i) $x^2 - 2x$
   j) $8p - pq$ k) $8x - x^2$ l) $ab - 12a$

Page 86   **Exercise 2**

1   a) a^3 b) $6a^2$ c) $16pq$ d) $21a^2$
   e) $15xy$ f) m^4 g) $48ab$ h) $48p^2$

2   a) a^2b b) $20a^3$ c) $14pq^2$ d) $8a^2b^2$

Page 86   **Exercise 3**

1   a) $6p + 12$ b) $20t - 40$ c) $21h + 63$
   d) $10d + 8$ e) $56k - 40$ f) $28 + 16p$
   g) $20 + 28b$ h) $12 - 6z$ i) $16 - 12m$
   j) $18 + 72v$ k) $6n - 36m$ l) $9u + 72v$

2   a) $6n - 18m$ b) $20u + 40v$ c) $35n - 42m$
   d) $3u + 24v$ e) $16x - 28y$ f) $6p - 33q$
   g) $16s - 96t$ h) $24x + 30y$

3   a) $-q - 2$ b) $-x - 7$ c) $-h - 3$
   d) $-g - 3$ e) $-4n - 8$ f) $-14 - 2r$
   g) $-24 - 40a$ h) $-20 - 5z$ i) $-6a - 24$
   j) $-7b - 14$ k) $-22 - 2c$ l) $-60 - 5d$

4   a) $-p + 3$ (or $3 - p$)   b) $-q + 5$ (or $5 - q$)
   c) $-r + 6$ (or $6 - r$)   d) $-s + 2$ (or $2 - s$)
   e) $-4u + 28$ (or $28 - 4u$)   f) $-24 + 2v$ (or $2v - 24$)
   g) $-56 + 8w$ (or $8w - 56$)   h) $-25 + 5x$ (or $5x - 25$)

5   a) $-m - 3$ b) $-n + 11$ c) $-p - 4$
   d) $-q + 7$ e) $-4r + 36$ f) $-26 - 2s$
   g) $-16 + 8t$ h) $-30 - 5u$ i) $-v^2 - 4v$
   j) $-v^2 + 5v$ k) $-12x + x^2$ l) $-4y - y^2$

6   a) $-30g + 18$ b) $-28v - 56$ c) $-10 - 8m$
   d) $-50 + 40v$ e) $-10 - 15n$ f) $-32z + 8z^2$
   g) $-12b + 6$ h) $-8y^2 - 24y$

Page 87   **Exercise 4**

1   a) $6z + 14$ b) $8c + 38$ c) $12u + 64$
   d) $5c + 19$ e) $9v + 57$ f) $8w + 22$
   g) $12b - 2$ h) $9t + 3$ i) $17m + 29$

2   a) $4p - 21$ b) $c - 17$ c) $4q - 16$
   d) $j - 7$ e) $4y - 18$ f) $14c - 27$

3   a) $8q + 29$ b) $-2c - 48$ c) $18q - 8$
   d) $-a - 14$ e) $17z$ f) $2q + 2$

4   a) $5z + 22$ b) $7c + 30$
   c) $7u + 31$ d) $12p^2 + 17p - 3$
   e) $14m^2 + 45m + 30$ f) $-7k^2 + 3k + 4$
   g) $42b^2 + 69b$ h) $-56t^2 + 81t + 4$
   i) $-19h^2 + 24h$

8.3 Factorising

Page 88   **Exercise 1**

1   a) $2(a + 5)$ b) $3(b + 4)$ c) $5(c + 3)$
   d) $4(1 + 3x)$ e) $3(5 + y)$ f) $7(4 + v)$
   g) $5(2d + 7)$ h) $4(2x + 3)$ i) $4(2c - 5)$
   j) $21(p - 4)$ k) $7(2 - x)$ l) $12(2x + 1)$

2   a) $5(a + 3b)$ b) $3(3c + 4d)$ c) $3(x + 4y)$
   d) $7(3u + v)$ e) $4(2c + 3f)$ f) $5(5d + 7e)$
   g) $4(3x + 4y)$ h) $3(x + 3y)$

3   a) $4(a^2 + 3b)$ b) $3(c + 5d^2)$
   c) $5(c^2 + 5f)$ d) $6(x + 2y^2)$

4   a) x b) $2y$ c) $8p$ d) $5n$
   e) $5d$ f) $8m$ g) $6a$ h) $2b$

5   a) $a(3a + 7)$ b) $b(4b + 19)$ c) $x(2x + 9)$
   d) $y(7 + 15y)$ e) $d(10d + 27)$ f) $y(4y + 13)$
   g) $y(11 + 3y)$ h) $w(22 + 5w)$ i) $x(4x - 9)$
   j) $q(21q - 16)$ k) $y(15 - 7y)$ l) $z(27z + 11)$

Page 89   **Exercise 2**

1   a) $5a(a + 2)$ b) $4b(1 + 2b)$ c) $3c(c - 3)$
   d) $9d(1 - 2d)$ e) $2f(3f + 1)$ f) $7p(p + 3)$
   g) $2y(1 + 9y)$ h) $3h(1 - 5h)$

2   a) $5c(2c - d)$ b) $10x(2x - y)$ c) $3x(3x + 2y)$
   d) $4x(3x + 2y)$ e) $2b(a - 3b)$ f) $3a(2a + 1)$
   g) $4x(y - 2x)$ h) $2b(a + 6b)$

3 **a)** $5p(2p + 3q)$ **b)** $4y(3x + 2y)$ **c)** $5a(3b - 4a)$
d) $6q(2q - 3p)$ **e)** $3a(2a + 3b)$ **f)** $4p(3q - 2p)$
g) $2a(4a + 3b^2)$ **h)** $8x(3xy - 2)$ **i)** $5ab(6b + 5)$
j) $14x(x - 2y^2)$ **k)** $4xy(3y + 2x)$ **l)** $2ab(4b + 5a)$

Page 89   Exercise 3 — Mixed Exercise

1 **a)** $2(x + 2y)$ **b)** $x(2 + x)$ **c)** $2x(1 + 2x)$
d) $8(x + 3)$ **e)** $3(2a + 3b)$ **f)** $x(7 - x)$
g) $y(7 - 4x)$ **h)** $pq(1 + p)$ **i)** $m^2(7n + 4p)$
j) $2y(2 - 3y)$ **k)** $4y(5 + 3x)$ **l)** $3p(3r + 2q)$

2 **a)** $7(4a - 5b)$ **b)** $5a(3b - 2a)$ **c)** $12(5x + 12y)$
d) $4rs(7t + 10r)$ **e)** $2abc(2c - 3a)$ **f)** $5q(p + 2r)$
g) $4m(5mn - 6)$ **h)** $23p(q - 4)$

3 **a)** $5pq(2q - 3p)$ **b)** $2cd(4d - 3c)$
c) $7mn(2m - 5n)$ **d)** $2pq^2(8 - 3)$ (or $10pq^2$)

Section 9 — Equations & Inequalities

9.1 Solving Equations

Page 90   Exercise 1

1 **a)** $x = 3$ **b)** $x = 11$ **c)** $x = 16$ **d)** $x = 26$
e) $x = 15$ **f)** $x = 6$ **g)** $x = 2$ **h)** $x = 11$
i) $x = -4$ **j)** $x = 26$ **k)** $x = -9$ **l)** $x = 52$
m) $x = 35$ **n)** $x = 49$ **o)** $x = 49$ **p)** $x = -1$

2 **a)** $x = 3$ **b)** $x = 2$ **c)** $x = 1$ **d)** $x = -5$
e) $x = -5$ **f)** $x = -8$ **g)** $x = -6$ **h)** $x = -2$

3 **a)** $x = 5$ **b)** $x = 18$ **c)** $x = -16$ **d)** $x = -8$
e) $x = 6$ **f)** $x = 9$ **g)** $x = 21$ **h)** $x = -11$
i) $x = 21$ **j)** $x = 22$ **k)** $x = -4$ **l)** $x = 15$

4 **a)** $x = -0.5$ **b)** $x = 8.9$ **c)** $x = -3.5$ **d)** $x = -2.4$
e) $x = -0.7$ **f)** $x = -3.6$ **g)** $x = -3.71$ **h)** $x = 5.45$

Page 91   Exercise 2

1 **a)** $x = 5$ **b)** $x = 3$ **c)** $x = 6$ **d)** $x = 11$
e) $x = 13$ **f)** $x = 1.5$ **g)** $x = 3.5$ **h)** $x = 6.5$
i) $x = 1.5$ **j)** $x = 0.2$ **k)** $x = 0.75$ **l)** $x = 4.5$

2 **a)** $x = 14$ **b)** $x = 18$ **c)** $x = 10$ **d)** $x = 12$
e) $x = 20$ **f)** $x = 8$ **g)** $x = 16$ **h)** $x = 18$

3 **a)** $x = -3$ **b)** $x = -4$ **c)** $x = -2$ **d)** $x = -10$
e) $x = -10$ **f)** $x = -1.2$ **g)** $x = -2$ **h)** $x = -0.2$

4 **a)** $x = -10$ **b)** $x = -3$ **c)** $x = -9$ **d)** $x = -5$
e) $x = 4$ **f)** $x = 8$ **g)** $x = -12$ **h)** $x = -15$

5 **a)** $x = 4$ **b)** $x = -0.8$ **c)** $x = 0.6$
d) $x = -0.068$ **e)** $x = -0.6$ **f)** $x = 0.075$
g) $x = -0.6$ **h)** $x = 0.7$

Page 92   Exercise 3

1 **a)** $x = 6$ **b)** $x = 40$ **c)** $x = 44$ **d)** $x = -18$
e) $x = 7.5$ **f)** $x = 1.2$ **g)** $x = -5.5$ **h)** $x = -6.4$

2 **a)** $x = -12$ **b)** $x = -30$ **c)** $x = -11$
d) $x = -1.5$ **e)** $x = -5.25$ **f)** $x = -4.62$
g) $x = -0.64$ **h)** $x = -15.75$

3 **a)** $x = 9$ **b)** $x = 15$ **c)** $x = 14$
d) $x = 3.6$ **e)** $x = 1$ **f)** $x = -0.15$

g) $x = -0.02$ **h)** $x = 1.26$

Page 93   Exercise 4

1 **a)** $x = 7$ **b)** $x = 10$ **c)** $x = 8$ **d)** $x = 4$
e) $x = -4$ **f)** $x = -5$ **g)** $x = -3$ **h)** $x = -2$

2 **a)** $x = 1$ **b)** $x = 2$ **c)** $x = 3$ **d)** $x = 2$
e) $x = -14$ **f)** $x = -30$ **g)** $x = -20$ **h)** $x = -10$

3 **a)** $x = 10$ **b)** $x = 7$ **c)** $x = 8$ **d)** $x = 3$
e) $x = -3$ **f)** $x = -6$ **g)** $x = -5$ **h)** $x = -5.5$

4 $x = 8$

5 **a)** $x = 12$ **b)** $x = 12$ **c)** $x = 72$ **d)** $x = 20$
e) $x = -16$ **f)** $x = 9$ **g)** $x = -40$ **h)** $x = -21$

6 **a)** $20 = 5x + 10$ **b)** $x = 2$

7 **a)** $x = 1$ **b)** $x = 4$ **c)** $x = -2$ **d)** $x = -9$

Page 94   Exercise 5

1 **a)** $x = 5$ **b)** $x = 7$ **c)** $x = 9$ **d)** $x = 2$
e) $x = -2$ **f)** $x = -3$ **g)** $x = -5$ **h)** $x = -7$
i) $x = 8$ **j)** $x = 6$ **k)** $x = 12$ **l)** $x = 13$
m) $x = 12$ **n)** $x = 20$ **o)** $x = 10$ **p)** $x = 18$
q) $x = -12$ **r)** $x = -7$ **s)** $x = -9$ **t)** $x = -30$

9.2 Solving Harder Equations

Page 94   Exercise 1

1 **a)** $x = 5$ **b)** $x = 1$ **c)** $x = 3$
d) $x = 2$ **e)** $x = 6$ **f)** $x = 3$
g) $x = 8$ **h)** $x = 5$ **i)** $x = 1$

2 **a)** $x = 5$ **b)** $x = 2$ **c)** $x = 3$
d) $x = 2$ **e)** $x = 7$ **f)** $x = 10$
g) $x = 36$ **h)** $x = 6$ **i)** $x = 9$

3 **a)** $x = 0.5$ **b)** $x = 4.7$ **c)** $x = -0.6$
d) $x = -2$ **e)** $x = 0.7$ **f)** $x = -2.4$
g) $x = 8$ **h)** $x = 6.3$ **i)** $x = -9$

Page 95   Exercise 2

1 **a)** $x = 4$ **b)** $x = 3$ **c)** $x = 12$
d) $x = 14$ **e)** $x = 10$ **f)** $x = 14$
g) $x = 10$ **h)** $x = 14$ **i)** $x = 3$

2 **a)** $x = -1$ **b)** $x = -2$ **c)** $x = 10$
d) $x = 0.5$ **e)** $x = 3.5$ **f)** $x = 1.3$
g) $x = -1.6$ **h)** $x = 2.2$ **i)** $x = 5.1$

3 **a)** $x = 5$ **b)** $x = -5$ **c)** $x = \frac{2}{3}$
d) $x = -2$ **e)** $x = 0.6$ **f)** $x = \frac{2}{7}$
g) $x = \frac{13}{18}$ **h)** $x = -\frac{2}{9}$

Page 95   Exercise 3

1 **a)** $x = \frac{4}{5}$ **b)** $x = 6$ **c)** $x = 5$
d) $x = \frac{10}{3}$ **e)** $x = \frac{6}{13}$ **f)** $x = -6$
g) $x = 8$ **h)** $x = -5$ **i)** $x = -10$

2 **a)** $x = 6$ **b)** $x = 8$ **c)** $x = -10$

d) $x = -\dfrac{20}{3}$ **e)** $x = -16$ **f)** $x = 60$

Page 96   Exercise 4

1   **a)** $x = 8$ **b)** $x = -1$ **c)** $x = 5$
    d) $x = 11$ **e)** $x = 8$ **f)** $x = 21$

2   **a)** $x = 13$ **b)** $x = 6$ **c)** $x = 4$
    d) $x = 5$ **e)** $x = 4$ **f)** $x = 4$

Page 96   Exercise 5 — Mixed Exercise

1   **a)** $x = -\dfrac{3}{4}$ **b)** $x = -\dfrac{1}{4}$ **c)** $x = -\dfrac{4}{5}$
    d) $x = -1$ **e)** $x = -6$ **f)** $x = -4$
    g) $x = -13$ **h)** $x = -7$ **i)** $x = \dfrac{64}{55}$

2   **a)** $x = 16$ **b)** $x = 9$ **c)** $x = 12$
    d) $x = 2$ **e)** $x = -\dfrac{5}{4}$ **f)** $x = \dfrac{9}{4}$

3   **a)** $x = 10$ **b)** $x = 54$ **c)** $x = 44.4$
    d) $x = 12.6$

4   **a)** $x = -7$ **b)** $x = \dfrac{12}{17}$ **c)** $x = 4$
    d) $x = 3$

5   **a)** $x = -17$ **b)** $x = -1$ **c)** $x = 1$

9.3   Writing Your Own Equations

Page 97   Exercise 1

1   **a)** 7   **b)** 15   **c)** 19   **d)** 29
    e) 11   **f)** 9   **g)** 36   **h)** 112

2   **a)** 8   **b)** 12   **c)** 10   **d)** 13.5

Page 98   Exercise 2

1   **a)** **(i)** $8x + 20° = 180°$ **(ii)** $x = 20°$
    b) **(i)** $7x + 110° = 180°$ **(ii)** $x = 10°$
    c) **(i)** $60x = 180°$ **(ii)** $x = 3°$
    d) **(i)** $10x + 40° = 180°$ **(ii)** $x = 14°$
    e) **(i)** $19x - 10° = 180°$ **(ii)** $x = 10°$
    f) **(i)** $13x - 15° = 180°$ **(ii)** $x = 15°$

2   **a)** **(i)** $10x + 16 = 146$ **(ii)** $x = 13$
    b) **(i)** $4x + 26 = 196$ **(ii)** $x = 42.5$

3   **a)** $6(x + 4) = 180$ <u>or</u> $6x + 24 = 180$ **b)** $x = 26$

4 $x = 18$

9.4   Solving Inequalities

Page 99   Exercise 1

1   **a)** $6 > 1$ **b)** $2 < 8$ **c)** $-1 > -3$ **d)** $-7 < 1$

2   **a)** x is greater than or equal to 1.
    b) x is less than 7.
    c) x is greater than -4.
    d) x is less than or equal to 9.
    e) x is less than 8.
    f) x is less than or equal to -5.
    g) x is greater than or equal to 3.
    h) x is greater than -4.

3   **a)** $x > 4$ **b)** $x \le 12$ **c)** $x \ge 8$ **d)** $x < 3$

4   **a)**

    b)

    c)

    d)

    e)

    f)

    g)

    h)

    i)

    j)

    k)

    l)

Page 100   Exercise 2

1   **a)** $x > 5$

    b) $x \le 9$

    c) $x \ge 16$

    d) $x < 26$

    e) $x \ge 30$

    f) $x > -3$

    g) $x < 2$

    h) $x \le -2$

2 **a)** $x > 17$ **b)** $x < 10$ **c)** $x \geq 1$ **d)** $x \leq 13$
 e) $x \geq 4$ **f)** $x > 13$ **g)** $x < -30$ **h)** $x \leq 5$

3 **a)** 6 is greater than x. **b)** $x < 6$
 c)
```
  2   3   4   5   6   7   8   9   10
←——+———+———+———+——(+)——+———+———+———+—
```

4 **a)** $x \leq 12$ **b)** $x > 4$ **c)** $x \geq 15$ **d)** $x < 14$

5 **a)** $x > 16$
```
  12  13  14  15  16  17  18  19  20
———+———+———+———+——(+)——+———+———+———+→
```

 b) $x \geq 16$
```
  12  13  14  15  16  17  18  19  20
———+———+———+———+——●———+———+———+———+→
```

 c) $x < 18$
```
  14  15  16  17  18  19  20  21  22
←——+———+———+———+——(+)——+———+———+———+—
```

 d) $x \leq 1$
```
  -3  -2  -1   0   1   2   3   4   5
←——+———+———+———+——●———+———+———+———+—
```

6 **a)** $x \geq 3$ **b)** $x < 5$ **c)** $x > 4$ **d)** $x \leq 3$
 e) $x < -4$ **f)** $x > -8$ **g)** $x \leq 3$ **h)** $x < 22.5$
 i) $x \geq 9.5$ **j)** $x < 7.5$ **k)** $x \geq -8$ **l)** $x \leq -0.75$

7 **a)** $x \geq 6$ **b)** $x < 10$ **c)** $x < 24$ **d)** $x \leq 35$
 e) $x < -8$ **f)** $x \leq 3$ **g)** $x \geq 11$ **h)** $x < -0.64$
 i) $x < 6.6$ **j)** $x \geq -1.2$ **k)** $x \leq 0.18$ **l)** $x < -0.69$

8 **a)** $x < 3$ **b)** $x \leq 8$ **c)** $x \geq 2$ **d)** $x > 11$
 e) $x \geq -12$ **f)** $x > 1$ **g)** $x < 2.1$ **h)** $x \leq 6.5$

9 **a)** $x < 1$ **b)** $x \geq 6$ **c)** $x > 22$ **d)** $x \leq 10$

10 **a)** $x \geq 14$ **b)** $x > 3$ **c)** $x < 16.8$ **d)** $x \leq 11.84$

Page 102   Exercise 3

1 **a)**
```
   0   1   2   3   4   5   6   7   8
———+——(+)——+———+———+———+——●———+———+—
```

 b)
```
  11  12  13  14  15  16  17  18  19
———+——●———+———+——●———+———+———+———+—
```

 c)
```
  -1   0   1   2   3   4  ·5   6   7   8
———●———+———+———+———+———+———+———+——(+)—
```

 d)
```
  24  25  26  27  28  29  30  31  32
———+——●———+———+———+———+——●———+———+—
```

 e)
```
   3   4   5   6   7   8   9   10  11
———+——●———+———+———+———+——(+)——+———+—
```

 f)
```
  34  35  36  37  38  39  40  41  42
———+——(+)——+———+———+———+——(+)——+———+—
```

 g)
```
  -1   0   1   2   3   4   5   6   7
———+——(+)——+———+———+———+———+———+——(+)—
```

 h)
```
  35  36  37  38  39  40  41  42  43
———+——(+)——+———+———+———+———+——●———+—
```

 i)
```
 -2.4 -2      -1       0       1   1.6
———●———+——————+———————+———————+——(+)—
```

2 **a)** $4 < x \leq 12$
```
   4   5   6   7   8   9   10  11  12
———(+)——+———+———+———+———+———+———+——●
```

 b) $6 \leq x \leq 16$
```
   6   7   8   9   10  11  12  13  14  15  16
———●———+———+———+———+———+———+———+———+———+——●
```

c) $-6 \leq x \leq -1$
```
  -7  -6  -5  -4  -3  -2  -1   0   1
———+——●———+———+———+———+——●———+———+—
```

d) $37 \leq x \leq 60$
```
  30  35  40  45  50  55  60  65  70
———+———+——●———+———+———+——●———+———+—
```

e) $2.6 \leq x < 7.2$
```
 2.5  3  3.5  4  4.5  5  5.5  6  6.5  7  7.5
———●———+———+———+———+———+———+———+———+——(+)—+—
```

f) $1.2 < x < 19.7$
```
   0   2   4   6   8   10  12  14  16  18  20
———(+)——+———+———+———+———+———+———+———+———+—(+)
```

3 **a)** $4 < x < 7$ **b)** $16 < x \leq 21$ **c)** $-3 < x \leq 5$
 d) $6 < x \leq 16$ **e)** $-3 \leq x < 4$ **f)** $5.6 < x \leq 8.4$

4 **a)** $2 < x < 4$ **b)** $4 < x \leq 10$
 c) $-7 < x \leq 12$ **d)** $4 < x \leq 4.6$
 e) $-3.3 \leq x < -2.1$ **f)** $\frac{17}{3} < x \leq 9$

Page 102   Exercise 4 — Mixed Exercise

1 **a)** $x > 15$ **b)** $x \leq 20$ **c)** $x \geq 6$
 d) $x < 28$ **e)** $x \leq 9$ **f)** $x \geq 15.98$
 g) $x < 26.24$ **h)** $x > 10.74$

2 **a)** $x \geq 21$ **b)** $x < 9.5$ **c)** $x \geq -\frac{56}{9}$
 d) $x \leq -0.9$ **e)** $x \leq 12$ **f)** $x > 75$
 g) $x \geq -20$ **h)** $x < -64$

3 **a)** $x < 5$ **b)** $x \leq -2$ **c)** $x \geq 1$
 d) $x > \frac{7}{4}$ **e)** $x < 0$ **f)** $x \leq -\frac{5}{12}$
 g) $x \geq -1$ **h)** $x > \frac{79}{46}$

4 **a)** $x < 20$ **b)** $x \geq 23.6$ **c)** $x \leq 30.6$
 d) $x > 18.8$

5 **a)** $-\frac{5}{2} < x < 1$ **b)** $-6 < x \leq 7$ **c)** $0 < x \leq 2$
 d) $-3 < x \leq 11$

9.5 Trial and Improvement

Page 103   Exercise 1

1 **a)** $x = 5$ or $x = -7$ **b)** $x = 4$ or $x = -7$
 c) $x = 8$ or $x = -12$ **d)** $x = 11$ or $x = -16$
 e) $x = 7$ or $x = -13$ **f)** $x = 10$ or $x = -17$
 g) $x = -1$ or $x = -7$ **h)** $x = -1$ or $x = -8$

2 **a)** $x = 7$ **b)** 15 cm, 7 cm

3 **a)** $x = 3$ **b)** $x = 2$ **c)** $x = 4$ **d)** $x = 7$

4 **a)** 3 seconds **b)** 7 seconds

Page 104   Exercise 2

1 **a)** 8.75 **b)** Greater.
 c) **(i)** Greater. **(ii)** Greater. **(iii)** Less.
 d) $x = 2.7$

2 **a)** $x = 4.6$ **b)** $x = 2.8$ **c)** $x = 8.2$ **d)** $x = 14.8$

3 **a)** $x = 4.3$ **b)** $x = 3.2$ **c)** $x = 5.8$ **d)** $x = 6.5$

4 **a)** $x(x + 7) = 100$ or $x^2 + 7x = 100$ **b)** $x = 7.1$

c) 14.1 cm, 7.1 cm

5 **a)** $x = 2.3$ **b)** $x = 4.1$ **c)** $x = 1.8$ **d)** $x = 1.1$

6 **a)** 2.3 seconds **b)** 5.5 seconds **c)** 17.7 seconds

Page 105 Exercise 3

1 **a)** 13.8125 **b)** Greater.
c) **(i)** Greater **(ii)** Less
d) The solution is closer to 3.27 **e)** $x = 3.27$

2 **a)** $x = 4.57$ **b)** $x = 2.77$ **c)** $x = 3.18$ **d)** $x = 5.71$

9.6 Equations and Inequalities Problems

Page 106 Exercise 1

1 **a)** $x = 4$ **b)** $x = 35$ **c)** $x = 23.5$ **d)** $x = 15$
e) $x = 9$ **f)** $x = -12$ **g)** $x = -3$ **h)** $x = -6$
i) $x = -63$ **j)** $x = -32$ **k)** $x = 5$ **l)** $x = -11$

2 **a)** $x = 4$ **b)** $x = \dfrac{3}{4}$ **c)** $x = 0$

d) $x = 9$ **e)** $x = -16$ **f)** $x = -31$

g) $x = \dfrac{63}{13}$ **h)** $x = 15$ **i)** $x = 1$

3 **a)** $x = \dfrac{51}{8}$ **b)** $x = \dfrac{46}{11}$ **c)** $x = \dfrac{81}{19}$

d) $x = \dfrac{35}{11}$ **e)** $x = -\dfrac{128}{21}$ **f)** $x = \dfrac{15}{2}$

4 £33.75 **5** 35 pence

6 **a)** $5x + 30° = 180°$ **b)**

7

8 $x = 30$ **9** $x = 31$ **10** $x = 3$

Page 107 Exercise 2

1 **a)** $x > 25$

b) $x \leq 8$

c) $x \geq -18$

d) $x > -10$

e) $x \geq 3.5$

f) $x < -10$

g) $x \leq 87.8$

h) $x < -4.23$

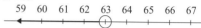

i) $x \geq 28$

j) $x < 12$

k) $x < 63$

l) $x \leq 7$

m) $x \geq 7$

n) $x < 800$

o) $x > 8$

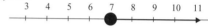

p) $x \leq 15$

2 **a)** $x \leq 11$ **b)** $x \geq 5$ **c)** $x < 13$ **d)** $x > 6$
e) $x > 25$ **f)** $x \leq 26$ **g)** $x < -2$ **h)** $x \geq -\dfrac{55}{6}$

3 **a)** $5 < x \leq 7$

b) $3 < x < 5$

c) $-1 \leq x < 3$

d) $-7 \leq x \leq -2$

e) $1 < x < 2$

f) $-4 < x \leq 7$

4 **a)** $x = 9.7$ **b)** $x = -2.8$ **c)** $x = 5.3$ **d)** $x = -1.5$
5 $x = 12.2$ **6** $x = 3.6$
7 **a)** $x = 1.8$ **b)** $y = 4.4$

Section 10 — Formulas

10.1 Writing Formulas

Page 108 Exercise 1

1 **a)** $c + 6$ **b)** $s - 3$ **c)** $p - 8$ **d)** $r + 20$

2 **a)** $d - 8$ **b)** $6 - s$ **c)** $2m$ **d)** $\dfrac{1}{3}c$

3 **a)** $2f$ **b)** $3f$ **c)** $3f - 6$

4 $3b + 5$ **5** $8h + 18$

6 **a)** $0.25n$ **b)** $0.25n + 7$

Page 109   Exercise 2

1 $C = 3h$ **2** $T = 2k$ **3** $P = 8w$ **4** $n = a + 2$

5 $d = r - 5$ **6** $C = F + 5.5n$ **7** $C = pt + 25$

8 $C = 0.22m + 10$

9 $C = (0.8 \times 60h) + 125$ <u>or</u> $C = 48h + 125$

10.2   Substituting into a Formula

Page 110   Exercise 1

1 **a)** 11   **b)** 4   **c)** 5   **d)** 42

2 **a)** -11 **b)** -1 **c)** -7 **d)** -4

3 **a)** 6   **b)** 2   **c)** 7   **d)** -1
   e) 8   **f)** 9   **g)** 7   **h)** 21

4 **a)** 42 cm^2 **b)** 48 cm^2
   c) 84 cm^2 **d)** 138 cm^2
   e) 222 cm^2 **f)** 246 cm^2

5 **a)** 59 °F   **b)** 42.8 °F
   c) 75.2 °F   **d)** 212 °F

6 **a)** 7.27 m/s   **b)** 28.6 m/s   **c)** 16.7 m/s
   d) 178 m/s   **e)** 8000 m/s

7 **a)** 12   **b)** 16   **c)** -5 **d)** 4
   e) 4   **f)** 12   **g)** 0.75   **h)** 36

8 **a)** 55   **b)** 5050   **c)** 500 500   **d)** 12 502 500

9 **a)** -8 **b)** -7 **c)** -12 **d)** -14
   e) -27 **f)** -1 **g)** -29 **h)** 90

10 **a)** 1.9   **b)** 8   **c)** -12.8 **d)** 31.68
   e) -32.768 **f)** -0.4 **g)** 25.6   **h)** 137.472

11 **a)** 3   **b)** $\frac{2}{3}$ **c)** $-\frac{4}{9}$ **d)** $-\frac{1}{4}$
   e) $\frac{5}{12}$ **f)** $1\frac{1}{12}$ **g)** $2\frac{2}{3}$ **h)** $\frac{1}{2}$

12 **a)** 100 °C   **b)** 18 °C   **c)** -40 °C **d)** 37 °C

13 **a)** 78.5 cm^2 (to 1 d.p.)   **b)** 38.5 cm^2 (to 1 d.p.)
   c) 387.1 cm^2 (to 1 d.p.) **d)** 128.7 cm^2 (to 1 d.p.)

14 **a)** 2.0 s (to 1 d.p.)   **b)** 1.4 s (to 1 d.p.)
   c) 1.0 s (to 1 d.p.)   **d)** 7.9 s (to 1 d.p.)

15 **a)** 12 m^2 **b)** 3 m^2 **c)** 12 m^2 **d)** 0.36 m^2

16 **a)** 226 cm^3 **b)** 1900 cm^3

17 **a)** 25.1 cm^3 **b)** 303 cm^3

18 **a)** 38   **b)** 267   **c)** 16.24
   d) 48.3159   **e)** -53 **f)** -120.6525

19 **a)** 44   **b)** 1241.5   **c)** 585.466
   d) 5866.476   **e)** -864.2602 **f)** 780.3752

10.3   Rearranging Formulas

Page 113   Exercise 1

1 **a)** $x = y - 2$ **b)** $x = b + 5$ **c)** $x = z - 7$
   d) $x = m - 2.3$ **e)** $x = p + 8.4$ **f)** $x = z - 12$

2 **a)** $x = z - r$ **b)** $x = 3y - 4r$ **c)** $x = 16r - 23t$

3 **a)** $x = \frac{z}{4}$ **b)** $x = \frac{p}{17}$ **c)** $x = \frac{r}{4.2}$
   d) $x = \frac{s}{3.7}$ **e)** $x = \frac{s}{6}$ **f)** $x = \frac{s}{3.5}$

4 **a)** $x = 8y$ **b)** $x = 17z$ **c)** $x = 8.6t$
   d) $x = 4m$ **e)** $x = 6.1n$ **f)** $x = 17.4p$

5 **a)** $x = \frac{abc}{2}$ **b)** $x = \frac{t}{y}$ **c)** $x = \frac{uv + y}{4.2}$
   d) $x = \frac{v}{7.3w}$ **e)** $x = \frac{vwy}{6}$ **f)** $x = \frac{2z + 4}{2.2y}$

6 **a)** $x = -\frac{p}{3}$ **b)** $x = -5q$ **c)** $x = -\frac{n}{6}$
   d) $x = -9m$ **e)** $x = -\frac{r}{2.1}$ **f)** $x = -2.5s$

7 **a)** $y = \frac{5}{4}a$ **b)** $y = \frac{4}{3}b$ **c)** $y = \frac{3}{2}c$
   d) $y = \frac{11}{7}d$ **e)** $y = \frac{3}{10}e$ **f)** $y = \frac{7}{20}f$

8 **a)** $s = y + 4$ **b)** $s = 11t$ **c)** $s = \frac{4}{3}d$
   d) $s = \frac{5}{4}m$ **e)** $s = -\frac{r}{16}$ **f)** $s = -\frac{p}{14.2}$
   g) $s = \frac{4}{5}a$ **h)** $s = -\frac{7}{6}b$ **i)** $s = -\frac{c}{11.6}$

9 **a)** $h = \frac{V}{\pi r^2}$ **b) (i)** 2 cm   **(ii)** 2.4 cm

Page 116   Exercise 2

1 **a)** $x = \frac{y - 3}{5}$ **b)** $x = \frac{z + 2}{8}$ **c)** $x = \frac{p - 18}{15}$
   d) $x = \frac{m - 3}{6}$ **e)** $x = \frac{n - 4}{5}$ **f)** $x = \frac{r + 8}{2}$

2 **a)** $y = 3z - 4$ **b)** $y = 4x - 7$ **c)** $y = 9s + 2$
   d) $y = 9.7t + 5.3$ **e)** $y = -3v - 11$ **f)** $y = 5w + 65$

3 **a)** $x = \frac{u}{4} + 2$ **b)** $x = \frac{v}{8} - 4$ **c)** $x = \frac{w}{3} + 4$
   d) $x = 8 - \frac{p}{6}$ **e)** $x = -\frac{q}{5} - 1$ **f)** $x = -5r - 5$

4 **a)** $y = \frac{p + 5}{4}$ **b)** $y = \frac{q - 4}{9}$ **c)** $y = \frac{r + 4}{21}$
   d) $y = \frac{s - 15}{8}$ **e)** $y = \frac{t + 8}{3}$ **f)** $y = \frac{u + 3}{13}$

5 **a)** $a = \frac{v - u}{t}$
   b) 7   **c)** 4.1   **d)** 9.81 (to 2 d.p.)

6 **a)** $c = \frac{5}{9}(f - 32)$
   b) (i) 10   **(ii)** $26\frac{2}{3}$ <u>or</u> 26.7 (1 d.p.)
   (iii) $-34\frac{4}{9}$ <u>or</u> -34.4 (1 d.p.) **(iv)** 0

7 **a)** $d = \sqrt{\frac{A}{21.5}}$ **b) (i)** 4 cm   **(ii)** 2.5 cm

8 **a)** $x = \frac{P}{4} - \frac{y}{2}$ **b) (i)** 2   **(ii)** 6

10.4 Formulas Problems

Page 117   Exercise 1

1 **a)** $c = w - 45$ **b)** 80

2 **a)** $h = \dfrac{m-1}{5}$ **b)** 7

3 **a)** £24   **b)** $n = \dfrac{C - 7.5}{0.06}$ **c)** 550 units

4 **a)** $C = 1.25n + 30$ **b)** £70

   c) $n = \dfrac{C - 30}{1.25}$ **d)** 40

5 **a)** $T = 35w + 25$ **b)** 207 minutes

   c) $w = \dfrac{T - 25}{35}$ **d)** 5.8 kg

Section 11 — Sequences

11.1 Sequences — Term-to-Term Rules

Page 118   Exercise 1

1 5, 9, 13, 17, 21   2 2, 4, 8, 16, 32

3 **a)** 100, 94, 88, 82, 76   **b)** 40, 20, 10, 5, 2.5
   c) 11, −22, 44, −88, 176

4 **a)** 3   **b)** 15, 18, 21

5 **a)** 2   **b)** 48, 96, 192

6 **a)** **(i)** Add 2 to the previous term.
       (ii) 11, 13, 15
   b) **(i)** Multiply the previous term by 2.
       (ii) 16, 32, 64
   c) **(i)** Multiply the previous term by 3.
       (ii) 324, 972, 2916
   d) **(i)** Add 3 to the previous term.
       (ii) 16, 19, 22
   e) **(i)** Subtract 2 from the previous term.
       (ii) −3, −5, −7
   f) **(i)** Add 0.5 to the previous term.
       (ii) 3, 3.5, 4
   g) **(i)** Multiply the previous term by 10.
       (ii) 100, 1000, 10 000
   h) **(i)** Divide the previous term by 2.
       (ii) 12, 6, 3

7 **a)** **(i)** Subtract 4 from the previous term.
       (ii) −16, −20, −24
   b) **(i)** Multiply the previous term by 3.
       (ii) −81, −243, −729
   c) **(i)** Divide the previous term by 2.
       (ii) 1, 0.5, 0.25
   d) **(i)** Multiply the previous term by −2.
       (ii) 16, −32, 64

8 **a)** Add 6 to the previous term.
   b) **(i)** 28   **(ii)** 34   **(iii)** 46

9 **a)** Multiply the previous term by 3.
   b) **(i)** 81   **(ii)** 729   **(iii)** 6561

10 **a)** 7, 13, 19, 25, 31, 37

   b) 9, 5, 1, −3, −7, −11
   c) −1, −3, −9, −27, −81, −243
   d) −72, −36, −18, −9, −4.5, −2.25
   e) 0.2, 0.8, 3.2, 12.8, 51.2, 204.8
   f) −63, −55, −47, −39, −31, −23

Page 119   Exercise 2

1 **a)** 1, 2, 3, 4   **b)** 22, 28, 35

2 **a)** **(i)** 1, 2, 3, 4   **(ii)** 19, 25, 32
   b) **(i)** 2, 4, 6, 8   **(ii)** 35, 47, 61
   c) **(i)** −2, −3, −4, −5   **(ii)** 0, −7, −15

3 **a)** 1, −2, 3, −4   **b)** 4, −2, 5

4 8, 13, 21

5 **a)** 1, 2, 3, 4   **b)** 120, 720

Page 120   Exercise 3

1 **a)** **(i)** Add an extra triangle to the previous pattern.
       (ii)
       (iii) 13
   b) **(i)** Add two extra squares, one on the right and
          one at the bottom of the shape.
       (ii)
       (iii) 34
   c) **(i)** Add an extra square to the left of the previous
          pattern.
       (ii)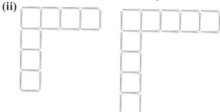
       (iii) 18

2 **a)**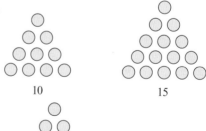

10   15

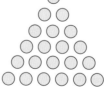

21
   b) The difference between terms increases by 1 each
       time, with the first difference being 2.
   c) 28

3 a) (i)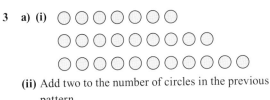

(ii) Add two to the number of circles in the previous pattern.

(iii) 13   (iv) 19

b) (i)

(ii) Add two to the number of circles in the previous pattern.

(iii) 14   (iv) 20

c) (i)

(ii) The number of circles added increases by 2 each time. <u>OR</u> For each square the number of circles is its position in the sequence squared.

(iii) 49   (iv) 100

11.2 **Sequences — Position-to-Term Rules**

Page 121   Exercise 1

1   a) 5   b) 7   c) 9   d) 11

2   a) 18   b) 16   c) 14   d) 12

3   −4, 3, 10, 17

4   a) 6, 7, 8, 9   b) 5, 8, 11, 14
    c) 2, 6, 10, 14   d) 4, 9, 14, 19
    e) 9, 8, 7, 6   f) −1, −5, −9, −13
    g) 2, 12, 22, 32   h) −10, −13, −16, −19

5   a) 2, 5, 10, 17   b) 3, 9, 19, 33
    c) 2, 11, 26, 47   d) 0, 2, 6, 12

6   a) 30   b) 40   c) 60   d) 220

7   a) 91   b) 70   c) 10   d) −20

8   a) (i) 16   (ii) 21   (iii) 111
    b) (i) 13   (ii) 23   (iii) 203
    c) (i) 29   (ii) 59   (iii) 599
    d) (i) 32   (ii) 52   (iii) 412
    e) (i) 95   (ii) 90   (iii) 0
    f) (i) 15   (ii) 0   (iii) −270
    g) (i) 492   (ii) 992   (iii) 9992

---

    h) (i) −10   (ii) 0   (iii) 180

9   a) (i) 8   (ii) 50   (iii) 800
    b) (i) 11   (ii) 53   (iii) 803
    c) (i) 11   (ii) 95   (iii) 1595
    d) (i) 6   (ii) 30   (iii) 420

Page 122   Exercise 2

1   a) 7   b) 7th

2   a) 3   b) 3rd

3   a) 7th   b) 9th   c) 6th   d) 8th

4   a) 7th   b) 4th

5   a) 8th   b) 7th   c) 6th   d) 4th

6   a) 3rd   b) 10th

7   a) 2nd   b) 5th   c) 7th   d) 9th

8   a) (i) 13   (ii) 201
    b) (i) 23   (ii) 399

9   a) 21   b) 55

11.3   **Finding a Position-to-Term Rule**

Page 123   Exercise 1

1   a) 4   b) $4n + a$ c) $a = 5$
    d) $4n + 5$

2   a) $6n + 1$ b) $7n − 4$ c) $4n$
    d) $10n − 4$ e) $5n$ f) $20n − 13$
    g) $40n + 1$ h) $8n − 5$

3   a) $2n − 3$ b) $3n − 5$ c) $4n − 13$
    d) $19n − 64$

4   a) $12 − 2n$ b) $6 − n$ c) $20 − 5n$
    d) $43 − 3n$ e) $80 − 10n$ f) $87 − 9n$
    g) $65 − 5n$ h) $108 − 8n$

5   a) $9 − 5n$ b) $9 − 3n$ c) $5 − 15n$
    d) $−12n − 27$

6   a) $6n − 2$ b) $5n + 2$

7   a) $3n + 1$ b) $3n + 2$
    c) (i) Each term in sequence B is 1 greater.
      (ii) The formula for sequence B is the formula for sequence A plus 1, i.e. $3n + 2 = (3n + 1) + 1$.

8   a) $5n + 1$ b) $5n + 2$

9   a) $17 − 4n$ b) $15 − 4n$

Page 124   Exercise 2

1    $2n + 1 = 54$
       $2n = 53$
        $n = 26.5$
   Since 26.5 is not a whole number, 54 is not a term in the sequence.

2    $3n − 1 = 80$
       $3n = 81$
        $n = 27$
   Since 27 is a whole number, 80 is the 27th term in the sequence.

3    $n = 11$

4 **a)** $5n - 1$ **b)** Yes, $n = 7$.

5 **a)** $6n + 6$ **b)** No.

6 **a)** No. **b)** Yes (27th). **c)** No.
d) Yes (77th). **e)** No.

7 **a)** Yes, $n = 13$. **b)** Yes, $n = 20$. **c)** No.
d) No. **e)** Yes, $n = 222$.

Section 12 — Graphs and Equations

12.1 Coordinates

Page 125   Exercise 1

1 **a)** **(i)** $(0, 0)$ **(ii)** $(2, 2)$ **(iii)** $(1, 3)$
(iv) $(0, 4)$ **(v)** $(4, 4)$
b) X-COORDINATE COMES FIRST

2 **a)** 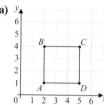 **b)**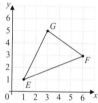

c) 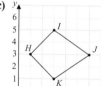 **d)**

3 **a)** **(i)** SQUARE **(ii)** CIRCLE **(iii)** CUBOID
b) **(i)** $(2, 1)$ $(-4, 1)$ $(4, -4)$ $(-5, 3)$
(ii) $(2, -4)$ $(5, -2)$ $(5, 3)$ $(-5, 3)$ $(-2, -4)$ $(-5, 3)$
(iii) $(4, -4)$ $(-2, -4)$ $(-4, 1)$ $(-4, 5)$ $(-3, -2)$ $(3, 3)$
$(4, 1)$ $(-5, 3)$

4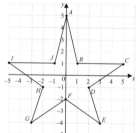

Page 127   Exercise 2

1 **a)** X: $(-5, 1)$, Y: $(3, 5)$ **b)** M: $(-1, 3)$
c) Use a ruler to check your diagram.

2 **a)** $(2, 2.5)$ **b)**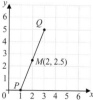

3 **a)** $(2, 3)$ **b)** $(3, 2)$ **c)** $(2, 2)$ **d)** $(4, 7)$

4 **a)** $(0, 2)$ **b)** $(-3, 4)$ **c)** $(2, 1)$
d) $(1, 1)$ **e)** $(-2, -6.5)$ **f)** $(-2.5, -1.5)$
g) $(-2.5, -1.5)$ **h)** $(-0.5, -4)$

5 **a)** $(0, 5)$ **b)** $(-3.5, 4)$ **c)** $(3.5, 3)$
d) $(-0.5, -2.5)$ **e)** $(0.5, 1)$ **f)** $(0.5, 0.5)$

12.2 Horizontal and Vertical Graphs

Page 128   Exercise 1

1 A: $x = -5$ B: $x = -2$ C: $y = 3$
D: $x = 5$ E: $y = -2$

2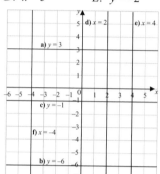

3 **a)** 0 **b)** $y = 0$

4 $x = 0$

5 **a)** 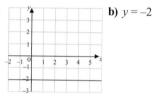 **b)** $y = -2$

6 **a)** 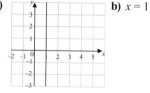 **b)** $x = 1$

7 $y = 8$ **8** $x = -2$

9 $x = 1$ **10** $y = 6$

11 **a)** **b)** $y = -1$

12 $x = 2$

13 **a)** 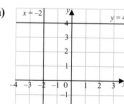 **b)** $(-2, 4)$

14 a) $(2, 4)$ **b)** $(-3, 7)$ **c)** $(8, -11)$ **d)** $(-5, -13)$

1 a)

x	0	1	2	3	4	5
y	2	3	4	5	6	7
Coords	$(0, 2)$	$(1, 3)$	$(2, 4)$	$(3, 5)$	$(4, 6)$	$(5, 7)$

b), c)

2 a)

x	0	1	2	3	4	5
y	-4	-3	-2	-1	0	1
	$(0, -4)$	$(1, -3)$	$(2, -2)$	$(3, -1)$	$(4, 0)$	$(5, 1)$

b), c)

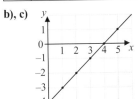

3 a)

x	-2	-1	0	1	2
y	-4	-2	0	2	4
Coords	$(-2, -4)$	$(-1, -2)$	$(0, 0)$	$(1, 2)$	$(2, 4)$

b), c), d)

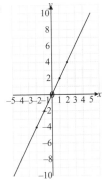

e) (i) $(4, 8)$ **(ii)** $(-3, -6)$ **(iii)** $(-5, -10)$

4 a)

x	0	1	2	3	4
y	8	7	6	5	4
Coords	$(0, 8)$	$(1, 7)$	$(2, 6)$	$(3, 5)$	$(4, 4)$

b), c)

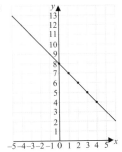

5 a) (i)

x	-1	0	1	2
y	2	3	4	5
	$(-1, 2)$	$(0, 3)$	$(1, 4)$	$(2, 5)$

(ii)

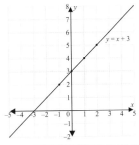

b) (i)

x	-1	0	1	2
y	4	5	6	7
	$(-1, 4)$	$(0, 5)$	$(1, 6)$	$(2, 7)$

(ii)

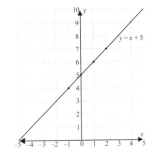

c) (i)

x	-1	0	1	2
y	-2	-1	0	1
	$(-1, -2)$	$(0, -1)$	$(1, 0)$	$(2, 1)$

(ii)

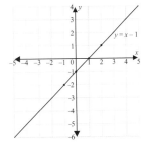

d) (i)

x	-1	0	1	2
y	-4	-3	-2	-1
	$(-1, -4)$	$(0, -3)$	$(1, -2)$	$(2, -1)$

(ii)

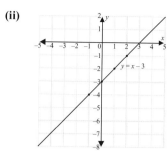

e) (i)

x	−1	0	1	2
y	−3	0	3	6
	(−1, −3)	(0, 0)	(1, 3)	(2, 6)

(ii)

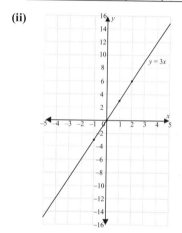

f) (i)

x	−1	0	1	2
y	−4	0	4	8
	(−1, −4)	(0, 0)	(1, 4)	(2, 8)

(ii)

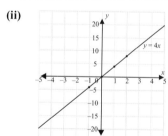

g) (i)

x	−1	0	1	2
y	−0.5	0	0.5	1
	(−1, −0.5)	(0, 0)	(1, 0.5)	(2, 1)

(ii)

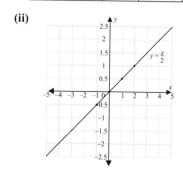

h) (i)

x	−1	0	1	2
y	−4	−1	2	5
	(−1, −4)	(0, −1)	(1, 2)	(2, 5)

(ii)

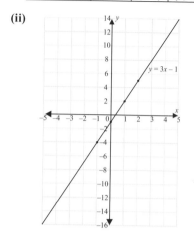

i) (i)

x	−1	0	1	2
y	3	5	7	9
	(−1, 3)	(0, 5)	(1, 7)	(2, 9)

(ii)

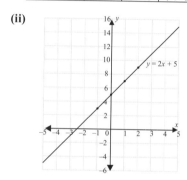

j) (i)

x	−1	0	1	2
y	−7	−3	1	5
	(−1, −7)	(0, −3)	(1, 1)	(2, 5)

(ii)

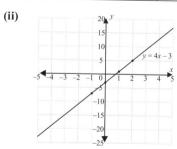

k) (i)

x	−1	0	1	2
y	4	3	2	1
	(−1, 4)	(0, 3)	(1, 2)	(2, 1)

(ii)

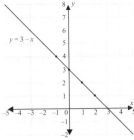

$y = 3 - x$

l) (i)

x	-1	0	1	2
y	5	4	3	2
	$(-1, 5)$	$(0, 4)$	$(1, 3)$	$(2, 2)$

(ii)

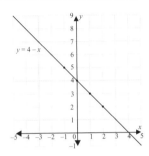

$y = 4 - x$

m) (i)

x	-1	0	1	2
y	8	6	4	2
	$(-1, 8)$	$(0, 6)$	$(1, 4)$	$(2, 2)$

(ii)

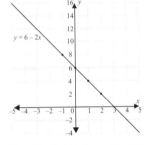

$y = 6 - 2x$

n) (i)

x	-1	0	1	2
y	11	8	5	2
	$(-1, 11)$	$(0, 8)$	$(1, 5)$	$(2, 2)$

(ii)

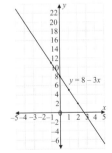

$y = 8 - 3x$

o) (i)

x	-1	0	1	2
y	3	1	-1	-3
	$(-1, 3)$	$(0, 1)$	$(1, -1)$	$(2, -3)$

(ii)

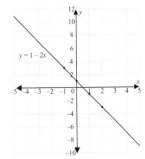

$y = 1 - 2x$

p) (i)

x	-1	0	1	2
y	5.5	5	4.5	4
	$(-1, 5.5)$	$(0, 5)$	$(1, 4.5)$	$(2, 4)$

(ii)

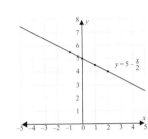

$y = 5 - \dfrac{x}{2}$

6 a)

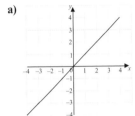

b)

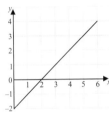

c)

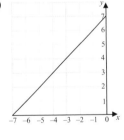

d)

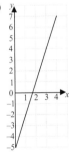

e)

f)

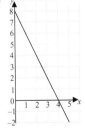

12.4 Gradients

Page 131 Exercise 1

1 a) 4 **b)** 3 **c)** Positive. **d)** $\frac{4}{3}$

2 a) 1 **b)** 4 **c)** –1 **d)** $-\frac{5}{3}$

e) $-\frac{3}{4}$ **f)** $-\frac{1}{3}$ **g)** $\frac{3}{2}$ **h)** 0

3 a) Negative. **b)** 4 **c)** –5 **d)** $-\frac{4}{5}$

4 a) $-\frac{2}{5}$ **b)** $-\frac{1}{2}$ **c)** $\frac{2}{3}$

5 a) (i) G: (2, –5), H: (6, 6) **(ii)** $\frac{11}{4}$

b) (i) I: (–10, 5), J: (30, –25) **(ii)** $-\frac{3}{4}$

c) (i) Line 1: K: (–8, –25) L: (8, 35)
Line 2: M: (–4, 30) N: (6, –15)

(ii) Line 1: $\frac{15}{4}$ Line 2: $-\frac{9}{2}$

6 a) **b)** 1

7 $\frac{1}{2}$

8 a) 3 **b)** 2 **c)** $\frac{2}{3}$

d) $-\frac{3}{4}$ **e)** $-\frac{1}{2}$ **f)** $\frac{3}{4}$

Page 133 Exercise 2

1 a) (i) 3 **(ii)** (0, 2) **b) (i)** 2 **(ii)** (0, –4)
c) (i) 5 **(ii)** (0, –11) **d) (i)** –3 **(ii)** (0, 7)
e) (i) 4 **(ii)** (0, 0) **f) (i)** $\frac{1}{2}$ **(ii)** (0, –1)

2 a) (i) –1 **(ii)** $(0, -\frac{1}{2})$ **b) (i)** –1 **(ii)** (0, 3)
c) (i) 0 **(ii)** (0, 3)

3 A and E, B and D, C and F

4 A: $y = -\frac{1}{3}x + 4$ B: $y = 3x$

C: $y = \frac{1}{3}x + 2$ D: $y = \frac{7}{3}x - 1$

E: $y = x + 2$ F: $y = -x + 6$

12.5 Quadratic Graphs

Page 135 Exercise 1

1 a)

x	–3	–2	–1	0	1	2	3
x^2	9	4	1	0	1	4	9
$x^2 + 2$	11	6	3	2	3	6	11

b), c)

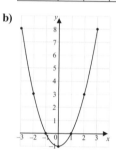

2 a)

x	–3	–2	–1	0	1	2	3
x^2	9	4	1	0	1	4	9
$x^2 - 1$	8	3	0	–1	0	3	8

b)

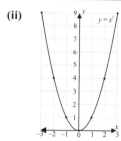

3 a) (i)

x	–3	–2	–1	0	1	2	3
x^2	9	4	1	0	1	4	9
x^2	9	4	1	0	1	4	9

(ii)

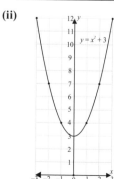

b) (i)

x	–3	–2	–1	0	1	2	3
x^2	9	4	1	0	1	4	9
$x^2 + 3$	12	7	4	3	4	7	12

(ii)

c) (i)

x	−3	−2	−1	0	1	2	3
x^2	9	4	1	0	1	4	9
$x^2 - 2$	7	2	−1	−2	−1	2	7

(ii)

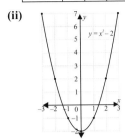

d) (i)

x	−3	−2	−1	0	1	2	3
x^2	9	4	1	0	1	4	9
$x^2 + 4$	13	8	5	4	5	8	13

(ii)

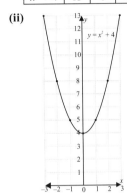

e) (i)

x	−3	−2	−1	0	1	2	3
x^2	9	4	1	0	1	4	9
$5 - x^2$	−4	1	4	5	4	1	−4

(ii)

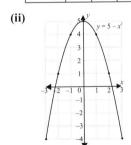

f) (i)

x	−3	−2	−1	0	1	2	3
x^2	9	4	1	0	1	4	9
$10 - x^2$	1	6	9	10	9	6	1

(ii)

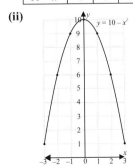

Page 136   Exercise 2

1 a)

x	−3	−2	−1	0	1	2	3
x^2	9	4	1	0	1	4	9
x	−3	−2	−1	0	1	2	3
$x^2 + x$	6	2	0	0	2	6	12

b), c)

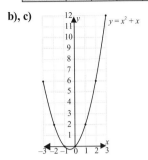

2 a)

x	−3	−2	−1	0	1	2	3
x^2	9	4	1	0	1	4	9
$-2x$	6	4	2	0	−2	−4	−6
$x^2 - 2x$	15	8	3	0	−1	0	3

b)

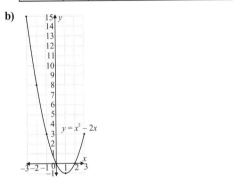

3 a) (i)

x	−3	−2	−1	0	1	2	3
x^2	9	4	1	0	1	4	9
$3x$	−9	−6	−3	0	3	6	9
$x^2 + 3x$	0	−2	−2	0	4	10	18

(ii)

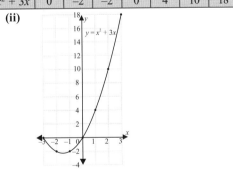

b) (i)

x	−3	−2	−1	0	1	2	3
x^2	9	4	1	0	1	4	9
$2x$	−6	−4	−2	0	2	4	6
$x^2 + 2x$	3	0	−1	0	3	8	15

(ii)

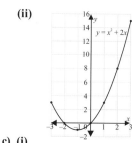

f) (i)

x	-3	-2	-1	0	1	2	3
x^2	9	4	1	0	1	4	9
$4x$	-12	-8	-4	0	4	8	12
$x^2 + 4x$	-3	-4	-3	0	5	12	21

(ii)

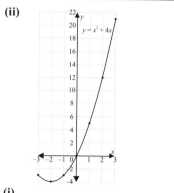

c) (i)

x	-3	-2	-1	0	1	2	3
x^2	9	4	1	0	1	4	9
$-4x$	12	8	4	0	-4	-8	-12
$x^2 - 4x$	21	12	5	0	-3	-4	-3

(ii)

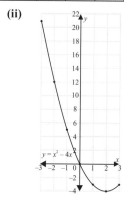

4 a) (i)

x	-3	-2	-1	0	1	2	3
x^2	9	4	1	0	1	4	9
$2x$	-6	-4	-2	0	2	4	6
5	5	5	5	5	5	5	5
$x^2 + 2x + 5$	8	5	4	5	8	13	20

(ii)

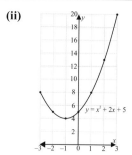

d) (i)

x	-3	-2	-1	0	1	2	3
x^2	9	4	1	0	1	4	9
$5x$	-15	-10	-5	0	5	10	15
$x^2 + 5x$	-6	-6	-4	0	6	14	24

(ii)

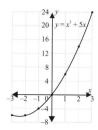

b) (i)

x	-3	-2	-1	0	1	2	3
x^2	9	4	1	0	1	4	9
x	-3	-2	-1	0	1	2	3
-3	-3	-3	-3	-3	-3	-3	-3
$x^2 + x - 3$	3	-1	-3	-3	-1	3	9

(ii)

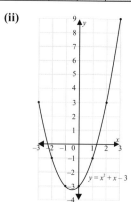

e) (i)

x	-3	-2	-1	0	1	2	3
x^2	9	4	1	0	1	4	9
$-3x$	9	6	3	0	-3	-6	-9
$x^2 - 3x$	18	10	4	0	-2	-2	0

(ii)

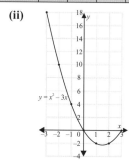

c) (i)

x	−3	−2	−1	0	1	2	3
x^2	9	4	1	0	1	4	9
$-3x$	9	6	3	0	−3	−6	−9
-2	−2	−2	−2	−2	−2	−2	−2
$x^2 - 3x - 2$	16	8	2	−2	−4	−4	−2

(ii)

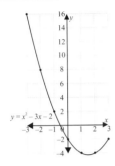

d) (i)

x	−3	−2	−1	0	1	2	3
x^2	9	4	1	0	1	4	9
$-2x$	6	4	2	0	−2	−4	−6
-3	−3	−3	−3	−3	−3	−3	−3
$x^2 - 2x - 3$	12	5	0	−3	−4	−3	0

(ii)

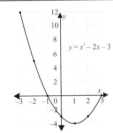

e) (i)

x	−3	−2	−1	0	1	2	3
x^2	9	4	1	0	1	4	9
$-3x$	9	6	3	0	−3	−6	−9
-1	−1	−1	−1	−1	−1	−1	−1
$x^2 - 3x - 1$	17	9	3	−1	−3	−3	−1

(ii)

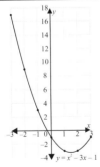

f) (i)

x	−3	−2	−1	0	1	2	3
$-x^2$	−9	−4	−1	0	−1	−4	−9
$-x$	3	2	1	0	−1	−2	−3
-1	−1	−1	−1	−1	−1	−1	−1
$-x^2 - x - 1$	−7	−3	−1	−1	−3	−7	−13

(ii)

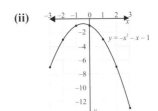

Page 137   Exercise 3

1 a) $x = -1$, $x = 1$
  b) $x = -1.41$, to 2 d.p. (allow $x = -1.4$ to $x = -1.5$)
     $x = 1.41$, to 2 d.p. (allow $x = 1.4$ to $x = 1.5$)
  c) $x = -1.73$, to 2 d.p. (allow $x = -1.7$ to $x = -1.8$)
     $x = 1.73$, to 2 d.p. (allow $x = 1.7$ to $x = 1.8$)
  d) $x = -2$, $x = 2$
  e) $x = -2.24$, to 2 d.p. (allow $x = -2.2$ to $x = -2.3$)
     $x = 2.24$, to 2 d.p. (allow $x = 2.2$ to $x = 2.3$)
  f) $x = -2.45$, to 2 d.p. (allow $x = -2.4$ to $x = -2.5$)
     $x = 2.45$, to 2 d.p. (allow $x = 2.4$ to $x = 2.5$)

2 a) $x = 0.21$, to 2 d.p. (allow $x = 0.2$ to $x = 0.3$)
     $x = 4.79$, to 2 d.p. (allow $x = 4.7$ to $x = 4.8$)
  b) $x = 1$, $x = 4$
  c) $x = 0.44$, to 2 d.p. (allow $x = 0.4$ to $x = 0.5$)
     $x = 4.56$, to 2 d.p. (allow $x = 4.5$ to $x = 4.6$)
  d) $x = 1.38$, to 2 d.p. (allow $x = 1.3$ to $x = 1.4$)
     $x = 3.62$, to 2 d.p. (allow $x = 3.6$ to $x = 3.7$)
  e) $x = 0.70$, to 2 d.p. (allow $x = 0.65$ to $x = 0.75$)
     $x = 4.30$, to 2 d.p. (allow $x = 4.25$ to $x = 4.35$)
  f) $x = 2$, $x = 3$

3 a) $x = -2.83$, to 2 d.p. (allow $x = -2.8$ to $x = -2.9$)
     $x = 2.83$, to 2 d.p. (allow $x = 2.8$ to $x = 2.9$)
  b) $x = -2.65$, to 2 d.p. (allow $x = -2.6$ to $x = -2.7$)
     $x = 2.65$, to 2 d.p. (allow $x = 2.6$ to $x = 2.7$)
  c) $x = -2.24$, to 2 d.p. (allow $x = -2.2$ to $x = -2.3$)
     $x = 2.24$, to 2 d.p. (allow $x = 2.2$ to $x = 2.3$)
  d) $x = -2$, $x = 2$
  e) $x = -1.73$, to 2 d.p. (allow $x = -1.7$ to $x = -1.8$)
     $x = 1.73$, to 2 d.p. (allow $x = 1.7$ to $x = 1.8$)
  f) $x = -1$, $x = 1$

4 a) $x = -1.84$, to 2 d.p. (allow $x = -1.8$ to $x = -1.9$)
     $x = 1.84$, to 2 d.p. (allow $x = 1.8$ to $x = 1.9$)
  b) $x = -1.10$, to 2 d.p. (allow $x = -1.05$ to $x = -1.15$)
     $x = 1.10$, to 2 d.p. (allow $x = 1.05$ to $x = 1.15$)
  c) $x = -2.79$, to 2 d.p. (allow $x = -2.75$ to $x = -2.85$)
     $x = 2.79$, to 2 d.p. (allow $x = 2.75$ to $x = 2.85$)
  d) $x = -2.14$, to 2 d.p. (allow $x = -2.1$ to $x = -2.2$)
     $x = 2.14$, to 2 d.p. (allow $x = 2.1$ to $x = 2.2$)

5 a) $x = 0$, $x = 5$
  b) $x = 0.70$, to 2 d.p. (allow $x = 0.65$ to $x = 0.75$)
     $x = 4.30$, to 2 d.p. (allow $x = 4.25$ to $x = 4.35$)
  c) $x = 0.21$, to 2 d.p. (allow $x = 0.2$ to $x = 0.3$)
     $x = 4.79$, to 2 d.p. (allow $x = 4.75$ to $x = 4.85$)
  d) $x = 1$, $x = 4$
  e) $x = 0.25$, to 2 d.p. (allow $x = 0.2$ to $x = 0.3$)
     $x = 4.75$, to 2 d.p. (allow $x = 4.7$ to $x = 4.8$)
  f) $x = 1.58$, to 2 d.p. (allow $x = 1.5$ to $x = 1.6$)
     $x = 3.42$, to 2 d.p. (allow $x = 3.4$ to $x = 3.5$)

6 a)

x	−1	0	1	2	3	4	5
x^2	1	0	1	4	9	16	25
$-4x$	4	0	−4	−8	−12	−16	−20
x^2-4x	5	0	−3	−4	−3	0	5

b)

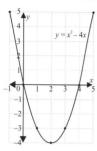

c) (i) $x = -0.65$, to 2 d.p. (allow $x = -0.55$ to $x = -0.75$)
  $x = 4.65$, to 2 d.p. (allow $x = 4.55$ to $x = 4.75$)
(ii) $x = -0.24$, to 2 d.p. (allow $x = -0.2$ to $x = -0.3$)
  $x = 4.24$, to 2 d.p. (allow $x = 4.2$ to $x = 4.3$)
(iii) $x = -0.45$, to 2 d.p. (allow $x = -0.4$ to $x = -0.5$)
  $x = 4.45$, to 2 d.p. (allow $x = 4.4$ to $x = 4.5$)
(iv) $x = -0.83$, to 2 d.p. (allow $x = -0.8$ to $x = -0.9$)
  $x = 4.83$, to 2 d.p. (allow $x = 4.8$ to $x = 4.9$)
(v) $x = -0.53$, to 2 d.p. (allow $x = -0.5$ to $x = -0.6$)
  $x = 4.53$, to 2 d.p. (allow $x = 4.43$ to $x = 4.63$)
(vi) $x = 1.37$, to 2 d.p. (allow $x = 1.3$ to $x = 1.4$)
  $x = 2.63$, to 2 d.p. (allow $x = 2.6$ to $x = 2.7$)

7 a)

x	−1	0	1	2	3	4
x^2	1	0	1	4	9	16
$-3x$	3	0	−3	−6	−9	−12
2	2	2	2	2	2	2
x^2-3x+2	6	2	0	0	2	6

b)

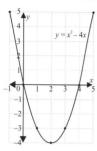

c) (i) $x = -0.56$, to 2 d.p. (allow $x = -0.5$ to $x = -0.6$)
  $x = 3.56$, to 2 d.p. (allow $x = 3.45$ to $x = 3.65$)
(ii) $x = 0.38$, to 2 d.p. (allow $x = 0.3$ to $x = 0.4$)
  $x = 2.62$, to 2 d.p. (allow $x = 2.6$ to $x = 2.7$)
(iii) $x = -0.79$, to 2 d.p.(allow $x = -0.7$ to $x = -0.8$)
  $x = 3.79$, to 2 d.p. (allow $x = 3.7$ to $x = 3.8$)
(iv) $x = -0.16$, to 2 d.p. (allow $x = -0.1$ to $x = -0.2$)
  $x = 3.16$, to 2 d.p. (allow $x = 3.1$ to $x = 3.2$)

8 a) $x = -2.30$, to 2 d.p. (allow $x = -2.25$ to $x = -2.35$)
  $x = 1.30$, to 2 d.p. (allow $x = 1.25$ to $x = 1.35$)
b) $x = 1, x = -2$
c) $x = -1.37$, to 2 d.p. (allow $x = -1.3$ to $x = -1.4$)
  $x = 0.37$, to 2 d.p. (allow $x = 0.3$ to $x = 0.4$)
d) $x = -1.78$, to 2 d.p. (allow $x = -1.7$ to $x = -1.8$)
  $x = 0.78$, to 2 d.p. (allow $x = 0.7$ to $x = 0.8$)

9 a) $x = -1.56$, to 2 d.p. (allow $x = -1.5$ to $x = -1.6$)
  $x = 2.56$, to 2 d.p. (allow $x = 2.5$ to $x = 2.6$)

b) $x = -2.19$, to 2 d.p. (allow $x = -2.1$ to $x = -2.2$)
  $x = 3.19$, to 2 d.p. (allow $x = 3.1$ to $x = 3.2$)
c) $x = -2.04$, to 2 d.p. (allow $x = -2.0$ to $x = -2.1$)
  $x = 3.04$, to 2 d.p. (allow $x = 3.0$ to $x = 3.1$)
d) $x = -1.92$, to 2 d.p. (allow $x = -1.9$ to $x = -2.0$)
  $x = 2.92$, to 2 d.p. (allow $x = 2.9$ to $x = 3.0$)

12.6 Graphs and Equations Problems

Page 139 Exercise 1

1 a), b) — this is a kite.

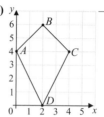

2 $(-1, 3)$

3 a) (i) 2   **(ii)** $(0, 3)$
b) (i) 3   **(ii)** $(0, 8)$
c) (i) 4   **(ii)** $(0, -5)$
d) (i) −1   **(ii)** $(0, 3)$
e) (i) 3   **(ii)** $(0, \frac{1}{2})$
f) (i) $-\frac{2}{3}$ **(ii)** $(0, -1)$

4 $x = 11$ **5** $y = 7$

6 AB: −1 CD: −2 EF: $\frac{2}{7}$

7 A: $x = -5$ B: $y = x^2$ C: $y = x$ D: $y = -4$

8 a) 5   **b)** 3   **c)** −1   **d)** −4

9 a) A: $(1, 5)$ B: $(4, 5)$ C: $(6, 3)$
  D: $(4, 1)$ E: $(1, 1)$
b) $(2.5, 5)$ **c)** $(5, 4)$ **d)** $x = 1$ **e)** −1

10 a)   **b)**

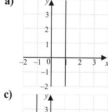

c)   **d)**

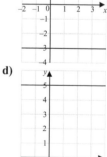

11 a)

x	−3	−2	−1	0	1	2	3
y	11	10	9	8	7	6	5
	$(-3, 11)$	$(-2, 10)$	$(-1, 9)$	$(0, 8)$	$(1, 7)$	$(2, 6)$	$(3, 5)$

b)

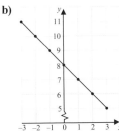

12 a)

x	-3	-2	-1	0	1	2	3
y	-4	-2	0	2	4	6	8
	$(-3,-4)$	$(-2,-2)$	$(-1,0)$	$(0,2)$	$(1,4)$	$(2,6)$	$(3,8)$

b)

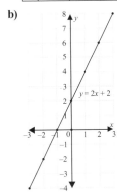

c) $x = 1.5$

13

14 $x = -2.8$, $x = 1.8$

15 a)

x	-4	-3	-2	-1	0	1	2
x^2	16	9	4	1	0	1	4
$4x$	-16	-12	-8	-4	0	4	8
$x^2 + 4x$	0	-3	-4	-3	0	5	12

b)

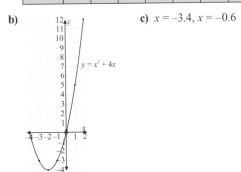

c) $x = -3.4$, $x = -0.6$

Section 13 — Real-Life Graphs

13.1 Interpreting Real-Life Graphs

Page 141   Exercise 1

For Questions 1-4, accept answers that are within £5 or €5 of the given answer.

1 a) €60   **b)** €290   **c)** €130   **d)** €340

2 a) £40   **b)** £170   **c)** £310   **d)** £370

3   £110

4 a) €490   **b)** £400   **c)** France

For Questions 5-8, accept answers that are within £1 or $1 of the given answer.

5 a) $16   **b)** $48   **c)** $70   **d)** $98

6 a) £6   **b)** £46   **c)** £34   **d)** £25

7 a) £36   **b)** £72

8 a) $64   **b)** $128

For Questions 9 and 11, accept answers that are within 10p of the given answer. For Questions 10 and 12, accept answers that are within 10 g of the given answer.

9 a) £1.80   **b)** £6.80   **c)** £1.10   **d)** £7.30

10 a) 280 g   **b)** 500 g   **c)** 120 g   **d)** 210 g

11 a) £7.20   **b)** £14.40

12   1.12 kg (or 1120 g)

13 a) 24 mph (*accept answers between 23.5-24.5 mph*)
   b) 43 km/h (*accept answers between 42-44 km/h*)

14   2.5 mph (*accept answers between 2-3 mph*)

15   Spain, by 5 mph (or 8 km/h) (*accept 4-6 mph or 6-10 km/h*).

Page 143   Exercise 2

1 a) D   **b)** A   **c)** C   **d)** B

2 a) Oven 1   **b)** Oven 2
   c) Between 60 and 80 seconds
   d) Between 144 and 156 seconds
   e) (i) 84 seconds (*accept answers between 82-86 seconds*)
   (ii) 150 °C

3 a) The water got steadily deeper for about an hour, then steadily shallower for about 6 hours. Finally it got steadily deeper for about 5 hours.
   b) 09.20   **c)** 1.2 m
   d) 13.00 and 17.45   **e)** 2 hours 15 minutes

4 a) (i) 5 cm   **(ii)** 5 cm   **(iii)** 5 cm
   b) (i) 10 cm   **(ii)** 4.5 cm   **(iii)** 2.5 cm
   c) The depth of water in vase P increases steadily while the depth of water in vase Q increases quickly at first then more slowly as the vase fills up. This means that when the vases are nearly empty the depth of water in vase Q increases quicker than the depth of water in vase P, but as the vases fill up the depth of water in vase Q increases at a slower rate than the depth of water in vase P.

Page 145   Exercise 1

Your answers to this exercise may differ slightly depending on the accuracy of your graphs.

1 a)

No. Days	1	2	3	4	5
Cost (£)	60	100	140	180	220

b)

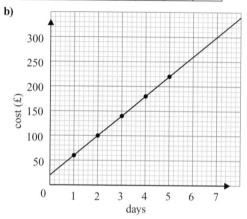

c) (i) £300   **(ii)** 6 days

2 a)

Weight (kg)	1	2	3	4	5
Time (minutes)	60	95	130	165	200

b)

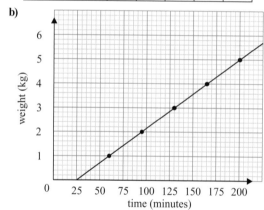

c) 2.4 kg

3 a)

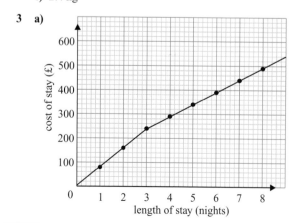

b) £390   **c)** 5 nights

4 a)

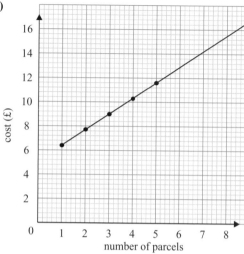

b) £15.50   **c)** 7 parcels

5 a)

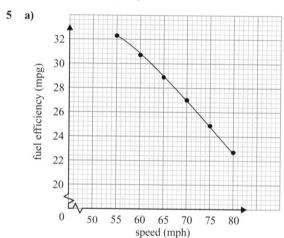

b) 25.6 mpg

6 a)

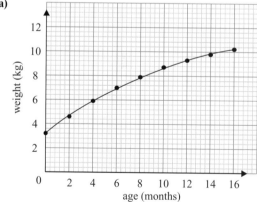

b) 0.9 kg

Section 14 — Angles and 2D Shapes

14.1 Basic Angle Properties

Page 147 Exercise 1

1 $a = 90°$ $b = 65°$ $c = 120°$ $d = 60°$
   $e = 327°$ $f = 70°$ $g = 270°$ $h = 123°$

2 $a = 18°$ $b = 56°$ $c = 140°$ $d = 40°$

3 $a = 127°$ $b = 28°$ $c = 113°$ $d = 62°$ $e = 107°$

Page 148 Exercise 2

1 $a = 35°$ $b = 60°$ $c = 33°$ $d = 45°$ $e = 60°$
   $f = 72°$ $g = 53°$ $h = 30°$

2 **a)** TRUE. Angle $EOB = 43° + 72° + 65° = 180°$
   b) TRUE. EOB is a straight line, and
        angle $AOB = 90°$, so angle $AOE = 90°$ too.
   c) TRUE. Angle $FOC = 25° + 90° + 65° = 180°$
   d) FALSE. Since FC is a straight line,
        $p = 180° - 72° = 108°$

3 $a = 50°$ $b = 90°$ $c = 55°$ $d = 100°$

4 Angle $AOB = 59° + 65° + 58° = 182°$ so AB cannot be
   straight

5 **a)** 70°, 40°, 30°   **b)** $m = 220°$

14.2 Triangles

Page 149 Exercise 1

1 **a)** Scalene; right-angled
   b) Equilateral; acute-angled
   c) Isosceles; acute-angled
   d) Isosceles; right-angled

2 $a = 53°$ $b = 22°$ $c = 15°$ $d = 16°$

3 $e = 73°$ $f = 41°$ $g = 52°$ $h = 49°$ $i = 131°$

4 $a = 20°$ $b = 10°$ $c = 60°$ $d = 60°$

5 $a = 30°$ $b = 120°$ $c = 70°$ $d = 45°$ $e = 36°$
   $f = 66°$ $g = 114°$

6 **a)** $x = 60°$ **b)** $y = 120°$

7 **a)** $p = 125°$ **b)** $q = 110°$

14.3 Parallel and Intersecting Lines

Page 151 Exercise 1

1 $a = 40°$ $b = 160°$ $c = 75°$ $d = 105°$ $e = 90°$
   $f = 90°$ $g = 90°$

2 **a)** $v = 44°$
   b) $w = 44°$ — it is an opposite angle (formed by two
        straight lines crossing) to the 44° angle v.

3 $a = 81°$ $b = 49°$ $c = 60°$ $d = 63°$ $e = 47°$
   $f = 70°$ $g = 54°$ $h = 48°$ $i = 78°$

4 $w = 64°$ $x = 64°$ $y = 52°$ $z = 76°$

Page 152 Exercise 2

1 $a = 120°$ $b = 72°$ $c = 35°$ $d = 98°$ $e = 82°$
   $f = 98°$ $g = 45°$ $h = 45°$ $i = 48°$ $j = 132°$

2 **a)** $x = 42°$
   b) x is alternate to an angle of 42° as the floors are
        parallel and the stairs are a straight line crossing
        them.

3 $a = 73°$ $b = 46°$ $c = 61°$ $d = 65°$ $e = 65°$
   $f = 50°$ $g = 116°$ $h = 64°$ $i = 52°$

Page 153 Exercise 3

1 $a = 135°$ $b = 72°$ $c = 111°$ $d = 100°$ $e = 128°$
   $f = 128°$ $g = 128°$ $h = 52°$ $i = 108°$ $j = 72°$
   $k = 132°$ $l = 48°$

2 $h = 141°$ $i = 39°$ $j = 39°$ $k = 105°$ $l = 75°$
   $m = 75°$ $n = 75°$ $o = 75°$ $p = 105°$ $q = 105°$
   $r = 78°$ $s = 102°$ $t = 102°$ $u = 78°$ $v = 102°$
   $w = 78°$ $x = 102°$

3 $y = 81°$

4 $a = 65°$ $b = 115°$ $c = 65°$ $d = 115°$ $e = 69°$
   $f = 69°$ $g = 111°$ $h = 111°$ $i = 69°$ $j = 114°$
   $k = 66°$ $l = 24°$

Page 154 Exercise 4 — Mixed Exercise

1 $a = 130°$, opposite an angle of 130°
   $b = 130°$, corresponding to a
   $c = 37°$, corresponding to an angle of 37°
   $d = 143°$, $d = 180° - 37°$
   $e = 143°$, corresponding to d
   $f = 143°$, opposite d
   $g = 143°$, corresponding to f
   $h = 37°$, opposite an angle of 37°
   $i = 37°$, corresponding to h
   $j = 60°$, opposite an angle of 60°
   $k = 60°$, alternate to j
   $l = 120°$, $l = 180° - k$
   $m = 55°$, corresponding to an angle of 55°
   $n = 125°$, $n = 180° - m$
   $o = 65°$, corresponding to an angle of 65°
   $p = 40°$, alternate to an angle of 40°
   $q = 75°$, $q = 180° - 65° - 40°$
   $r = 115°$, corresponding to an angle of 115°
   $s = 115°$, corresponding to an angle of 115°
   $t = 58°$, supplementary to an angle of 122°
   $u = 40°$, $u = 180° - 30° - 110°$
   $v = 52°$, $2v = 180° - 76° = 104°$ so $v = 52°$
   $w = 52°$, alternate to v

2 $w = 48°$, opposite an angle of 48°
   $x = 48°$, corresponding to w
   $y = 84°$, $y = 180° - 48° - 48°$
   $z = 84°$, opposite y

14.4 Quadrilaterals

Page 155 Exercise 1

1 $a = 112°$ $b = 92°$ $c = 90°$ $d = 70°$ $e = 109°$

Page 155 Exercise 2

1   2 E.g.

3 a) They are the same length.
   b) 90°
   c) (iii)

Page 156 Exercise 3

1 a)   b) E.g.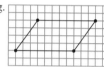

2 $a = 122°$ $b = 72°$ $c = 108°$ $d = 118°$ $e = 62°$
   $f = 51°$ $g = 129°$ $h = 70°$

Page 157 Exercise 4

1 a) d b) Q c) S
2 $a = 113°$ $b = 111°$ $c = 90°$ $d = 70°$ $e = 99°$

Page 158 Exercise 5

1 a) parallel   b) two pairs   c) one pair
   d) one pair   e) 360°
2 $a = 120°$ $b = 120°$ $c = 60°$ $d = 74°$ $e = 116°$
   $f = 56°$

Page 158 Exercise 6 — Mixed Exercise

1 a) parallelogram b) rectangle   c) kite
   d) trapezium   e) square
2 a) square, rhombus
   b) square, rectangle
   c) square, rhombus, rectangle, parallelogram, kite
   d) square, rectangle, parallelogram, rhombus
   e) square, rectangle, parallelogram, trapezium,
      rhombus
   f) trapezium
3 $a = 128°$ $b = 116°$ $c = 82°$ $d = 60°$ $e = 120°$
   $f = 114°$ $g = 230°$ $h = 130°$ $i = 62°$ $j = 118°$
   $k = 62°$ $l = 54°$ $m = 54°$ $n = 36°$ $o = 77°$
   $p = 103°$ $q = 77°$
4 138°   5 both 80°
6 both 127°   7 both 110°

14.5 Interior and Exterior Angles

Page 160 Exercise 1

1 a) 360°   b) 900°   c) 1080°   d) 1260°
2 a) 720°   b) 1440°   c) 1800°   d) 3240°
3 a) One triangle is partly outside the original shape.
   b)

   c) 720°   d) 265°
4 $a = 118°$ $b = 247°$ $c = 210°$
5 a) 900°   b) 128.57°
6 a) 135°   b) 140°   c) 144°
7 a) 100°
   b) No — not all the interior angles are equal.

Page 161 Exercise 2

1 a) $a = 72°$ b) $b = 108°$
2 a) (i) 51.43°   (ii) 45°   (iii) 40°
   b) (i) 128.57°   (ii) 135°   (iii) 140°
3 $a = 54°$ $b = 56°$ $c = 74°$ $d = 135°$
4 a) 53°   b) 40°   c) 35°   d) 40°
5 a) 8 sides, Octagon
   b)

   c) 135°   d) 1080°
6 a) (i) 6 sides   (ii) 120°   (iii) 720°
   b) (i) 4 sides   (ii) 90°   (iii) 360°
   c) (i) 9 sides   (ii) 140°   (iii) 1260°
   d) (i) 3 sides   (ii) 60°   (iii) 180°
   e) (i) 36 sides   (ii) 170°   (iii) 6120°
   f) (i) 40 sides   (ii) 171°   (iii) 6840°
   g) (i) 60 sides   (ii) 174°   (iii) 10 440°
   h) (i) 72 sides   (ii) 175°   (iii) 12 600°
   i) (i) 90 sides   (ii) 176°   (iii) 15 840°
   j) (i) 120 sides (ii) 177°   (iii) 21 240°
7 $x = 10°$ $y = 100°$ $z = 20°$

Page 163 Exercise 3

1 a) [grid figure] tessellates

   b) [pentagon figure] does not tessellate

c)  tessellates

d) tessellates

2 a)

b)

c)

d)

3 a) E.g.

b) E.g.

c) E.g.

d) E.g.

4 a) E.g.

b) E.g.

c) E.g.

d) E.g.

5 You need one of each of the four 'types' of corner on your quadrilateral meeting together for the tessellation to work (and this works for any quadrilateral).
For example:

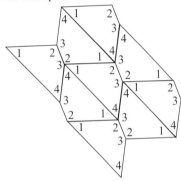

Page 164   Exercise 1

1 a) 1 line of symmetry

b) 1 line of symmetry

c) no lines of symmetry
d) no lines of symmetry
e) 2 lines of symmetry

f) 1 line of symmetry

g) 5 lines of symmetry

h) 4 lines of symmetry

Answers **359**

2 a)  2 lines of symmetry

b) 2 lines of symmetry

c) no lines of symmetry

d) 1 line of symmetry

e) 5 lines of symmetry

f) 6 lines of symmetry

g) 7 lines of symmetry

h) 8 lines of symmetry

1 a) 2   **b)** 6   **c)** 1   **d)** 2
   e) 1   **f)** 1   **g)** 2   **h)** 2
   i) 3   **j)** 7

2 a) rotational symmetry order 4

   b) rotational symmetry order 1

   c) rotational symmetry order 1

   d) rotational symmetry order 1

   e) rotational symmetry order 5

f) 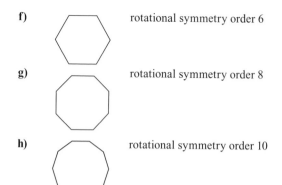 rotational symmetry order 6

g) rotational symmetry order 8

h) rotational symmetry order 10

Page 166   Exercise 3 — Mixed Exercise

1 a) (i) 3 lines of symmetry
     (ii) rotational symmetry order 3
   b) (i) no lines of symmetry
     (ii) rotational symmetry order 1
   c) (i) 4 lines of symmetry
     (ii) rotational symmetry order 4
   d) (i) 1 line of symmetry
     (ii) rotational symmetry order 1

2 a) B   **b)** A   **c)** D   **d)** C

3   **4**

5   **6**

14.7 Angles and 2D Shapes Problems

Page 167   Exercise 1

1 $a = 18°$ $b = 62°$ $c = 53°$ $d = 127°$ $e = 127°$
    $f = 45°$ $g = 186°$ $h = 94°$ $i = 72°$ $j = 59°$
    $k = 75°$ $l = 58°$ $m = 47°$ $n = 47°$

2 $r = 82°$ $s = 103°$ $t = 59°$ $u = 62°$ $v = 28°$
    $w = 71°$ $x = 95°$ $y = 92°$

3 $o = 28°$ $p = 56°$ $q = 118°$ $r = 103°$

4 a) A, B, C, D, F, G
   b) F   **c)** B   **d)** A, G

5 $a = 58°$ $b = 70°$ $c = 66°$ $d = 294°$ $e = 66°$
    $f = 66°$ $g = 114°$ $h = 114°$

6 $a = 61°$ $b = 119°$ $c = 43°$ $d = 43°$ $e = 98°$
    $f = 98°$ $g = 91°$ $h = 91°$ $i = 89°$ $j = 78°$
    $k = 78°$ $l = 102°$ $m = 58°$ $n = 125°$ $o = 55°$
    $p = 35°$ $q = 33°$ $r = 327°$

7 No. Angle BAC + Angle $ACD = 178°$ not 180°

8 a) 720°   **b)** $x = 70°$

9 a) 540°   **b)** $y = 110°$

10 $w = 270°$ $z = 117°$

11 $p = 34°$

12 a) $a = 105°$ **b)** $b = 165°$ $c = 146°$

13 a) $x = 60°$ **b)** $y = 120°$

14 $x = 45°$ $y = 90°$

Section 15 — Units, Measuring and Estimating

15.1 Reading Scales

Page 169   Exercise 1

1 a) A 3 cm   **B** 7 cm   **C** 9.5 cm
  b) A 10 cm   **B** 45 cm   **C** 75 cm
  c) A 4.2 cm   **B** 4.4 cm   **C** 4.8 cm
  d) A 28 cm   **B** 46 cm   **C** 52 cm

2 a) 7 mm   **b)** 4 mm   **c)** 8 mm

3 4.5 cm

4 2 m, 4.5 m, 3.5 m

5 a) 3.5 kg   **b)** 9 g   **c)** 18 kg
  d) 45 g   **e)** 0.5 kg   **f)** 8 tonnes
  g) 5.3 kg   **h)** 20 tonnes   **i)** 4.35 kg

6 160 g   **7** 65 ml

8 a) 5 l   **b)** 400 ml   **c)** 22.5 cm³
  d) 3.75 l   **e)** 4.5 ml   **f)** 0.25 cm³
  g) 0.55 l   **h)** 0.75 cm³

Page 172   Exercise 2

1 a) lower bound = 9.5 cm, upper bound = 10.5 cm
  b) lower bound = 14.5 g, upper bound = 15.5 g
  c) lower bound = 22.5 km, upper bound = 23.5 km
  d) lower bound = 17.5 l, upper bound = 18.5 l
  e) lower bound = 56.5 mm, upper bound = 57.5 mm
  f) lower bound = 132.5 ml, upper bound = 133.5 ml

2 a) lower bound = 172.5 cm, upper bound = 177.5 cm
  b) lower bound = 885 km, upper bound = 895 km
  c) lower bound = 227.5 g, upper bound = 232.5 g
  d) lower bound = 62.5 l, upper bound = 67.5 l
  e) lower bound = 2050 l, upper bound = 2150 l
  f) lower bound = 19 m, upper bound = 21 m

3 5.75 cm³   **4** 10.5 m, 10.7 m

5 a) 24° C
  b) Yes, the minimum possible temperature is 21.5° C

6 Yes, the maximum width of the table is 96 cm

7 95 g, 105 g   **8** 10 cm (175 cm – 165 cm)

15.2 Converting Metric Units — Length, Mass and Volume

Page 173   Exercise 1

1 a) 20 mm   **b)** 3000 ml   **c)** 4100 mg
  d) 15 cm³   **e)** 126.7 ml   **f)** 2000 m
  g) 250 cl   **h)** 2300 kg

2 a) 4 m   **b)** 3.4 km   **c)** 0.5 m
  d) 3 kg   **e)** 2 l   **f)** 0.5 l
  g) 0.246 tonnes   **h)** 5 l

3 a) 0.2 cm   **b)** 3000 g   **c)** 12 700 ml
  d) 37.9 cm   **e)** 3 tonnes   **f)** 0.4 g
  g) 0.123 l   **h)** 0.05116 kg   **i)** 1.2 l
  j) 2.7165 m   **k)** 0.0223 g   **l)** 1.05 m

4 a) 1200 g   **b)** 40 servings

5 6 bottles

6 a) 500 cm   **b)** 5000 mm

7 a) 20 000 cm   **b)** 600 000 g   **c)** 400 000 cm
  d) 231 000 mg   **e)** 62 000 mm   **f)** 3400 mm

8 a) 0.001 m   **b)** 0.003 kg
  c) 0.15 l   **d)** 0.001532 tonnes
  e) 0.01005 km   **f)** 0.003023 kg

9 6

10 a) 500 laps   **b)** 200 km

Page 174   Exercise 2

1 a) 78.5 l   **b)** 7.54 tonnes
  c) 5801 cm   **d)** 23 240 m
  e) 3.575 kg   **f)** 1395 cm
  g) 1250 ml   **h)** 723.5 cm
  i) 1204 kg   **j)** 13 111.1 m

2 3800 g   **3** 1600 m

4 0.05 kg   **5** 741.4 kg

6 Yes. Their total weight with equipment is 0.2262 tonnes.

Page 174   Exercise 3

1 8 days

2 14.8 km

3 7 packs to make sure there is enough

4 a) 750 l   **b)** 267 days

5 a) 1.6025 kg   **b)** 8 people

15.3 Converting Units — Area and Volume

Page 176   Exercise 1

1 a) 2000 m × 3000 m = 6 000 000 m²
  b) 2 km × 3 km = 6 km² × 1 000 000 = 6 000 000 m²

2 a) 20 mm × 40 mm = 800 mm²
  b) 800 ÷ 100 = 8 cm²

3 a) 2600 mm²   **b)** 36 000 m²
  c) 170 mm²   **d)** 10 500 cm²
  e) 70 000 m²   **f)** 12 000 cm²

4 a) 0.84 cm² **b)** 0.175 m² **c)** 290 cm²
   d) 3.15 km² **e)** 85 cm² **f)** 0.17 m²

5 3 bottles

6 33.24 m²

7 a) 85 000 cm² **b)** 8.5 m²

8 a) 6.5 cm² **b)** 650 mm²

9 a) 1 200 000 mm² **b)** 10 000 000 cm²
   c) 0.0605 m² **d)** 0.0673 km²
   e) 50 m² **f)** 5 000 000 mm²

Page 177　Exercise 2

1 a) 1.5 m × 3 m × 2 m = 9 m³
   b) 150 cm × 300 cm × 200 cm = 9 000 000 cm³
      9 000 000 ÷ 1 000 000 = 9 m³

2 a) 1 000 000 m³ **b)** 15 000 mm³
   c) 200 000 cm³ **d)** 55 mm³
   e) 1 200 000 000 m³ **f)** 17 600 000 cm³
   g) 435 000 000 m³ **h)** 6 700 000 000 m³
   i) 0.045 mm³

3 a) 0.134 m³ **b)** 16 cm³
   c) 0.003 m³ **d)** 453.6 cm³
   e) 0.00000015 km³ **f)** 0.091475 cm³
   g) 0.0000359 m³ **h)** 131.4 cm³
   i) 0.0000179 km³

4 0.002 m³

5 a) 595 cm³ **b)** 140 cm³ **c)** 455 000 mm³

6 35 771 complete bricks

7 482485.5 mm³

8 a) 40 glasses **b)** 525 000 mm³

9 a) 1125 m³ **b)** 1 125 000 000 cm³
   c) 1 125 000 litres

10 a) 560 000 cm³ **b)** 560 000 000 mm³

15.4　Metric and Imperial Units

In this topic there are sometimes alternative answers, depending on which conversion factor is used to convert between the metric and imperial systems.

Page 178　Exercise 1

1 a) 24 inches **b)** 12 feet **c)** 4 pints
   d) 56 pounds **e)** 72 pints **f)** 10 800 feet

2 a) 2 pounds **b)** 4 stone **c)** 5 yards
   d) 5 feet **e)** 4 gallons **f)** 3 stone

3 a) 10 cm
   b) 84 g (or 85 g / 86 g)
   c) 9 l
   d) 64 000 g (or 62 720 g / 63 000 g / 63 636 g)
   e) 450 cm **f)** 40 km **g)** 6.75 cm
   h) 2.57 l (or 2.53 l) **i)** 207 cm

4 a) 5 miles **b)** 100 pints (or 101 pints)
   c) 2 stone **d)** 2 feet **e)** 10 inches
   f) 10 miles **g)** 2 ounces
   h) 16.5 pounds (or 16.4 pounds / 16.7 pounds)
   i) 30 miles

5 4 laps

6 a) 5 jugs **b)** 0.15 l (or 0.19 l)

7 56.25 mph **8** 562.5 miles

9 a) 1620 cm **b)** 16.2 m

10 a) 2.25 kg (or 2.24 kg / 2.27 kg / 2.29 kg)
    b) 3.3 m **c)** 6.4 kg (or 6.3 kg)
    d) 13 500 ml (or 13 680 ml)
    e) 18 m **f)** 8.25 m
    g) 9120 ml (or 9000 ml)
    h) 160 kg (or 157 kg / 158 kg / 159 kg)

11 a) 1.4 pints
    b) 0.5 stone
    c) 0.1875 miles
    d) 1 stone
    e) 48 ounces (or 47 ounces)
    f) 4.9 pints (or 5 pints)
    g) 352 ounces
      (or 350 ounces / 356 ounces / 357 ounces)
    h) 3 feet

Page 179　Exercise 2

1 a) (i) 68 ounces **(ii)** 4 pounds 4 ounces
   b) (i) 30 ounces **(ii)** 1 pound 14 ounces
   c) (i) 96 ounces **(ii)** 6 pounds (and 0 ounces)
   d) (i) 175 ounces **(ii)** 10 pounds 15 ounces
   e) (i) 35 ounces **(ii)** 2 pounds 3 ounces

2 a) 6 feet 8 inches **b)** 1 foot 9 inches
   c) 5000 feet **d)** 2 feet 6 inches
   e) 2 inches

3 No, Maddie is too short at 132.5 cm.
   (Or convert 140 cm to 4 feet 8 inches.)

4 No, they need 784 g / 787.5 g.
   (Or convert 750 g to 1 pound 11 ounces.)

Page 180　Exercise 3 — Mixed Exercise

1 a) 3.5 m **b)** 7 kg **c)** 10 miles
   d) 9 l **e)** 1.5 kg **f)** 5 stone
   g) 160 stone **h)** 10 l

2 £35.91 (or £36.39) **3** 2 litres

4 550 miles (or 543 miles)

5 a) 1540 ml (or 1525 ml)
   b) 20 kg (or 19.7 kg / 19.8 kg / 19.9 kg)
   c) 17.97 m **d)** 50.89 km
   e) 10.9 kg (or 10.8 kg) **f)** 730 cm
   g) 5815 ml (or 5781 ml) **h)** 723.5 cm

6 No, their total combined weight is less than 740 kg.

15.5　Estimating in Real Life

Page 181　Exercise 1

1 a) centimetres (or millimetres)
   b) grams **c)** metres
   d) millimetres (or centimetres)
   e) tonnes **f)** kilograms (or grams)
   g) kilometres

2 **a)** probably between 2 m and 3 m
  b) between 4 m and 5 m
  c) around 2.5 m
  d) between 1.5 m and 2 m
  e) between 20 cm and 25 cm
  f) between 200 l and 300 l

3 around 7 m   **4** between 2 m and 2.5 m

5 length ≈ 11 m, height ≈ 3.6 m

6 The dinosaur is about 3 times as tall as the chicken and 7 times as long. So if you reckon the height and length of an average chicken are around 30 cm, the dinosaur will be around 0.9 m tall and 2.1 m long.

7 The rhino is about 6 times as tall as the cat. So if you reckon the height of an average cat is around 25 cm, the rhino will be around 1.5 m tall.

Section 16 — Speed, Distance and Time

16.1 Speed, Distance, Time Calculations

Page 182 Exercise 1

1 **a)** 15 km/h   **b)** 20 km/h   **c)** 30 mph
  d) 4 m/s   **e)** 6000 km/h   **f)** 35 mph

2 **a)** 40 km/h   **b)** 16 km/h   **c)** 25 m/s
  d) 0.1 cm/s   **e)** 600 mph   **f)** 7800 m/s
  g) 1.5 m/s   **h)** 1.25 m/s

3 **a)** 20 km/h   **b)** 6 km/h   **c)** 12 km/h
  d) 3 km/h   **e)** 2.5 km/h   **f)** 14 km/h

Page 183 Exercise 2

1 **a)** 40 km   **b)** 50 miles   **c)** 500 m
  d) 72 km   **e)** 135 m   **f)** 175 miles

2 **a)** 2 h   **b)** 5 s   **c)** 3 s   **d)** 2.5 h
  e) 0.5 s   **f)** 0.25 h (or 15 minutes)

3 120 miles   **4** 980 miles   **5** 0.16 s

6 5 hours   **7** 6 minutes   **8** 1.875 miles

Page 183 Exercise 3 — Mixed Exercise

1 4 m/s   **2** 25 m   **3** 2.5 h   **4** 28 m/s

5 405 cm   **6** 0.75 s   **7** 4.05 km **8** 0.05 m/s

9 0.008 m/s **10** 22.5 seconds

16.2 Distance-Time Graphs

Page 184 Exercise 1

1 **a)**   **b)**

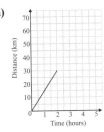

c) **(i)** 70 km   **(ii)**

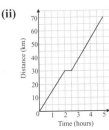

2 **a)**   **b)**

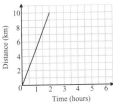

c)

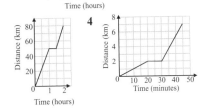

3   **4**

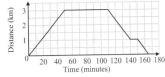

5

6

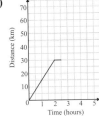

7 **a)** **(i)** 1 hour   **(ii)** 50 miles
  b) 1 hour
  c) **(i)** 11:00 am   **(ii)** 2 hours

8 **a)** The person travels 5 km in 2 hours. They rest for 1 hour. They then continue their journey for another 1 hour, during which time they travel a further 3 km. They then stop for 30 minutes. Finally, they travel back to their starting point in 1.5 hours.

  b) The person travels 1 km in 1 hour. They rest for 30 minutes. They then continue their journey for another 30 minutes, during which time they travel a further 0.5 km. They then stop for 15 minutes. They then continue their journey for 30 minutes, and cover a further 2 km, before stopping for 15 minutes.

Answers   363

c) The person travels 35 miles in 45 minutes. They rest for 45 minutes. They then travel 15 miles in 30 minutes back towards their starting point before stopping for a further 30 minutes. They then continue their journey away from the starting point for another 20 miles, which takes 30 minutes.

Page 186   Exercise 2

1 a) The second stage, since the graph for that part of the journey is steeper.
  b) (i) 2 km   **(ii)** 4 km/h
  c) 12 km/h

2 a) Between 13:30 and 14:30, since the graph between those times is steepest.
  b) (i) 1 hour   **(ii)** 3 km   **(iii)** 3 km/h
  c) 2 km/h   **d)** 4.5 km/h

3 a) (i) 40 km/h   **(ii)** 33.3 km/h (to 1 d.p.)
  b) and **d)**

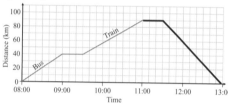

  c) 1.5 hours

4 a)

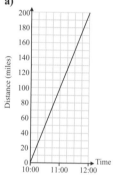

b)

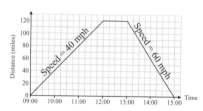

Section 17 — Pythagoras, Bearings and Scale Drawings

17.1 Pythagoras' Theorem

Page 188   Exercise 1

1 a) 5 cm   **b)** 13 mm   **c)** 30 cm
   d) 34 m   **e)** 6.71 cm   **f)** 73.54 m
   g) 2.5 m   **h)** 7.75 cm   **i)** 6.36 km
   j) 13.57 mm   **k)** 1.39 m   **l)** 3.30 m

2   10.63 cm

3 a) 8.60 cm   **b)** 11.70 cm   **c)** 6.58 mm

4 6.65 cm   **5** 216.33 m   **6** 25 m

7 1110 m   **8** 5.98 cm

9 a) 8.38 cm   **b)** 4.19 cm

10 6.40 units   **11** 30.46 cm

Page 190   Exercise 2

1 a) 5 cm   **b)** 5.66 cm   **c)** 8.49 mm
   d) 24 cm   **e)** 40 cm   **f)** 25.61 mm
   g) 4.53 m   **h)** 14.77 km   **i)** 3.89 cm
   j) 174.28 mm   **k)** 9.00 m   **l)** 247.18 cm

2 a) 7.94 cm   **b)** 11.53 m
   c) 10.53 mm   **d)** 14.53 cm

3 15.99 cm   **4** 0.79 m   **5** 3.20 m   **6** 8.66 cm

7 18.73 cm   **8** 12.36 m   **9** 1.88 m   **10** 747 km

11 111 km   **12** 0.57 m

Page 191   Exercise 3 — Mixed Exercise

1 4.37 m   **2** 94.58 km   **3** 10.89 m   **4** Yes

5 2.12 m   **6** 100 m   **7** Yes   **8** 1.96 m

9 3.8 m   **10** 8.66 cm

11 a) 8.06 units   **b)** 4.47 units   **c)** 6.71 units

12 $GE = 3$ m, $GD = 4.24$ m

13 a) 9 m   **b)** 22.5 m   **c)** 13.5 m

14 931   **15** 18.97 units   **16** Marrow, by 0.12 km

17 24.97 m   **18** 10.52 cm

19 a) 19.09 m   **b)** 18.57 m   **20** 10.42 cm

17.2 Scale Drawings

Page 193   Exercise 1

1 a) (i) 2 km   **(ii)** 3 km   **(iii)** 11 km
     (iv) 1.5 km   **(v)** 0.25 km   **(vi)** 0.125 km

   b) (i) 10 cm   **(ii)** 16 cm   **(iii)** 28 cm
     (iv) 7 cm   **(v)** 1 cm   **(vi)** 1.4 cm

2 a) 700 km   **b)** 150 km   **c)** 80 km
   d) 622 km   **e)** 301 km   **f)** 430 km

3 a) 3 cm   **b)** 12 cm   **c)** 20 cm
   d) 0.5 cm   **e)** 0.2 cm   **f)** 0.3 cm

4 a) 5.4 m by 3 m   **b)** 6.4 m by 4.4 m
   c) 3.7 m by 2.8 m **d)** 1.8 m by 2.7 m

5   1 cm : 40 km   **6**   **a)** 1 cm : 3 km   **b)** 21 km

7   **a)** 8 cm   **b)** 36 cm
    c) 42 cm   **d)** 23.6 cm

8   1.6 cm

9   **a)** Width = 57 cm, Depth = 30 cm
    b) Width = 66 cm, Depth = 45 cm

10   **a)** 1 cm : 50 m   **b) (i)** 75 m   **(ii)** 125 m

Page 194   Exercise 2

1   **a) (i)** 7 m   **(ii)** 24.5 m   **(iii)** 77 m
      (iv) 34.65 m   **(v)** 50.75 m   **(vi)** 89.95 m

    b) (i) 2 cm   **(ii)** 2.5 cm   **(iii)** 0.5 cm
      (iv) 0.6 cm   **(v)** 2.7 cm   **(vi)** 0.42 cm

2   **a)** 3 m   **b)** 8.25 m   **c)** 4.125 m
    d) 5.925 m   **e)** 18.075 m   **f)** 12.9 m

3   **a)** 0.3 m or 30 cm   **b)** 1.4 m or 140 cm
    c) 0.84 m or 84 cm   **d)** 0.12 m or 12 cm
    e) 1 m or 100 cm   **f)** 0.43 m or 43 cm

4   **a)** 2 m   **b)** 1.4 m   **c)** 1.28 m   **d)** 0.96 m

5   2.68 cm

6   **a)** 4 cm   **b)** 6 cm   **c)** 20 cm   **d)** 1.2 cm

7   **a)** 7.5 cm   **b)** 11.25 cm   **c)** 4.5 cm

8   **a)** 1 cm : 1.5 km   **b)** 1 : 150 000

9   **a)** 1 cm : 15 m   **b)** 4 cm

10   **a)** 1 : 600   **b)** 7.2 m   **c)** 0.75 cm

11   **a)** 1.2 km   **b)** 3 km   **c)** 2.64 km

Page 196   Exercise 3

Your answers to this exercise should be accurate
scale drawings with the measurements shown.

1
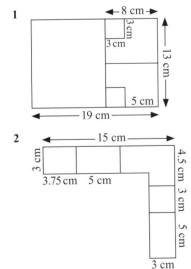

2

3   **a)**
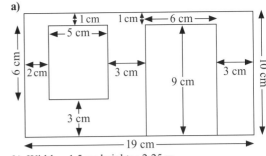

    b) Width = 1.5 m, height = 2.25 m.

4   **a)**
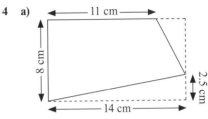

    b) 14 m - 15 m

17.3   Bearings

Page 197   Exercise 1

1   **a)** 090°   **b)** 045°   **c)** 180°   **d)** 270°
    e) 225°   **f)** 315°

2   **a)** 062°   **b)** 130°   **c)** 227°   **d)** 301°
    e) 071°   **f)** 113°   **g)** 187°   **h)** 288°

3   065°

4   **a)** 21°   **b)** 23°   **c)** 75°
    d) 63°   **e)** 45°   **f)** 48°

5   **a)**
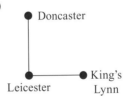

    b) 090°
    c) (i) 180°   **(ii)** 135°
    d) (i) 270°   **(ii)** 315°

6

7 **a)** 030° **b)** 169° **c)** 348°
d) 101° **e)** 249° **f)** 309°

Page 198 Exercise 2

1 038° **2** 305° **3** 130°

4 203° **5** 281°

6 **a)** 020° **b)** 130° **c)** 260°
d) 297° **e)** 195° **f)** 279°

7 **a)** 32° **b)** 032°

8 **a)** 270° **b)** 090°

9 **a)** 135° **b)** 315°

10 **a)** 112° **b)** 292°

11 **a)** 055° **b)** 143° **c)** 244° **d)** 326°
e) 235° **f)** 323° **g)** 064° **h)** 146°

Page 200 Exercise 3

1 **a) (i)** 250 km, 050° **(ii)** 190 km, 125°
b) 340-350 km

2

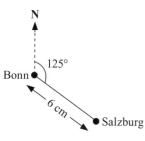

3

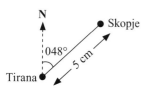

4

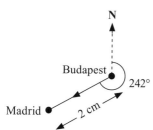

5

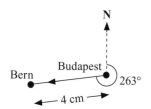

6 **a) (i)** 300 km **(ii)** 450 km **(iii)** 580 km
b) (i) 060° **(ii)** 140° **(iii)** 290°

17.4 Pythagoras, Bearings and Scale Drawing Problems

Page 200 Exercise 1

1 309 km

2 **a)** 180° **b)** 270° **c)** 225°

3 **a)** 1 : 10 000 **b)** 70 m **c)** 308 m

4 **a)** 1 cm : 1 km **b)** 14.9 km **c)** 310°

5 **a)**

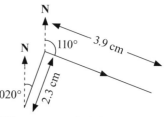

b) 90° **c)** 453 m

6 **a)**

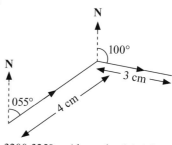

b) 3200-3250 m (shown by 6.4-6.5 cm on diagram)
c) 255°

7 **a)** 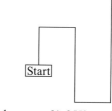 **b)** 22-23 m

8 **a)** 1344 km **b)** 255°

Section 18 — Constructions

18.1 Circles

Page 202 Exercise 1

1 **a)** 6 cm **b)** 4 cm **c)** 70 mm **d)** 56 mm

2 **a)** 4 cm **b)** 5 mm **c)** 9.5 mm **d)** 2.4 cm

3 **a)** 8 cm **b)** 12 cm **c)** 60 mm **d)** 50 m
e) 5.6 m **f)** 9.2 mm **g)** 7.4 m **h)** 98 mm
i) 110 m **j)** 8.4 mm

4 **a)** 1 cm **b)** 6 cm **c)** 7 m **d)** 14 mm
e) 0.7 cm **f)** 1.4 m **g)** 28.5 mm **h)** 2.15 cm
i) 0.4 m **j)** 0.01 cm

5 Measure your diagrams — they should be as follows:

a)
4 cm
8 cm

b)
5 cm
10 cm

c)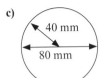
40 mm
80 mm

d)
3 cm
6 cm

e)
3.5 cm
7 cm

f)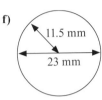
11.5 mm
23 mm

Page 203 Exercise 2

1 **a)** chord   **b)** diameter   **c)** tangent
    d) radius   **e)** sector   **f)** circumference
    g) arc   **h)** segment

2 *A*: radius   *B*: diameter   *C*: circumference
    D: tangent   *E*: sector   *F*: segment

3 Your diagram should look something like this:

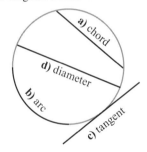

a) chord
d) diameter
b) arc
c) tangent

18.2 Lines, Angles and Triangles

Page 204 Exercise 1

1 **a)** 40°   **b)** 3.9 cm - 4 cm   **c)** 4.9 cm - 5 cm
    d) 65°   **e)** 4.4 cm - 4.5 cm   **f)** 2.9 cm - 3 cm
    g) 120°   **h)** 4.8 cm   **i)** 1.8 cm

2 **a)** and **b)**

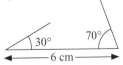
30°
70°
6 cm

3 **a)** and **b)**

130°
170°
8.5 cm

4 **a)**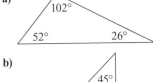
102°
52°
26°

b)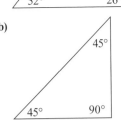
45°
45°
90°

Page 205 Exercise 2

1 If you've drawn the triangles accurately, your answers should be as follows:
    a) *l* = 5.0 cm - 5.1 cm   **b)** *l* = 6.1 cm - 6.2 cm
    c) *l* = 8.8 cm - 8.9 cm   **d)** *l* = 5.6 cm - 5.7 cm

2 **a) (i)**
C
A 55°
35° *B*
4 cm

(ii)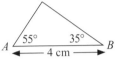
C
A 22°
107° *B*
8 cm

(iii)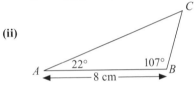
C
A 65°
30° *B*
6.5 cm

(iv)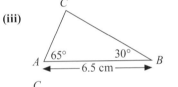
C
120°
28° *B*
A 7.2 cm

    b) (i) 3.2 cm - 3.3 cm   **(ii)** 3.8 cm - 3.9 cm
      (iii) 5.9 cm - 6.0 cm   **(iv)** 11.7 cm - 11.8 cm

3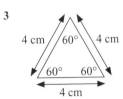
4 cm 60° 4 cm
60° 60°
4 cm

4 3.5 km - 3.6 km

Page 206 Exercise 3

1 If you've drawn the triangles accurately, your answers should be as follows:
a) l = 13 cm
b) l = 5.5 cm - 5.6 cm
c) l = 4.8 cm - 4.9 cm
d) l = 110 mm

2 a) (i)

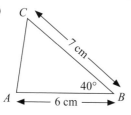

(ii)

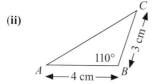

(iii)

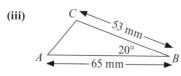

(iv)

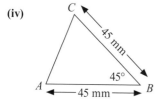

b) (i) 4.5 cm - 4.6 cm **(ii)** 5.7 cm - 5.8 cm
(iii) 23 mm - 24 mm **(iv)** 34 mm - 35 mm

3

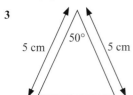

4 a) and **b)**

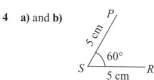

c) 120°

d)

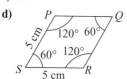

5 a)

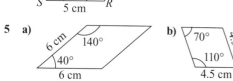

b)

Page 207 Exercise 4

1 Measure all 3 sides of your triangles and check the lengths are correct.

2 Measure all 3 sides of your triangles and check the lengths are correct.

3 Measure all 3 sides of your triangle and check the lengths are correct.

4

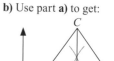

18.3 Constructions

Page 208 Exercise 1

1

2

3

4 a)

b) Use part **a)** to get:

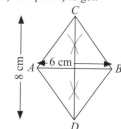

5 a)

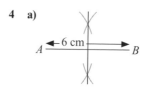

b)

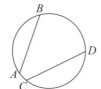

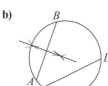

c)

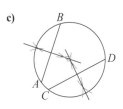

d) They meet at the circle's centre.

Page 209 Exercise 2

1 a)

b)

c)

d)

e)

f)

g)

h)

2 a)

b)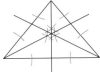

They intersect at a single point.

3 a)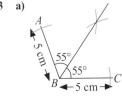

b)

ABCD is a kite.

Page 210 Exercise 3

1

2 <u>or</u>

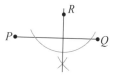

3 a), b) and c)

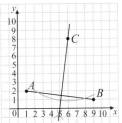

4 a)

b)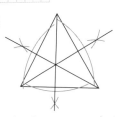

They intersect at a single point.

5 a)

b)

c) *FG* = 4.9 cm, area = 12.3 cm²

Page 211 Exercise 4

1 Measure the length of *AB* and the size of the angle in your diagram to check they are correct.

2 Measure the 3 sides and angles in your triangle to check they are correct.

Page 211 Exercise 5

1 Measure the length of *AB* and the size of the angle in your diagram to check they are correct.

2 Measure the length of *AB* and the sizes of the 3 angles in your triangle to check they are correct.

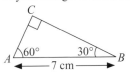

3 Measure the sides and angles in your triangle to check they are correct.

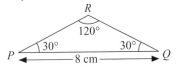

Page 212　Exercise 6

1　Measure your angle to check that it is a right angle.

2　Measure the sides of your rectangle and check the lengths are correct. Measure each angle to check they are right angles.

Page 212　Exercise 7

1　Measure your angle to check that it is 45°.

2　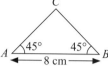

Measure AB to check the length is correct. Measure angles CAB and CBA to check they are 45°.

Page 213　Exercise 8

1　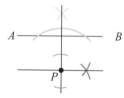

2　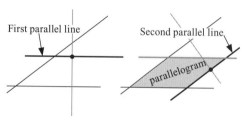

3　a)　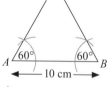　　b)　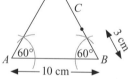

c)　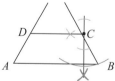

Page 213　Exercise 9 — Mixed Exercise

1　a)　　　b)　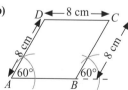　

2　a)　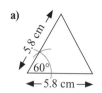　　b)　

3　a)　　　b)　75°

4　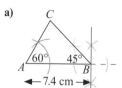

Construct an angle of 60°. The bisect that angle once to get an angle of 30°. Then bisect this angle of 30° to construct an angle of 15°.

18.4　Loci

Page 214　Exercise 1

1　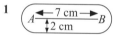

2　a)　　　b)　

3　

4　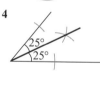

5　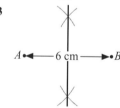

6　a)　$P \bullet\!\!\longleftarrow\!\!-5\text{ cm}\longrightarrow\bullet Q$

b)　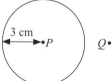

c)

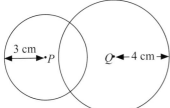

d) The points marked with dots are both 3 cm from P and 4 cm from Q.

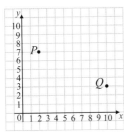

7 a)

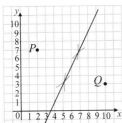

b)

8 a)

b)

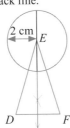

9 a)

b) Locus of points shown by black line.

1 a) $P \bullet\!\!\longleftarrow\!\!\text{---}\,3\text{ cm}\,\text{---}\!\!\longrightarrow\!\! \bullet L$

b)

2 Location of treasure marked by the dot.

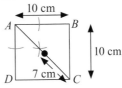

3 Location of bonfire marked by the dot.

4 a) $A \bullet\!\!\longleftarrow\!\! 5\text{ cm}\,\longrightarrow\!\! \bullet B$

b) Shaded area shows where they could meet.

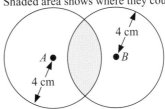

5 Shaded regions show where the dog can move.

a)   **b)**

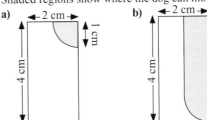

Section 19 — Area and Perimeter

19.1 Rectangles and Triangles

Page 216   Exercise 1

1 a) 12 cm	**b)** 28 m	**c)** 20 cm
d) 20 cm	**e)** 43 m	**f)** 90 mm
g) 16.8 cm	**h)** 31.8 mm	**i)** 25.9 m

Page 217   Exercise 2

1 a) 50 cm^2	**b)** 18 m^2	**c)** 16 mm^2
d) 33 m^2	**e)** 121 cm^2	**f)** 10 mm^2
g) 6 cm^2	**h)** 176 cm^2	**i)** 25 cm^2

Page 218   Exercise 3 — Mixed Exercise

1 a) (i) 9 cm   (ii) 4.34 cm^2
   b) (i) 8.4 mm   (ii) 3.41 mm^2
   c) (i) 7.2 cm   (ii) 3.24 cm^2

2 a) (i) 16 cm   (ii) 16 cm^2
   b) (i) 28 m   (ii) 48 m^2
   c) (i) 76 mm   (ii) 345 mm^2
   d) (i) 68 m   (ii) 289 m^2
   e) (i) 53 m   (ii) 95.46 m^2
   f) (i) 22.8 mm   (ii) 21.6 mm^2

3 a) (i) 24 cm   (ii) 26.8 cm^2
   b) (i) 26 m   (ii) 26.95 m^2
   c) (i) 42.8 mm   (ii) 65.8 mm^2
   d) (i) 30 mm   (ii) 25.6 mm^2
   e) (i) 31.5 m   (ii) 50 m^2
   f) (i) 36 m   (ii) 40.15 m^2

4 a) 407 m^2 b) 81.6 m

5 a) 5.88 m^2 b) 9.8 m

6 27

7 a) 67.5 m^2 b) 0.25 m^2 c) 270

8 a) 100 cm   b) 1416 cm^2

Page 219   Exercise 4

1 a) 68 m^2 b) 108 m^2 c) 148 mm^2

2 a) (i) 50 cm   (ii) 136 cm^2
   b) (i) 30 cm   (ii) 47 cm^2
   c) (i) 92 mm   (ii) 334 mm^2

3 a) 56 m^2 b) 75 cm^2

19.2 Other Quadrilaterals

Page 220   Exercise 1

1 a) 28 cm^2 b) 8 m^2 c) 48 mm^2
   d) 54 mm^2 e) 630 m^2 f) 47.56 mm^2

2 50.84 cm^2

3 The square has the larger area. The vertical height of
   the rhombus (a special type of parallelogram) is less
   than 6 cm, so its area will be less than the area of the
   square.

Page 221   Exercise 2

1 a) 28 m^2 b) 90 mm^2 c) 40 mm^2
   d) 19.475 cm^2 e) 313.95 mm^2 f) 0.1375 cm^2

2 90 m^2

3 They have the same area, since they have the same
   vertical height, and ½(9 + 3) = 6.

Page 222   Exercise 3 — Mixed Exercise

1 a) 22 cm^2 b) 210 m^2 c) 937.5 mm^2
   d) 288 mm^2 e) 50.6 cm^2 f) 5.25 m^2

2 116.16 cm^2

3 a) 1800 cm^2 b) 1200 cm^2

Page 223   Exercise 4

1 a) 82.5 cm^2 b) 139 mm^2

2 a) (i) 96 mm^2 (ii) 46 mm
   b) (i) 89.25 m^2 (ii) 34 m
   c) (i) 336 m^2 (ii) 88 m
   d) (i) 810 m^2 (ii) 150 m

19.3 Circumference of a Circle

*The answers in this topic have been calculated
using the π button on a calculator.*

Page 224   Exercise 1

1 a) 25.1 cm   b) 37.7 cm   c) 6.3 cm
   d) 31.4 cm   e) 94.2 mm   f) 15.7 mm
   g) 22.0 m   h) 28.3 cm

2 a) d = 4 cm, so C = 12.6 cm
   b) d = 3 mm, so C = 9.4 mm
   c) d = 5 cm, so C = 15.7 cm
   d) d = 1 m, so C = 3.1 m
   e) d = 3.4 cm, so C = 10.7 cm
   f) d = 2.6 mm, so C = 8.2 mm
   g) d = 5.2 m, so C = 16.3 m
   h) d = 22.2 mm, so C = 69.7 mm

3 a) 12.6 cm   b) 25.1 mm   c) 28.3 m
   d) 18.8 cm   e) 69.1 m   f) 138.2 cm
   g) 88.0 km   h) 219.9 mm   i) 7.9 m
   j) 11.9 cm   k) 0.6 km   l) 19.8 mm

Page 225   Exercise 2

1 a) 10.3 cm   b) 66.8 mm
   c) 10.3 m   d) 36.0 cm

2 a) 16.3 cm   b) 61.1 mm   c) 15.9 cm
   d) 32.1 mm   e) 50.1 mm   f) 13.4 cm

Page 226   Exercise 3

1 9.4 m   2 62.8 cm   3 78.5 cm   4 144.5 m

5 264 cm   6 110 mm (or 11 cm)   7 35.8 km

8 a) 345.6 cm   b) 172.8 cm

9 2857 m (to nearest m)   10 703 m (to nearest m)

11 50.3 m   12 8.1 m   13 25.1 cm

19.4 Area of a Circle

*The answers in this topic have been calculated
using the π button on a calculator.*

Page 227   Exercise 1

1 a) 12.6 cm^2 b) 314.2 mm^2
   c) 28.3 m^2 d) 2827.4 mm^2

2 a) r = 4 cm, so A = 50.3 cm^2
   b) r = 25 mm, so A = 1963.5 mm^2
   c) r = 3.5 m, so A = 38.5 m^2
   d) r = 6 mm, so A = 113.1 mm^2

3 **a)** 113.1 mm² **b)** 78.5 cm² **c)** 50.3 m²
d) 132.7 cm² **e)** 56.7 mm² **f)** 9.6 m²
g) 113.1 km² **h)** 380.1 cm² **i)** 5.3 m²
j) 1520.5 mm² **k)** 1.1 mm² **l)** 3.5 m²

4 38.5 m²   **5** 50.3 cm²   **6** 132.7 cm²

7 40.7 m²   **8** 2.0 km²   **9** 21.2 cm²

10 **a)** 5.3 cm²
b) A 2p coin has the greater area (of 5.3 cm², the combined area of two 5p coins is 5.1 cm²).

11 The circle, with an area of 452.4 mm².
(The rectangle has area of 440 mm².)

12 39.3 cm²   **13** 3.1 cm²

Page 229   Exercise 2

1 **a)** 77.0 cm² **b)** 139.3 mm² **c)** 59.3 cm²
d) 22.3 cm² **e)** 116.5 cm² **f)** 146.3 mm²
g) 158.5 cm² **h)** 178.5 mm² **i)** 10.3 cm²

2 9.8 m²   **3** 2.4 m²   **4** 28.3 cm²

5 1714.2 m²   **6** 1.9 cm²   **7** 15.7 m²

8 **a)** 353.4 cm²
b) 3646.6 cm²

19.5 **Area and Perimeter Problems**

The answers in this topic have been calculated using the π button on a calculator.

Page 230   Exercise 1

1 **a)** 11.3 m² **b)** 2128.3 mm² **c)** 216 mm²

2 **a)** *P* = 12.6 cm; *A* = 10.3 cm²
b) *P* = 754.0 m; *A* = 27 879.6 m²
c) *P* = 15.1 cm; *A* = 6.6 cm²

3 **a)** 36.2 cm² **b)** 34.8 cm²

4 1608.5 m²   **5** 120 cm²

6 They both have the same area (= *a*²).

Page 231   Exercise 2

1 40.7 m **2** 14.3 cm **3** 3.0 cm **4** 9.2 feet

5 5.1 km **6** 25.5 m

Page 231   Exercise 3

1 4.9 cm **2** 3.0 m **3** 6.3 m **4** 17.5 m

Section 20 — 3D Shapes

20.1 **Nets**

Page 232   Exercise 1

1 **a)** 6 faces, 8 vertices, 12 edges
b) 5 faces, 6 vertices, 9 edges
c) 4 faces, 4 vertices, 6 edges
d) 5 faces, 5 vertices, 8 edges

2 **a)** Cube **b)** Triangular Prism
c) Tetrahedron **d)** Square-based Pyramid
e) Cylinder

3 *A*, *B* and *C*

Page 233   Exercise 2

1 **a)** **(i)** 0 **(ii)** 4 **b)** **(i)** 6 **(ii)** 0
c) **(i)** 1 **(ii)** 4

2 8

3 No, a cuboid has 6 faces but this net is made up of only 5 rectangles.

4 No, a cube has 6 faces but this net is made up of 7 squares.

5 **a)** Square-based Pyramid

b) Cuboid 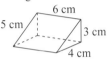 **c)** Triangular Prism

6 **a)** 2 **b)** 2 **c)** 2 **d)** 0

7 **a)** 1 **b)** 1 **c)** 1 **d)** 0

8 *C*

Page 234   Exercise 3

1 **a)** E.g. 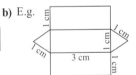 **b)** E.g.

2 **a)** E.g. **b)** E.g.

c) E.g. 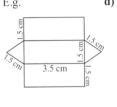 **d)** E.g.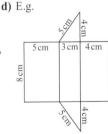

e) E.g. 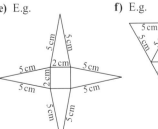 **f)** E.g.

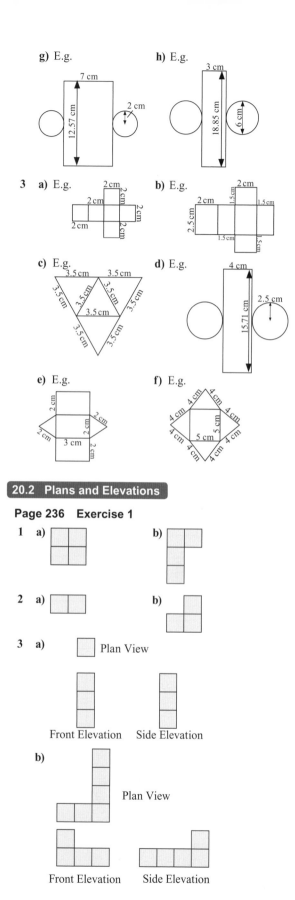

g) E.g.

7 cm
12.57 cm
2 cm

h) E.g.

3 cm
18.85 cm
6 cm

3 a) E.g.

2 cm
2 cm
2 cm
2 cm
2 cm
2 cm

b) E.g.

2 cm
2 cm
2.5 cm
1.5 cm
1.5 cm
1.5 cm
1.5 cm

c) E.g.

3.5 cm
3.5 cm
3.5 cm
3.5 cm
3.5 cm
3.5 cm
3.5 cm
3.5 cm
3.5 cm

d) E.g.

4 cm
15.71 cm
2.5 cm

e) E.g.

2 cm
2 cm
2 cm
2 cm
3 cm
2 cm

f) E.g.

4 cm
4 cm
4 cm
4 cm
4 cm
4 cm
4 cm
4 cm
5 cm
5 cm

20.2 Plans and Elevations

Page 236   Exercise 1

1 a)   **b)**

2 a)   **b)**

3 a)   Plan View

Front Elevation   Side Elevation

b)   Plan View

Front Elevation   Side Elevation

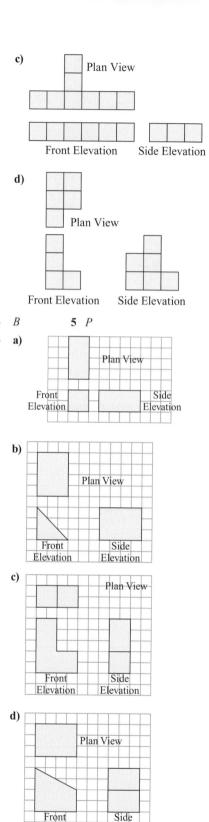

c)   Plan View

Front Elevation   Side Elevation

d)   Plan View

Front Elevation   Side Elevation

4 *B*   **5** *P*

6 a)   Plan View

Front Elevation   Side Elevation

b)   Plan View

Front Elevation   Side Elevation

c)   Plan View

Front Elevation   Side Elevation

d)   Plan View

Front Elevation   Side Elevation

e)

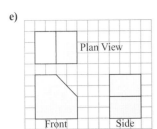

f)

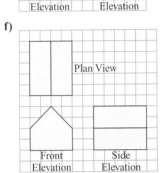

g)

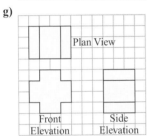

h)

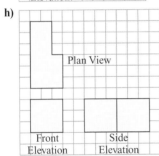

Page 237   Exercise 2

1 a)

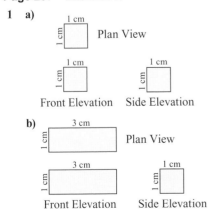

b)

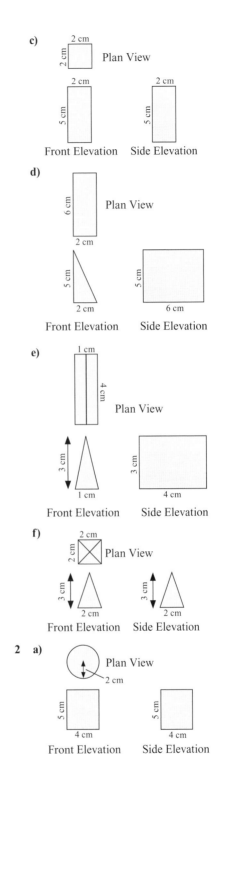

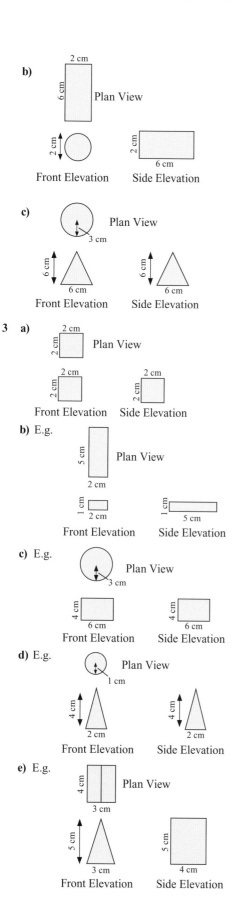

b) Plan View — 2 cm, 6 cm

Front Elevation — 2 cm, circle

Side Elevation — 2 cm, 6 cm

c) Plan View — circle, 3 cm

Front Elevation — 6 cm, 6 cm

Side Elevation — 6 cm, 6 cm

3 a) Plan View — 2 cm, 2 cm

Front Elevation — 2 cm, 2 cm

Side Elevation — 2 cm, 2 cm

b) E.g.

Plan View — 5 cm, 2 cm

Front Elevation — 1 cm, 2 cm

Side Elevation — 1 cm, 5 cm

c) E.g.

Plan View — circle, 3 cm

Front Elevation — 4 cm, 6 cm

Side Elevation — 4 cm, 6 cm

d) E.g.

Plan View — circle, 1 cm

Front Elevation — 4 cm, 2 cm

Side Elevation — 4 cm, 2 cm

e) E.g.

Plan View — 4 cm, 3 cm

Front Elevation — 5 cm, 3 cm

Side Elevation — 5 cm, 4 cm

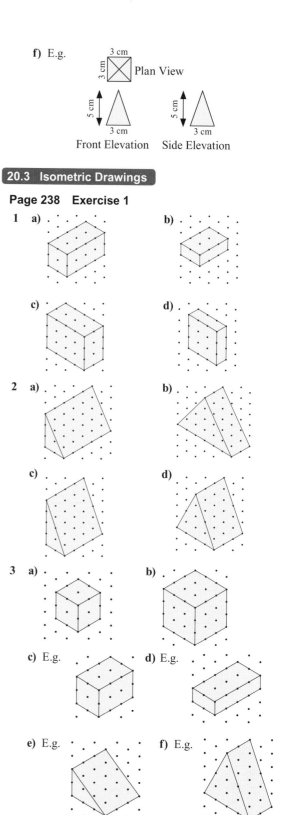

f) E.g.

Plan View — 3 cm, 3 cm

Front Elevation — 5 cm, 3 cm

Side Elevation — 5 cm, 3 cm

20.3 Isometric Drawings

Page 238   Exercise 1

1 a)   **b)**

c)   **d)**

2 a)   **b)**

c)   **d)**

3 a)   **b)**

c) E.g.   **d)** E.g.

e) E.g.   **f)** E.g.

4 a)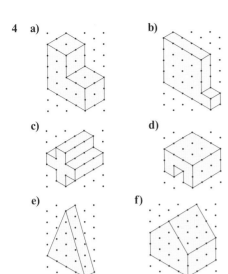

b)

c)

d)

e)

f)

Page 240   Exercise 2

1 a) 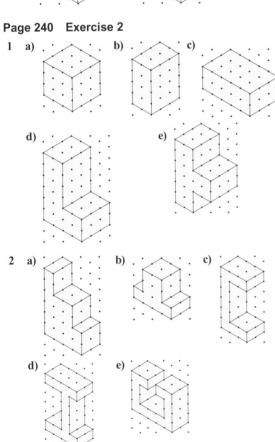 b) c)

d) e)

2 a) b) c)

d) e)

3 a) b) c)

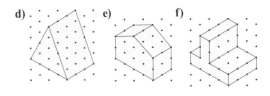

d) e) f)

Page 241   Exercise 1

1 a) 1 cm³
  b) (i) 5 cm³   **(ii)** 4 cm³   **(iii)** 8 cm³   **(iv)** 7 cm³

2 a) 30 cm³   **b)** 10 m³   **c)** 28 cm³
  d) 84 mm³   **e)** 27 cm³   **f)** 64 m³

3 a) 6 cm³   **b)** 24 cm³   **c)** 70 m³
  d) 1600 cm³   **e)** 31.5 cm³   **f)** 756 m³
  g) 130 mm³   **h)** 35.136 mm³   **i)** 200.564 cm³

4 32.768 mm³   **5** By 0.06 m³ (box *A* is bigger).

6 No.   **7** 3312 cm³

8 a) 20 cm³   **b)** 6 cm³

9 1.2 cm

10 a) 0.45 m³   **b)** 0.225 m³   **c)** 0.4 m

Page 243   Exercise 2

1 a) 6 cm³   **b)** 54 cm³   **c)** 9 m³
  d) 12.25 cm³   **e)** 16.1875 mm³   **f)** 105.56 mm³

2 a) 28 cm³   **b)** 30 cm³
  c) 22.5 cm³   **d)** 15.71 cm³ (to 2 d.p.)

3 a) 60 cm³   **b)** 66 cm³
  c) 33.93 cm³ (to 2 d.p.)   **d)** 101.2 cm³

4 a) 624 cm³   **b)** 8.463 m³
  c) 904.78 m³ (to 2 d.p.)   **d)** 282.74 mm³ (to 2 d.p.)
  e) 18.9 m³

5 a) 14.4 m³   **b)** 80 cm³   **c)** 33 mm³   **d)** 9 m³

6 a) 30 cm³   **b)** 60 cm³   **c)** 80 cm³   **d)** 51 cm³

Page 244   Exercise 1

1 12 cm²   **2 a)** 1 cm²   **b)** 6 cm²

3 a) 4 m²   **b)** 24 m²

4 a) 8 m²   **b)** 12 m²   **c)** 6 m²   **d)** 52 m²

5 a) 54 cm²   **b)** 38 cm²   **c)** 23 m²
  d) 57.5 m²   **e)** 390 mm²   **f)** 31.6 m²
  g) 1.2 m²   **h)** 140 m²

6 a) 150 m²   **b)** 216 mm²   **c)** 48 m²
  d) 135.5 m²   **e)** 64 m²

7 a) 11.69 m²   **b)** 3 tins

Page 246 Exercise 2

1 a)
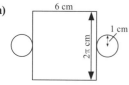

b) Circular faces have area 3.14 cm²
Rectangular surface has area 37.70 cm²
c) 44.0 cm²

2 a)
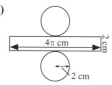

b) Circular faces have area 12.57 cm²
Rectangular surface has area 25.13 cm²
c) 50.3 cm²

3 a) 31.42 cm²   b) 226.19 m²   c) 276.46 mm²
d) 131.95 m²   e) 12.82 m²   f) 51.90 mm²
g) 8.17 m²   h) 207.35 m²

4 a) 113.1 m²   b) 471.2 mm²   c) 1694.1 cm²
d) 1537.9 m²   e) 2.5 m²

5 a) 19.10 m²   b) 2 tins

6 a) 98.14 m²   b) 883.3 m²

7 3.27 m²

Page 247 Exercise 3 — Mixed Exercise

1 a) E.g.   b) 72 cm²

2 a) 113.10 cm² b) 226.19 cm²

3 a) 54 cm²   b) 40 cm² c) 72 cm²   d) 78 cm²

4 a) 12 m   b) E.g.

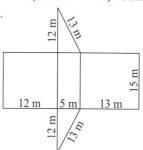

c) 510 m²

5 a) Your drawing should look like this:
Measure the lengths on your
drawing to check it is correct.

b) 3.4 m   c) 46 m²
d) £28   e) £51

Page 248 Exercise 1

1 a) E.g.
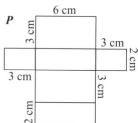

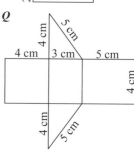

b) P
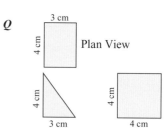

Front Elevation   Side Elevation

Q

Plan View

Front Elevation   Side Elevation

c) P
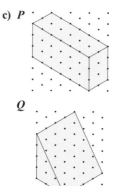

Q

d) P 36 cm³   Q 24 cm³
e) P 72 cm²   Q 60 cm²

2 a) E.g.

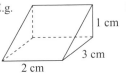

b) 42.41 cm^2

3 a) 512 cm^3 **b)** 12 288 cm^3

4 a) E.g.

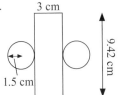

b) E.g.

5 a) E.g.

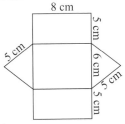

b) 4 cm

c)

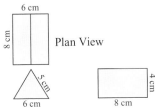

Plan View

Front Elevation   Side Elevation

d)

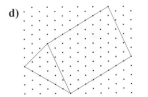

6 a) 22 619 cm^3 **b)** 283 cm^3 **c)** 80 jars

7 a) 9 cm^2 **b)** 3 cm   **c)** 27 cm^3

d)

8 a) 473.09 cm^3 **b)** 29.6 cm × 22.2 cm × 11 cm
   c) 7228.32 cm^3 **d)** 1551.2 cm^3

9 a) 1244.07 cm^3 **b)** 215.98 cm^3
   c) 1028.1 cm^3 **d)** 4.29 cm^3 **e)** 240 sheets

10 a) 16.00 mm   **b)** 2238 mm^2
   c) 10 000 mm^3 **d)** 2146 mm^3

Section 21 — Transformations

Page 250   Exercise 1

1 a)
b)
c)
d)
e)
f)
g)
h)

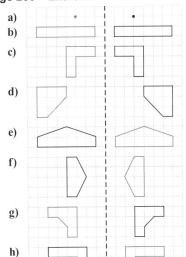

2 a) b) c) d) e)

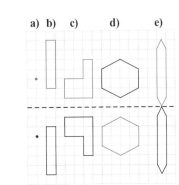

3

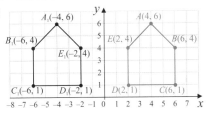

Page 251   Exercise 2

1 a), b)

$A_1(-4, 6)$ $A(4, 6)$
$B_1(-6, 4)$ $E(2, 4)$ $B(6, 4)$
$E_1(-2, 4)$
$C_1(-6, 1)$ $D_1(-2, 1)$ $D(2, 1)$ $C(6, 1)$

c) The x-coordinates become negative in the reflected
shape, and the y-coordinates stay the same.

2 a)

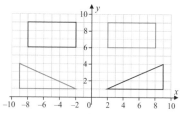

b)

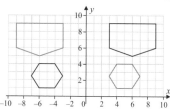

3 a) (i)

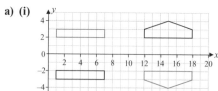

(ii)

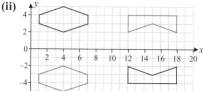

b) The sign of the y-coordinate is reversed (so a positive y-coordinate becomes negative, and a negative y-coordinate becomes positive), while the x-coordinate stays the same.

4 a) $(1, -2)$ **b)** $(3, 0)$ **c)** $(-2, -4)$
   d) $(-1, 3)$ **e)** $(-2, 2)$

5 a) $(-4, 5)$ **b)** $(-7, 2)$ **c)** $(1, 3)$
   d) $(3, -1)$ **e)** $(4, -8)$

6 a), b), c)

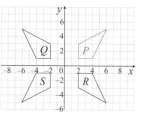

d) The y-axis.

Page 252   Exercise 3

1 a), b), c)

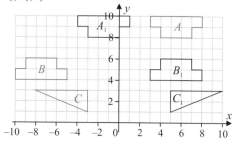

d) $y = 7$

2 a), b), c), d)

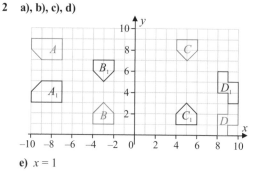

e) $x = 1$

Page 253   Exercise 4

1 a), b)

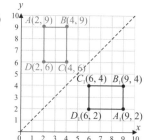

c) The x-coordinate becomes the y-coordinate, and the y-coordinate becomes the x-coordinate.

2 a)

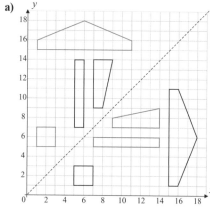

b)

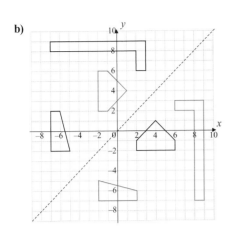

3 **a)** (2, 1)   **b)** (0, 3)   **c)** (4, −2)
    d) (−3, −1)   **e)** (−2, −2)

21.2 Rotation

Page 254   Exercise 1

1 **a)**

    b)

2 **a)**

    b)

3 **a)**

    b)

    c)

    d)

4

    a)
    b)

5 **a)**

    b)

c)

6
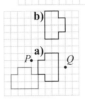
    b)
    P **a)** **Q**

7
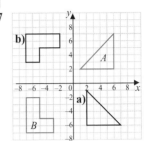
    b)
    a)
    B

8
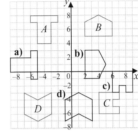

9
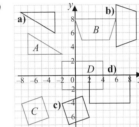

10 a), b), c)

11 a), b), c)
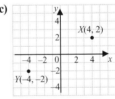

12 $D_1(6, 2)$, $E_1(6, −5)$, $F_1(1, −5)$

Page 257   Exercise 2

1 **a)** Rotation of 90° clockwise (or 270° anticlockwise) about the origin.
    b) Rotation of 90° anticlockwise (or 270° clockwise) about the origin.

2 **a)** Rotation of 180° about the origin.
   b) Rotation of 180° about (0, 2).

3 **a)** Rotation of 180° about (0, 3).
   b) Rotation of 90° anticlockwise (or 270° clockwise) about (0, 2).

4 **a)** Rotation of 90° anticlockwise (or 270° clockwise) about (–1, 7).
   b) Rotation of 90° clockwise (or 270° anticlockwise) about (1, –2).

5 **a)** Rotation of 180° about (0, 6).
   b) Rotation of 90° anticlockwise (or 270° clockwise) about (–2, 7).
   c) Rotation of 90° clockwise (or 270° anticlockwise) about (1, 8).

6 **a)**

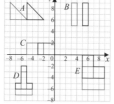

   b) Rotation of 90° anticlockwise (or 270° clockwise) about (–2, 1).

21.3 Translations

Page 258 Exercise 1

1 **a)** 1 to the right, 1 up   **b)** 2 to the right
   c) 3 to the right, 1 down   **d)** 2 to the left, 6 up
   e) 3 to the left, 2 down   **f)** 5 to the left

2 **a)** 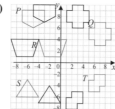 **b)**

3 **a), b)**

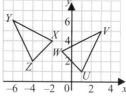

   c) The x-coordinates of the image points are always 10 less than those of the original points.
   The y-coordinates of the image points are always 1 less than the originals.

4 **a)** (3, –3)   **b)** (6, –4)   **c)** (7, –6)
   d) (2, –9)   **e)** (0, 1)   **f)** (5, –6)

5 **a)** (–2, 4)   **b)** (–1, 9)   **c)** (–6, 5)
   d) (3, 2)   **e)** (–5, –3)   **f)** (–7, 8)

6 D_1(–1, 3), E_1(1, 0), F_1(2, 2)

7 P_1(–3, –4), Q_1(1, –3), R_1(–1, –1), S_1(–4, –2)

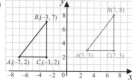

Page 259 Exercise 2

1 **a)** $\begin{pmatrix} 1 \\ 2 \end{pmatrix}$ **b)** $\begin{pmatrix} 1 \\ -2 \end{pmatrix}$ **c)** $\begin{pmatrix} -2 \\ 0 \end{pmatrix}$ **d)** $\begin{pmatrix} 0 \\ -3 \end{pmatrix}$

   e) $\begin{pmatrix} -4 \\ -3 \end{pmatrix}$ **f)** $\begin{pmatrix} 6 \\ 7 \end{pmatrix}$ **g)** $\begin{pmatrix} -5 \\ 2 \end{pmatrix}$ **h)** $\begin{pmatrix} 0 \\ 6 \end{pmatrix}$

2 **a)** 2 units to the right, 3 units down

   b) $\begin{pmatrix} 2 \\ -3 \end{pmatrix}$ **c)** $\begin{pmatrix} 2 \\ -4 \end{pmatrix}$

3 **a)** $\begin{pmatrix} 4 \\ -3 \end{pmatrix}$ **b)** $\begin{pmatrix} 9 \\ 0 \end{pmatrix}$ **c)** $\begin{pmatrix} -5 \\ -3 \end{pmatrix}$

   d) $\begin{pmatrix} 4 \\ -5 \end{pmatrix}$ **e)** $\begin{pmatrix} -13 \\ 5 \end{pmatrix}$ **f)** $\begin{pmatrix} -9 \\ 2 \end{pmatrix}$

4 **a)** $\begin{pmatrix} 0 \\ -5 \end{pmatrix}$ **b)** $\begin{pmatrix} 8 \\ 0 \end{pmatrix}$ **c)** $\begin{pmatrix} 13 \\ 1 \end{pmatrix}$

   d) $\begin{pmatrix} -8 \\ 0 \end{pmatrix}$ **e)** $\begin{pmatrix} -13 \\ -6 \end{pmatrix}$ **f)** $\begin{pmatrix} -8 \\ 5 \end{pmatrix}$

5 **a)** **b)** $\begin{pmatrix} 3 \\ 4 \end{pmatrix}$

6 **a)** $\begin{pmatrix} -1 \\ 2 \end{pmatrix}$ **b)** $\begin{pmatrix} 1 \\ -2 \end{pmatrix}$

Page 261 Exercise 3

1 **a)** $\begin{pmatrix} 3 \\ -5 \end{pmatrix}$ **b)** $\begin{pmatrix} -3 \\ 5 \end{pmatrix}$

   c) The x and y coordinates have changed signs.

2 $\begin{pmatrix} -1 \\ 4 \end{pmatrix}$

3 **a), b), c), d)**

4 D(0, –4), E(–3, 0), F(4, –2)

21.4 Enlargements

Page 262 Exercise 1

1 **a)** **b)** **c)** **d)**

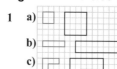

2 **a)** **b)** **c)**

3 **a)** 5 cm / 5 cm (square) **b)** 10 cm / 5 cm (rectangle)

c) 7.5 cm / 10 cm (triangle) **d)** 5 cm / 5 cm / 10 cm / 10 cm

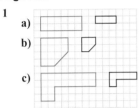

Page 262 Exercise 2

1 **a)** **b)** **c)**
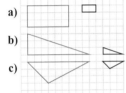

2 **a)** **b)** **c)**

3 4 cm   **4** 3 cm × 7 cm

Page 263 Exercise 3

1 **a)** **b)**
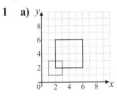

c) **d)**

2 **a), b), c), d)**
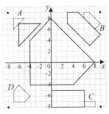

3 **a), b)**

4 **a)** **(i)** 4 units **(ii)** 4 units **(iii)** 4 units **(iv)** 4 units
   b) **(i)** 8 units **(ii)** 8 units **(iii)** 8 units **(iv)** 8 units

c)
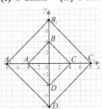

5
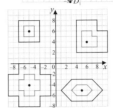

6 **a), b)**
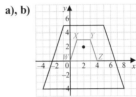

7 **a)** **(i)** 3 units **(ii)** 3 units **(iii)** 0 units
   b) **(i)** 6 units **(ii)** 6 units **(iii)** 0 units

c)
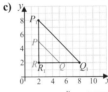

8
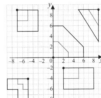

9 **a), b)** **c)**

Page 265 Exercise 4

1 **a), b), c), d)**
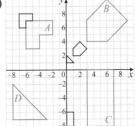

2 a), b), c), d)

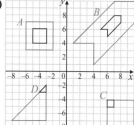

Page 266 Exercise 5

1 a) Scale factor 2, centre (2, 10)
  b) Scale factor 2, centre (6, 10)
  c) Scale factor 3, centre (11, 9)

2 a) Scale factor 2, centre (1, 1)
  b) Scale factor 2, centre (6, 5)
  c) Scale factor 3, centre (5, 4)

Page 266 Exercise 6

1 a) perimeter of *WXYZ* is 8 units

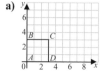

  b)

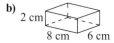

  c) perimeter of $W_1X_1Y_1Z_1$ is 16 units

2 a) 36 cm   **b)** 100 m   **c)** 180 m

3 a) area of *ABCD* is 9 square units

  b)

  c) area of $A_1B_1C_1D_1$ is 36 square units

4 a) 16 cm^2 **b)** 36 cm^2 **c)** 135 m^2 **d)** 40 cm^2

5 a) 12 cm^3
  b)   **c)** 96 cm^3
  2 cm 8 cm   6 cm

6 a) 40 cm^3 **b)** 64 cm^3 **c)** 27 cm^3
  d) 216 m^3 **e)** 500 m^3

Page 268 Exercise 1

1 a)

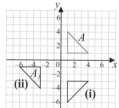

  b)

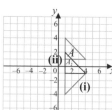

2

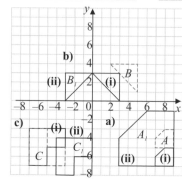

3

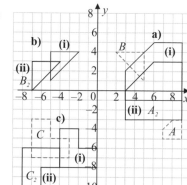

4 a), b) (i)   **(ii)**

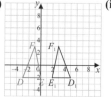 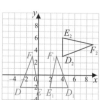

  c) (i)

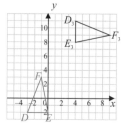

(ii)

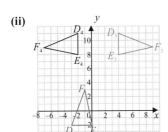

5 a)

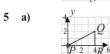

b) (i)

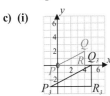

(ii)

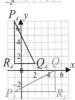

c) (i)

(ii)

Page 270   Exercise 2

1 a)

b)

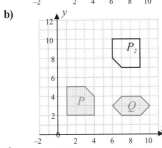

c)

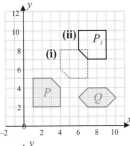

d)

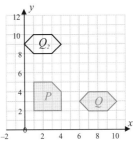

e) P_1 and P_2 are identical, and Q_1 and Q_2 are identical.

2

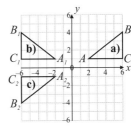

d) Rotation of 180° about (0, 0)

3

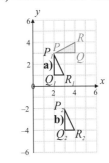

c) Rotation of 90° clockwise about (0, 0)

4

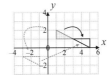

Rotation of 180° about (3, 1)

21.6 Congruence and Similarity

Page 271   Exercise 1

1 A is congruent to G, B is congruent to J,
   C is congruent to F, D is congruent to H,
   E is congruent to I.

2 a) D **b)** H **c)** I **d)** N **e)** Q **f)** V

Page 272   Exercise 2

1 A, C and F are similar
   B, E and K are similar
   D, G and I are similar
   H, J and L are similar

2 a) A and B **b)** D and F **c)** H and I
   d) J and L **e)** M and N **f)** Q and R

1 a) All the angles in one triangle are the same as the angles in the other triangle.
   b) All the sides in one triangle are in the same ratio as the corresponding sides in the other triangle.
   c) All the angles in one triangle are the same as the angles in the other triangle.
   d) Two sides in one triangle are in the same ratio as the corresponding sides in the other triangle and the angle between them is the same in both triangles.

2 a) Similar — the angles are the same in both triangles.
   b) Similar — corresponding sides are in the same ratio.
   c) Similar — 2 corresponding sides are in the same ratio and the angle between them is the same.
   d) Not similar.
   e) Similar — 2 corresponding sides are in the same ratio and the angle between them is the same.
   f) Not similar.

Page 275   Exercise 4

1 a) (i) $100°$ (ii) $55°$ b) $110°$
2 a) (i) angle ABC (ii) angle ACB
      (iii) angle BAC
   b) $1:3$
   c) (i) 7.5 m   (ii) 4 m
3 a) 6 cm   b) 10 cm   c) 5 cm
4 a) 1.5 m   b) 5.4 m   c) 3.6 m
5 a) $34°$
      It forms a pair of opposite angles with angle ZXY.
   b) angle XRQ
   c) $1:2$
   d) (i) 8 m   (ii) 7 m
6 $a = 110°$, $b = 45°$, $c = 25°$,
   $d = 25°$, $e = 5.385$ cm, $f = 8$ cm

Section 22 — Collecting Data

22.1 Using Different Types of Data

Page 276   Exercise 1

1 a) Primary data   b) Secondary data
2 Primary data   3 Secondary data
4 Primary data
5 a) Data needed — girls' answers to some questions about school dinners.
      Method of collecting — e.g. Nikita could ask all the girls in her class to fill in a questionnaire.
   b) Primary data

6 a) Data needed — colours of cars passing Dan's house in the 30-minute interval.
      Method of collecting — e.g. Dan could observe cars passing his house and note the colour of each car in a tally chart.
   b) Primary data
7 a) Data needed — daily rainfall figures for London and Manchester last August.
      Method of collecting — e.g. Anne could look for rainfall figures on the internet.
   b) Secondary data
8 a) Data needed — the distance an identical ball can be thrown by the boys and girls in his class.
      Method of collecting — e.g. Rohan could ask everyone in the class to throw the same ball as far as they can. He could measure the distances and record them in a table, along with whether each thrower was male or female.
   b) Primary data
9 a) Data needed — one set of data consists of the temperature readings in Jim's garden taken at 10 am each day. The other set consists of the Met Office's temperatures recorded for Jim's area at the same time.
      Method of collecting — e.g. Jim could collect the data from his garden by taking readings from a thermometer. He can get the Met Office temperatures from their website. He should record both temperatures for each day in a table.
   b) Data collected in Jim's garden is primary data. The Met Office data is secondary data.

Page 277   Exercise 2

1 Discrete   2 Qualitative
3 Discrete   4 Discrete
5 Continuous   6 Continuous
7 Qualitative   8 Continuous
9 Continuous   10 Qualitative
11 a) One set of data consists of the average number of chocolate bars eaten each week by each pupil. The other set consists of the times it takes these pupils to run 100 metres.
   b) Gemma could ask each pupil how many chocolate bars they eat on average each week.
      She could time how long it takes each pupil to run 100 m and record the data in a table, along with the chocolate bar data.
   c) The chocolate data is discrete data, and the running times data is continuous data.
   d) Both sets of data are primary data.

Page 278 Exercise 1

1 a) There is no tally column.
The rows do not cover all the possible answers.

b) The tally column is very narrow.
The rows do not cover all the possible results.

2 a)

Programme	Tally	Frequency
Drama		
News		
Sit-com		
Reality		

b)

Visits	Tally	Frequency
0		
1		
2		
3		
More than 3		

c)

Destination	Tally	Frequency
UK		
Europe		
USA		
Asia		
Other		

d)

Breeds	Tally	Frequency
0		
1		
2		
3		
4		
5		
More than 5		

3 a) E.g.

Brothers/Sisters	Tally	Frequency
0		
1		
2		
3		
More than 3		

b) E.g.

Transport	Tally	Frequency
Walking		
Car		
Train		
Bus		
Bicycle		
Other		

c) E.g.

Fruit	Tally	Frequency
Apple		
Orange		
Banana		
Peach		
Other		

d)

Days	Tally	Frequency
28		
29		
30		
31		

Page 279 Exercise 2

1 a) There is no row for someone who went to the cinema 0 times — the lowest possible answer is 1.
The classes are overlapping.

No. of trips	Tally	Frequency
0-10		
11-20		
21-30		
31-40		
41 or more		

b) There are gaps between data classes.
The classes do not cover all possible results.

No. of people	Tally	Frequency
0 - 5000		
5001 - 10 000		
10 001 - 15 000		
15 001 - 20 000		
20 001 - 25000		

c) The classes are overlapping.
There are not enough classes.

Time (t mins)	Tally	Frequency
$t \leq 1$		
$1 < t \leq 2$		
$2 < t \leq 3$		
$3 < t \leq 4$		
$t > 4$		

d) There are gaps between classes.
The classes do not cover all possible results.

Weight (w kg)	Tally	Frequency
$w \leq 3$		
$3 < w \leq 3.5$		
$3.5 < w \leq 4$		
$w > 4$		

2 a) E.g. $5 \leq h \leq 10$ $10 < h \leq 15$ $15 < h \leq 20$, $20 < h \leq 25$ $h > 25$

b) E.g. 0-4   5-8   9-12   13-16   17-20

c) E.g. $w \leq 180$ $180 < w \leq 190$ $190 < w \leq 200$, $200 < w \leq 210$ $w > 210$

d) E.g. $v \leq 260$ $260 < v \leq 270$ $270 < v \leq 280$ $280 < v \leq 290$ $290 < v \leq 300$

3 a) E.g.

Time (t hrs)	Tally	Frequency
$t \leq 5$		
$5 < t \leq 10$		
$10 < t \leq 20$		
$20 < t \leq 40$		
$t > 40$		

b) E.g.

No. of pairs	Tally	Frequency
0 - 4		
5 - 8		
9 - 12		
13 - 16		
17 or more		

c) E.g.

Length (s cm)	Tally	Frequency
$s \leq 15$		
$15 < s \leq 20$		
$20 < s \leq 25$		
$25 < s \leq 30$		
$s > 30$		

d) E.g.

Distance (d km)	Tally	Frequency
$d \leq 5$		
$5 < d \leq 10$		
$10 < d \leq 20$		
$20 < d \leq 40$		
$d > 40$		

Page 280   Exercise 3

1 a) There are not enough hair colour data classes.
The age classes overlap. The data is for adults and
does not need a data class for 0-15 years.

b) E.g.

Hair Colour	Age in whole years				
	18 - 30	31 - 45	46 - 60	61 - 75	76 or more
Blonde					
Light brown					
Dark brown					
Ginger					
Grey					
Other					

2 a)

Crisp Flavour	Male or female	
	Male	Female
Plain		
Salt and Vinegar		
Cheese and Onion		
Prawn Cocktail		
Other		

b)

Season	Gender	
	Male	Female
Spring		
Summer		
Autumn		
Winter		

c)

Music	Age Group	
	Adult	Child
Pop		
Classical		
Rock		

d) E.g.

Time spent (t hours)	School Year				
	7	8	9	10	11
$t \leq 1$					
$1 < t \leq 2$					
$2 < t \leq 3$					
$3 < t \leq 4$					

3 a)

Cats or dogs	Male or female	
	Male	Female
Cats		
Dogs		

b) E.g.

TV time (t hours)	Age Group	
	Adult	Child
$t \leq 1$		
$1 < t \leq 2$		
$2 < t \leq 3$		
$3 < t \leq 4$		
$t > 4$		

c) E.g.

Transport	School Year				
	7	8	9	10	11
Walking					
Bus					
Car					
Bicycle					
Train					
Other					

d) E.g.

Height (h cm)	No. of fruit portions eaten				
	0 - 2	3 - 4	5 - 6	7 - 10	11 or more
$h \leq 120$					
$120 < h \leq 140$					
$140 < h \leq 160$					
$160 < h \leq 180$					
$h > 180$					

Page 281   Exercise 4

1 E.g.

No. of people	Tally	Frequency
1		
2		
3		
4		
5 or more		

2

Hair rating	Age Group	
	Adult	Child
1		
2		
3		
4		
5		

3 E.g.

Pocket Money	Tally	Frequency
0 - £2.00		
£2.01 - £4.00		
£4.01 - £6.00		
£6.01 - £8.00		
£8.01 or more		

4 E.g.

TV time per week (t hours)	Sport time per week (s hours)			
	$s \leq 5$	$5 < s \leq 10$	$10 < s \leq 20$	$s > 20$
$t \leq 5$				
$5 < t \leq 10$				
$10 < t \leq 20$				
$t > 20$				

Page 282 Exercise 5

1 E.g. one from: it's too vague / it's hard to answer because there are no options or time span given / it could be difficult to analyse the data because the answers could all be different.

2 It's a leading question, so the results could be biased.

3 E.g. this might be a sensitive issue for people, so there should be options where people can tick a range of weights rather than stating their exact weight.

4 It's a leading question, so the results could be biased.

5 E.g. this might be a sensitive issue for people, so there should be options where people can tick a range of amounts rather than stating their exact salary.

6 There is no tick box for 'no pets'.

7 The tick boxes don't include all possible options. There should be an 'other' option.

8 The tick boxes overlap.

9 Jay's question is better. E.g. two from: Amber's question is too vague because people will have different ideas about how to answer (e.g. "1 hour", "a lot") / Amber's question has no time span / Amber's data could be difficult to analyse because there are no options to limit the answers / Jay's question is clearer because it has a time span / Jay's question covers all possible options / Jay's data will be easier to analyse since there are only 5 options to choose from.

Page 283 Exercise 6

1 The tick boxes should be changed so they don't overlap. E.g. *How much time do you spend reading each week on average?*

1 hour or less ☐
More than 1 hour, but no more than 2 hours ☐
More than 2 hours, but no more than 3 hours ☐
More than 3 hours, but no more than 4 hours ☐
More than 4 hours ☐

2 There should be a tick box added for "other", and possibly more options e.g. "Documentary" or "News". E.g. *What's your favourite type of TV programme? Tick one box.*

Comedy ☐   *Soap* ☐   *Reality* ☐   *Sport* ☐
Documentary ☐   *News* ☐   *Other* ☐

3 A box for "Neither" or "Don't Care" could be added. E.g. *Which type of film do you prefer — horror or thriller? Horror* ☐   *Thriller* ☐   *Neither* ☐

4 Reword the question so it is not a leading question. E.g. *Do you think the gym should open a squash court or a tennis court?*

Page 283 Exercise 7

1 Provide options for the different modes of transport, including "other", and make it clear that one answer only is to be selected.
E.g. *"What is your main means of transport to school? Please tick one box only."* You could include boxes such as "Car", "Bus", "Walking", "Train", "Bicycle" and "Other".

2 Include a time span and tick boxes which cover all possible answers and do not overlap.
E.g. *"How much time do you spend, on average, doing household chores each week?"*
You could include boxes such as "None", "Less than 2 hours", "2 - 4 hours", "More than 4 hours".

3 Include a time span and tick boxes which cover all possible answers and do not overlap.
E.g. *"How many times, on average, do you use the gym each week?"*
You could include boxes such as "I don't use the gym", "Less than once a week", "1-2 times", "More than 2 times".

4 Include a tick box for each day of the week, and make it clear that more than one can be selected.
E.g. *"On which day(s) of the week do you usually shop at the supermarket? You may tick more than one box."*

5 Include tick boxes to cover all possible opinions.
E.g. *"What do you think about the length of the dance class?"* You could include boxes such as "Much too short", "A bit too short", "About right", "A bit too long", "Much too long".

Page 284   Exercise 1

1   E.g. It would take far too long to time all 216 pupils, and a smaller sample would create less disruption in the school routine.

2   E.g. It would be highly impractical and time-consuming to interview everyone in the town.

3   E.g. It would take a long time to test all the matches, and Jim wouldn't have any matches left to use at the end of it.

4   E.g. Kelly's sample is far too small and her results could easily be very unrepresentative of the whole audience.

5   E.g. There is a random element to the results of tossing a coin, so different samples will usually give different results.

6   Alfie's sample was bigger and would be expected to be more accurate — therefore, "chocolate" is more likely to be the most popular flavour.

7   E.g. Nikhil's idea is best, as only tasting one cake would not be accurate, and tasting 50 out of the 200 would take too long and use up a quarter of their cakes.

Page 285   Exercise 2

1   Barry's friends could easily have similar opinions about the film.

2   Animal rights activists are more likely to want vegetarian food, so the sample will be biased in favour of vegetarian food.

3   People using the library on a Monday are unlikely to want it to close on a Monday, so the sample will be biased away from a Monday closure.

4   People at work probably won't be able to answer the phone in the afternoon, so the only replies they will get will be from people who don't work, home workers, and people with the day off.

Page 285   Exercise 3

1   E.g. The dentist could assign each of the adult patients on his database a number, generate 20 random numbers with a computer or calculator, and match the numbers to the patients to create the sample.

2   E.g. The teacher could put all the names of Year 7 pupils into a hat, then mix them up and pick 50 at random.

3   E.g. The manager could assign each of the female members on her database a number, generate 40 random numbers with a computer or calculator, and match the numbers to the members to create the sample.

Page 285   Exercise 4

1   George's sample will be a much higher percentage of the total number of pupils, and Stuart's sample is not random. For example, it could be a group of friends who may all support the same football team.

2   E.g. Seema's sample, being taken on a Sunday morning, may include a lower than usual percentage of churchgoers (if they are at church at the time) or a higher than usual percentage (if they are going to/from church). It would be better to conduct the survey on a weekday evening when far fewer people will be at work or at (or going to/from) a place of worship. Also, people chosen at random in the street may not even live in that street. So instead, Seema could pick 20 house numbers from her street at random and knock on the doors, asking one person from each house.

3   E.g. The management could select 20 employees from each branch by assigning each employee at the branch a number, generating 20 random numbers using a computer or calculator, and matching those numbers to the numbered employees.

4   E.g. If the factory runs for 24 hours a day, test one freshly made component roughly every 30 minutes (or at 50 random times throughout the day).

Section 23 — Analysing Data

23.1   Using Lists and Tables

Page 286   Exercise 1

1   a)

Type of Music	Tally	Frequency
Classical	I	1
Indie	III	3
Pop	IIII IIII	9
Rock	III	3
Other	IIII	4

b) **(i)** 1   **(ii)** Pop   **(iii)** 20

2   a)

Weight (g)	Tally	Frequency
117	III	3
118	II	2
119	II	2
120	IIII	4
121	IIII	4
122	I	1

b) 120 g and 121 g

3 a)

Age (years)	Tally	Frequency
0-9	ＨＴ ＩＩ	7
10-19	ＩＩＩＩ	4
20-29	ＨＴ Ｉ	6
30-39	ＨＴ ＩＩＩ	8
40-49	ＨＴ ＩＩＩ	8
50-59	ＨＴ ＩＩＩＩ	9
60-69	ＩＩＩ	3
70-79	ＩＩＩＩ	4
80-89	Ｉ	1

b) The 50-59 age group is the most common.

4 a)

Mark	Tally	Frequency
20-29	ＩＩＩＩ	4
30-39	ＨＴ ＩＩＩＩ	9
40-49	ＨＴ	5
50-59	ＩＩＩ	3
60-69	ＨＴ ＨＴ	10
70-79	ＩＩＩ	3
80-89	ＨＴ ＩＩ	7
90-100	ＨＴ ＩＩＩＩ	9

b) 29

c) No, because the grouping used means the table doesn't show how many students in the 50-59 group scored less than 55 (and so failed), and how many scored 55 or over (and so passed).

23.2 Averages and Range

Page 287 Exercise 1

1 a) 8 **b)** 6 **c)** 8
2 58 **3** 78 seconds **4** red

Page 288 Exercise 2

1 a) 5 **b)** 6 **c)** 13
2 a) 3.8 **b)** 16.5 **c)** 3
3 58 **4** 81 seconds **5** 7
6 16.9

Page 289 Exercise 3

1 a) 5.6 **b)** 6.33 (to 2 d.p.) **c)** 13.125
2 a) 3.68 **b)** 18.075 **c)** 3.125
3 60.2 marks (to 1 d.p.)
4 83 seconds
5 a) mean = 3.25, median = 2.5, mode = 2
   b) mean = 3, median = 3, mode = 3
6 10 **7** 15.3

Page 289 Exercise 4

1 a) 5 **b)** 7 **c)** 9

2 a) 4.1 **b)** 6.19 **c)** 1
3 52 **4** 17 seconds **5** 2 or 11

Page 290 Exercise 5

1 a) 1 **b)** 2
   c) (i) 5 **(ii)** 8 **(iii)** 7 **(iv)** 5 **(v)** 2
   d) 45 **e)** 27 **f)** 1.67 (to 2 d.p.)
2 a) 4 **b)** 3 **c)** 3.07 (to 2 d.p.)
   d) 4
3 a) 18.5 °C **b)** 18.5 °C
   c) E.g. The student's garden has experienced some fairly typical June temperatures for the UK.

Page 292 Exercise 6

1 a) 16-20 **b)** 11-15 **c)** 12.2
2 58.5 g
3 a) 11-15 hours **b)** 11-15 hours **c)** 11.0 hours

Page 292 Exercise 7 — Mixed Exercise

1 a) (i) 138 cm **(ii)** 137 cm **(iii)** 142 cm
   b) 33 cm
2 a) (i) £5.04 **(ii)** £5.00 **(iii)** £5.00
   b) £1.58
3 a) (i) 6.49 cm **(ii)** 6.35 cm **(iii)** 4.3 cm
   b) 4.7 cm
4 a) 0 **b)** 20 **c)** 1
   d) (i) 20 **(ii)** 1 **e)** 3
5 a) 3 **b)** 2.7 **c)** 3
   d) More goals were scored on average than in the previous year.
6 a) 1.61 m - 1.70 m **b)** 1.61 m - 1.70 m
   c) 1.70 m

23.3 Two-Way Tables

Page 293 Exercise 1

1 a)

	Walk	Car	Total
Boys	12	6	18
Girls	16	3	19
Total	28	9	37

b)

	Walk	Car	Total
Boys	16	9	25
Girls	18	4	22
Total	34	13	47

c)

	Walk	Bus	Car	Total
Boys	9	5	3	17
Girls	5	8	6	19
Total	14	13	9	36

d)

	Walk	Bus	Car	Total
Boys	10	12	8	30
Girls	11	15	4	30
Total	21	27	12	60

2 a)

	Germany	France	Spain	Total
Male	16	7	12	35
Female	18	4	16	38
Total	34	11	28	73

b) 4   **c)** 16   **d)** 28

e) 38   **f)** 73

3 a)

	Chocolate	Crisps	Jellies	Total
Male	3	5	10	18
Female	3	7	2	12
Total	6	12	12	30

b) 12   **c)** 2   **d)** 16.7% (to 1 d.p.)

4 a)

	Red	Black	Blue	White	Total
Cars	8	7	4	3	22
Vans	2	2	1	10	15
Motorbikes	2	1	1	2	6
Total	12	10	6	15	43

b) 1   **c)** 15

d) (i) 51.2% (to 1 d.p.)   **(ii)** 34.9% (to 1 d.p.)

(iii) 27.9% (to 1 d.p.)

23.4 Bar Charts, Pictograms and Histograms

Page 295   Exercise 1

1

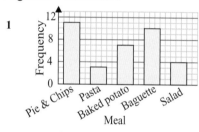

2

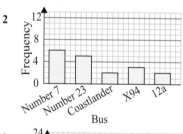

3

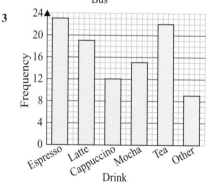

4

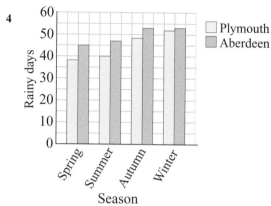

5

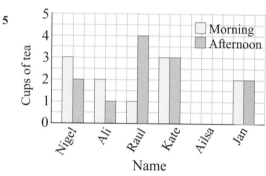

Page 296   Exercise 2

1

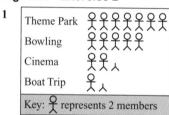

2 a) (i) 40   **(ii)** 30 (or "approximately 30")

b)

Monday	▷☐◁ ▷☐◁ ▷☐◁
Tuesday	▷☐◁ ▷☐◁
Wednesday	▷☐◁ ▷☐
Thursday	▷☐◁
Friday	▷☐◁ ▷☐◁ ▷☐
Saturday	▷☐◁ ▷☐◁ ▷☐◁ ◁〜
Sunday	
Key: ▷☐◁ represents 20 packets of sweets	

3 a) 10   **b)** Number 1   **c)** 39

Page 297   Exercise 3

1

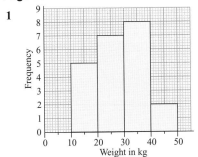

2

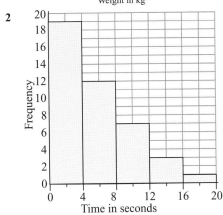

3 **a)** 17   **b)** 2   **c)** 3-4 km

Page 298   Exercise 4

1

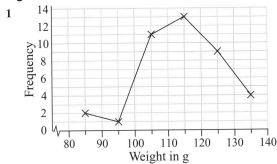

2

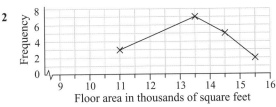

3 **a)** 3   **b)** 0 to 0.5 hours

4 **a)** 1   **b)** 0 - 5 minutes   **c)** 19

Page 299   Exercise 1

1 **a)**

4	1	8			Key: 4	1 means 41
5	1	4	9	
6	5	5	9	
7	4			
8	0	6	9	

Key: 4 | 1 means 41

b)

1	2	5	5	7
2	4	6	7	
3	1	6	9	
4	1	1		

Key: 1 | 2 means 12

c)

4	2	6	
5	4	9	
6	3	6	7
7	1	4	
8	3	7	
9	4		

Key: 4 | 1 means 41

2 **a)**

3	1	4				
4	0	4	9	4		
5	3	7	9	4	1	7
6	0	1				
7	7	1				

Key: 3 | 1 means 3.1

b)

20	3	5				
30	1	4				
40	2	9	9	4	3	2
50	0	1	3			
60	6	8	1			

Key: 20 | 1 means 201

3

0	0	0	0	1	3	6
1	1	3	6			
2	0	5	7			
3	1	6	8			
4	1					

Key: 0 | 1 means 0.1 cm

4 **a)** 51, 58, 63, 67, 67, 73, 74, 76, 78, 78, 82, 87, 87, 91, 93

b) 211, 213, 213, 215, 218, 222, 224, 224, 231, 239, 242, 251, 253, 255, 259

Page 300   Exercise 2

1 **a)** 32   **b)** 20   **c)** 27

2 **a)** 61   **b)** 7   **c)** 6

3 **a)**

10	2	6			
11	4	7			
12	4	8	9		
13	1	3	6	9	9	9
14	2				
15	4				
16					
17	3				

Key: 10 | 1 means 10.1 seconds

   b) 13.9 seconds   **c)** 7.1 seconds   **d)** 7

Page 301   Exercise 3

1

						Set 2		Set 1					
9	8	5	3	3		1	2	8			
7	5	3	2	2		2	4	8	9		
				2		3	2	3	7	8	
						4	1	8			

Key: 1 | 2 for Set 1 means 12
       1 | 2 for Set 2 means 21

2 **a)** **(i)** 72 bpm   **(ii)** 77 bpm
   b) These people's average heart rate was greater after exercise.

3 **a)**

					London		Dundee							
			9	7	4	0	1	2	3	3	4	5	6	7
8	6	5	3	2	2	1	1	2	5	9				
				4	1	2	3							

Key: 1 | 2 for London means 21 °C
       1 | 2 for Dundee means 12 °C

   b) The average temperature in London was higher.

23.6 Pie Charts

Page 302   Exercise 1

1 **a)** 60   **b)** 6°
   c) Black 150°, Silver 102°, Red 48°, Other 60°
   d)

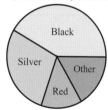

2 **a)** 36
   b) Carlisle 130°, Kendal 90°, Millom 80°, Bristol 60°

c)

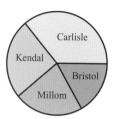

3

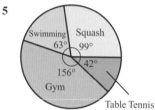

4

5

6 **a)** 48
   b) Plain 135°, Salt and Vinegar 97.5°, Cheese and Onion 75°, Other 52.5°
   c)

7

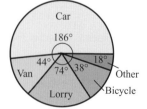

8

9

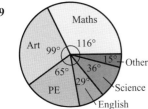

Page 304 Exercise 2

1 Set 1 : Q   Set 2 : P   Set 3 : S   Set 4 : R

2 a) $\frac{1}{3}$ **b)** Hamsters **c)** 24 **d)** 3

3 a) Pepperoni **b)** $\frac{1}{4}$ **c)** 60 **d)** 6

4 a) Yes **b)** Yes
   c) No. The pie charts do not represent times, just the proportion of homework tasks set for each subject.

5 a) 50+ **b)** $\frac{1}{10}$ **c)** 120
   d) (i) 24 **(ii)** 12
   e) 40
   f) 15

23.7 Line Graphs

Page 306 Exercise 1

1 a) 16:00 **b)** 19:00

2 a) £9000 **b)** £7000 **c)** £4000 **d)** 4 years

Page 307 Exercise 2

1
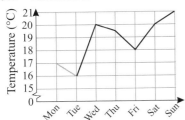

2 a)
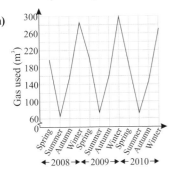

   b) The graph seesaws up and down with the seasons, indicating the family uses more gas when it gets colder.

3 a)
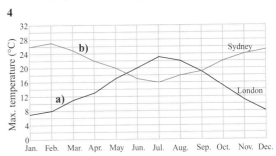

   b) There was a steep rise in the percentage of students who own mobile phones, from almost no one in 2000, to almost everyone in 2010.

4
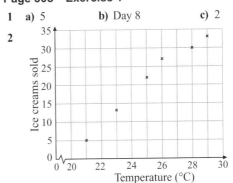

   c) The London graph peaks in July, when the Sydney graph is at its lowest. The Sydney graph peaks in February, when the London graph is very low. Warmer temperatures in one city correspond to lower temperatures in the other city.

23.8 Scatter Graphs

Page 308 Exercise 1

1 a) 5 **b)** Day 8 **c)** 2

2
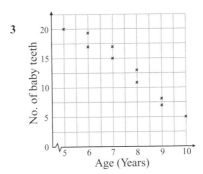

3

Page 309   Exercise 2

1 **a)** Negative correlation.
   b) No Correlation.
   c) Positive correlation.
2 **a)** Positive correlation — as it gets warmer, people will probably be more likely to buy ice cream.
   b) Negative correlation — as it gets colder, people will probably be more likely to buy hot chocolate.
   c) No correlation — there probably isn't any connection between how hot it is and how much bread people buy.
   d) Positive correlation — as a child grows, he or she gets taller.
   e) Positive correlation — most people will probably drive more slowly in an area with a low speed limit.

Page 310   Exercise 3

1 **a)** Yes, the points will lie close to a straight line.
   b) No, the points are randomly scattered.
   c) Yes, most of the points will lie close to a straight line.
2 **a)** Negative correlation <u>OR</u> the more time spent watching TV, the less time was spent on homework.
   b) 1 hour   **c)** 1.5 hours
3 **a)** Positive correlation <u>OR</u> the higher the tree, the wider the trunk.
   b) 65 cm   **c)** 20 m
4 **a), b)**

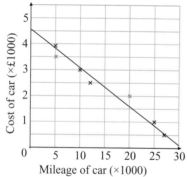

   c) About £2300.

5 **a), b)**

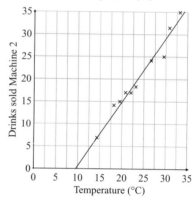

   c) Machine 1: 20 drinks. Machine 2: 22 drinks.

Section 24 — Probability

24.1 Probability — The Basics

Page 312   Exercise 1

1 **a)** B: spinning more than 2
   b) B: picking a spade
   c) A: the day begins with S
2 2, 1, 4, 3
3 **a)** Evens   **b)** Impossible **c)** Impossible **d)** Evens
   e) Certain **f)** Unlikely   **g)** Evens   **h)** Likely
4 **a)** C   **b)** D   **c)** B   **d)** A
5

f)	**d)**	**b)**	**c) e)**	**a)**
Impossible	Unlikely	Evens	Likely	Certain

6 **a)** A   **b)** L
   c) P: 1   A: 2   R: 1   L: 3   E: 1

Page 314   Exercise 2

1 **a)** D   **b)** C   **c)** A   **d)** B
   e) E
2 **a)** C   **b)** A   **c)** D   **d)** B

3   c) (i)   c) (ii)   b)   a)

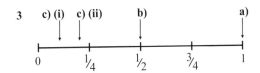

0      $\frac{1}{4}$ $\frac{1}{2}$ $\frac{3}{4}$ 1

24.2 Calculating Probabilities

Page 315   Exercise 1

1   **a)** 2   **b)** 52   **c)** 10   **d)** 8
    e) 7   **f)** 365 (or 366 for a leap year)

2   **a)** 6   **b)** $\frac{1}{6}$ **c)** $\frac{1}{3}$

3   **a)** $\frac{1}{6}$ **b)** $\frac{1}{6}$ **c)** 0   **d)** $\frac{1}{3}$
    e) $\frac{1}{3}$ **f)** $\frac{2}{3}$

4   **a)** $\frac{1}{9}$ **b)** $\frac{2}{9}$ **c)** $\frac{4}{9}$ **d)** $\frac{5}{9}$

5   **a)** $\frac{1}{4}$ **b)** $\frac{1}{3}$ **c)** $\frac{2}{3}$ **d)** $\frac{3}{4}$

6   **a)** $\frac{1}{8}$ **b)** $\frac{3}{16}$ **c)** $\frac{1}{16}$ **d)** $\frac{1}{8}$
    e) $\frac{3}{8}$ **f)** $\frac{3}{8}$ **g)** $\frac{15}{16}$ **h)** 0

7   **a)** $\frac{1}{4}$ **b)** $\frac{1}{13}$ **c)** $\frac{1}{2}$ **d)** $\frac{1}{52}$
    e) $\frac{3}{4}$ **f)** $\frac{2}{13}$

8   **a)**   **b)**   **c)**

The unmarked sections can be any number different from the ones already shown on the spinner.

Page 316   Exercise 2

1   **a)** $\frac{1}{12}$ **b)** $\frac{1}{366}$

2 $\frac{1}{39}$

3   **a)** $\frac{1}{9}$ **b) (i)** 7   **(ii)** $\frac{7}{18}$

4   **a)** $\frac{1}{100}$ **b)** $\frac{1}{100}$

5   It takes no account of how good the team is or how good their opponents are. The three outcomes are not equally likely.

Page 317   Exercise 3

1   **a)** Yes   **b)** No   **c)** No

2   **a)** Yes   **b)** No   **c)** No   **d)** No
    e) No   **f)** No

3   0.8   **4** $\frac{3}{8}$ **5**   75%

6   0.55   **7**   0.26

8   **a)** 0.55   **b)** 0.8

Page 318   Exercise 4

1   0.3

2   **a)** 0.3   **b)** 0.9

3   0.45   **4** $\frac{3}{8}$

5   40

Page 319   Exercise 5 — Mixed Exercise

1   **a) (i)** $\frac{2}{5}$ **(ii)** $\frac{1}{3}$ **(iii)** $\frac{2}{3}$
    b) (i) $\frac{5}{18}$ **(ii)** $\frac{13}{18}$ **(iii)** $\frac{2}{3}$

2   **a)** $\frac{3}{8}$ **b)** $\frac{7}{8}$

3   **a)** $\frac{1}{2}$ **b)** $\frac{1}{3}$
    c) These are not mutually exclusive outcomes that cover all the possibilities. (The two events aren't mutually exclusive, because if 6 is rolled, then both events have happened. And the outcomes 1 and 5 are not included in either event.)

24.3 Listing Outcomes

Page 320   Exercise 1

1   **a)**

1st coin	2nd coin
Heads	Heads
Heads	Tails
Tails	Heads
Tails	Tails

    b)

Dice	Coin
1	Heads
1	Tails
2	Heads
2	Tails
3	Heads
3	Tails
4	Heads
4	Tails
5	Heads
5	Tails
6	Heads
6	Tails

2

1st ball	2nd ball
Green	Green
Green	Blue
Blue	Green
Blue	Blue

3

1st spin	2nd spin
Blue	Blue
Blue	Purple
Blue	Orange
Purple	Blue
Purple	Purple
Purple	Orange
Orange	Blue
Orange	Purple
Orange	Orange

4 a)

Burger	Drink
Hamburger	Cola
Hamburger	Lemonade
Hamburger	Coffee
Cheeseburger	Cola
Cheeseburger	Lemonade
Cheeseburger	Coffee
Veggie burger	Cola
Veggie burger	Lemonade
Veggie burger	Coffee

b) $\frac{1}{9}$ **c)** $\frac{1}{3}$

5 a)

1st spin	2nd spin
1	1
1	2
1	3
2	1
2	2
2	3
3	1
3	2
3	3

b) $\frac{1}{9}$ **c)** $\frac{1}{3}$

6 a)

1st toss	2nd toss	3rd toss
Heads	Heads	Heads
Heads	Heads	Tails
Heads	Tails	Heads
Heads	Tails	Tails
Tails	Heads	Heads
Tails	Heads	Tails
Tails	Tails	Heads
Tails	Tails	Tails

b) $\frac{1}{8}$ **c)** $\frac{3}{8}$

Page 321   Exercise 2

1 a)

	1	2	3	4	5	6
H	H1	H2	H3	H4	H5	H6
T	T1	T2	T3	T4	T5	T6

b)

	Red	White	Blue
Red	RR	RW	RB
White	WR	WW	WB
Blue	BR	BW	BB

2 a)

	1	2	3	4	5	6
1	2	3	4	5	6	7
2	3	4	5	6	7	8
3	4	5	6	7	8	9
4	5	6	7	8	9	10
5	6	7	8	9	10	11
6	7	8	9	10	11	12

b) 36

c) (i) $\frac{5}{36}$ **(ii)** $\frac{1}{36}$ **(iii)** 0   **(iv)** $\frac{7}{12}$
   (v) $\frac{5}{18}$ **(vi)** $\frac{1}{2}$

3 a)

	B	G	G	Y
B	BB	BG	BG	BY
G	GB	GG	GG	GY
Y	YB	YG	YG	YY

b) (i) $\frac{1}{12}$ **(ii)** $\frac{1}{6}$ **(iii)** $\frac{1}{3}$ **(iv)** $\frac{1}{2}$

Page 321   Exercise 3

1 a)

	1	2	3	4	5	6
A	A1	A2	A3	A4	A5	A6
B	B1	B2	B3	B4	B5	B6
C	C1	C2	C3	C4	C5	C6
D	D1	D2	D3	D4	D5	D6

b) (i) $\frac{1}{24}$ **(ii)** $\frac{1}{24}$ **(iii)** $\frac{1}{12}$ **(iv)** $\frac{1}{8}$
   (v) $\frac{1}{8}$ **(vi)** $\frac{1}{6}$

2 a)

		Asha's score (2nd number)				
		1	**2**	**3**	**4**	**5**
Hayley's score (1st number)	**1**	1, 1	1, 2	1, 3	1, 4	1, 5
	2	2, 1	2, 2	2, 3	2, 4	2, 5
	3	3, 1	3, 2	3, 3	3, 4	3, 5
	4	4, 1	4, 2	4, 3	4, 4	4, 5
	5	5, 1	5, 2	5, 3	5, 4	5, 5

b) $\frac{2}{5}$ **c)** $\frac{4}{25}$

Page 322   Exercise 1

1 a) $\frac{17}{50}$ b) $\frac{33}{50}$

2 a) Red $\frac{49}{100}$, green $\frac{17}{50}$, yellow $\frac{2}{25}$, blue $\frac{9}{100}$
   b) Perform the experiment more times.

3 a) $\frac{13}{50}$ b) $\frac{9}{50}$
   c) Jason's should be more accurate as he has
      performed the experiment more times.

4 a) (i) 0.452   (ii) 0.237   b) 0.089

5 $\frac{5}{6}$

6 a) $\frac{8}{15}$ b) $\frac{7}{15}$

7 $\frac{2}{5}$

8 Lilia could examine the recent records of her team's
   previous matches against a similar level of opposition,
   count the number of wins and divide it by the total
   number of matches in those records.

Page 323   Exercise 2

1 a) 15   b) 45   c) 75   d) 750
2 a) 20   b) 20   c) 60   d) 100
3 a) 20   b) 100   c) 160
4 12

Page 324   Exercise 3 — Mixed Exercise

1 a) Blue 0.22, Green 0.21, White 0.18, Pink 0.39
   b) Blue 0.25, Green 0.25, White 0.25, Pink 0.25
   c) The spinner seems biased as the relative
      frequencies for white and pink are a long
      way away from the theoretical probability.

2 a) 20 times.
   b) The dice may be biased as the number 4 comes up
      much more than expected.
   c) Perform the experiment more times.

3 a)

	Amy	Steve	Hal
No. of tosses	20	60	100
No. of heads	12	33	49
Relative frequency	0.6	0.55	0.49

   b) Hal's should be the most accurate, as he has
      performed the experiment the most times.
   c) The coin seems fair, as the expected frequency of
      heads is 0.5 and Hal's results are very near that.

Index